I0815842

"The collection, translation, and publication of Johann Georg Hamann's *London Writings* fills in an important gap in our knowledge of this orthodox Lutheran theologian's spiritual awakening, which occurred in England just at the time that the Evangelical revival was gaining momentum. These writings remind us that traditional Protestant theology was making a comeback in an age dominated by Enlightenment deism and are a significant witness to a movement that is too often overlooked. An essential resource for all who are interested in this crucial period in the development of modern evangelicalism."

—GERALD BRAY, research professor of divinity,
Beeson Divinity School

"Reading the reflections of Christians from the past is an excellent way to strengthen us in times of doubt and uncertainty. Hamann's reflections on Scripture, God's grace in Christ, and the church's hymnody offer readers a wonderful way to think deeply upon the truths of Scripture. Deep currents of thought run through this book—currents that can slake our thirst for Christ and refresh our hearts as we live the Christian life."

—J. V. FESKO, Harriet Barbour Professor of Systematic
and Historical Theology, Reformed Theological Seminary,
Jackson, Mississippi

"Hamann was a rare bird: in many ways ahead of his time yet returning to the abandoned wells of Christian orthodoxy. To friends like Kant, he was a traitor to the Enlightenment and he was mostly sidelined in his day. Romantic writers picked up on Hamann's 'metacriticism' of the Enlightenment yet looked for a 'new mythology' to satisfy their spiritual longing. All of this makes for a fascinating episode. More importantly, Hamann offers resources for engaging both rationalists and 'spiritual but not religious' outlooks today. This expert translation of his *London Writings* gives us access to the piety that inspired Hamann's innovative philosophical and hermeneutical labors."

—MICHAEL S. HORTON, J. Gresham Machen Professor of
Theology and Apologetics, Westminster Seminary California

"This wonderful translation of Hamann's *London Writings* exposes readers to a central theme of his life: the passionate encounter with the word that reads us and our world. Here we see Hamann captivated by the perplexing simplicity of God's word, modeling true enlightenment that sees through a glass darkly."

—TYLER WITTMAN, associate professor of theology,
New Orleans Baptist Theological Seminary

"The German idealist tradition has made skeptics of us all, and its influence continues to be felt everywhere. But perhaps an early voice offers a way through the mire of the subjective turn. These writings from Hamann show a philosopher wrestling to know—to know God in faith and certainty. One is struck by how Hamann comes to Holy Scripture to hear God's voice and to discover vital wisdom for life in God's world. Accordingly, Hamann models for us a type of anti-modern offramp for philosophy, rebuffing the Enlightenment drive to leave the word immanentized and lifeless. These *London Writings* offer the philosopher and thoughtful Christian alike a constructive vision of what it means to encounter God transformationally and with surety—as he has revealed himself in Scripture—and to therefore set such knowledge as the proper foundation of any philosophy or science."

—DENNIS GREESON, dean of the Alexandrian Institute

THE COMPLETE

LONDON WRITINGS

THE COMPLETE LONDON WRITINGS

MEDITATIONS ON THE GOODNESS AND MERCY OF GOD

JOHANN GEORG HAMANN

JOHN W. KLEINIG (TRANSLATOR)

GENE EDWARD VEITH JR. (EDITOR)

The Complete London Writings: Meditations on the Goodness and Mercy of God

Lexham Academic, 1313 Bay St, Bellingham 98225
LexhamPress.com

Print ISBN 9781683598268
Digital ISBN 9781683598275

Lexham Editorial: Todd Hains, Gene Edward Veith Jr., Ethan McCarthy, Kelsey Matthews, Mandi Newell
Cover Design: Jonathan Myers
Typesetting: Jessi Strong

25 26 27 28 29 30 31 / IN / 12 11 10 9 8 7 6 5 4 3 2 1

TABLE OF CONTENTS

Introduction: "The Sage from the North" ix

Hamann and His London Writings ix

The Origin and Purpose of the London Writings xiii

The Nature of the London Writings xviii

The Key Metaphors and Themes xxv

The Publication of the London Writings xxxix

Chronology of Hamann's Life xliii

London Writings

1. On the Interpretation of Sacred Scripture 1
2. Biblical Meditations of a Christian 5
3. Thoughts on the Course of My Life 325
4. Thoughts on Church Hymns 371
5. Deuteronomy 20:11–14 together with Romans 10:4–10 425
6. Fragments 435
7. Meditations on Newton's Essay on Prophecies 449
8. Further Thoughts on the Course of My Life 457
9. Prayer 469

Select Bibliography 477

Subject and Author Index 481

Scripture Index 493

INTRODUCTION: "THE SAGE FROM THE NORTH"

The greatest sages, like true prophets, are seldom appreciated or understood by their contemporaries. They may have some immediate impact, often for the wrong reasons, and gain some followers, who tend to use them to promote their own causes. But they are seldom understood and little appreciated because they are usually out of step with their times and their own cultural context. So their significance only becomes evident after their death, as times change and the dominant culture is more attuned to their insights. Then their guidance is welcomed for personal reorientation in a changed world, like a map for travel in an unknown land. The new mentality provided by their wisdom helps people locate themselves in that new territory.

Johann Georg Hamann may rightly be regarded as such a sage. One of his earliest disciples, Carl von Moser, called him the sage from the north. And Hamann was happy to accept that designation, not because he considered that he was a sage in the contemporary sense of the word as a moral philosopher, but because the German *Magus* identified him with the Magi, the wise men from the East in Matthew 2:1–12. Like them, he followed the star that led him to worship Jesus as the promised Messiah. So, for example, in 1784 he signs off a letter to his friend Kraus with an ironic self-appellation that alludes to both these sages from the East and the tax collector Matthew: *magus in telonio*, "sage at the tax booth."[1] Like his hero Socrates and the apostle Paul, he spoke of his ignorance to people who claimed to have sure

1. Arthur Henkel, ed., *Briefwechsel* (Wiesbaden: Insel Verlag, 1965), 5:291. Hamann's letters were published in Wiesbaden by Insel Verlag in two stages as *Johann Georg Hamann, Briefwechsel,* the first from 1955–57 and the second from 1965–79. Volumes 1–3 were edited by Walther Ziesemer and Arthur Henkel, and volumes 4–7 by Arthur Henkel. From 1767 to his retirement in 1787, Hamann worked for the Prussian Government, first in its General Excise Department and then in its Customs Office.

and certain knowledge of themselves and the world. Like them, he prized the unsettling folly of true wisdom. And that is nowhere more apparent than in his *London Writings.* They show us something of his wisdom and its unlikely provenance. From them we may understand why Hamann has recently been considered an intellectual and spiritual guide by an increasing number of thinkers in a variety of fields.[2]

One might think that Hamann would be of little interest to English readers in this new millennium, considering his difficult style and how little of his work has been translated into English. He was a minor civil servant who spent most of his life in the remote province of East Prussia, far from the political, cultural, and intellectual centers of his day. In his spare time he published a series of obscure works in which he engaged with some of the leading lights in German-speaking central Europe. Many of them were fascinated by him, even though they did not quite know what to make of him and his writings. He was far too much out of step with his times to be at all directly influential on the mainstream of scholarship and debate. His influence, such as it was, was largely secondhand and indirect through those who had benefited from his provocations. Yet even they tended to cherry-pick some of his insights and use them to pursue their own concerns.

He did have a widespread and indirect influence on three strands of German and central European culture that are of some academic interest. It can be discerned in philosophy via Herder, Kant, Hegel, Jacobi, and Kierkegaard; in literature via Goethe and German Romantic writers such as Jean Paul; and in Lutheran theology via the confessional revival that came in the wake of the French Revolution and the Napoleonic wars with August Vilmar and Wilhelm Loehe. But it did not go much further than that. Only a few specialists were interested in some aspects of his life and work for historical reasons. Even in Germany there was so little interest in him that only some of his works were issued forty years after his death, and his

2. The best English introduction to the *London Writings* is provided by John R. Betz, "Hamann's London Writings. The Hermeneutics of Divine Condescension," *Pro Ecclesia* 14, no. 2 (2005): 191–216. Betz is also the author of a comprehensive study of Hamann's thought and its importance today: *After Enlightenment: The Post-Secular Vision of J. G. Hamann* (Oxford: Wiley Blackwell, 2012).

complete works were only published by Joseph Nadler in a comprehensive critical edition after the Second World War, from 1949–1957.[3]

Even though Hamann had no direct cultural, intellectual, and theological influence on the English speaking world, he has suddenly become much better known and more highly regarded in current academic discourse. This has come in two stages. The study of Hamann by English scholars began in the two decades after the Second World War in connection with the existential philosophy of Kierkegaard and the neoorthodoxy of Karl Barth and has continued into the new millennium in connection with what is now called postmodernism.[4] In this new context his work has become increasing relevant and useful.

The reason for this growing engagement with Hamann is obvious. It stems from the apparent triumph of what is now called postmodernism with its hermeneutics of suspicion about the Enlightenment faith in human reason and its dominance in all areas of life. Thus John Betz makes this claim for Hamann and his present appeal:

> He was arguably the most brilliant critic of the Enlightenment, the Socrates of Königsberg, the German translator of Hume, the first to read and "metacritically" deconstruct Kant's *Critique of Pure Reason,* in short, probably the most interesting and radical thinker the ranks of Lutheran orthodoxy ever produced.[5]

That claim is rather provocative. While Hamann is widely acknowledged as a critic of the Enlightenment, the Lutheran theological foundations for his metacritical project are either overlooked out of embarrassment or else disregarded in a vain attempt to appropriate him.

---

3. Joseph Nadler, ed., *Johann Georg Hamann: Sämtliche Werke*, 1–6 (Wien: Herder Verlag, 1949–57).

4. For Kierkegaard, see Walter Lowrie, *Johann Georg Hamann: An Existentialist* (Princeton, NJ: Princeton Theological Seminary, 1950), and Ronald Gregor Smith, *J. G. Hamann: A Study in Christian Existence with Selections from His Writings* (London: Collins, 1960). For Barth, W. M. Alexander, *Johann Georg Hamann: Philosophy and Faith* (The Hague: Matinus Nijhoff, 1966). See Walter Leibrecht, *God and Man in the Thought of Hamann* (Philadelphia: Fortress, 1966) for an excellent assessment of Hamann as well as for a critique of his appropriation by existentialism and neoorthodoxy. For postmodernism, see Oswald Bayer, *A Contemporary in Dissent: Johann Georg Hamann as a Radical Enlightener* (Grand Rapids: Eerdmans, 2012), and Betz, *After Enlightenment*, 2012.

5. Betz, "Hamann's London Writings," 191–92.

Contemporary interest in Hamann focuses on him as a critic of the Enlightenment with its rationalism and its promotion of individual autonomy. Broadly speaking, scholars paid attention to four main topics of Hamann's writings: the correlation of language and thought;[6] the nature of people as embodied beings with integrated physical, mental, and spiritual powers;[7] the role of the senses and the perceptive imagination in all human knowledge;[8] and God's self-revelation as Father, Son, and Holy Spirit by condescension in creation, redemption, and the inspiration of sacred Scripture.[9] The key to his thinking on these topics and all his other concerns is provided by his *London Writings*, for all the issues that he later pursues less directly and more enigmatically in his literary work are already expressed embryonically and explicitly in them. They show us the whole man with his whole vision of human life with God in its cosmic context.

The growing interest in Hamann's criticism of the Enlightenment has led to an increased appreciation of his *London Writings* for their articulation of foundations for his life and thought as a man of letters. Like the *Confessions* of Augustine, they are not just of value historically but also existentially for orientation in our so-called postmodern context. Thus Oswald Bayer and Bernd Weissenborn quite rightly claim: "*The London Writings* are a religious, cultural, literary-historical, philosophical, and theological source that is first-class in its significance."[10] Since up to now we have had no complete translation of these writings in English, this publication serves to fill that gap.

---

6. See Leibrecht, *God and Man*, 39–55; Terrence German, *Hamann on Language and Religion* (Oxford: Oxford University Press, 1981); James C. O'Flaherty, *"Language and Reason in the Thought of Johann Georg Hamann," Lutheran Quarterly*, no. 4 (1988): 457-75; Katie Terezakis, "Words and the Word: J. G. Hamann, Trojan Horse at the Gates of the Enlightenment," *Edinburgh Critical History of Christian Theology*, Daniel Whistler, ed. (Edinburgh: Edinburgh University Press, 2017).

7. See Leibrecht, *God and Man*, 83–144, and Julia Goesser Assaiante, *Body Language: Corporeality, Subjectivity, and Language in Johann Georg Hamann* (New York: Peter Lang, 2011).

8. See Hans Urs von Balthasar, *The Glory of the Lord: A Theological Aesthetics* (Edinburgh: T&T Clark, 1986), 3, 239–78, and Knut Alfsvåg, "Imagination and Critique in the Work of Johann Georg Hamann," *Mishkan*, 80 (2019): 68–80.

9. See Leibrecht, *God and Man*, 33–38, Alexander, *Johann Georg Hamann*, 25–37, and John R. Betz, "Hamann's London Writings," and "Glory(ing) in the Humility of the Word: The Kenotic Form of Revelation in J. G. Hamann," *Letter & Spirit* 6 (2010): 141–79.

10. This and subsequent quotations are translated from Oswald Bayer and Bernd Weissenborn, eds., *Johann Georg Hamann. Londoner Schriften, Historisch-kritische Neuedition* (München: C. H. Beck, 1993), 10.

Despite their historical significance, these reflections by Hamann are, for me, much more personal than academic, because they teach me, and others like me, how to read the Bible as my story, a story which interprets me and my life, the story that shows me who I really am rather than who I fancy I am. In the present cultural context with its disdain for the Christian faith, Hamann's remarks address my spiritual ignorance and personal blindness. They bamboozle me and confound my expectations; they expose my fashionable prejudices and pretensions and subvert my secular mentality with its moralistic self-righteousness; they present me with a new, whole vision of myself as God sees me and invite me to embark with him in a journey of self-discovery by my discovery of God by listening to him. They do not just call me to reconfigure myself and transform the way I live, but actually reorient and reform me. In a social culture that prizes its supposed 'wokeness' and takes pride in its assumed rational expertise, Hamann's confessions and meditations bring me down to earth and humble me. They address God's self-revealing words to me personally to awaken, enliven, and enlighten me, in body and mind, in soul and spirit, by faith in God's hidden glory and gracious presence with me. They open my eyes to see myself and others and the world around me as God does.

"THE STORY OF MY OWN LIFE" THE ORIGIN AND PURPOSE OF THE *LONDON WRITINGS*

Hamann lived from 1730 to 1788 and spent most of his life in the city of Königsberg, the German-speaking administrative and academic center of East Prussia, which has been renamed Kaliningrad and is now part of Russia. Born to parents of modest means, he had a rather conventional Lutheran upbringing with a father who was largely orthodox in orientation and a mother who was influenced by Lutheran pietism.

He studied theology and the law in the local university, where he became a fashionable advocate of the Enlightenment with his two best friends, Christoph Berens and Johann Gotthelf Lindner. He admits that his own interest lay elsewhere than in the study of theology and law: "What took away my taste for theology and all serious subjects was a new inclination that awoke in me for antiquities, for critical analysis; for the fine, decorative arts as well; for poetry, novels, philology; for French authors and their talent for writing, painting, portraying, pleasing the imagination, and so on."[11] Due to his haphazard attendance of classes, his pursuit of extracurricular activities, and a speech impediment that precluded a career as a pastor or a lawyer, he failed to graduate. Yet all the time he kept on reading widely and voraciously.

After employment as a tutor for two German noble families from 1752 to 1756 in what is now Latvia, he was employed in Riga as a secretary of a merchant firm owned by the family of his best friend Christoph Berens and sent on a secret trade mission to London to negotiate a trade deal for the firm between Russia and England in 1757. When that failed, he lived rather dissolutely, fell into the bad company of a fashionable homosexual circle, and got deep into debt. Lost and lonely, he suffered from ill health from overindulgence, deep depression from his friendless social isolation, and spiritual desolation. Then, befriended by a devout Christian couple who provided cheap accommodation for him early in 1758, he went into social seclusion. He began to read some of the many books he had bought and found little consolation in them for his great distress. The most significant of these was a collection of religious poetry by Edward Young (1681–1765) called *Night Thoughts*,[12] which he learned about from reading *Meditations and Contemplations* by James Hervey (1714–1758). Young's combination of devout piety and deep emotion touched him. On impulse he bought an English Bible and set out to read it on March 13, "with more attention, in a more orderly way, and with more hunger."[13] And the more he read, the more he experienced its divine content and effect.

For the first six days, its impact on him was largely intellectual, giving him a deep awareness of the Bible's unity in Christ and his redemption of the human soul. As Hamann read it intently and attentively, he became aware of the veil over his reason and his heart, a veil that had closed this book to him, a veil that had made him blind and deaf to it.[14] Then, on Palm Sunday, March 19, 1758, it struck him that as he was reading the Bible God

11. "Thoughts on the Course of My Life," 339.

12. "Biblical Meditations," 8.

13. "Thoughts on the Course of My Life," 362.

14. "Thoughts on the Course of My Life," 362.

was speaking to him personally.[15] Instead of analyzing it critically, he began to meditate on the Bible as it critiqued him and his rationalism. On that day he began to read it for a second time in a new way, and wrote down the results of his meditations in a kind of spiritual journal that he called "The Biblical Meditations of a Christian." On Friday evening, March 31, in the week of Easter, he fell into a deep reverie as he was reading Deuteronomy chapter 5, which reported that the Israelites at Mount Sinai heard God speaking the Decalogue face to face with them. Here is how Hamann describes what happened to him then:

> I recognized my own offenses in the history of the Jewish people. I read the story of my own life and thanked God for his forbearance with this his people, because nothing but such an example could justify a similar hope for me. ... In the midst of these reflections, which seemed rather mysterious to me, I read the fifth chapter of the Fifth Book of Moses[16] on the evening of 31 March and fell into deep meditation. I thought about Abel and God's word about him: "the earth had *opened its mouth* to receive your *brother's blood*."[17] I felt my heart thump, I heard a voice groaning and wailing in its depths like the voice of blood, like the voice of a murdered brother, who wanted to avenge his blood, even though I, at times, did not hear it and continued to shut my ears to it. It said that this was what made Cain restless and unable to escape.[18] At once I felt my heart flowing, it poured itself out in tears, and I could no longer hide from God that I was the killer of my brother, the murderer of his only begotten Son.[19] Despite my great weakness, despite the long resistance which I had, until now, put up against his witness and his tender touch, the Spirit of God kept on revealing to me, still more and more, the mystery of divine love and the benefit of faith in our gracious, only Savior.[20]

15. "Biblical Meditations," 6–9.

16. That is, Deuteronomy. The fifth chapter of Deuteronomy repeats the Ten Commandments.

17. Gen 4:11.

18. Gen 4:12. Here Hamann diverges from Luther's translation by replacing *flüchtig*, fleeing, being a fugitive, with *unflüchtig*, unable to flee, unable to escape.

19. John 1:14.

20. "Thoughts on the Course of My Life," 363–64.

In that momentous upheaval, that dramatic spiritual awakening, Hamann was convicted of two things: his own sin of fratricide and God's grace for him as the murderer of his Son. Then in his broken heart he heard how the blood of Jesus, which called out to God for vengeance, was also proclaiming God's grace and love to him there. That broke his blind, hard, rocky, misguided, stubborn heart, and he surrendered it to God for recreation by his Spirit. God poured him out, he says, "from one container into another."[21]

Hamann's awakening with its spiritual transformation may seem to be too sudden to be credible. Yet that is not so at all! On the one hand, his personal, moral collapse prepared him physically, mentally and morally for it. It turned him in his despair away from himself to Jesus as his only hope for recovery. On the other hand, the extent of his biblical knowledge and the depth of his theological insights were grounded in his initial study of theology as well as Greek and Hebrew at high school and the university before he switched over to law. His spiritual awakening therefore transformed his former theoretical knowledge of Christian doctrine by his personal experience of it.

After that event Hamann continued to read the Bible receptively and recorded the fruit of his meditations in an outburst of creative energy. Then, when he had completed the "Biblical Meditations," he recorded the "Thoughts on the Course of my Life" from April 21–25; followed by "Thoughts on Church Hymns" from April 29 to May 6; a sermon, "Deuteronomy 30:11–14 together with Romans 10:4–10," on Sunday, May 7; "Fragments" on May 16; and the undated "Meditations on Newton's Study on Prophecies" as well as the first part of "Further Thoughts on the Course of my Life" before he left London by sea on June 27 and arrived at Riga on July 16. There he added some further thoughts on his life and an undated personal prayer of supplication and intercession for his own devotional use.

This collection of documents that make up the *London Writings* were never meant for publication, nor did Hamann ever publish them. He wrote them primarily for himself as a personal account to document his spiritual reorientation. But he also intended to share some if not all of their contents with his father and brother, as well as his two best friends Berens and

21. "Thoughts on the Course of My Life," 365.

Lindner, to explain how and why he had changed.[22] We do not know what his father and brother thought of them, but we do know that his best friend and employer Berens was most alarmed when he read what Hamann had written. In fact, Hamann's *Schwärmerei*, his tasteless, irrational religious fanaticism nauseated Berens. This is how Hamann defends himself against Berens's charges of neurotic, self-righteous misanthropy in a letter to his brother:

> God does not wish to hear us, to receive us, and to know us except in his Son. ... I write to you not as an enthusiast [*Schwärmer*], not as a Pharisee, but as a brother, who could not love you as long as he did not know and love God; but who now wishes you well with all his heart, and since he has learned to pray, will not forget to pray for you too. ... One's heart loves one's brothers through God alone. ... If we do not know Jesus, we have come no further than the pagans. As the apostle James says, all miracles, all mysteries, and all works of faith and true religion are united in the worthy name by which we are called Christians. This worthy name, by which we are called, is the only key of knowledge, which opens the heaven and the hell, the heights and the depths, of the human heart. ... Now I live in the world with pleasure and with a light heart, and know that godliness holds promise for this life and the life to come, and that it is useful for all things (1 Tim 4:8). Since I have come to know God's Word as the medicine, as the wine, which alone is able to make our heart glad and our face to shine with oil, as the bread that strengthens the heart of man, I am neither a misanthrope, nor a hypochondriac, nor an accuser of my brethren, nor an Ishmael of divine providence.[23]

The result of that clash with Berens was that Hamann failed to gain permission to marry Berens's sister Katharina and ceased to be employed by the Berens family merchant firm in Riga.

In late 1759 Hamann returned to Königsberg to live with his widowed father and his housekeeper Anna Regina Schumacher, an uneducated

---

22. "Thoughts on the Course of My Life," 365.

23. Henkel and Ziesemer, ed., *Briefwechsel*, 1, 242–43. This translation is taken from Betz, *After Enlightenment*, 32–33.

peasant girl who eventually became Hamann's common law wife. There he lived until his retirement in 1787. After a period of extensive reading and intense study to consolidate his spiritual reorientation, some short-lived jobs, and further travel, he eventually gained steady employment as a civil servant with the Prussian government. He began to work as a clerk in the taxation office in 1767 and then became the superintendent of the customs office from 1777 to his retirement in 1787.

Hamann's career as a man of letters began in 1759. It was triggered by the negative reception of his *London Writings*. His best friend, Christoph Berens, was so disgusted by Hamann's religious fanaticism and its apparent rejection of reason that he enlisted the help of their mutual friend, the philosopher Immanuel Kant, to knock some sense into Hamann's brainwashed mind and reclaim him to their common cause. That project was an utter failure. It was, in fact, counterproductive, for it showed how little they had in common spiritually, even though they seemed to be very much on the same page intellectually. This effort was the catalyst for Hamann's first major publication, the *Socratic Memorabilia,* and his subsequent work as an ironic, provocative critic—or, to use his own term, a *metacritic* of what we now know as the Enlightenment.[24]

"THIS ORBIT AND ITS COURSE"[25] THE NATURE OF THE *LONDON WRITINGS*

On a cursory reading, it is hard to discover the nature and unity of the *London Writings*. They vary so greatly in every respect that it is not obvious what kind of texts they are and how they cohere. Each is written in a different genre for a different purpose. They differ greatly in length, from two pages, in the case of "On the Interpretation of Sacred Scripture," to 256 pages, in the case of "Biblical Meditations." Taken together, the *London Writings* are what we would now call a spiritual journal—the product of reading the Bible and in one case a theological text, as well as the product of meditation and prayer. All of them are personal devotional exercises.

24. For a more extensive summary of Hamann's life and career as a man of letters, see James C. O'Flaherty, *Johann Georg Hamann* (Boston: Twayne, 1979), 17–33.

25. See "Thoughts on the Course of My Life," 370.

It is also hard to discover any external and internal coherence in these nine disparate devotional documents. To be sure, there are common themes and concerns that recur without any formal correlation. As F. H. Jacobi, one of the first readers who recognized their unique value, observed, there is also a common spirit that pervades them. Yet, more evidently, there are two markers which show how they are interrelated.

The first and most obvious of these are the chronological notes, which relate most of the writings sequentially to three months in Hamann's life before and after his so-called conversion, the spiritual reorientation of his soul around God and his word. Thus, after commencing with a new way of reading the Bible on March 13, 1758, he writes the "Biblical Meditations of a Christian" from March 19–April 21. After that, he pens "Thoughts on the Course of my Life" from April 21–24 and composes his "Thoughts on Church Hymns" from April 29–May 6. Then he starts work on "Fragments" on May 16 and continues his autobiographical journal on May 29. So the writings are all related to his personal, spiritual transformation over that period in his life.

There is also another deeper chronology along with this outward chronicle of events, a chronology that has to do with the parallel, more hidden dimension to his inner life. This is shown by Hamann's correlation of his reading and writing with certain significant times in the liturgical calendar. Thus he begins his meditative reading of the Bible on the Monday after Judica, the Fifth Sunday in Lent, and starts writing his "Biblical Meditations" on Palm Sunday. He interrupts their sequence with an extended meditation on the Sermon on the Mount on Maundy Thursday, passes over Exodus entirely, and considers Leviticus on Good Friday. Then on Friday, March 31, in the week of Easter, he comes to Deuteronomy 5 and experiences his spiritual awakening on the evening of that day. On Saturday, the eve of the Fifth Sunday after Easter, he begins his "Thoughts on Church Hymns" and interrupts them on Ascension Day to pen a moving meditation on a Christian's involvement in Christ's condescension and exaltation. Then come the composition of "Fragments" on Tuesday in the week of Pentecost and the continuation of his journal on the Monday after Trinity Sunday. In this way, Hamann reconnects his life once again, after some interruption, with the life of the church and the life of Christ. His spiritual reorientation results in the exercise of liturgical piety. That is evident in his report of his association with the German Lutheran congregation in London and its Pastor J. R. Pitius,[26] as well as his participation in the Lord's Supper in his home congregation on the second Sunday in Advent after a session of private confession with Pastor Essen on the previous evening.[27] It is also evident in his numerous reflections on a wide range of Lutheran hymns.[28] As a result of his spiritual reawakening, he is once again at home in the liturgical life of the Lutheran Church.

In a letter to Lindner on March 9, 1759, Hamann claimed that in his spiritual life he was nourished by three books: the Bible, the hymnal with its liturgical texts, and Luther's Small Catechism.[29] He alluded to God's command to the prophet Ezekiel to eat the scroll that God had set before him and fill his stomach with it (Ezek 3:1–3). When the prophet ate that scroll, it tasted as sweet as honey. In an echo of this symbolic event, Hamann claimed that these three books were his *Leibbücher,* his "body-books," and his *Magenbücher,* his "belly-books." They sustained him bodily with God's Spirit and fed him physically with heavenly food. They were the mainstay of his piety, an incarnate piety that was as physical as it was spiritual, a scriptural, catechetical, liturgical piety that he had previously learned in its outward observance at home, at school, and at church, and now appropriated inwardly for himself.

So, taken as a whole, the *London Writings* are devotional texts, the product of intense meditation on God's word and reception of it in ardent prayer. They document the U-turn in his life from fashionable rationalism to orthodox Christianity. The turning point came for him with intense prayer for God's help in his distress. Thus Hamann says:

> In the tumult of all my passions, which so overwhelmed me that often I could often hardly breathe, I kept on praying to God for a friend, a wise, sincere friend, such as I could no longer envisage. Instead of that, I had tasted, tasted enough, the bitterness of false friendship and

---

26. "Thoughts on the Course of My Life," 370, and "Further Thoughts," 457.

27. "Further Thoughts," 463.

28. See "Thoughts on Church Hymns," 371–423.

29. Henkel and Ziesemer, *Briefwechsel*, 1, 293.

> the unlikelihood of a better friendship. A friend who could give me a key to my heart, the thread that would lead me out of my labyrinth, was a wish that I often had, without understanding and discerning its content rightly.[30]

In answer to those prayers, he was transformed in two ways. On one hand, as he described it, the inner veil that had previously covered his heart and blinded his reason was removed.[31] He began to hear what God was saying to him, see what God was showing him, and receive what God was giving him as he read and meditated on God's word. On the other hand, he became aware of another threefold kind of speaking in his own heart: the voice of his murdered brother Jesus interceding for him like an angel with God the Father; the voice of the Holy Spirit that prompted and helped him to pray as it prayed on his behalf; and the voice of his own conscience, his heart, in its groaning and sighing.[32] So he became a man of prayer by meditating on God's energizing, life-giving, enlightening word and receiving the Spirit of prayer.[33]

Since Hamann discovered for himself how the inspired word of God inspired him with the Holy Spirit, who, in turn, inspired him to pray to God the Father in the name of Jesus with the help of the Holy Spirit,[34] meditation on God's word and prayer are the two main drivers in the composition of these texts. This is reflected in their arrangement and sequence. They begin with a reflection on how to read the Bible followed by meditation on the whole of it in the light of his own experience,[35] and they end with a comprehensive petitionary and intercessory prayer.[36] But they do not just end in prayer. Again and again, the various meditations turn into short exclamatory prayers[37] as well as extended intercessions and supplications.[38]

30. "Thoughts on the Course of My Life," 362.

31. "Thoughts on the Course of My Life," 362.

32. "Thoughts on the Course of My Life," 363–64.

33. See "Biblical Meditations," 154.

34. See "Thoughts on the Course of My Life," 363–64.

35. "On the Interpretation of Sacred Scripture," 1–2, and "Biblical Meditations," 6–15.

36. "Prayer," 469–75.

37. See, for example, pages 7, 15–16, 63, 90, 91, 113, 339, 345, 433 of this volume.

38. See pages 81–82, 90, 91, 327, 367, 403–5, 466–67, 471–76 of this volume.

An understanding of the *London Writings* as a spiritual journal helps explain four of their noteworthy features. The first is the recurrence of emphatic textual devices, such as underlining certain words, phrases, and sentences and the sidelining of paragraphs and sentences for later reconsideration. The use of underlining and sidelining mark significant passages for further reflection and meditation, and this translation renders them with italics.

The second feature is the repeated use of unmarked scriptural quotations and allusions. They require readers to identify them, read them carefully in their context, and consider how they apply. This causes the readers also to meditate on God's word, the word of the Spirit, so that it will produce what God desires to impart to them or do for them. The Spirit transforms the analytical, critical reader into a receptive reader and hearer.

The third feature is the common use of exclamation and exclamatory sentences to evoke consideration, amazement, and astonishment in the reader. The most common device is the use of a "how" clause or sentence, as in "How good is that!" or "We see how good that is!" These exclamations incite a mental or emotional response. Most commonly, Hamann uses them to evoke the sense of sight and the insights that come from perceptive seeing. Since these exclamations seem rather odd to our ears, I have translated many of them by adding "We see how," or using some other verb of perception.

The fourth related feature is the recurrent appeal to the imagination with biblical imagery that engages the five senses physically and mentally, with particular emphasis on the sense of sight.[39] Hamann repeatedly shifts his and our attention away from the abstract, general ideas in the text to its concrete pictures, its particular imagery, hence his fascination with narrative rather than intellectual explanations,[40] as well as his musings on the stories in the Bible and their application to the story of his own life. Thus Hamann does not speak about these meditations as reflections on biblical texts but as *Betrachtungen*, contemplations of them. As he reads the Scriptures, he

39. The term that Hamann uses for imagination is *Einbildungskraft*, distinguishing it as a perceptive power from fantasy, the ability to visualize what does not exist. For a useful discussion on the role of imagination in Hamann's thinking, see Knut Alfsvåg, "Imagination and Critique in the Work of Johann Georg Hamann," *Mishkan* 80 (February 2019): 68–80.

40. "Biblical Meditations," 12–15.

focuses on their divinely inspired imagery, their symbolism and typology, because it shows how God reveals himself to sensory people analogically in sensory terms. He meditates on the Bible's use of sense-images, the *Sinnbilder* in them,[41] for the revelation of the mysteries that the Holy Spirit reveals to the soul, things that are grounded in sensory perception and yet transcend all human conception, things that engage and yet surpass human imagination even when they speak most directly to the needy human soul. Thus he maintains:

> I confess that the understanding of this book and faith in its contents can therefore be gained by no other means than through the same Spirit who inspired its authors and that his unutterable sighs which he creates in our hearts are of the same nature as the inexpressible images that are scattered throughout Holy Scripture with a greater richness than all the seeds of the natural world and its realms.[42]

For Hamann, the images in the Bible are far richer and much more productive for the enlightened imagination than all that we perceive in the natural world. They are not disclosed by the exercise of natural reason, but discerned by the sighs for what they offer and display. By the sighs that are produced by the Holy Spirit, the reader seeks and gains enrichment from them. It is as if the visual depiction of plain nutritious food not only aroused the appetite for it, but also satisfied the appetite. In keeping with his goal of giving what people need rather than what they fancy, God shows his glory and his grace to them in humble, physical imagery,[43] in what seems trivial and insignificant, lowly and foolish, dishonorable and tasteless to intellectual and spiritual snobbery.[44]

---

41. The German term *Sinnbild* is now almost only taken to mean a symbol, but Hamann still uses it more literally and concretely for a "sense-picture," an image perceived by one or all of the five senses.

42. "Thoughts on the Course of My Life," 366.

43. "Fragments," 442.

44. See also "Biblical Meditations," 204–5: "Scripture cannot speak to us humans except in parables because all our knowledge is sensory and figurative. ... Apart from this consideration, we see that God was pleased to hide his counsel with us and reveal as much to us as is necessary for our redemption and our comfort, but, at the same time, in a way that would deceive the clever people of the world, its masters. Thus, as the apostle says, God has made the worthless, despised things, yes, the things that are nothing, instruments of secret counsel and hidden will."

Our access to what the divinely inspired Scriptures offer us depends on our imaginative empathy, our ability to put ourselves in the shoes of its authors and to see them with their eyes. That ability is received through prayer for the Holy Spirit and his enlightenment. Thus Hamann maintains:

> As readers we need to put ourselves with our perceptions into the perceptions of the writer that we have before us and to match his frame of mind as much as possible. We can gain this for ourselves through the felicitous power of the imagination, by which a poet or a historian tries, as much as possible, to help us.[45]

To read the Scriptures with that kind of imagination, we need to pray for the same Spirit that inspired them. We need to have the right frame of mind—a spiritually enlightened imagination. By faithful contemplation of the imagery in the Scriptures, readers learn to see themselves as a whole in relation to God and others in the visible and invisible world. They become truly enlightened as they see what the text is saying to them and about them. And more than that! Their whole self, their whole body and soul with all their senses, is renewed and nourished, enlivened and energized, enlightened and transfigured. Thus while many of his contemporaries tried to construct a comprehensive system of knowledge out of their calculations and abstractions, an encyclopedic system that explained everything, Hamann pursued a vision of human life in its cosmic context as revealed by God and his Spirit through three books: the book of God's word, the book of nature, and the book of human history. And the key to that vision was God's word, for apart from it neither nature nor history could be deciphered—let alone each human soul in its misery and glory! By God's word we not only see what God says but we come to see everything in its light. With God as its center, the human soul regains its proper orbit, like the earth and the moon around the sun.[46]

---

45. "Biblical Meditations," 8.

46. See his claim in "Thoughts on the Course of My Life," 370: "If our soul first finds its center in him, then it no longer abandons him in its motion. It remains true to him, like the earth with the sun, and all other inclinations are governed, like the moon, by the original, proper influence of this orbit and its course."

The basic contours of Hamann's vision are painted in radiant shape and vivid color in a sermonic meditation on 1 Corinthians 4:9 for Ascension Day in the 'Thoughts on Church Hymns."[47] It is a vision of the exalted Lord Jesus and the exaltation of Christians with him and his human nature in a dramatic enactment in the theater of the cosmos and the new stage of the human soul for display to the world, the angels, and all humanity. It is a vision of human humiliation and transfiguration in and through God's incarnate Son. That vision undergirds and pervades all his published works, which begin with the admission of his ignorance in *Socratic Memorabilia* (1759) and culminate in the acknowledgement of his hidden participation in God's glory in *Disrobing and Transfiguration* (1786).

"AN ARCHIPELAGO"[48] THE KEY METAPHORS AND THEMES OF THE *LONDON WRITINGS*

Unlike many of his contemporaries, Hamann is not a systematic thinker, nor does he privilege systematic thought with its abstractions as a superior kind of knowledge.[49] He is, if you like, not concerned with the big picture provided by a comprehensive theory, a geometrical model, or an encyclopedia, but with little pictures full of particular, relevant details that are perceived by the eyes and discerned by the imagination. Yet what he says does have an intricate, organic coherence, like the apparent disorder in the natural world. Thus, what he says about the Scriptures also applies to what he himself has written:

> All methods of interpretation should be regarded as the handcarts of reason and its crutches. The imagination of a poet has a thread that is invisible to the common eye and appears to be a masterpiece to experts. All hidden artifice is governed by the nature of the

47. "Thoughts on Church Hymns," 398–405.

48. "Socratic Memorabilia," 2, 61, with an English translation from Gwen Griffith Dickson, *Johann Georg Haman's Relational Metacriticism* (Berlin: Gruyter, 1995), 379.

49. See his letter to Lindner, 1759, Henkel and Ziesemer, *Briefwechsel* 1, 29–30, 431: "I am not up to universal 'truths, fundamental principles, systems.' Instead I am up to crumbs, fragments, whims, thoughts."

> imagination. In this respect Sacred Scripture is the best example and finest touchstone for all human criticism.[50]

We cannot therefore discover the big picture Hamann sees apart from its partial disclosure in the little pictures he paints for us.

Hamann once noted that the things he had written were like islands in an archipelago.[51] Even though he as a writer did not build bridges to take us from one thought to another, we must nevertheless presuppose that they have an invisible connection, hidden, as it were, under the sea. As readers we must make our own mental bridges between them by ascertaining how they belong together and why. So, like the editor of the collection of sayings in the book of Proverbs, Hamann does not tell us what to think, but makes us think about something critically, constructively, and practically, within a given frame of reference.

Hamann, somewhat ironically, referred to his *London Writings* as a *Geschmier*.[52] This unflattering German term combines three pictures: the scrawling of an unpracticed writer, the daubing of paint by an apprentice painter on a canvas, and the greasing of the wheels of a carriage or a cart to make it run more smoothly. The image that is most revealing for me is of Hamann as a painter. In the *London Writings* he uses words to paint a picture of his impressions, so that we not only see what he sees, but also see as he sees. But that requires a discerning eye and a sharp mind with an enlightened imagination.

Since Hamann is not an abstract, systematic philosopher but an intuitive, analogical thinker,[53] it would be unhelpful and presumptuous to isolate some ideas and themes from the abundance of thoughts and pictures on many different topics in the *London Writings,* as if they were the key to understanding them. Instead of doing that, I shall highlight four key biblical metaphors and analogies that govern what Hamann says in his written meditations on the Bible and his life as a Christian.

---

50. "Biblical Meditations," 297–98.

51. "Socratic Memorabilia," 2, 61.

52. See his letter to Lindner on March 21, 1761, in Henkel and Ziesemer, *Briefwechsel* 2, 75.

53. See the perceptive discussion by O'Flaherty, *Johann Georg Hamann*, 82–99.

The first metaphor is the picture of God as an author, the writer of a story.[54] Since he is the creator of heaven and earth, he is not just one of many authors but the only true author. He is the author of two great books: the book of nature, which includes the book of history;[55] and his own book, the Bible, the book of God.[56] While God is the anonymous author of the first book, he puts his name to the second book, even though he coauthors it with certain chosen human writers who write it under the inspiration of his Holy Spirit. It is therefore also the book of the Spirit, for he is the Spirit of this word.[57] Since these two books tell the same story from two different points of view, they do not contradict each other.[58]

By itself, the book of nature is sealed because it does not show how God is its author and the actor in it. The other book, God's own book, unseals the book of nature. It discloses the heart of nature and the heart of God as its creator.[59] Even though both books are commentaries on God's word,[60] the book of nature requires God's written word to unlock it and open it up for people to see it as God's creation. Hamann says:

> All natural phenomena are dreams, visions, riddles, which have their meaning, their secret sense. The book of nature and the book of history are nothing but ciphers, hidden signs, which require the same key that interprets Holy Scripture and is the purpose of its inspiration.[61]

The same Spirit that created the natural world and inspired the Bible unseals the book of nature for the human observer.[62]

In his book, the Bible, God does not present himself as its omniscient author who is remote from the plot of the story and uninvolved in its

54. "On the Interpretation of Scripture," 1; "Biblical Meditations," 8–11.

55. "Biblical Meditations," 8-9, 137, 153, 191; "Fragments," 442–43

56. "Thoughts on the Course of My Life," 362–63.

57. "On the Interpretation of Scripture," 1; "Biblical Meditations," 111–12, 178, 307.

58. "Biblical Meditations," 8–9.

59. "Biblical Meditations," 153–54.

60. "Fragments," 442.

61. "Fragments," 448.

62. "Biblical Meditations," 191.

implementation. He is the central character in his book, the main actor and speaker in it, even though he is not presented as such but only as one of many actors. This how Hamann invites us to envisage the involvement of the Triune God in that story:

> Consider how God the Father has humbled himself by not only forming a lump of earth but also giving it a soul with his breath. Consider how God the Son has humbled himself—he became a man, became the least of all people and took on the form of a servant; he became the most hapless of them; he was made sin for us; in God's eyes he was the sinner of the whole people. Consider how low God the Holy Spirit has condescended by becoming a historian of the smallest, most contemptible, most insignificant incidents on earth, so as to reveal the mysteries and ways of God to mankind in its own speech, its own history, and in its own ways.[63]

In the Bible God reveals the highest mysteries in the most lowly, least divine, and most human terms, for the main character in it is Jesus, God's incarnate Son, the perfect man who is God's image and likeness and also the worst of all sinners, because he bears the sins of the world. Jesus translates what God has to say into ordinary human speech, using language that he himself has borrowed from us. This means that even though the Bible is God's book, it is open to human criticism for its supposed omissions and apparent imperfections.[64]

The setting of the action is on two stages. On one hand, the general action of the story is set on the world as its stage with Jesus as the main character and all the angels and all people as spectators, actors, and scriptwriters.[65] On the other hand, that general action is matched by what happens personally in the soul of the believer.[66] Hamann says:

63. "Biblical Meditations," 118.

64. "Biblical Meditations," 9–10.

65. "Thoughts on Church Hymns," 398.

66. For a discussion of this theme, see Oswald Bayer, "God as the Author of My Life History," *Lutheran Quarterly* 15 (2001): 45–58.

> I am convinced that every soul is a stage for the great wonders that are contained in the history of creation and the entire Holy Scripture. The course of the life of every Christian is included in the daily work of God, in his covenants with people, in transgressions, warnings, revelations, miraculous preservations, and so on. For a Christian, who has passed from the death of sin into a new life, can the preservation of Jonah, the raising of Lazarus, the healing of the cripple, and so on be conceived as greater miracles? Does not the Savior himself say: "Which is easier, to forgive sins or to say: take up your bed and walk?"[67]

These two plots come together in Jesus and his redemption, for "all history, all miracles, all the commandments and works of God converge at this central point, in order to lead the human soul out of the slavery, bondage, blindness, folly, and death of sin to the greatest happiness, the highest blessedness, and a reception of such good gifts that their greatness, when they are revealed to us, must shock us more than our own unworthiness or the possibility of making ourselves worthy of them."[68]

The second metaphor is the picture of divine condescension. The German term for this is *Herablassung*. It describes an act by which a person in a high position with superior knowledge and power leaves that place to sit down on the ground with lowly people to interact with them in their own terms, like a mother with her baby. That is what the Triune God does for the benefit of human beings, without showing off to them and patronizing them in any way. The paradigm for this is the story of the tower of Babel in Genesis 11:1–9.[69] Even though the human race wanted to ascend into heaven on the tower of reason to make a great name for itself, the Triune God descends from heaven to earth to meet with them there. His condescension is the only means by which they can approach him.

The Bible tells the great story of divine condescension, the condescension of God the Father in creation, God the Son in his incarnation, and God the Holy Spirit in the inspiration of the Bible. In his notes on how to interpret

---

67. "Deuteronomy 30:11–14 together with Romans 10:4–10," 432–33.

68. "Thoughts on the Course of My Life," 362–63.

69. "Biblical Meditations," 36–37.

the Scriptures, Hamann maintains: "The inspiration of this book is as great an act of self-effacement and condescension as the creation of the world by the Father and the incarnation of the Son."[70] In the condescension of each separate person of the Trinity, the other two persons are also involved. So, for example, Hamann claims that God the Father was pleased to see himself humbled together with the other persons of the Trinity by his condemnation of his Son in our place and the bestowal of his righteousness and holiness on us, so that there is now no condemnation for us.[71]

God condescended in the creation of Adam. God, as it were, got his hands and mouth dirty by forming him from clay and breathing his own life-breath into him.[72] He interacts with people through people. He condescended to engage personally in his conversation with Abraham in Genesis 18 in order to satisfy his desire for a son, instruct him in his will, and make him an intercessor.[73] With Jacob he condescended to comply with Jacob's conditions for his acceptance of him as his God, without requiring any commitment from him until he had earned the right to it by blessing Jacob with earthly possessions.[74] But, above all else, God condescended by sending his Son and the Holy Spirit as his gift for all people, so that God was humiliated by the shameful death of his only begotten Son for their sin at the instigation of the devil, as well as by the proclamation of his murdered Son as the Prince of Life though the twelve apostles.[75]

The Son condescended to engage with people on earth by his incarnation as a man and his death on the cross. Since that is the heart of the matter, Hamann focuses his attention on it with this challenge: "Consider how God the Son has humbled himself—he became a man, became the least of all people and took on the form of a servant; he became the most hapless of them; he was made sin for us; in God's eyes he was the sinner of the whole people."[76] He could not go any lower than that for us. And it was all for our

70. "Interpretation of Sacred Scripture," 1–2.

71. "Biblical Meditations," 54–55.

72. "Biblical Meditations," 14–15.

73. "Biblical Meditations," 42.

74. "Biblical Meditations," 45–46.

75. "Biblical Meditations," 109–10.

76. "Biblical Meditations," 118.

benefit. He humbled himself to exalt us. Hamann gives this graphic account of that great exchange:

> As the God who condescended to be like us in every way had no place where he could lay his head, and did not enjoy the comforts that the animals looked for in their nests and holes, so the Man had to be raised above all finite creatures, exalted and glorified in God himself. God became a son of man and an heir of his curse and death and fate, so that the man would become a son of God, an only heir of heaven, as closely united with God as the fullness of divinity dwelt bodily in Christ.[77]

This emphasis on the condescension of God's Son is not unique to Hamann. It is quite in keeping with his Lutheran heritage, even though that teaching was largely ignored by his contemporaries who had no interest in and little comprehension of such paradoxes.

The self-effacement and condescension of the Father in creation and of the Son in the incarnation corresponds with the condescension of the Spirit in the inspiration of the Bible.[78] This emphasis comes in large part from Hamann himself. He makes it part of his Trinitarian confession of faith in his biographical sketch where he says: "I confess that for us the Holy Spirit has published a book for his word, in which, like a fool or a madman, yes like an unholy and unclean spirit, he turned proud reason's children's stories, trivial, contemptible events, into the history of heaven and God (1 Cor 1:25)."[79]

In a completely tasteless reversal of expectations, the Holy Spirit chooses to reveal the things of God physically and vernacularly. He discloses the highest mysteries to ordinary people in a lowly way with what seems trivial and insignificant,[80] foolish and insane, dishonorable and despicable to his critics. He translates the language of God and the angels in heaven into humble, vulgar human discourse. God acts in this way because he does not

77. "Thoughts on Church Hymns," 400.

78. Hamann even goes so far as to speak of the incarnation of the Spirit as comparable to the incarnation of God's Son in this way: "God's Spirit, revealed in his word as self-subsisting—in the form of a servant, is flesh—and dwells among us full of grace and truth" (449–50).

79. "Thoughts on the Course of My Life," 336–37.

80. For further discussion about God's choice of apparent trivia to reveal his mysteries, see "Biblical Meditations," 34, 53; "Thoughts on the Course of My Life," 46–47, 68, 165, 369–70.

want to communicate information about himself to satisfy the idle curiosity of philosophers. Instead he uses human words as a physical means of grace to rescue imprisoned people, enlighten blind souls, and confound proud unbelievers.

Hamann explains this most vividly in his notes on the interpretation of the Bible which introduce his *London Writings*.[81] He gives three instances, which show three aspects of this endeavor. Just as Jeremiah was rescued from the muddy cistern that imprisoned him by some old rags that were tied together to form a rope to lift him up out of it (Jer 38:11–13), so people are saved from their spiritual imprisonment by the unpretentious words of God. They are not rescued by looking at these rags but by relying on the help that they offer. Just as Jesus used a salve from spittle and dust and a pool of water to give sight to a man who had been born blind (John 9:6), so the Holy Spirit uses ordinary words and the water of baptism to give spiritual enlightenment. Just as David averted the threat from Achish the Philistine king of Gath by scribbling like a slobbering madman on the doors of the city gate (1 Sam 21:13–15), so the Holy Spirit confounds the critics and enemies of Jesus by deluding them with what look like the scribblings of a spiritually insane person.

What is God's purpose in all this? Hamann maintains:

> God's Spirit has done everything to make us attentive to his speech, to take our reason captive, to win it or confound it. We are too dull to understand all these reminders, or else we despise God's kindness, so that his condescension is completely misunderstood by everybody. We do not take pains to examine what kinds of treasures lie hidden under their manifold coverings and in the earthen jar. Moreover, he wants to let us realize that he has more to show us than the dress that people see him in, and that he has made himself unrecognizable in order to ambush their enemies.[82]

By their condescension and engagement with human beings in human terms, the three persons of the Trinity put on human dress in order to hide themselves from human misconception and misappropriation. This is done

81. "Interpretation of Sacred Scripture," 2.

82. "Biblical Meditations," 154.

for two reasons: to make people faithfully attentive to God's word in order to receive the spiritual treasures that are hidden for them under its human trappings, and to ambush his enemies. God puts on human clothes in creation, redemption, and communication to win human reason for obedience to him or confound it in its unbelief.

By his condescension God accommodates himself to human limitations, weaknesses, and needs. He meets with human beings where they are, to show his love and deliver his gifts to them in a human way. Hamann says:

> God has accommodated and lowered himself as much as possible to human inclinations and notions, yes even to human prejudices and weaknesses. This hallmark of his love for humanity, which fills the whole of Holy Scripture, is the cause of mockery by weak minds who presuppose that they will find some human wisdom in the divine Word, or some satisfaction for their curiosity, their wit, and some agreement with the taste of the time in which they live or the sect to which they belong. No wonder that they find themselves deceived in their conception! No wonder that the Spirit of Scripture is dismissed with the same indifference![83]

The third recurrent metaphor in the *London Writings* is the picture of a spiritual battle that is waged in three locations: in the whole cosmos, on earth in human history, and in the human soul. While much of Hamann's depiction of this battle is conventional, the use of this picture has an apologetic edge to it, because the rationalists of his day were particularly critical of the biblical teaching about the devil as God's opponent. Since they were moralists in their disposition and self-presentation, they interpreted that teaching symbolically as moral instruction about the battle between virtue and vice. At the same time they claimed the moral high ground for themselves and their cause by criticizing the supposed immorality of many things that were depicted in the Old Testament.

In contrast to them, Hamann shows how the Scriptures depict a far greater battle than that. The battle between light and darkness is, in fact, the cosmic battle between God the Creator and Satan the destroyer, the spiritual

83. "Biblical Meditations," 11.

battle between the Holy Spirit and the evil spirit, the earthly battle between the children of God who trust in him and the children of the devil who do not believe in God but rebel against him. It is the battle in human history between the serpent and the offspring of the woman that God himself had prophesied in Genesis 3:16.[84]

Even though the spiritual dimension of life on earth is hidden from human sight, this battle is waged visibly on earth in all human history, from the conflict between Cain and Abel to the conflict between Jesus and his opponents, until it reaches its conclusion with God's final judgment at the end of the world. Hamann therefore maintains: "The hostility of the serpent's offspring against the blessed offspring of the woman runs through all Sacred Scripture with its explanation of the first prophecy and a continual affirmation of it until the time of fulfillment."[85] The spiritual nature of that conflict remains hidden until the Holy Spirit reveals it to believers through the Scriptures. The Spirit shows that what appear to be personal, social, political, and international hostilities are also part of a greater invisible spiritual battle between God and the devil.

God's decree in Genesis 3:16 provides the readers of the Bible with an important key to the story of the whole Bible and their part in it. On one hand, they can thereby distinguish themselves from those people who are the offspring of the Serpent. Yet Hamann does not identify the offspring of the Serpent with any particular nation or race, but with all those who are God's enemies. And that includes those Israelites who are hostile to God and his faithful servants. In all the stories about the people of faith from Abel to the disciples of Jesus, we can see how Satan attacks God's people to destroy their faith in him. In God's defeat of his enemies, we have a preview of the blessings that they will receive from Christ's victory over the Serpent and his offspring.[86] The victory of the woman's offspring over the Serpent's offspring is therefore "the guiding thread of divine revelation."[87] From these stories they can also see how God uses believers to pass judgment on Satan

84. "Biblical Meditations," 88–89. The *London Writings* are full of allusions to this text, which shows how significant it is for Hamann.

85. "Biblical Meditations," 168.

86. "Biblical Meditations," 104–5.

87. "Biblical Meditations," 224.

and his subjects.[88] In his wisdom, God himself even uses the snares that Satan sets for human beings to catch him by redeeming a host of them in a miraculous way, for, by accusing and condemning the sinners that God had pardoned, Satan passes judgment on himself.[89] So, the human family is the tree of knowledge for the spirit world, since by the fall of mankind they too fall and discover their own downfall.[90]

On the other hand, Christians can also discover the nature and destiny of Satan from his human underlings. They "must always consider the offspring of the Serpent and the Serpent himself together with each other."[91] Since each fallen person is a symbol of the fallen angel, the nature and activity of the devil and all evil spirits are revealed in their human subjects. They share the same mentality and the same condemnation by God for the same rebellion against him. God's wisdom has created people as "envoys of higher spirits"; the evil spirits tempt them just as they themselves are tempted, while devout believers enjoy God's grace in defiance of their enemy.[92]

The Holy Spirit provides a human window into the invisible context for all human life on earth through the story of the mysterious battle in the Scriptures between the woman's offspring and the Serpent's offspring. Hamann gives this summary of that encompassing reality:

> So in the Sacred Scriptures God has gathered fruit from our own soil. He has made a choice from it and has turned the perceptions of our own nature, the events that occurred to our own people, into previews, taskmasters, teachers, comforters, and spies. God has allowed everything to happen through people on earth that has happened in heaven and will happen in hell. God has made everything visible that will happen invisibly. In the present times he lets that happen which has happened in the most distant past and that which will happen in the most distant future.[93]

88. "Biblical Meditations," 1-9, 145–47, 230–31.

89. "Biblical Meditations," 204–5.

90. "Biblical Meditations," 119–20.

91. "Biblical Meditations," 119.

92. "Biblical Meditations," 181.

93. "Biblical Meditations," 116–17.

The rationalist readers of the Bible fail to see what it says. They fail to grasp that its imagery is meant to disclose what is invisible in external, sensory, visible terms. So, for example, while they seek to extract the moral kernel in the sayings of Proverbs, the Wisdom of Solomon, and the story of Job, they do not discover the connection of visible things, like the crocodile in Job 41 and the ant in Proverbs 6:6–9, with invisible, spiritual things.[94]

The fourth metaphor that pervades the *London Writings* is the biblical picture of divine advocacy, the speaking of Jesus and the Holy Spirit for people in their hearts.[95] This carries great weight for Hamann, because it is the key to his understanding of his singular spiritual reorientation in London[96] and to his regular devotional life of meditation and prayer.[97] Hamann's use of this image presupposes that, spiritually speaking, each human soul is by nature both deaf and dumb. By itself and unaided by God's word, the soul is unable to articulate what it feels and what it needs from God. It is so burdened and tongue-tied that it cannot pray, let alone articulate its utter woe and its deepest needs. The best it can do is to resort to inarticulate groans and sighs. Like the abyss of the primeval world, in its natural state the soul is shapeless and void, so dark that no one but God can look into it and see what is there.[98] God does not just see but hears the soul's inarticulate cries, just as a mother hears and interprets the cries of her infant child:

> God hears us cry out when the devil seems to titillate us in the midst of our sins. God hears our cries when the sleep and intoxication of sin let us think about nothing but ourselves. He thinks about us even more. He knows our neediness. This need of ours is the cry which God needs to hear us. How wretched would the young ravens themselves be if God would wait so long as to provide their food only when they were starving and began to cry out to him for it. Nothing would grow old enough in the world to be able to use its voice. We would

94. "Biblical Meditations," 204–5.

95. In his discussion of this complex reality, Hamann recalls Job 33:23–28; Rom 8:26–27, 33–34; Heb 7:25; and 1 John 1:9–2:2.

96. "Thoughts on the Course of My Life," 363–64.

97. "Prayer," 469–75.

98. "Biblical Meditations," 102.

> go hungry before our tongue would learn to stammer. As a mother understands the speechless cry of her child, so God feels our hunger and thirst, our nakedness and impurity.[99]

In that situation, Jesus comes to aid the soul with his Holy Spirit to bring light into the deep darkness and order into the inner chaos. He comes in the guise of a voice that arises in the human soul,[100] a voice that Satan tries to silence.[101] Hamann describes it in this way:

> The Word, God's Son, the object of our faith is near—in the mouth! We cannot pray except in his name and in the Spirit of his mouth. Yes, this same Spirit that teaches us to pray gives us the food for our souls and the hunger for him in the divine Word. The Spirit forms him in *our heart*, acts so that Jesus may gain shape there, prepares the heart and voices the sighs that we do not utter and we are unable to utter. So that One is in our mouth and heart in whom we live and move and have our being, and only his Spirit can make the testimony of his love for humankind and our salvation in him so understandable and pleasing to us that we hear it in faith and live by faith according to it.[102]

The voice that is heard in our heart is in fact the combination of three voices: the voice of Jesus, the voice of the Spirit, and the voice of our own conscience. But the main voice is the voice of Jesus. He is our advocate, our inner spokesman, our speech therapist.

By his voice in us, Jesus becomes our advocate, the advocate that the Israelites longed to have, so that they could rightly fear and love God.[103] Jesus turns our sighs into words and our groans into prayers that please him because they ask for what he wants to give us. The voice of Jesus is the voice of his blood that cries out for God to avenge his murder. But in an amazing

---

99. "Biblical Meditations," 106.

100. Hamann says: "Great God, our corrupt nature, in which You have desired to unite and also create heaven and earth, is only all too like chaos in its shapelessness, emptiness, and the darkness that covers the abyss from our eyes, the abyss that is only known by You. ... Through the Spirit from Your mouth and Your Word, turn this waste earth into good, fruitful land, a garden of Your hand" ("Biblical Mediations," 102).

101. "Biblical Meditations," 101.

102. "Deuteronomy & Romans," 432–33.

103. "Thoughts on the Course of My Life," 363.

reversal of expectations, Jesus does not cry out for God's vengeance on us but on himself as our substitute. He therefore sprinkles our hearts with his blood, which cries out to God for pardon and grace and assures us of that. Hamann concludes:

> When we get to know ourselves, when we come to see ourselves almost as we really are, how we then wish, plead, fear for ourselves. How we then feel the need for all that God, without us knowing it, being interested in it, and asking for any of it, has never grown tired of presenting to us, offering to us, and encouraging us, yes, frightening us to receive. Then we hear the blood of the Redeemer crying out in our heart. We feel that the bottom of it has been sprinkled with the blood that was shed for the reconciliation of the whole world. We feel that the blood of vengeance cries out for grace on our behalf.[104]

As our advocate, he does not plead our innocence but his guilt, the guilt that he bears on our behalf before God the Father with the penalty he paid for us by his death. So in answer to his pleading, God has this to say to the human heart, the guilty conscience that fears God's punishment:

> Hear in your heart, in its depths, when My presence comes close enough to you, how the Israelite, an angel, groans, an angel who acknowledges that he is guilty, who beseeches me for grace. I will hear his voice (Deut 5). His words please me. He is an angel who cries out, like the earth which opened its mouth to receive the blood of Abel.[105]

Here the mention of Jesus as an angelic mediator and intercessor recalls Job 33:23–28.

As Hamann notes in his account of his spiritual upheaval, he also heard another voice besides the voice that was "groaning and wailing" in the depths of his heart like the voice of his murdered brother Jesus. It was a voice that reduced him to tears of repentance, the voice of the great Interpreter who translated those sighs and groans into human speech: God's Spirit who "kept on revealing" to him, "still more and more, the mystery of divine love and

104. "Biblical Meditations," 101–2.

105. "Biblical Meditations," 99.

the benefit of faith in our gracious, only Savior."[106] He discovered that the Holy Spirit was "the Spirit of prayer,"[107] the Spirit who did not just help him to pray that night in London but did so regularly. In his consideration of Solomon's prayer of dedication for the temple, he has this to say:

> We, however, can all pray, and must all pray, like Solomon, because this Spirit of prayer is the indispensable blessing and fruit of the faith that the Holy Spirit works in us. The prayer of our King and great High Priest makes all our sighs, no matter how broken, how truncated, how short they may be, just as full, as rich, as powerful as Solomon's rich, royal offering that God accepted.[108]

The intercession of Jesus and the Spirit were so important for Hamann that in his daily prayers he included a petition for Jesus to intercede for him before the Father as well as for the Holy Spirit to prompt him to address God as his Father from his heart, as Jesus did, and turn his inarticulate sighs into heartfelt prayers.[109]

"A REAL TREASURE" THE PUBLICATION OF THE *LONDON WRITINGS*

Like their eventual publication, the survival of Hamann's *London Writings* was somewhat haphazard and accidental. They could easily have been lost for posterity were it not for a rather impulsive decision by his son Michael not to destroy them after the death of his father.

Hamann never intended to have his *London Writings* published. They were written mainly for his own benefit as a kind of journal to document his spiritual enlightenment and transformation.[110] But he also wished to share them with his father and brother as well as his two best friends, Christoph Berens and Johann Lindner, to explain how and why he had changed.[111] We

106. "Thoughts on the Course of My Life," 364–65.

107. See "Biblical Meditations," 122, 136; "Prayer," 154, 171, 473.

108. "Biblical Meditations," 154–55.

109. "Prayer," 473.

110. "Biblical Meditations," 7–8; "Thoughts on the Course of My Life," 365.

111. "Thoughts on the Course of My Life," 365.

do not know how they were regarded by his father and brother, but we do know that his friends were not at all impressed by what he had written. Berens was so disgusted at Hamann's religious fanaticism that he seems to have destroyed his copy. But not so Lindner.

Oddly enough, Hamann himself most likely valued these "scribblings" so lightly that he seems to have either lost his copy or had not even kept a personal copy for himself. Whatever the case, in 1761 Hamann discovered that he no longer possessed these writings when he was sorting out and tidying up his rather extensive library. He then remembered that he had earlier on sent a package to Lindner with all that he had written in London. He therefore wrote to ask Lindner to return the manuscripts, which Lidner did. From then on, they remained in Hamann's possession, though in some disarray, as he himself noted. He left them behind in that state when he traveled to Münster with his son in 1777.

After Hamann's death in 1788, his grief-stricken nineteen-year-old son, Michael, came upon that package when he was sorting out and making an inventory of what his father had left behind. But he failed to recognize its significance, nor was there any reason why he could or should have done so. But he did not discard what was in the package. Instead, on impulse he sent these handwritten papers to his father's friend, the philosopher Friedrich Heinrich Jacobi, for his opinion of them and his decision on what to do with them. Jacobi at once realized how valuable they were. He understood that they belonged together as a single coherent composition and kept them for himself and his friends. He gives this account of them and their value in a letter to the theologian Johann Friedrich Kleuker, a mutual friend, when he sent the manuscripts to him:

> I have now received a complete work by him [Hamann] on the Bible which he wrote over five weeks in London in 1758. During these five weeks he read the whole Bible and wrote down this thick book of his meditations on it. Then immediately after that, he wrote an account of the course of his life up to this time with its complete change of mind. ... As well as that, the meditations [on church hymns] and some short outlines that were made soon thereafter are a real treasure, at least for me. Everywhere in them I find the same spirit, the same

> mentality, the same convictions. The key to it all is God's Spirit which a person must receive. With the Spirit we discover the most persuasive proofs just there where we otherwise see the most insoluble doubts.[112]

Kleuker arranged for two copies to be made, one that ended up in the national library in Berlin via Johann Gottfried Herder, and the other that was lodged in the university library of Keil. Hamann's original text passed from Jacobi to Friedrich Roth for its publication and then via Roth's son to Karl Hermann Gildemeister, and from him to the university library in Königsberg. They are the three basic manuscripts of what we now know as the *London Writings*.

The story of the publication is far too complex and piecemeal to cover in this introduction. Despite his best intentions, Jacobi never found the time to have the *London Writings* published. He agreed to let Friedrich Schlegel publish the introduction to the "Biblical Meditations" up to his comments on Genesis 1:31 in 1813 in his periodical called *Deutsches Museum*, the German Museum. Then Friedrich Roth took over from Jacobi. After Roth had published some extracts from Hamann's "Biblical Meditations" in 1816 to commemorate the tricentenary of the Reformation,[113] he published the first edition of Hamann's works in seven volumes from 1821–25, which contained about a quarter of the material from the *London Writings*.[114] But neither Roth nor Hamman's other nineteenth-century editors ever published the whole of them. Despite increased interest in Hamann as a philosopher rather than a theologian, later scholars continued to pick some bits from what he had written and to ignore other parts. It was only in 1934 that Erwin Metzke identified the collection of documents as a whole and examined all its parts. His prizewinning study on *J. G. Hamann's Place in the Philosophy of the Eighteenth Century*[115] paved the way for the first complete publication of the *London Writings* by Josef Nadler, his monumental critical edition of Hamann's works in six volumes from 1949 to 1957.[116] Nadler's

112. Quoted in BW, 16. My translation.

113. Friedrich von Roth, ed., *Johann Georg Hamanns Betrachtungen über die Heilige Schrift* (Altdorf and Nürnberg, 1816).

114. Friedrich von Roth, ed., *Hamann's Schriften*, vol. 1–6 (Berlin, 1821–24), and vol. 7 (Leipzig, 1825).

115. Erwin Metzke, *J. G. Hamanns Stellung in der Philosophie des 18. Jahrhunderts* (Halle, 1934).

116. Josef Nadler, *Johann Georg Hamann. Sämtliche Werke*, 1–6 (Vienna, 1949–57).

work was complemented and corrected by publication of a new historical critical edition of the *London Writings* in a single volume in 1993 by Oswald Bayer and Bernd Weissenborn. Their meticulous study, with its up-to-date introduction and its textual apparatus and explanations, provides the text for this translation. It is distinguished by their recognition of the pivotal significance of Hamann's so-called conversion in London, their conviction of the work's inner unity, and their appreciation of its theological insights.

Interest in Hamann has gradually grown in the English speaking world since the Second World War. It was stimulated by the pioneering work of Walter Lowrie,[117] James O'Flaherty,[118] and W. M. Alexander.[119] These studies were accompanied by the first publication of selections from Hamann's writings in English by Ronald Gregor Smith.[120] That included some parts of the *London Writings* with extracts from "Biblical Meditations" (118–37) and "Thoughts on the Course of my Life" (140–57), as well as the whole of the "Fragments" (160–73). But apart from that, there has been no translation of this seminal work into English. This book aims to fill that gap with the hope that it will show how most of Hamann's later ideas are adumbrated here, for it is now increasingly acknowledged that the *London Writings* provide the theological key to his vision of life. While parts of my translation have been influenced by Gregor Smith, my understanding of the text depends in large measure on the textual apparatus and explanations provided by Bayer and Weissenborn as well as the perceptive analysis of John Betz.[121] They show what real treasures of wisdom and understanding are to be found in these "scribblings."

117. Walter Lowrie, *Johann Georg Hamann: An Existentialist* (Princeton: Princeton Theological Seminary, 1950).

118. James C. O'Flaherty, *Unity and Language: A Study in the Philosophy of Johann Georg Hamann* (Chapel Hill: University of North Carolina Press, 1952). See also his *Johann Georg Hamann* (Boston: Twayne Publishers, 1979).

119. W. M. Alexander, *Johann Georg Hamann* (The Hague: Martinus Nijhof, 1966).

120. Ronald Gregor Smith, *J. G. Hamann (1730–88): A Study in Christian Existence, With Selections from his Writings* (London: Collins, 1960).

121. Betz, "Hamann's London Writings," 2005.

CHRONOLOGY OF HAMANN'S LIFE

CHILDHOOD: 1730–1746

- Birth in 1730 in the city of Königsberg, the administrative, trading, and intellectual center of East Prussia
- Older son of a Lutheran middle class family whose father, the son of a Lutheran pastor in Lausitz, was a surgeon and the manager of the city bath house
- Haphazard primary and secondary education, with matriculation from the Kneiphof Gymnasium in 1746

TERTIARY STUDY IN THE UNIVERSITY OF KÖNIGSBERG: 1746–1752

- Study of theology before switching to law, without formal graduation
- Friendship with Johann Christoph Berens and Johann Gotthelf Lindner
- Collaboration with a circle of friends to produce *Daphne*, a weekly journal for women
- Departure from the university without an academic degree

EMPLOYMENT AS A HOUSEHOLD TUTOR FOR MINOR GERMAN NOBLE FAMILIES: 1752–1756

- Tutor for the young Baron Budberg in Kegeln, a feudal estate near Riga in Latvia
- Tutor for the two sons of General Witten in Grünhof, a feudal estate near Mittau in Courland
- Ongoing contact with the Berens family in Riga
- Death of mother in early 1756

EMPLOYMENT BY BERENS FAMILY IN RIGA: 1756–1759

- Commission as an agent for the Berens merchant firm on a secret trade mission to London
- Travel from October 1756, with visits to Berlin, Lübeck, Hamburg, and Amsterdam along the way, and arrival in London on April 18, 1757
- Failure of the trade mission, followed by six months of aimless dissipation that led to severe debt
- Stay with Mr. and Mrs. Collins in Malborough Street from February 8, 1758
- Beginning of a meditative reading of the Bible on March 13, 1758
- Writing of "*Biblical Meditations of a Christian*" from March 19 to April 21, with his personal enlightenment on March 31
- Writing of "*Thoughts on the Course of My Life*" from April 21 to 25
- Writing of "*Thoughts on Church Hymns*" from April 29 to May 6
- Writing of "*Deuteronomy 30:11–14 together with Romans 10:4–10*" on May 7
- Writing of "*Fragments*" beginning on May 16
- Writing of further "*Thoughts on the Course of My Life*" from May 29, 1758 to January 1, 1759
- Return by sea to Riga from June 27 to July 16, where he stays with the Berens, falls in love with Katharina Berens, and is refused permission to marry her
- Return to Königsberg to live with and care for his father

LIFE AS A MINOR CIVIL SERVANT AND MAN OF LETTERS: 1759–1787

- Composition of *Socratic Memorabilia* (1759), his first major published work, in response to attempts by Kant and Berens to reclaim him to rationalism from orthodox Christianity
- Period of intensive reading and study to consolidate his Christian convictions
- Work for the Prussian government in the Department of War and Crown Lands at the end of the Russian occupation in 1763, until he resigns in 1764 to care for his father after his father had a stroke
- Travel outside of Prussia in search of employment
- Editor of *Königsbergsche Gelehrte und Politische Zeitungen* from 1764–1775
- Common law, de facto marriage to his father's housekeeper Anna Regina Schumacher (1736–1789) after his father's death in 1766
- Birth of four children: Johann Michael (1769), Elizabeth Regina (1772), Magdelena Katharina (1774), and Marianne Sophie (1778)
- Employment as clerk and translator by the General Excise Department of the Prussian Government in 1767
- Promotion as the Superintendent of the Custom's Office in 1777 until his retirement in 1787
- Travel to Münster in 1787 to visit Princess Gallitzin and other supporters, where he dies in 1788

1

ON THE INTERPRETATION OF SACRED SCRIPTURE

The title of this pamphlet leads us to expect a set of hermeneutic guidelines for the analytical exegesis of the Bible. Instead, we receive guidance on how to meditate on and receive spiritual help from the Bible. Hamann does not set out his principles for the cognitive analysis of the Scriptures but graphically explains why a humble heart is the only proper frame of mind for reading the Bible, which is even more misinterpreted and misapplied by its philosophical critics than Aesop's fables about animals would be if the animals were able to read them. A humble, receptive heart alone does justice to the Bible's miraculous inspiration by the condescending Holy Spirit, and to the Spirit's paradoxical revelation of God's wisdom and power through what seems to be foolish and weak. What the Scriptures have to say for our salvation and our spiritual enlightenment appears to be just as stupid to unbelievers as the feigned madness and scribblings of David, the fugitive from Saul in the court of Achish, the Philistine king. This word of the Spirit is an unlikely means of grace, like the rags that were used to rescue Jeremiah from his muddy prison and the pool of water with spittle and dust that Jesus used to give sight to a blind man.

God an author! (The Creator of the world and the Father of humanity is denied and criticized; the God-man was crucified; and the Inspirer of the divine word is mocked and slandered.) The inspiration of this book is as great an act of self-effacement and condescension as the creation of the world by the Father and the incarnation of the Son. Thus a humble heart is the only proper frame of mind for reading the Bible and the essential preparation for doing that.

The Creator has been denied, the Redeemer has been crucified, and the Spirit of wisdom has been slandered. The word of the Spirit is just as great a work as the creation of the world, and just as great a mystery as the redemption of mankind. Yes, this word is the key to the work of the former and the mysteries of the latter. Thus it is the epitome of atheism and witchcraft to assume God's blindness in revelation, and it is an act of sacrilege to scorn this means of grace.

As little as an animal is able to read the fables of Aesop, Phaedrus, and LaFontaine, or even if it were able to read them, it would not be able to make such beastly judgments on the sense of the stories and their applicability as people have made in criticizing and philosophizing about God's Book.[1]

We all lie in just as muddy a prison as Jeremiah. Old rags served as ropes to pull him out of it; he was indebted to them for saving him. He was not rescued by looking at them, but by the services that they offered and the use that he made of them (Jer 38:11–13).

Our Redeemer used a pool, for which he prepared the salve for
Gen 2:7 the eyes from his spittle and the dust of the earth, to give sight to a man who had been born blind (John 9:6).

And who can, without fear and trembling, read the story of David in the court of the king of Gath, who distorted his gestures, acted as if he were mad, scribbled on the doors of the gate, and slobbered on his beard, without hearing, in the judgment of Achish, an echo of the thinking of the unbelieving smart alecks and sophists of our time (1 Sam 21:13–15)?

---

1. Aesop, a Greek author who lived during the sixth century BC, collected and published more than six hundred fables for entertainment and instruction, many of them stories about animals. Phaedrus, a first century AD Roman author, translated Aesop's fables into Latin verse and published them together with other instructive satirical fables in a number of different books. The French writer La Fontaine collected fables from many different sources, reworked them into witty French free verse and published twelve books of fables from 1668 to 1694.

Who would, like Paul in 1 Corinthians 1:25, be so bold as to speak of God's weakness? No one except the Spirit who searches the depths of the godhead could have disclosed to us this prophecy, which has, more than ever before, been fulfilled in our own times, the prophecy that not many who are wise according to the flesh, not many who are mighty, not many who are of noble birth, are called to the kingdom of heaven, and that the great God has desired to reveal his wisdom and power by deliberately choosing what is foolish in the world to shame the mighty. God chose what is lowly and despised, yes, things that are not, in order to bring to nothing things that are, things that boast of what they are. *1 Cor 1:28*

2

BIBLICAL MEDITATIONS OF A CHRISTIAN

PALM SUNDAY, MARCH 19, 1758

LONDON

Here we have the heart and soul of the London Writings. This comes first, after the introductory thoughts on sacred Scripture, because God's word produced Hamann's spiritual reconfiguration. His meditation on the Bible led to his spiritual awakening and transformation from a rationalist intellectual to a faithful confessor of the Triune God.

The original title was "The Diary of a Christian." By changing the title to "The Biblical Meditations of a Christian," Hamann shifted attention away from himself to the Bible. His choice of the German term Betrachtungen, which means contemplations or observations, emphasizes his visionary engagement with it, or rather its visionary impact on him and his imagination as he meditated on it. He did not meditate on the Bible analytically and cognitively to further his knowledge of its content, but devotionally and contemplatively, to see what God was saying to him as he read it. He considered it typologically by noting prophetic allusions to Christ and his present work in the church and the life of each Christian in its stories. He therefore read the Bible in order to be enlightened by the Holy Spirit and gain insight into God's dealings with him and all people.

In the first published edition of this work, Roth inserts the following summary passage by Hamann, written on a loose leaf from this time as an introduction: "Every Bible story is a prophecy that is fulfilled through the centuries and in the soul of every man. Every story bears the image of man, a body which is also dust and ashes and nothing with sensible letters, but also a soul, the breath of God, the life and the light that shines in the darkness and cannot be grasped by the darkness. The Spirit of God is revealed as something self-subsisting—in servant form, is flesh—and dwells among us full of grace and truth." The passage reappears in an expanded version as the introduction to the "Meditations on Newton's Essay on Prophecies."

Once it is understood that Hamann does not seek to interpret the text exegetically, we can make sense of its unsystematic, haphazard character, with his attention to what may appear to be insignificant texts and apparent neglect of other more significant passages. They record his personal "impressions." As he reads, he meditates on those parts that strike him, that address him personally, or challenge him intellectually as a child of the Enlightenment. They identify his blind spots in order to grant him deeper and more accurate insight into the spiritual realities they portray.

Today with God's help I have begun to read Holy Scripture for the second time. Since my circumstances make it necessary for me to live in the loneliest wilderness where I sit and watch like a sparrow on the rooftop, I find, in the company of my books which occupy me and exercise my thoughts, a remedy for the bitterness of many sad meditations on my past follies, as well as on the misuse of the blessings and opportunities which God in his providence has so
Ps 102:6–7 graciously wished to single me out to receive. The prospect of a barren desert where I see myself deprived of water and ears of grain is nearer to me now than ever before. The academic disciplines[1] and my rational friends seem, like Job's friends, to test my
Job 16:20 patience rather than comfort me. They make the wounds of my

1. The German term *die Wissenschaften* does not just refer to what we now call "the sciences" but includes all intellectual disciplines.

experience bleed instead of easing their pain. While nature has put some salt in every body that chemists know how to extract, God's providence, it seems, has put a moral element in all adversities that we are to dissolve and separate from them, an element that we can profitably use as a remedy for our natural sicknesses and mental ailments. If we overlook God's presence by sunshine in the pillar of cloud, then his presence shines more visibly and impressively for us by night in the pillar of fire. *Exod 13:21–22*

As I look back on my whole life, my utmost confidence in his grace is justified. Even in my present state I myself recognize a loving Father who warns me with earnest glances, yet allows me to come to my senses, like the prodigal son, a Father who will respond to my penitent return to him, not only by withholding the punishment that I deserve, but also by his gracious forgiveness and unexpected welcome. *Jer 3:4, 19; Luke 15:11–32* Neither my evil will nor the lack of opportunity stopped me from falling into far deeper misery and far heavier debt than I now find that I am in.[2] God! We are such miserable creatures that even our lower level of trouble is a reason for thanksgiving to you. God! We are such unworthy creatures, since nothing but our unbelief can shorten your arm, limit your generosity in blessing us, and curtail it against its will. *Luke 17:10; Isa 59:1*

If temptation[3] has made me attentive to the word, I can credit it to the writings of the spiritually gifted Hervey,[4] which he owed to the *Night Thoughts* of the venerable "swan" of

2. This refers to his impoverished state and the debts that he had incurred.

3. Here the German word for temptation is *Anfechtung*, which interprets temptation as a spiritual attack by the devil. This statement is an allusion to Luther's translation of Isa 28:19b: "Denn allein die Anfechtung lehret aufs Wort merken": "For only temptation teaches to attend to the word." The literal sense of this Hebrew clause is: "And there will be only trembling to discern what is heard."

4. Here Hamann refers to the Anglican clergyman James Hervey (1714–58). In 1748 Hervey published a widely read book in two volumes called *Meditations and Contemplations* (John & James Rivington, 1748). Hamann read this work as early as 1756 and it influenced him greatly in his *London Writings*.

this island.[5] My reading of this devout scribe has so often
impressed the divine character of the Bible on the feeling of
my soul with just the same liveliness as the newly replanted
Neh 8 city of Jerusalem heard the law of Moses from the lips of Ezra.
Hervey has motivated me in my decision to write down my meditations from my repeated reading of Holy Scripture and gather together the impressions that this or that passage in it has awakened and produced in me. The impartiality of a critic and the respectful simplicity of a Christian heart may guide me equally in this.

The great Author[6] of these holy books intends to make every
honest reader of them *wise for salvation* through faith in his
2 Tim 3:15 Redeemer. The holy men under whose name they have been preserved were moved by the Holy Spirit. Divine inspiration was
imparted to them as they completed their writings, so that they
would be useful for teaching, for reproof, for correction, and for
instruction in righteousness (2 Tim 3:15, 16; 2 Pet 1:21). God cannot
withhold these effects from anyone who prays for them, because
Jesus has promised the Holy Spirit to all those who ask the heav-
Luke 11:13 enly Father for him. As readers we need to put ourselves with our
perceptions into the perceptions of the writer that we have before us and to match his frame of mind as much as possible. We can gain this for ourselves through the felicitous power of the imagination, by which a poet or a historian tries, as much as possible, to help us. This rule with its requirements is just as necessary for this as for other books.

I would like to make a few general remarks about divine revelation as they occur to me. God has revealed himself to human beings in nature and his word. We have not yet analyzed the similarities and connections between both of these revelations so extensively and explained so clearly, nor have we penetrated into this

5. This refers to *The Complaint: Or Night-Thoughts on Life, Death and Immortality* by Edward Young (1681–1765). When Hamann calls him "the swan" of Great Britain, he praises him as a great lyric poet. The emblem for lyric poets was the white swan with its beauty and purity, its ability to fly by gliding on the air, and its freedom from earthly constraints.

6. By his use of a term which means both originator and author, Hamann refers to the Holy Spirit.

harmony, so that sound philosophy could open up a wide field for itself. In countless instances both revelations must be rescued in the same way from the greatest objections to them. Both revelations explain and support each other; they cannot contradict each other, no matter how much the interpretations of our reason would like to claim that they do. Rather, it is the greatest contradiction and abuse of reason when reason itself wishes to reveal anything. A philosopher who puts the divine word away from his eyes in order to please reason is like the Jews who seem to cling more rigidly to the Old Testament the more obstinately they reject the New Testament. In them the prophecy was fulfilled that what was meant to confirm and complete their other insights is an offense and foolishness in their eyes. The study of nature and history are *1 Cor 1:18–25* the two pillars of true religion. Unbelief and superstition are based on shallow physics and shallow history. Nature is as little subject to blind accident or to eternal laws as all events can be explained in personal and political terms. Newton is deeply moved as a historian by the wise omnipotence of God and equally so as a scientist by God's wise government.[7]

God reveals himself—the Creator of the world an author! What kind of fate would his books have to experience? To what kind of strict judgments and what kind of sharp-witted literary critics would his books be subject? How many miserable scorners of religion have enjoyed their daily bread from his hand? How many strong spirits,[8] like Herostratus,[9] have arrogantly and shamefully looked for some kind of immortality[10] which they, on their death

7. Sir Isaac Newton (1643–1727) was a pioneer in mathematics, physics, and astronomy. He was both a brilliant scientist and a devout student of theology with a special interest in prophecy and eschatology. In his day science was understood as natural history.

8. Or "freethinkers." Many philosphers of the French Enlightenment, such as Voltaire, regarded themselves as *esprits forts* ("strong spirits")—daring intellectuals who took pride in their atheism.

9. In AD 356 Herostratus burned down the great temple of Artemis in Ephesus, so that he would by this act gain immortal fame. Subsequently the citizens of Ephesus decided never to mention his name.

10. Hamann's corrections and insertions in the last part of this sentence make it difficult to construe its exact meaning.

bed, foreswore to God, their God, and begged for a better kind of immortality by their repentance?[11]

God is used to seeing his wisdom criticized by the children of men. The staff of Moses was not in any danger even though it was
Exod 7:8–12 encircled by the staffs of the wise Egyptians that hissed at it. These masters of a thousand arts were finally compelled to recognize the finger of God in a most contemptible insect and give way to the
Exod 8:16–19 prophet of the true God. Thus the notion that the highest Being has himself honored these humans with a special revelation seems to be so strange and extraordinary to these dimwits that together with Pharaoh they asked what this God wanted and why he had
Exod 5:2 come to visit them. But this notion of revelation must necessarily be combined with consideration of those who benefit from it. God desired to reveal himself to *people*; he has revealed himself through *people*. The means by which God made this revelation beneficial for them and won them for it, the means by which he spread, propagated, and preserved it among them, had to be based most appropriately on human nature and his wisdom. Any philosopher who wished to criticize or correct God in his choice of all these circumstances and ways by which God communicated his revelation would always act more reasonably if he trusted in his own judgment about it less, so that he did not run into the danger of that royal astronomer who regarded the Ptolemaic system and his explanation of the movement of the stars as the true construction of the heavens.[12]

If God had intended to reveal himself to human beings and the whole human race, then the folly of those who wish to make a limited

11. The text of this section is uncertain because it is full of possible variations that are written over and under the main line. Another translation based on a different combination of phrases is as follows: "Who in the agony of death begged God their God for a better kind of immortality."

12. Here Hamann refers to Alphons X, the King of Leon, Castille, and Galicia (1221–1284), a well-known medieval astronomer and astrologist.

taste[13] and their own judgment[14] the touchstone for the divine word is even more evident. We do not speak about a revelation that Voltaire,[15] a Bolingbroke,[16] or a Shaftesbury[17] would find acceptable, revelation that catered best to their prejudices, their wit, their moral, political, magical[18] fancies, but about a disclosure of truths whose certainty, credibility, and importance are of concern to the whole human race. People who are confident enough in their own insight to be able to make do without divine instruction would have found faults in any other revelation and would have need of none. They are the healthy people who need no physician. *Luke 5:31*

God has certainly found it most suitable for his wisdom to bind this nearer revelation of himself first to a single man, then to his family, and finally to a particular people, before he allowed it, as he wished, to become more general. We may no more fathom the reasons for this choice than why it pleased him to create in six days what his will could have done just as well in a single moment. *See Deut 4:7; Ps 145:18; 148:14; Rom 10:8*

Furthermore, God has accommodated and lowered himself as much as possible to human inclinations and notions, yes, even to human prejudices and weaknesses. This hallmark of his love for humanity, which fills the whole of Holy Scripture, is the cause of mockery by weak minds[19] who presuppose that they will find some

13. Like *bon sens*, sound reason, *bon gout*, good taste, was a key axiom of the Enlightenment.

14. This is another axiom of the Enlightenment.

15. The French philosopher, historian, and writer Voltaire (1694–1778) was a leading figure in the Enlightenment and a teacher of Frederick the Great.

16. Viscount Bolingbroke (1678–1751) was a leading English politician. He was dismissed from the government of George I in 1714 for his support of the exiled Stuarts and lived in France until 1725. There he joined with Voltaire, who influenced him in his best-known work, *Letters on the Study and Use of History* (1735), which Hamann translated into German and published in 1774.

17. The English philosopher, politician, and moralist Anthony Ashley Cooper, the Third Earl of Shaftesbury (1671–1713) was influenced by Seneca, Cicero, and Plato in his secular thinking and by Socrates in his skeptical writing. Hamann valued him so highly that he translated his *Letter Concerning Enthusiasm* (1708) into German during his time as a tutor in Latvia.

18. Or "epic." The writing of this word is hard to decipher.

19. Literally, "weak heads." This sarcastic term refers to the so-called freethinkers, the "strong spirits" who take pride in their "strong heads."

human wisdom in the divine word, or some satisfaction for their curiosity,[20] their wit, and some agreement with the taste of the time in which they live or the sect to which they belong.[21] No wonder that they find themselves deceived in their conception! No wonder that the Spirit of Scripture is dismissed with the same indifference![22] Yes, no wonder that this Spirit seems just as dumb and useless as the Savior was to Herod, who, despite his great curiosity and desire to see him, soon sent him to Pilate with something more than cold
Luke 23:7–11 indifference!

Who would have imagined that we would want to look for the history of the world in the Books of Moses?[23] Many people seem to slander Moses only because he does not provide them with resources to explain, complete, or refute the fables of Herodotus.[24] How ridiculous—how incredible would this history of the primeval world probably appear to them, if we had it as completely as they would like it to be?

These books had to be preserved by the Jews. So many particular details must have applied so closely to this people that they were taken in by their content. In itself the history of this people is of greater significance for our religion than that of all other peoples is for us, because God shows us the saddest picture of our corrupted nature in the stubbornness of this nation and the greatest proofs of his patience, righteousness, and mercy in guiding and ruling it. In short, he shows us the most sensory revelation[25] of his attributes.

Why has God chosen this people? It was not on account of their
Deut 7:7; 9:4–6 superior qualities. The freethinkers may contrast their stupidity and

20. For Hamann idle intellectual curiosity was a prominent characteristic of the Enlightenment, a trait that they shared with the Athenians in Acts 17:19-21. The German term *Neugierde* describes the desire for what is new.

21. Here Haman debunks the claim that fashionable taste can determine what is right or wrong, true or false.

22. Hamann also provides "with the greatest indifference" as an alternative reading.

23. This is the traditional term for the Pentateuch.

24. Herodotus (ca. 480–425 BC), a Greek historian, is regarded as the father of Western history, even though his *Histories* are an odd mixture of fact and fantasy.

25. Here Hamann refers to God's disclosure of himself to all the five human senses.

wickedness with other peoples as much as they like. Has God not chosen to propagate the gospel in the same way through ignorant and unimpressive instruments in the eyes of the world? Who can fathom his counsel in this?

So even though a Voltaire and a Bolingbroke found so little to complete and explain the early history of the nations in the first five chapters of the First Book of Moses,[26] its disclosures are of even greater significance for the human race in general.

There has been no lack of good intentions among the philosophers to explain creation in terms of some natural events. It is therefore no wonder that they have credited the same idea to Moses and expected natural explanation rather than a story. I say a story. A story, which must be gauged according to the comprehension of the people and, to some extent, be understood in connection with the concepts of the times in which he wrote, can give little satisfaction to minds that demand an explanation, minds that prefer that a matter should be comprehensible rather than true. We know that the desire to investigate future events has misled people into many follies and that this desire has given them confidence that they were capable of achieving this. They considered that they had the means to satisfy their inquisitiveness with the stars, the flight
of birds, and so on. The lust to know things that are too high for *Ps 131:1*
us, things that are beyond the range of our sight, things that are unfathomable on account of the same weakness which makes the future so dark for us, has led people into just as many ridiculous methods and errors. Such people deserve to be called experts and philosophers as rightly as gypsies, astrologers, and so on may be called fortune tellers.

Let us compare natural events with natural events and miracles with miracles if we wish to make a judgment of them.

26. Here Hamann refers to Bolingbroke's "Letters on the Study and Use of History" (London 1735), 5–32.

It would be just as ridiculous to demand that Moses should explain nature with Aristotelian,[27] Cartesian,[28] or Newtonian[29] concepts as to demand that God should have revealed himself in general philosophical language, which has been the philosophers' stone[30] for so many learned minds.

To say that Moses wrote only for a vulgar crowd is to judge him in either a meaningless or ridiculous way. Does the sun arise so early in summer only for farmers because the lazy townsperson and the lascivious courtier can do without it for so much longer, or because they have no need for it at all?

After Paul had been caught up into heaven, he could find no words to explain and elucidate the concepts that he had brought
2 Cor 12:2–4 back with him from the third heaven. Just as our ears cannot hear unless they are touched by the sound in the air, and all intelligible hearing depends on vibration in the air which is neither too strong nor too weak, so it is with what we conceive. Our mental conception depends on physical images. Where these are absent for us and where we cannot awaken them in others, [nothing can be conceived].[31] We see how difficult it is to translate figures of speech and idioms of one language into another. The more people differ in their way of thinking, the more we are forced to resort to variations and substitutions, or, I might say, approximations. How then must a story be constructed that makes those things that are far beyond the scope of our concepts understandable and comprehensible to us?

With what humility, what mute attentiveness and deep awe, must we accept what the Creator of the world wants to tell us about the mysteries of the great week in which he worked at creating our
Gen 1:1–2, 4 earth. As short as the story is about the production of a work that

27. This refers to the geocentric explanation of the universe by the great Greek philosopher, Aristotle.

28. The French philosopher and scientist René Descartes (1596–1650) attempted to explain the universe in mechanical, mathematical terms.

29. Newton is considered the father of modern science.

30. According to alchemy, this was a mineral that could turn base metal into gold and heal all diseases.

31. This implied main clause is missing in the German text.

met with his approval when it came to be, a work that he found worth preserving for so long, a work that he reserved as a bare scaffolding for a higher building for him to erect in a most festive fashion,[32] it must be equally significant in our eyes. As much as he condescended for us to understand the little that is possible, necessary, and profitable for us, so widely does his work also surpass our powers of comprehension.

GENESIS 1:5, 8, 10

God *named*—here the use of the first names and words are ascribed to God.

GENESIS 1:20

Abundantly. This abundance is decreed especially for the waters. The fulfillment of the divine command is in the next verse. This abundance is still evident in nature.

GENESIS 1:22

God's blessing over the inhabitants of the sea and the air has to do with their increase in number. Their increase least hinders the increase of people on earth. Moses always mentions them before all other living creatures, just as he first mentions the Spirit of God moving over the waters at the beginning of his story. *Gen 1:2*

GENESIS 1:26

What a disclosure in human nature! How festively the Triune God prepares himself before he undertakes the construction of man. How often does Moses, and the Spirit of God through him, find it necessary to repeat this assurance that God created man in his own image, in the image of God, in God's likeness. Here reason falls down. God's decision to redeem fallen man and restore this image rests on this basis. How much my redemption has cost! Nevertheless, you, unfathomable God, have held that this race *Gen 1:27; 5:1; 9:6* *1 Cor 6:20*

32. This alludes to God's promise of a new creation through Jesus, the second Adam.

Matt 20:28 was worth the payment of this costly ransom. Our great worth in redemption is the reason for the worth that you conferred on us and intended for us in creation. In order to restore this likeness, *Phil 2:7; 1 Tim 3:9* God had to take on our human likeness. Both are equally great mysteries of faith.

GENESIS 1:28

Ps 82:6 Subdue the earth. See Ps 115:16. Be the gods of the earth. Preserve the holiness in your world that dwells with us in heaven. Assert your dominion with the dignity which we have granted to you in creation, especially over the creatures that been made subordinate *See Luke 10:17; also Phil 3:21; 1 Pet 3:22* to you. Spirits that would never have gained their existence if God had not granted it to them rose up against his throne and ended their bliss. Watch out that the spirits subordinate to you do not use the same craftiness, power, or wickedness against you that brought them to disgrace with God. Watch out on behalf of those who are there on your account.[33]

GENESIS 1:31[34]

Reason must be satisfied with the judgment of the philosopher Socrates[35] on the writing of Heraclitus: "Since what I understand is excellent, I therefore infer the same for what I do not understand."[36] Only God's own testimony[37] can assure us completely to what extent our insight into nature is insufficient. God passes this judgment after he had examined every part of creation closely. He declared that *Gen 1:4, 10, 12, 18, 21, 25* for him every part was good. But the correlation of all these parts gives them the highest good and perfection. And God saw everything that he had made and behold, it was *very good*.

---

33. This seems to refer to those creatures that human beings are meant to rule.

34. Two of the main manuscripts of "Biblical Meditations" begin here.

35. The German has "that philosopher."

36. This quotation comes from "The Life of Socrates" by Diogeges Laërtius (II.22). Heraclitus of Ephesus (ca. 535–476 BC) was an early Greek philosopher. Most of what he wrote was lost apart from some excerpts and fragments. Hamann was interested in his teaching on the role of the Logos in the world and in the dynamic polarity and unity of opposites.

37. This refers to God's testimony in the Scriptures.

GENESIS 2:3

God created in order to make.[38] Matter and form. He created what exists and its purpose, so that nothing becomes something and this something becomes all that he wills. How can we express in words what we are not able in the least to imagine for ourselves? Here we must regard ourselves like those who are denied the sense of hearing in birth. They must be taught painstakingly to pronounce certain words that they themselves cannot hear and to some extent, through lip-reading, replace their deafness by sight.

GENESIS 2:7

From God's construction of Adam, as described by Moses, we have a measure by which we judge our human nature. Even though the structure of our body is a work of art that has been wonderfully made, here God, as it were, fails to remind us of his wisdom in making it. He finds it more necessary to refer us to the dust of the earth which he has made into this masterpiece of the physical world. For a similar reason Moses seems to speak about the creation of sky with such a common and insignificant image of them as lights. *Gen 1:16* Yes, he even lingers on the sun and the moon as two great lights, the greater to measure the day and the lesser to measure the night, so as to keep the Jews safe from the natural idolatry of the stars and especially from those that strike the eyes most of all. I think that this observation has been made by others. It shows how God adapts himself in his revelation to human concepts and times and considers its general use in the application of trivial details that serve to arouse the scorn of some people. If our body is dust, how should our love and care for it be fashioned? From the dust God has made such a miraculous machine, a mirror of the greater world, just as in his first miracle our Savior turned water into wine that surpassed the first wine. See what conclusions David draws from the creation of humanity in Psalm 100:3 and 103:14.

---

38. This is a literal translation of the Hebrew text that is usually translated as "God created and made."

In contrast with this, the breath of life in our nostrils is a breath of God. So Moses describes as an effect of God's breath that which is the surest sign of the union of the soul with the body. The mysterious nature of the human soul, its importance, and its dependence on its Author are described with a very sensory and simple picture. Longinus admired Moses for permitting God to speak so that what he says happens.[39] In the story of Moses the creation of Adam offers a far more mysterious and ceremonious act than a mere word. God's decision is introduced first. God takes the trouble to *form* the dust of the earth. In comparison with this, the rest of the creation seems to be a hasty act. The greatest mystery reaches its conclusion when God breathes on what he had formed. This breath is the goal of the whole creation, just as our glorified Savior shares the fruits of his great redemption with the same picture of his mysterious breathing on his disciples (John 20:22). The expression that Moses uses for the soul includes a sense picture for its spiritual life. Just as the union of the body and the soul is bound up with the breath of bodily life, so that both end at the same time, so the spiritual life is in union with God, and spiritual death is in the separation of both. While the gift of our breath is from God and remains in his hand, its use depends on us. Let us never forget that the existence of our nature which we receive from the breath of life belongs closely to God and is closely related with him. It cannot therefore be complete and happy by any other orientation, and any deviation from it is opposed to our nature and our happiness. Our soul does not just depend on his word but also on his breath. He can neither destroy it, nor can he countenance the debasement of what he has made in his image, something that has such a close connection with his infinite being. We need his assistance in our deeds, just as much as we need breath for our vitality and activities. We cannot forget ourselves without dishonoring God; we cannot harm ourselves without grieving God; we cannot participate in his

39. Dionysius Longinus, a pagan author from the first half of the first century AD, wrote a tract on "The Sublime." In chapter nine he refers to the Jewish story of creation by God's spoken utterance.

will without participating in his happiness; we cannot do his will without also delighting him by our participation in his happiness. Who would have believed, had God himself not told us, that the primeval world wounded him and pained his heart? Who would have believed that he gains his fame from our obedience and the enjoyment of his glory in our fellowship with him and participation in him? The seventeenth chapter of John is a commentary on human creation,[40] because it must be considered together with its redemption if we are to judge and admire both in their proper light by their correlation (Ps 104:29–30).

Gen 6:5–7

GENESIS 2:8, 9, 15

God made man the lord of the whole earth. It would take centuries before the blessing with its commission to fill the earth could be accomplished. Here we see two persons on a piece of land that now nourishes and contains countless people. If Adam could have understood the greatness of the planets as we now do, how would he have judged the desolate space which seems to be as good as useless? We are now no longer prone to the prejudices and errors into which he could have fallen. We see the earth fuller than Adam could even have foreseen or imagined from God's words of blessing about him and his family in the future, fuller even than Abraham with the promise that he received about his offspring. So Peter quite rightly calls God a faithful and trustworthy Creator in 1 Pet 4:19.

Gen 12:1–3; 15:5; 22:17

God restricts the place of residence for the human beings to a special location on earth and devotes special attention to it. Even though the whole earth was made very good through its creation, this did not satisfy the love and care of their Father. He *plants* a *garden*. He lets its soil produce excellent trees through which he tries to please the senses and provide useful nourishment for human beings. He officially appoints Adam as their attendant and warden. How much pleasure Adam had in his easy work of maintaining what

40. This chapter records the prayer of Jesus as high priest, his prayer of consecration for himself and his disciples, so that in union with him they may share in his life, sonship, and glory in the presence of his heavenly Father.

God had established, let me say, with beautiful diligence,[41] for our pleasure and what we need in our *greatest relationship* with him. Here there was no talk about *daily work* that a master imposes on us, nor about the labor that we need to do for his blessing, so that he can feed us and let us sleep under his roof and so on, nor about any need to earn our daily bread. Speechless creation seems to do this of its own accord. How could Adam hold back from tending those trees and attending to them, might I say, from loving the trees that wooed his eyes, his smell, and his taste, so that he took delight, as it were, in tasting their beauty and transformed his natural need into the greatest benefit by the sweetness of their powers (Ps 78:72)?[42]

How different is the judgment that sin brings in its wake. Instead of a gardener in the garden that God had so pleasantly and carefully planted, Adam becomes a painful worker of the ground that had
Gen 3:17–19 been cursed because of him. Thorns and thistles instead of those trees that were pleasing to see and good to eat; the grass of the field instead of this divine orchard. Worry at the sight of unproductive agriculture, worry that will not let him taste his bread or else makes its taste bitter and sharp for him.

We can see how the story of Moses about the state of innocence and the state of the fall from it basically belong together. They are both connected together with each other as exactly as I have noted about the correlation of human creation and redemption.

GENESIS 2:18

It is not good for a man to be alone. Thus God's wisdom in its ways and its decisions for people is always based on what is best for them. Would he have permitted their fall, if their redemption would not have given them greater blessings, privileges, and rights than creation itself or their innocence? So the assets of fellowship have become rank and wild liabilities. Help in the state of marriage

41. This refers to God's creation of trees that were not only good for food but also pleasant to the eyes (Gen 2:9; 3:6).

42. The point of this reference to David in Ps 78:72 is uncertain. It may imply that Jesus, the new David, our Good Shepherd, delights us in a similar fashion.

has been distorted into a new curse for human life, a new burden and impediment. This was also the reason for human displacement from the Garden of Eden into a field of thistles and thorns.

GENESIS 2:19–20

Here Adam tries out the knowledge that God had given him (Ps 94:10). God named the light "day" and so on. Here he lets Adam name the animals. Like the trees of Paradise, the animals of Paradise differed from the others on earth. I believe that this difference has not been noted as much as it should have been. This observation could serve to determine our understanding of verses 4–6.

Gen 1:5

GENESIS 2:21–23

Like the dead that David mentions in Ps 88:10, Adam wakes up in order to praise God. With the same joy we will wake up from the deep sleep of death and see the transformation of our bones and flesh like Adam with his rib. That's how the sleep of his beloved will be (Ps 127:2).

GENESIS 3:3

We are so prone to lapse from far too much repression of our desires into complete surrender to them. These are the utmost limits where superstition and unbelief get lost and join together (Prov 30:6).[43] This is seen in the threats that fence off the law of Moses (Deut 4:2) and the revelation of the new covenant by the prophet John (Rev 22:18).

GENESIS 3:7–8

Fear, the shame of a bad conscience, the folly and the inadequacy of our reason to make up for the evil in our heart and cover it up are painted in this part of the story with such accuracy, simplicity, and profundity that no human brush can match. Our difficulties in understanding the conditions of the fall into sin all flow from

43. The reference to Prov 30:6 speaks about gaining supernatural knowledge from heaven or earth apart from God's words.

the prejudices that we have about the wisdom of Adam and the
misconceptions that we have about the wisdom of God. This is
the childhood of the human race in which it had innocence. God
would have preserved it in order to educate his creatures in it, so
Eph 4:11–16 that under his nurture they would grow up into the glorious height
of faith which our Savior compared to the relation of a mustard
Matt 13:31–32 seed to a full grown tree. The restlessness of a bad conscience is
like those emotions that we call shame and fear. Here we abandon
all secondary concepts and look at emotions of the soul by themselves. Our words are allegories and pictures of our thoughts. Our inclinations and affects are as similar to Adam's as our clothes are similar to his, even though we are not dressed like him. Our first parents lost God's image through their unhappy fall into sin. With David they could say: "I was so foolish that I knew nothing; I was like a beast with you" (Ps 73:22). So their thoughts were like the thoughts of an ostrich which God mentions in Job 39:14–17 and introduces in order to shame human beings. They were deceived like this dumb bird which lets itself be caught when it sees a skin like its own and believes that it cannot be seen when it sees nothing. This was the shame, the fear, this instinct to conceal themselves. Their own bodies stood in the way for them. They wished that they could remove themselves from their own eyes. They covered themselves with the broadest leaves that they could find in order to remove themselves from their own sight. They thought that God was like
Gen 3:5 them (Ps 50:21). Instead of becoming like the gods, they believed
that God was just like them. With that, their eyes were opened,
and every evildoer has this knowledge of the consequences of his
actions which our parents had from their fall into sin. Thus Cain's
Gen 4:13–14 eyes were opened to the greatness of his sin.

GENESIS 3:9, 13

God hides those attributes from them which could be frightening to them as sinners. Here he discards his omniscience and condescends to Adam's blindness: "Adam, where are you?" He asks Eve what she has done. He softens his righteousness to let them see his

conciliatory character, his forbearance, his grace, and his patient nature more clearly. His anger does not come from the heart against us poor people. The suffering that he had to inflict on our race in Adam was nothing compared to the compassion that he promised for him according to the multitude of his mercies (Lam 3:32, 33). Our Savior gave the disciples on the road to Emmaus a gentle indication of God's disposition to us people (Luke 24:32). I make a comparison with this story so as to explain how the snake flatters our first mother and what a sorry state she was to herself in her own eyes. See how God shuts the eyes of his disciples and believers for a while, in order to set their hearts alight through their ears with an
even greater flame. He opens their eyes; they recognize him, and he *Luke 24:32*
ceases to be seen by them as the impact of his appearance remains fixed in their souls, giving them joy and comfort.

GENESIS 3:16

Like the pain and sorrow with which Adam had to eat the fruit of
the earth, God prophesied the pain of Eve from the fruit of her body. *Gen 3:19*
"I will," says God, "greatly increase your pain and your conception." We know that pain naturally grows and increases with the number of children for all mothers. She had to depend on her husband just as he depended on the produce of the earth and the cultivation of soil from which he was taken (Gen 3:23). Adam was made from the
dust of the earth and the judgment on him made him, as it were, its *Gen 2:7*
vassal. Eve was made from the rib of the man and the judgment on *Gen 2:21–23*
her made her subject to his will. The story of Moses gives us the reason for human and social inequality.

GENESIS 3:21

God made coats of skin for these fallen people and clothed them. We know what prophetic comfort and revelation lies in this small detail from the story of Moses and God's account of it which no freethinker but only a Christian can feel. Its application and the secret understanding of it may even have been a mystery for David when he reflected on God's writings. There are beautiful things in this account which escape the finest taste of a Longinus[44] and the greatest rabbi, but the commonest and simplest Christian can feel. There are mysteries in it which bewilder and confuse all human understanding.

From this concern of the Most High to clothe human beings David may have derived the confidence that he expresses in Psalm 57:2: "God who performs everything for me."[45] "Why do you worry about nourishment and clothing," says our Savior. "Your heavenly Father knows that you need all this" (Matt 6:28, 31, 32).

GENESIS 3:24

This flaming sword that turns about in all directions to guard the way to the tree of life is an excellent picture for the nature of the law which Paul expounds so profoundly in the Letter to the Romans.

GENESIS 4:1

How many parents, especially mothers, have deceived themselves in assessing their children like Eve whose high hopes for Cain came to nothing. His bad behavior may have resulted from the pampered upbringing which he received in keeping with the preconceptions of his mother, and it may have annoyed him that his mother's favorite was viewed with indifference by God. The pride which is so usual for children that are favored more than their siblings seemed to have made Cain fond of power over his brother. He therefore often had good reason to oppose Cain's will, and in many cases even Eve herself was not able to blame her younger son for that. The good conduct of Abel and the misbehavior of Cain may have tipped the understanding of Eve in favor of Abel, however much her heart sided with Cain. God's words in 4:7 give us the motive for this: "If you would do what is right, would you not have the eminence that

44. See footnote 39.

45. Here Hamann follows the English text of the KJV.

makes you jealous?[46] Your parents would love you much more, and you will be regarded by your Creator with the same eyes as Abel. Because you do what is evil, you are shunned by people and by God. This is the reason why your brother cannot give as much room for your intentions and desires as you wish, why he cannot comply with the dominance that you presume to exercise over him." Since Abel was a shepherd, a dog may, already then, have performed the tasks that these creatures carried out especially for people in this occupation. The sin that lies at the door would therefore be a natural picture that made excellent sense, because such a dog would frighten off strangers and stop them from coming too close to their master. The evil heart of Cain was like a similar nasty dog that Abel had to be on guard against, the reason why he did not come too close to him, but instead approached him coolly and cautiously. An outburst of anger which is aroused at once by something that is said and takes revenge relentlessly without reflection is like this kind of animal that does not know the difference between a thief and a friend of its master but greets them both with the same barking. *Gen 4:2*

GENESIS 4:2

Here already we find the diversity of human occupations and workplaces. Age most likely seems to have been the reason for this. Since looking after sheep was easier work than farming, it was more suitable for Abel.

GENESIS 4:4

"Faith," says Paul, "made Abel's offering more acceptable to God." *Heb 11:4* Without doubt the faith that made such a difference in God's acceptance is the reason why the two offerings are compared. Thus Moses pays more attention to Abel's offering. It was an offering of firstborn *animals*; he offered *the fat* from them.

46. Here Hamann gives his own paraphrase of the enigmatic Hebrew text. Its literal translation is: "If you do well, there is lifting up."

GENESIS 4:9

Here God appears for the second time as a judge. Just as he had
Gen 3:9 asked Adam, "Where are you?" so he here asks Cain, "Where is
Abel, your brother?" Just as Adam combines his disobedience with
Gen 3:10–12 ingratitude, so his son combined murder with lies. The rebel against
society obtained forgiveness just like the rebel against God. The
sentence of death that both deserved was carried out on neither of
them. The commandments of the second table of the Decalogue
Deut 5:6–21 are based on the first. So unbelief and superstition circumvent all
certainty and tranquility in the human social order. While unbelief is the theoretical enemy of humanity, superstition is its practical enemy. Heathen temples were full of incredible false gods; our times have produced some enthusiasts[47] in unbelief who, like papists with Mary, pay homage only to reason.

GENESIS 4:10–14

Gen 3:17–19 The curse that Adam's sin against God had brought on the ground
is replicated by Cain's sin against his brother. Even though Adam's work would be hard, nevertheless God's blessing would reward it with its fruits. The work of Cain would be, to some extent, in vain, or without the result that his father could expect for himself from it. The ground would withhold its strength from him. The more communally people live, the more they can enjoy the produce of the land and soil that they farm together. The more strictly they fulfill their duties to each other in their community, the easier it is for them to satisfy their needs and the more they benefit from their strength. Disunity weakens community and diminishes the value of its natural assets. It turns fruitful land into a wilderness and impoverished inhabitants into fugitives that seek to gain nothing, so that they would have nothing to lose.

---

47. The German word here is *Schwärmer*, "gushers." Luther used this term for religious "enthusiasts" who wrongly held that they were filled with God apart from any external mediation. Here Hamann implies that the contemporary rationalists were, in fact, "believers" who worshipped reason as their idol, the false god that filled their minds.

We see the unhappy results of a bad conscience that numb and befog our reason laying us open to the fury of the most disordered and gruesome emotions. Adam was frightened and ashamed of himself before God. He wanted to be invisible. His own body annoyed him. He blamed God for giving him a helper that he had received from his Creator with such delight and interest as a part of his own nature. He wants to escape God's omnipresence and omniscience with fig leaves and shady trees. By his despair Cain renounces divine mercy. He forgets God's right and power to punish him and is only afraid of the vengeance of his fellow creatures. He begs his Judge, his true Judge that he ignores, for nothing except to be kept safe from them. Cain seems to intimate that his crime is too great to be forgiven by human beings. He does not regard his condition as a fugitive and wanderer as the result of his evil deed but as an arbitrary punishment by God which therefore seems to be too harsh for him because in this state he must succumb to the first person who meets him. In every feature of this description of Cain by Moses, we see a picture of the unhappiness that we fall into through our wrongdoing. Those who deliberately become an enemy of community cannot expect to receive the benefits from it. Nature withholds the strength from such a miserable person that it shares with others. What an influence unsociable passions have on human health, human posture, and human perceptions. If a peaceful heart which can only come from virtue makes for living well continually, then an evil heart is a poison that embitters all our food and robs its natural vitality. This mental unease makes us unsteady. Our fear shows us enemies all around us where there are none, and it gives us an excuse to treat all people as such. Every evildoer is stupid enough to buy a stay of execution from the devil and to fear hell less than the sword of the judge.

Gen 3:10

Gen 2:18, 23

Gen 3:7–8

GENESIS 4:15

How ridiculous is the curiosity to guess what the sign of Cain was! If Moses had told us, how many interpretations would have been given of it! Since nothing has been disclosed to us of it, restless people have made up for the lack of it. Clearly enough, we see a sign of the great covenant which concerns nothing less than the preservation of the human race and its habitat.[48] How indifferently we regard it, even though the reason for this sign is revealed to us and is so important to us.

GENESIS 4:17

The first city was built by Cain. Apparently, he gave up farming the land because he experienced the effect of God's curse on this work. The fear from his bad conscience made him look at everything with hostile eyes. He used all his reason and his abilities to create a safe place against his fear. The neglect of agriculture and the unruly passions that were produced by leisure, together with the distractions by which it tried to make up for its empty time and empty heart, spread through his descendants. The discovery of music made some people soft and lascivious. Presumably, the discovery of metals led soon enough to weapons with which by practice they secured artificial strength and superior power against animals and their fellow citizens. Early on, the weakness of one and the power of another gave rise to tyrants and slaves, ambitious giants and lascivious weaklings. The descendants of Cain seem to have given up farming. It seems that animal husbandry was their
Gen 4:20 only occupation. On account of the few buildings that they set up on the land, they became nomadic families who were comfortable with living in tents. Perhaps Jubal's sons were neither shepherds nor farmers, but were supported by them for the pleasure and amusement that they provided these workers, just like the sons of Tubal-Cain for the protection of both shepherds and farmers from the
Gen 4:22 weapons they invented. In our thoughts we always need to picture the human race in its childhood. We know the power of youthful passions. So each person can judge what they were like for the first people and especially for the coarse descendants of Adam as their

48. This most likely refers to God's covenant with Noah.

idleness increased and got out of hand (Luke 17:27; Matt 24:38), as the wickedness of their tyranny transgressed all limits (Gen 6:4).

GENESIS 4:24

Without doubt this speech by Lamech has been retained as an example of the mentality that governed his descendants. We see how all perceptions of human love are stifled by the desire for revenge, and how, on account of God's patience with Cain's crime, this desire for revenge hardens and boasts about a greater, much more privileged freedom to commit its own crime. How necessary it is that crime must be punished on earth, so that all the wheat is not choked out by weeds. It is also necessary that any government *Matt 13:37–41* is committed to do what is right for a society, and that, even if God could disown his own holiness with regard to the sins that people committed against himself, he must unleash extraordinary punishments against them to preserve them. Lamech's conclusion, which he seems to suppose is a natural law is this: if Cain who killed his innocent brother was avenged seven times, then Lamech would be avenged seventy-seven times, because he killed a man for wounding him and a young man giving him the bruise that he, no doubt, showed his wives. He considered it right for them to allow him to *Gen 4:23* vent his rage without setting any limits to what it wanted. Had not God perhaps intended to avenge Abel's murder by the sacrifice of all the firstborn males under the law? *Exod 13:1–2, 11–17; 23:19*

GENESIS 5:1–6:3

If we consider the construction of our body with the number of years that we live, it seems that its fragility and weakness correspond exactly to its lifespan. The genealogy in this chapter shows how long the life of the first people lasted in contrast with ours. It also shows how all the things that we number in the course of nature and count as its laws depend directly on God.

Which natural law is more universal and certain than that each person must die? Yet even this law was waived by the will of the Most High in the case of Enoch. Just as people often set their nature *Gen 5:21–24* against their reason and will and make their customary activity a matter of necessity, so worldly wisdom has often wished to set nature against its Creator and spoken of unnatural and supernatural works. God has performed so many miracles, we could rather say, that we should regard nothing as natural. What is there in nature, in the most common and most natural occurrences, that is not a miracle for us, a miracle in its strictest sense?

GENESIS 5:21, 24

Enoch walked with God. He regarded his life as a journey, a way by which we must come to our homeland, God's dwelling place. This happy pilgrim chose as his fellow traveler and companion, his guide and his leader, the Lord of eternity where by faith he hoped
Heb 11:5, 13–16 and sought to lodge with him. He found a shortcut that is unknown to everyone but only revealed by God to two men who were dear to him (Heb 11:13).[49]

GENESIS 6:1–4

The sensuality and attendant debauchery of people is here designated as a crime that God's Spirit was no longer able to keep in check.

While a part of the human race abandoned themselves to bestial lasciviousness, a few arose who in their pride and conceit set themselves up as gods and apparently began to be adored as such by those enslaved to their lusts. The name that they made for themselves by their deeds, their ambitious work to gain fame, seemed to be something supernatural for the weaklings who found their greatest happiness in indolence and luxury. What a source of vices and atrocities is here uncovered for us! We see people who had been made in God's image transformed almost into beasts and demons, people who no longer had any knowledge of God and used all their abilities to grieve him, people who had the will of fallen angels without their power. In his omniscience God was best able to foresee

49. The other man was Elijah, who, like Enoch, was taken up from this life without dying (2 Kgs 2:1–11).

this. So he told Noah in 6:13 that he was well aware of this frightful outcome. In his compassion he let them perish, because, apart from the Flood, their violence and wickedness would have wiped them out, but without any deliverance, without any possible help. In order to preserve the deliverance of the human race, he had to implement such an extraordinary measure, such a universal punishment on them. So in the foresight that comes from experience, a gardener makes a final attempt to prevent a tree from withering up entirely, by chopping it off down to its roots. *Matt 3:10*

GENESIS 6:11–12

God looks down on the earth (2 Chr 16:9). But not with pleasure as he saw the new earth coming from his hand. All that had formerly been very good has been corrupted. *Isa 65:17; Rev 21:1* His purpose in creating human beings, the great blessedness that he had intended for them in the world and in him, this divine way which human ways were meant to follow,[50] had been corrupted, without leaving any trace of it any longer. The narrow way which was supposed to lead people to heaven was overgrown; it was no longer traveled by anyone, *Matt 7:14* and it had been lost. However, the road to hell was so broad that the whole earth, so to say, traveled on it. Was this the purpose of creation? Did God have this in mind when he formed man and breathed in him the breath of life? *Gen 2:7* No, but the carnal-minded man made it, so to say, impossible for God himself to help him. *Rom 8:5* And his wisdom found no other means to once again renew his way and to pave it anew than the extermination of this brood which did not any longer want to know God's will. They cast his warnings and threats to the wind. They scorned heaven into which he had, by a *miracle*, transferred Enoch on account of the footsteps by which *Gen 5:24* he showed that path to his contemporaries and his descendants as well as the destination to which his footsteps had brought him. They were as unnaturally indifferent to the fate of future generations as an ostrich with its young, because they welcomed their own demise, *Lam 4:3*

50. Here Hamann notes the two possible interpretations of the phrase in 6:11 as "His way" (KJV; ESV) and "its way," the way of all flesh (RSV; NIV).

mocked Noah, and confidently and defiantly awaited the fulfillment of God's wrath. Thus the purpose of the great flood was to restore God's way on earth (Jer 6:19). On the one hand, he let the unhappy world see its captivity once for all time, handing it over to Satan's power, and showing it the outcome of its ways and the payment *Gen 5:32; 6:18* for its wickedness once for all time. On the other hand, in order to impress the frightful example of their fellow creatures even more deeply on them, he convinced eight souls of his existence, his holiness, and righteousness, and revealed himself to them as the Lord, Judge, and Savior of men.

GENESIS 6:17

Gen 6:17 God says, "Behold, I, even I." Despite this repeated, emphatic assurance that God had brought on a flood of waters, it has occurred to some natural scientists and intellectuals to make this event easier for God's omnipotence by their explanations.[51] They fancied that this would have happened apart from God's will, yes even apart from the occasion that human sin provided for him to carry out his will, or else that by themselves God's will and its power seemed for them to be insufficient if they could not imagine that it was reasonably possible or even easily done. Reason, it seems, could not, any earlier, have discovered that the story of the flood was true, nor could it have rescued the reputation of Moses any better until it excluded God's freedom as much as possible from the story or belittled his omnipotence by making it subject to human means. They presuppose the construction of the earth under certain conditions and the advent of a certain comet, in order to deduce the inundation of the earth by these two things as necessarily as the alternation of day and night from its revolution around its axis. Under these conditions the philosopher rejoices in his happy rescue of the Author of the divine story and cries out with the surveyor of antiquity who

51. Here Hamann most likely alludes to the speculations of the English mathematician and theologian William Whiston (1667–1752).

demanded a place for a lever to shift the earth from its central position:[52] "Give me this kind of planet that I have described for you, a planet created before the flood, and this kind of comet which God then had at hand, and I will have enough water to put the earth fifteen cubits under water, and let it emerge again by itself in the form that you now see it."

GENESIS 8:7–11

The story of the three birds corresponds far too closely with the blessings that Noah gives to his three sons not to prefigure them. Ham was the raven that did not return, but, as soon as it left the ark, excluded itself from it, like Ham's descendants from the blessing of the other two brothers. Like the dove that flew back to the ark after Noah had stretched out his hand, which helped it come back to him in the ark, God persuaded Japheth to dwell in the tents of Shem (Gen 9:27). The last dove with the olive leaf is Shem, whose descendants would be promised the blessing of all nations and the prince of peace. For Ham the raven see Gen 9:22. *Gen 12:3; 18:18; 22:18; 26:4; 28:14; Isa 9:6*

GENESIS 9:1–16

God makes a twofold covenant with the human race in particular and with it and the whole animal creation in general. Not without reason God repeats five times that the latter covenant has to do with people as well as with every living creature (9:10, 12, 15, 16, 17). I am surprised that the closer interest which God takes in the animal world has been ignored, and that he wants people to pay more attention to it in order to understand it.

The reasons for this are perhaps explicable from God's special covenant with human beings. Here we first discover that, instead of the rule that was given to them over the animals in creation, the fear and dread of them was put on living creatures. Second, they obtain the freedom to nourish themselves from the animals. Third, their *Gen 1:28; Gen 9:2* *Gen 9:3*

52. This refers to the Greek mathematician Archimedes (287–212 BC), who worked out the physics of the lever and is reputed to have said: "Give me somewhere to stand and I will move the world."

Gen 9:4–6 (see Lev 17:11) blood had to be a substitute for the blood of human beings. God provided the blood of the animals as a ransom from them for their own life. Should not the Spirit of religion extend to the lower creation in us, so that the blood of those animals which have nourished us would be a substitute for the human race for so many centuries? Do we Christians not also enjoy the flesh and blood of the Passover Lamb who has purchased and redeemed us with his divine blood? *1 Cor 5:7; 1 Pet 1:18–19; Rev 1:5; 5:9*

GENESIS 9:26–27

Here we see the forefather of the human race drunk from the vintage of his own vineyard, in a sleep that accompanied his intoxication, in a state that a sober person or also a wide-awake intoxicated person would have been ashamed of. Ham sees his nakedness and all its attendant circumstances as a kind of enjoyable spectacle, from which we may conclude that he apparently reports this to his two brothers to let them see the show that he had enjoyed. How well this behavior of Ham foretells the corruption of his descendants! In them we encounter human nature in the same sorry, shameful state, in the intoxication of its desires, in the insensitivity of the most disgusting vices and crudest idolatry in which they, like sleeping drunkards, have, for many centuries, been lying and still lie buried. For the Romans Africa was the homeland of what was atrocious; in this the human race seems to have copied its senseless inhabitants eagerly and outdone them.[53] But with what godly wisdom the behavior of Shem and Japheth portrays the customs of their descendants. Since they failed to share in the detestable excesses that the Canaanites particularly enjoyed, they, instead, tried to cover

53 Hamann understands this story theologically and spiritually rather than morally and genetically. For him, Noah is the father of the human race in its fallen state. His drunken sleep discloses human nature in all its shameful nakedness. Like his spiritual descendants, Ham regards his father's nakedness as a spectacle for enjoyment, a pornographic spectacle that intoxicates its voyeurs, desensitizes them spiritually and corrupts them with sexual idolatry. On the other hand, Shem and Japheth deal with it appropriately by averting their eyes from it and covering it, so that Noah's human dignity is restored in a prophetic enactment that prefigures the redemption of all Noah's descendants. That includes the descendants of Ham. Hamann therefore discounts the racial misapplication of the 'curse of Ham' genetically to black Africans. He challenges his reader to consider whether they may be spiritual heirs of Ham.

up what was abhorrent and weak in human nature, like their father here with clothing. Just as Noah lay drunk and naked in their midst and was only a little less visible, so it was too with their pursuit of knowledge and virtue. They could not restore their intoxicated, sleeping, naked nature to the wakeful, sober state of Noah when he walked with God. They fancied that it would be sufficient and all that they could do, to cover him with clothing, just as their first parents did not know how to find any better help than fig leaves.

Their imperfection and inadequacy are expressed even more beautifully and sensuously by two particular features. They "walked backward" (Isa 44:25). The wisest heathen were nothing better than people walking backward. Their faces were averted so that they could not see the nakedness of their father. They had no knowledge of the great disgrace and deep misery of fallen human nature. Can someone like Blackmore, who has impressed the learned world with his enthusiasm for ancient mythology,[54] show us an allegory which has clothed such important truths, not just important but also prophetic truths, in such simple, lively, varied, and amazingly similar pictures and colors? When we also consider the three words which he utters, after waking up from his intoxication and catching sight of the clothes which he discovered had covered him in his sleep, we see the sudden transformation of a drunken, insensible man, lying completely and disgracefully naked, waking up as an angel. He seems to be more than a man. He sees far over the centuries into the future. He beholds the inhabitants of Africa in the same light as we still see them. Enraptured, he speaks of God's blessing and the participation of the gentiles in it. Even more than that, like a god he determines the fate of the nations with his curse and blessing. He exercises his power over the nations of the earth and speaks as a judge of the earth (1 Cor 6:2). Which human tongue has ever included such a stream of knowledge with so few words as Noah does here, and in an event which looks so simple and yet explains so many deep mysteries? When we have admired Shem and Japheth

54. This refers to Richard Blackmore and his work *The Creation: A Philosophical Poem* (London, 1712).

enough with the cloak on their shoulders and their uncertain steps as they walked backward with their faces turned away, we will be able to recognize the God of Shem in chapter 16 of Ezekiel with so much more admiration and love.

The more we consider the words of Noah together with his story, the richer our meditations on them both will be. Here we see Shem and Japheth doing the same thing. The God of the younger brother Shem would be invoked only by Jacob. The Jews under the law and the gentiles under the light of reason are completely equal before God. Both revelations, the revelation of the law and the revelation of nature and the conscience, were insufficient for their salvation. This rested alone on the divine Fulfiller and Satisfier of the law, on the Light of the gentiles, on the God of Shem who would persuade Japheth to dwell in the tents of his younger brother (Mark 9:5, 6).

Matt 5:17; Isa 42:6; 49:6; Luke 2:32

GENESIS 11:1–9

The whole earth had a common language and a common speech. God had not just maintained a common language but also a common way of speaking subject to the natural variability of all human things. This is even more surprising because language depends so much on ways of thinking and customs. In the course of their development, both of these ran so wild and became so opposed, even though the sound of it did not change its form.

Here we find an unusual unity among human beings, the unity that gained its strength from folly and the evil thoughts of the heart. For only in this are people perfectly *equal* and perfectly *united* in their human nature. "Come! Come!" So verses 3 and 4 begin. One city and one tower whose top reaches up into heaven. One name that will result for us from that, and so on. For this eternal enterprise, from which they expected to gain such great fame for themselves, they used fragile bricks rather than stones that would be more likely to last and loose slime rather than firmer cement.

I doubt whether all the sons of Shem took part in this famous construction of folly. It may be that the example of their scattering and dispersal gave all the others reason to fear what they wanted to prevent through their project.

God realized that this unity in the human race was a disadvantage to them. The leprosy of human nature was too infectious for it to be expedient to lock them all up in the circle of a city wall and under one roof. The vassals of Belial[55] would have made his dominion heavier and stronger through their union under him (Matt 12:25).. Thus the confusion of language was carried out by God as a solemn decree of the Trinity and as the only means to deal with the misadventure in which they became their own master builders.

Just as I have noted that human beings would probably have wiped themselves out even without the Flood and that in view of this the Flood should not at all be regarded as a punishment but as a benevolent act, so the dispersal and the *misunderstanding* of a sadder kind from this unity would have occurred, like a storm after a time of calm, as something that God brought about as a miracle in their midst.

Moses describes God's zeal in curbing the resolve of these people with the same word that they had expressed theirs: "Come!" The deity speaks in plural form in order to confront this united people. "Come!" says God. "We want to condescend from heaven. Let Us go down." This is the means by which we have come closer to heaven: the condescension of God to earth. Not by the tower of reason, whose top reaches heaven! Not by its bricks and slime with which we think that we can make a name for ourselves! Not by its banners which are supposed to serve as a sign for the erring crowd! Each person understands his own speech, and no one understands the speech of another person. Descartes understands his reason, Leibnitz his reason, Newton his own reason.[56] Do they therefore understand each other better? We must learn their speech to

55. Literally "worthlessness" in Hebrew. See 2 Cor 6:15 for the use of this derogative term for the devil.

56. These three scholars were pioneers of the Enlightenment. See footnote 7 for Newton and footnote 28 for Descartes. Leibnitz (1646–1716) was a German polymath who was famous for his discovery of calculus, his teaching on theodicy, and his efforts to unite the Lutheran and Roman Catholic churches.

distinguish their concepts; we must check their subject matter; we must examine the purpose of their system, the foundation for it, the goal that they pursue, and the place where they end. We must not act according to the promises or prejudices which they impose on us as principles, experiences, and conclusions. And so on.

When God lifted his curse on the earth and its soil, he presumably also foreordained the unification of mankind with a single language and a single knowledge of the truth. The spread of the gospel is the means to unite our hearts, our senses, and our reason. By the destruction of Babel, the prophets of the Old and New Testament give us hope that, like the Jewish diaspora, the dispersal of the human race would also come to an end. The preservation and government of the world will remain a continuous miracle as long as that, until the *mystery of God* is finished (Rev 10:7).

GENESIS 12:10–20

It is clear that this part of Abraham's life resembles the story of God's people. Like the children of Israel, famine drives him into Egypt. Just as they owed their life to their brother, so Abraham asks his wife to pass him off as her brother, because nothing apart from this title seems to give him security for his life. Through this he has success in Egypt. His departure from Egypt is so similar that I need not dwell on it any longer.

GENESIS 13:8

Compare this with Acts 7:25, 26. As Abraham was inclined to go
Gen 13:9 out of the way for his brother's son, so Moses had to separate him-
Exod 2:11–15 self from his people for fear of Pharaoh. Abraham's rescue of Lot
follows soon after this, just as the Israelites were rescued by the
Exod 12:1–18, 27 same Moses who wanted to remedy their disunity with each other.

GENESIS 13:17

Abraham's faith probably provided him with the energy and vigor for God to commission him to inspect this land as his own: "Arise, walk up and down through the whole land, in the length and breadth of it." Who can doubt that Abram's faith burned in equal measure from the fire of these promises? We can read about the effect of them on David's soul in Psalm 60; cf. Psalm 108.

GENESIS 14

This chapter is full of the most extraordinary events in the life of Abraham. The alliance of four conquerors! The subjugation by them of five neighboring kings for twelve years, before they tried to shake off their yoke and rebel against their tyrants! The amazing success of the four kings with their weapons against all who stood in their way! Their pride in attacking and also overthrowing their rebellious vassals! The five conquered princes seem to have deserved the disaster that happened to them and their subjects whose goods and foodstuff the victors took away with them. I say, they appear to have deserved the disaster because of the previous testimony to their wickedness in chapter 13. We shall find even stronger proof *Gen 13:13*
of it in what follows. Among the booty that they took from Sodom and Gomorrah was Lot. A fugitive brings Abram news about his fate. He led his servants into battle, triumphs over these successful tyrants and recovers all their booty, his brother Lot, his possessions, his women, and his people. We cannot read the elated description of this campaign of Abram by the prophet Isaiah and the moving use of it by God without delight (Isa 41).

After this, two utterly unlike persons who claim our attention by their difference and contrast appear in the story of Moses. One of the saved kings confronts Abram in order to demonstrate his gratitude and offer all his possessions, pleading only for the release of his captured people in exchange for them.

The second is Melchizedek, King of Salem, to whom Abram offers a tithe of all the booty for the blessing that he had received from him.

The reticence of Moses in his mention of this king, despite his importance as a person and the office that he attributes to him, shows how God limits himself in using Moses only as a writer of the history of the Jewish people and his rule over them from their cradle

onwards. Paul could tell the Hebrews what God did not at all wish
Heb 7:1–10 to explain to them through Moses on account of their weakness. A
Jew had to regard the law as the only true religion, the only divine
service. We, however, should not think that the law was necessary
in God's sight as the only condition for pleasing him. God most
likely had people who truly served and honored him in the line of
Japheth and Shem, people who tried to preserve the knowledge and
faith of Noah, for we here discover a priest that belonged to this
Ps 110:4 order. Yet it pleased God to call idolatrous Abram to himself and to
Josh 24:2–4 grant him special favors. He made him a great nation on account of
the promises that he had given to him and the faith with which he
had received them, to take his descendants under his special rule
Gen 12:1–3 and care. It pleased God to instruct us sufficiently about the good
deeds that he showed to his people and to demonstrate the same
from them to him; and all this to prepare the world for the Messiah
before he came, and when he had come, to convince it, much more
emphatically, about the truth of this event.

I am using this particular case to give a correct idea of the purpose of God's revelation. It had to be spread out through the Jews. It had to make them as interesting as possible by the exact description of the life story of their ancestors that was meant to fascinate them with the most trivial details and by all the means that could engage the interests of a nation and draw it to himself. It is therefore just as foolish to look for a history of other nations in the books of Moses, except where its connection with other nations makes it absolutely necessary, as to look for the complete elucidation of a divine system in a revelation that occurred for humanity, because it
1 Pet 1:12 contains things that make the angels eager to look into. And he has made so many events prophetic for faith as well as instructive for morality; that is, they prefigure future events and teach his general will, so that we can arrange what we do in the future according to it.

Here the victory of Abraham undoubtedly prefigures the victories of his descendants under Moses and Joshua. Thus Melchizedek as a person pointed the Jews to a Priest and King to whom Moses and Joshua were to show honor and pay homage. We, praise God, recognize this Melchizedek in the bread and wine that he gave and from the seventh chapter of the Letter to the Hebrews. Abraham's unselfishness and conscientiousness about the oath that he had made was an example of their father Abraham that the Israelites do not copy.

GENESIS 15

"I am your shield and very great reward. To take away your fear, trust in my omnipotence," God wants to say. "Trust in my love, my truth and faithfulness. I present myself to you. The use of my attributes shall, as it were, be in your hands. You shall use them as a shield. I will withhold my righteousness for a long time, until I let you participate in my secret decrees. My conciliatory character will remain asleep in me unless Abram's words and complaints awaken it. You will teach me righteousness; you will teach me grace.[57] All danger ends when this life ends; it is only here that you need a shield, and only here that you need to use me as a shield. It will not be enough for me to reward you as an infinite God rewards a finite creature by loving as he loves himself (that is all that can be said and still be true), but I myself will be your very great reward."

Moses seems to be so moved by this promise of God and believes that he provides people with such unexpected joy by it that he puts this promise up front and then gives a detailed account of the occasion for it together with an extensive description of God's appearance. These words seem to me to be part of that. The fear of Abram seems to be explained in 15:12 and 15.

As careful as Abram is here in 15:11 in guarding the signs of God's covenant and driving away every bird that wants to approach them, so God wants to fulfill the terms of covenant. (Might not our Savior allude to this instance in the story of Abraham when he says in Matt 24:28 that wherever a corpse is there the vultures will gather?)

57. This is a truly amazing assertion about Abraham as an intercessor and God's condescension in speaking to him as in Gen 18:16–21. God's conciliatory character remains asleep until, like the psalmist in Ps 35:23; 44:23; 59:4–5, Abraham's prayers awaken it and determine how it is to be shown in any given situation, such as was the case with his intercession for Sodom in Gen 18:22–32.

GENESIS 18

In all likelihood we may regard this appearance of God as the one *John 8:56* about which our Savior said that Abram rejoiced in that day. Here Abram addresses God with the appropriating word of faith. He races; he commands Sarah to hurry; he runs to the herd, picks a tender, good calf, and prepares it quickly.

Who can remain unmoved to read about God's condescension in his address to Abram in 18:17–19? We see how he accommodates himself to human passions, and how circumspectly he instructs *Gen 14:8–17, 21–24* Abram. Here the Redeemer of Sodom is its advocate.God had given this people an example of better morals with Lot as their neighbor. He had punished its princes and subjects with slavery, with warfare. He delivered them again, delivered them at no cost to them through Abram. Yet they showed no gratitude to Lot for the liberation through his friend nor the least regard for his better morals. How often God repeats to Abram what he says just as emphatically through the prophets: "I do not desire, I do not desire the death *Ezek 18:23, 32; 33:11* of a sinner."

GENESIS 19

Human beings do not want to be preserved. They had 120 years in vain before the Flood. The angels came in vain to rescue Lot's sons-in-law. They regarded the offer of rescue as a ridiculous matter, a joke. When men are miraculously preserved, how little are they, like Lot's wife, concerned to do the least that is required for their preservation!

When will people learn that their life, their true existence, their happiness, and everything depends on God's commandments *Matt 19:17* (19:26)? With the author of the Wisdom of Solomon 10:7 we may regard the people of Sodom as an example of an unbelieving soul or punished disobedience. Here, however, I cannot refrain from adding a special observation about God's judgments. How closely God keeps his eyes, as it were, on those who have seen his judgments when he lets them escape from them! How severely he avenges the disrespectful insensitivity, curiosity, or malice of those who see their fellow creatures under God's special judgment! Lot's wife wanted to have the credit in her family of giving the most accurate description of this event. She may have hesitated in order to remain behind, so that she would have enough time to observe it undisturbed and quite alone. The others did not think of doing so from obedience to the angel's command and maybe from fear. She did not consider God's wrath nor the misfortune of her former townsfolk. How fitting for such a mentality is her transformation into a rigid pillar of salt! In this chapter we also discover how quickly this example of disobedience in his family was forgotten by Lot, as well as how Lot's daughters were punished for their lechery. *Gen 19:30–38*

GENESIS 22

The previous chapter gives us evidence of motherly love in 21:16 so that we will be even more amazed at the victory of Abraham over his natural tenderness.

Moses, it seems, passes quickly over what happened in so many centuries where the main events were a reproach to humanity. Adam's life was not at all noteworthy apart from the outstanding proof of his ingratitude and disobedience. Abraham's whole life is so much more noteworthy as a practical example of human obedience that touches God himself. The blessing of his descendants, yes, the blessing of the whole human race, is promised to him on account of his obedience. God seems to have waited for this example of human obedience in order to match it with the full height of divine love and goodness. In God's eyes this act made him worthy to be the father of Isaac, the forefather of David, and, as the end and climax of it all, the forefather of the Messiah.

GENESIS 23

In this chapter we find a valuable picture from antiquity of how solemn contracts were sealed and what customs prevailed among them for their wellbeing. The money that Abraham pays for the future possession of the land purchases a field for a tomb that was worth what he paid. Thus Abraham bought a cemetery in the land

of promise, the promised land for the Israelites, where nothing belonged to their family except a grave. Thus earthly Canaan was the land where the ashes of their father rested. It was a shadow of
Heb 10:1 the land that their souls had entered.

GENESIS 24

Who could fail to notice the faithfulness of Abraham's upright, devout servant? He prays, "O God of my master, give me success today not for my own sake but so that my master may receive new evidence of your kindness and favor. Graciously grant that I may deliver it to him with my own hand" (24:12). The emotions that his amazement and attentiveness aroused in him (24:21). The joy and thankfulness that breaks out from his devotion (24:27). The modesty and humility of this upright servant (24:30) who was proud of his master's confidence in him (24:10, 30). His zeal in declaring his commitment to his master's concerns (24:49). And his impatience in hurrying back to give him an account of the successful outcome. Is this not a picture of God's servants, and especially Moses, through whom God wished to rule his people?

GENESIS 25

How brief Moses is in reporting those things that are not part of his plan. He seems to introduce them only so as to allude to this.

In 25:5, 6 Abraham gives all that he has to his promised son without treating his other sons unjustly. He distributes gifts to them and sends them away with presents. This simple account sheds many rays of light on the picture that Isaac's obedience presents and the payment and privilege that our divine Redeemer has gained for those who belong to him (Ps 8:6).

In this deed of Abraham, we see an allusion to God's stewardship of the Jewish people with regard to other nations. When he made the Jews heirs of a great promise, he did not forget the other nations. Like Abraham he was rich enough to satisfy them with other gifts which were probably just as significant in their eyes as the privilege of Isaac in succession to him. Don't we discover that Esau sold his birthright as the firstborn son for a stew of beans? Gen 25:29–34

GENESIS 27

We should be amazed to see how God is involved in all trivial circumstances and prefers to reveal his reign in the common events of human life rather than rare and extraordinary events. We see how he controls the prejudices, the errors, and the good and evil inclinations of people. He directs them according to his design and also carries it out so splendidly through them for themselves despite all human hindrances. While we ignorant, poor people think of nothing but how to satisfy our petty passions and carry out our projects, God deals out his own design like a pack of cards into our hands. A Rebekah works with that design as if it were her own, and an Isaac, despite his reluctance, his cautious concern to protect himself against deception, must put his hand to it. It was in vain that Isaac *trembled strongly with great trembling*; in vain that one violent shudder after another overcame him. Jacob says, "I have blessed him: yes, he shall be blessed." It was in vain that Esau, who had despised his birthright, now perceives the greatness of the blessing that he had forfeited.

We cannot read about his sorrow and despair unmoved, as he now laments about the blessing that he had lost. He suffers continually from the delusion that this blessing depends on his father. It was in vain that Esau turned his pain into deadly hatred and waited only for the death of his father to kill his brother. It seemed as if he hoped to find a kind of comfort in the murder of his brother.

GENESIS 28:6–9

Do we not see how God's gracious election is justified by his rejection of Esau? His envy at seeing that his brother was loved and obedient motivates him to do whatever he can to grieve his parents. Moses is just as frank in mentioning God's patience and

condescension, his forbearance[58] with the weaknesses and transgressions of the patriarchs. Who is not surprised to see how Jacob is caught up in such a weak understanding of God's omnipresence after the extraordinary manifestation that he had seen in the dream? Instead of loving the place where God had given him so many gen-
Gen 28:17 erous promises, he regards it with fear and trembling. He is horrified to discover that he is so close to God's house and standing in the gates of heaven.

GENESIS 28:20–22

Who is not astonished at God's condescension when we hear Jacob's conditions for accepting God as his God? Who is not astonished at how God is pleased not to demand faith from him any sooner than when God would have, as it were, earned the right to do so through the fulfillment of everything that Jacob recognized as necessary for his temporal success?

GENESIS 29

The life of the patriarchs is full of allegories for Jewish history. This means that in his government of what happened in their lives God has given a model of his plan for the Jews. Laban's contradictory, ungrateful, deceptive, and harsh encounter with Jacob depicts in a very sensory way how the Jews would later treat God. Who does not see in Jacob's agreement what we see as a shadow in Isaac when he became silent?[59] "Give me my wife, for my time is completed" (29:21). He has to put up with another seven years.

GENESIS 29:31

Human hatred moves God to do what is good, more good, greater good than the evil that all mortals can do to harm us, yes, more good than all people together can do for us. Do we still want to have any doubt about God's rule, when Scripture regards all great

58. Hamann provides "overlooking" as an alternate reading in superscript.

59. This may refer to the silence of Isaac in Genesis 22:9–10 or 24:62–67.

events, all important affairs, as insignificant, in order to show us how God's attention extends to the most trivial movements of our souls, such as Isaac's love for wild game (25:28), to Jacob's pea stew (25:29), to Jacob's cushion of stone (28:11), and the colors of Laban's livestock? He prizes these proofs as alone worthy of his revelation, these proofs of his foreknowledge of the emotions that he arouses in the hearts of princes and their ministers, in order to produce revolutions in the kingdoms of the world, those proofs, I say, that are mostly as foolish as these. So, on one hand, Jacob's life is a preview of all the afflictions that God's people would fear and from which they would be redeemed. On the other hand, in his dealings with Laban, his life is an example of God's patience with their ingratitude. God's word is like a flaming sword that turns around in all directions, or like a light that contains all colors in itself.

Gen 3:24; Heb 4:12; Rev 1:16; 2:16

GENESIS 33:2, 14

We see the law of love in Jacob's arrangement of the order for the company, and, more remotely, in the pace of its movement as he wants to lead it. He says, "I will lead my people on slowly, following in the footsteps of my work and in the footsteps of my children."[60] It was God's love that let the two maidservants go first[61] and made his revelation through his Son come last at the rear of all the rest as his dearest work for them.

Because of human weakness, did not God's work require that he proceeded with this revelation so slowly, so comfortably? Which Christian knows God so poorly that he would think that he was delaying it, let alone blame him for its delay?

GENESIS 33:19

Here Jacob purchases a tiny piece of land to set up his tent in a land which, according to the promise, would belong entirely to his descendants. God also purchases the Jewish people as the one spot

60. The Hebrew noun used here means both work in its usual sense, and occasionally livestock that is the product of human work.

61. This refers to God's revelation through the law and the prophets in the Old Testament.

in the whole earth with the intention of convincing all nations that they would be as dear and close to him as they were. Just as the Jews had an equally valid right to the whole land as Jacob had to this spot, so the right of all nations is comparable to the right of this single man. A piece of land to set up a tent! How perfectly this corresponds with earthly Canaan, the tabernacle, yes even Solomon's temple, in comparison with the glory that would arise and has arisen
Isa 40:5; 60:1 for the whole world. *The Spirit of prophecy is the testimony of Jesus* (Rev 19:10). This rule serves as the cornerstone for the whole of the Holy Scriptures and must be the touchstone of all interpreters.

GENESIS 34

This chapter is quite significant. It shows that circumcision does not make anyone a Jew, that this sign of the covenant was not the covenant itself, and that this covenant consisted only of Abraham's blessing which should only belong to his family. By their execution of the circumcised men of Shechem, Simeon and Levi seem to contradict the bias of the Jews for circumcision. After this event and the reason for it, the emphasis in 34:31 is on God's accusations against the Jewish church by its portrayal as a prostitute.

GENESIS 37:33

Jacob says, "This is my son's robe! A wild animal has devoured him." Just as the aged Jacob identified the robe with his son and tied the fate of both together in his thoughts, so the Jews thought they had destroyed the whole Redeemer by destroying that man. What blindness! When the children of Israel no longer had this brother, they went hungry. These brothers could just as rightly say to Joseph as Abraham had said to Sarah, "Let me be your brother, so that it may go well with me on your account and my soul may live because of you" (Gen 12:13). They begrudged him what they had proposed to do with his robe. It is my son's robe, it was the human nature of the Redeemer, it was his body, it was the heels
Gen 3:15 by which the serpent had stung him. Here we see how the true perpetrators of the supposed murder that Jacob accepted as a fact,

could not, in their conscience, regard themselves any better than that. Yes, they declared themselves to be such by doing what they did to deceive their father, so that he would not conclude anything better than Joseph's death. When we see this and them comforting their father, is it not like when we see the Jews eating the Passover lamb so soon after they had slain the Lamb for the world? Jacob grieved for his son and asked for no other comfort than in the grave of his murdered son who was nevertheless on the way to make his old days happy.

Gen 37:35

John 1:29; 6:33, 51

GENESIS 38:9

Like the sin of Simon, the sin of Onan has been turned into the common noun. Yet onanism has as little to do with him[62] as simony with the gain of a spiritual office through bribery. Undoubtedly this event served even more to sharpen the observance of the law that was based on it.[63]

Acts 8:18–24

There is no historian like Moses who so often and so naturally develops the reason for actions. In a masterly manner he discloses the hand by which all things are so necessarily interwoven and interdependent on each other. As we read this chapter from verse 1 to 26, we see what a string of events is threaded together with such skill, and, even more, how they are soldered together in an extraordinary way. He begins with Judah's acquaintance with an Adullamite. This is connected with Judah's marriage; the marriage of his oldest son with his lapse into a wicked act; with his terrible judgment on his stepdaughter whom he wanted to have burnt to death; with his recantation of that judgment; and even with his great confession: "This sinful woman whom I had sentenced to death by burning is more righteous than I." We note how the Adullamite was an intermediary, an accomplice in his transgression, a follower of his shameful behavior and an eyewitness of all its specific circumstances. We note that the seal, armband, and staff that Judah had

62. Onanism became the technical term for masturbation. But Onan withdrew from Tamar before orgasm to prevent her from becoming pregnant.

63. This refers to the law in Deut 25:5–10 for a levirate marriage.

left in the hand of this righteous prostitute testified against him. We note how she presents him with proof of his shameful behavior, just as he and his brothers had sent the robe to convince Jacob that his son had been murdered.

While the judgment of Judah that he passed on Tamar is similar to that of David, his daughter's response was similar to its application by Nathan (2 Sam 12:5–7).

GENESIS 38:28–30

God sifts the ways of people, yes, the steps that they choose to take. Since Judah intends to save his son Shelah, he was lured by Tamar to take his place. We have seen how completely Judah was convinced he was the father of the children whose mother he wanted to offer
Gen 38:24 up in fire. In this we discover God's government most powerfully in a situation that hardly seems to deserve our attention, a situation where God confounds the understanding and word of the midwife and allows her to be deceived. Not the one who put out his hand first! Not the one that she wanted to distinguish with a scarlet thread more surely as the oldest child! Not her assurance that he was the oldest! Just when she says it, the unborn child pulls his hand back in in keeping with God's will. Just when his hand is pulled back in, the other brother is there. Why all these details about the birth of one child? Because this child would belong to the forefathers of the Messiah!

GENESIS 39:5

God blesses the house of the Egyptian because of Joseph. Thus his choice of Abraham's family was also for the benefit and advantage of other nations. God's partiality for the Jews has all too often been exaggerated, because their good fortune was meant to be regarded as nothing but the means to extend it generally to the whole human race. Since God so often blessed the earth through the ancestors of the Messiah, we can expect just as much for ourselves after his coming. If Joseph's life had such an influence on the house of his master and, ultimately, on the whole land in which he resided as an alien, what can his promised presence with us Christians to the end of days accomplish? *Matt 28:20*

GENESIS 39:12[64]

We have seen Joseph's robe in his father's hand. Here we find his cloak in a woman's hand, a cloak that bore testimony to his innocence but now became the reason for his harsh imprisonment as a punishment for a crime that he could not have committed, yes for an act that was its opposite. This part of Joseph's life prefigures the life of our divine Redeemer in a new way: his innocence of heart and the wickedness of his accusers was the true cause of his punishment too. When we compare the correspondence of this preview with our Savior, we must not be surprised that, at the very hour that Jesus was taken captive, there was a young man who could remind his enemies and disciples of Joseph's flight (Mark 14:52). We should not be surprised that the evidence of Joseph's innocence in the hand of a woman served as proof of his crime, while, in contrast, in the story of our Savior a woman had to give testimony to the innocence of the accused man through a *dream*.[65] *Matt 27:19* Just as the woman here misled the man to an unjust judgment, so Pilate's wife there tried in vain to frighten him to pass a righteous judgment through a dream.

GENESIS 40

Do we not see in Joseph's two fellow prisoners the example of two murderers, one that was accepted and the other that was rejected? *Luke 23:23, 39–43* The ingratitude of people is shown by looking at the butler who forgot Joseph's request in 40:14, which was so much like that of the thief on the cross (Luke 22:43). Are we not all like the butler in this? Strictly understood, must we not owe our life and the happy state that we enjoy to our Savior, like the butler in 41:13? We forget him. The awareness of our sins that wakes our conscience is able to

64. Hamann misidentifies this as 26:12. We have corrected it here for clarity.

65. This word is underlined twice for greater emphasis.

restore the remembrance of him for us all and make us acceptable to him. I remember my own sins (41:9). Joseph is much like the Redeemer in his dignity and appearance. I have set you over everything (41:43); bow the knee (41:44, 45); the new name, so usual for the patriarchs, is received from God as a blessing. All nations come to Joseph (41:55, 57).

Matt 15:32–39 Like our Savior's miracle to satisfy the hunger of those that followed him, the famine in all the world apart from the land where Joseph was is an unnoticed miracle, because his time may have made Egypt so famous and all the surrounding countries needed to nourish themselves with Egyptian bread. *Gen 41:54–57*

The story of Joseph is like those pictures that look directly at us from whichever side we look at them. So we glimpse the glances of our Redeemer which radiate from his life.[66]

GENESIS 32:10

Old people usually have keepsakes from their youth, most of all those who have been temporally blessed by God. They retain tokens of their poverty as family heirlooms that remind them how different times now are from what they once were. They revere them as special marks of their love for their children. Judah may have retained his staff for this reason. This may have been the staff that he gave as a pledge to Tamar, the staff that bore witness to his sin (38:18, 25).

GENESIS 38

Like Cain, Onan thought, "Am I my brother's keeper?" He, the second son of Judah, represents the human race and thus too the person in whom our sin is punished and atoned for, so that the youngest brother would be preserved. We waste the seed of the *Gen 3:15; Luke 8:11* woman and the seed of God's word. That is why our Savior compares his generation with Sodom. We see God's rejection of Israel *Matt 11:23* and the Jews in Onan's punishment. The story of Judah also mysteriously foreshows God's wisdom and love in sending his Son.

66. This section is followed by three additional, retrospective sets of sketchy afterthoughts that Hamann did not incorporate in their proper places in the preceding text.

Both these acts had to do with the youngest son of creation.[67] Like Judah in this story, God is therefore presented as a widower. God passes the same judgment on himself that Judah made on Tamar, because his Son was not just a man but sin itself. The sentence of *2 Cor 5:21*
death that would be carried out on him would, humanly speaking, have turned God's righteousness into unrighteousness if he had not forgiven us, just as Tamar was found to be innocent.

GENESIS 12:7, 8; 13:4, 18

Just as God's Spirit counts and records all the acts of devotion, every altar that Abraham built, so, subsequently, the assurance by our Savior of the joy in heaven over a repentant sinner becomes apparent throughout the history of the old covenant. *Luke 15:7*

GENESIS 13:9

Abram had separated himself from his father's relatives and kinsfolk. Here we have a new separation. This proves the observation *Gen 12:1–4*
that God uses this law in the creation of the world as well as in its government and follows it in order to do all things *well.*[68] *Gen 1:31*

GENESIS 13:10, 14

Lot lifts up his eyes in order to make a choice. Happy the person God commands to do this so as to show him what he has chosen, or, as the prophet says (Ezek 20:6), what he had *explored* for them.

GENESIS 20:6

We see how what we ascribe to the goodness and innocence of our hearts is God's grace that keeps us from sinning, when we are unaware of our danger, by difficulties, by often fanciful notions,

---

67. Hamann coins this curious term in contrast with Jesus as "the first born of creation" (Col 1:15), as well as its Omega (Rev 1:8; 22:13). Just as Perez, the youngest son of Judah, became the ancestor of David and Jesus, so Jesus, the firstborn Son of God, the Alpha of creation, became the second Adam, the youngest, last-born son of creation.

68. See God's acts of separation that are mentioned in Gen 1:4, 6, 7, 14, 18, as well as all the other acts that are not specified as such, like the land from the sea, the trees from the plants, the birds from the fish, humans from the animals, and women from men.

and by the tiniest circumstances that we would otherwise not heed, yes, circumstances that would more likely inflame and incite us to fulfill our desires.

GENESIS 22:13

Just as an animal is a substitute for Isaac's offering, so all offerings
Heb 4:14; 7:26–27 are substitutes for the great offering of our High Priest. What could teach the Jews the true meaning and purpose of the sacrificial service better than this story of Abraham? With the money from the
Matt 27:2–10; Acts 1:18–19 betrayal of Jesus a grave was also purchased.[69]

GENESIS 23

Just as the possession of a grave in the promised land was the pledge for the possession of the whole land, so the grave in which Christ was laid and from which he arose is a guarantee of our resurrec-
Matt 27:59–60 tion and of heaven.

GENESIS 25:30

The concupiscence and lustfulness of Esau is expressed quite naturally: "Let me eat up, gulp down, or feed on the *red* stuff, the *red* stuff."[70]

GENESIS 27:43

Just as Jacob had to escape from his brother, so Israel had to evade the Edomites when they refused to let them go through their territory (Num 20:21).[71]

---

69. Here the emphasis is not on the betrayal of Jesus by Judas but on the purchase of a cemetery for paupers by his death, just as Abraham purchased a grave for his wife and himself from the Hittites in Hebron.

70. Here Hamann attempts to give the crude sense of the Hebrew verb and Esau's somewhat inarticulate demand.

71. This comparison hinges on the fact that the Edomites were the descendants of Esau.

GENESIS 31:14–16

We see here how temporal gain makes God's will agreeable to us. If we blind people learn to recognize the worth, the profit for our souls, and the goods that God has stored, kept, and prepared for us, how much more should his gracious will then constrain us.

GENESIS 31:20

Here keeping silent about a matter that we should have spoken about and disclosed is called theft—*and Jacob stole away the heart of Laban*—by not telling him anything, and so on.

GENESIS 31:35

Rachel's[72] excuse points forward to the incarnation of Christ. Just as Jacob, unwittingly, sentenced Rachel to death, so God too like- *Gen 31:32*
wise passed judgment on his Son by condemning this man. The righteousness of Jacob is a preview of the righteousness that our dear Savior gained for us poor people. We hear how Jacob insists on his innocence with his former master and blood relative. So faith may say to God, "Where are my sins, the sins for which you want to punish me? Is there anything to be punished, anything to be condemned in me? Yes, is not my whole life much rather an act *Rom 8:1*
of faithful and pleasing service in your eyes?" We Christians know that all the greatness of this righteousness and all the radiance of holiness covers us only through the merit of Jesus Christ. Like the other persons of the praiseworthy Trinity, God the Father must take delight in seeing himself humbled. Like unrighteous Laban here, there are many actual examples of this in Scripture, such as Judah, Saul, and so on.

GENESIS 31:39, 40

Just as all our sins are accounted to our Savior, so all his merit is ours—his poverty, his destitution, his suffering, the death that he suffered, his hunger and thirst. We benefit from all that; we have

72. Hamann's mistaken reference to her as Rebekah has been corrected.

suffered all that; we are innocent and should expect an account from God for that. Can a greater exchange, a greater swap be imagined than that? Is anything more amazing than the union of Jesus Christ and God with us, since He, as it were, has made himself nothing as a man, in order to raise us to sit on God's throne and seat with such boldness and so many privileges?

Phil 2:7–8; Eph 2:9; 3:12

O you unfathomable spring!
How will my weak spirit,
No matter how high it aspires,
Be at all able to fathom your depths?
Everything else has its time;
God's love, *infinite, incomprehensible love,*[73] is eternal.[74]

GENESIS 33:14

... *in* ***step*** *with the work (or herd) that goes before me and in* ***step*** *with the children*—that's how the word *foot* must be translated here. So too in Gen 30:30, Jacob says to Laban, "The Lord has blessed you with my foot or by accompanying it. That is, he was there with the first step that I took in your house and all the steps that I have taken in it."

GENESIS 38:5

Judah was absent at the birth of his younger son. We may suppose that he was not particularly satisfied with his wife, since he left her in that situation and was absent then.[75]

---

73. Hamann inserts the phrase "infinite, incomprehensible love" in this line.

74. Hamann paraphrases the last part of the third verse from Paul Gerhardt's hymn "Sollt ich meinen Gott nicht singen?," "I will sing my Maker's praises" (LW 439). The English translation there is:

O Lord, spring of boundless blessing,
How then could my finite mind
Of your love the limit find
Though my efforts were unceasing?
All things else have but their hour,
God's great love retains its power.

75. The reason for this deduction is that Judah did not name him like his firstborn son, but she did so.

GENESIS 38:9

Envy was the reason for Onan's sin and Satan's sin. Because he envied human happiness that he was not allowed to share, he gets them to spoil the means for their salvation and the sources for their life.

GENESIS 40:8

This question is a shining example of Joseph's faith. The certainty that he was in favor with God assured him that he would obtain everything that also belonged to him.

GENESIS 41:9

Pharaoh's frivolous, forgetful butler was reminded of Joseph when he remembered his sins. How pleasing it is to remember Jesus, who slips from our minds in good days, when our sins wake up for us through our conscience and the awareness of their consequences and penalties.

GENESIS 41:32

Double repetition makes a prophecy and divine decree certain and inevitable. How important our redemption must then be, how unalterable and eternal its gain, since Holy Scripture does nothing else but repeat this story in pictures.

GENESIS 43:8[76]

Jacob lets Judah's proposal put the brakes on him.[77] This shows that his family would bring the Savior of souls into the world.

GENESIS 45:1

Just as Joseph made himself known to all his brothers, so after his resurrection our Savior appeared to no one except his disciples. *Matt 28:8–17*

76. This corrects a mistaken reference to 40:8.

77. This rather obscure comparison refers to the brakes on a horse-drawn carriage that slowed it down to prevent an accident. Just as Benjamin's presence with his brothers would save the family of Jacob, so the presence of Jesus would save the world.

GENESIS 45:12

Joseph uses the same reasons to provide a foundation for their faith
John 20:20, 25 as our Savior does.

GENESIS 45:24

Here Joseph shares the same royal command of brotherly love with his brothers before their departure as our Savior did before the end
John 13:34–35 of his life.

GENESIS 3:12

The word that you gave me,[78]

> The gifts that from your hand
> I should have gratefully received,
> They have turned me away from you.
> —Alas, God! Is your Spirit still in me?[79]

GENESIS 18:1

... *in the heat, on the plain, at the door of the tent, lifting up the eyes and seeing.* All these are sensory images for the frame of mind in which our Lord appears to us—in sincere candor, in simplicity, in seclusion from the world, in the longing of faith.

GENESIS 18:6–8

Abram hurries to Sarah in order to welcome God and offer hospitality to him—Abraham runs to the herd, chooses a tender, good calf, and gives it to a young man to be prepared. The law and the divine word first prepare us for our conversion by making us pleasing to the Lord in Christ, who must be formed in us through the Holy Spirit and presented to God, like the tender, good calf by the young man.

---

78. Hamann turns Adam's words to God about "the woman that you gave me" into an allusion to God's command in Gen 2:16–17 in a lament at his own rejection of God's word and abuse of the Spirit's gifts through it.

79. Here Hamann quotes the first four lines from verse 8 before the first line of the hymn: "Ach Gott! Ist noch dein Geist bei mir," written by Ulrich, Duke of Braunschweig-Wolfenbüttel (1633–1714). For the whole hymn in German, see the Breslau Hymnal of 1903, number 1535.

ON MAUNDY THURSDAY[80]

I will lift up my eyes to the mountain that the Lord who made
heaven and earth ascended. Mount Zion is like a beautiful branch *Ps 121:1, 2; Matt 5:1;*
that comforts the whole land. It is not at all like the mountain in *Ps 48:2; Isa 4:2*
the wilderness that he descended to preach the curse of the law in
a thunderstorm (Heb 12:18–21). When he had taken his seat, his *Exod 19:16–18;*
disciples came to him, these elders of their nation and the whole *Deut 4:11*
human race. He opened his mouth to let streams of milk and honey
flow out from it. Let us hear the glorious things that were preached *Ps 87:3*
on this mountain. Here God, who had spoken at many times and *See Exod 3:8;*
in many ways in the old covenant, speaks in his Son, summons *Song 4:11*
us by him here onto this mountain, and opens up the long-locked *Heb 1:1–2*
treasures of his manifold wisdom and its mysteries for us here. The *Eph 3:10*
One who sat here sits at the right hand of the Majesty on high. He *Ps 110:1;*
has become much superior to the angels because he has inherited *Heb 1:3–4*
a much more excellent name than the mediators who delivered the
shadow of the law. *Gal 3:19; Heb 10:1; 2:2*

What a masterpiece of *teaching* and *eloquence* reigns in this discourse! Such humble-minded understanding and such a gentle-
minded heart! Your clothing is nothing but myrrh, aloes, and cassia
as you enter the ivory palaces in your beautiful splendor. Those who *Ps 45:8*
know themselves will easily picture for themselves those who heard
Jesus speak. People with hearts that were slow to hear and believe; *Luke 24:25*
people who were besieged by more prejudices than the mountains
around Jerusalem. In his presentation the Teacher must take his *Ps 125:2*
direction from the map of the land, the high hills and the valleys,
to prepare a smooth way for his entrance and his kingdom. *Isa 40:4*

Here in Matthew 5:2–3 Heumann violates the text in two ways that I shall note.[81] For him, "them" refers more directly to the crowds

80. This excursus, which interrupts the journey through the Bible, is a meditation on some parts of the Sermon on the Mount in Matthew 5–7. Composed on March 23, 1578, it is written on four sheets of paper.

81. Christoph August Heumann (1681–1764) was a notorious professor of literature and then of theology in Göttingen who championed a Reformed understanding of the Lord's Supper and a rationalistic interpretation of the New Testament. Here Hamann interacts with Heumann's *Erklärung des Neuen Testaments*, which appeared in 12 volumes from 1750–63.

of people than to the disciples. With this observation he fancies that he has kindled a brighter light for the understanding of the whole sermon. But those who are *closest* to Jesus are always the focus of his words. To be sure, he does speak in the hearing of the whole crowd, but he speaks especially into the hearts of each disciple that the Father has given him. Heumann links "blessed" (μακαριοι) directly to "in spirit" (τω πνευματι) and translates the phrase "mentally happy." But the order of words and letters yields a much richer and more accurate sense: "Blessed are the poor in the Spirit."

The introduction in which Jesus courts the favor of his hearers is a continuous contrast of the Mosaic and philosophical, the Jewish and the gentile or Greek way of thinking. The gospel redeems from the curse of the law and makes truly *blessed* people. This blessedness is not sensuous and apparent but is higher than reason and contrary to all human rules.

Agur feared poverty and riches. The Jews waited for the restoration of Solomon's times at the coming of the Messiah when silver
1 Kgs 10:21 would be held to be of no value. They took comfort in him, like
Lamech with Noah, without thinking of the flood that God would
Gen 5:28–29 bring over them in his time. In 5:5 "the meek," the gentle-minded,
calm, patient, kindly people, are contrasted with the *conquerors*. The
history of *Caesar* and *Augustus*, which were a living example then,
illustrates the *antithesis* of this claim. Devout Jacob, who remained
Gen 25:27, 29–33 in his tents, inherited the blessing of a firstborn son. The human
race is divided into two parties in their understanding of happiness, one half that wants to *inherit* it and the other half that wants to *earn* it. The Jews said, "It must come to us; we are the children of Abraham." The gentiles claimed divinization as the reward of the virtues and deeds. The former appealed to the truth of God; the latter to their righteousness or favor.[82]

The first seven Beatitudes are presented somewhat indefinitely and generally. Both the first and the eighth have the same

82. The word is *Gnade*, which means "grace" or "favor." Here Hamann seems to refer to those who regarded themselves as the favorites of the gods, people who had ingratiated themselves to them.

conclusion: *the kingdom of heaven is for all these,* or *for such.* They all speak of a single truth that is described and expressed in innumerable ways. The general formula is something like "*Blessed is the Christian.*" Here we have the seven characteristics, seven marks, of true Christianity. All kinds of blessedness are united in the kingdom of heaven, which has been prepared since the beginning of creation *Matt 25:34* and at whose revelation the end of all things will happen.

We can easily imagine how the hearers felt about this introduction. What powerful paradoxes in relation to the teachings of their faith! What a play on words! What dark ambiguities in the concepts of this teacher! Was it possible for an uninitiated hearer to understand what was meant by the poor, or by speaking about *divine* sorrow? Could this crowd make any sense of hunger and *2 Cor 7:10* thirst for righteousness, when his friends, after a much longer and more intimate association and acquaintance with his idiom and speech, fell into such a gross misunderstanding when he spoke of leaven? Could not the greatest teacher of these inconvenient truths *Mark 8:14–21* have helped them out with a much polished presentation? Was not *this* and the choice of his messengers and ambassadors why he and his truth would have such little success with his people and his family? Alas, if only he, in our days, would rend heaven and come down among us, how reasonable, how divine, how harmonious *Isa 64:1* all his words would appear to us! His teachings, which struck the simple, carnal Jews as ivory castles in the air, would, in our philosophical times, be regarded as the most correct, well-grounded, and straightforward theories. Even though all centuries had taken offense at him, ours would not have taken offense because he would present all revealed truths as the natural consequences of the simplest principles of reason with its systems.

Since Jesus knew the souls of his disciples and hearers, we can to some extent conceive how bitter his teaching office became for him, and what work it meant for him. They comprehended none of his words, understood nothing that he said. He was never clear enough for them. When he dared to speak the truth, his life was in danger. They refuted him with stones, or else they forsook him. It *John 8:9, 59*

would not have been so inconceivable to believe in the Antipodes
in former times as the Jews who looked for a universal monarchy
must have thought it absurd that the people that Jesus described
for them should be considered blessed and children of the king-
Matt 13:38; see 8:12 dom.Jesus was the only person on whom God's Spirit rested, just
as Gideon's fleece alone lay drenched with dew on it, while all the
Isa 11:2; land was dry around it. How wretched it is to live in such a desolate
John 1:32–33; Judg 6:39–40 wilderness with people, so separated from them as our High Priest
Heb 7:26 from sinners, distressed by their thoughts, words, and deeds, having
to deal with them. In such a situation the heart burns, but with little
desire to open one's mouth and waste one's words. A lover walks
around in the forests and among the rocky crags with similar imag-
inary projections.[83] "I will make your face like a flint," says God to
Isa 50:7 a prophet. Love conquers everything, even the strongest locks and
bolts of silence; it opens our mouth even if we know that stones
and trees are our hearers.

The first sermon of a Savior was: "Repent, for the kingdom of
Matt 4:17 heaven is at hand." That is, "Change your mind." Would people
not have ignored this condition as something trivial? What cranky
notions must the message of the kingdom's arrival have aroused in
the Jews? What kind of Muslim fancies, rebellious thoughts, dreams
of security and hope? Our Teacher knows all the carnal, malignant
misconceptions that his truth must put up with in our minds. Yet
that does not deter him from passing it on to us. It may be an aroma
2 Cor 2:16 of life to life or an aroma of death to death. It may be peace or a
Luke 2:35 sword through our souls. That is how his heavenly Father is glorified and his will is done.

LEVITICUS 1[84]

All the offerings had to be taken from the domesticated animals that served as human food. Among the birds there were the doves.

83. Hamann uses the Greek rhetorical device *prosopoeia*, by which a poet presents an imagined person speaking to an audience of inanimate things.

84. The meditations on Leviticus most likely and rather significantly begin on Good Friday.

LEVITICUS 3:11

Moses has written for us that God rested after the creation of the world and enjoyed the same refreshment from his work that we enjoy from and in our rest. Here we discover the great mystery that is expressed in the peace offerings and offerings for atonement. God declares that they are his food; their sweet aroma must be his food.[85] The fat of this offering belongs to the Lord (Lev 3:16). How quickly the rest that God enjoyed after his creation was disrupted by the fall of mankind! How often it caused him regret and pained him in his heart! How often have we been eager to provoke his wrath, *Lev 3:5, 16* while he held it back so that it did not break out! How painful it was for him to let it be revealed to us in order to prepare us to be redeemed! Were these the fruits that God should expect from the work of his hands which he could regard as the recompense for his creation? The recompense was nothing but our blessedness, which was why he had created us. Thus, just as the atoning punishment for our sins and the impurity of our nature would be figuratively removed in God's eyes in the burnt offerings, so he would see the *See Lev 1* life of the new creature in these peace offerings, his reawakened *See Lev 3* image restored and blooming in holiness. This is God's food that we humans offer him. He looked for wine from the grapevine; the *Isa 5:2* gardener brought him sour wine mixed with gall. This is what his *Matt 27:34* Son drank for him on the cross. Dear God, how wonderful you *Matt 27:48* are in your redemption, in your being, in your attributes! Nature disappears at your word. Here is the Holy of Holies. The whole of creation is only a forecourt compared to what we see in this word of yours. Thus every sin offering and guilt offering was also a burnt offering and peace offering. This means that atonement was not *See Lev 4:1–5:13; see Lev 5:14–6:7* just made for the omission of what was good and the commission of what was evil, but it also signified the lack of the good that was required in us. An employee who does nothing already fails to do his duty. If he, instead of doing what he should do, does the opposite, his guilt is even greater. If the employer wanted to acquit him

85. The Hebrew term is literally a soothing aroma, an aroma that gives rest.

for the lack of service and its damage, he would be bound to offer an even greater satisfaction for what was required in his service.
Lev 7:20–21 We may not approach God in an unclean state or with empty hands (Exod 23:15).

LEVITICUS 6

We see how God regards all injustice against our neighbor as sin against himself, because his image must be holy for us in our brother. Moses here includes the disavowal of what was entrusted to us for safekeeping. (Here I understand *"taking in hand" as all kinds of theft that are not violent,* thefts that require physical and mental craftiness or the retraction of a verbal undertaking that had been made with a handshake).[86]

LEVITICUS 10[:9–10]

Could drunkenness have been the reason for the foolhardiness of Aaron's two sons since God thereafter enjoined on him abstinence from wine and strong drink, so that you may distinguish between holy and unholy things?

LEVITICUS 12

Human nature is so corrupt and unclean that the conception and birth of a person is not without blemish. The acts that belong to the propagation of our race are like the toil of a farm hand who wanted to cultivate the field of his master in order to produce weeds
Matt 13:24–30 instead of wheat.

LEVITICUS 13:12–13

It is a well-known characteristic of skin diseases that the more they appear on the outside, the less dangerous they are, because by this the spread of the poison weakens. The more the surface of the body is covered with it, the more the inner parts are relieved of it. Was

86. Here Hamann explains the rather obscure Hebrew expression "the placement of the hand" in 6:2, a technical commercial term for a "deposit" (ESV) or a joint investment.

not the leprosy of tax collectors likewise cleaner in the eyes of the Physician of our souls than the Pharisees and the scribes? *Matt 9:12*

In this sickness the color of the hair was a much more decisive characteristic than the sight of a watery discharge for our physicians. *Lev 13:18–44* Both are natural anomalies. This sickness was infectious. Since it may have been the only kind of plague to which the Jews could be exposed, and since the whole community could be endangered by one leper, we see why God treats it with such great care and entrusts its diagnosis to his priests.

LEVITICUS 16[:9–10]

The one on which the Lord's lot fell had to be slaughtered. The other one was let loose in the desert, in the wilderness.

LEVITICUS 16:31

Who is able to endure a Sabbath of solemn rest with the grief that the Jews were supposed to inflict on their souls? The apostle explains this sorrow for us. *2 Cor 7:10*

LEVITICUS 16:33

What could give us a greater grasp of God's holiness and make it easier for us to grasp through the law than that atonement needed to be made for the sanctuary itself, the altar and the tent of meeting? Their holiness was like the light of the moon and the planets, reflected light.

LEVITICUS 18:1–5

Here these frequent repetitions are not insignificant. Believe that *Lev 18:2, 4, 6, 21, 30* I am your Lord and your God. Therefore do not let prejudice and precedent become your law makers and do not believe that they will excuse the transgression of my will and justify you in my eyes. In this we hear how divine omniscience and its words are both commands and prophetic oracles. The Jews should not discount the perfection of the law by thinking that their forefathers and they themselves have previously lived without it. But they should also not build on its perfection so completely that it would never end and its observance would continue even when God would usher in a further revelation of his name. Do not believe that your conduct according to the law and its present restrictions of your conduct will satisfy my wisdom and my will in the future!

The Jews transgressed both of God's commandments. They followed the ways of the land into which God brought them, and they forgot that the Lord was their God. They used the example of false gods to make a new law book. In contrast to this, after the birth of
1 Tim 3:16 Christ and his revelation in the flesh, they followed the ways of the
land and the laws that had so long governed them. They adhered
1 Pet 1:18 to the way of life they had inherited from their fathers.

Keep my laws, because in them I have revealed myself as your Lord and God. These laws and ordinances are a memorial in my eyes, a sketch of the greater redemption that I will accomplish than what you have seen in the land where you lived so long as slaves and the fulfillment of greater promises than those you will now enjoy by the occupation of the land into which I will bring you. Therefore keep my commandments for their own sake and because they come from me.

Keep these commandments for your own sake. The human being[87] who walks in them will have life, because I am the Lord of
Rom 10:5; Gal 3:12 human beings.

LEVITICUS 18:22, 23

It is noteworthy that while God calls the sodomites in human families a sexual abomination, he gives such a mild name to the mixing[88] of a man with an animal. The reason for this law is the key to all the laws of Moses on marriage.

87. Or "man." Here the Hebrew text uses the term *adam* to show that this applies to every person rather than just the Jews.

88. The Hebrew term for this refers to the confusion of divinely created classes or kinds of creatures.

LEVITICUS 18:24–25

We see how God gives an account of his judgments and ways to people. It was not God's partiality for the Jews but the voice of nature, the disgust of the ground that wants to spew out its filthy inhabitants. It was not his honor that these false gods ascribe to the demons, but the sins which cry out mutely that called God to sweep away these nations like rubbish and remove them from the sight of his whole creation.

Who is not able, without horror, to recognize, in the spread of these sins, the abhorrent Machiavellianism[89] of the enemy of God and humanity, the intent of this liar and murderer to wipe out the whole human race and transform the drive for human preservation and reproduction gradually into inclinations that are quite opposed to the human race and destroy it? If the devil had been successful in what he intended, he would not have needed to teach Pharaoh to bribe the midwives and turn those who were meant to assist in human birth and foster it into assassins.

John 8:44

Exod 1:15–22

Since God is so gracious, he does not want to reveal to us the great danger that we face from the destroyer; instead, he wants to reveal much more his love for us, the excellence of his nature and the glory of his attributes, in order to draw us to himself more through our fear of him than our fear of the power of our mutual enemy. How is it possible that people could by themselves fall into such aberrations, unless the cunning adversary made use for himself of our stupidity and weakness, with all the advantages that he had over us as a rebellious, fallen, vengeful, crafty spirit, with all the advantages that not only his invisibility but also his skill in telling lies, blatant lies, and in disguising himself as an angel of light gave him?

2 Cor 11:14

He used the same trick that he used to ruin the temporal life of people against their spiritual life. Its root is the divine word. He tries to undermine it. He uses the cleverest, most witty heads to make it ridiculous. Since our reason was meant to be impregnated, if I might say so, with the seed of God's word and meant to live in intimacy

89. Nicolo Machiavelli (1469–1527) published a famous political treatise called *The Prince* (1532) as a handbook for despotic rule without the restraint of any moral principles.

with it, in submission and love like a husband and a wife under one roof, he has not just continually tried to discover disagreements between them both and to separate what God has joined together. He has also, in our times, tried to bring about a formal divorce between them and to flatter reason with systems, dreams, and so on, in order to curb truth and virtue, and gradually thereby make it possible for him to confuse the difference between truth and lies.

LEVITICUS 19:5

God's religion is a great promoter of freedom. The only means to please him is a free will offering. That's why all free Christian states should be intent on spreading and explaining his doctrine. Sin
John 8:34 makes us slaves. Whoever hates a tyrant and loves freedom should profess allegiance to God's flag, in order to share in the great, glorious victory that he has promised over the worst tyrant, the most
1 Cor 15:57; Heb 2:14–15 despotic usurper.

LEVITICUS 19:19

In history as well as in the laws of Moses, God has shown that his attention extends to the smallest things. By his deep condescension God may have wished to teach us humility by his own example. But God knows our nature and how often it can be folded into little things and sustained by them. Furthermore, he has wanted to inculcate this attention to them, because the temptation of insignificant and even innocent things is most successful in misleading us into the greatest error. Thus the misuse of God's name eventually makes us indifferent to God himself, so that we can gradually become indifferent to something shameful by speaking about it and finally fall in love with it. On the other hand, these little things have a prophetic significance and involve great things in their fulfillment. The Bible is a much too important book to the devil for him not to read it. How it must annoy this proud spirit that God does not honor him by naming him as the author of the fall into sin, but instead lets Moses speak about the snake as an animal that was more cunning
Gen 3:1 than the other beasts of the field! How that addition must grieve him

after God had created the beasts of the field! God owed him more respect than that because he had been created with more excellent qualities! With what reverence we should receive the Bible, the masterpiece of divine wisdom, the book that prizes all the miracles alike which are contained in it, a book that is meant to be a light for the path for the simplest people and a riddle for the angels of a much higher rank! If the devil were not a liar and the free thinkers knew his opinion and thoughts about this book, how ashamed they would be for making themselves so ridiculous to him. How little of God's first judgment for the punishment of the fall was the devil able to imagine! How incomprehensible it may have seemed to him! He knew God. Even though the woman's offspring seemed to be ridiculous to him, he was afraid of it, and this fear moved him to use so many strategies to divert humans from reproduction and to murder children. We must regard many prophecies in this light. His superior intelligence was more of a disadvantage to him, because it made him shortsighted in many things where human understanding had more use of its own shortcomings. It was a new affront to his pride that a simple Jew with his faith could see more accurately than his falcon's eye.

Ps 119:105; 1 Pet 1

Gen 3:15; Rev 12:17

LEVITICUS 19:29

The thoughtlessness and corruption of parents, particularly their own indifference to the sixth commandment, has produced its greatest effect in making prostitution common. The more corrupt parents are, the more prostitutes there are; the more prostitution prevails in the land, the more dissoluteness and wickedness takes the upper hand. What deep insights this provides for the government to preserve the morals of their state!

LEVITICUS 19:33

Since, as we discover, foreigners are so often remembered in sacred Scripture, God seems to have good reasons to commend this duty to the Jews and to welcome them. The nomadic life of their forefathers gave rise to the spread of God's name, which may be a reason why the devil is enraged against foreigners. God let several of Israel's forefathers go on journeys for the same reason.

Let me make still another observation. The union of people with each other was a deep-seated project of Satan in order to make his dominion over them easier and more permanent and his enslavement more onerous through natural corruption. So we see how God made his solemn decision to forestall his purpose. Even though universal blindness would cover the human race, it would not be in the same degree with all nations and composed of the same errors. Every race now cultivates the soil of its weeds as it fancies. Consequently, in their judgments and tendencies people would necessarily begin to diverge sharply in keeping with the natural riches of their soil, no matter how bad its growth itself was. Yet nothing is more beneficial for reason than the comparison of different opinions and tendencies, and nothing is more detrimental for the destruction of obvious absurdities and gross vices. From this we can see that, as detrimental as the combination of degenerate people would be for them, so their reunion would be beneficial, after their customs, ways of thinking, and so on had come to be different. We know how many discoveries we owe to travels, and that we cannot travel without observing the natural diversity of lands and their inhabitants. In more recent history we have seen that virtuous citizens were exiled into misery, since one person would not exile himself from the others and since he had not sought a nation that was more suitable and similar in his way of thinking. Evil allows for no system.[90] It asserts itself, and its connection with others is often little better than the haze from a fog. Thus the author of evil cannot act coherently. Like a sly minister of state, he employs every means, every strategy, to help himself escape embarrassment, even if he too had to contradict all that he just had said and done just one minute earlier. He is only intent on doing evil. When we act according to our inclinations, our evil inclinations, we often stand by ourselves in the light. Our enemy has, most likely, had this experience of us

90. This is an ironic assertion about the disorder and incoherence of evil and evildoers.

often enough. That may have cost him much effort to coax some gentiles to side with him, to keep them in good spirits, and so on. How petty this enemy has become in the eyes of the true Christian! Thanks be to God who gives us the victory through our Lord Jesus Christ. Amen. *1 Cor 15:57*

LEVITICUS 23:7

Hard labor was imposed on Adam as a curse, a punishment for his fall into sin. His rest with God was interrupted through it. The sweat of his brow was meant to prefigure the sweat of blood that our sins cost to our Redeemer and the hard labor that we imposed on him through them. The Sabbath and the festivals were therefore a foretaste of our liberation from the forced labor of our sins. *Gen 3:17–19; Gen 2:3* *Luke 22:44*

LEVITICUS 23:11

God is satisfied with a handful from our harvest. He accepts what he owns as a gift from us.

LEVITICUS 26:13

I have restored your erect posture which distinguishes you from the animals and which you lost under the yoke of sin and idolatry. The divine image had become so indiscernible up to even its least traits and its external features. God had to teach people to stand erect again. He had to stoop to perform the little services of a nurse until they grew up, in order to lead them into all truth through his Spirit. *John 16:13* This is the full growth that Paul speaks of, which we can attain only through revelation and faith. *Eph 4:15* This was the time when the prophecy was fulfilled that there would no longer be any children that grow old among mankind. *Isa 65:20*

LEVITICUS 26:15

To spurn God's ordinances and to heartily abhor his commands. No one has known the human heart except he who made people and had to redeem them (Zech 11).

LEVITICUS 26:16

The loss of what we worked hard to get always affects us deeply. But nothing makes our tears more bitter and no sorrow eats away at the heart more than when we see our enemies scornfully devour what we had hoped to enjoy in peace. "You prepare a table before
Ps 23:5 me in the presence of my enemies," says David. My enemies will see how you will serve up the best of your goods just for me and how I will feast on them and your grace, while every morsel that I swallow will fire up their hunger even more and enflame their futile anger even more.

LEVITICUS 26:17

In verse 8 we hear how five men would be so strong that that they would put a hundred to flight and a hundred so strong that they would put ten thousand to flight. They would fall by your sword without seeing my arm, which they thought would only be strong enough to destroy them. They would fall before your eyes. How feeble you will be. You will flee when no one chases you; you will regard your own shadow as a pair of enemies.

LEVITICUS 26:18

Dear God, let us kiss your rod in all your punishments. When your
Ps 32:4 hand seems to lie too heavy on us, let us always consider that you have the right and enough power to punish us sevenfold for our sins.

LEVITICUS 26:19

God gives some power to us. He knows the pride of human power and on what it relies. How tame a mighty man becomes when God does nothing more than put him on shorter rations.[91] That proud man who regards the sky and the earth as his property becomes a fool, a slave to his belly. If you think that the sky is yours, if you think that you have created it, says God, I will turn it into iron. With what authority and power God uses reason to convict a person! He adds, the abilities that I have given you cost my omnipotence so little that

91. Literally, "than raise his breadbasket a little higher."

I can easily tolerate their loss. Yes, I will give you greater powers to show you that my power is as nothing when it is employed by your hands, by your disobedient and unclean hands. You will sense my powers in you. I will let you use them for yourselves, and when you wait for some effect, you will be amazed that they accomplish nothing. If I give you gold, it will turn into smoke in your crucibles. The devil took away the golden earrings of Israelites to give them a golden calf in return. This calf is ground to dust by Moses, and they, if they are at all able to recognize any of it, drink their god as putrid, stirred up, muddy water.

LEVITICUS 26:22

It is better for the earth to be filled with wild beasts that devour your children and your livestock than for you to become like them and be child murderers. I myself will do what you intend against me and what you wish to unleash against yourselves in self-deception under the impulse of Satan. In every wild beast you will see your tempter, not in a snakeskin but in his true guise as a roaring, hungry *Gen 3:1* lion (Ps 22:13; 1 Pet 5:8). He seeks to exterminate the offspring of the woman in your children. He cannot tolerate your livestock, *Gen 3:15; Rev 12:17* because I have accepted their blood for yours. He seeks to weaken you by decreasing your number, so that it is so much easier for him to devour you. He wants to make your roads deserted and, most of all, abolish your companionship with the spirits that Jacob saw descending and ascending in the service of mankind. *Gen 28:12; Heb 1:14*

As divine as all these images are in their spiritual sense, we see their literal sense fulfilled in those lands where the prince of this world still exercises his visible dominion: (1) wild beasts in greater *John 12:31; 14:30; 16:11* numbers with greater fury, venomous snakes, and so on; (2) parents with no love for their children who offer them up by selling them as slaves; (3) nourishment with horse meat, fish, and so on from the lack of livestock; (4) depopulation; (5) little connection of people with each other, no trade, no association of people with each other.

In 26:14 it merely says: "If you will not listen to me." That is the beginning of sin. After that we deny God completely; we regard him as an enemy that we want to get rid of entirely. We set out to attack him (26:15). That is why Satan took away the earrings of the Israelites to make false gods from them.

We do not listen to God; we neglect his word. This is the momentous beginning that Satan makes, the entry of his rhetoric by which he gains a favorable hearing for himself. First, he leads us into one of his ways that are the opposite of God's ways and then into more of them. After that, he makes our life ungodly, inhuman, and bestial. Finally, he imprints his image on us and turns us into devils.

We see how God always walks close behind a person and follows him along all the crooked ways that lead into the murderer's cave of this miserable enemy. We see how God's power is doubled for us in our danger, just as his grace increases the more people draw near to him and lets them taste more and more of his sweetness, unlocking treasure upon treasure and raining down on them blessing upon blessing.

LEVITICUS 26:25

The sword of a pestilence will seek you out in fortified cities and the sword of warfare outside them. In our times God's grace and forbearance employ the latter more than the former. In many cases warfare is a worse judgment of God than pestilence because it provokes people to hatred and vengeance against each other. Because God suffers with them, he regards famine as his last resort in judgment. We see how God is touched and moved by this miserable trouble from his description of it. The rapid onset of a pestilence itself relieves the judgment. The commotion of warfare and the fury of vengeance distract people from heeding the peril for their souls.

LEVITICUS 26:29

Here God depicts the worst famine with images that appeal first of all to our human senses. We see how loathsome the enemy must be in our eyes who makes such punishments the goal of his enticements. Scripture presents the devil to us as the seducer and hangman of the human race. Here we see him quench his hunger on our own flesh and blood. Yet that is not enough for him. Who is able to read the following verse without horror? He wants to make us as rotten as he himself is, so that God's soul is as disgusted with us as with him and damns us like him. This shows us, as our Savior, Moses, and the prophets declare, that the devil wants to bring us to the place where God's mercy ends, the place where the worm in him and his servants never dies and the fire is never quenched. *Mark 9:48*

LEVITICUS 26:31[–33]

Your sanctuaries will be made desolate. Our bodies are God's temples, says Paul. *1 Cor 6:19* God says, "I will not smell the aroma of your offerings. I will be deprived of your deeds which should have been pleasing and perfect for me through your spiritual life, your deeds which needed to be washed with the blood of my Son to make them holy. *Rom 12:1–2; 1 Cor 6:11; Rev 1:5* The earth will be devastated. Your enemies that live among you and the devil that now believes and shudders will now shudder at my judgment on you and him. *Lev 26:32; Jas 2:19* I will give the gods of the gentiles as booty for you and will draw out my sword that would eternally forbid the way for you to the tree of life and pursue you." *Lev 26:33; Gen 2:9; 3:24; Rev 2:7; 22:2, 14, 19*

LEVITICUS 26:34–35

Who is able to hear God's lament at the transformation of his Sabbath without astonishment when we think of the great Sabbath that was his goal in his institution of the earthly Sabbath? *Heb 4:1–11* The following verses are a prophecy of the judgments on both the Jews and the whole earth. Just as God's Spirit wanted to reveal himself to all nations in his revelation to a single nation, so he has likewise revealed himself at all times to the end of the world. Only our Redeemer, who is God, whose presence fills all places and all centuries, could say, "I am with you always to the end of the world." *Matt 28:20* God's Spirit has given us the same testimony about his divine attributes through the inspiration of his word in which the truths of the Spirit reveal his eternal omnipresence and omniscience. *Ps 139:7–12; John 14:17; 1 Cor 2:9–10*

Just as the sun shines every day and rises for all nations, so the light of God's word is in God's world. It is written for all people and all times. Its Author calls all people by name. He knows all the events in the world with their time, their interconnection, their place, and their smallest, their very smallest details. He has given his word to us serfs of Satan as a charter of truth, to keep us safe from the craftiness by which Satan seeks to dupe our blindness and exploit our gullibility. In the presence of our enemies, Moses has to repeat for us a thousand times that God is the Lord, that God, the Lord of the whole world, is our Lord, and that our Lord is one God. He is our God, our gracious, abundantly gracious God, who can and will do even more than he has promised, even though his promises are so infinitely and amazingly great. His enemy has never had any right to claim us poor people, let alone now that we are the redeemed of the Lord.

God's Spirit does not just give us his word as documented evidence *Eph 6:17; John 8:44* against the lies of the tyrant but also as a sword in our hands against all his weapons. With it we can, without fear, tread safely on his head because his sting has been lost in the heels of the woman's *Gen 3:15; Rev 12:17* offspring, and we shall see the wounds of Jesus on his glorified body just as we by faith see them, already now, like his disciples with physical eyes. He lets us touch them, he lets us use our feeling to *Luke 24:39; John 20:27; 1 John 1:1* help us, when we do not dare to trust our eyes alone. Who would not melt with love and gratitude for the three witnesses that we have in heaven and the three witnesses that we have on earth for who he is and what he does?[92] Jesus built the ark to rescue us from the *Gen 6:14–22; 1 Pet 3:18–2* peril of water. He built the tent of meeting to reconcile us with his blood. He grants us his Spirit because he is the Spirit of truth and has *John 16:13* made us children of his Father and his Holy Spirit so that we might become heirs of his Father's kingdom and to make us one from all *Rom 8:14–17; Gal 4:5–7; John 17:21* this, like the Father in the Son and the Son in the Father. Deliver us

92. See the Western variant reading for 1 John 5:7–8 as given in the NKJV: "For there are three that bear witness in heaven: the Father, the Word, and the Holy Spirit; and these three are one. And there are three that bear witness on earth: the Spirit, the water, and the blood; and these three agree as one."

from the evil one, for yours is the kingdom and the power and the glory forever. Amen. *Matt 6:13*

LEVITICUS 27:10

It could be said that God regards the offerings and vows of a poor person with great deference. No matter how damaged the offering was that could be paid to fulfill a vow, he did not need to look around for a better one in order to make a better payment for his promise through a substitute, so that a more expensive offering would make up for the damaged one. If such a substitute was made, then both animals were holy to the Lord. Because God reckons the righteousness of his Son as our own righteousness, so, despite the imperfections that characterize it, our righteousness is as holy to him as that of his Son (27:33).

LEVITICUS 27:24

What condescension of the highest Lawgiver that he puts the observance of human ordinances on the same footing for his people! What an excellent hint that the Spirit drops for us here that it is impossible for God to deviate from the laws of holiness and the eternal laws of nature and annul any of them. Thus our divine Redeemer submitted himself to the orders of worldly authority and its terms for his own service.

DEUTERONOMY 1:33

God's presence was more visible in fire by night with the dim knowledge of him before and after the giving of the law, whereas with the light of the gospel he now puts an end to miraculous deeds and leads us into the cloud.

DEUTERONOMY 1:36–38; CF. NUM 13:30; 14:24

Caleb is always introduced by himself.[93] He alone silences the people; he alone may enter the land. On the two occasions where his name is not expressly required for the understanding of the story, Joshua is omitted. Who cannot but see that Joshua is thereby distinguished in Scripture as a type of our Savior? We see that he was made sin on our account and can be reckoned with the rebels. Yet at the same time we see that he has done too much to only quiet the grumbling of the people together with Caleb, and that Caleb would be brought into the promised land under him and by him.

DEUTERONOMY 2:4

Here we see where Edom's courage and defiance originated (Num 20:18, 20). We see how often Satan now trembles with fear at God's children and tries to intimidate them.

In this chapter there are outstanding proofs how the offspring of
Gen 3:16 the serpent,[94] despite its enmity against God's people, received their land from his hand, lived under his government, and enjoyed the truth and faithfulness of his promises. Yes, we see how he himself protects and preserves them from his own people, because Satan would readily devour everything through his servants in as much as God has cleared and still clears a place for him on earth.

When we consider God's flock among a large number of such nations that were skilled in warfare, nations who had exterminated
Deut 2:10–12, 20–23 other nations before them with numerous and famous giants, we understand what Paul says in 1 Cor 1:27–28.

DEUTERONOMY 2:24–25

Who does not wake up with surprise to see Moses suddenly break out from the accuracy of a historian and a reporter into prophetic ecstasy with the ardor of a commander in chief? As mere human

93. This is only so in these cases.

94. In the Old Testament Edom is regarded figuratively as the archetypal enemy of the people of God.

beings we can appreciate the beauty of this, which is just as evident to someone like Longinus as to a Christian.[95] But a Christian discovers something more. God would not have included this jubilation of Moses in his word, had this victory not been a preview of the great victory that we all share. Through this war-cry Moses *1 Cor 15:57*
summons us to the banner of our Savior to fight and gain the victory under him, so that we may share in its rich booty together with him. Before our Savior set out against this enemy, he crossed the Kidron Brook. The day of his resurrection was the day of which *John 18:1*
Moses here speaks by the Spirit, when the king of hell would be delivered into his hands and ours. He gave his disciples power over snakes and vipers. He gained the authority for them to spread *Luke 10:19*
the gospel among all nations. He made Satan tremble who tried *Matt 28:18–20; Mark 16:15*
in vain to pour out his wrath against the apostle through nothing else than the viper's brood of his children. Here we find the messengers—they come with words of peace—they know no other *Jas 2:19; Matt 3:7; Deut 2:26*
enemies than those that the Lord commands them to slay. They are not conquerors. The whole spirit of the gospel appears in the words of Moses: the kingdom of Jesus is not of this world. His *John 18:36*
disciples should not share in the goods of this world, even though they all belonged to God, and the liberality of its prince. They were not supposed to share in the fame, the glory, the pleasures, the excesses of the children of mankind. They looked for nothing except the King's Highway to travel through the land of Satan to the promised land. They should not deviate to the right or to the left— *Num 20:17; 21:22; Deut 2:27*
yes, the teaching of the cross; here they should purchase all the goods of the world that they consumed; here they should sow with *Deut 2:6, 28*
tears—they should travel by foot, while the children of the world *Ps 126:5*
would possess and enjoy horses and treasures, power and wealth. God himself would protect the disciples, if they would covet the inheritance of the world's children, because they were on the way to their heavenly inheritance. What a religion! What a God who

95. See note on 39n18.

reveals himself! What a new creation is the Christian! And what a monster is the person who refuses to be a new creation!

DEUTERONOMY 2:31

What is to be done for the possession of Canaan after the victory that our Savior has won? Begin and take possession, you man, so that you may be an heir.[96] Take hold of it with the hand of faith. Take and eat, take and drink what your Savior has bequeathed for
Matt 26:26; 1 Cor 11:2 you as the booty of his victory. You wear a sword at your side that Satan has already tasted, a sword that he truly fears. Show it to him,
Eph 6:17; Rev 12:11 use it against him when he harasses you, when he intends to dispute your enjoyment of the table that God has prepared for you or the
Ps 23:5 estate that he has made available for you. As long as you remain on the King's Highway and do not turn to the right or the left, he has no power over you. As long as you are in your vocation and in the place that God has allotted to you, consider yourself God's knight who carries out his feudal duty to his Lord, a knight of God, who does not betray you and sell you to his enemies.[97]

DEUTERONOMY 3:21

Our religion has seen a happy victory over kings that prefigure the victories that it will have over all the kingdoms of Satan. It has triumphed over Israel according to the flesh and the idolatry of the lands that have had Rome as their head. The descendants of Esau and Lot, the kingdom of Ishmael, and Babylon, the oldest and most enduring work of Satan, have not yet fulfilled their time. God has promised and announced that they will come to a terrible end, and our descendants will see that what the Lord our God did before the eyes of our fathers with these two kings will be done to them.[98]

---

96. Here Hamann reflects on a rather unusual Hebrew idiom which combines an imperative of a verb with its gerund infinitive: "Possess by possessing" or "Possess for possessing." He construes the idiom as a play on the verb which can mean to inherit land as well as to take possession of it.

97. See Kierkegaard's "Knight of Faith" in *Fear and Trembling,* which begins with an epigraph from Hamann.

98. The two kings are Sihon (2:26–37) and Og (3:1–11).

We can see how great our enemy is that our Savior has overcome, from the fear that we, like grasshoppers, would naturally
have of this giant, had God our Lord not fought against him and
had he, who had promised his presence with us always in this
world until its end, not determined that he would fight for us. *Num 13:33;*
This fierce lion will be like the grass of the field that the ox licks *Matt 28:20*
up (Num 22:4). *1 Pet 5:8;*

O Lord our God, all that you have shown of your greatness and *Isa 11:5; 66:25*
your mighty hand to your servants and Christians, all that you give
them to hope for, is only the beginning, the *Alpha* of your divine
name and your divine works. When our Savior's prayer is learned *Deut 3:24*
by us, when this prayer is prayed in faith by your Israel, when your
will is done on earth as in heaven, then we shall see perfectly that
you are the greatest God on earth as in heaven. You seem to ques- *Matt 6:9–13*
tion your own greatness, infinite God, your greatness in heaven,
until we understand that you are as great on earth as you will be
on our behalf and must be for your own sake. If you were not the
most long-suffering, most patient, most tolerable God for us poor
people, the God who creates when he speaks and gave nature time *Ps 33:9*
from morning to evening to do his will, how would things be for
us, yes for the tyrant himself whom we would prefer to you? It is
due to your forbearance with us that he is not yet judged, not yet
thrown into the pit of hell that will burn forever, forever for him
and his offspring. *Rev 20:10*

What Moses, your faithful servant, your great Eliezer,[99] had to
pray for, you give without prayer to every Christian. From across *Deut 3:23–25*
the Jordan through which our Savior waded so that its flood waters
came up to his soul[100] and through which you led your people
with dry feet, you showed Moses the good land, the lovely hill
and Lebanon. It is not enough that you have given us a foretaste *Ps 69:1–2;*
of the powers of the future world and your fruit from heaven in *Deut 3:25*
your word by the witness of your Spirit in our hearts and the sign *Heb 6:5*

99. This name means "God is my help." It was also the name of Abraham's steward (Gen 15:2; see 24:2) and the second son of Moses (Exod 18:4; 1 Chr 23:15, 17).

100. In Hebrew the word for soul is also the term for a person's throat.

of the covenant by which the Lord, your Son and our Lord, pledged *Rom 6:5; Matt 26:28* himself on earth. It is not enough that from its entrance you show every Christian the land that he enters, the land where our friends the prophets and apostles have been and where such a great multitude will follow after us. You do not just show us the land but also the lovely hill, your stronghold, and Lebanon, the cedar forest, the armies of angels planted around your throne[101] that you use to *Heb 1:14; 12:22–24* minister to people and your church. Yes, just as Solomon used the cedars of Lebanon in the temple for your name, so their services are already here at our disposal in us and our own homes, in our *1 Kgs 6:9–16* ways and all the steps that we take on them.

DEUTERONOMY 4

What a splendid chapter! Every word that proceeds from God's mouth is a whole creation full of thoughts and emotions in our souls. Wisdom and understanding that the demons envy and respect us *Deut 4:6* for, if we keep the commandments! Regardless of the light that God sheds in our souls through his word, he himself wants to be near to *Deut 4:7* us. He is where his word is; he is where his Son is. If his word is in us, his Son is in us; if his word is in us, the Spirit of his word is in us. How can God the Father do without us when we have robbed him of his best fellowship? His Son leaves heaven, makes himself desolate and empty, and comes into our hearts, not just to make a paradise of them, as from the waste and empty earth, but also to pitch the tent of heaven itself. O how holy should this lump of earth be for us where God deigns to set up his tabernacle because *John 14:23; Rev 7:15; 21:3* our poor spirit dwells under it. May God be highly praised from eternity to eternity.

Amen!

Oh God! How can I write down what my heart feels, what my heart declares! If John had written as a man, he would never have finished writing. He speaks the truth of his heart that if everything

101. The cedar was the king of the trees that grew on Mount Lebanon, the king of the mountains. So cedars were emblems of the king of Israel who reigned with God on his earthly mountain and the angels who reigned with God on his heavenly mountain.

were written in detail as clearly for us men as we here already see the light in the darkness, the books would be too many for the whole world. If everything were written down, the whole world would have no room for these books.

John 1:5; 1 John 2:9

John 21:25

DEUTERONOMY 4:12

You saw no likeness to anything except his voice; you saw his voice.[102] Speech itself becomes almighty when God uses it for himself. You saw no other likeness, says God, than this repeated word by which I have revealed myself, the word of my Spirit, and the word that was in the beginning and is God himself. What mysterious revelations! They are a likeness for us, a voice of God! How will the revelation be when we see him face to face?

See Deut 4:15

John 1:1

1 Cor 13:12

DEUTERONOMY 4:13

No more than Ten Commandments, and no more than three for himself and seven for our neighbor![103] God, how unsearchable you are, how unfathomably gracious!

Rom 11:33

Here we see how loathsome idolatry is! How was it possible that man could be so stubbornly enamored with it? How was it possible to continue in the one true offering for our fallen nature when God's enemy did not just want to mock mankind but also its Creator, when he had not just stripped it naked, but also laughed at its nakedness? Thanks be to God that this pleasure was spoiled for him! Thanks be to God who gives us the victory over him through our Lord Jesus Christ!

1 Cor 15:57

102. Here Hamann follows Luther's literal translation of the Hebrew text: "But you saw no form except the voice." All current English translations avoid this paradoxical assertion of seeing a voice by saying that there was only a voice (NIV; TEV) or they heard only a voice (KJV).

103. Hamann follows the Roman Catholic and Lutheran tradition of numbering the prohibition of adherence to other gods and idolatry as a single commandment and treating the prohibitions of coveting as two separate commandments.

DEUTERONOMY 4:32

How can we, when we consider our own idolatry, be amazed at the blindness and hardheartedness of the Jews without shame, slander, and fear? Do we, we who are Christians, we to whom God has revealed so much infinitely more, not live in the same idolatry as the Jews, in the same unbelief that entangled them, and in the same blindness that covers them despite the testimony of their senses, the testimony of Moses and the express will of God through commandments, benefactions, and punishments? Alas, O God! If their judgment was so terrible, what will ours be? If Jerusalem fell into such ruin, what will the fall of Babylon be like?

Heb 4:12 Since God knows us, he divides joints and marrow. No matter how much he does, how much he promises, how much he threatens, how much he carries out both of these as he wills, we do not believe in him. We do not believe in him. Since you do not believe in me, I no longer demand that of you, says God (4:32). Ask the times before you, as long as you can still ask, if what I told you is true. Ask your neighbors, as far as you can ask, if what you have experienced has happened. If their reports agree with my word, then at least believe in yourselves. However much the spirit of deception has marred and scarred the history of the world and has tried to bribe
1 Kgs 22:21–23; see 2 Cor 4:4 its subjects, our neighbors, to claim their allegiance, all his tricks must indeed come to nothing. They themselves must testify to the
Exod 8:18–19 truth against themselves, like the Egyptians magicians, or they must
Mark 14:55–59 betray themselves with their own lies which contradict each other.

DEUTERONOMY 4:33

The revelation and appearance of God in the burning bush, which burned and yet was not burnt up, is one of most comforting and
Exod 3:2–3 powerful episodes in the story of Moses. The goodwill of him who dwelt in the bush (Deut 33:16) preserved this wonderful bush. The people of Israel and the human family are this bush that God's wrath should have burned up. Yet he speaks from the midst of the fire of his wrath to preserve men from consumption by it. He spoke by his Spirit, obtained through his Son. What a great mystery

that excited the curiosity of Moses, not just his but also that of the angels, says St. Peter (1 Pet 1:12)! Our life depends on this point. Hearing it preserves us. Faith in his Son and his word does not just preserve us from an eternal, terrible death; it also gives us a new, better, imperishable life.

DEUTERONOMY 4:34

Almighty God makes a trial;[104] the only wise God performs an experiment! All these things were nothing but preludes, an experiment, trials of an infinitely greater redemption: almighty God tried! The enemy of God and of mankind exercises his power over us unhappy people to show us what kind of a god he is for us. He uses all his conjuring tricks to alienate us from ourselves, so that we do not know ourselves and are not aware of ourselves. So, since Satan dupes us with lies and craftiness, God transforms himself into a man who accommodates himself to our senses, our reason, our inclinations, and our weakness. Thus God says, "Ask the days that are past. Ask everything around you and what is now present, before you believe me. Be as cautious as you can be with my testimony. I only require a free will offering from you, your reasonable service of God." Even though Satan always tries to stir up people against God, he does not once disclose him to them as his enemy and theirs. God wants to attract them to himself in love. If indeed they have no capacity for this love, he would rather attract them out of fear and shame towards him and out of love for their self-preservation than that they should be afraid of the devil. Even more than that, despite the security that covers people with their blindness for the cruelty and craftiness of the serpent, he repeats nothing so often as: "Fear not! Take heart! Yes, despite your partiality for my enemy, despite your hostility towards your Friend and Benefactor,

104. Here Hamann meditates on the singular use of this Hebrew verb, which usually refers to people testing God (e.g., Deut 6:16) or God testing people (Deut 8:2, 16), for God's engagement in a kind of test run, in which he tries out something tentatively before its full enactment.

I will not stop being your Friend and Benefactor. I will not take vengeance on you, but on him."

Even though you may not thank me for it or may yourselves not know it, you will be protected from him. Yes, even if your enemy *Luke 22:31* would fall at my feet and ask for you in order to sift you, he will remain unheard. He will be dismissed because I will lose none of *John 17:12; 18:9* you except the one who wants to be lost, the one who makes it impossible for me to rescue him, the one who has no desire to fix his eyes on the serpent, the bronze serpent that would heal him from the sting of the hellish, fiery serpent. One glance that you *Num 21:8; John 3:14–15; Ps 121:1* grant me, the lifting up of your eyes to me, for I bless the whole of nature with my glance, the glance that the seraphim long to *Isa 6:2–3; 1 Pet 1:12* see. See how much good your glance at me, which I beg of you, promises for you.

God attempted to *go.*[105] The redemption of the world is a greater work than creation. God spoke, "Let there be light and it was light." In order to make Adam, he stooped down, looked for a clod from the earth, built it, and blew the breath of life into it. This is the creation; this is the creation of a new person. This is the redemption. His whole work in the old covenant consisted in his coming down to earth. The God who owned the whole earth looked for a clump of earth. He found it in Shem, in Noah, in Abraham, in Israel. He built it through Moses and the prophets, and after this clump of earth had been built, he completed it through the Spirit of his Son, *Gen 2:7; John 20:22* through the breath of his mouth. This was the creation of Eve: a long sleep, a rib which he took from the human race, a helper whom he presented to himself in the person of his Son in order to *Gen 2:18, 21; Hos 2:21–22* betroth him to mankind in righteousness and holiness.

God attempted to go and took for himself a people from the midst of the peoples, just as he took a clump of earth from the midst of the earth and a rib from the middle of Adam's body. Like the creation of the world, this gives us, even more gloriously, a preview of the eternal creation. The first three days of God's work

105. The NIV omits this verb entirely.

were nothing but acts of separation—light from darkness, water from water, sea from dry land. The third day's work[106] was two lights to give light to mankind, the one in the night of the day with a borrowed light, the law, the other to rule the day, the sun of righteousness from which the law derives its splendor. Both of the last days were nothing but the fruit and completion and blessing of the other days; and the last work, the goal of the last work was the Man who was meant to enjoy all that had cost God six days, who through God's image was established as the Lord of the whole creation. Holy, holy, holy is God; all lands are full of his glory. Your will be done on earth as it is in heaven! Amen.

Gen 1:3–5, 6–8, 9–10

Gen 1:14–19; Mal 4:2

Gen 1:20–31

Isa 6:3; Gen 2:1–3; Gen 1:28; Ps 8; 2 Cor 4:4; Col 1:15; Heb 1:3; Matt 6:10

1. TEMPTATIONS[107]

We sense the influence of these from the existence of the highest God as well as from the existence of his enemy. This runs through all of Holy Scripture, which is the greatest revelation that we have of both heaven and hell. Both we and our enemy depend on God. Both of us were created by him who created heaven and earth. As the rank of Satan is greater among the spirits, so his freedom must be much greater. The greater the gifts that he received as a star, so much greater is his wickedness and the darkness into which he fell, so much greater is his will, so much more power he has to do harm than we have. The more power God lets him have over us, the more power we permit him to have over us, the more territory we take away from God and clear out for the enemy, so much harder our temptations make us, so much more mistrustful of God we become, so much more like the pillar of salt that is set up as a sign for us in the case of Lot's wife, so much more inattentive to God's influence we become, so much less we feel the hand of God, God's outstretched arm, and become so much riper for the *great terror* of the judgment. This outstretched arm is his declaration of war. From this trial comes the decision whether we acknowledge

Isa 14:12–14; Rev 9:1–2

Gen 19:26

106. Hamann either mistakenly refers to this as the work of the third rather than the fourth day or else thinks of three daily works with the production of vegetation as the second work.

107. This refers both to how we are tempted by the devil and tested by God.

God's influence more than that of a creature, a corrupt creature,[108] the decision whether God will be for us or against us.

2. SIGNS: REVELATIONS OF THE DIVINE WILL

See how, like Scripture, the whole of nature is full of signs in which God's gracious will is shown and the destructive purpose of the tempter goes out and about. Temptations and signs are always joined together from God's side and the side of his enemy. In all temptations, in all signs, we discover the enmity of the serpent's
Gen 3:15 offspring against the offspring of the woman, the liar and murderer
John 8:44; 15:26; 16:13; Rom 8:6 against the Spirit of truth and peace, the corrupter against the Creator and Preserver of the world. We discover the Householder
Matt 13:27–28 with the good seed and the weeds of the enemy.

3. WONDERS

These are creative acts by creatures done in the name of the true God who wants to reveal the characteristics of his will, its power and its severity, the powerlessness of the adversary, the limits of human beings, of each false god, and of the whole natural world. They show us that God is the Lord over heaven and earth, over the prince of this world and the spirits of the air, and over the hosts that
Deut 10:14; John 12:31; 14:30; 16:11; Eph 2:2; Ps 103:20–21 do what he commands, with pleasure and gratitude and vigor. These are miracles by which he announces the purpose of his decrees, their wisdom, the mysteries of his being, his name, and his will, which are above all finite reason and contrary to all the thoughts of people and angels. By them he performs his will gloriously. By them he creates what is good and governs what is evil.

4. WAR

This is the war between light and darkness until God separates them; the war between the waters above and the waters below until God creates a barrier that is to separate the water in the air and water under it; the war between the sea and the dry land until

108. This refers to Satan as a spirit that God created.

God gathers the waters under the sky and lets the land appear. Gen 1:6–10 And he gives each of these separated domains a special name. It is the war between the children of God and the children of humanity whose mixture was an abomination in God's eyes, the mixture that he avenged through the mixing of the whole earth;[109] the war between the offspring of the woman and the offspring of the serpent; the war between God who created heaven and earth and a Gen 3:15 creature that was more cunning than all the beasts of the field. It Gen 1:1; 3:1 was a war that resulted in so many alliances that God made with people, as if this God were not strong enough to fight against his own enemies; a war in which mankind was to be the booty and was set up as the only victor and beneficiary of it and all the goods that would be looted from the enemy, provided that mankind possessed the booty together with God—provided that he would believe that God was God and the Lord was the Lord—and instead of regarding us by ourselves and at the mercy of mere creatures, he himself became a man to convince people of this, yes to atone for the grave breaches of peace that they had perpetrated against God. O God, what depths; tremble, O man, if you want to come too close to this bush that burns and is not burnt up! How great is the good will of Exod 3:2 him who dwells in that bush, who has chosen to endure the fire that should have consumed us! He has refined and cleansed us all with this great, wonderworking, charitable ordeal by fire, so that we can draw near to God through his infinite accomplishment, feel nothing but his influences for what is good, overcome all the temptations of Satan, believe nothing but the signs and wonders of his law, and possess wisdom and knowledge to oppose the juggling tricks that Satan uses to bewitch our senses, reason, and heart and destroy them through the Word of truth which has been given to us. He has 2 Cor 6:7; 1 John 2:14; given us the victory through our Lord Jesus Christ. He can extin- 1 Cor 15:57 guish all the arrows of Satan, which he no longer fires away at us

109. See page 88. Here Hamann alludes to the violation of sexual boundaries between fallen angels and human beings and between the descendants of Seth and the descendants of Cain that resulted in corruption of the whole earth and the flood in Gen 6:1–13.

Eph 6:16; Gen 10:9 as an armed warrior but as a willful hunter of the Lord, who can turn them back on him with greater danger for his own snake skin.

5. A MIGHTY HAND

His enemies experience this, and his friends see how his grace hovers over them and covers them, how it stretches over them in blessing and suppresses our enemies in punishment. If God's enemies do not believe in his hand, he stretches out his arm. God does not need to do anything more to let them experience all that they are able to bear, in order to shatter his enemies and keep his children in safety and rest. When his enemies have enough of his arm, his friends shall enjoy it completely; he and all heaven shall belong to them.

6. THE GREAT TERRORS[110]

Sinners and rebels will be shocked at the judgment that God pours out on them when he casts them out into the pit that he has prepared for them. God's children will be shocked by the grace of their Lord who has chosen to redeem them from it. They will be even much more shocked by all the good things that God has reserved for them, the good things that no eye has seen, no ear has heard,
1 Cor 2:9 and can come into no human heart. Grant that to me, my Savior, for the sake of your love. Amen!

DEUTERONOMY 4:37

Gen 3:15; Rev 12:17 He loved your fathers, not according to the flesh—the offspring of the woman is the firstborn of creation. Note how every passage in
Col 1:15 the Scriptures looks back behind it and forward from it, how the work of creation is based on the work of redemption, and vice versa, how Abraham is to bless all nations and how he himself receives
Gen 12:1–3; 18:18; 22:18 this blessing through his blessing.

110. Hamann formats this in a different way by including no number but the sentence: "The last are the great terrors."

DEUTERONOMY 4:39

We see how the entire duration of time is nothing but an eternal *today*. The whole of time may make up a single day in God's economy in which all hours cohere and are included in one morning and one evening. The coming of our Savior marks the middle of the day. The creation of the world which cost God six days will last no longer than *today*. God, what is eternity, and what is its Lord! How many millions of days has that taken, how many millions of revolutions has the earth made before it has reached those that it makes today, and how many millions will follow them which you have all numbered, just as all those that have passed have been numbered! Just as this eternity of days which have been and will yet be in the world are nothing but today for you, so the present day is an eternity for me. Yes, the present moment is an eternity for me. Lord, your word makes us wise, even if it teaches noth- *2 Tim 3:15*
ing more than to number our days. What kind of nothing, what *Ps 90:4, 12*
smoke, what poisonous nothing are they in our eyes when reason numbers them! What kind of everything, what treasure, what an eternity, when faith numbers them! Lord, teach me to number my days that I may become wise! Everything is wisdom in the order of nature, when the Spirit of your word unlocks our spirit. Everything is a labyrinth, everything is disorder, when we want to look at it by ourselves. We are more wretched than blind when we despise your word and look at nature with Satan's deceptive glasses. Our eyes have the sharpness of an eagle, gain the light of angels when we see everything in your word—yourself, loving God, heaven and earth, their fullness, the works of your hands, the thoughts of your heart towards both and in both.

DEUTERONOMY 4:40

The Christian alone is a man, a father, a master of the animals. He alone loves himself, those who are his, and his goods, because he loves God who loved him when he did not yet exist and when he did exist, he existed as his enemy. My Lord and my God! *Rom 5:9*

"Prolong the days of your life"—is anybody so almighty that he can prolong them? Does God regard us for himself? How wisely God has hidden the future hour from us, since we know nothing of the future world. The Christian alone is a lord of his days, because he is an heir of the future. Our time is so connected with eternity that they cannot be separated without blowing out the light of life from them both. No matter how unlike they are in their nature, what joins them together is the soul with its human life, just as human life is made up by the conjunction of the soul with the body. That is the reason why the life of a person is called his blood in the
Lev 17:11 Scriptures. In the sinner the gift of life costs him his blood; in the believer the gift of life is the blood of the Redeemer. So too all those
1 Pet 1:18–19 that he has purchased through his blood. The unconverted person is like a sacrificial animal that has to pay for its own life and the life of the Savior with his own blood. The believer is the righteous Israelite whose blood the great sacrifice of the world's Redeemer has paid for, the believer who now participates in all the treasures that are bound up with his own life and the transfigured life of the world's Redeemer.

Out of love for his descendants, God moved Abraham to keep the covenant. Here he recalls his love for the patriarchs. How excellent is the new covenant which discloses the Messiah as our brother, so that we may serve, fear, believe, and trust God out of brotherly love.[111]

DEUTERONOMY 7:22

Just as God always shows that he is righteous in his ways, so he did not wish to uproot the inhabitants of Canaan all at once, because the Israelites were not strong enough to settle the whole land all at once. God had also chosen a larger place for them to live in than that which Israel could fill at once and settle properly. Here the Spirit of God that hovers over the darkness and is upon the surface of the

111. After this meditation on Deut 4, Hamann's dramatic spiritual awakening occurred on the evening of Friday 31 March as he meditated on Deut 5:5 in conjunction with Gen 4:8–10. See his account of this in "Thoughts on the Course of my Life."

depth of our heart gives us a still more significant disclosure of our Gen 1:2
nature. Our situation, our being, and the condition for our existence that had been set for the first man make testing utterly necessary. Without this testing in which the tree of knowledge would Gen 2:17
be replaced for the Israelites by the Canaanites and their gradual extermination, the dominion of the serpent would increase. The story of Job is the most outstanding explanation of the fall into sin and human redemption.

DEUTERONOMY 8:1

God's commands do not just make us alive when we are dead, but they also make our life fruitful in good works.

Rev 20:10, 14, 15

DEUTERONOMY 8:2

Why is there this wilderness that brings us into the land of Canaan? God has revealed everything in his word. He is rich in it, much richer than in nature. It is to humble us—to test us—and to know what is in our hearts.

We see how short this humiliation lasts, how necessary it is for us, and how gloriously it will serve us in that great victory that
we will take part in over God's enemies. What does this humilia- 1 Cor 15:57
tion consist of? He has made us lower than the angels. This great Ps 8:5
Father, who did not at all need to make us, takes an interest in everything that he cannot immediately give us and wants to repay it a hundredfold, since we are at home with him and he knows that
we lack it here on our journey through the wilderness. We are earth, Matt 19:29
and this earth is joined with an immortal spirit. This spirit suffers through its union with the former limitations which are at times like fetters for it. That is how hunger is. God uses this natural need
to test us. "I am suffering yours in addition to ours," says our Peter. 1 Pet 4:13; 5:9
Who would believe that when he lets us suffer just a little hunger, anyone would be afraid that he would let him starve to death? Yes, who would not be even more amazed if that person, instead of asking God for bread, would become impatient and disobedient by heeding his rebellious impulses and letting them rise up against

God? Why must these arise? So that we will recognize what is in our hearts and are able to oppose this evil, correct it, and, if possible, reconcile God with us.

"I humbled you," says God to Israel and to everyone, "through your lack of knowledge and goodness. I tested you through this lack in order to feed you with manna, with a wisdom that is heavenly, so that you may know that people do not live by bread alone. It is
Deut 8:3; Matt 4:4 by every word that comes from God's mouth that people live." How graciously God has tried to attract us to himself through temporal favors. He wants to use our temporal privation to warn us of spiritual hunger, and the poverty of our nature to lead us to the riches and the treasures of his love and grace!

DEUTERONOMY 10[:18]

God sees us as orphans and our souls as widows because we have disinherited ourselves through sin, lost the love of our Father and the love of our bridegroom. He regards us as aliens on earth who
John 12:31; 14:30; 16:11 are oppressed by its prince, Satan. Loving God, what pictures you use to portray your loving heart for us! God so, so loved the world
Jer 3:4, 19 that he gave his only begotten Son that whoever believes in him
John 3:16 should not perish but have everlasting life.

He will pronounce judgment over the tyrants who oppress his orphans and widows. He loves the alien; he gives him food and clothing.

DEUTERONOMY 11:14

Here God gives the gracious promise of the early rain and the later
Heb 6:4–5 rain, the powers of the Holy Spirit. When the heavens shut up this rain, the land ceases to produce fruit. The coming of the Messiah is most likely the early rain and the pouring out of the Spirit the later rain.

DEUTERONOMY 16:3

How beautifully the repentance of the new covenant is portrayed as unleavened bread, the bread of affliction.

The Feast of Weeks is a preview of the fruits of redemption and the church which God would found through his blood (Matt 9:37–38). Hence the weeks of Daniel! *Dan 9:24; Acts 20:28*

DEUTERONOMY 19:15–21

The law against false witness is very comforting for us Christians, since the accuser of our brothers is afraid of it and will get the death *Rev 12:10* that he intended for us. In the book of Job we see how much he reflected on this law and what use he made of it.

DEUTERONOMY 20:1–4

In Hebrew we have "hurry on," "make haste," instead of "tremble." This term combines both ideas in an outstanding way. Who is faster than a fearful person? The most fearful animals are also the swiftest. How unexpectedly the fear of God throws us into his very arms! That is why we should fear what is evil. We do not distance ourselves from our sins for the love of God unless we think of him as children do. When we try to distance ourselves from this snake hole, we do not bump into anyone else except the very God who is only jealous when he sees us in the clutches of an enemy.

DEUTERONOMY 20:5–9

We may compare the conditions for an Israelite soldier with our Savior's parable of the marriage feast in Luke 14:16–24.

DEUTERONOMY 23:15–16

This is a law by which we copy Satan, who is not just content to accuse us but also to denounce us.

DEUTERONOMY 24:5

This is why our Savior compares his disciples to the guests of the bridegroom who may not mourn like the Baptist's disciples. *Matt 9:15*

DEUTERONOMY 24:6

Neither the upper nor the lower millstone may be taken in pledge, because the use of the mill depends on both and neither can do without the other, and a person's life depends on bread. How cruel Satan is in his dealings with us! He does not just try to hoodwink our senses but also our reason.

DEUTERONOMY 24:7

We clearly see how Satan immediately receives his judgment for many sins, like here with the law of kidnapping and the sale of a kidnapped person. We see how God not only intends to judge Satan on our account but also through us, because our obedience shames and condemns his disobedience. That is the reward for our obedience and its fruit as well.

DEUTERONOMY 25:3

When we consider the cruelty in the story of Job, we discover what God's Spirit tells us here: your brother will be degraded in your sight. We hear his friends and how they misuse the greatness of his calamities in order to debase him so much more.

DEUTERONOMY 25:13, 14

The spiritual sense of this law should be considered. How miserly we are in our duties to God; how wasteful we are in the service of Satan. How heavy is the weight by which we weigh our failures; how light the weight by which we weigh our neighbors. The full, fair weight, the full, fair measure is nothing but God's word and his
Matt 7:3; Rom 8:9; 1 Cor 3:16 Spirit that dwells in us through it.

DEUTERONOMY 27:17

This is what will happen when we become like the offspring of the serpent with all the curses that we have brought on ourselves
Gen 3:14–19 through him. He is the one who removes our boundaries as neighbors of lowly status. He is the one who uses our ignorance to lead
Gen 3:5–6 us astray. He is the one who had no pity on us when he saw us

as aliens, remote from God and cut off from his grace. He is the one who desired to pollute and violate the human souls that God the Father, the Creator, had sought out as his bride. He is the one
who took on the form of a wild animal to seduce us. He kills his *Gen 3:1–2*
neighbor in secret. He accepts a bribe to kill innocent people. (Job; *Deut 27:24, 25*
Abimelech's covenant with Abraham.) *Gen 21:22–26*

DEUTERONOMY 28:13

The realm of darkness is itself an appendage to creation. God wants to make us the head of it. Our whole nature, says God, is to remain over heaven, not at all under it.[112]

DEUTERONOMY 28:26[–51]

This explains why Abraham drove away the birds in Genesis 15:11 and why God made the covenant with him. We have so often discovered the eternity of hell in Moses and discover it here once again. In it there will be no one who will curtail the power of Satan over us. A wretched person will then gain all his wishes to belong completely to the devil, and that undisturbed and unhindered.

God, with what horror we read of these curses that were carried out on Israel, Christians, and every unbelieving sinner. Madness—blindness, mental confusion—God will show you what you have done to him. He wanted to be betrothed to you, but you have given your love to Satan. He has built a home for you in which you will not dwell; he has planted a vineyard, the fruit of which you will not enjoy. Yes, your soul will feel despair like a man who has been betrayed by his wife, the owner of a house who has been evicted from his own house, and the father of a family who is not allowed to eat the fruit of his own garden.

---

112. This enigmatic remark is best taken together with verse 12, which refers to the bounty that God sends in blessings on his people from heaven. God's people are not just exalted with Jesus over the nations but also over all creation so that they are not subject to it or anything in it.

Who is to blame that the seed of the divine word has produced so little? The locusts, the foreigner who steals it from your hand (v. 38).

All these curses uncover for us the soil of our natural corruption and the punishment that we deserve when we cultivate it, when we want to relinquish our soil to be sown by the enemy rather than
Matt 13:1–9 with good seed.

We borrow a little mud from Satan, a little honor, and hand over our conscience and rational powers to him for it. Instead of that, God intends to make us so rich that he must give us good promises to gain something from our possessions.

Satan is the enemy of old age—we see how he tries to dishonor and mock it—and a child-killer (v. 50). In verse 51 we have *he* as if the enemies were a single person.

DEUTERONOMY 30:11[113]

We discover what mysteries of our nature are elucidated for us in God's word. Without it, the whole person appears to be nothing but earth, without form, empty, and darkness on the face of the
Gen 1:2 deep. Here is a deep that finite understanding cannot fathom, a deep on which the darkness lies, whose surface our eye is not even allowed to distinguish. If we wish to know anything, then let us ask the Spirit who hovers over this deep, who can transpose this unformed, empty, dark, mysterious world into beauty, fullness, clarity, and glory which, by contrast, makes the rest of creation appear to lose its radiance.

The commandment that God gives us is not hidden—it is not far from us. The word is near to you, O man—it is in your mouth! Yes, it is in your heart! So that you cannot excuse yourself by the difficulty of doing it or the freedom of not doing it. The commandment is fixed in your nature, woven into your being, so that both of them

113. This is a key text for Hamann's understanding of how God's word that is spoken to its hearers becomes his word that speaks to and for them in their hearts. He provides a much more extensive meditation on it later in the *London Writings* in "Deuteronomy 30:11–14 together with Romans 10:4–10."

must cease to be, if you should disown this word with your mouth or break it. This word is set so near to you that it costs less to satisfy it than the easiest necessity of your temporal life. Think of the breath that goes from your mouth and who has breathed it into you. Do not consider it to be of little significance because it seems easy for you to draw it into and push it out from you. Hear in your heart, in its depths, when my presence comes close enough to you, how the Israelite, an angel, groans, an angel who acknowledges that he is guilty, who beseeches me for grace. I will hear his voice (Deut 5).[114] His words please me. He is an angel who cries out, like the earth which opened its mouth to receive the blood of Abel. He knows the blood that was shed for him[115] (his generation) and fears my vengeance despite your clamoring hardness and complacency.

See Job 33:23–28

Gen 4:10–11; Heb 12:24

DEUTERONOMY 31:30

Moses spoke the words of this song into the ears of Israel, until they were finished, and the Spirit of God spoke them into the hearts of Israel, until they were filled.

DEUTERONOMY 32:5

Each one has acted falsely. They are his children and do not want to be that any longer. That is their blemish; a crooked and twisted generation.

Acts 2:40; Phil 2:15

DEUTERONOMY 32:6

God is a father who has *purchased* us. This is the refrain of the entire sacred Scriptures from the first verse of Genesis: "In the beginning God created heaven and earth." "Hear, O heavens, I will speak. Hear O earth, the words of my mouth." The end comes with the Hallelujah and the revelation of John in accord with it.

Gen 1:1

Isa 1:2

Rev 19:1–8

114. In this dense, difficult comment Hamann seems to regard Jesus as a second Moses, a mediator and intercessor. Unlike Moses who was not allowed to offer his life to atone for Israel's transgression at Mount Sinai (Exod 32:30–34), Jesus is the angelic intercessor who atoned for the sins of the world by his death and now lives to intercede for sinners at the right hand of God the Father (Rom 8:34; Heb 7:25).

115. That is, for Abel. Grammatically, it could also refer to the angel.

DEUTERONOMY 33:6[116]

Like Cain, who as an older brother in the order of creation killed
Gen 4:8 his younger brother, so, I believe, Reuben represents the tempter.
He defiled his father's bed. God regarded the sin of the serpent
Gen 3:14–15 with the same eyes. If we extend this judgment to the offspring of the serpent, it is easy to understand it ... Let him live ... Let him not die ... but his reign must be destroyed through Jesus Christ. This is the reason why Judah follows after Reuben here, just as in Genesis 11 Moses combines the tower of Babel and the genealogy of its destroyer.

DEUTERONOMY 33:7

Do we not hear the kneeling, trembling, blood-sweating Savior in
Luke 22:44 the prayer of Moses for Judah?

DEUTERONOMY 33:8

God tested us through hunger and fed us with manna. He tested
Exod 16; 17:1–7; John 4:16; 6:32–51; 7:37–38; 1 Cor 10:4 us with thirst and gave us to drink from the rock of living water.

DEUTERONOMY 33:9

The Spirit of the religion that Christ preached disowned father and
Mark 14:29; Luke 14:26 mother, brother and friends—and that for faith.

Here we find no trace of Simeon. Only eleven were named by Moses, as though he wished to announce beforehand, through his silence, what the twelve apostles, the founding fathers of the new covenant, would experience when one could not share in the final
John 13:21–30; Luke 24:50 blessing of the Savior as he ascended into heaven.

DEUTERONOMY 14:7–8

Those who hear the word but do not do it are like the animals who chew their cud but do not have a cloven hoof. Those who have a cloven hoof but do not chew their cud are the Pharisees who have outward righteousness, meritorious works, ordinances, and washed

116. Hamann mistakenly ascribes this and the next three verses to chapter 32.

hands with an unclean, ghastly heart, who are uncircumcised in spirit and without faith and love, whitewashed graves with unclean carcasses lying in them. *Matt 23:27*

DEUTERONOMY 24:6

Satan does not just overpower our sense organs and our lower mental powers but also our reason. The life of our Savior and his miraculous acts of healing consisted, for the most part, in the redemption and restoration of the upper and lower millstones. Their recombination sets the condition of our nature and the movement of our life.

DEUTERONOMY 28:68

Egypt is a symbol of hell. Through our journey in the wilderness, we were brought out from it. God warned that the children of Israel would be brought back to it again by ship. Then no further deliverance would occur. That is why we, so often, see our Savior preaching from a ship. *Mark 4:1–2*

DEUTERONOMY 29:11

In the Scriptures the good angels are usually understood as drawers of water, just as the hewers of wood can also be taken to portray the evil angels. Here the sojourner in the camp alludes to the spiritual world, the army of guardian spirits.

JOSHUA 1:18

Here we have a new example how God commands in advance what a person who has been left to his own devices would regard as necessary and his own responsibility. Thus in the abyss of our heart, there is a voice that Satan himself does not let us hear, but which God hears and to which he also seeks to pay attention. When we get to know ourselves, when we come to see ourselves almost as we really are, how we then wish, plead, fear for ourselves. How we then feel the need for all that God, without us knowing it, being interested in it, and asking for any of it, has never grown tired of

presenting to us, offering to us, and encouraging us, yes, frightening us to receive. Then we hear the blood of the Redeemer crying out in our heart. We feel that the bottom of it has been sprinkled with the blood that was shed for the reconciliation of the whole world. We feel that the blood of vengeance cries out for grace on our behalf.[117] All the miracles of Holy Scripture happen in our soul. Great God, our corrupt nature, in which you have desired to unite and also create heaven and earth, is only all too like chaos in its shapeless-
Gen 1:2 ness, emptiness, and the darkness that covers the abyss from our eyes, the abyss that is only known by you. ... Through the Spirit from your mouth and your word, turn this waste earth into good, fruitful land, a garden of your hand.

JOSHUA 5:9

Egypt is often taken to represent hell. Was not the neglect of circumcision a reason why the deceiver so tempted the Jews in the wilderness and with God's permission had so much influence on their hearts?

JOSHUA 5:12

Since God wants to be served alone and share his glory with no creature, so it is with his word. It alone wants to be tasted and enjoyed because it replaces everything else. It disappears as soon as a person returns to the old food from his land and soil. Spirit
John 14:17; 15:26; Luke 15:16 of truth, let me never return to the husks of this world after I have sucked your honey, the honey from the rock and the oil from the flinty rock (Deut 32:13).

JOSHUA 11

Who can read about the splendid victories of Joshua in his apparent flight from Ai so as to conquer with his ambush and the spear
Josh 8:1–29 that he stretched out against Ai, and not think rapturously about the Hero who put all our invisible enemies to flight?

117. See Hamann's previous meditation on Deut 30:11.

JOSHUA 11:15

Here we discern how perfectly our Savior fulfilled the law, just as Joshua did everything that Moses charged him to do and the Lord had commanded Moses. In chapter 8 we saw how Joshua read out all the words of the law aloud to the people and pronounced the blessing and the curse over the assembly (8:34–35).

In the division of the land, we see that a tree of knowledge remained for each tribe, a touchstone for the faith and obedience and a stumbling stone for unbelief and disobedience. Reuben, Gad, and the half tribe of Manasseh lived together with the Gerushites and the Maachites (13:13).

Josh 13:8–19:51

Gen 2:17

Isa 8:14; Rom 9:32–33

See also Josh 17:12–13; compare Exod 23:29–30; Deut 7:22

During the time of Joshua, Judah was not able to drive out the inhabitants of Jerusalem (15:63).

Ephraim did not drive out the Canaanites from Gezer (16:10).

JUDGES 1:7

Why does Satan keep count of the bread crumbs that we gather under his table? To turn us kings into his serfs. He succeeds in this because he mutilates our natural powers. He cripples our hands and our feet. Our Savior has paid him back for that. Our Hero from the tribe of Judah has deprived him of more than his thumbs.

JUDGES 1:12

Since the story of Achsah is retold in the sacred Scriptures, it is undoubtedly prophetic. What was the blessing from the victory of our Othniel except the rich outpouring of the Holy Spirit to water the land that our Savior did not just buy but also consecrated and sanctified with his blood.

Josh 15:16–19

JUDGES 1:21

Just as the Jebusites live with the children of Benjamin in Jerusalem, so we see from Job how Satan appears among the angels.

JUDGES 1:24, 25

God uses even his harshest judgments as means of grace and mercy. When Jericho was destined by God for destruction, God's wisdom ruled the heart of a prostitute. She served his spies with her good will in word and deed. Therefore she and her whole house were preserved. *Josh 2; 6:25*

Here we see a fortunate man who preserved himself and his family in a similar way.

In this we have the great mystery of God's wisdom. Through the least of his enemies God chooses to avenge himself on his greatest enemies. He gives us grace in order to let them experience his harshest judgment. He offers us nothing less than his grace with our life, which stands in his hand, which we have forfeited.

JUDGES 2:10

That generation did not acknowledge the Lord, just as Egyptians and Pharaoh did not acknowledge Joseph and his accomplishments. *Exod 1:6*

JUDGES 2:14

The more we consider the craftiness of the serpent's offspring, their rage, and the use that God has made of his freedom as well as his dominion over them, the more we will feel gratitude for the offspring of the woman and his blessing. He always sought to bind up and heal the poison of the serpent's frequent bites until he came to crush its head. *Gen 3:15; Rev 12:17*

We cannot read the story of the judges without amazement. We read how in God's hand every person became a hero to defeat his enemy. We read how by faith Ehud, whose right hand had been shot off, had to pull out his dagger from his right thigh with his left hand and was not able to retrieve his dagger from the belly of his obese opponent. We read how by faith Shamgar fought against Acher.[118] *Judg 3:15* *Judg 3:19–23, 31*

118. Here Hamann seems to construe the Hebrew preposition "after" as a proper name and the Hebrew verb "was" as "killed." This comment and many others show that Hamann had a copy of the Hebrew Bible with him in London.

We read how one woman had to serve by appointing a judge and another by executing a godless prince. *Judg 4:4–24*

Just as we best recognize the loathsomeness of sin in the suffering of Jesus, so in the previews of our blessing we also see pictures of the tyranny of the serpent overcome by him. What terrible enemies, who, even if God takes away their greatest power, are still terrible, enemies who seem to be born for murder, enemies who come as God's agents, enemies who secretly catch us out and try to separate us from the help of our Creator and his angels. They use the weapon of their hatred with such rage against us that they thereby forget their own self-preservation. When they have murdered us, they seek to lock us up above as prisoners of war. What enemies that we can rout with one ox goad! What a cruel woman, *Judg 3:31* who, under the guise of a hospitable, peaceful, agreeable wife, runs out to meet us, offers her tent, covers us, gives us milk rather than water to drink, and covers us up again, a woman to whom we are foolish enough to confide our fears and appoint her to stand on guard against our danger, while she has no other intention, with her friendliness, care, and attendance, than to see us sound asleep, in order not only to pierce our head with an iron peg but also to pin it tight to her ground and soil! Thus God defeated Satan through *Judg 4:17–22* his own agents, through the craftiness that he taught them, through the falsehood that he had taught them in his school, through acts of cruelty that he had hardened them to do. Thanks be to God who has given us the victory, the glorious victory through our Lord Jesus Christ! *1 Cor 15:57*

The peg of a tent—a venomous sting, a device of hell—with a hammer in the hand, with might and main. His own power does not seem to be sufficient to kill us. He daily looks for more power from God, a stronger hand, yes, a hammer for us! He sneaks around—he strikes the place that he knows is most dangerous—he pins us to the ground while we sleep, while we are exhausted by the curse that he has helped us to load on ourselves. He cannot now prevent God's blessing, no matter how hard he tries to thwart its fruit.

JUDGES 6:6

So often we read that Israelites cry out, Moses cries out, the earth cries out, the blood cries out. As little as God needs ears to hear, so little does he need a voice for him to hear us. His omnipresence, his omniscience are his ear and his eye. His mercy and wisdom provide a voice for all creation. Each part of it has its own voice. That is, each part needs God's generosity for its success. Each part has its own limits that God must maintain. Each has its own measure that it must fill. God hears us cry out when the devil seems to titillate us in the midst of our sins. God hears our cries when the sleep and intoxication of sin let us think about nothing but ourselves. He thinks about us even more. He knows our neediness. This need of ours is the cry which God needs to hear us. How wretched would the young ravens themselves be if God would wait so long as to provide their food only when they were starving and
Job 38:41; Ps 147:9 began to cry out to him for it. Nothing would grow old enough in the world to be able to use its voice. We would go hungry before our tongue would learn to stammer. As a mother understands the speechless cry of her child, so God feels our hunger and thirst, our nakedness and impurity. He has provided for all things before we knew any of these needs, before we even begrudged him a good word about them, yes without even very few people thanking him for it and hearing his cry by which he offers his heaven to us, shows
Matt 16:19 us the keys of heaven and the smoke of hell so that we may more safely escape it.

JUDGES 6:11

How necessary are the persecutions of the church to maintain the ardor and life of men! How hungry we are for God's word when we have to enjoy it secretly, like Gideon threshing his wheat in the grape press. It tastes the best for us in the wine press of the cross. Thus we see why the Midianites are good for God's people, why the Lord let them live in their land, and so on.

JUDGES 6:37, 39

When the whole earth knew nothing of God's word, the promised land was watered so richly with it. Just as this dew of the Spirit was spread over the whole land, so Israel in the flesh was like Gideon's fleece.

JUDGES 7:5

Only the person who receives Jesus, like the Canaanite woman, the tax collector, unclean people, sick people, and sinners, is a worthy soldier of God. While a Pharisee bends his knee and drinks, a thirsty sinner falls down flat and outstretched on the earth to be so much more like the current of living water that flows for him.

JUDGES 7:17

Look at me and do likewise. Believe and follow me. That's the voice of our Savior who through Gideon gave courage, spirit, life, and victory to the Israelites who lapped up like a dog.

JUDGES 7:16

Trumpets in every hand—watchfulness with the pledge of the Christian's redemption: the sword of the Lord and of Gideon. *Judg 7:20*

Empty earthen jars with torches and firebrands in them. These firebrands must now scare our enemies. We throw our earthen, empty jars at them and feed them with dust and clay and shards, because they wanted to oppress us and extinguish the divine light in our souls. *Judg 7:19*

JUDGES 8:18

Who hears Gideon speaking to Zebah and Zalmunna without hearing the voice of the woman's offspring, after his glorious victory, pronouncing a judgment over the offspring of the serpent, the prince of the air and of this world? The men of Succoth are so like the Pharisees and scribes that we would expect to find the same punishment for them.

Gen 3:15; Rev 12:17; Eph 2:2; John 12:31; 14:30; 16:11

Judg 8:4–7; 13–16

In Jether's silence we discover the weak faith of the disciples of
Judg 8:20 Jesus, their faint-heartedness and uncertainty.

JUDGES 8:21

Ornaments like the moon. Ordinances that copy the law, errors instead of the light of nature that Satan spread among the Jews and heathen and hung especially on his camels, the Pharisees, scribes, Greeks, and philosophers of this world.

JUDGES 8:27

We discover that earrings were used to make the golden calf in the
Exod 32:1–6; Judg 8:24–27 wilderness and the ephod of Ophrah, because Satan steals our ears from God and uses them to make us unbelieving and disobedient to God. Since the great danger of losing something is connected with its worth, our redemption, like all God's good deeds, not to mention the greatest of them, can become a snare for a crafty enemy to draw us into his kingdom. Note how all this shows up in the imperfection of these prefiguring pictures as well as the most perfect Savior who
2 Cor 5:21 was made sin for us by God.

JUDGES 10:15

Whose hair does not stand on end when he hears how the Israelites, these covenant-breaking, ungrateful, unfaithful Israelites, themselves in their own name call on the Lord: "We have sinned!" This confession is already a relief. "God, do to us whatever seems good in your eyes. This will be an utter relief instead of the sin that oppresses us and the enemies, the cruel enemies. We want nothing from them except to be delivered from them. We want to fall into your hands. Your wrath cannot be as terrible as their maliciousness."

JUDGES 10:16

God, what language your Spirit speaks! What thoughts are your thoughts! The soul of the Lord was cut short at the misery of Israel, his breath like a cross. God feels human sympathy when someone wrestles with him. He forgets that he is God. He forgets his omnipotence and cannot prevail against that person. He has yielded so much power to him over his love that the whole of creation almost regards it with envy and as a weakness of the great God for this perverted generation. *Gen 32:22–31*

In the book of Judges we find that God's ways and judgments are justified, so that it looks as if God had included the mentality of people with all their sin in the plan by which he punished and shamed and would finally judge their deceiver through the wretched people that he deceived. Israel lamented that it had to wipe out a tribe for the abominable deed that had been done in it. *Judg 21:6* Satan takes delight in hounding people, accusing them, slandering God to them and them to God, *Rev 12:10* tormenting those who are weaker and less than him with the power that he has over creatures and laughing at their torment.

JUDGES 4:15

The devil gives his children a coach and horses, so that they unlearn and forget the use of their own feet. When the need arises, how little help there is for them in their own feet that have, for so long, not seemed useless to them, how unnecessary, how detrimental, all the benefits are that deprive us of our natural advantages. How cruel and crafty the enemy of humanity is with all the tendencies that he inspires, and how self-seeking and how ruinous are his gifts.

JUDGES 19:22

In this shocking story there is also a figure of redemption, even though its meaning is manifold, like the manifold wisdom of God's Spirit.

The old host of the Levite offers up his daughter and the concubine of his guest. For me the Levite with his concubine seems to represent the union of the divine and human nature. "Are you God's Son?" *Matt 4:3; 26:63* This question was the eternal foundation of the spirits of darkness—and this agrees with the loathsome intention of

2 Cor 6:15 the sons of Belial[119]—to get us to acknowledge the devil. The old
host offers the concubine of his guest as if he were her husband,
and her husband abandons her to the whims of the sons of Belial.
We see how God has condescended by the gift of his Holy Spirit
and his only begotten Son! We see how he was humbled in both
through our sin and its instigator—his Son to the point of death
Phil 2:8 on the cross![120] We see how he has sent out the proclamation of
Acts 3:15 this murdered prince of life, this executed, only begotten Son and
heir of glory, through his twelve apostles into the world, in order
Eph 2:2 to gather men and take vengeance on the spirits of the air through
their conversion.

In this story there is also God's judgment of the Jewish people.
God abandoned his people to the hardening of their hearts to gain
Rom 11:11–12, 25–32 a greater advantage for them through their hardness of heart. The
spirit of unbelief deprived the Jews of all awareness of life in God.
Isa 65:12 When God called them, there was no one who answered him.
Thereafter he carried out his judgment on the corpse of the Jewish
people and scattered them in all the world. In the following chapter
we see a preview of the rejection of the Jewish people in the anni-
hilation of the tribe of Benjamin. The Rock of Rimmon provided
Judg 20:47 security and preservation for a remnant. See Song of Songs 2:14.

RUTH 1:1

There was a famine in the land. We should regard all the situations
where God lets us feel our needs and our natural limits as trials that
Deut 8:2 God uses to show us what is in our hearts, so that through his grace
he can separate what is displeasing to him, so that we can examine what our heart brings up on the touchstone of Scripture and assess the veins of our treasure in their ore according to its goodness. When we do not feel our natural needs, we are like stagnant

119. This designation, which means worthlessness in Hebrew, is a contemptuous name for the devil.

120. In his use of this somewhat shocking analogy Hamann does not assert that the divine nature of God's Son abandoned his human nature to the devil. Instead he claims that God the Father allowed his Son to be put to death in his human nature by the devil who in this way wanted to tear the Son's human nature from his divine nature.

water that deposits slime and mud where it is retained and begins to stink and become foul.

In his wonderful wisdom God has set up a wonderful harmony, such an extraordinary union and partition too between the powers of the body and the soul, between the waters above and the waters below, that they complement each other, are ready to serve each *Gen 1:7* other, and discover their connection in their separation. God has given the sense of hunger to our body so that we may assume the same need in our spirit. Yes, the hunger, care, and aridity in our spiritual life may make our body very weak, very greedy. With *Ps 42:1; 63:1* their senses Moses, our Savior, and his disciples experienced the nourishment that we feel with the fulfillment of God's will. So a true Christian, the longer and more he reads it, discovers how different God's wonder-working word is from other books. He feels that the Spirit of the word melts in his heart so that its aridity is refreshed as with a dew from heaven. He proves for himself how it is alive, *Deut 32:1–3* powerful, and sharper than any two-edged sword, which penetrates to the division of soul and spirit, bones and the marrow in them, and sifts the thoughts and impulses of the heart. He proves *Heb 4:12* that he lifts up his face in it and uncovers it to him in whose eyes everything is manifest, to whom everything is bare and naked. He *Heb 4:13* proves that he is the Spirit that hovers over the depths of all creation with whom we have to do, and whose voice we ask for and *Gen 1:2* hear in sacred Scripture.

What a comforting story is found in this book! The whole Bible could be preserved alone through this book. In it there is for us nothing more than the comfort of a foreign, deserted, exiled widow, who, however, remained loyal to her mother-in-law and followed the reapers on the field of her lover, who was promoted from her *Ruth 2:2–3* ephah of wheat to be a spouse and bride of her blood-friend and lord. We must feel so sorry for the human race and young people *Ruth 2:17; 4:13* that are led about so far and wide to glean wisdom, taste, and virtue. Yet, instead of the harvest that they hoped for, they finally find dry stubble in their barns that we try so painstakingly to fill and die from hunger and thirst at the overflow from them. In this book the mysteries of God alone are revealed, the fullness of the earth and the abysses of hell and all that is constructed from them, the riddle of the human heart that is so hard for us to solve and yet so easy when *Judg 14:18* we plough with the cow of the strong Hero, when we, like Samson's enemies, consider it with his lover and, with her help, seek to dis- *Judg 16:4–22* cover the secret of his strength and the meaning of his parables.

You, my soul, are the Moabite woman, who must leave her fatherland, her friends, her childhood home, and the vipers' brood of liars and murderers. You must go hesitantly into a foreign land. You must think, like Naomi, of the bounty that you have lost and feel and bewail your poverty and the hostility of him who has *Ruth 1:20–21* made you so poor. Go gleaning ears of grain in the fields of him who will look on you with grace, him whose reapers have the same compassionate heart as their master and carry out his commands *Ruth 2:1–9* about you. He will comfort you. He will pass on to you some parched grain and dip your morsel into his wine. Yes, it is not too inconvenient for him to attend to it himself, to pass it on to you yourself and put it in your mouth, the more humbly you seem to *Ruth 2:14* keep your distance from him. You will eat, be satisfied, and have something left over. Without your knowledge he will instruct his servants to forget handfuls deliberately for you, so that you have so much more to glean, so that you may not just have enough to eat but have some to take home with you, to comfort your forsaken *Ruth 2:18* mother-in-law and refresh her with it. Be sure that you do not to go to any other field, but wait patiently for the harvest time of his reapers. Beware of the malice of your neighbors! Don't let their mockery mislead you, but stay faithfully with his maidservants *Ruth 2:8–9* as one of them! Wash yourself, anoint yourself, and put on your *Ruth 3:3* dress. Rather, let yourself be washed, anointed, and dressed with *Isa 61:10; Eph 4:24* the cloak of his righteousness and holiness. Lie down at his feet; confess that you are his maidservant; confess that you want him to hide your nakedness with his wide blanket, the state of naked- *See Exod 22:26–27; Deut 24:12–13, 17; Gen 3:1* ness that a merciless creditor, your neighbor, your fellow creature, the crafty beast of the field, has brought on you. How great will his lovingkindness finally appear, since he has made such a great beginning with his graciousness to you! Ask the Spirit, who knows you and knows him; he is your confidant and his confidant; he is at home in the foreign land where he has brought you. Follow his counsel and trust in his testimonies by which he has sent you back with gifts from his hand, so that you do not appear empty from him. Be still, my daughter, until you see the outcome of it all, for *Ruth 3:15* the Man will not be satisfied before he has completed this matter and accomplished it. Already today! *Ruth 3:18*

Hear him as he talks in his gates. He is already speaking about you to the elders and all the people. He summons them to show that everything belongs to him. He has bought everything, paid for everything, paid generously for everything that belonged to your fathers, to your sons. He says that you, the daughter of Moab, have not been purchased by him to be a maid but his wife! He will revive the name of the deceased man on his estate, so that the name of your deceased husband will not be cut off from his brothers and cease to exist. He will have a place in the gates of his city, his fatherland, his kingdom, a place that the name of your dead husband will inherit and possess through the name of your eternally living Husband and Friend. Hear the blessing of the people and the elders in the gates of heaven about your renewed privilege. Hear the blessing *Ruth 4:11–12* over the Son from your body, the Heir of your blessedness, that will be spoken by your sisters to your faithful mother, the nurse of your newborn child. *Ruth 4:14–16 See also Matt 1:5–6*

May you be praised, most loving God, for the blessing that you have spoken on my so foreign, unclean soul, however poor it may still appear to you. Do not take any rest until you have completed the great work that your grace has begun with me through your Holy Spirit, for the sake of your Son, my Mediator and Savior, Jesus *Phil 1:6* Christ. Amen! Amen!

How delightful to the human taste are all the sentiments[121] of the simple, country life, this first age of the world, the childhood of

121. The German word *Empfindung* is a key term in Hamann's understanding of human experience. It covers sensation as the impact of something on the five physical senses, the perception of it with the imagination, and sentiment as the proper emotional reception of it.

the earth! What expertise, except the pen of the ready scribe who
Ps 45:1 let the soul of David overflow with great emotions and thoughts, could have inspired it? What expertise could have attained this truthfulness without artifice and embroidered the plot of this story with an abundance of prophetic features, depicted it outwardly and inwardly with equal beauty and sewn in color with the kind of fine detail and symmetry that the created world gives us but a foretaste? Who cannot be led to reflect that if a mere human heart is filled with emotion at the character of Ruth, Boaz, and Naomi, then God is pleased to preserve these human sentiments so as to restore them through the recreation of the human heart and make them more perfect, yes, what's more, that he has turned these human events into the pattern for heavenly decrees and mysteries.

He says,[122] "This is how you people on earth have behaved with each other now and then. The least sensitive among you is touched just to perceive these sentiments in his fellow creatures. I have let these sentiments and the reasons for them pursue you, in order to redeem you and make you happy. Just feel it, you poor people. If you are to be and want to be like this, my Spirit must prepare your heart and fashion truth in your understanding and lovingkindness in your will, which only my will and my word can impress on you and enliven for you."

1 SAMUEL 2:12–17

In the presentation of Eli's children, we once again find the starkest
Gen 3:15 description of the serpent's offspring. Like the angels of a higher order, they should have been like priests for us and, at the very least, not desecrated the offerings that we made to God in our naiveté and weakness. Here we see how Satan removes the best part from a human offering for God by stealing as much as he can with his three-pronged fork through his servants. The three prongs of this
1 John 2:16 fork are the lust of the flesh, the lust of the eyes, and the pride of life. In the parable of the sower, our Savior explains this fork with three

122. This has been added to show that what follows is what God says. In this paragraph God is the speaker.

prongs: they are the birds by the pathway, the stony land, and the thorns. Whereas this enemy uses power and threats in his robbery of God and human beings, God requires everything willingly from us. This is one of the reasons that make it hard for most people to shake off his yoke.

Matt 13:1–9

As in the book of Ruth where the reapers are named in the same way, young men often appear as representatives of the angels.

Ruth 2:5, 6, 9, 15, 21; 1 Sam 2:13

1 SAMUEL 3:2, 3

All the little details of the time that God called Samuel are prophetic. Eli was lying down in his place, his eye had begun to grow dim so that he could not see, before the lamp of God went out, in the temple of God where the ark was and where Samuel lay down, where they had been brought to rest. Judah came to an end, just as so many other human kingdoms have perished. So God also let his state perish, but in an extraordinary way: it had to do with his place. Prophets had stopped speaking—the law itself was suppressed with human ordinances—before the lamp of the Lord with the temple and the law had gone out completely, because the Savior had fallen asleep and had been woken up again, at that time Samuel was called by God.

2 Kgs 25:1–21

Matt 8:23–27

1 SAMUEL 3:11–14

All the judgments against Eli apply both to the seducer and the serpent's offspring. See 1 Sam 2:31–33. In particular, verse 14 is a wonderful prophecy that sacrifices would cease and that subsequently he who would himself be the sacrifice would forever be the judge of both Eli and his household. He would judge him forever for the iniquity that he knew because his sons had made themselves cursed and he had not even frowned at them for that. When we connect the traces in the sacred Scriptures, we discover specific allusions that cannot be explained by anything else than the bondage and power of the spirits under which we stand, like the animals given under our dominion. Both, however, belong to the prince of the world. We discover that these spirits, which God had given as our guardians

Gen 3:15

John 12:31; 14:30; 16:11

or princes, whose immature dependents or subjects we are, have not fulfilled the terms of the compact by which God had ceded us *Gal 4:1–3; Gen 4:9* to them. Cain said, "Must I be my brother's keeper?" God does not condemn him to death; he lets him be a fugitive. He builds cities; *Gen 4:12–17; Eph 2:2* he discovers arts and crafts. Is not all this like the spirit of the air? Just as God lets us regard what he gives us as our property, so the devil likewise considers the earth and human beings as his own. Like us, he forgets that he has received it from God and that he has not received it from God for harm to himself and others, but for the benefit of himself and others. He forgets that God regards love for *Matt 22:36–40* our neighbor as a part of the love that we owe to him. This implies that God always associates our herd with us and the herds of our *Gen 10:9; Exod 10:9, 24–26; 12:31–32; Deut 12:6 Judg 9; John 12:31; 14:30; 16:11* enemy with his herds.[123] That is why Nimrod is called a mighty hunter of the Lord. Like Abimelech, he is the prince of the world. Just as a hunter treats the animals that live on his land, so Satan regards people; he carries out his pleasure and cruelty on them. That is why God himself became a man and encountered them, just as Satan has encountered us. Satan[124] encountered Jesus as a stranger; he let him hunger and thirst; he made the world a prison for him. ... From this we see all that Satan should have done for us, all that he promised God and had failed to do. From this we see why Satan tries to egg on people against God. We see the tyranny that he exercises on us and God's forbearance with us, the choice of the ways that he goes with us and are so opposed to the violence of Satan. God gives us light so that we may recognize and love him. He reveals that he is Lord of all. He reveals that it grieves him to see us abused and that, if we wish, we will have satisfaction against our enemy and a rich reward with him. So in the sacred Scriptures God has gathered fruit from our own soil. He has made a choice from it and has turned the perceptions of our own nature, the events that occurred to our own people, into previews, taskmasters, teachers, comforters, and spies. God has allowed everything to happen through people on

123. This most likely refers to Num 31:28–30 with its law that some of the cattle taken as booty from Israel's enemies were to be given to the Levites.

124. Hamann writes "he" instead of Satan and later "him" instead of Jesus.

earth that has happened in heaven and will happen in hell. God has made everything visible that will happen invisibly. In the present times he lets that happen which has happened in the most distant past and that which will happen in the most distant future.

1 SAMUEL 4:13

I have noted how the time when God called Samuel corresponds exactly with the time when our Savior came into the world. How often Samuel went to Eli before he came to God. How faithfully he reported to Eli what God had revealed to him. Here we see the capture of the ark, the cessation of the law. We see Eli sitting on a seat *by the road* and waiting foolishly for what the whole city already knew—he broke his neck. We have the destruction of the Jews who sat by the road, their foolish reliance on the ark, and the end of the Jewish kingdom. Yes, what's more, we also have the first example of the indifference of a Jewish woman to a son. The midwife called to her in vain—she did not answer, nor did she set her heart on him. The offspring of the woman had come when the ark was captured and Eli broke his neck.

1 Sam 4:18

1 Sam 4:20

Gen 3:15; Rev 12:17

1 SAMUEL 7:15

Only of Samuel is it said, "He judged Israel all the days of his life." The prophet asks, "Who can number them? Who can measure their length?"

Ps 90:12–15

1 SAMUEL 8

What we here find out about Samuel's sons, we also find out about the sons of God in Genesis 6:2. They reject Samuel; they do not let God's Spirit punish them. When we have God as our gracious Judge, instead of his enemy, our condition is like the freedom from the tyranny of its kings that Israel enjoyed under the judges. God was too bad for them; Samuel's authority was too simple. We prefer the pomp of Satan displayed in debts, in borrowed, stolen trifles. He takes the children of his subjects in order to maintain his imposing court, yes, let me say, the care of his horses, his footmen. He steals

the best vineyards of his subjects, a tenth of their grain and sheep to
1 Sam 8:11–18 make himself full and fat and spend the rest on his courtiers. He is unaware of the voice of the Israelites, the voice of the human race. Since we believe more in our darkness, this shuts our eyes to the light that our nature wants to shed on our wishes and the things that we wish for.

1 SAMUEL 9, 10

Consider how God the Father has humbled himself by not only
Gen 2:7 forming a lump of earth but also giving it a soul with his breath. Consider how God the Son has humbled himself—he became a man, became the least of all people and took on the form of a servant; he became the most hapless of them; he was made sin for us;
Phil 2:7–8; 2 Cor 5:21 in God's eyes he was the sinner of the whole people. Consider how low God the Holy Spirit has condescended by becoming a historian of the smallest, most contemptible, most insignificant incidents on earth, so as to reveal the mysteries and ways of God to mankind in its own speech, its own history, and in its own ways.

Imagine this mystery! Suppose that you wished to make yourself understood to a nation that was born deaf and blind, a nation whose eyes were blinded and ears locked shut by sorcery. No one but God could speak to such a nation, no one except the One who made the eyes and the ears; no one except he who was greater than all the magicians of Egypt, who confounded all their power with
Exod 8:15 his finger, would be able to reveal himself to that kind of nation.

Nature is full of glory. But who can survey it? Who understands its speech? It is lifeless for the natural person. But Scripture, God's word, the Bible, is more glorious, more perfect. It is the wet nurse that gives us our first food, the milk that gradually makes us strong
1 Pet 2:2 enough to walk on our own feet. It removes the magic spell of Satan over our senses and our reason. It transforms the din of wild passions in our soul that make us so deaf that we are no longer aware of ourselves into stillness, peace, eternal heavenly peace.

By the events in the life of a Moabite woman, the Holy Spirit tells us the story of our human nature, the human soul.[125] In the advice and comfort, the tenderness and hidden guidance of her mother-in-law, he tells us about his own direction of human beings. Thus we see the same thing in the story of Saul in a new light, with a new taste for us, and in new dress. So too the natural world! God lets people see and taste his goodness in a thousand guises, in a thousand changes which are nothing but the outer shells of his goodness that flows through the whole creation as the basis for its existence and its blessing. Let us consider all Scripture as a tree which is filled with fruit, each and every one with its own seed, a rich seed in which lies both the tree itself and its fruit. This is the tree of life with leaves that heal the nations and the fruit that nourishes the soul. *Gen 2:9; Prov 3:18; Rev 22:2*

1 SAMUEL 9:2

How well the superiority of man over all other creatures on earth is expressed by the description of Saul—from his shoulders upward he was taller than everyone in Israel—this is also the difference between every human being and the firstborn of creation. We must *Col 1:15* always consider the offspring of the serpent and the serpent himself together with each other. Furthermore, we must consider that *Gen 3:15* the human family seems to be the tree of knowledge for the spirit world, for just as man fell through this tree, so the spirits fell through *Gen 2:9; 3:1–7* mankind. Shall we go up or down as trees? (Judg 9:9, 11, 13). There are many mysteries that we do not need to discover which God lets us uncover through a magnifying glass, mysteries that he has withdrawn from natural sight. In compassion God has not chosen to reveal all the power that Satan presumes to have over us under the pretext of his right, nor all the danger. It is enough for us that we are completely convinced that God is his Lord and the Lord of heaven and earth. It is enough that even though there was a time *Matt 11:25* when it seemed to be ridiculous to Pharaoh that a God whom he did not know should require him, the great King of Egypt, to let

125. The Moabite woman is Ruth.

a people go whom he regarded as his slaves, there soon came a day when Pharaoh himself drove out his slaves as free people and *Exod 14:27–28* received his judgment in the sea. It is enough that we know that the Lord of heaven, the only God, is our Lord and God. He has done even more for us. He has ransomed us from the tyrant. Even though there was a time when we knew and had *no other father than the devil*, we, thank God, have now left this family and friendship. We no longer know our father or mother. We tell him that we have never seen him. We do not know our brothers, nor does he know his own children, for we are now the people of the Savior, his broth- *Rom 8:17* ers, God's heirs and fellow heirs with Christ. Thus here in Saul's father we can recognize the Spirit who calls our Savior the Father *Heb 12:9* of the human race and especially those who are unbelievers. For a while he sends a person the wrong way after his donkeys and has more love for them than his unhappy children. We discover Saul about to return home to his father and express feelings of childish love against this tyranny, while in his servant we hear him who led, advised, and comforted the human race, as represented by Naomi, and here in the image of a servant takes an interest in mankind. He brings Saul to Samuel, the man of God, who is held in high honor in his Father's house, whose words are true, who alone is the way *John 14:6* by which we come to God.

Saul's servant did all this, as the agent of the Holy Spirit. When we, with Saul, admit our poverty because our spirit is empty and we have nothing to give, this faithful servant says, "See, a quarter of a shekel is here in my hand! I will give it to the man of God to show us the way." The Spirit prepares us. He helps us acknowledge our needs and enables us to appear before Jesus. He himself puts the down payment for us in his hands and tells him that we wish to know the way. Instead of the joy that Saul expected to find for himself in the midst of the lost donkeys of his father, he sees himself, on the hill of the city, in the midst of its young maidens and virgins who draw water. Who cannot but discern that these are the spirits that minister to people with their graceful figures, their virginal purity, and their services that allow nothing to be too bitter for them to do for people? They are especially devoted to refreshing souls and ensuring that there is no lack of natural refreshment and moisture which they depend on for their survival and fruitfulness. Who does not discern the same joy in their address that Jesus attributes to the angels over a repentant sinner? Every word that they say is repeated by the prophets and explained by Jesus. See Samuel coming to meet Saul.

Heb 1:14

Luke 15:7, 10

Already before the human race existed, God had recognized and accepted its Savior. The Lord opened Samuel's ear a day before Saul came. He still comes just like that to meet every sinner who comes together with the Holy Spirit. Even though Saul had been revealed to Samuel, the Lord tells Samuel as he sees him, "This is the man of whom I spoke to you! He it is who will rule over my people." The Spirit of God is not satisfied with the witness of his divine Word in which the Savior is present everywhere and where everything is full of the Redeemer, but he brings him for us into our souls. With his finger he points to him and says, "See, this is Boaz, this is Joseph, your Jonathan—into his hands his Father has given everything, heaven and earth. He wants to make you a fellow heir with him of everything." Saul comes closer, and he asks about the seer's house. When we seem to speak to a stranger and when we first wish to see the house of a prophet, we are speaking to the Lord of the house with the very Spirit of all the prophets. Go up before me, for you shall *eat today*. Only in the company of the Spirit can we participate in the table of Jesus. It was this, this Spirit, who has raised the human race of the Messiah up on high where we follow him with those who are his to enjoy the marriage supper of the Lamb. *You shall* eat, and tomorrow I shall let *you* go.

Matt 28:18; Rom 8:17; Luke 24:15–27

1 Pet 2:9; Eph 2:6; Rev 19:9

How moving is Samuel's explanation for the sinner and the whole sinful race! For whom is the whole, highly praised Trinity more engaged, yes, the whole of heaven is more concerned, than for you, a sinner, and all your sinful brothers? Here the evangelists are the best interpreters, and our Savior always has the story of Saul before his eyes in his parables.

Samuel speaks with Saul on the roof of the house. In Hebrew it is not Samuel who speaks, but the text says that "they spoke with Saul";[126] there was an intimate fellowship with him on the roof of the house. They get up early. At daybreak Samuel calls Saul on the roof of the house and says: "Up, that I may send you away." Saul rose up, and they both, he and Samuel, went away from home. Here in Samuel's fellowship with Saul we see the mystery of God's incarnation. They got up *early*; through prophets and miracles God continually prepared the human race for this last, great event. Finally, God called his Son—and with this call came the dawn from on high; the day of salvation broke for the human race. This call consisted of the life, death, resurrection and ascension of our Savior. All this cost God a *call*, whereas the whole creation has cost him only *a word*. Samuel sends Saul as he himself goes with him. Saul was already on the roof of the house. Yet here Saul arises.[127]

With God there is no time, no difference between his persons and acts. Everything is present; for him yesterday is today; for him tomorrow is today. It is astonishing how the Holy Spirit uses the confusion, the apparent disorder of our concepts to make what is mysterious intelligible for us, what is divine, high and incomprehensible, something that neither our reason nor even the angels can do. Despite this apparent topsy-turvy disorder, there is the greatest order in its fulfillment and greatest clarity in the contemplation of what belongs to our faith. This single passage shows us that God is one God, that the persons of the Godhead comprise this unity in God. It shows us that all three persons were revealed at the beginning of the human race for the redemption of mankind and employed all means, so that fellowship with Saul might occur on the roof of the house. God took upon himself our human nature—a wonder that surpasses all concepts and thoughts—this, to be sure, was fulfilled in time, but was already present in God's eyes with the first day of the earth. That is why he went out to draw

126. Hamann takes this plural as an allusion to the three persons of the Holy Trinity.

127. Here Hamann refers to use of the Hebrew verb for "arise" in 9:26b as an allusion to Christ's resurrection from the dead.

people to himself, why He, so to say, rose up early. It shows us that God and God's Spirit accept the validity of the Son's sacrifice. It shows that through his calling God's foreknowledge[128] was carried out and sealed, and that God therefore took him back to himself and poured out the Spirit as the seal of reconciliation. Saul arises—God the Son came into the world. That is why God the Father and God the Holy Spirit did not abandon the earth. And just as the Savior finally came to the city before he was taken up into heaven, so he left his disciples by themselves, in order, thereafter, to pour out his Spirit with his gifts and powers. This is what Samuel says, "Let the servant go on a little before us!" So he went ahead. "But you stay here, so that I may show you God's word." After that the anointing of Saul and the apostles occurred.

Who but almighty God could have made it possible to make so many mysteries intelligible to us that we poor blind people could have some idea, an idea about what is so infinitely high and remote beyond the horizon of human reason? We ourselves are shocked at the height to which the God's Spirit has brought us, since we seem to have climbed nothing more than an easy hill, a hill that costs us no effort to climb, a hill where his association, the manner of his association with us, deceives all our senses.

1 SAMUEL 10:1

Here Samuel symbolizes the Holy Spirit just as he had prefigured the Redeemer. That is why it says in 7:17, "he returned to his home." As our Redeemer, he ascended into heaven and sent the Holy Spirit to anoint us and to give us the kiss of peace. This sending of the Holy Spirit was connected with signs and wonders.[129] The first sign that the Holy Spirit performed in the souls of the apostles and first Christians was the conviction about the person of Christ and

128. The literal sense of the German term *Vorsehung* is fore-vision, the preview of what will happen.

129. Here Hamann alludes to the text of 10:1b in the LXX: "Has not the Lord anointed you to be a prince over his people Israel? And you shall reign over the people of the LORD and you will save them from the hand of their surrounding enemies. And this shall be the sign to you that the LORD has anointed you to be prince over his heritage" (ESV).

his validity with the Father who once again acknowledged people as his children.

God is everywhere on every hand, in heaven and on earth, in the miracles of Moses and the obstinacy of Pharaoh. He let the serpent speak and Adam eat. He sent Israel into Egypt and led it out glori- *Eph 2:3* ously from it. He made the children of his wrath and the children of his grace. Since God has his prophets, his churches, his altars, so he has allowed some for Satan. Since he has sent his apostles to lead people to the light, since he seeks to redeem people through the offspring of the woman, so Satan too has his apostles, his offspring *Gen 3:15; Rev 12:17* that go out from him in order to bring everything back to him.

The first sign was the two men by Rachel's tomb who testified *1 Sam 10:2* that the donkeys had been found and his father had missed his son. He is concerned about him: "What shall I do about my son?" This was the first blessing from the anointing of the Holy Spirit. God convinces us in our soul that he has once again found us, and that it has cost him his Son to receive us as his children and the brothers of his Son. He works repentance in us, the godly grief over the sacrifice that our sins had cost for God who gave up his Son for *2 Cor 7:10; John 3:16* us, to redeem and rediscover the dullest and slowest spirits that he had created.

1 Sam 10:3–4 The second sign is the plain of Tabor—the plain of the mountain that we Christians ourselves ascend after our Savior was transfig- *Matt 17:1–9* ured on it. In the foreground we see two people because the third is joined with Saul. Here all three approach the sinner; they greet him with peace. The reconciled Creator carries the offerings of the old covenant as symbols of the propitiation of his wrath. The Son of God carries the bread of life, the first nourishment for our souls, and does not permit the old covenant to enjoy the last bread, his own body, or the wine of the Holy Spirit. Yet all three of them greeted the believers of the old covenant with peace and gave them two loaves of bread.

1 Sam 10:6–7 The third sign is the gifts of the Spirit—joy, gratitude, faith, the freedom of the conscience—the new and certain spirit that the Spirit creates in us, the Spirit that was accompanied in the early church by his miraculous gifts. *Ps 51:12* *Mark 16:17–18; Acts 2:43; 4:30; 5:12; Heb 2:4*

1 SAMUEL 10:11, 12

The people said, "What has come over the son of Kish? Is Saul among the prophets?" This was the envy of the angels.[130] One of them answered the rabble of the spirits: "Who is the father of the prophets? Who is the father of the spirits, even the evil spirits? Can he who created the angels turn people into angels?"

So this proverb arose. It became a matter of discussion in the world of the spirits: "How can this be? Does our God wish to make himself so common and take people, the sons of Belial, as his race, *2 Cor 6:15* put his Spirit on them, and hear his praise from their unclean mouths? How should we, for an hour, be considered equal with these creatures? Should they be superior in rank to us?" With so much warrant we may therefore believe that God intended to test the angels through us and us through them. We may believe that *1 Cor 6:3* their fall is greater than ours and that they became even greater enemies of humanity, the more they became God's enemies. We may believe that this, perhaps, was the reason for God's amazing decision that Hannah celebrated in her song: "The pillars of the earth are the Lord's, and on them he has founded the world." God *1 Sam 2:8* has set the laws that he has given to the sun beam as the foundation for the movement of the sun itself. God resolved to show the size of his finger with insects. Yet the same God who punished the *Exod 8:16–19* Egyptians with his finger, killed their firstborn and the firstborn of their cattle with his outstretched right hand, and led the Israelites out on dry land through the Red Sea in which he drowned Pharaoh. *Exod 11:5; 14:15–29*

The same Israelites who had rejected God received a king from God. Thus our sin brought us into heaven through the great sacrifice that our Savior paid it. Thus the rejection of God by our older brothers and fathers has made us kings and gained the highest rank for us in heaven. *Eph 2:6; 2 Tim 2:12; Rev 1:6; 5:10; 20:6*

130. This refers to the fallen angels.

1 SAMUEL 10:22

See, he has hidden himself under the trash from the house, the rubbish. Since God had called humanity to the highest place of honor, his Son concealed himself. He polluted himself before God with the trash from his own household. Since our Redeemer was God, he hid himself in the form of a wretched person in order to make himself thereby the King of the whole world.

1 SAMUEL 10:25–27

This is the mysterious book of the Lamb, the unsealing of which John describes in his Revelation. It is the last thing, the judgment when our Savior sends each person into his home, the blessed of the Lord into the house of the Lord and the godless into the realm
Rev 20:10, 14, 15 of Satan or, much rather, into the lake of fire. Here we also discover the little bands of our Savior whose hearts God touched to follow
2 Cor 6:15 him and the rejection of these by the sons of Belial. 1) There is their unbelief by which they despise him and his teaching and deny his commission by God as well as his divinity itself. 2) There is the atonement for unbelief through his suffering, death, and judgment. They despised him before his resurrection and did not believe when he had risen and his victory was preached to them. When he was proclaimed as the Son who sat at the right hand of the Father, they did not want to pay homage to him. So he became *like one deaf to them*. He too did not hear them. That is the judgment, the final verdict on unbelief and its father, the verdict on Belial and his children, the obduracy for which Jerusalem was destroyed.

1 SAMUEL 18:4

The friendship of David and Jonathan prefigures the union of divinity and humanity in Jesus and the communion that we enjoy through it. God's Son unclothes himself like Jonathan. He does not just give people his own clothes but also his victorious sword, his bow, and
Eph 6:14, 17 his belt.

1 SAMUEL 19:13[131]

This pillow of goats' hair is a picture for the sacrificial service of the Jews. It was put in a bed for a sick person to make atonement for him, so that through it he, like David, would escape. So just as David was rescued through the love of the king's daughter for him, our souls are set free through our love for God's Son.

1 SAMUEL 20:1–17

We see how the Trinity and the unity of the divine and human nature in Christ are given to our human reason through our senses in the Holy Scriptures. In verse 8, David as the human nature speaks to Jonathan: "Your hatred brought your servant into a divine covenant with you.[132] Would you now kill me if anything villainous is found in me? Yes, you are God's son. Why do you want to bring me to your angered father?" Immediately after this, in verse 14 we hear Jonathan, like the human nature, pleading for grace from David (v. 14), so that he would not die. He pleads for his house, for he considers all David's enemies cut off by the Lord. He asks that through David's enemies and by their hand God would promote the covenant that he made with the house of David, and that God would maintain and affirm this covenant by their downfall.

1 Sam 20:12–17

1 SAMUEL 20:18

How prophetically the new moon portrays the time when our Savior was sacrificed, and the three days portray the time when he hid himself. His royal seat would remain empty because he had gone to the sacrifice for his house (20:29, 18). Saul states the reason for this: "He is not clean; surely he is not clean." He has borne all our sin. Saul's wrath is against his son. The father hurls a spear at him as a sign that David is indeed a son of death in his eyes.

1 Sam 20:26; Isa 53:4

2 Sam 12:5

131. Hamann has 1 Sam 19:12 rather than 19:13.

132. It is hard to work out exactly what is meant here by Jonathan's hatred. Hamann may consider Jonathan as a representative of his human father who represents God. Jonathan brought David to Saul who tried to kill him in rage with his spear (1 Sam 19:7–10).

1 SAMUEL 20:35–36

Jonathan himself shot the arrows for the death that his father had intended for David; so God himself reconciled himself to us in Christ. The boy did not know the meaning of the arrows that he gathered, nor did he, without him who was over him and who had shot them beyond him, any longer see anything more than
1 Sam 20:37–39 one who belonged to this world. Thus, without knowing what they were saying, the Jews cried out, "His blood be on us and our chil-
Matt 27:25 dren." They saw the blood of the crucified Redeemer and the physical agony that they had inflicted. But they did not see the anguish that their sin and God's wrath had heaped on him. This was the arrow that was beyond them, the arrow that had been shot over their heads, the arrow that they could not see. Jonathan gives these arrows and his weapons to his attendant to carry and instructs him: "Go! Carry them into the city." So our dear Redeemer has given us the weapons of his mighty victory and all the fruit of his redemption to us as our own, so that we can appear before God and his throne with them as our very own.

1 SAMUEL 21:9

"There is nothing like it," says David about the sword of Goliath.
Eph 6:17; Eph 6:16; cf. Ps 11:2; 64:3 This is the sword of the Spirit. The Spirit of God has wrapped up the arrows of Satan that he aims at people through sin, as it were, in a cloth behind the ephod, so that we can put the enemy to death with his own poison. The Holy Spirit has become a historian of foolish, yes sinful human deeds, in order to dupe people, like David with Achish.[133] Like the Spirit of purity and wisdom, David disguised his appearance; he scribbled signs on the *doors* of the *gates*. The Holy Spirit is not just satisfied to speak and write as a man—but as less than man—as a foolish, mad, yes raving man. He, however, poses as such only in the eyes of God's enemies—paints the doors of the gates with signs that Achish could not decipher, signs mistaken as the handwriting of an idiot—even more than that, he let his spittle

133. The following meditation explains the brief comment on this incident in the previous section "On the Interpretation of Sacred Scripture."

run down his beard. He seems to contradict and defile himself by what he had been inspired as God's word—the lies of Abraham, the incest of Lot, the disguise of a man after the heart of God into the form of a person who was held to undergo God's greatest punishment, a person who has been robbed of the use of his reason as the unique human prerogative. This is the sword of Goliath by which David overcame the Philistines. This is the sword of our enemy, which God's enemy has prepared, in a cloth behind the ephod as a holy weapon for David's victories. My God, it is through your counsel, which reason cannot admire enough, silently admire and honor enough, that your wisdom has turned human folly, human sin, into our taskmaster to bring us to Christ, to our glory in Christ. My God, how could pride enter the human heart? The whole of Scripture is written in a way that you yourself have chosen to humble yourself so as to teach us humility, to bring to nothing the pride of the Philistine who regarded the wonderful things that you wrote with your pencil on the doors of the gates, for heaven and earth to see, so that all who went out and came in could read them, as the writing of a mad man. You did this, so that the sons of the serpent would lose the wisdom to bind the blessed offspring of the woman because they too regarded him as mad. You did this so that your apostle would have to be accused publicly of madness, because through him your Spirit spoke words of truth and sanity.

Gen 19:33–36 20:3

1 Sam 13:14

1 Sam 17:51

Gal 3:24

Gen 3:15; Rev 12:17; Mark 3:21–22

Acts 26:24–25

1 SAMUEL 22:2

How could the scribes see our Savior in the midst of sinners, tax collectors, sick people, wretched people, and blame him for that, without thinking of David becoming the captain of all those of his people who were distressed, indebted, and depressed?

Luke 15:1–2

1 SAMUEL 22:22

Matt 2:16–18 Like the slaughter of children in Bethlehem, the city of the priests and
its people prefigure the martyrs that God, for the sake of Jesus, would
give to Doeg the Edomite[134] to offer up, just as Satan enjoyed arous-
ing the whole Jewish nation through their disunity and their blind
obstinacy by which they brought the vengeance of the Romans on
themselves and God confirmed his own righteousness and the truth
of his promises. David's flight to Moab with his father and mother
Matt 2:13–15; alludes to the flight of Jesus to Egypt. His return from there and the
forest of Horeth appeared to be the wilderness where the Spirit of
1 Sam 22:5; 23:15–18; Matt 4:1 our Savior led him to expose him to the temptations of Satan.

1 SAMUEL 23

The incarnation of God is shown in a lovely way through his con-
finement in a first city with gates and bars and an enemy around it
1 Sam 23:7 who wants to surround it and besiege it.[135] Our Savior triumphed
over the army of his enemies and broke up the gates and bars of hell.

1 SAMUEL 24:2

The Rocks of the Wild Goats seem to hint at the places in the land
of the Jews where Jesus stayed. So too the errors of the Pharisees
and their pride in their own righteousness and the teaching of the
Mark 7:1–13 gospels which God sets against their statutes.

1 SAMUEL 24:11

David removed the corner of Saul's robe. God, how great are your mysteries! Is anyone allowed to approach them? Our Savior was God and man. Does it not seem that his divinity opposes his Father because the Father's righteousness wanted to punish the sins of mankind in him? Was this not a temptation, one of the greatest temptations that beset our Savior? Was not this why Satan tormented and oppressed him severely, so that his patience as a man

---

134. Like Doeg, King Herod was an Edomite.

135. By the mention of a first city, Hamann does not refer to Keilah but to the womb of the virgin Mary.

might thereby cease? Through the mouths of the Pharisees and the people, he always called out to him, "If you are God's Son, then come down." As God, our Savior, as it were, had God in his power. *Matt 27:40* He did nothing more than steal the corner of his cloak from him to cover the nakedness of people and thereby convince God that he should forgive them. Thus in Judah the Father cried out, "My daughter, you are more righteous than I am." Thus in Saul the Father *Gen 38:26* cries out, "My Son, you are more righteous than I am." We see our *1 Sam 24:17* Redeemer before his pursuing, incensed Father and our King, the promised King David, fall down with his face to the ground. How can we not humble ourselves and bow down before our Jonathan, our David, and God our reconciled Father?

God does not cover up the ways of evil that he permits in creation; he covers up the ways that he intends to go.[136] Everything evil is something good; it is a divine means which is covered for us. It is his infinite wisdom which, like his clothes, covers up his feet, his steps and ways.

1 SAMUEL 24:12[137]

God, who does not tremble at your word? You sinners, hear your David speaking to God. I cut off the corner of your robe, but I did not kill you. To approach a holy God in sin means to believe that he is unholy and to oppose him who has condemned us as a righteous Judge. It means that we want to call into question his sword of righteousness and rob him of it, to do away with him by it. God would have had to do away with himself, he would have had to destroy his own being or torture it eternally, if he had denied, or changed, his righteousness and holiness in human sight. God therefore had to be reconciled through a person who not only spared his life, but who, in doing this good deed, also removed the corner of his robe, in order to cover the shame of sin with it. The Holy Spirit has not revealed more in any story than in the story of David. These

136. This alludes to the Hebrew text in 24:3, followed by the KJV, which speaks about Saul "covering his feet" as a euphemism for relieving himself.

137. Hamann cites 24:11.

mysteries alone unlock eternity for us who see the sparks from it darting around in a dark place in our souls. The pillars of the earth
1 Sam 2:8 are the Lord's, and on them he has founded the world. Our astronomers know how small the earth is compared to the world. Hannah may not have known it, but the Spirit knew that people would have some idea of their smallness through this relationship, for with the Spirit nothing is small, nothing is big. Yes, when he deals relatively, it is reversed. Something small is great for him; something great is small. He impoverishes those who are full and lifts the beggar from the stinking dump of ashes. Take comfort, sinful soul, in the pillars of your righteousness! God would become a sinner, God himself would annihilate himself and everything, everything would perish, before he would suspend the least part of the atonement that our Savior offered to God as a man. If it were possible for him not to
Heb 10:15–18 forget our former guilt, then we would be more righteous than God himself. Do you now understand that the pillars of the earth are the Lord's and he himself has founded the world on them?

1 SAMUEL 25:22

The human race is described as a person who urinates against the wall; he pollutes the wall that covers him and provides protection.[138] In the lowliest images, the lowliest of them, there is a sense, a meaning that is unlocked when we read them with simplicity and humility, the same simplicity and humility that the Spirit of God had employed when he revealed himself to man through it. The man who intended to overthrow a wall with his impurity and thought that his urine could be enough to undermine it, would be regarded as a fool. Thus the power of sin, even when the Philistines, the Amalekites, and the Goliaths among the spirits want to unleash it against the Creator, is nothing more than the urine of a man against a wall.

138. This reflection is based on the Hebrew description of an adult male as one who urinates against the wall, an image preserved in the KJV.

1 SAMUEL 25:29

David used the sword of the giant Goliath to kill him and the Philistines. Here we discover an explanation for the stones in his slingshot. They are the souls of his enemies, the spirits themselves who were God's enemies. God sets them against the first mutineer[139] as witnesses of his sin; in this way he turned him into *stone*, like Abigail with her *Nabal*. Her booty is the blessing of those purchased, those redeemed by God.[140] This chapter is the story of human redemption. It includes our sin, God's judgment on us and our tyrant whose temptation we have followed, our repentance, our faith, our riches and reception of it, and the whole of our religion. It keeps on adding new details to present the whole of it in a brighter light. Wisdom, who has made the earth her colony, turns the smallest point of it into a miniature earth which nourishes her inhabitants and citizens.[141] It is just as true that the thoughts of Scripture are as many as the stars of the sky and the sand of the sea. God compares both in human eyes to contrast them with the blessing of the woman's offspring. We can take them both together to contrast them with the fruitfulness of the seed of the divine word.

1 Sam 17:51
1 Sam 17:40, 49
1 Sam 25:27
Gen 15:5; 22:17
Luke 8:11; 1 Pet 1:23

1 SAMUEL 26:3, 4

David sees Saul and also sends spies to discover what he sees. Is not God's Spirit, who tears down the high places of our reason in order to impart a heavenly vision instead, present everywhere? He seems to confuse our reason by letting light shine in it and separating the darkness from it.

2 Cor 10:4–6
Gen 1:4

1 SAMUEL 27:12

Out of ignorance Achish accepts David and declares him to be his best, only servant. Our Savior must have been just as valuable to the seducer who considered him to be his most faithful servant.

---

139. That is, the devil in his rebellion against God.

140. In the Hebrew text of 25:27, the present that Abigail brought to David is called her "blessing."

141. This reflection is based on the description of Abigail as a woman with sound reason (25:3) and good judgment (25:33).

1 SAMUEL 28

The resurrection of our Savior is foretold in the reawakening of
Samuel (28:11–12). We have a man with Saul (28:8) and a god
coming up out of the ground (28:13). We see how humanity speaks
with God, with the King, the Father, the righteous God who turns
1 Sam 28:15–19 sin into a tyrant because it makes his Son a sacrifice for sin. Saul
1 Sam 28:20 was powerless from horror and hunger. People had aroused God's
wrath. They had robbed him of the fruit that he expected from his
creation of them. Here the humanity of Jesus Christ, which was
united and reconciled with his divinity, prepares a fattened calf for
him and his attendants. This is the marriage feast of the Lamb. It
will be a very great feast in heaven in which God, after such a long
fast and such futile longing to find the lost son once again and enjoy
Luke 15:11–32 his new life, will hope to eat the fruit of his creation and new creation that he had hungered for so greatly. Holy, holy, holy is God!
Isa 6:3 All lands are full of his glory. Amen!

1 SAMUEL 29

More and more I see how the covering[142] is lifted that the Philistine
gave to Sara to remove the sight of her beauty from himself and
Gen 20:16 those around her. God and the Spirit do not have to reveal the word.
They lift the veil that shuts our eyes, the veil that with God's per-
2 Cor 4:3–4 mission Satan has spread over the beauty of the sacred Scriptures,
so that our eyes do not see through it and the glances of this Sara
Exod 34:33–35; 2 Cor 5:13 cannot converse with our souls.

1 SAMUEL 29:5

Saul struck down a thousand, David ten thousand. God purchases ten thousand souls by the example of his righteousness that he had to employ against a thousand. By the example of Lot's wife, who became a pillar of salt, he purchased all those who were touched by her example of punished unbelief and disobedience.

---

142. Or "veil." Here Hamann alludes to "the covering of the eyes" in Gen 20:16, which is the idiom for the public proof of Sarah's innocence by the payment of compensation for Abimelech's apparent besmirchment of her honor.

He gave David five stones in his sling, Nabal's five souls[143] which turned into stone at the judgment on their disgraceful behavior, in order to kill giant Goliath with them and to plunder his armor, horrify the Philistines with his head, and give joy to the Israelites. *1 Sam 17:40* *1 Sam 25:37* *1 Sam 17:54*

1 SAMUEL 30:2

In the Scriptures women represent human souls.

1 SAMUEL 30:11

We cannot but be moved by the misfortune of the young Egyptian, the misery that the cruelty of his master had caused, and David's generosity. In this little episode there is, as in a grain of seed, the whole tree of our faith and life.[144] They found an Egyptian—who and where? The ministering spirits, the Lord's young men, the heavenly virgins who draw water.[145] In the field—who would have looked for him there? If he had still been by the road, then he would have been exposed sooner to the compassion of those who passed by. But the Amalekite cared so little for those who fell sick from working for him that none of them would become healthy again. He put them out of the way so that no one would take them up and have mercy on them. They brought him to David. The obedience of these spirits was David's obedience who always took advice from the ephod of the Lord, even though he himself was its creator.[146] They gave him bread—without receiving any services from him like an Amalekite master, without questioning whether it would help him or whether it be worth wasting bread on a man who was about to die under their care. What expression of gratitude does God require from us for his spiritual bread? Take and eat, take and drink. *1 Sam 30:7–8; see 1 Sam 23:6, 9; 1 Sam 30:11; Ps 51:12* *Matt 26:26*

The Egyptian did just that. How revived was he? His spirit returned, he feels new life, new blood, a new heart, yes, a new

143. This may be an allusion to the five proverbial stages of human life.

144. At this point Hamann adds "1.)," but he fails to complete the list.

145. This slightly disjointed passage has been rearranged by the addition of "who and."

146. Since David did not create the ephod, this must refer to the Lord God who instructed Moses to make it (Exod 28:6–14).

spirit that returns to him with greater strength than that which had
1 Sam 30:12 left him. What a cruel Amalekite! He did not leave his servant, his
sick servant, a piece of bread or a drop of water. He left him alive
so that he, with his living body, would feel the death from the lack
of them. For three days he had the feeling of hunger, the feeling of
thirst, as the proof of his existence. Bread and water are best for
quelling hunger and quenching thirst. When the Egyptian felt them
no more, he enjoys a tasty morsel—and all at no cost, even though
he is not David's servant but a servant of his enemy, even though
David does not intend to make him his servant or require his services as payment for his good deeds. All that David demands from
his enemy, the slave of his enemy, is an honest confession from
the heart in answer to these two questions which the whole Bible
intends to make easier and more certain for a person: "To whom
1 Sam 30:13 do you belong, and from where, why, for what purpose are you?"
The whole Bible teaches us nothing more than to answer our God
with the same feeling and to teach us just the same answer that
experience had put in the mouth of the young man. The general
confession of our inherited sins and repentance for our specific
sins, which both join together in the fire that we ourselves light
where the seducer leaves us in the lurch because he himself must
soon thereafter be thrown into it and is about to have the same sen-
Rev 20:10 tence. After this repentance, David encourages trust, faith after his
redemption, after the vengeance that he will exact for this Egyptian
on his tyrant and maniac. Our faith which God foresaw was his signpost. It showed the Egyptian the way to the victory that our Savior
gained for us, and the same faith that we have received with him
as the signpost for victory should also be our signpost; it should
give us the victory and a right to share the plunder. This chapter is
inexhaustible in comfort and spirit, light, and grace.

1 SAMUEL 31

Here we see the death of our Savior, its full sufficiency in the eyes of God's righteousness, and the unity of God the Father and God the Son. Saul goes on his last military campaign. Saul falls into great danger; the archers find him; they find him vulnerable at his heels. Saul says to his armor-bearer, "Draw your sword!" The armor-bearer is shocked at this command; Saul takes a sword and falls on it; his armor-bearer falls with him. I have the power to lay down my life. The death of the armor-bearer of divine wrath could not *John 10:18* rob Saul of his life; he laid it down for his enemies and his sheep. This armor-bearer falls by himself. O death, where is your sting! O hell, where is your victory! Thanks be to God who has given us the victory through our Lord Jesus Christ. *1 Cor 15:55, 57*

Just as every letter in the book of nature proclaims the wise Creator and every line in the history of the nations proclaims the just Ruler, so every sinner in the sacred Scriptures calls for and proclaims the Redeemer of the world for all people.

Here the punishment of Saul's body by the Philistines prefigures the death on the cross. They nail him to the wall of Beth-shan. Saul's bones were buried. But, before that, they had to pass through fire. So our Savior descended through the grave into hell and came back from hell to make his grave the grave for our sins and our punishment.

2 SAMUEL 1

At the end of the last chapter in 1 Samuel we saw how Saul died, and his bones were burnt and buried. Here we see his death from a different point of view. I have already compared the deception of eyes in the case of the Ptolemaic astronomers[147] with the deception of our reason in its observation of the Scriptures. We see them standing still, reversing, and making crooked movements, without our natural eye being able to give a reason for it all. The Spirit himself, who has given the eye, must open it. He lends us the telescope of faith. Then these bright spots that seem to run about all over the place, like sparks from a stoked fire, become clear worlds and suns

147. Claudius Ptolemy (AD 100–160) was an influential astronomer who proposed a geocentric model of the universe in which the sun and the planets moved around the earth as its stationary center.

that run their course set for them according to wise laws and reach
Ps 19:6 their predetermined goal, like a champion runner.

The messenger of death pleads guilty of it. The joy that he hoped to bring to David and the reward that he intended to get from it turned into a confession of a most gruesome murder and sentence to death for it. How could the Jews think of Gilboa without the similarity in sound, which so often results in the conjunction of the remotest ideas and perceptions, reminding them of Golgotha! Saul fell by a sword. Here we see him leaning on a spear. Is this not the spear that the unbelieving Jews and gentiles brought away from the death of our Redeemer? Is not this the spear in the hand of the Roman, the spear which performed a great miracle that was so important that John could not affirm its truth enough to make
John 19:34–37 people pay attention to it?

Let us not lose a single word of Saul as he dies (1:9). He calls his murderer; he asks him, and after he has heard his answer, he speaks to him again: "*Stand* by me, I beg you, and kill me because *my coat*
See 1 Sam 31:9–10; John 19:23 *of mail, my seamless robe* prevents me, so that *all my life is still in me.*"

Who is strong enough to weigh and winnow these heavy words? The innocence of Jesus, by which he provoked death, was his coat of armor that, as it were, made his death impossible, no matter how mighty it was and no matter how great the sin of the world was that provoked it. This coat of mail was the godhead united with innocence. This seamless robe preserved his life completely, even after the wound that Satan, sin, and death had inflicted on him. So God, our blessed Savior, could not receive the wages of sin without transforming righteousness itself into cruelty in God, yes, without pleading for this cruelty as a grace, as the only grace. Stand by me and kill me. What was impossible for God, and what was an atroc-
2 Sam 1:14 ity for David, the Amalekite could do by killing the Lord's anointed. The Amalekite[148] showed it to him as an act of grace. He stood by Saul, he killed him, he stole his crown and bracelet, and brought it to God the Father of the slain Lamb, to the slain Lamb himself.

148. Hamann says "he." In this section Hamann regards the Amalekite as an instrument of God the Father and Saul, who had been anointed king, as a type of Christ.

What a terrible, astonishing judgment! What horror awaits those who will wake up, wake up from death, and see him whom they had pierced, him whom they thought they had pierced to death, with the crown on his head that they had intended to steal from him, and the bracelet on his hand, the flock of his right hand whose redemption had cost him so much!

Rev 5:6, 9, 12

Ps 95:7; Matt 25:33; Rev 1:16; 2:1

2 SAMUEL 1:18

This Amalekite was the arrow. The bow that shot this arrow was the people of Israel, and this truth, this deed, "this bow," was to be taught to them in the lamentation that David composed.[149] Since God's Spirit inspires the Book of the Just, David points to the evangelists and apostles whose writings contain the life and teaching of the righteous. In this Book of the Just we discover the miracle[150] of Joshua in the death of our Savior and the interpretation and fulfillment of this profound lamentation which the Holy Spirit gave by inspiration to David. Every syllable of this divine, heavenly funeral lamentation is explained in the New Testament.

2 SAMUEL 2:19[–28]

Here Asahel pursues Abner, just as the conscience pursues the murderers of our Savior and every sinner who, like Abner, takes part in the insurrection and rebellion against David. The punishment by which Abner takes revenge on Asahel and tries to free himself from persecution by him disconcerts and halts everyone who saw the murder of Asahel. We hear Joab speaking peacefully to Abner and turning away from the pursuit of him as soon as he had explained himself to him.

2 Sam 2:26–28

149. In verse 18 the Hebrew text reads: "and he said that the Bow should be taught to the children of Israel as written in the Book of the Just." The name for the song seems to be "the Bow."

150. Or "wonder." This alludes to the only other mention of the Book of the Just in Josh 10:13. It records Joshua's command for the sun to stand still so that he could defeat his enemies. This miracle stands in contrast with the eclipse of the sun during the passion of Jesus (Matt 27:45). In Hebrew the name for Jesus is Joshua.

2 Sam 3:31–34 It seems that in David's lament over the death of Abner we may see the tears of our Redeemer over the destruction of Jerusalem *Luke 19:41–44* and the downfall of the Jewish nation. We may see that Asahel was *2 Sam 3:8–11* God's Spirit who had to pursue Abner, Ish-bosheth's commander. We may see that, like this nation, Abner suppressed the witness of the Spirit and murdered his witnesses, the apostles, and that God also used this Abner as an instrument to draw all of Israel to himself and make the whole earth his possession. David did not accept *2 Sam 3:6–21* Abner apart from Michal. So the Jews would be received into grace through their acceptance of the Redeemer. The jealousy of Joab at the acceptance of Abner, who had killed his brother, shows the *2 Sam 3:22–27; Rom 11:28* enmity of the Jews at the status of the gentiles. We see how their vengeance against the teaching of the gospel in seeking to persecute Christians fell on their own heads. It was punished by God and was *1 Thess 2:15–16* set as a new sign of the Last Judgment.

So, like the murder of Asahel, the assassination of Abner was the rejection of the Holy Spirit, which David pronounced as a curse *2 Sam 2:23; 3:27–29, 38–39* on Joab for the sin of hardheartedness and its terrible penalty. Here in the case of Joab we see the enemy of humanity and especially redeemed humanity who made use of everything to extirpate and eradicate the new church of Jesus Christ. To this end he used Jews and gentiles. But God used all his hostile, murderous thoughts as a means for carrying out his work. He let Asahel die in order to use Abner for David; for he was held in high regard by the people and *2 Sam 3:6–19* had now publicly begun to announce his support for David. Since God wanted to show that Abner's help was not needed for him to establish David's kingdom, he let Abner be killed by Joab and Joab's house bear the curse for everything, so that the king's will would be shown to be right and he would be praised by all the people, by friends and by foes.

2 Cor 6:15 In this way the children of Belial, the Philistines, would be laid low by their own weapons. As God's enemies they would contend for his glory, experience their downfall in their strength, and become *Rom 1:22* fools in their wisdom.

In the description of Asahel and Abner, we see a depiction of the Holy Spirit. The former pursues a person in every step that he takes; he does not turn aside to the right or the left. He does not pay attention to any human threats and does not leave him until that person does away with him with his own hand, with the butt of the spear, through contempt for him and slander against him. Abner *Matt 12:31–32* had the testimony of the Spirit, but Joab slanders him. Joab regards his warnings and his zeal as the tricks of a traitor who observes the ways by which we go out and come in, in order to betray us. He misrepresents our only human Friend as our enemy and murders him as such. *2 Sam 3:17–30*

David's lamentation is therefore the dirge for the rejection of the Jewish nation after they slandered and rejected, yes, even stoned the Holy Spirit, just as they would have Jesus crucified. The curse *2 Sam 3:33–34; 2 Sam 3:29, 36–37* of Joab and his house confirms this even more, because all sicknesses are spiritual deficiencies and maladies that God's Spirit remedies, so that we come back to God—impurity, leprosy, trust in vain help, the aroma of death in what has been given for our life, *2 Cor 2:16* and a famine for souls, a complete drought of the land, without *Amos 8:11* sowing or dew. *2 Sam 1:21; 1 Kgs 17:1*

Abner's sin was the sin of those who murdered Jesus; Joab's sin was the obstinacy of those who did not just reject Jesus but also the messengers and witnesses of Jesus. That is why God forgave Abner's sin but laid such a heavy curse on Joab. Abner's sin was condoned by God for the confirmation and fulfillment of Scripture. That is why we find Ish-bosheth's head in the tomb of Abner as evidence of his innocence in contrast with the cut off hands and feet of those who executed him as a martyr. *2 Sam 4:5–12*

It seems that Satan received power to execute so many judgments on earth because he pretended that as its prince he would *John 12:31; 14:30; 16:11* avenge the death of devout Jesus and would sift his disciples. All *Luke 22:31* the blood that he shed in these judgments of God fell on his head, while all the good reports that he brought to God of his obedience and allegiance to the Redeemer of men were judgments against him. For he is not yet in the place for the Last Judgment. The

Rev 20:1–15; 1 Cor 6:3; see Rev 20:7–10

Book of Revelation tells us that his judgment will occur at the same time as ours; yes, it tells us that the believers will judge this proud Philistine.

2 SAMUEL 5:6

Matt 8:17; 2 Pet 1:4; Col 3:10; Gen 20:16; Matt 22:29

The more I read, the greater my wonder, the greater my devotion, the greater my thanksgiving for my Creator, my Savior, my dear Companion and Comforter! What a hard condition was set for the conquest of Jerusalem! Unless you are able to make all the blind see and all the lame walk, that is, unless you are a god, you will never enter our city. How otherwise did our Savior prove this sign literally than through the fulfillment of this miracle that he performed by travelling through the whole land of the Jews? The blessing of our salvation depends on the healing of our blindness, the removal of all our diseases, our participation in his divine nature that he wants to create in us, the renewal of the divine image and the complete radiance that he wants to put by it into us. Here we openly see how Abimelech paid for a covering over Sarah. We see that the Jews were handed over by God to a spirit of hardheartedness, so that they did not understand the power of God or the Scriptures.

2 Sam 4:5–12; 1 Sam 5:4–5

We see how Satan derives the strength of his power from our blindness and infirmity. He knew that he would always remain the master of mankind as long as they did not see God, as long as they saw God as their enemy and him as their god, and as long as they had no ability to approach him. Hence thumbs of the hands and the feet as the punishment of Dagon and of Rimmon's sons are all previews of the judgment that Satan will experience and of the sins that he has committed against us.

2 SAMUEL 5:8

Luke 23:9; Matt 27:14

To attract attention, this verse has one of the lovely things that are found in silence, in verbal reticence. How amazed Herod and Pilate were that Jesus did not deign to give them an answer! So our dear God is also at times silent with those whom he favors and befriends.

This silence is at times a herald of an unexpected, unusually gracious revelation and disclosure of his blessing. When did he give greater proof of his love for men than when he kept silent?[151] On that day David said: "Whoever climbs up the water gutter[152] and strikes down the Jebusites as well as the lame and blind that are hated by David's soul," because they had said, yes these blind and lame people had said: "He shall not come into the house."[153] *Isa 53:7*

David himself does not know what he should give to the person who would share in this victory. Because he promises him nothing,[154] and his grace will also surpass even the hope of greatest faith, he lets him hope for everything.

These were not the blind and the lame that our Savior came to heal but those blind and lame people who, like the Pharisees, thought that they could see and had no need of any physician. *John 9:39–41; Matt 9:12*

What was the reason for this blindness and lameness and the extraordinary delusion by which they saw nothing but the sickness that itself was in them? It was the water gutter of Satan. They had forsaken God, the living fountain, and dug wells for themselves that Satan filled with his gutters. Satan boasted about this wretched artifice and held that it was indestructible. In its construction he spent all the tricks and deceptive arts of his architecture. Nothing except a god was strong enough to destroy it and annul the inferences of this magician by which he deluded the senses and harassed the necessities of men.

151. The text is silent about the reward that David offers and the actual conquest of the city.

152. While Hamann follows Luther in his interpretation of this obscure term as roof gutter from its only other occurrence in Ps 18:42, most modern translators regard it as a water-shaft under the city.

153. In what follows Hamann gives his own translation of the rather difficult Hebrew text which sounds as if David is about to announce a reward but instead only gives the condition for it. He seems to say, "Anyone who strikes the Jebusites and lame and blind that are hated by David's soul by climbing up the water shaft." In keeping with verse 6, Hamann regards 8b as a statement by the blind and lame that prohibits the entry of David into the city of Jerusalem.

154. The KJV rectifies the omission of a reward by adding: "he shall be chief and captain" from 1 Chr 11:6.

2 SAMUEL 5:23

Here we see that a rustling sound in the tops of the certain trees is a sign of the hour when God would go on ahead to strike down his enemies and the enemies of Israel. I do not know whether the name in the Hebrew text and the Septuagint refers to the same
Luke 19:4 tree that Zacchaeus climbed to see our Savior. Zacchaeus, without doubt, gave himself away by the noise which drew the eyes of Jesus up on high. The visit in his house was a solemn occasion, and the beginning of his passion was connected with his departure from the
Luke 19:11–48 house of Zacchaeus. The assurance that Jesus gave to the house of Zacchaeus was a word of promise about which his enemies grumbled and from which this rich tax collector enjoyed comfort. By it Jesus declared that he sided personally with sinners and classed the grumblers with the crowd of his enemies that he now traveled to Jerusalem to defeat. The subsequent events in the story of David makes me even more sure that this noise in the top of the trees relates in both cases because the defeat of the Philistines was followed by the
2 Sam 6:1–4 return of the ark, the outburst against Uzzah, God's frightful threat
2 Sam 6:6–10 against David himself, and the blessing of Obed Edom from which
2 Sam 6:11–12 David withdrew himself, just as Zacchaeus received the grace that the Pharisees refused and grumbled about as an offensive visit and an ignorant action of our Savior. Michal's judgment about David's joy at bringing the ark into his house corresponds with the grum-
2 Sam 6:20 bling of the Pharisees.

2 SAMUEL 9:6

Do we not hear the king addressing Mephibosheth, the same King that addressed Mary when she mistook the risen Jesus for the
John 20:15–16 gardener?

2 SAMUEL 9:8

This is an emphatic picture of the grace that God shows to the sinner by serving a cripple, a dead dog, an unclean animal that is therefore dead.

2 SAMUEL 9:10

Why had God given Ziba fifteen sons and twenty servants? To cultivate the land and soil much better, so that the one who was lame in both his feet could enjoy its fruit. Thus the riches of the children of this world are meant to provide for the poverty of the children of the light. *Luke 16:8*

1 KINGS 3:16

Let us not admire the wisdom of Solomon but the wise mercy of God who has rescued us from the peril of eternal death. This story is one of those with infallible eyes. We will note what they see in a few places. There are two women who belong to the same equally sinful class and live in the same house. One of them becomes a mother before the other. The first one kills her child, gets up in the middle of the night to steal the living child of her neighbor, and put her dead child in its place. She breastfeeds the stolen child, as if it were her own.

This is the story of the serpent and our childhood, better, the childhood of the human race. God made us the visible lords of the earth, which, however, also had its invisible princes. All the visible works of God are signs and expressions of his attributes. So, *Gen 1:28; Ps 8* it seems, the whole bodily nature is an expression, a parable, of the spirit world. All finite creatures are only able to see the truth and essence of things in parables. Thus, just as the sickness of our body expresses the corruption of our soul, so the fallen person is a symbol of the fallen angel, and his fall is the natural consequence *Isa 14:12–20* of that angel's fall.

Here we see two unclean spirits, two unchaste spirits that have grieved God's holiness, desecrated his honor, and tempted his righteousness. We have the mother and the child who was smothered by the mother. This angel, the spirit of this earth, pretends to be the nursemaid, the foster mother of mankind, a mother who tells God about the care that she would provide for mankind. The star

of dawn was meant to be the father and lord of human beings,[155] just as Adam[156] was the father and master of the visible earth. But both were to remain God's creatures whose success, of necessity, depended as much on God as their existence. Just as Adam considered it a yoke that a single tree was the obstacle for him to be the universal master of the whole earth and held false ideas about
Gen 2:17; 3:6 the use and beauty of the tree, so too, it seems, it went with the seducer. He was offended that he had to be the father and master of the earth and that he had to take care of this man on it. Yet this man was supposed to be obedient to God in only one respect, but not at all to Satan. We see the purpose of Satan in the counsel that Ahithophel gave to Absalom. To bring the subjects of your father
2 Sam 16:21 completely over to your side, says the serpent, commit a crime that will make all your supporters so detestable in God's eyes that they may never again dare to forsake you and hope for grace from him, but cling to you, because they will openly see that their preservation depends of yours and that, without you, they would be too weak to protect themselves.

He, therefore, tried to make people rebels against God, so that they would repudiate God and surrender to him. So, because human beings had forsaken God as their Overlord and had thrown themselves into the arms of a king who was a serpent, so God, as it were, renounced his right over them. To protect them from his own righteousness, he accepted them as subjects, slaves of a higher spirit. He wanted to allow and oversee that spirit's engagement with human beings and direction of them but reserved the right to overthrow and judge him through his own subjects. We poor slaves were too weak to set ourselves free from the yoke of the seducer whom we ourselves had chosen as our master because he had ingratiated himself with us in the guise of a family member, a beast of the field, to get us to renounce obedience to God and listen to his voice. God's judg-
Gen 2:17 ment was pronounced on us: "You shall surely die." He, therefore,

---

155. This is an allusion to Lucifer in Isa 14:12–20 and Rev 9:1–2. Before his fall he was an archangel, if not the archangel.

156. Or "the man."

could not undertake to do anything else than fulfill this judgment. As aliens we were deceived, but God had mercy on us and directed his righteous judgment on the deceiver, the seducer, who rejoiced in his robbery and anticipated the enjoyment of his hellish plan in the kingdom that he intended to found with us.[157]

We discover so many alliances of God with people in the sacred Scriptures that we can likewise presuppose the same with higher spirits. So we discover that Satan appeared in the time of Job and received permission from God to rob him of everything. God only reserved for himself the power over his life. All the alliances that Abraham made with the surrounding princes and his own descendants that resulted in battles and victories and established their righteousness are symbols of the alliances and the limits that God set for Satan on this fallen earth. God made him its prince and kept back nothing more for himself than one man and his descendant as his possession, whom he therefore announced as the Conqueror of the serpent's offspring. Just as Satan began to gain complete dominion over mankind by helping them to discard obedience to God's only commandment from their eyes, so he, to assert his dominion, deliberately and specifically, had to make that unique Man, whom God had selected for himself to redeem mankind, the target of his tyranny against them. Thus he used every possible means to get rid of all suspected people. He, as it seems, always used good intentions to cloak his cruelty and seduces people so that he can accuse them. He accused them before a righteous God so that he could condemn them. How faithfully his image has been set up in the schools for politics. No title is needed where the similarity is so true to life. Meanwhile, God allowed him to establish kingdoms and devise sciences. Yes, God relinquished to him all the benefits and gifts of nature to distribute them to people, as if they came from his hand and the whole earth bowed its knee before him, because he had bribed them with God's gifts and stolen their hearts through his rebellious, dissembling behavior. So in all the glory that he claimed

Gen 3:15; John 12:31; 14:30; 16:11

157. Literally, "with our seed."

for himself he was also not secure against the unique Man, against the unique race that God seemed to have reserved for himself. He did not want to cede to the Lord the fountain of the whole earth, for which God would pay so much that he nourished it and its land for the sake of all his children. So just as we hear Abimelech telling lies, speaking deceptively, and talking ambiguously, so Satan was against
Gen 20:1–18 God. He was a traitor of his King and a traitor of his own race.

Satan smothered his own offspring and oppressed them with the sentence of death that he brought on them because his mind was always fixed on him whom he had to regard as an enemy of his race. So he also tried to steal this unique race of God. To that end he used midnight to nourish God's inheritance with his adder's milk as
See Ps 140:3 if it were his own and wanted to substitute his own dead race for it.[158]

This, therefore, was the purpose of the many temptations that the Jewish people underwent with the result that it was hard for God himself to rule and God became fed up with them. Satan had drawn good hope from the wrath that he heard from God's prophets. He intended to nourish the Jewish faith and quench the law of Moses with ordinances, with the blindness and wickedness of the princes and teachers of the people, so that through the nourishment that he gave to the offspring that did not belong to him, it would become so much easier for him to alienate them from God. But among his offspring he sought to lavish knowledge, sciences, great sham virtues, power, might, and pomp, so that this offspring would be regarded as God's offspring and his favorites.

Satan made the corruption of the Jewish nation so deep-rooted, with such rank growth, that their sins gave him an excuse to hasten the judgment on this nation and require it as a matter of necessity, an inescapable sacrifice of divine righteousness. He employed midnight and sleep to carry out his purposes. The time of ignorance
Acts 17:30 that God allowed for a while on earth was a bad time for him. He believed that God no longer remembered his promises and was

158. After the preceding disgression, Hamann returns to the parable of the two prostitutes in 1 Kgs 3:16–27.

fast asleep for his people, because he saw that he had more subjects among them than God.

When the second woman got up in the morning to feed her child, she saw that it was dead. But when she looked at it that morning, she saw that it was not her son that had been born to her. Thus Adam also saw that all his children were smothered until the new Adam appeared and came into the world wonderfully as a living man, a new man, an innocent man. Satan wanted to claim him likewise for himself as his descendant. He tried to steal him and is pleased with the happy charade of a contest between the Snake-treader and himself when they both appeared before God. We see God's sword drawn over the living son who seems to face a much more terrible end than the squashed, smothered son. Satan divulges that he could steal the fruit but not the heart of a mother and that he falsely claims the privileges and rights of a mother in order to act as the murderer of his own children and the executioner of his neighbor. "Give her the living child, and do not put him to death." *1 Kgs 3:27*

We have a wretched mother who sees the sword of righteousness stretched out over her own child and another death of it in the surrender of her offspring, which was the only way that it could be preserved.

It does not belong to me, nor my neighbor; it belongs to your sword—divide the child with it.

Here we see that our preservation from the sentence of death that God threatened depended on the generosity of the tender mother who deferred to the false mother, so that, in the moment of divine wrath, her own child would instead escape. We see that this surrender lasted for just a moment, only long enough for our enemy to clearly admit that he had neither the right nor the love of a mother but confessed that he was a prostitute, a false witness, a murderer. This means that he as good as draws the sword away from the child on to himself. Solomon is satisfied that he has discovered this cruel mother and exposed her to public disgrace. The mere preservation of the child—his restoration to his proper mother whose heart burnt for her son when she heard Solomon's first judgment; the assurance of his life and the King's public recognition of her as his mother—this was all that Solomon had to do. He does not consider that he needs to judge the other party because she had already passed judgment on herself.

1 KINGS 5:5

And behold I say that I will build.[159] In our speech we express ourselves by saying, "I think! I propose!" Let all earthly history be as mere dreams, thoughts, and fancies for us. Instead let all thoughts be *words* to God's glory, and all good *words* still better works. Let us also imitate our Father in heaven; every good thing that occurs to us happens according to our word, our approval, our will. For it is his word, his approval, his will that gives us the thought and power to do what is good. If we do not let this good will, which he speaks to us as his word in our ears, be all-powerful and strong in us, our power over it also ceases. Because the bow is slack and the hand that shoots it is weak, our prayer comes back dead to us. So every Christian must have Solomon's mentality: "Behold, I think; I say; I do—this or that duty, this or that vow"; then everything becomes possible for him, because only faith can produce this peace, this unity in our thoughts, words, and deeds.

1 KINGS 5:6

It is wonderful how often the Holy Spirit hints that God seems to give up his right to own the serpent's offspring. He lends them out to their masters and pays them with earthly and temporal blessings. He pays them well for the services that they provide for his race. All his laws that he gives to foreigners rest on this notion, because he insists that the earth should be nothing but a wilderness for us by which we enter into the promised land on the King's way, the way that he himself had purchased and established at such great cost. He insists that the inhabitants of the land are children of Belial

Num 20:17; 21:22

159. Literally, "I am saying to build." Here Hamann reflects on the rather odd Hebrew idiom which conflates thinking with speaking, speaking with planning, and planning with doing.

and their king is the prince of the air. So, in the sight of the world's children, he has made his band as naked and bare as possible, like human beings in creation, without earthly wisdom, earthly goods, and earthly honors, very bereft of these things in contrast with the others. He has allowed his own enemy to sift and separate his band and has defeated the mightiest giant through a little troop, by means that seemed to wage war contrary to all reason, yes, by what seemed to be a mere shadow in the far distance.

Deut 13:13; 2 Sam 23:6; 2 Cor 6:15 Eph 2:2

Col 2:17; Heb 10:1

1 KINGS 5:7

Satan seems to be so pleased, so satisfied, so devoted to everything that he could employ for his own use and his own purposes. From the example of Hiram we may see how dissatisfied he is with the outcome, how ungrateful he was for the fulfillment of the conditions that he had previously accepted with such great pleasure.

1 Kgs 9:12–14

1 KINGS 5:18

Both Solomon's carpenters and Hiram took part in building the temple and the citadel of Zion. Light and darkness, earth and water were equally necessary for God's creation of the earth. It did not receive its threefold life[160] and the fruitfulness to maintain it any earlier before the separation and division of these opposite, original elements. For this purpose, both must be necessary, just as God was pleased to use his own and foreign artisans for Solomon's building.

Gen 1:4–10

1 KINGS 6:7

This was God's order for construction: all the stone was prefabricated and ready before it was brought into its place. No one did anything else than wait for the moment that it appeared in the world. God did not want a hammer or an axe or iron to be heard in his house. These tools belonged to the structural engineering of the tyrant who crippled, blinded, and frightened us even more with the din of his power and tried to drive us into a state of horror and

160. That is, vegetable life, animal life, and human life.

fear with clattering of his workmen. Thus this great temple came to be, even though no one saw or heard it being built. In the same *Matt 12:6* way, its Lord came into the world. Silently and without the least din from his tools, he built a dwelling place for himself on this earth that would cast Babel down to the ground and would thereafter be *Matt 16:18; John 1:14; Rev 21:3* planted on the rock on which the fortress of heaven is founded.

1 KINGS 7

These two chapters are full of speaking and living images which, in part, appeal to the senses, the senses of a Christian. Others, however, are additional decorations of God's work, like those that were between the lion and the ox of the stands for the basins (7:29), or like pictures that were put on a blank surface of their panels to fill it up in a pleasing way so that the eye would not find any empty space (7:36).

Hiram, the artist, was the son of a Jewish widow, and his father was a man of Tyre, a worker in bronze (7:14). All people had forfeited their inheritance as children of God. Thus the human race had become an orphan through its fall into sin, and God complains about it like a formerly married man[161] who had divorced his wife. Despite his love for this divorcée, he was not able to disarm his own arm of righteousness. So, even though he once again accepted *Gal 4:4* the human family in the blessed offspring of the woman, all other human families were slaves of his enemy, as stepbrothers of his Isaac before his birth. He had to banish them because they offended him in his legitimate Son, because they were sons of the condemned *Gen 21:1–20* woman, the prostitute, the divorcée, the servant girl. Esau was also *Gen 27:34–40* blessed on account of Isaac and Abraham. So we see that the heathen received every good thing—their existence, their wealth, their virtues, their insights into nature—from the Giver of every good *Josh 1:17* gift. They were all gifts of the Spirit that the serpent's offspring enjoyed on account of the previous friendship with God that had been disrupted by the fall. He, therefore, was the Spirit of wisdom

161. German, "widower."

in Israel and in Tyre. He taught Moses the secret story of creation *1 Kgs 7:14* and redemption and the tablets of the law, God's commandments. He sang in Moses and narrated in him. He blessed and cursed by him according to the word of the Father and goodwill of his Son from whom he proceeded. He assisted the artisans of Tyre in their *John 14:16–17, 26; 15:26* work with bronze and filled them with wisdom, understanding, and inventiveness. They acquired them only as gifts from him in order to impart their work in bronze.

Hiram's inheritance from his mother's side was divine, the same that the Israelites received. Their father according to the flesh gave them the produce and treasure of his land. Their maternal inheritance they then squandered except when the Spirit of widows and orphans deemed them worthy of special enlightenment and extraordinary grace, just as Hiram here came to King Solomon and completed all his work. *1 Kgs 7:40*

In 7:45 we, however, see that Hiram is an image of the Holy Spirit himself, just as Solomon is an image of our Savior. If we *Matt 12:42* believe that we see the precious works of Hiram complete and reckon that we look at the vessels for the Lord's house that Hiram made for King Solomon gleaming and polished in their hands, we will be brought back unwittingly in time by God's Spirit. In the plain of the Jordan the king cast all these precious vessels in the thick clay of the ground. Do we not here see God breathing the breath *1 Kgs 7:46* of life again into the nostrils of a clod of clay, a better, polished, and renewed life? "Is there any God like our God?" says Moses repeatedly. "Is there any people like Israel?" he also says. Is there *Exod 15:11; Exod 33:16; Deut 4:7–8, 33–35* is any book, yes, even the book of nature, like the one that alone can unveil for us the veil of nature and its heart, yes, the heart of its Creator? How is it possible for any Christian to put this book, *Isa 25:7; 2 Cor 3:12–18* carelessly and irreverently, below other books without committing the sin of idolatry?

1 KINGS 8:1

Solomon assembled! Before King Solomon in Jerusalem. Here Solomon is contrasted with King Solomon. God's Spirit has done everything to make us attentive to his speech, to take our reason *2 Cor 10:5; 1 Cor 1:18–2:15* captive, to win it or confound it. We are too dull to understand all these reminders, or else we despise God's kindness, so that his condescension is completely misunderstood by everybody. We do not *Col 2:3* take pains to examine what kinds of treasures lie hidden under their *2 Cor 4:7* manifold coverings and in the earthen jar.[162] Moreover, he wants to let us realize that he has more to show us than the dress that people see him in, and that he has made himself unrecognizable in order to ambush their enemies.

1 KINGS 8:9

Nothing in the ark except the Ten Commandments! All the imagery of the old covenant and pictures that foretold redemption had disappeared because King Solomon himself was present.[163]

All the splendor, all attention to God's architecture and the wealth of the king, disappears when we see Solomon standing *1 Kgs 8:22* before the altar and spreading out his hands toward heaven. The *Zech 12:10; 1 Kgs 8:23–53; Rev 15:8; compare 1 Kgs 8:10–11* Spirit of prayer flows from his heart and fills his mouth as the smoke filled the temple. We do not need to build, nor are we able to build a temple like Solomon. Our temple, of which this one was but a shadow, has already been made. Yes, our heart is more pleasing to *Heb 10:10; Isa 57:15; Eph 3:17* God than this temple. He fills it just as visibly with his presence; and its darkness is not so thick for us Christians as it was for the *Exod 20:21; 1 Kgs 8:12* Jews. We, however, can all pray, and must all pray, like Solomon, because this Spirit of prayer is the indispensable blessing and fruit of the faith that the Holy Spirit works in us. The prayer of our King and great High Priest makes all our sighs, no matter how broken,

---

162. The mention of a jar may allude to the jar for the manna that was hidden with the ark in the Holy of Holies (Exod 16:33–34).

163. This seems to refer to Aaron's staff and the jar of manna that Moses was told to put in the ark (Num 17:10; Exod 16:33–34).

how truncated, how short they may be, just as full, as rich, as powerful as Solomon's rich, royal offering that God accepted. At times God gives us the grace that we can occasionally pray with the same span of breath and the same fullness and warmth of the heart that we hear Solomon pray.

Rom 8:26–27; 9:24; Heb 7:25

This prayer shows us one of the scrubbed and polished vessels that Hiram made and the king cast in the thick clay of the ground. This prayer, the reading of it and meditation on it, must be more precious to us and give us more delight than looking with our own eyes at the whole temple, the House of the Forest of Lebanon, and all the glory of Solomon in a vision and enjoying the freedom to walk around in them.

1 Kgs 7:1–7

1 KINGS 10

I believe that we can read a description of our times in the conclusion of this chapter. A general knowledge of God, which is not, like the early church, made of gold but of baser goods that are detrimental to the glory of the gospel. The king's merchants may be the commerce that has been made of pastoral ministry. The distribution of horses and chariots is the attempt to spread religion through conquests, through wars and trade. Solomon's polygamy in his later years is the division of Christian sects.

See 1 Kgs 10:14–11:18

1 Kgs 10:15

1 Kgs 10:26–29

1 Kgs 11:1–8

1 KINGS 11

The whole of sacred Scripture is the Book of the Acts of Solomon and the Book of the Upright. Everything was made through him and for him. The deeds of his reign and redemption, written in this book, are the acts of our Solomon.[164] The whole of Scripture is the biography of this unique, upright Man who came into the world to mend the crooked ways of men and restore the royal way through his suffering and life.

1 Kgs 11:41

Josh 10:13; 2 Sam 1:18; John 1:3; Col 1:16

Isa 40:3–5; 62:10–12

164. Our Solomon is Jesus (Matt 12:42), the teacher and embodiment of divine wisdom.

1 KINGS 15:23[165]

He had diseased feet. This remark is meant to surprise us by its oddity. It, however, affirms that just as God can speak to us only through bodily, sensible signs, so he has expressed the corruption of our souls through the corruption of the body. Yes, I have already said that Satan has projected many perceptions of the soul onto the body and has tried to suppress both conjointly through his craftiness. Our need to cleanse our bodies points us to the stains that our spirit suffers from thoughts, impressions, and so on. Idle people eat and drink more than others. Sick people are more impatient and allow themselves greater license to sin with resentment, dissatisfaction, distractions. Yes, even more than that, why has God connected kinds of sin with certain kinds of sickness, as if these bodily ailments would be necessary for us to restrain the passions that were the reason for them? The bad-tempered person, the drunkard, the whoremonger, the rich person, the poor person, each has the diseases that correspond with and resemble the sins of their class, age, the use of their possessions, the use of their reason, and so on. Asa, who had diseased feet, sought help from physicians (2 Chr 16:12). We may remember that this
1 Kgs 15:18–19; 2 Chr 16:2–3 same Asa sought help from his covenant with the king of Syria. Thus, like Pharaoh who did not have himself punished enough by the staff of Moses but employed the assistance of his magicians to
Exod 7:8–8:19 reproduce his plagues, Satan knows how to deceive us.

1 KINGS 17

Who can read the list of kings in Israel and review it without dismay and shock that God's Spirit was its historian? He included their names and incorporated their deeds in his word to provide evidence of sin's atrocity and the book of judgment in which all our deeds are written. How solemnly the prophet Elijah appears in the midst of ungodly people with his display of greater authority and greater power with his word than all their idols and idolaters can boast of!

165. Hamann wrongly cites 15:24.

1 KINGS 19

The God who had storm, earthquake, and fire as his messengers chooses a still soft voice as a sign of his presence. Elijah—who had heard and felt the storm, the earthquake, and the fire, unmoved—hears this voice and hides his face in his cloak. This is the still soft voice that we hear with trembling in God's word and in our (trembling) hearts.

2 KINGS 10:32

How much patience had God had with Israel; only now does he *begin* to exterminate them—no, to cut off its extremities, its outcrops and its border. So God begins with his fire on the borders of the camp, its outskirts (Num 11:1).

2 KINGS 12:3

Here we come upon the high places on which the people continued to sin ... These are the high places that John had previously
left in place, to level them through the preaching of repentance
and prepare the way of the Lord. Only faith and the preaching of *Luke 3:3–6*
the gospel can tear down the high places that the apostle speaks
about. This kind of idolatry therefore had to do with the corrup- *2 Cor 10:4–6*
tion of the human nature under the influence of Satan. It could not
be removed through the law but only through the revelation of our
Savior in the flesh. *1 Tim 3:16*

2 KINGS 17:9

Which historian has such an extensive knowledge? These secret sins against the Lord are as countless as the public sins. Rather, the public sins are often most secret. Satan transforms things that are not right before God into fashionable, beneficial behavior, indifferent, equivocal matters. These high places were secret sins. In all their towns ... in all the powers of our soul, from the tower of the night watchman—from the abilities of our senses that we have in common with the animals, to the fortress of a fortified, walled town—to the knowledge by which we not only differ, and God wants to distinguish us, from the animals, but also from godless people and the demons themselves.

2 KINGS 17:35

The fear of other gods, their outward paraphernalia, is already idolatry, let alone the service, the alliance that we make with them through sacrifice.

2 KINGS 19:3

Hezekiah could not have chosen a stronger picture to portray his anguish and the anguish of the people than the pangs of a woman giving birth to a child. She does not have enough strength to deliver her unborn baby, she feels her own powerlessness, she feels more powerless than the children themselves that merely struggle in vain to break out by themselves.

2 KINGS 22:7

I am not able to read this report of the ongoing payment of all those who work in the house of the Lord and the honesty of their paymasters who were not required to account for their expenditure without supposing that here is a parable of God's grace to the Jews and all the rest of the people who then lacked the knowledge of God and are still excluded from it. God will not hold them accountable for that. He will accept their faithfulness in fulfilling their civic responsibilities and the precepts of natural conscience as a valid effort. Since he has not granted them a special revelation of his will and his attributes, he will not use the same plumb line for them that he uses to
Amos 7:7–8 judge his people. Not only human beings but also their seducer can expect a varied sentence and judgment. The person who is in the town and the person in the field receive the same punishment but
Matt 24:17–18 in a different way. I believe that there is a great difference between them, threatened as they both are with punishment. I assume that the difference between the one who urinates against the wall and the
1 Kgs 14:10; 21:21; 2 Kgs 9:8 one who is imprisoned indicates a difference of persons. The first one is free; he is able to pour out his impurity where he wishes. He

only needs to choose the right wall, which a sick person—a praying Christian, and Hezekiah—turns to face, a wall which is not available for the others (2 Kgs 20:2). The person who is locked up in a narrow prison has nothing but four walls around him. He probably does not know or see the wall that he pollutes.

2 KINGS 22:14

We see how the Holy Spirit veils himself and his works in human hearts. We see how he has never become tired of producing good emotions in us. We see how he, at times, creates good opportunities for this and offers himself with the means to sustain them. Here we come upon him as a prophetess whose grandfather on her husband's side was a *keeper of clothes*.

2 KINGS 23:34; 24:17

Here the enemies of Israel give its last and second to last kings other names, even though God gave the first and third ancestor new names. A king of *Egypt* was the first tyrant of Israel; a king of *Babylon* was its last tyrant.

2 KINGS 24:4

The innocent blood that was shed destroyed Jerusalem here for a while and the second time for ever. Thus the first destruction was nothing else than a prophecy of the second destruction. And the sin that caused it was the same.

Matt 27:24–25; Luke 11:47–51;

2 KINGS 24:14

Only the poorest people were preserved. Do we not see a pointer to Christ and his gospel everywhere? We see how God has given people a certain kind of omniscience because he lets the past happen again and because what happens is nothing but a sketch for the future. More correctly, the plan for the whole of time has a central point where all lines, all figures, correlate and converge. The building consists of one story; the laws for its arrangement are simple. The present is its front. Its front surface area is open to us, but the main body, including the sight of its back part, is concealed. The past and the future are just this side that we see in profile, foreshortened. Every movement of the eye gives us another dimension or a picture of it in another dimension. All of them are shortened forms of the whole; they all give us some idea of its perfection and beauty.

2 KINGS 25:[4–]5

All the soldiers fled—at night, by way of the gate, between two walls, which is near the king's garden. They escape. Every detail shows us
Matt 7:13–14 the narrow gate that our Savior speaks about.

The king goes the way to the plain, the broad way, the wide gate, and he becomes a captive of his enemies.

2 KINGS 25:15

In Hebrew the repetition of the same word is very significant. It indicates that something is certain, great, good.[166] We should assess the repetition of the same events exactly like the repetition of the same words as an indication of their certainty, greatness, excellence, and perfection. The idioms of ancient languages are closest to how we actually think and feel. We should therefore remain as close as possible to them in our translations of the sacred Scripture. Since *strong* speech is better than correct speech, we should make more room for the language in which Scripture is written and translate its words more faithfully. Contrary to all rules and, in this case, unnecessarily, we Lutherans have adopted the translation "*Vater unser*."[167] In the Psalms there were some beautiful anomalies that contradicted the rules of syntax. So too in Job and the Prophets! A sweet fragrance, a restful fragrance, mutilates and suppresses Scripture. If the language is appropriate, there is a lively sense that is explained by God's Spirit in so many other places.

---

166. Here Hamann refers to the use of the Hebrew expressions "gold gold" and "silver silver."

167. In English "Father our." Luther's translation of the Lord's Prayer echoes the Latin text which reverses the normal German grammatical order.

2 KINGS 25:27[–30]

God performed a miracle personally with Jehoiachin himself so as to confirm and prefigure the certainty of redemption. He lifted up his head out of prison, he spoke kindly to him, he set him on a throne above the thrones of his neighbors, he changed his prison clothes, he gave him bread—continually, in his presence—all the days of his life. For greater certainty and an abundant supply, a set allowance was provided for him; a continual allowance was arranged and regularly presented day by day, all the days of his life. Was the king of Babylon able to do this and did he have to do this at God's will? Are the ravens, at God's will, so compassionate and full in the worst drought that they can feed a prophet? What would God himself do? *1 Kgs 17:4–7* What would our Savior do? What is Babylon's monarch compared to him? What is Jehoiachin compared to the least Christian who trusts in his Redeemer?

1 CHRONICLES 4:9–10

Here Jabez appears, like Melchizedek, without father, without mother, without a genealogy.[168] Enoch and Elijah were lifted up *Heb 7:3* beyond death and taken alive into heaven. Was it not possible for *Gen 5:24; 2 Kgs 2:11* God to perform a similar miracle with regard to his birth? Did not Melchizedek and Jabez prefigure the birth of our Savior and his coming into the world, just as they both prefigured his departure?

1 CHRONICLES 5:1–2

Here we see how Reuben is a parable of the darkened morning star whose throne became empty in heaven.[169] We see that Judah, *Isa 14:12–20; Gen 49:9* the lion,[170] merely exercised his power to grant the right of the first born to Joseph, the youngest son, and that Judah became the head *Gen 48:8–20*

168. These remarks rightly note that the story of Jabez is an anomaly in its context, a short aetiology inserted in a chain of genealogies. It explains the meaning of his name from its supposed derivation from the Hebrew term for pain. This story seems to have been inserted here to show how prayer can override the destiny forecast from an unfortunate name. Like Jabez, Jesus gained blessing from the pain of his suffering.

169. The reference is to Lucifer.

170. This refers to Judah as the father of the Messiah and his representative.

of creation to install the youngest son of creation on the peak of

Eph 1:22; compare Col 1:18; Rev 1:5 glory and perfection.[171]

1 CHRONICLES 10:13

Our offense was that we did not observe God's command but followed the deceptive conclusions of a sorcerer. Thus disobedience

1 Sam 15:23 is called the sin of sorcery.

1 CHRONICLES 12:18

The Spirit *clothed* Amasai. God's Spirit was the one who clothed

Gen 49:9 our naked parents with the skins of animals.

1 CHRONICLES 12:32

An understanding of the times provides us with the understanding

Ps 31:15 of our duties. Only the Lord of time knows them; so he alone can tell us how important the moment is that he gives us. The present moment is like a dead torso, without head or feet; it always stays where it lies. The past must be revealed to us, and the future likewise. With regard to the past, our fellow creatures can help us a little; the future is completely undisclosed. Even the breath of the next hour is its own master; at the very least the future depends on the previous hour as little as a breath can govern the one before it and the one after it. Every moment in time is perfectly rounded. The line that comes from it depends on the thread that Providence has drawn through it. Neither Providence nor our weak eyes permit us to observe its precise combination for ourselves. This thread makes the coherence of moments and parts of time so firm and inseparable, so inter-grown, that everything consists and seems to consist of one piece.

1 CHRONICLES 19:[5]

Remain in Jericho until your beards have grown and then return. Thus, it seems, the souls of people had to remain until the promise

Gal 4:4 of the woman's offspring was fulfilled and he who brought back the

171. Jesus, the lion of Judah, enthrones the church as God's youngest son together with him (Eph 2:6).

captives redeemed them from their captivity. So, perhaps, the souls of the children, yes, our souls too, may have a Jericho where they stay until God gathers them all, ripe and mature, freed from disgrace, for the day of the great judgment and the universal harvest of the earth and brings them into his barns. Yes, he allows the whole earth to have time to recover from the scorn of the seducer before he brings home all his banished, disgraced children and avenges them through the repudiation and overthrow of the serpent. David *Rev 12:9* himself remained in Jerusalem while Joab led his campaigns (20:1).

1 CHRONICLES 21:1–2

Satan incited David; David used Joab—the king's word was meant for Joab, and God's for Satan. You, God, govern everything when Satan stands up to seduce, when he believes that he wins the victory with David, and David supposes that he has the power to command Joab. You, therefore, are the great Lord, the First and the Last of all. The king's word was abominable to Joab. Satan recounted David's *Rev 1:8; 1 Chr 21:4* sin to you as an abominable deed, and in your eyes his accusation was the greatest abomination. No one understands you; you survey all people and all their acts.

1 CHRONICLES 21:11

Choose, O man, how gracious God is with the person that he punishes by putting him in charge of his penalties and allowing him to choose. Satan believes that he remains unpunished; he will therefore have to receive his punishment without any choice.

1 CHRONICLES 21:12

Three years, three months, three days—we see how God's wisdom measures out the times. We see how David teaches us to be afraid of the longest punishment. The sufferings of the present time are not worth comparing with the glory that will be revealed to us; the punishments of the present time are moments compared with the years of eternity. We see how David teaches us to avoid the drought of God's blessing, with the lack of bodily necessities being a symbol of the spiritual drought and the starvation of the soul being the greatest evil. We see how well David knows people, their hostility, the agents and instruments of wickedness and hatred. The Lord's sword is lighter, swifter, and more merciful than the hunger that experiences natural needs without the benefits and means of nourishment by which God quenches it; more merciful than the intent of our enemies, who are not content to grate on us for a while but seek to embitter and poison all the days of our lives, our enemies who let us experience that their peace is as cruel as the wrath of their warfare.

So let us like David acknowledge no one except God as Judge
and Lord. God relents, he calls out to the angel wielding the sword:
1 Chr 21:15 "It is enough!" He makes him stand still by the threshing floor, the
work place for our temporal nourishment, as a sign that he wants
to make peace with us as a gracious, amiable, blessing God, a sign
that he has not struck us out of hatred, like a farmer treading his
harvest down with his feet, but only to winnow the straw from the
grain so that he can enjoy it. How could Satan hear David pray
without sensing his own evil heart ... "What have these sheep done,
whose keeper you were meant to be?" Satan has to hear this from
1 Chr 21:17 the person that he had accused and slandered. God seems to have
selected all examples of sinful people to shame this enemy. The
generosity of Ornan, who required nothing for his threshing floor,
contrasts with the selfishness of Satan, who sold off his subjects and
1 Chr 21:23 the earth to God and intended to cheat God himself.

1 CHRONICLES 23:5

Four thousand shall praise God with the instruments that I made to praise him. God's Spirit has revealed himself to people through people. He, therefore, has made himself as human as possible for the weakness of their nature. Does it not appear that he wants to copy their distractions and has, in some instances, almost forgotten himself in them? We see how God's Spirit has let a word drop[172] that he should have spoken through the mouth of the historian by

172. See Deut 32:2 for the use of this idiom to introduce a prophetic speech.

saying: "With the instruments that I have made."[173] He is the Spirit who has taught us to call on God in spirit and truth, who prepares our mouth to laud and praise God, who tunes David's harp and delights God with his psalms. He seems to be somewhat jealous of his honor and lets it be noted by us humans, the angels, and himself that he is the God who makes the voice of clay, earth, and ashes as pleasing and melodious as the jubilation of the cherubim and seraphim. God, how gracious you are! Sheer grace! It is amazing thatyou became a man to please us. You seem to be God only for our sake. How great is our ingratitude when we forget this and live and die apart from you.

John 4:24

1 CHRONICLES 23:11

We see how God's Spirit has found it worthwhile to record the smallest arrangements that were made in his service and has noted the smallest details (1 Chr 12). That is just the way that he works in our souls. Those who feel God's Spirit in themselves will certainly feel him in the Scriptures. He knows how to use the smallest matters that we encounter to edify people—to support, delight, comfort, warn, and speak to them. It is true that he intended to please no other people than believers, true Christians, through his divine word. The unbeliever is not his concern. No matter how simple or learned he may be, the Spirit is sealed off from him. The believer is his intimate confidant. He is allowed to taste for himself some of the simplest and most profound understanding, with the same pleasure, in the same measure, with the same riches of heavenly wisdom and supernatural grace.

1 CHRONICLES 26:1

The whole service of God in the Jewish church—the sacrifices, the songs, the temple, the harps—were all prophetic. They were all symbols of the divine service that we Christians would offer through

173. The insertion of the first person pronoun rather than the use of the third person as usual in the narrative gives the perspective of God's Spirit speaking directly through David as a prophet rather than indirectly through the chronicler of these events.

faith in his Son by our thoughts, words, and deeds, with our whole body and every member of it, with every instrument of our calling, our pleasure, our conduct, and our devotion. All the life and the divine service of every Christian, all his deeds, are prophetic. They are prophecies of the heavenly service that we should and will offer to God before his throne in the midst of his angels and to the Lamb
Rev 7:9–12 of God in the midst of his witnesses and brothers. Thus the mantle
2 Kgs 2:8, 13–14; Exod 4:1–5, 17, 20; 7:5–12, 15–20; 8:5–6, 16–17; 9:22–23; 10:12–15, 21–23 of the prophets and the staffs of his servants were miracle-workers.

2 CHRONICLES 18

How detrimental fellowship with the world is for a devout person. No matter how well it receives him, it is always self-seeking. The devout person always thinks that he must acknowledge the world's good acceptance through compliance with its will.

2 CHRONICLES 18:20–21

This vision of Micaiah is extraordinary. We observe the Lord on his throne, perplexed about how he should overthrow a godless person. God hears the thoughts of his creatures. Finally, a spirit comes forward, stands before the Lord and says: "I will deceive him. I will go out and be a lying spirit in the mouth of all the prophets." Who does not see God's omnipotence bound, as it were, by his other attributes? Even the downfall of a godless Ahab is in his eyes a righteous judgment that he is loath to undertake. He must bring about his own overthrow. Because he had no interest in God's laws, so, it seems, God will not even have any interest in the penalties against those who transgress them. Here we see a spirit who stands before God without acknowledging his holiness, without making it the guideline of his thoughts. He takes the complete freedom to fulfill God's commands, to dictate them to God, a lying spirit—a lying spirit in the mouth of the prophets—a shameless boxer with
2 Chr 18:23 the hand of Zedekiah, an advisor of Ahab who told him to disguise
himself in order to see Jehoshaphat captured and struck dead in his
2 Chr 18:26 place—perhaps he also prompted the king of Syria to think that only
the king of Israel should be targeted. So it looks as if the lying spirit

wanted to deceive God himself. The Lord helped Jehoshaphat, it is said, and *a man* drew his bow in his *innocence*[174] and struck *the king* of Israel, despite his disguise, despite armor, between *its scales*. *2 Chr 18:33*

Here God strikes Ahab through an innocent man. He does not need a lying spirit to hit him or recognize him, no matter how much Satan has disguised and covered him.

From this example we therefore see how this lying spirit understands God's commands, how he carries them out, how he misuses them, how he acts against the Lord and his people in violation of the covenant, how he regards people, and how he tries to clear away the good people in favor of all the others.

2 CHRONICLES 21:9–10

The godless man sees all his underlings and allies rise up against him and get him to experience his own disobedience through theirs. Our reason, our desires, our needs, nature, time, life itself all oppose us. How opposite is the peace of a Christian with God and himself.

2 CHRONICLES 26:10

We often discover that the taste of people is recorded in sacred Scripture. Uzziah, Azariah, loved agriculture.

2 CHRONICLES 28:20

We see how the help and comfort of the world is here portrayed by Tiglath-Pileser. He made Ahaz less successful. He embarrassed him even more, without strengthening him in the least, without giving him the least help. Even though Ahaz paid him richly, he did not help him at all.

2 CHRONICLES 28:22

The godless make good deeds more arrogant and punishments more sacrilegious. As King Ahab was, so the prince of the world is in all his children. *John 12:31; 14:30; 16:11*

174. The Hebrew term also means simplicity and ignorance.

2 CHRONICLES 30[:6–10]

How touching is this royal pastoral letter by which Hezekiah summons the people to the Passover. Do not be like your fathers and brothers who sinned against the God of their fathers. We see how the fathers of the human race are distinguished here, as the off-
Gen 3:15 spring of the woman and the offspring of the serpent. Do not be stiff-necked—give your hand to the Lord, and enter his sanctuary.

How shocking the ridicule and scorn and mockery of the reader of the letter. This is the reply that Satan prompts us to make to the invitations of God and his Spirit. He gives us the shameless voice of a prostitute.

2 CHRONICLES 32:8

And the people *leant, relied* on the words of Hezekiah.

2 CHRONICLES 32:21

Here, presumably, the angel was the same as the lying spirit and God's slanderer. With the king of Assyria he saw the penalty of his own judgment, the sword of his human children by which he would fall.

EZRA 4:1

The hostility of the serpent's offspring against the blessed offspring of the woman runs through all sacred Scripture with its explanation of the first prophecy and a continual affirmation of it until the
Gen 3:15; Rev 12:17 time of fulfillment. The enemies of Judah and Benjamin begin with smooth words. They want the people who had been exiled and transplanted to imagine that they sought their God just they did and offered sacrifices to him. They appealed to a mighty King who had brought them there and compared his authority with Cyrus.

EZRA 4:4

The people of the land, the inhabitants of the earth, its prince—the strong one in his generation—*weakens* the hands of the people of Judah. He makes them disheartened, disconcerted, disunited, doubtful, sluggish. He *disturbs* them and unsettles them in their work—he *hires* counselors against them. His right hand is filled with bribes, which he knows how to press on a Balaam, yes, even on God's people. He waits for a good time, a right opportunity, and then he writes an *accusation* against the inhabitants of Judah and Jerusalem. God's Spirit has uncovered all states and kingdoms, *Ezra 4:6–16* all the lies and snares of hell, so openly that we can anticipate the smallest movement of this cunning foe.

EZRA 4:11

The men this side of the river[175]—who want to help the men on the other side because, like them, they also served their god—now describe their undertaking as an insurrection, a danger to the welfare of the state and the monarch. The devil has so often employed this reason in the most ridiculous way to deceive people. Certainly, out of political craftiness he tried to suppress the teaching of Jesus and to indict him as a dangerous enemy of Roman power and the Jewish state—just as he knows how to flatter the self-interest of the aristocracy and teaches them to base their power on the oppression of their subjects with taxes and levies. Just as he knows how to use history and historians, as his own testimony, to confirm his own slanderous accusations.

EZRA 4:22

Why should something damaging arise to harm the kings? Quite the same spirit dominates the written petition and the subsequent reply of Artaxerxes. Let the subjects bleed; let the guilty suffer with the innocent. A king must be ready not only to wish for the complete submission of his people, but also to be able to use the axe on their necks, so that he may no longer fear anything to damage and harm him. Those who brought the report to Artaxerxes regarded it as their duty to offer this to him since *they had been salted with the salt of his court and palace*. Since the salt that they received for their livelihood was the salt of the king and his court, it would therefore

175. The river is the Euphrates. Judah and Jerusalem belonged to the Persian province of Trans-Euphrates (Neh 2:7).

be improper for them to condone the king's dishonor by this people
Ezra 4:14 and their undertaking without acting.

EZRA 7:6

Whatever people can give us, whatever good thing our neighbor can do for us, depends on the hand of the Lord our God on us. The more gracious God is with us, the more right we have to what belongs to God and what he rules over, and the more he makes room for us in the heart, the will, the inclinations of our neighbor. It is not his good heart, his good will, our merit, our cleverness that makes our neighbor well-disposed to us, but the hand of the Lord our God on us. This belief and this truth is so very useful for the whole of human life. It makes us brave, confident, and content in all our undertakings because all our purposes and inclinations relate only to God.

EZRA 7:9

The foundation for our going out, for the beginning that we make
in our vocation and its completion, our return home after our daily
work is done, all depend on the *good hand of our God* on us. We must
be convinced that our God is the Ruler of the whole world. By faith
we must sense our participation in his grace and presence. But we
must also, at the same time, so take our steps and go our ways that
the shadow of the divine hand on us is like a guide and the cloud
Exod 13:21 that led Israel in the wilderness. We must always take pains to travel
under it, never beside it to the right or to the left. Just as the men
Matt 2:2 from the east saw the star over the house, so we must endeavor to
see God's hand continually over our heads. How was the hand of
God, his God, on Ezra? Because the law of God was never out of
his hand (7:14), and God's law is his wisdom (7:25).

EZRA 7:23

Why would there be vengeance or wrath against the king and his sons? How excellent is the politics that teaches us to fear God, which makes the realm and those who come after us the focus of its concerns and dealings (cf. 4:22)!

EZRA 8[:24–30]

The book of Ezra is a prophecy of the works of the Holy Spirit by which he endeavored to build and establish the new church of Christ. The offerings that Ezra here weighed out for the twelve chief priests are the gifts of the Holy Spirit that were distributed to the apostles and the first Christians. The hand of God on me is the laying on of hands by which God's Spirit is distributed.

Acts 2:1–4; Heb 2:4

Acts 8:18; 9:17; 19:6; 2 Tim 1:6

EZRA 8:29

We have a special responsibility for the gifts of the Holy Spirit.

EZRA 9

The most excellent gifts of the Holy Spirit shine out in Ezra, most of all the gift of prayer, which must have been so natural for him in all his undertakings that he breaks out in a prayer in the middle of his account after recounting the king's charter and mandate for him. In this chapter we find longer prayer with all the vigor of repentance, the fear of the Lord, and hearty devotion poured out in it. The second gift of the good Spirit in Ezra is the taste, the zeal, the feeling of God's word. His speech, his deeds, his whole disposition seems to be permeated with it. So too everyone who *trembled at the words of the God of Israel* (9:4). The Spirit of the old covenant, which is, as Paul describes, a spirit of the fear of slavery, is evident in Ezra.

Zech 12:10

Ezra 9:5–15

Neh 9:20; Ps 143:10

Rom 8:15

EZRA 10:44

We see how sin suppresses and corrupts all natural inclinations. Out of love for their wives and children, the Israelites did not want to enter the promised land. Here the love for their wives and children does not prevent them from taking foreign wives and falling into the very sin that they had to repent of with such difficulty.

Num 14:3

NEHEMIAH 1:3

The wall is God's law and our obedience to it that protects from the accusations of our conscience and our enemies. The gates by which we were meant to enter heaven were changed into the gates of hell. An eternal fire had consumed them.

NEHEMIAH 1:4

The news that is heard of our sin and of our demolished walls—the report of the fire that has consumed our gates—puts us down, throws us to the earth, casts us down to the ground, and lays us on
Gen 3:19 the soil from which we were taken and to which we must return, squeezes out tears from us, gives us a heavy, burdened, disconsolate heart, deprives us of the zest for life and our existence, which we no longer find worth living, which is a curse in our eyes, and drives us to the prayer in which we acknowledge God as our Lord, our Judge and our Redeemer.

NEHEMIAH 1:5

Then we recognize God's truth, the holiness of his covenant, grace, and mercy, the need to love him and keep his commandments, because he is a great and awesome God.

NEHEMIAH 1:6

Then we call on him for his attention, for an open ear and an open eye which our hearing and sight have found shut for so long, so that they could be touched by nothing except the punishments that afflicted us and the enemies who inflicted their reproaches on us.

NEHEMIAH 1:8–9

Then God's word, despite its terrors, is more precious and valuable. Yes, its terrors themselves comfort us more when our own heart distresses us and our enemies dishearten us.

NEHEMIAH 1:10

Then our eyes are open to the blessing of being God's servants, his people, the greatness of his redemption and its power. Then the fear of God is our only wish, all that our heart desires. We desire to find grace and compassion in the eyes of the man who is our God and King. God's Spirit, the lawgiver in Ezra and the cupbearer in Nehemiah, teaches us to pray like this.

NEHEMIAH 2:1

Do not grieve the Holy Spirit. The Spirit of joy and comfort whom God the Father never sees sad, becomes sad on our account, on account of our sadness, on account of the reproaches of our enemies against us, on account of our misery in lying waste, our punishment that God's wrath has turned into a fire that does not let us approach him, a fire by which all fellowship, all access to him is cut off. *Eph 4:30*

NEHEMIAH 2:2

Nehemiah is afraid that the king should consider him prone to sorrow in his presence. It is an offense against the Highest Majesty that makes everything joyful to show a sad face, a downcast heart, and divulge how the wine which he should receive from our hand is changed into vinegar and gall. Be afraid, you sinner, when you consider that you darken the joy of enthronement before God, that you possess the power to make God himself sad. How can this strike the sinner who is able to think of Golgotha without being overcome with anguish? *Matt 27:34*

NEHEMIAH 2:3

The city where my fathers lie buried lies in ruins. The earth where God himself lived as a man, died, and was buried, is ruined. It still looks just as it was then, when I hovered over the face of the waters.[176] It is waste, empty, and dark over the deep. The grave of the fathers, the death of Adam, is visible in its rubble—the punishment of sin, the fire of hell, still burns at the gates. *Gen 1:2*

NEHEMIAH 2:4

Before Nehemiah answers the king, he prays to his God, the God of his fathers, the God of the city on which his name rests. We cannot answer God any earlier, appear before his judgment, do justice to his questions, and expect his grace for ourselves, before conversing with the Spirit of his Son and claiming a favorable hearing and

176. The Spirit speaks in this sentence.

pardon, grace, and freedom by faith in his intercession and reliance
Rom 8:26–27 on it. Here we also see with what conditions the Spirit of God was
John 15:26 sent to us and proceeded from the Father and the Son. The King and
the humanity that was crowned in God's Son made the Spirit their envoy and the restorer of God's people. Nehemiah could not undertake his journey without the King's letters. With these he obtained divine authority, and these royal letters are God's word that the Holy Spirit brought with him from the throne of heaven to earth.

NEHEMIAH 2:7

To show the unity of the divine persons, we always find that the works by which they reveal themselves are interchanged in Scripture. The Triune God created the world, but God the Father owns the work of creation in a special way for himself. The Triune God was the redeemer of the world, yet God's blessed Son alone became a man and suffered on our behalf, even though the fellowship of the other two persons was not thereby excluded from the work of our redemption. The Holy Spirit takes an especially prominent part in it. These letters to the governors of Beyond the River are the revelations through Moses and the prophets that go alongside and accompany the promise of his coming until its fulfillment. Through the later letters to the Keeper of the King's Forest, we understand the revelations of divine redemption to our souls
that prepare for the birth of Jesus in our hearts in a special way by
Luke 1:35 him who overshadowed Mary and by whose power she received
the promised Son. This divine Spirit builds us up as temples of God
1 Cor 3:16; 2 Cor 6:16 and Christ, and his gracious operations are here compared with the
timber needed by Nehemiah who himself represents the Redeemer:
timber as beams for the gates of the fortress that belongs to God's
Neh 2:8 house—to restore the entrance from earth into heaven, to reestab-
lish the entrance of God in our hearts, the fellowship of the soul
with God—timber for the wall of the city, so that God's kingdom
may no longer dwell among us in a tent, but be set in a fixed place,
2 Sam 7:5–16 a secure place against all the attacks of our enemies, timber for the
house that Nehemiah would dwell in. This was the overshadowing

of the Holy Spirit in Mother Mary and in every soul where God would dwell.

NEHEMIAH 2:10

The whole of sacred Scripture teaches us who this Sanballat and Tobiah are. We discover the same dismay that they felt because a man would come, and had come, to promote the welfare of the human race, in Abimelech, Esau, Pharaoh, the Philistines, and, finally, in the scribes and Pharisees and the eyewitnesses of Babylon.

The entire second half of the chapter describes the incarnation of Jesus Christ, the redemption, in clear and bold outlines that, like the rays of the sun, convince the eyes of faith.

Our Savior came at night, which was revealed to the shepherds and the wise men from the East, the former through the song of the angels and the latter through the star, in the night when the *Luke 2:8–14; Matt 2:1–2* Jewish people were wrapped in the darkness of Satan—by the Valley Gate. In the utmost humiliation, the way of all flesh, in poverty and penury—from the Dragon's Spring and the Dung Gate—he became *Neh 2:13; Phil 2:7–8* a man, born under the curse that God had put on the childbearing of the woman, and his mother had as much need for the Day of *Gen 3:16* Purification as every sinful mother. *Luke 2:22–23* Thus in his childhood he saw the misery of our nature and so shared in our weakness that he felt it all and was able to have so much more sympathy with us. *Matt 8:17; Heb 4:15* Few people kept him company. He did not disclose himself to the world. For a while he was quite alone and people saw nothing of him except as a man, just as Nehemiah only had an animal under him. Finally, his disciples themselves were the mild, despised, sluggish creature on which he would make himself the King of the world.

He observed human nature in the scribes and the Pharisees, who were supposed to be the custodians of the spring of living water and the King's Pool, which had been dug for people in the *Neh 2:14; Jer 17:13* law of Moses. It was for him as it was for Noah's dove: he found no place to put his feet. *Gen 8:9*

His last journey, the last observation that he made of human nature, was over the Brook of Kidron, the brook of death and the

Neh 2:15; John 18:1 wall of hell. He left the world, as he had entered it, through the gates of the valley and returned, without the leaders of the people, the Jews, the priests, and the nobles knowing anything of it.

NEHEMIAH 2:13

We may properly understand passing through the Dragon's Spring as the temptation of Satan and through the Dung Gate as the abuses of the Mosaic law, because this was most likely the gate where the impurities of the sacrificial animals were brought out.

After this inspection, which Nehemiah had undertaken in a secret journey, he revealed himself and the building began. Then God's Spirit was poured out, who was to lead the disciples into all
John 16:13; Acts 2:33, 47; 4:4; 5:14; 6:7; 9:31 truth, and the church of God was built.

NEHEMIAH 2:19

This is the laughter of hell. This mockery, this accusation of sin and rebellion, was the suffering of our Savior and his apostles and all true Christians.

NEHEMIAH 2:20

This is the wealth of our faith and also the judgment on our enemies. We have a share in Jerusalem. Jesus is our brother and the Father
John 3:35 has placed everything in his hands. We have a right in Jerusalem—on our account he suffered, died, is God from eternity to eternity. We have a greater memorial than the pillar of Absalom that was
2 Sam 18:18 set up in the King's Valley, a monument before God in his glorified body, in his incarnation, in the inscription of his wounds that
Phil 3:21; John 20:20, 24–27 he suffered for us, in the down payment of the Holy Spirit that he poured into our souls.

2 Cor 1:22

NEHEMIAH 4:17

Just as the Israelites had to eat the Passover Lamb as travelers with
Exod 12:11 their staffs in their hands, so the rebuilders of Jerusalem had to build and work as soldiers with their swords in their hands.

NEHEMIAH 4:18

God's Spirit gives us the signal of the trumpets in his word to keep us vigilant and praying in our calling.

NEHEMIAH 4:21

From the rising of grace, like the sun in our souls, to the night of the grave and the sight of the starry sky seen by the dying Christian whose sleep is, like Jacob's, a revelation of the angels and God's morning star. *Gen 28:10–17; 2 Pet 1:19; Rev 22:16*

NEHEMIAH 5

Ezra had described the transgression of his people with foreign wives, which had to do, mainly, with the pollution of the early church. Nehemiah describes for us how the Jews oppressed each other. Both are parables of the violence and injustice that the seducer perpetrates against our souls. Moses only divorced foreign wives. Nehemiah puts away the fields and vineyards that our enemy had gained for himself in the guise of a brother. *Ezra 9:1–2; 10:1–17; Rev 2:14, 20–22; 14:4* *Deut 7:3–4; compare Exod 34:11–16*

NEHEMIAH 5:15

The godless themselves, the servants of Satan, are the tyrants of the believers and their unjust lord's governors.

NEHEMIAH 5:19

God's Spirit searches out those human deeds everywhere that have the most to do with Satan, that shame him the most and have drawn our sighs at his tyranny most of all to him. By our sighs the vengeance that God wants to wreak on Satan has been nothing but our own example, our own life, our own prayer, despite the blindness that he imposes on us and the corruption with which he tries to make us like himself.

NEHEMIAH 6

What can be a clearer prophecy than that the spirit who was at work in these three men is the same as with the Pharisees and scribes? *Neh 6:1* How often they came under the guise of peace to catch out our

Savior and lie in wait for his life! Is not the fifth occasion when the servant of Sanballat with a direct accusation and its content that there was a king in Judah fulfilled in the history of our Savior? We see how they try to make Nehemiah's hands weak and tired, how they hired enemies for him from his own people. Jews and gentiles took oaths against Nehemiah. Here in 6:18 we discover the same abuse of the land acquired in marriage as in the history of our Savior.[177]

Neh 6:7

Neh 6:8–9

NEHEMIAH 7:3

The gates of Jerusalem were not to be opened until the sun burned hot. When this time was fulfilled, our Savior came into the world. When this time was fulfilled, he entered Jerusalem as a king shortly before his passion. When this time was fulfilled, the Spirit of God was poured out for the proclamation of the gospel to Jerusalem and the whole world.

Gal 4:4

Matt 21:10

Luke 24:45–49; compare Acts 2:1–4

NEHEMIAH 8:1, 3

The people walk about in the street before the Water Gate to hear the law. Ezra reads it in the street before the Water Gate. The Spirit who gathered the people was the Spirit of the word and the Spirit of purification and ablution in the water of Holy Baptism.

Titus 3:4–7; compare Eph 5:26; Heb 10:22

NEHEMIAH 8:5

When Ezra opens the book of the law, the people stand up. When the Spirit opens up its sense, we see how erect a person seems. The Spirit lifts up his head, draws his ears to him, raises up his hands on high, and permits us to cry "Amen! Amen!" with a full heart.

NEHEMIAH 8:10

The joy of the Lord is our strength. It gives us power to walk our way, to eat the fat from his blessing, to drink his grace, and a generous heart that provides a portion to those who had nothing

177. This seems to be an allusion to King Herod the Great, an Edomite who was related by marriage to the Jewish priestly aristocracy.

prepared for them. The understanding of God's word stills our hunger and thirst, makes us rich with love, and fills the heart with great joy (8:12).

NEHEMIAH 9

We see how the book of Nehemiah prays compared to Ezra. Here we have a foretaste of the spirit of the gospel. This is not just the spirit that is oppressed under the law in Ezra but the spirit that tastes of the fruit of the new covenant with God's cup bearer.[178] It is the key to the whole story of Moses, the greatest miracle, and the core of divine revelation in the Old Testament.

NEHEMIAH 9:21

You did not become dissatisfied with the mantle that covered the nakedness of the people before the wrath of your righteousness, and you did not take away from them the power that they needed for the strenuous way of the law. In the Scriptures clothes are to be understood as the righteousness of faith and feet as the power for the spiritual life and the righteousness of life and conduct.

NEHEMIAH 9:29

They presented a quivering shoulder that drew back from him.[179]

NEHEMIAH 9:30

Nevertheless, you spread yourself over them for many years—the basic sense of this word must indicate something that goes beyond our powers, that spreads further than we can.[180] My God, what a notion! You violate yourself by stretching your grace as far as our sins make it necessary.

178. This alludes to the words of Jesus in Mark 14:23–25 about the cup of his blood in Holy Communion.

179. This is a literal translation of the Hebrew text.

180. Here Hamann gives a literal translation of an unusual Hebrew idiom of a stretched heart for exercising patient forbearance.

NEHEMIAH 9:32

It has not just cost God's mercy much to protect us, to preserve us, for such a long time from his righteousness. We must also beg God to regard our punishment as greater than it is. He must, as it were, bribe his truth for him to spare us. More correctly, God should avenge the forbearance that we have required from him and the compassion that we have begged from him on the enemy who has egged us on against him and destroys and disgraces us through his temptations and his cruelty when we succumb to them. This is also how 9:36–37 is to be understood.

NEHEMIAH 13:2

Perhaps Satan tempted our Savior with the same purpose as the
Num 22–24 Ammonite and Moabite tempted Balaam through an error, or per-
haps the whole story of Balaam is much more a type of our Savior's
Matt 4:1–11 temptation in the wilderness.

NEHEMIAH 13:8

This situation alludes to the expulsion of buyers and merchants by
Mark 11:15 our Savior in the temple.

NEHEMIAH 13:26

Solomon drew God's wrath on himself by his foreign wives. The sins that were foreign for him were punished in our Solomon. He bore the idolatry of our souls and experienced God's wrath for it.

ESTHER 1:15

Here we see the reliance of Ahasuerus on the council of his seven
wise men. In his vision Micaiah saw how God also asked a similar
question and agreed with the thoughts of the angel.[181] Here we see
2 Chr 18:18–22 the exertion of the Holy Spirit for human souls and their Savior both
in the affection of Mordecai for an orphan and in the extraordinary
Esth 2:7–10 inclination of Hegai. It is amazing that God provides so many acts of

181. Hamann refers incorrectly to 2 Chronicles 11.

redemption for the Jewish people to confirm the great, final act for the redemption of their souls and the whole human race. Mordecai's first service was his discovery of the conspiracy of the two chamberlains; the second, his relationship with Esther. *Esth 2:22*

Wisdom seems to have created the human race as envoys of higher spirits. The evil spirits tempt them just as they themselves are tempted. The devout believers enjoy, and have always enjoyed, God's grace in defiance of the enemy of humanity. Yes, what made Mordecai so hated in Haman's eyes[182] is indeed the touchstone and the revelation that God so graciously accepts.

How accurately the mentality of pride, this devilish vice, is depicted in Hamann[183] with its attention to scandalmongers and flatterers (3:5). Pride is the presumption that everyone alike should honor us and bow down before us, the zeal for petty aspects of wellbeing. Presumption is the most extravagant of all passions by which pride tries to gain satisfaction for itself. It is a despicable kind of vengeance that must only punish the person who insults us or seems to humiliate us. It is vengeance that must be so public, cruel, and unjust that the whole kingdom must speak about, be alarmed by it, and wonder at its perpetrator with horror. Respect for those above us, the duties of our station, even self-interest, are sacrificed for our vengeance. The wellbeing of the land and enthusiasm for the honor of the king and what is best for him are misused as a cloak for it. Heartlessness to good deeds and insensitivity to the need of others are the two main traits of pride (3:11, 15).

Pride finds all the reasons that motivate others to pursue pride as evidence of its own worth. Pride considers that they cannot possibly have anything else in mind than its vindication. This constant admiration of itself makes it blind, rash, and ripe for its impending fall (chapter 5).

---

182. The thing that made Mordecai so hated was the disclosure that he was a Jew (Esther 3:4–6).

183. Here and below, Hamann begins spelling the name of the villain of the Esther story like his own name with a double "n," even though he is always called "Haman" in Hebrew as well as in both the KJV and Luther's translation. Hamann would later joke about his illustrious ancestor who was hanged. See his satirical letter "*To the Witch at Kadmanbor.*"

The more advantages pride enjoys, the more insatiable it becomes. The more joy it seems to have in the moment that it receives them, so much more it is punctured by the least thing that gets in its way. No matter how thoroughly Hamann reports all his success to his wife and friends, bolstered by it, he nevertheless still admits that it means nothing to him as long as a gatekeeper of the
Esth 5:9–13 royal castle does not bow his knee before him.

Pride is so stupid. It admires every suggestion which flatters what it likes and follows it blindly. How foolish pride is in its choice of trivial things by which it distinguishes itself, such as gallows fifty cubits high in 5:14.

The king sought help in getting to sleep by having the history of his kingdom read to him. Hamann sought to get to sleep by the
Esth 6:1–4 implementing his attack that brooked no delay and gave him no rest.

We see how pride is inclined to exclude everything else and only focus entirely on itself. We see what an enemy of humanity it is, a tyrant who deceives himself and turns this delusion into a law for him to show and employ its power (6:6).

We can follow the ebb and flow, the battle, the vehemence of the passions in the breast of this ambitious murderer and scoundrel. We can consider the blindness and horror of his case. We can consider how God's government turns out so splendidly in so many extraordinary circumstances that are so remote, and in the moment when they converge. We can analyze the whole story of redemption. If that is so, how should not the story of the gospel itself and the revelation and transfiguration of all divine attributes and decrees concerning the pillars of the earth on which they are grounded by
1 Sam 2:8 the incarnation of God fill us with feelings of gratitude, the joy of faith, comfort, and hope?

JOB 1:10

From the mouth of the enemy himself we hear how necessary God's hedge is around us and our property so that our evil neighbor and animals do not harm us, what a thorn such a fence is in the eyes of the enemy, and how he tries to overcome it under the pretext of something good. The reason for his insistence here is that the service we offer to God is self-serving and merely sensual.

Furthermore, here we see that, at least in Old Testament times, Satan had the freedom to appear among the angels in God's presence. Even if that was restricted after the victory of our Savior, we *Rev 12:7–9* have no reason to exclude it completely. On the contrary, he still seems to have a seat in heaven that he will have to vacate for us in a terrible way at the judgment of the world, so that he is now *John 12:31* already terrified to see the Son of Man and true God seated at the right hand of the Father.

Satan's going to and fro on the earth and his walking up and down on it seems to be a duty from his position. 2 Chronicles 16:9 says of God: "The eyes of the Lord *run to and fro*, over and over, through and through the whole earth, in order to show himself strong, with all his power, on behalf of those who hearts are perfect toward him, for him to hold strongly to them and remain with them."[184] So Satan goes up and down on the earth and spends the most time with those whose hearts are turned to God and belong to him. Those who are devout are a bare thorn in his eyes. They stand in the way of his complete rule over the earth. They acknowledge another Lord apart from him. They do not bow their knee to him. He therefore regards them as a handful of rebels. In every possible way he tries to dupe them, swallow them up, oppress them, plunder them, and make them impatient and alienated from God. What a comfort! Although the adversary goes up and down like a fierce lion, the eyes of the Lord run to and fro, over and over, yes, *1 Pet 5:8* through and through! He shows himself strong on behalf of those whose hearts are perfect toward him. This is the fence around them, around their house and around all that they have, all around them.

Apart from some minor details, our first parents were in the same dilemma as Job. Did not God, when they fell, let them tear down the hedge around the happiness and life of human beings? Was not Satan's unbelief confirmed through this trial, which seemed

184. Here the Hebrew verb means both to show oneself strong and to act with strength.

to be so successful for him, and did not the weak virtues of human beings, therefore, like the miracles, serve to punish the seducer and refute him?

We should regard all temporal punishments as rods which the adversary of humanity tries to steal from God by stealth, hiding his hatred of people under a love for righteousness and perfection. How necessary it is for God to curtail his power! How inclined Satan is to expand it! Hence the divine law to give no more than forty lashes
Deut 25:3 to a brother, so that he would not be degraded in their sight. We see how Job became degraded in the eyes of his wife and friends and how Satan tried to degrade him in his own eyes and in God's eyes.

JOB 1:13

How quick Satan is to make use of the permission that he had received. How very keen he is to test Job. We see how clever he is in carrying out all punishments most frightfully, without letting Job have any time to recover, beginning with a little blow and ending with the heaviest blow, choosing the time for it when Job's sons would be enjoying themselves, to unsettle conscientious Job by making him suspicious of God and his own children.

JOB 1:15, 17

Satan pays for the bold, murderous attack and robbery by the Chaldeans and Sabeans with Job's property, just as he may have incited them through it to commit this crime. He kills all the servants, and his pity in preserving only one person is an even greater atrocity because that survivor had to be its messenger.

JOB 1:16, 19

Satan borrows the terrors of nature so as to make his judgment on Job so much more impressive. With fire he consumes the sheep as the foremost animals for offering, as if the offering of them belonged to him and as if the offerings that Job brought to God for his children were a robbery from him; a storm, a great, strong wind that tears the mountains and breaks the rocks in pieces as Elijah heard it, a storm in which the Lord was not (1 Kings 19:11), strikes the four corners of the house, so that it collapsed on the young people, and only one person was preserved to bring this news likewise to Job.

The sequence of his judgments and mighty deeds was so arranged that the four messengers of each disaster had to follow each other as quickly as possible, so that Job would have no time to hear out a single person but only saw the truth of what had happened from the horror of his face, from the fear with which he had escaped his fate and told that he was the only survivor.

JOB 1:20

We see how happily and impatiently Satan seems to wait for the effect of his miracles. How long the time takes for him: Job stands up, now he will break out, he still remains silent. Job stands up and tears his robe—this was a stark gesture of grief that belonged to the outward well-being of a mourner. He shaves his head, he falls on the ground, and performs all the symbolic acts by which he was accustomed to show his reverence for God. How Satan must have been amazed, shaken, and blanched/shamed[185] when he heard the outburst of words from Job.

JOB 1:21

What lack of interest in all the earthly goods on which Satan builds his power and by which he wields all his dominion and witchcraft over stupid, foolish mortals! We see how strong Job's reason was in turning a mere hint of nature into such a strong peg for his faith. He says, "Naked and destitute I came from my mother's body, and naked shall I return to it again. This nakedness with which I came into the world arouses God's pity in order to give me more, infinitely more, than I need. Now he puts me back again into that nakedness and lets me return to it again.[186] Since he has given to me, he has a right to take away. Yes, he may even exercise the same right to give

185. These are two words in the sentence, given by Hamann as alternate readings.

186. Here Hamann refers to his destitute state in London.

me greater riches that I know so little about, in the same condition that I know so little about and is so strange to me as when this clod of earth was in my mother's womb—He will reveal himself, just as he has, until now, revealed himself to me. Yes, he will reveal more to me in this second nakedness in which he has now put me than in the first. May his name be blessed. May his unsearchable will be accepted and acknowledged with thanksgiving, with faith and humility."

JOB 1:22

In all this Job did not sin, nor did he charge God with folly. Satan seems to take such an interest in the government of this world in order to mislead people by their faith in God's attributes and his providence, so that they think everything happens accidentally or so necessarily that nothing can be thwarted, or that God's rule is sleepy, unjust, haphazard, and erratic. Satan puts these foolish thoughts into our hearts to attach and ascribe them to God's
Job 2:9–10 rule. This was what he attempted to do with Job's wife in order to defame and belittle God and slander his ways and providence among sinful people. In his second attempt he used Job's friends to debase human nature, to magnify the corruption that he himself had planted in it, to impress the justice and holiness of God on us as his only attributes, to depress us, confuse us, and bring us to despair through partial knowledge and insights, through deformed and isolated truths, through reasons that have been separated and
Job 2:11–13 torn from the context of divine wisdom and economy. Thus Satan
Gen 3:12 excused himself in Adam, "the woman that you gave me"; and he
Gen 4:13 humbled Cain, "my sin is greater than your forgiveness."

JOB 2

We see how Satan's rage increases with Job's virtue and steadfastness. He asks God to give him a greater sign for his unbelief. How great and terrible will be the judgment of this adversary. He has made us disobedient and foul in God's eyes. This too seems to be something petty to him. He seeks nothing so much as to make God unmerciful, yes, if it were possible, if he could get his way, unrighteous. He seeks to make the righteous God unrighteous towards the weakest, the most wretched of his creatures, who as outcasts and oppressed, as orphans and strangers, could of course be the first to pervert his righteousness and falsely gain his compassion.

JOB 2:3

God first maintains Job's upright piety, the purity of his heart, even though "*you*[187] *incited me against him*, so that I would *swallow* or *devour him*" (2:3).[188]

JOB 2:8

A piece of broken pottery—Lazarus had dogs to lick his feet. Poor Job had nothing but a piece of broken pottery,[189] a dubious, imperfect, dismal wick of reason, a broken reed as his support, something natural in appearance that was uncertain, dead, and cold, like the fickle paleness of the moon.

Isa 42:3; Matt 12:20

JOB 2:9

To torment Job, Satan employed the aid of everything that belonged to flesh and blood, to flesh and bone, to the weakness of our nature. He used his wife to relieve him of the only remedy which he demanded of Job and the only counsel that he offered by which, if accepted, she sided with Satan. When Job rejected Ahithophel's advice,[190] Satan dispatched three of his well-intentioned friends to comfort him and help him to lament, so that he would feel his misery and pain even more and give up hope of his recovery, since God must be just and Job must have earned this punishment through his sins. Yes, if he would not acknowledge

187. That is, Satan.

188. In Hebrew the verb that is usually translated by "destroy" means to "swallow" or "devour."

189. Hamann imagines that this bit of pottery comes from a clay lamp.

190. David's trusted counselor, Ahithophel, betrayed his master by joining Absalom's conspiracy against him and later committed suicide (2 Sam 17:23).

this, if he would not accept Satan's blows as God's chastisements that he deserved, he would bring down even more punishments on himself.

JOB 2:13

How much it pains us to have witnesses of our unhappiness, who, as soon as they see us and do not recognize us, cry out louder than we ourselves do and then, all at once, become silent. Job's piece of broken pottery gave him more relief than this silence, their mute staring at him. We may indeed find in the whole story of Job an account of ourselves and our own misery.

For seven days God let us lie in the deep humiliation that our sins had brought us before he shared with us a rather imperfect
Exod 24:15–18 kind of comfort through the revelation of his law, until he himself
Job 38:1; 42:10, 12 appeared, to instruct us, like Job, and bless us twice as much.

JOB 3

Should Satan get his way, then we would all sit like Job and regard our existence, our life, human emotion, as a curse. The wretchedness of Job disappears when we compare him with the rich man in
Luke 16:22–31 hell. Job sits in darkness. He does not know the hand that strikes him, the enemy that has deprived him of what belongs to him, the
Job 2:7 enemy that torments him with such excruciating, festering sores. He has an innocent, honest conscience. He, at least, has a piece of pottery to relieve his itching pain. Under the complete power of Satan, the sinner looks at the fire of hell in a dreadful light, the presence of the dreadful enemy whom he has served, and sees that he is now betrayed and tormented by him. He feels the furies of his conscience. His whole life, with all its blessings, rather than the day of his birth, has become a curse. Every moment, from the first to the last, is a century of sin and evil and the punishment for them. He suffers from thirst but is not able to quench it. He suffers torment and is not able to ease it in the least, even with a drop of water.

JOB 3:3

Let the day perish on which I was born! Job saw that there was nothing to blame for unhappiness except the fate of human birth. This fate seemed to be so terrible to him that all the troubles of human life were as nothing compared with it. Because he saw the reason for that apart from God, he cursed it, no matter how it would turn out. We must regard Job as a devout man who nevertheless seemed to hope in God only for this life and therefore considered that he was less fortunate than other mortals. God is so gracious that he has heard all our wishes in our misery and fulfilled them in advance by sparing us and removing so many curses that he could have put on us, that we ourselves know we have earned and deserved. How terrible and dreadful is the journey of a devout person without the comfort of divine revelation, which is a lamp to our steps, a warning to our enemies, and a message of our peace *Ps 119:105*
with God. If God chastises us, we see the hand that beckons us, *Rom 5:1–11*
apart from the fatherly rod with which it is armed. But if we fall into Satan's hands, he first makes us suspicious of God and then unacquainted with him in order to hide him completely and overshadow the soul with his darkness.

JOB 3:14–19

What makes the fate of human life so sad, and what are the troubles that Job discovered in it? Kings and counselors who built desolate places for themselves, princes that have gold, who fill their houses with silver, stillborn embryos that are not given the time to be what they should be, children who do not come to see the light, the wicked who are never at rest, the weary who can gain no strength, prisoners who hear nothing but the voice of the oppressor, great and small, masters and slaves who punish each other. *Job 3:14–19*
How Job expresses the weariness of life in his praise of the grave! We see the same too in the curse of his birth: darkness, where we have no light, imperfection that prevents God from taking part in the government of human lives, the light that falls back on all that

he created seems to have been extinguished in mankind. All those things that can make a day dreadful and a night frightful are combined in human life.

Reason shows us nothing more than what Job saw: the misfortune of our birth, the advantage of the grave, and the uselessness and inadequacy of human life—because we have no insight and feel passions and urges in us that we do not know the purpose of.

JOB 4

By the speeches of these three friends Satan has no other purpose than to rob him of a naturally good conscience by presenting him with a one-sided notion of God.

JOB 4:7

How can the innocent person suffer and perish when God rules the world?

JOB 4:17[–18]

God requires such righteousness and holiness of us that even his servants cannot have any confidence in depending on their service, nor his angels in depending on their own insights.

JOB 4:19[–21]

How can you people live/stand[191] before him? Do you not see from daily experience how you perish without him being concerned for you? What does your reason help you when it dies without wisdom in you?

FINISHED APRIL 9, 1758

I have stopped writing down my thoughts from reading the book of Job because they seemed to stray too far from its meaning and the understanding of it is too difficult. God will give me the grace to comprehend it better with the repeated reading of his word.

191. These are alternate readings.

So as not to lose what I have gathered and felt after its completion, the following thoughts will suffice for me:

1. In it we find the Spirit of the other books of sacred Scripture, the Spirit who explains himself everywhere through himself and gives his testimony of redemption through Christ everywhere as the purpose of his divine revelation. For us he described the Seducer as a mere snake in the story of the fall into sin, and here we find *Gen 3:1–7* his appearance among the angels sketched out just as simply and objectively.

2. The speeches of the three friends teach us how insufficient faith, or the knowledge of God's name, is that is based on his general attributes. Yes, they teach us how we can misuse them so badly through their improper application in particular cases, and how, instead of justifying God's wisdom and holiness, we can deny them. They teach how human compassion for the weakness and suffering of our neighbor is more acceptable to God than the justification of his ways. They teach how God is pleased with trust in his grace, conciliation, and love for humanity. They teach how dear it is to him when a devout Christian judges God's heart after his own heart.

This is what made Job's faith strong and gave him such an extraordinary revelation in his heart of God's mysteries that he could not possibly regard his punishments and troubles as God's will. He was not able to doubt that God was pleased with the uprightness and innocence of his heart, the honesty and simplicity by which he always tried to serve him and hung firmly on him, even in the middle of the ash heap. He did not allow either the great trial and affliction of God or the condemnation of his friends to assail him. He assumed that an enemy, a tyrant, had turned God and the world into his enemies and mustered them against him. He wished for nothing except to be able to speak with God about it. God heard this wish of his and with it the wish of the whole human race.

What a sealed book is nature itself without interpretation by his Spirit and its Creator! How many things Job mentioned to justify himself, things that must have occurred to Satan himself in his heart? How this spirit, who was allowed to stand before God, must have been shamed by the frankness, the steadfastness, and the testimony of Job's generosity to strangers, sufferers, widows and orphans, and so on, the generosity of an unhappy man whom Satan had, by his cruelty, put in such a wretched state?

We see how Job's assumption in 9:24 is affirmed by God's disclosure of his ways in 38:11, 22–23, 38–41. There are so many creatures on earth, which God has put under the dominion of human beings, all the creatures who do not listen to their voice and submit to their yoke that God also regards as a necessary part of the animal kingdom. However stupid the ostrich may be, she, when she is aroused,
Job 39:18 derides the horse and its rider. The description of the horse is not
just a painted picture in which nothing but its nature is copied in
poetic colors, but all its traits are found in the archetype of the mon-
Job 39:19–25 ster that God wants to show Job in pictures. Have you clothed its
neck with thunder?[192] Just as the devil is usually compared everywhere with the birds of the air, so there is the hawk, the eagle, whose
Job 39:30; Luke 17:37 last trait our Savior applies to himself. God reveals himself nearer
and nearer to Job (40:11, 12, 14). Behemoth is the first of God's ways (40:19). And above all he is confident that he can draw the Jordan in his throat (40:23). He is the king of all the high children of pride (41:4, 22, 24, 25, 31, 34).

We see that by his strong faith Job understood God's parables
from his answer: "Who is the person that hides his counsel with-
Job 42:3 out wisdom?" How should the all-wise God not know why he permits the power of this crocodile? From the repentant remorse with which Job humbles himself before God, we see how touched Job was by the danger in which God preserves a weak person from much stronger, invisible enemies than if the crocodile and Behemoth were his table guests and bedfellows. Nothing but the person of Elihu is still incomprehensible and obscure to me.

192. See Job 39:19 in KJV and NKJV. Modern translations take the Hebrew word here as the term for the horse's "mane'" rather than "thunder."

PSALM 1:1

The counsel of the wicked, the way of sinners, the seat of scoffers.

PSALM 2:3

What is the counsel of the realm of darkness, and what is the actual intention of the sinner? It is to break up the bonds by which the Creator and his Anointed One bind him and to cast off the cords of the Lord and his Anointed One. God bound Adam with the command: "You shall not eat from the tree of knowledge"; to attach him even more to it, God added a second bond to it with the threat of death. If you want to revoke obedience to me, then, at least, do not deny the love that you owe to you yourself. For these are tied together so exactly that it is impossible to separate them from each other. Satan discredits these bonds and cords for men as painful fetters and convinces them to cast them off. A mad delusion that is punished like the wickedness of Hananiah. We break a wooden yoke in exchange for an iron yoke (Jer 38).[193]

Gen 2:17

Matt 22:37–39

Jer 28:10–14

PSALM 2:7[–8]

This is the warrant for the claims of every believing soul, the warrant that God's Spirit publicly proclaims and seals in our hearts: "The Lord has said to me, 'You are my son; today I have begotten you (John 1:12–13; James 1:18; 1 Pet 1:23). Ask of me, and I will give the gentiles for your inheritance and the uttermost ends of the earth for your possession. You shall break them with a rod of iron; you shall dash them to pieces like a potter's vessel'" (Luke 10:20). The whole life of a Christian consists of a constant battle against the temptations of sin, the world, and flesh and blood, which he overcomes and tramples with his feet. In all these cases God's word is fulfilled that we would tread on serpents and adders and touch them unharmed. In Christ's kingdom to which we have been called, the kingdom which will shine completely bright in us after we have died, this inheritance of the gentiles and the possession of the uttermost

Luke 10:19; Mark 16:18

193. Hamann mistakenly cites Jeremiah 38.

parts of the earth, the judgment on God's enemies and our tempter and accuser, will be fully disclosed.

PSALM 3:3

You are the Raiser, the Lifter Up of my Head. God alone must give us the erect, upright posture that distinguishes us as human beings. God alone is able to raise the downcast state of our spirits. The Lifter Up of the Head is in its basic sense nothing but a term for the Redeemer, who again restores us lost people, like the Pharaoh's
Gen 40:20 butler, just as Evil-Merodach lifted up the head of Jehoiachin from prison (2 Kgs 25:27–30).

PSALM 3:5

This verse is certainly a prophecy of the death and resurrection of Jesus and of those who believe in him. Just as our natural sleep is in itself prophetic, so our Savior expressly refers to this concept as a key to the language of the Holy Scriptures.[194] The last verse of the
Ps 4:8 following psalm is to be understood in this sense. Since the service of God in the Jewish law and the Jewish church was so different from the preaching of the kingdom of heaven, so we cannot assume anything else than that a different management of God takes place after death, a supposition that seems to be confirmed by many passages in the Holy Scriptures. They rest from their labor just as we Christians rest from it. In this our destiny is the same. But is not the day of rest for the Jews of a different kind than the Sabbath that we Christians celebrate?

PSALM 4:1

You have extended me, made space for me or made me greater than I am, given me more courage, patience, hope and comfort by the cross than what the natural man is able to receive. How mysterious is God in his love! Even though we do not know it, the cross serves to give us our high status, our greatness, and our strength.

---

194. See the reference of Jesus to the death of Lazarus in John 11:11–13 as a sleep from which Jesus would awaken him.

PSALM 4:4

Converse in your own heart on your bed and be still. What is the voice in our own hearts that we call the conscience, or the whisper of reason, or our guardian angel? God's Spirit dresses himself up with our own voice, so that amazed we see his address to us, his counsel, his wisdom welling up out of our own hearts of stone. On our bed! The story of the evangelists often tells us that sick people were brought to Jesus and healed on the bed where they lay. They tell us that our Savior so often said, never in vain, "Take up your bed."

Matt 4:24; 9:32; 12:22; Mark 1:32; 8:22; 9:17–20; Matt 9:2; Mark 2:3–4

Matt 9:6; Mark 2:9; John 5:8

PSALM 5:3

In the morning! We see that the sunrise from on high and the dawn of salvation, as well as eternity, is to be understood here, because our return to God is our birthday in heaven. The next verse shows even more clearly that this morning alludes to the revelation of Christ in the flesh and the righteousness that was gained through this man.

Luke 1:78; 2 Pet 1:19

1 Tim 3:16

PSALM 5:6

In the psalms and the Old Testament, the bloodthirsty and deceitful man is always the spirit who was a liar and murderer from the beginning.

John 8:44

PSALM 5:10

Pronounce them guilty, O God! The prince of this world came upon an innocent man as a murderer on one who did not belong to him.

John 12:31; 14:30; 16:11

PSALM 141:5

Let my prayer, says David, also come to belong to the calamities of my enemies.[195] This is one of the most subtle descriptions of a Christian's victory over his enemies as well as of the embarrassment of the godless when they are punished for their wickedness. It is a common thought, since it is said that the sighs, the tears, of

195. This is a literal sense of a difficult verse that has perplexed translators and commentators.

this innocent person oppress this evildoer. David's enemies do not just teach him to weep but also even more to pray, and the power of this prayer and its loveliness was, in the eyes of his enemies, a fearful punishment that was added to the rest of their misfortune. When we go to the origin of these perceptions in such cases with the godless, they arise (1) from revenge, because the prayer of the devout person has hastened their misfortune, (2) from fear and envy in finding that Providence is on the side of the innocent person whom they have oppressed, (3) from shame and despair at seeing themselves robbed of this means for their establishment of what they like to enjoy.

PSALM 142:4

David is in trouble. He looks around himself on his right hand and sees no one who wants to recognize him. What he had regarded as a refuge disappears from him in the moment that he wants to grasp it or use it for himself—even those from whom he had expected more have no true concern for his life and his welfare. This is the reason why the help of such people, which is more for show than genuine intention and human love, is so null, so void. This comes, in part, as a new stage in the sad experience that David has in his misfortune of such people who engage with their neighbors and friends in an apathetic way, without any ardor and fervor.

PSALM 144:8, 11

Their right hand is a right hand of falsehood; that is, their strength, their understanding, their wit rest on lies and deception.

PSALM 146:4

We should not put our hope in people. Their life is so frail that their breath which they now exhaust in promising us hills of gold leaves them all too soon. Yet their thoughts are much more mortal and vanish much more quickly than their days. Perhaps, the good sentiments and intentions that they have for us perish in sin, because we, at least, doubted their sincerity. In this way David here contrasts the vanity of human thoughts and intentions with the vanity of human life in order to nullify our confidence in people even more.

PROVERBS 1:7

The fear of the Lord is the epitome of knowledge—not just human knowledge but all knowledge that the highest angels themselves are able to have. From whom do we have the power to see, to hear, to judge, to experiment, except from the Lord? And everything that can be an object of these powers is also his. From whom can we get the safest guideline for building up and furnishing our knowledge and the deepest plumb-line for reaching the depths of his wisdom except from him? To whom will the Lord more gladly entrust what belongs to him than to those who fear and love him? What else is religion than the clear, sound reason which has been choked and grown wild through the fall into sin, which God's Spirit, after pulling up the weeds, preparing the soil, and consecrating it once again for the seed from heaven, seeks to plant and once again restore in us?

PROVERBS 1:8

How corrupt we humans are! We are able to block our ears to this loving, gentle voice, which does not cry out with the commands of a lord, the laws of a judge, but calls to us like a father, like a mother, a voice that wants to win us, despite our unworthiness and misbehavior, by calling us a son, the title that she confers on us.[196] To flatter us even more in our weakness, she puts her words in the mouth of the greatest king that the earth has seen.[197] So as not to frighten us by her majesty, she borrows a human appearance, earthly majesty.

196. In Proverbs wisdom is personified as a gracious lady who offers her patronage to the student she instructs.

197. Here and in what follows wisdom is personified as a noble woman.

PROVERBS 1:9

She does not put a yoke on us, but jewelry, a simple headdress, chains for us to wear as an adornment, a mark of distinction to show that we are children of a king who belong to a royal family,
1 Pet 2:9 people of high rank.

PROVERBS 1:10

This sympathy that hides our true danger from the power of Satan, as much as possible, and us as nothing but Satan's instruments in whose use God has curtailed his wrath as an equal proof of his grace, is shown for us through all of Holy Scripture. What kind of sinners these are we can deduce from the description that strips off
Matt 7:15 their snakeskin and sheepskin and shows the wolf, the crocodile,[198] so starkly to us that we cannot fail to recognize it.

PROVERBS 1:15[–19]

Despite their frightful company, we have to force ourselves to keep our feet away from their footprints. So the warning is repeated about their inclinations. Their feet run and make haste to evil, they race to shed blood—should we be more naïve than the animals? A net is spread in vain in the sight of every bird that has wings. Self-preservation is an inviolable law for every creature. Should reason be of less use to us than a bird that would make use of its wings, even if it had only one? They lie in wait for their own blood and set an ambush secretly with each other for their own lives. These are the ways of every one that is greedy for stolen loot. It costs its possessor his own blood; he has to pay for it with what is best in his life.

This same point is repeated again in chapters 12–19 where Satan is presented as a wicked person who speaks arrogant, defi-
Prov 2:16–19; 5:1–14; 6:23–36; 7:4–27; 9:13–19 ant, foolhardy things, the wicked person whose ways are darkness, the crooked ways of a serpent—in the guise of a forbidden woman, as is common in the Scriptures, a flattering prostitute who

198. Hamann mentions leviathan, the Hebrew term for a crocodile in Job 41:1 as well as for the mythological chaos monster in Job 3:8 and Ps 74:14 that was identified with Satan in Isa 27:1.

has forsaken the guardian of her youth and the covenant of her
God. God's judgment on the serpent and its offspring is also pro- *Prov 2:17*
nounced on them in 2:22. *Gen 3:15*

PROVERBS 1:20–22[199]

This is a prophecy that was completely fulfilled, particularly in the incarnation of our Savior, by himself and the dispersion of his disciples and evangelists.

PROVERBS 1:33

Those poor lands that are now overwhelmed by war, or a traveler who walks on an unsafe road where he must expect hungry wolves and murderous robbers, come to know what is meant by a secure place of residence, not just a safe place to reside but also to be at rest from the fear of anything bad and evil. So much trouble never happens to a person except what he has feared for himself. The most secure evildoer knows the fear of sin from an anxious conscience. Even devout Job was unsettled in the midst of his success by fear from the trouble that happened to him (Job 3:25).

PROVERBS 2[:2–5]

Our hearing—our inclination and desire to hear! A cry for knowledge, a loud voice, an earnest prayer for it—seeking for it as something valuable—rummaging around for it as something that escapes our eyes unless we pay all possible attention to it.

PROVERBS 2:6

The same God that breathed the breath of life in us, from his mouth *Gen 2:7*
come knowledge and understanding. The Spirit that comes as breath from his mouth created the whole world and keeps *our soul in life* (Ps 66:9).[200] The life of the soul consists alone in his wisdom and

199. Hamann wrongly cites verse 23.

200. The Hebrew phrase can be construed either as either "in life" or "among the living."

knowledge. Without them, it is not much better than the breath that steams from our nose. Yes, it is blood in God's eyes.[201]

PROVERBS 3:2

Length of days and a long life and peace—in the old covenant length of years is often understood as eternity or the life to come. Taken together, both concepts can allude to a happy eternity, or else the first can refer to the length of a temporal life and the second to eternal life.

PROVERBS 3:16

We must take length of days, riches and honor as they are all understood in the gospel, because wisdom here is understood as the original word of God as well as the Holy Scriptures. The faith that God's Spirit works through his word, faith in Jesus Christ, is also understood here as wisdom.

PROVERBS 3:20

By his wise counsel the depths were broken open and the clouds dropped down their dew. He will reveal the severity of his righteousness with the same wisdom as he shows the wonder of his grace. He punished the first world with the waters from the depths and blessed the descendants of Noah by sending the promised Redeemer and the Holy Spirit. *Gen 7:11; 9:8–16*

PROVERBS 3:22

Gen 9:4; Lev 17:11 The life consists in the blood—your life is blood; it is forfeited; it is a token of eternal death. Your life is blood; you have been redeemed through the precious blood of the divine Savior. *1 Pet 1:19* Your righteousness before God is valid only in Christ. Through his death he has preserved us from death. This then is so when in the name of Wisdom our Savior promises *life to our soul* in his teaching. In Scripture the

201. This is a cryptic reference to God's assertion in Leviticus that the life of a person is in his blood.

neck mainly represents the will;[202] hence a stiff-necked person, a person with an unbroken will. His life and death and all that he has accomplished is ours in God's eyes. His perfect holiness is reckoned to us. It says, *grace for your neck*; the decoration and beauty of a holy life is vested on us as something Christ has earned for us. From him we receive the powers of the Spirit to fulfill our duties, powers that not only order and secure our whole way of living, but also our end, transforming death itself into a sweet sleep.

PROVERBS 3:27

All the following rules of Solomon stress those duties in which Satan hurts us most and in which our life is the greatest reproach to his wickedness. Through them we first distinguish ourselves from his basic ordinances and tendencies, and in them we are also able to recognize his influences most certainly.

PROVERBS 4:12

How much happier is the pious person than the sinner! He walks in the ways of a God who is *truth* and *grace*, and Wisdom is pleased to *lead* him on a straight, right, just pathway. Here we find a safe pavement, a firm, broad basis. If we walk or run on it, we do not need be afraid of any danger. By contrast, how unsafe it is to entrust oneself to the will-o'-the-wisp of a malicious magician, who at each moment deceives our senses. All at once he turns the widest plains into the narrowest, most dangerous mountain tracks. He makes a pleasing amusement for himself by rolling a block between the feet of those who run on his wide highway so that he can see them fall over.

PROVERBS 4:18, 19

These two descriptions reveal the blessed Offspring of the woman *Luke 1:42*
and his manifestation as well as the end of the serpent's offspring. Scripture is the shining light by which we see the path of the righteous

202. The Hebrew word for a soul is also the term for the throat (e.g., Isa 5:14) and the neck (e.g., Ps 105:18) as well as for desire (e.g,. Song 1:7) and will (e.g., Gen 23:8).

Man shine more and more until he breaks out in the dawn from on
Luke 1:78 high, which came to enlighten and redeem the whole world. While
Exod 10:21–23 Goshen enjoys the bright sunshine, Egypt lies in darkness. This is
the unique trick of the serpent's reign, so that sinners may not see what they fall over. They would be frightened, they would turn away from him, and he would lose all his subjects. The sinner himself will stumble on this darkness and be wrecked by it, just as this was also fulfilled.

PROVERBS 4:22

We all miss out on life and health. No one can expect spiritual life and eternal life without this wisdom. No one can be healed from the sickness and leprosy of the soul and from eternal death apart from this physician and the medicine for it.

PROVERBS 5[:1–6]

As Job unlocks nature for us and God teaches us in that book how we should regard the works of his creation in a reflected light, so in Proverbs Solomon gives us the key to what we call the world at large with its customs and its business. Saul is among the prophets;
1 Sam 10:11; Num 23:11 Balaam, who sets out to curse, blesses Israel. So among the children
of the light Satan himself is a teacher, a prophet, and the head of
Job 40:19 God's ways, like Behemoth. We discover how accurately the character of the seducer is here depicted and expressed by Solomon in the picture of a prostitute and adulteress. What a strong sketch is drawn by the one who knows our hearts! Her ways are changeable
Prov 5:6 so that you are unable to recognize her. This is the great magic of courtesans. Like silk cloth, they glitter with all colors and please the eye through the illusion by which we are entertained. They engage the eye with continual anticipation and amusement, so that we are unable to think for ourselves because constant distraction stops us from paying any attention to ourselves and other things.

PROVERBS 5:9

The seductive serpent has destroyed the honor that we should have
Rom 3:23 had from God and has tried to make us subject to his cruelty.

PROVERBS 5:15[–18]

The example of Abraham who quarreled with Abimelech over the well that he had dug, as well as the example of Isaac, explain these passages. Wisdom seeks to take the place of the faithless one in our souls. She offers herself as the rightful, chaste, tender owner of our hearts, as the one who was the bride of our souls in the state of innocence, who had to pay so much to assert her rights and gain our corresponding attraction through her steadfast love and the corresponding gift of our obedience through her obedience to the point of death, even death on the cross.

Gen 26:17–22; Gen 21:25–31

Phil 2:8

PROVERBS 5:22, 23

These sentences of judgment always apply to the whole of hell from its prince to every mortal sinner.

PROVERBS 6:1

Our peril and obligation to escape it are presented to us graphically in the picture of a poor debtor and guarantor who is harassed by a cruel creditor. All the passages that speak about indebtedness refer mainly to the concept of redemption.

PROVERBS 6:6[–11]

Here temporal diligence and laziness in our dealings is a symbol of spiritual sloth and the postponement of repentance, a symbol of sleepiness in God's service. The traveler is the one who goes up and down on the earth, and the armed man is mentioned by our Savior. Our poverty in God's Spirit will be completely exhausted by our association with a traveler who gets on our back. Then the evil in us will gain the upper hand and power over us to such an extent that we become as powerless against it as a naked, starving beggar against a well-armed man.

Job 1:7; 2:2

Matt 12:29; Mark 3:27

PROVERBS 6:12, 13

The main means by which Satan propagates sin is alluded to here: he *enters* with a defiant mouth, with arrogant *words*; speech and conduct, teaching and life, words and deeds are the same in kind.

He winks with his eyes; he speaks with his feet; he teaches with his fingers. He has made a pact to do evil and spread evil with his whole body and every member of it, by commands, tricks, indulgence, example, and all kinds of unspoken incitements.

Perversity, malicious arrogance, is in his heart—the aim of his thinking and doing is nothing but harm and unhappiness. The troubles of others are his joy and entertainment (Prov 2:14; Job 41:22).

PROVERBS 6[:16–19][203]

The birth, the fruit of his heart and his inventions that he brings forth from himself, is warfare, dissension, disunity. In the seven things that are an abomination in God's eyes, the following verses describe the wicked one even more clearly, the father and king of all sinners who works and exercises dominion over the earth through them.

PROVERBS 6:21

Scripture cannot speak to us humans except in parables because all our knowledge is sensory and figurative and, in all cases, understanding and reason turn the images of external things into allegories and signs of more abstract, more spiritual, higher concepts. Apart from this consideration, we see that God was pleased to hide his counsel with us and reveal as much to us as is necessary for our redemption and our comfort, but, at the same time, in a way that would deceive the clever people of the world, its masters. Thus, as the apostle says, God has made the worthless, despised things, yes, the things that are nothing, instruments of secret counsel and
1 Cor 1:27–30 hidden will. He himself even uses the snares that Satan had set for human beings to catch him. Yes, in his wisdom God even wanted to see him judged through those that he had seduced, through his own underlings, by redeeming a host of them in a miraculous way.

I repeat this observation so often to myself because it has become the main key to discover the Spirit, majesty and mystery, truth and grace, where the natural person has discovered nothing but a poetic
See 1 Cor 2:14 in the KJV figure of speech or rhetorical trope or idioms of the parent language,

203. Hamann mistakenly cites 6:22.

the times, the people, petty rules of business, Sirach's moral sayings in the Wisdom of Solomon.[204] So we abide by the revelation
that God gave to Job with the oddities of the physical world, with *Job 38:4–38*
the animals and the description of them, with Leviathan, with the
ant. Instead of looking for the kernel in this shell, we look for the *Job 38:39–*
connection of this visible monster or these visible acts of God with *39:30; 40:15–41:34;*
invisible, spiritual things. That's how we must understand the heart *Prov 6:6–8*
and the neck here. So too the following verse. Walking is the activ- *Prov 6:22*
ity of our temporal life; sleep is a picture of death; waking up is the
state of resurrection. How accurate, how appropriate these words
are then in this sense, while they remain obscure allegories if they
are understood in sensory terms.[205]

PROVERBS 6:27, 28

Here, as in so many passages in the Pentateuch and the historical
books, we find clothes associated with feet. Your clothes did not
wear out and your feet did not become swollen. I have already *Deut 8:4*
remarked on the understanding of this passage. Clothes refer to
the righteousness that was foreshadowed by the blood of the sacrifices and fulfilled by the death of our High Priest. We have the
loss of our clothes through participation in sin, which uncovers
our nakedness before God. We appear before him in the disgrace
and abomination of our inherited nature, which cannot escape his
wrath and his righteousness.

The feet stand for the powers of the spiritual life, the holiness and the gifts of Christian virtues that the Spirit of God produces in us. Our participation in sin makes us unfit for spiritual life with God. It cripples our powers and allows us to be plundered by Satan.

---

204. This could refer to one of two books in the Apocrypha, the book that is called by this name which Hamann assumes was written by Ben Sirach or, more likely, the book in it that is called "Ecclesiasticus" which was written by him.

205. Hamann rejects a reading of the Bible that is limited to what can be known empirically by the five natural senses. He instead advocates an analogical, figurative, typological approach that discloses and discovers its deeper, invisible, spiritual sense that transcends its natural, historical setting.

Here sin is aptly compared with coals, burning coals, fire, as the punishment for sin that pitches us into hell. Thus, we must, in all cases, recognize the serpent in the image of the adulteress and prostitute to get the fullest possible sense of the words.

PROVERBS 6:29, 30

Here we see how all the laws of Moses have a greater extent than only what human nature, or the Jewish nation in contrast with all other nations, considers for itself. The thief that is mentioned here is not just required to restore what he has stolen, in keeping with the law of Moses, but must pay it back sevenfold; that is, the greatest amount, which is greater than what we can imagine. He, however, had to be caught for this theft, and he was caught, because he wanted to rob and kill an innocent, righteous man, because he regarded the Most High as his subject and abused him as such.

PROVERBS 6:34

God has attached jealousy like a torch[206] to his commandments to warn people,[207] and this jealousy for human souls will bring down the same frightful sentence on their heads that Ahasuerus passed on the enemy of his wife and her family (Esth 7:8).

PROVERBS 7

The sad tenderness of a widow, who cannot regard the son from her body without sympathy at the death of his father and her husband, coos just like a turtledove in every address that Wisdom makes to the people.

PROVERBS 7:4

The blood friendship that God wanted to have with our human race is also referred to here. The fellowship of the Holy Spirit which would be the result of our Savior's brotherly love, is also contained

206. The Hebrew word for the husband's anger in 6:34, his fury, refers to its burning heat.

207. This may allude to Luther's relocation of God's warning in Exod 20:5b–6 as the conclusion of the Decalogue in his Small Catechism.

in these words. This is the faith in Jesus that says: "*You* are my Lord and God." The faith that *you* are my brother and high priest can *John 20:28* only be worked in us when we call on his relative, the Spirit that proceeds from the Father and the Son, call on him in the name of Jesus as his friend and our friend. Our safety against the forbidden *John 15:26* woman, against the serpent who flatters with her words and against her offspring, depends only on this.

PROVERBS 7:6–23

The beauty of these allegorical stories is unfathomable. How many different points of view! How graphically they are all depicted! What riches, what soulfulness, what light there is in every part and in the arrangement, the unity of it all!

Wisdom spies on the ways of people with the attentiveness of a girlfriend, a lover of the human race. She singles out young people and tells us the pitiful story of an unhappy young man who fell into the clutches of this prostitute, her unworthy fellow paramour. She hears the silent whispering of the heart; her eyes see in black, dark night! How accurately the greatest allurements of voluptuous lust, the most refined and most acute whispering that is able to cater to sensual taste, are strung together here, to display the whole power of our seducer, which so few people have the opportunity to plead as an excuse. Her outward appearance, her craftiness, her demeanor, her flightiness, her shamelessness in pressing her favors and bamboozling people through the stimulus of flesh and blood, the eloquence of her glances—she *showed a strong face,* she tried, with each ploy, to provide every possible benefit for her brazen conquest of him. The eloquence of her tongue that begins with her and borrows the appearance of prosperity and virtue, the frenzy of passion is a sham to cloak her shamelessness. She expends everything, her effort, her treasures. She promises safety and employs so many tricks against an inexperienced, ignorant, naïve young man that he is unable to resist any longer and is quite incapable of any deliberation and reflection.

PROVERBS 7:22[–23]

Once the serpent has made the silly man witless and thoughtless by all its tricks, by all its sophisticated eroticism, its victory costs nothing more. He proceeds anxiously without knowing where he is led. He makes a sudden decision and tries to carry out his decision as quickly as possible. In the light of this passage, we see the dominion of Satan over worldly things and those who receive them from his hand. He feeds them, he fattens them, in order to slaughter them. He turns people into fools so that he is able to act as a taskmaster over them. These pictures are not strong enough to portray our blindness to us. Our danger is even greater. The arrow of our enemy will not even give us time to become fat. It will pierce our liver before we notice it. Yes, we ourselves rush into the snares that he sets for us. He does not even have to aim at us, nor does he even need to expend an arrow on us. We rush into the snare because we do not know that it has been set for our life.

PROVERBS 8:13

God has had to pretend to be frightful and fearful to a human being to do what is evil for him.[208] God has had to deny his own love, so that a person would love himself and fear whatever intends to harm him. Thus, God has charged the consequences of sin to his account and taken what is evil under his rule, to separate it even more from us and give us even more horror of it by commanding us to fear it on his account rather than because of the devil.

PROVERBS 8:20, 21

Here the merit of our Savior is expressed by his fulfillment of God's law.

PROVERBS 8:29

When God established the foundations of the earth, he made a decree for the sea that its waters should not transgress his com-
Job 38:11 mand. In Holy Scripture the sea seems to be a symbol of hell and

208. This pronoun refers to God even though grammatically it could also refer to a human being.

Satan. Thus in connection with his prophetic miracles, our Savior is called the man whom the sea and waves obey. That is why it is said that Leviathan makes the deep boil like a pot; he makes the sea like a pot of ointment, because a chemical reaction produces the strongest fire and chemists produce the greatest reaction though fire. In this connection God has set the sand as a limit for the wild sea (Jer 5:22) and often repeats that he would bless Abraham and his family like the sand, not just in its number but also as the means by which the power of the sea and Leviathan would be wrecked and their waves would be broken. It is just as certain that the Flood belonged in the plan for redemption, and that God's covenant after it was a reason for the even greater covenant that was mediated by our Savior. This is why Wisdom attributes a special part in this work to herself.

Matt 8:27

Job 41:31

Gen 22:17; 32:12; Isa 48:19; Hos 1:10

Gen 9:9–17

Heb 9:15; 12:24

We see how extensively the following verses reveal the person, the divinity, the love for humanity of our Redeemer. See too 21:1.

PROVERBS 9:1

Here we have the seven pillars that appear throughout the whole of Holy Scripture and are revealed most fully in the Revelation of John.

Rev 3:12; 1 Sam 2:8; Job 9:6; 26:11; Ps 75:3

PROVERBS 9:2

She has slaughtered her victim; she has slaughtered a great and chosen victim. This is my body which is slaughtered for you! She has poured out, she has filled her wine; this is my blood that is shed for you! She has set her table; everything is ready; come to the wedding. She has sent out her maids, her angels, her messengers of peace. The cook of this splendid meal may be understood to be the same cook as in the story of Samuel (1 Sam 9:23–24).

Luke 22:20

Luke 14:17; Matt 22:4

PROVERBS 9:17

The devil has put a surprising backup in our nature by which he at long last tries to assert himself. He greatly abuses our greatest asset; I refer to our freedom. Every commandment seems to violate our hearts and arouse our imagination, which knows how to make something attractive, beautiful, delicious, voluptuous from the most trivial thing as soon as it is forbidden, a mere invention of our deceived fancy, and vanishes as soon as it becomes available to everybody. The mob (I refer to the mob of hell, the monsters of sin) goes so far that in their taste nothing except sin can season the enjoyment of the most innocent things. This is the salt that is so necessary for their nourishment that they cannot live without it; by it they dedicate each act as an offering to hell. Bread of secret things[209]—the daily bread of the sinner is from those things which they would be ashamed of doing publicly, which they must not dare to divulge to their own conscience or their closest friend. He does not steal wine because it is delicious or water because he is thirsty, but because it is not tasty nor does it taste better unless he first breaks the seventh commandment and refuses obedience to God with it.[210] Hence Satan provides a special sweetness for him in the water that he gives, so that he would not die from thirst. It is not the delicacies that he eats in secret, but bread that he turns into a reproach, a shame, a curse for him, before he discovers that it is good for him.

We come across people for whom this is not literally true; but we do not have to apply this only to them. It was not just the flesh-
Exod 16:3 pots of Egypt but the contempt for the manna, and not just that, but a plague of Satan in the souls of the Israelites that was revealed by their hunger for meat as an infectious disease through a boil on
Num 11:4–6, 31–34 the skin. God says, "My people have committed two sins; they have forsaken me, the living fountain, and drink from puddles that they
Jer 2:13 have dug for themselves."

God has put a hunger in our souls for knowledge, a longing to know, a restlessness when we see that we are in a dark and gloomy place. He has put the thirst of desire in our souls, so that we yearn and cry out for something good which we as little know how to name as a deer for fresh water, something good that we nevertheless

209. This is a literal translation of the Hebrew phrase.

210. See Exod 20:15. This refers to the prohibition of theft according to the Lutheran and Roman Catholic way of numbering the Ten Commandments.

recognize and gulp down into us as soon we come across it. Just as we find a rich provision for our temporal hunger and thirst in nature, which considers and caters for every taste, so God has also prepared truth and grace, bread and water, manna and wine to nourish and strengthen our souls. Satan does not grant us this; he produces countless devices, fashions, prejudices to promote his stolen water as a sweet palliative for all human desires, like a quack salesman, and to recommend his secret bread, his bread of secret things, as a pleasant means to satisfy our hunger. We see how the enemy of our souls presents miserable, tasteless, yes, poisonous means for the nourishment of the desires that God has given us, desires that can therefore only be satisfied from his hand and with his food.

PROVERBS 10:8

A stupid person, a fool of lips[211]—See also 10:10. I surmise that in the first passage we have a hypocrite whose honesty is only in his mouth. In 10:10 we have a blatant evildoer who discards every show of honesty and uses his tongue just as maliciously as he blasphemes with his life. The hypocrite and the mocker reach the same end. The person who winks with his eye, who is underhanded in promoting evil, without openly declaring that he is in favor of it, will be embarrassed by it. Only the person who walks uprightly is secure; on the other hand, that person who perverts his ways will be found out, will betray himself, and fall on his own sword. *Prov 10:9; 1 Sam 31:4–5*

PROVERBS 10:11 WITH 10:6

Here is how I understand 10:6. When blessing rains down over the head of the righteous person, when each person desires the same prosperity and wellbeing, then the godless person is speechless; his violence shuts his mouth. Whereas the mouth of the righteous person flows like a spring of life that offers itself to all, whereas it makes the meadows and fields fruitful and waters animals and

211. A literal translation of the Hebrew idiom for a silly chatterbox.

people, the mouth of the godless pours out its own violence. The
Lev 13:45 leper had to put a cover over his mouth—the example of Cain and
Gen 4:8–9 Abel can also serve to explain these two sayings. The first person in 10:6 says, "I do not know." The second person in 10:11 says in his heart, "I will kill my brother." The greatest power of passion is divulged in silence; thus, silent rage is the most violent rage. Once Satan has exhausted his lies, he becomes a murderer, or, at least, an
John 8:44 assassin. Yes, he only uses his mouth to wrap up and strap up his murderous rage. See 18:4.

PROVERBS 10:12

Love covers up all sins. Therefore God is love. That is how God
1 Pet 4:8; Jas 5:20; 1 John 4:8, 16; John 3:16 loved the world. The high-priestly prayer of our Savior, the royal commandment of love, the letters of the apostle of love,[212] the whole life and suffering of our Savior are an exposition of these
John 17; Matt 7:12; Luke 6:31; compare Jas 2:8 words.

PROVERBS 10:18

The story of Job and the story of the fall show us this fool who
Gen 3:1 wanted to be more cunning than all the beasts of the field and forgot that he had been created as a seraph.

PROVERBS 10:19

In the multitude of words there is no lack of sin, but he who restrains his tongue is wise. How inexhaustible are the proofs of this common truth! A rich person tries in vain to satisfy the poverty of his greed with his many possessions. The world makes no soul rich; instead it makes it always poorer, always thirstier; the more it has, the more it lacks. Thus, the richest spirit is the poorest; the unhappiest spirit is the greediest. Words are rich with the world's treasures. They are the small coins of wisdom; the mass of them becomes heavy, useless, and worthless for us. All the needs of human life and human nature are similar to each other; they are scouts that should discover

212. That is, the letters of John.

a remote land for us. Hunger is not given to us, so that we should do nothing but eat. Shame and nakedness are not given so that we should merely supply clothes for ourselves. The tongue is not given so that we should do nothing but speak. The body is not given so that we should work with it for nothing except our daily bread or attend to nothing except its idleness. God has given us so many needs; he has subordinated them in such a way that nature by itself can teach us their worth, the order in which we should satisfy them. Despite that, custom, fashion, folly, and sin itself in all its possible guises have disrupted and perverted this order. So Satan knows how to feed us words rather than truth. We see how he has filled the belly of reason and puffed it up so long with this east wind (Job 15:2).[213] The Christian religion therefore bridles our tongue, the loquaciousness of sin in us, so strongly by showing us *Jas 3:1–12*
how God will judge every evil idle word. In which societies is there *Matt 12:36*
more sin than where it is a disgrace to be silent and it is considered to be good manners and a skill for living to speak about nothing? We see how customs have been corrupted by this freedom of association. We see how languages have made it hard for us to avoid what is necessary and useful with useless and futile activity. Which writings should be taken into most consideration for their choice and richness of speech? The emptiest, the most tasteless, the most sinful! Thus, the excellence of an outstanding work is characterized by excluding, as much as possible, everything that is unnecessary, by saying the most in the fewest words and the strongest things most simply. Thus, brevity is the mark of a genius even in human creations; and everything big, all excess, is a learned sin. Is not sin itself the mother of speech just as clothes are a result of our nakedness? Would God's Spirit have needed so many books, repeated himself so many times, used such a cloud of testimonies and witnesses, if our sin itself, the magnitude of our unbelief, had *Heb 12:1*
not made it indispensable?

213. This presupposes the literal translation of this verse: "Should a wise man utter wind-knowledge, and fill his belly with the hot east wind?" In Israel the hot wind that came from the desert in the east scorched the land and never brought any rain.

PROVERBS 10:26

If we wish to understand this splendid saying, we must let the disciples on the road to Emmaus interpret it, because in them we see the
Luke 24:25 sluggishness of faith, the sluggishness of the heart for wisdom. This sluggishness dulled their taste for what they found in the prophets and Moses, so that they did not understand the power of God's word. Like smoke, it hurt their eyes. They were sad because they looked at the death and resurrection of Jesus through a fog, which gave them both a reason for sadness. When this sluggishness was removed by the preaching of Jesus, we see how their hearts burned, and with what joy their feet ran (Luke 24:33). They got up that very hour to return to Jerusalem. The Scriptures were opened to them.
Luke 24:45 The Savior was visible to them. Their sense of taste and the insensitivity of their teeth was healed together with this sluggishness of heart, and their eyes did not weep with wet tears, nor did they feel any pain, nor did they peer through the darkness of the smoke.

PROVERBS 10:29[214]

The way of the Lord is strength for the upright, but destruction (downfall, hell, and death) for the workers of iniquity. The more God reveals himself, the closer the devout person sees himself to the source of his happiness, and the more eager he is to reach it. The more God reveals himself, the closer he brings the sinner and corrupter to the goal that he has chosen for himself, and the more appalled he is at the outcome of his own ways, at the payment for
Rom 2:5 the unrighteousness that he has heaped up for the day of wrath.

PROVERBS 11:8

How splendid the sense of this saying is when we always follow the victory of the woman's offspring over the offspring of the serpent as
Gen 3:15; Gal 3:16, 29; Rev 12:17 the guiding thread of divine revelation. We have become righteous through the death of Jesus, and our enemy, the wicked one, is in

214. Hamann mistakenly cites 10:28.

our place. He himself suffers what he intended for us. "'Vengeance belongs to the Lord, I will repay,' says the Lord." *Deut 32:35; Rom 12:19*

PROVERBS 11:11

What does the mouth of the wicked one do? He is the accuser, the slanderer, the denigrator of our brothers. *Rev 12:10*

PROVERBS 16:6

Through grace and truth, unrighteousness (transgression) is purified. While the former moves our heart, the latter convinces our understanding.

PROVERBS 25:17

Seldom set your foot in your neighbor's house, lest he have too much of you and hate you. Does not God seem to go around with us as our neighbor? He alone is near to those who pray to him, those who call on him for his presence with them. *Deut 4:7; Ps 145:18* He lets people carry on their business and pursue their trade in the world as if they did not matter to him, as if they were their own masters, while the adversary unsettles the devout and the godless indiscriminately, like those who withdraw in order to trouble everything and rule everything.

PROVERBS 25:25

How pleasing should the reports in Scripture from our heavenly homeland be for us? How eagerly should we desire to read the news of peace that God's messengers have brought back to us? *Isa 52:7; Nah 2:1*

ECCLESIASTES 1:5

The sun crawls back to the place where it arose! I think that in 1:3 the seducer is often understood to be included with humans. This is one of those books in which Solomon seems to copy his father in making himself strange and contemptible to the Philistines. *1 Sam 21:10–15*

ECCLESIASTES 1:4

The earth remains forever. Scripture so often speaks about its pillars, its cornerstone and its enduring foundation, that I do not apply the understanding of this truth to the body of the earth, but to its inhabitants and the mystery of their deliberate preservation by God, so that, even if their races would also perish, the whole human race would be preserved in its stump and grow from an implanted twig into a tree of the Lord that was higher than the chopped down trunk. Thus the sun is mentioned for the same reason as in Psalm 19.

Isa 11:1; Rom 11:1; compare Rom 11:17–24; Isa 6:13; 10:33–34; Ezek 17:22–24

Here Solomon seems to make a sharp distinction between God's works and human works when he shows the transience and weariness of human works. So he mentions the first of God's works that are the opposite of human works. The sun rises and sets; even though it rises every day, we never get sick of it. Does not this cycle of things that continually renew themselves and set out to replace themselves make it possible for us to see the human race in the same state as before the fall?

ECCLESIASTES 1:13

All human wisdom, all reason, works hard and is anxious and troubled by the gain from its work. The further reason sees, the greater is the labyrinth in which it gets lost, the labyrinth where it, like Solomon, begins to draw conclusions that, at least, help it to get up and not despair completely. Everything is futile; everything distresses the spirit instead of easing and appeasing it.

ECCLESIASTES 1:15

Reason works like an eye with a magnifying glass by which the softest skin becomes disgusting, the tastiest meal a heap of worms, and the finest work of art a slapdash botch-up. We see how impossible it is to remedy all the inequalities in human society; we see an overwhelming number of deficiencies and shortcomings in it. Yes, the dullness and limits of our senses and intellectual powers cause us to find blemishes in beautiful things because we only ever see everything piecemeal.

ECCLESIASTES 1:17[–18]

One of the most refined tricks of the seducer by which he has tried to construct a more refined philosophy is the notion that the happiness of human life consists of a mixture of wisdom and folly, dissipation and concentration, the notion that the whole art of living and enjoying the world depends on the skill of weighing them off properly against each other and mixing them with each other. This is so because there is much grief and sorrow in too much wisdom; that is, too much reflection makes us depressed, helpless in the eternal whirlwind of folly.

ECCLESIASTES 2:2

The more we deviate in pleasure, the closer it comes to loud laughter, the more we feel that we are in a kind of frenzy and madness that is even obvious to a cold-hearted observer. All the more refined kinds of pleasure depend on the imagination; they are shadow pictures from this magic lantern that are so diverse that one person is always surprised at the taste of the other one.

ECCLESIASTES 2:10

Here we once again find a trace of divine goodness. Despite the futility of all lusts and the bitter after-taste that they leave behind, despite the futility of all our works, a kind of joy, a spice of pleasure, has still been put in our work, in our occupation, and especially in useful occupations that catch our eyes and receive approval from us and other people, occupations that satisfy us more than the work itself, because we ourselves often do not notice what was so enjoyable to us while we were doing it with our own hands.

ECCLESIASTES 2:12

It is truly surprising that wisdom and folly, like worldly goods, actually differ so infinitely, and that worldly goods are hardly differentiated here. The wise man is dissatisfied with himself, and the fool is dissatisfied with the created thing that he has misused to serve himself. It is surprising that they both, with such different resources, reach exactly the same end in such different ways.

ECCLESIASTES 2:18

Solomon hated all his work because he had to bequeath it to a person that he did not know and who would have control over it. How it must have pained God to see this earth, this home for humanity, under the dominion and in the clutches of the corruptor and hear a person groan over the life that he had breathed in him as a pledge of a higher, better life.

ECCLESIASTES 2:24

Even though the world understands this saying and carries it out crudely, it remains the best portion that reason can choose: eating created things and the blessings of nature, alternating work with pleasure, and, in view of future things, choosing to enjoy all that Providence intends to give us. Yet how few are able to join this party. It depends upon a lucky throw of dice from nature or from education. Without it, the mind is not able to have this contentment. It depends on a modest livelihood, a livelihood that does not tempt
Prov 30:8–9 us to become richer or make us uneasy about becoming poor. Yet it is also even more what Solomon says in Proverbs 16:33: "The lot is cast into the lap, but the whole order of it is from the Lord." Where does more chance, more randomness, more blind luck, more confusion, and more intermixture appear? Yet this is God's order. Every number and every blank lot lies there according to laws; it lies in its own place. Thus, with the best portion that a rational person can grasp, everything likewise depends on God's hand.

ECCLESIASTES 2:25

Who has more right to claim all people as an offering for himself than God? Who has more right to hasten the revelation of his name, save his honor, discredit his enemies, annihilate the blots on his creation, renew everything once again through fire and retire from his

work with the enjoyment of the bliss that he had at the beginning? *2 Pet 3:7, 9*
It is the glory of God to conceal a matter. *Prov 25:2*

ECCLESIASTES 2:26

All the futility, all the labor, all the exertions of people for wisdom, success, and rest that lead them, by so many different ways, to death, where every difference that they try to achieve on earth ends, are not intended by God for those who are devout. They are a curse that sin has put on humanity, which God, however, chooses to turn into a blessing for those who belong to him. These busy, restless creatures gather and collect for those who are good in God's eyes. Through the work of the sinner, these will freely receive what the sinner seeks and never finds, what he works for and cannot enjoy: wisdom, knowledge, joy.

What is God's word, and how is the wisdom, knowledge and joy that is contained in it received? Is it not the honey that is built up by bees in a slain animal? Whose are the stories that it passes *Judg 14:8*
on to us as examples of the labor of sin, of futility, and of folly that people have incurred? God's wisdom has even included this folly in his plan in order to destroy it, and he clothed his own wisdom with human folly. *1 Cor 1:27–28*

ECCLESIASTES 3:1

Here we find a list of contradictory things and activities that occur in human life. Since they cannot possibly exist at the same time, they require their own separate time. The most suitable, best moment for each of them has been determined, and a time has been set for every purpose that will actually be accomplished.

ECCLESIASTES 3:11

The beauty of things is in this moment of their ripeness that God waits for. If anyone were to taste the leaves or flowers of a cherry tree, he would make a wrong evaluation of it. If anyone were to judge the cool shade of trees in winter weather and by their appearance in this season, he would make a rather blind evaluation of them. Yet we likewise pass judgment on God's government and its purposes.

ECCLESIASTES 3:14–15

In its limits of place and time, every finite thing has eternity before it and behind it, whereas with God what happened in the beginning is present and what will happen at the end of time and days is present. How is it possible that, if all things are present in God's sight, the most trivial different thing could occur that he did not know about? How should we not fear God, who has not just seen and known us since yesterday and the day before that, but since the beginning, when he created heaven and earth? Whatever is, is present before God, and what will be is as if it has been before him. He is not just Lord of the past but also of the future, since that which has been carried away in the stream of time returns and reappears at his summons. This is incomparably more appropriate for God's greatness than the coherence, the necessary coherence of all things, since this coherence exists even more by means of God's freedom and the omnipotence of his will.

ECCLESIASTES 3:19

Just as a person and an animal are here contrasted with each other, so I consider the same for similarities between the angels and people.

ECCLESIASTES 4:8

Insatiability, the greed of Satan, is often enough presented to us as his main sin.

ECCLESIASTES 4:13

The kings of the earth are often called the viceroys of the prince.[215] This passage seems to refer much more clearly than many others to Satan. The poor, wise child is the one in the manger in Bethlehem that the wise men came to worship, and the old, silly Herod was

215. That is, Satan, the prince of this world.

the best copy of Satan. How was it that, like Joseph, this poor, wise child was raised from the prison of the sinful earth and from death and hell to the throne of heaven, in order to depose him who was born as a prince and ruler in the name of his human subjects and to hand back to them the booty that he had gained from him and divide it with us? Both the following verses are obvious prophecies of Christ's kingdom, his humiliation, and the spread of his offspring.

Matt 2:1–12; Gen 39:22–41:57

ECCLESIASTES 5:1–6

The offering of fools seems to correspond with the prayer of the Pharisees. They pray with their lips, but their heart is far from them.

Isa 29:13; Matt 15:8

ECCLESIASTES 6:2

All the riches, all the honor that the fallen spirit obtained, shall be ours. Yes, whatever he intended to steal from us shall be repaid to us sevenfold. The following verse is also a prophecy of the judgment that awaits the old, foolish king of sinners and must fall on him.

We may adduce from 6:5 how badly he will be tormented by his knowledge of himself, the memory of his good fortune and the awareness of the loss that he has suffered.

ECCLESIASTES 6:8

I assume that the wise people are to be understood here as those who are cunning, and the foolish, poor mortal as a devout person.

ECCLESIASTES 7:16

We see this righteousness, this wisdom of Satan, in his children, in the scribes and the Pharisees, and how he used them against Jesus. Satan seems to turn God's holiness and his zeal for it into a sword by which he wears out people and claims that their protection and support is unjust with God. He turns their excessive evil and folly into the different severity of divine vengeance, in order to hasten the day of their judgement. Nevertheless these two reasons that he boasts of are meant to move people to return to God and fall on the accuser himself. From this seed of the venom that Satan had prepared for human beings, the devout person would emerge as a new person who would fear God and destroy the accusation of his enemy.

ECCLESIASTES 7:20–22

Gen 3:15 All these warnings seem to apply especially to the offspring of Satan. We see how hidden the transition is by which God's Spirit shows us that our sin is the source of all futility, folly, and wickedness. And we also see the wonderful resolution of all doubt by breaking out from it as a result of all his reflections. He concludes that God makes a person upright, and that everything that is not genuine, good, very important, is an invention, a fanciful artifice of a stranger.

ECCLESIASTES 8

This chapter gives us a great light. Thus, our misery is so great because no one can foresee the judgment of Satan and the time for his judgment. Just as no one has the power to resist death, so the time will also come for the king of the earth. Then it will be of no help to him to lay down his weapons, and he will feel weaker than a mortal person. Just as one person rules over another for a while
Prov 8:9 to his own hurt, so this too will be the fate of Satan. What is called vanity in many places would be better understood as an illusion, a mere mirage, an empty delusion that misleads us and does not intend to enlighten us.

ECCLESIASTES 8:15

When we hear that Solomon commends eating and drinking, we must regard this advice as in Esther 3:15 where the king and his favorite sat down to drink. We must regard this advice exactly like Esther's invitation to her meal, which made her enemy so proud
Esth 5:1–7:10 and brought about his downfall.

ECCLESIASTES 9:4–6

I assume that the dead must here be understood in the same sense as when our Savior says: "Let the dead bury their dead." Thus the lions are all those who had the sentence of eternal death spoken over them. They remain ignorant of God's decree about the salvation of human beings. They can no longer expect any other reward than what they receive as temporal goods in the world. Their love, their hatred, their envy, which they inflict on the devout and by which they intend to oppress them, does not come into any consideration for them. Their right to receive all that would happen in the future for their redemption, their transfiguration, is annulled.

ECCLESIASTES 9:11

Judgment and time will make the swift shamed, the strong weak, the wise poor, and so on. *1 Cor 1:27–28*

ECCLESIASTES 9:12

Here a person is mentioned rather than the father of humanity, the one who was seduced rather than their seducer, because both belong to the Lord and would both receive his judgment.

ECCLESIASTES 9:14–15

Without any doubt, this is the story of our redemption.

ECCLESIASTES 10:19

Here money is to be understood as the ransom that was not only paid for human souls but also for the whole of creation and all the benefits that they enjoy.

ECCLESIASTES 12

This is a description of the Last Day and all the signs that would come before it. Hence, we have so many similar pictures in our Savior's description of the destruction of Jerusalem and the world and with the plagues in the revelation of John. Then the dust, the flesh, the mortal person who sought the same nourishment as the serpent, would receive his judgment, and the devout person would return home to God.

It also contains a prophecy for the days of the Savior and the work of redemption as the days that would not please sinners or

their seducers, the days in which Satan would unleash his final
Rev 12:17 power and rage against the children of God through his offspring.

SONG OF SONGS

In Ecclesiastes, God's Spirit has turned the sadness of deep-thinking reason into the kernel of his revelation. Here he uses the delight of the strongest and softest emotion that people are capable of feeling, the emotion that, like reason, is subject to just as great misuse and that all too often becomes a sword and the deadliest and most nauseous cup of poison in the hand of a frenzied person.

ISAIAH 1:31

The strong man shall be like tinder and his work (what he has created) like a spark, and both of them shall burn together, unquench-
ably. What eloquence in expression! What sense there is in the
judgment that God pronounces on sinners and the author of their
sin. Satan wants to turn people into the dead instruments for his aim
Isa 14:13–14 to build ladders from them to mount onto the throne in heaven. Yet
Satan himself becomes tinder, and the work of his hands becomes a
spark. They burn, they both burn, and no one who wants to quench
it can quench it (Eccl 8:9).

ISAIAH 2:4

The powers that God has put in us changed all our sins into rebellious weapons against God. After God made peace with men, they are instruments of divine housekeeping and are adapted to our soil, to produce the fruits of peace for God.

ISAIAH 4:1

Was this the reason why, at the time of Christ, many possessed
people cried out to him, "You, son of David, why have you come
Matt 8:29 to torment us before the time?" Presumably, Satan also used the
souls of those who have died as his instruments. These may be the
Isa 3:12 children that helped to oppress Israel.

ISAIAH 5:26

This, of course, refers to locusts. They, however, are also the same locusts that John announces in his revelation. *Joel 1:2–7; 2:1–11* *Rev 9:3*

ISAIAH 7:4

They were nothing but a black stump of smoking firebrands and thus belonged to one body and head. See 7:8–9.

ISAIAH 7:6

We see how the destroyer always tries to make breaches[216] in God's works and gain control of his church for his own benefit.

ISAIAH 21:16

What is the year of a hired hand? He certainly measures his time exactly so that he does not have to serve too long.

ISAIAH 25:11

Is there not a similarity to the death on the cross in this comparison?

ISAIAH 41:2

Called him to his foot:[217] this may refer to the words: "Walk before me and be devout."[218]

ISAIAH 51:9

From this passage we see how all the conquests of the Jews prefigured the promised land. The dragon is Egypt and Pharaoh. Here the crocodile is called a dragon.[219]

---

216. This idiom describes breaking though a city wall in order to invade and conquer it.

217. Hamann presupposes the following literal translation: "Who has awoken the one from the east in righteousness? Who has called him to his foot?"

218. See Gen 17:1 in its German translation.

219. Hamann identifies Rahab with the "dragon," the water serpent, the mythical sea monster (Job 9:13; 26:12; Ps 89:10), and the dragon with the "crocodile" as the emblem of Egypt (Ps 87:4; Isa 30:7).

ISAIAH 30:23–24

The rich pasture for the herds, the seasoned fodder for the oxen and young donkeys. Thus, the prosperity of animals depends on *Rom 8:22* our virtues and vices: our vices squeeze out sighs from a creature; our virtues display blessings to them. By a miracle the donkey of a prophet received the gift of speech, to blame selfish Balaam for the undeserved blows that he dealt out unsympathetically on *Num 22:21–34* it. Do we human beings consider the services that the irrational creatures offer to us on account of the wise order of nature? Do we not abuse our dominion over them? Do we not imitate the seducer and corruptor of our race who brought the curse on the *Gen 3:15* offspring of the serpent? Does not Providence, which watches *Ps 146:9; Luke 12:6, 24* over sparrows and hears the cry of the ravens, give us a better example? In the laws of Moses, we find a trace of what we owe to *Deut 5:14; 25:4; Prov 12:10* animal creation. The righteous person has mercy on his animal.

In Sparta the cruelty of a child to a bird was punished. Our cockiness and innate wickedness corrupt the habits of tame, domestic animals; because of us they have to lose their instincts and adopt bad behavior that is unnatural for them. We increase their savagery, we turn them into our neighbor's enemies, we mock their weakness, just as we do with the handicaps of our fellow human being. When you consider your subjects, think, as David did of his: "What have *2 Sam 24:17* these sheep done?" Like the magicians of Egypt, acknowledge the *Exod 8:16–19* finger of God even in the most despicable insect. Do not despise these unspoken ethical teachings because their charade of virtues puts you to shame. Their activities are mirrors of your passions, like Aesop's fables, natural symbols that instruct you playfully as they dress up for us with what is pleasant, useful, and attractive. Hear with horror how your Father, who teaches oxen to recognize the manger of their Lord, has to complain about your ingratitude, and learn to recognize the voice of your Shepherd *Isa 1:3; John 10:1–21; Luke 2:7* and follow him who left heaven to be born for your sake in a stable and a manger.

JEREMIAH 1:18–19

We see what danger a devout person is in and how much miraculous work God must do to sanctify him and to preserve and protect his anointed one. We see how much unrecognized good God does for us, how much strength he gives us that we regard as our own strength because we can use it as our own.

JEREMIAH 2:11

It is certainly one of the miracles of darkness how faithful all nations were to their idols and how unfaithful the only nation that knew God always was to him. How emphatically Jeremiah cries out: "Be appalled at this, you heavens, and be dreadfully shocked, be waste and desolate." *Jer 2:12*

JEREMIAH 2:31

Have I become a wilderness to Israel, or land of darkness? Why then does my people say, "We are lords (we have dominion); we will come no more to you"? What can language express more boldly than when God compares himself with the wilderness where they would have died from hunger and thirst, had the Lord not been their Leader; yes, even more than that, with the land itself where they experienced the horrors of slavery that had given so much unease to Abraham in a mere dream? *Gen 15:12–14* Is God a desert for us? Is he a land of darkness for us? Does he let us be without bread, water, wine, and a travel guide who transforms the wilderness of this world into a short ascent for us? Is the yoke that he has put on us as heavy as the yoke of Egypt that he has broken? *Matt 11:29–30* Is there a mightier God than he whose wrath inflicted so many plagues and sicknesses on Egypt? *Exod 7–11* What garden and what sweet, beautiful things does Scripture prepare for us with God's commandments and ways? What land of light do we see in them?

JEREMIAH 7:28

Here truth is depicted as the fruit of our mouth, or as a limb from it that has withered and so falls from its body or is shaken off from it.

JEREMIAH 7:30

Dan 9:27; 11:31; 12:11; Matt 24:15; 1 Cor 6:19; 1 Thess 2:3–10

This is the sin of Satan and the wicked angels: they have set up their abominations in our hearts, which God has chosen as his temples. All Scripture gains a large vista when we see the author and disseminator in all sins and the judgments that were pronounced over the nations and people extended to the spiritual world, just as we must look for the blessed offspring of the woman in all its stories and promises.

JEREMIAH 23:12

Their way will be slippery—in darkness they will not have time to keep their balance, but they will be *driven*—and therefore fall.

JEREMIAH 32

This record of the purchase made by Jeremiah is quite like the sealed and open record that we have of God's promise in Holy Scripture, the record that the Spirit has kept and preserved in an earthly container for so long.

JEREMIAH 38:11

Old discarded cloths, rotten rags, were the ropes with which Jeremiah was pulled up from the slimy prison.[220] An Ethiopian was his redeemer and advocate with the king.

EZEKIEL

This prophet provides us many examples of God's attention to the current opinions, preconceptions, and principles of people, which are taken up as proverbs (11:5; 12:22; 16:44; 18:2, 25).

EZEKIEL 18:14

The purpose of this case is quite unusual. The example of an ungodly father is most often meant to encourage a son to examine himself, to see—and consider—and not to do the same as him.

---

220. See the first of the *London Writings*: "On the Interpretation of Sacred Scripture."

EZEKIEL 24:27

Every sinner sees so many signs that remain mute and are incomprehensible to him until he experiences the punishment that he deserves. Then they begin to speak and cease to be mute; then we recognize hundreds of events and examples in our lives as signs, eloquent signs that are meant to help us to acknowledge the providence and name of God.

EZEKIEL 25:3

We find that Solomon's saying in Proverbs 24:17–18 is confirmed in so many instances. This malicious delight is one of the first sins by which we divulge the offspring of the murderer. It is so inherent to our nature that it seems to reign in us as a human instinct. It should be regarded as the grin or sense of humor of the murderer. *John 8:44*

EZEKIEL 26:2

Here in the name of Jerusalem, we see a prophetic spirit, a spirit that Tyre could not possess but which we can credit to the enemy of the Jewish people.[221] It prophesies that Jerusalem was meant to be the gateway of the people, and that God himself constructed and established a way to heaven through it for the human race.

EZEKIEL 26:10

His horses will be so many that the dust which they stir up will cover Tyre. Yes, her walls will tremble at the noise of the horsemen, the wheels, and the wagons. The hooves of many horses will trample the streets down, treading them deeper—what supernatural eloquence!

EZEKIEL 27

The chapter provides a unique, most outstanding fragmentary account of the early history of trade.

---

221. That is, Satan. Here Hamann repeats his claim that unbelievers and God's enemies, such as Caiaphas in John 11:49–51, can be unwitting prophets. See [6] "Fragments" § 3.

EZEKIEL 27:28

The *waves*[222] will *tremble* at the sound of the cry of your pilots (sailors). How much danger there is when a sailor falls down from his ship. It is a misfortune that is able to touch these coarse men and turn them into women, men who try hard to refrain from cursing even when they are in danger of shipwreck.

EZEKIEL 28

Tyre is such an important subject of the prophet because its fall [foreshadows] Leviathan, the dragon in the sea (Isa 27:1). The legion of demons that Jesus cast out went into pigs to drown them-
Mark 5:11–13 selves with them. In the Scriptures the sea often seems to be a symbol of hell's dominion. The following chapter depends on this interpretation.

EZEKIEL 29:3, 9

We find just what Abraham, and Isaac too, tried to guard from the
Gen 21:25–34; 26:17–22; compare Gen 13:5-12 Philistines and Lot's shepherds in the well.[223]

EZEKIEL 29:14, 15

How true this prophecy has become with regard to Egypt and with regard to the visible dominion of Satan, whom God has defeated and shamed by so many miracles as clear signs of the great miracle and the main victory?[224]

Who is not amazed that in their wars and conquests and in their victories and devastations the greatest nations of the world have proved to be nothing else than prophets of invisible things, a puppet show of God's providence, for him to reveal himself to the faithful through these signs! This consideration should make the work of redemption very important for us in human eyes. We must view

---

222. Hamann derives his noun, which is commonly used to describe the belt of common pastureland around a city, from a verbal root that is used to describe how water is tossed up by a storm in Isa 57:20 and Amos 8:8.

223. They protected the well so that Satan would not take possession of it and pollute its water.

224. This refers to Christ's death and resurrection.

the whole earth only as a celestial globe of the astronomers and its entire history as a map or a mathematical diagram for an exercise of the higher art of measurement and motion.

EZEKIEL 31:8–9

Who cannot but see that here God's garden is heaven or the whole of creation with the cedars as their highest spirits?[225]

EZEKIEL 33

In all these revelations of God's will that have been given to humanity, we too discover his judgment on those angels who fell from the original holiness and radiance into rebellion and sham appearance. Should we not therefore conclude that this Bible, which was given to the Jews and to the whole human race in them, is also God's law for the angels, especially those who are engaged in the rule of the earth and its inhabitants? All the sins that God holds against Israel then receive their great weight. Should we not think that God has given the angels time to take stock of themselves, or that he, at least, permits them to fill their measure before they receive their judgment?

Jude 6; compare 2 Cor 11:14

Ps 82:1–6; compare Ezek 28:2, 6, 9

EZEKIEL 33:32

We must not listen to the voice of the Holy Spirit in God's word like the voice of a nightingale, to please our taste. We must tremble at it. Like Ezekiel we must let it delight our heart so that it may make us strong, faithful, and undaunted in performing our duties and our divine vocation.

Isa 66:2

EZEKIEL 34:4

All these requirements are the duties of the angels and messengers among men. All these are reproaches for those spirits that seduce us, the spirits that resort to trickery to charm our hearts, so that it becomes so much easier for them to steal the flock. Violence—cruelty—like gods. Meanwhile, the one true God

Ps 82:1, 6; compare Ezek 28:2, 6, 9; John 1:14

225. The cedar was the king of the trees that grew on Mt. Lebanon, the king of the mountains. So cedars were emblems of the angels who reigned with God on his heavenly mountain.

becomes a man, and, in wresting with a man, he confesses that he has been unmanned and overcome. He uses truth and grace as the only means to win human beings.

Gen 32:25–26; John 1:17

EZEKIEL 37:6

How hard it is to convince people of the basic, easiest, and most comforting truth that God is the Lord! God has performed so many signs for the nations in heaven and on earth. He has confirmed many promises and warnings, all with this seal: "You shall live, you dry bones that death has made so ghastly and dry because you did not want to acknowledge your Creator and Designer and Preserver as your Lord and God. Despite this annihilation, this transformation into dry bones, you will be clothed—with sinews, with flesh, with skin, animated with new breath. Yes, you will live in order to acknowledge that *God* is the *Lord*."

EZEKIEL 43:19 WITH 44:9–16

The rejection of the Jewish people and the end of God's purpose for them to represent the firstborn of humanity is implied in this rejection of the Levites and the acceptance of sons of Zadok in their place. Only the sons of the Righteous One will be the Lord's priests in the new covenant. It is worth noting that 44:11 expressly restricts the work of Levites to the slaughter of the burnt offering and the offerings of the people as a directive for them about how their purpose and the purpose of their service as God's housekeepers for the revelation of religion and his name to all the world would be completed.

Exod 4:22–23; Ps 89:27; Col 1:15

EZEKIEL 44:18

This happens because sweat is the curse of sin, and it is meant to remind us of the sweat of death, the drops of blood, that Jesus sweated for us in the garden.

Gen 3:19; Luke 22:44

EZEKIEL 44:31

It is worth noting that even our food must be sanctified by an act of murder, an act of murder performed by human hands so that it can be enjoyed. But nothing that had been torn by wild animals or anything that had died naturally.

Everything that has life must first die before it may be used for human enjoyment, most of all, the highest degree of enjoyment. Why were people given permission to eat living animals after the fall? Because the sentence of death over Adam's family had been carried out. God wanted to enjoy the fruits of human beings even more and also permitted them to have greater enjoyment of living creatures.

DANIEL 1:2

God suffered because the vessels of his holy temple had been brought into the treasury of Babylonian idols, just as he had suffered because his people had been handed over to the carcasses[226] that Satan had given them for their service instead of the service of the true God.

DANIEL 1:4

We see how eager the corrupter is to choose the best for himself, to steal the best from God, in order to educate it in his folly and the speech of his country. For three years he fed them with the king's food and wine so that they might stand before him after that short time in their life.

DANIEL 1:8

We see how God prospers all good resolutions by which we devote ourselves to him and separate ourselves from the service of the world, despite all the difficulties that scare us away from him. He showed Daniel favor and tender love through the chief of the eunuchs. He persuaded him to consent to the test that the young man proposed—he let this test turn out well through an extraordinary miracle. *Dan 1:12–16*

226. This is an allusion to Lev 26:30 with its sarcastic reference to pagan idols as dead carcasses.

DANIEL 1:15

God makes his vegetables and his water more nourishing than the king's dishes and flasks. The young men were not just more lovely in form and better in appearance, but their flesh was also healthier and plumper than all those who enjoyed the king's food. Whenever God blesses the bread and water of moderation and childlike gratitude, we can do without much and thrive on it with much to relish. The four young men did not just acquire the language and erudition of the Babylonians, but *God* also gave them knowledge and skill, that is, living theology and living, active, effective, practical knowledge in *all* learning and wisdom, in letters and in spirit—yes, supernatural,
Dan 1:17, 20 heavenly, divine insight into historical events and prophetic dreams.

DANIEL 1:19

God fulfilled the purpose of the Babylonian king and his steward. They *stand before the king*, not in his service and at his disposal but to discredit his service and his purposes.

DANIEL 2:1

How easy it is for God to unsettle us, to wake us up from the sleep of complacency and futility—a dream, a vision of the night—yes,
Job 33:15 even more so, by forgetting it.

DANIEL 2:4

No matter how far all human ability extends, these are the limits that are set for the greatest minds.[227] To discover means to *construct*! All that we can do is to interpret our own dreams and the dreams of others. What knowledge of *something in the future* can we expect from those who needed the mystery of the previous night to interpret it? How can they foresee tomorrow who cannot review a dream from yesterday and today, yes, those who use this dream as the data to work out what will happen in the future?

227. Literally, "greatest spirits," a term that was used for the leading thinkers of the Enlightenment in France and Germany.

DANIEL 2:5

Why else do we lose sight of what is in the future than because we let the past slip away from us? A yesterday, yesterday now lost, makes our present today restless and useless for the knowledge of eternity, for the wisdom to escape future troubles.

How unfortunate we are to serve a tyrant who turns impossible things into laws for our vocation and into conditions for our preservation! How gracious is the God who uses even our dreams to warn us, the God who recalls the past for us and permits us to see into the future, the Lord who has all times in his power and uses all *Eccl 3:15*
times to do what is best for us and reveals himself to us in everything for our salvation, the God who allows Nebuchnezzar, one of *Ps 31:16; Rom 8:28*
the greatest monarchs, to dream about what the least Christian can learn from his dream.

DANIEL 2:11

Here we have the testimony of Satan himself to the truth by the mouth of his sages and greatest sorcerers, his testimony to the greatness and love of our God, the only God who dwells in the flesh and reveals himself in the flesh (1 Tim 3:16). *John 1:14*

DANIEL 2:14

We see how God uses only one of his chosen people to preserve the whole race of sinners and worldlings, yes, even Satan's favorites, while this murderer does not spare or protect his own sons from his own murderous rage.

DANIEL 2:15

God is a long-suffering God. He gives us time. Even though his will is mighty in doing all that he thinks, he is not over-hasty. Centuries have not been too long for him to put up with human beings and their wickedness and follow up on them; yes, to stretch out his hand all day long to a rebellious people. Blessed be the name of God from *Isa 65:2*
eternity to eternity. He alone has wisdom and power (2:20), and he graciously gives both to his creatures (2:23).

DANIEL 2:23

Since a Christian regards every possession as a gift from God, he
is not envious or selfish by regarding what he receives as his own
property and claiming the credit of it for himself. He does not do
anything good only by himself; he never receives anything good
Dan 2:24 only for himself. Daniel petitions the eunuch. He thanks God in
the name of his Anointed One.

DANIEL 2:25

Arioch brought Daniel before the king in haste. A true Christian
does not know the impetuosity of human passions, the impetuosity
of their judgments (2:12), the impetuosity by which good people,
like this eunuch, are often carried away in doing commendable
deeds. Daniel took time to thank God. He engaged in his prayer
about God's greatness with pleasure, with delight, with forgetfulness of himself—he turns Arioch away from the execution of the
Dan 2:24 murderous command, he frees the sages from blame and speaks in
Dan 2:27 defense of them, he gives God the glory and discloses this God to
Dan 2:28 the monarch before he interprets his vision of the night for him. He
corrects the bias from the preference that God had shown him from
the thoughts of the monarch, and prepares him for the application
that he would make of the dream in keeping with God's purposes.

DANIEL 2:31

People have found four empires in in this dream. I believe that it may refer entirely to the same empire. Yet since they foresee nothing but God's rule over the earth, the spirit of this dream must presumably reach further and include a more sublime meaning.

DANIEL 3:5, 7, 10

Here we see the arts and crafts in their full bloom and their most
characteristic employment that Moses describes for us in the fourth
chapter [of Genesis] right after the murder by Cain and his settle-
Gen 4:17–22 ment. We also see how Satan tried to work in a systematic way
by establishing the huge nocturnal image with a golden head and

mish-mash of all metals, an image whose feet, however, appeared to promise nothing eternal.

DANIEL 3:15

How quickly Nebuchadnezzar seems to have forgotten the God of gods and King of kings to whom he had paid such deep homage for the revelation of his dream in Daniel's eyes. Who does not see that this is the king of Babylon whose kingdom God has reserved for destruction at the end of the world? *Rev 17–18*

DANIEL 4

The mysteries of this miracle will, without doubt, remain shut for the human race until its last days are unsealed. Here we discover that the depiction of Nebuchadnezzar as a tree and the application of this picture to him is a sign that God rules over the kingdom of men and gives it to whom he wills and is able to set over it the worst of men. Nebuchadnezzar's transformation and restoration, *Dan 4:17* with the excellent characteristics of reason and devotion that he attributes to God, seem to me to relate also, in part, to the human *Dan 4:33* race. They explain the four living creatures of Ezekiel, because Nebuchadnezzar appears as a man, as a lion in his reign, as an ox in his transformation, as an eagle with hair and nails at the point in time when God restores him. He seems to think like a cherub from God when we compare him with his former state. Daniel's answer in 4:19 is noteworthy. It shows that Nebuchadnezzar must *Dan 4:33–37; Ezek 1:5–10; Dan 4:19–27* be an image of both the human race and the seducer. It shows that while he would be restored as an image of mankind, the dream itself and its fulfillment would fall on him whom Nebuchadnezzar also represented, the one who hated God and mankind, the one who is their common enemy.

DANIEL 7:15

Here the body is called a *sheath* in Aramaic.[228]

228. This is found in the part of the book of Daniel that is written in Aramaic.

HOSEA 4:1

There was no truth, nor sympathy, mercy and *love for the neighbor,*[229] nor *knowledge of God* in the land. All three are connected with each other and follow one another, with the last as the beginning. Wherever we have the greatest confluence of people, these three sources of happiness are in many ways buried more quickly. In 4:12 it is said: "My people seek advice from a piece of wood and their staff gives them revelations"; it is their prophet, for the spirit of prostitution, of apostasy from God, leads them into these errors.
Hos 4:13 They offer incense under trees, because their shade is good. In gratitude to the shade of the tree, they show it divine honor and forget the living God, his judgments, his name, his prophets.

HOSEA 11:4

All sacred Scripture and the life of every person should be regarded as the exposition of this saying.

JOEL 1:4

We see what tiny despicable enemies, what insects God needs to wear us down! Vermin that we tread down with our feet are God's generals that wage his wars against the rebels that are their masters.

JOEL 1:10

The new wine is put to shame.[230] A shame-filled person does not show himself; he hides himself as much as he can. He dare not speak or move. He is silent and awkward, without lips, without spirit and life. The oil is dull and sickly; it is colorless and powerless.

JOEL 1:12

Human joy gladdens and enlivens the whole creation! Sadness in the heart deadens its colors and dulls its melody. The sharpness of our perception depends on emotions, and the enjoyment of our

229. Sympathy, mercy, and love are all translations of the same Hebrew noun.

230. Hamann derives this causative Hebrew verb from a root which means "to be ashamed" rather than a similar root which means "to dry up."

senses, the fire of our imagination, the richness and fruitfulness of our thoughts depend on joy.

JOEL 2:23

The former rain is the teacher of righteousness.[231] Thus, we see the rain everywhere in Scripture as a symbol for spiritual blessing and divine teaching.

JOEL 3:13

We see how the measure of wickedness is connected with the fullness of temporal abundance. The most fruitful years are prophets of famine, while the wealth of a nation, its full bloom, is a sign of its end and downfall.

JOEL 3:15

Locusts, caterpillars, sun, moon, and stars—everything belongs to our God. At a wink from him they grow dark and become great armies (2:25), like the conquerors from the cold, northern lands (2:20).

AMOS 1:1

The words of the prophets are not like human breath. They are visible, *convincing*, certain testimonies. For those who hear and understand them, they are a light, manifestations of God, his holy name and his wonderful works (1:3, 6, 9, 13; 2:1, 4, 6).[232] Here the God who did not want to destroy Sodom and Gomorrah for the sake of ten righteous people, who commissioned Jeremiah to discover a *Gen 18:32*
single person in Jerusalem so that he could forgive the whole city (Jer 5:1), is so rigid in his threats that no more than three or four sinners and criminals would be found in the nations that he would punish. Should we not regard all the judgments that he allowed to come upon the human race as forced utterances of his righteousness,

231. The Hebrew noun here is the term for both "the teacher" (NIV) and "the former rain," the early rain which falls at the break of the summer drought in late autumn (KJV; ESV).

232. This remark explains how Amos is a visionary prophet, a seer (7:12), who beholds what God says to him (1:1). He sees (9:1) what God shows him in his word (7:1, 4, 7; 8:1).

because he discovers that those whom he uses to execute it are abominable in his eyes if they carry it out without compassion and mercy? It is never his will to uproot them completely; in all such cases of divine wrath the destroyer misuses his license to use God's sword—with cruel *instruments*, flails of iron (1:3), in the *extent* of it, with complete captivity (1:6), without remembering the covenant and the treaty of brotherhood (1:9). Let us, at least, think about the horror of our vengeance after it has been satisfied and how God acts in a human way to get us to repent of the evil that our wrath has induced us to commit, even when it is rogues such as our servants that we punish. Let us beat our own breast and remember that they are our brothers who thus remind us of our own sins. They remind us that we should not be diabolically minded against our neighbor and corrupt all our natural sentiments by knowing no end for our wrath, never allowing our vengeance to cease even against those whom we should have least reason to treat in this way but should instead fulfill our duties to them quite differently (1:11). They remind us of the purposes and the use of all these means and hellish passions, the insatiable greed to possess and be the lord of the whole earth, princes of this world (1:13).

AMOS 2:1

A godless person sins against another, becomes his executioner, and
so brings down the same sentence of death on himself. Satan himself
hounds sinners into hell to burn them finally in it. If God so punishes
Compare Luke 23:31 the dry tree, what will happen with the green tree? If God so strikes
the gentiles, how will his sinful people stand before him? If he afflicts
people who are dust and ashes, how will he chastise the rebels
against his throne who also stand before his tribunal like angels of
darkness? What does a person enjoy on this earth compared with
the happiness of heaven; a poor, naked person, to whom God gave
clothes of skin out of pity for him when he drove him from Eden,
the person to whom he here out of pity gives a pair of shoes for as
Amos 2:6 long as he wanders around in the wilderness of this world? Yet not
once does our enemy grant us this. He crawls after the dust of the
Amos 2:7 earth on which the head of the poor person rests. Could we have a

more vivid description of the murderous rage of Satan than this? This life has been assigned to him as prey by God. He will receive the dust to eat from which mankind is made.[233] The time becomes too long for him to wait for that; he does his level best to bring each person as quickly as possible into the earth. To please him, God, the tender-hearted and long-suffering, has to shorten the way of a mortal person because he could never be righteous enough in the eyes of our accuser. In the same way, we hear Satan panting after Job's possessions. He also demands to have the disciples of Jesus in order to sift them like wheat. Not satisfied with the souls that he leads away from God, he sets traps for the devout on all sides and tries to seduce the virgins that God has chosen into unchastity and adultery in order to desecrate the holy name of God in their souls and in all the earth. In many passages in sacred Scripture, money lenders are pictures of Satan; that is why Jesus drove them from the temple. Satan takes away what is necessary for life from God's children in order to give it back to them from his hand, provided that they, in turn, pledge themselves to him. All these are the temptations of the flesh by which he tries to get people to side with him.

Rev 12:10; Job 1:9–19

Luke 22:31

Amos 2:7

Amos 2:8

Christians are therefore taught to call on God for their daily bread and shun the table of Nebuchadnezzar. See Proverbs 29:13: "The poor man and the money lender meet together; the Lord gives light to the eyes of both."

Matt 6:11; Dan 1:8–16

AMOS 4:2

Your posterity with fishhooks[234]—comparisons of the sea with the realm of Satan pervade the whole of sacred Scripture.

AMOS 4:6

Cleanness of teeth from famine ... and the lack of bread—the expression is very beautiful both in its natural similarity and its figurative sense.

233. Hamann assumes that the dust which the serpent was given to eat is the dust of people who have died (Gen 3:14, 19).

234. See the KJV for this translation.

AMOS 4:7

God withheld the rain three months before the harvest. The prophets and revelations had to cease for a short time before the coming of the Savior.

OBADIAH

The entire prophecy against Edom, which has to do with the judgment that would come on the prince of the world, announces the
John 12:31; 14:30; 16:11; Obad 1 salvation of mankind. We see the pride of the corrupter, his cruelty in swallowing the entire human race, his craftiness in trying to keep his murderous rage secret and hidden, his downfall through the children of his own kingdom, his sins against people that he
Obad 3–16 was to blame for! Mount Esau shall be judged—through saviors
Obad 21 that shall go up to Mount Zion—the kingdom shall be the Lord's. Deliver us from the evil one; for yours is the kingdom, the power,
Matt 6:13 and the glory, forever and ever. Amen.

JONAH 1:3, 5

The freight of this single passenger cost the sailors so much anxiety and the loss of their cargo.

JONAH 1:6

While everything was in turmoil, all tongues cried out, and all the hands of those who were not the reason for the storm were at work, the one man, on whose account God had roused it, was sleeping.

How true it is, as Solomon says in Proverbs 16:1, that the thoughts of our hearts and the speech of our tongue are God's work to make sure that we do not overlook the reason for our own acts, the purpose of our own ways, and the meaning of our words. It is also true that God says more through our lips than our souls think. Did the captain of the ship here know what he was saying as little
Mark 9:5–6 as Peter did on Tabor? We hear and speak truths when we dream, and we hear and speak dreams, nonsense, trifles with all the effort and attention of someone who is awake. Lot said to his son-in-law: "The Lord is about to destroy this city; escape, if you want to save

your life." They stared at him as if their old father-in-law were childish. In Jonah's answer there seems to be just as great a confession of faith as his heart had felt or as he wished to express in words. It deserves to be compared with Peter's confession of faith in Christ. *Matt 16:16*

JONAH 1:9

I am a Hebrew—a servant, a purchased subject of the one true God; that is my status, my name, my family and origin, my vocation—and on that account I fear God the Lord. I know, believe, and fear no one else than the only God, and he is my Lord—the Lord, the God of heaven—in it are all perfections that befit the highest, infinite, only Being; as long as he is the God of heaven and Lord, no greater Being could be imagined than this; it is not possible that he would lack anything; nothing would exist that did not come to be through him; what would be worth enough that the Lord of heaven would be concerned with it and interested in it? The Lord, the God of heaven, whom I fear, has made the sea on which I now find myself as a paying passenger, a stranger, yes, a runaway slave; and the dry land where I as a man am actually at home and belong, where I was commissioned with a message and where I took a forbidden way to escape from it. He has made the sea and the dry land.

With this faith Jonah acknowledged his danger and presented himself as an offering to the sea and a redeemer of his ship from the sea that tried in vain to wreck the ship. His offering held the *Jonah 1:12* ship in the midst of its raging waves and also kept it back just as powerfully from the shore where it tried to land. Now a great tyrant *Jonah 1:13* of the sea arises, a giant fish that the Lord had prepared. It swal- *Jonah 1:17* lows up Jonah, and the prophet travels in its wide entrails and the chambers of its belly through the wide realm of the deep. He sinks to the roots of the mountains and comes to the bars of the earth. *Jonah 2:6* The dwelling place of the prophet is a temple for him, the belly of the fearful monster a house of prayer. Disobedient, simple Jonah, who believed that he could escape from God on land and chose a ship to escape so much more quickly from God's presence, praises God. He glorifies his power over everything and his grace and

announces the miracle of his redemption with his mouth and in
Jonah 2:9 his body. Where? In the heart of the sea that God had made, on
Job 40:19–24 its ground floor, in the jaws of Leviathan that God had prepared,
Jonah 2:10 the Lord spoke to the fish, and it vomited him out on dry land. As prophetic as Jonah's confession of faith was, so literally he had to see it fulfilled and confirmed.

The whole of nature does not have a more vivid metaphor for the offspring of the serpent, the frightful, proud spirit that rages against the human race, than the sea. This creature of God seems to be animated with continuous panting and breathing, like the puffing, laboring breath of a giant that is weighed down by the burden of the serpent like a flowing mountain. It is therefore the best image for the spirit world in so far as it is set in contrast with the dry, dead land. Furthermore, when we consider its great extent over the earth and the many scattered islands, we see many more similarities to the human race and in particular the church of God from these points of view. Foul salt—the spice and spirit of the whole natural world is tainted in it—makes it impossible for people to drink; it has the taste and effect of poison. Nevertheless, this water is changed into dew and rain and a sweet spring for us. Without it the earth and plants and animals and people would be nothing and could be nothing. While the sea seems to swallow up the streams and rivers without rising any higher, the benevolent sun steals the imperceptible evaporation from it and turns it into new treasures of water for the dry land and blesses its inhabitants with its booty. Yes, the sea itself must spit out its treasures and cast them on the shore along with its own fruits. The weak inhabitant of the land knows how to master its rage and rule over the sea and its subjects. Yes, he uses what seems to have been made as a wall that separated human races as a bridge. This insolent creature, the sea, is pulled up and down from the moon, like a puppet with fishhooks in its nose, in order to remind it of its similarity through a satellite of the earth.

It has been revealed to us that, just as the seducer has become
Job 38:8–11; Ps 104:6–9; 148:6; Jer 5:22 the tyrant of the human race, the sea has become the master of the
dry land; but it has also been revealed that the boundaries of land

and the power of both have been fettered, the sea by sand and Satan by the seed of the *woman*. It has also been revealed to us that the sea would dry up and the deep pit would become the prison for the enemy of humanity.

Gal 3:16; Rev 12:7–17

Rev 20:2–3, 10; 21:1

In Jonah we see two acts of redemption, from the power of the sea and from the power of the fish. We have been redeemed through water and the blood, and this double redemption from the flood of sin and the jaws of hell is the work of the Lord, the God of heaven, who has made the sea and the dry land, heaven and earth. God has revealed himself in two ways to the world like Nineveh, by the *miracle with its prophet* and by his preaching. In God's will the mission of Jonah, his first mission, was thwarted and delayed by the disobedience of the prophet and the people through whom God chose to reveal himself, to make his second mission and the actual advent of the prophet so much more blessed. The narration of his amazing story may have contributed much to the power of his preaching and the conversion of the people.

John 19:34; 1 John 5:6

Matt 12:38–41; 16:4

Jonah 3:1–2

JONAH 4:1, 2

Who cannot but be shocked to envisage God's forbearance with us sinners in our anger at it because it preserves our neighbor, while we remain alive through the miracle of it, shocked that we blame God for the attributes that are our only protection and comfort? We want to teach him to be righteous—we blame him for our own life and flee from him, yes, we despise him, just because he is forbearing, gracious, slow to anger, and abounding in philanthropy, and relenting from disaster for people who do nothing but evil, who think of nothing but evil, who wish for and extort nothing but evil from him.

Exod 34:6; Titus 3:4

JONAH 4:5

God, what a monster is our heart! How vilely your image is distorted in us. How disgusting we must be in your eyes.

Instead of praying for the preservation of our neighbor, we take pleasure in being complacent spectators of his downfall, in comfort and at leisure, and in their proximity we wait impatiently for the fulfillment of your frightful judgment as a show, a feast for our eyes.

JONAH 4:6

Here the same God who threw out a great wind from himself and arranged for a great fish also prepares a plant, a shady plant for Jonah—how childish his joy is at it! The same God also prepares a worm, and prepared a silent[235] east wind in order to kill Jonah's darling plant with the worm and let him feel the lack of it and the *Jonah 4:7–8* heat of the air. Who is able to read about God's philanthropic judgment, about the patience of his wisdom, without being moved and enchanted by it? The whole story of this prophet, its brevity, its fullness, its digressions in explaining events and customs, its amazing attention to great and little things, its variety and elegance, turn this book into a significant model, just as the prophet himself was *Matt 12:39–40; 16:4* supposed to prefigure the greatest sign and model.

MICAH 7:1

Nothing can be more moving than this parable of the prophet! God, the Lord of his people and the land that he had given to them, *Deut 26:2, 10* reserved the first fruits for himself.[236] He waits in vain for them, he himself goes out to glean what his servants may have discarded or left lying. In this we can imagine the sadness of our Savior who had, for so long, prepared people for his advent through his prophets and had worked to make them humane towards God his Father through his Spirit. Finally, he himself came to see how they had forgotten to devote the first fruits to him. How did he find his vineyard? How empty, how hungry they left him, without compassion, without the least gratitude to him! Who has done more good on the earth as a mere man, and whose remembrance, as a mere man, if one were

235. The sense of this Hebrew adjective is a matter of conjecture. It could mean that the wind was "silent," which is how Hamann understands it, or "scorching." In his subsequent reflection on Haggai, Hamann nuances his interpretation by imagining the east wind as a furtive enemy that sneaks up on Jonah to attack him unawares.

236. Here Hamann takes the "first-ripe fruit" of the fig trees to represent all "the first fruits" that were offered to God as the owner of the land.

to exclude God and our great Mediator, is more despised? Whose name are people more ashamed of than Jesus, whereas wise Socrates and Plato are named with triumph and reverence?[237] Whose life have they tried harder to slander, to disguise and darken with lies, while they tried so lovingly and conscientiously to discount the most trivial accusations against the heathen as slander?

MICAH 7:2

If we examine ourselves and ask the Spirit, the Author of Scripture, about the state of our heart, we will discover how true all the disclosures of the human heart are in the sacred books.

MICAH 7:3

They do evil with both hands—*first of all.* They demand bribes—the great people are not ashamed to express the evil of their soul with the mouth; they do not have enough shame to keep it secret. It is a weakness to hide its indecency and vileness. An open acknowledgment of vice replaces repentance and remorse.

NAHUM

Next to the wealth of God in nature, which arose from nothing, there is no creation that is greater than that of human apprehension and perception of heavenly, divine mysteries, this supreme power of human language to apprehend and perceive the thoughts of cherubim and seraphim. How the impressions of our senses swell, how they glow, how they are intoxicated with the feeling and vision of faith and the Spirit! Every single grape of the divine word is a whole vintage for a Christian. Miracles are all daily events, hourly experiences of life in God. It is as impossible for a Christian to doubt God's word as for a baptized heathen to believe in it. What belongs

237. These two Greek thinkers are the two founding fathers of western philosophy. Socrates, who lived from 470–399 BC, was championed by Hamann's intellectual contemporaries for his rational pursuit of truth. In his *Socratic Memorabilia* Hamann turns the tables on them and uses him as a figure to critique their certainties through Socrates's conviction of his own ignorance. His student Plato (c. 428–348 BC), the teacher of Aristotle, used him as the key figure in his dialogues.

to religion is more than the witness of the senses and reason. It requires a more certain seal[238] than the approval of these immature, bribed watchmen that tell us what they see in their sleep.

HABAKKUK 2:3

God's revelation to his *speaking, true* witnesses sets the end of the appointed time. Yes, its *certainty* is the reason for its tardiness and postponement. Because it will certainly, unfailingly come, says the prophet, what the unbeliever regards as delay or deception will happen soon enough.

ZEPHANIAH 1:3

Here the birds of heaven and the fish of the sea once again represent the angels of corruption.

ZEPHANIAH 1:6

The distraction and negligence of those who do not seek the Lord and investigate his will is just as sinful as the apostasy of those who have received his self-revelation and known him.

ZEPHANIAH 1:9

Those who fill their masters' houses with violence and deceit—that is why the heathen consider it best to believe that the gods are not concerned about anything except their rule of the world, and that they must be the authors and supporters of evil (see 1:12).

ZEPHANIAH 2:3

We see how God always keeps good, devout people in his sight. We see how he comforts them and gives them hope. He may not want you to notice when his wrath judges the world relentlessly. He will act as if he cannot find you. You will be hidden from him.

---

238. See 2 Cor 1:22, Eph 1:13, and 4:30 for this reference to the seal of the Holy Spirit.

ZEPHANIAH 3:7

Human evildoing seems even to surpass God's omniscience. He who sees the entire future finds that he is, as it were, mistaken when he wants to foresee the behavior of the sinner. A fearful person becomes as fearless as a lion when it comes insulting God. When God punishes him, a sensitive person becomes unfeeling and shakes off the blows of the Almighty like a dog. A lazy person outdoes the most industrious manager when he has the opportunity to travel on forbidden roads, the path of death and hell.

ZEPHANIAH 3:9

A *pure lip*, with which all will call on the name of the Lord, and the earth will *serve* him with *one shoulder*.[239]

HAGGAI 1:5, 6, 9

Godliness holds promise for this life and the future life. How soon human blindness would cease if people were able to consider their own ways and set their hearts on this promise. It would be so easy for them to build their own houses and maintain what they have built. Yes, what's even more than that, to have enough, to have more than enough—to receive and enjoy the blessings of nature with contentment and thanksgiving, to multiply them through moderation, to make them useful and taste God's generosity in every creature. *1 Tim 4:8* *Ps 34:9*

What is the reason for meager harvest from much sowing, the hunger and thirst that can never be satisfied, the cold that our clothes cannot banish from us, and the *moneybag with holes* that we think will keep our wages? It is the lack of divine growth, and this fails because God and his service seem to be an optional task, an unnecessary thing, something superfluous. Yes, unfortunately, a hindrance to our occupation. This lack of religion and Christianity in people actually produces disordered desires, which see so much and believe that they receive so little, desires that quickly turn the little they have into chaff through a hundred little pleasures and snacks,

239. Hamann gives his own literal translation of the Hebrew text.

through all kinds of extravagances, carelessness, and follies. These *Ps 1:4* are the bag with holes and the chaff that God claims to blow away. This loving Friend of humanity cares about our business, our money box, like a tender father. He observes whether we have a little shelter in the shade or in the sun. For us he himself plants a pumpkin to delight us; but he also prepares a worm to attack it and a sneaking east wind[240] that is supposed to warm the top of our head to test our patience and make us more ready for his blessings, to delight us *Dan 4:7–8* with better things than the mere shade of a plant from the ground.

MALACHI

This prophet is distinguished by the frequent use that he makes of questions and answers. He calls the one who questions the awaker (2:12).[241] Here God puts the questions in the mouth of Israel and the prophet, and he himself gives the answer.

1. How has God loved us? (1:2)
2. How have we despised his name, and how have we defiled God and made him unclean? (1:6, 7)
3. Why? Why is our offering an abomination in God's eyes? Why does he threaten us? Why are God's judgments announced to us? (2:14)
4. How have we wearied God's patience and forbearance? (2:17)
5. What have we said against God? How are we arrogant? (3:13)

We see that our Savior has clothed the Last Judgment with similar questions and answers. His coming in the flesh was the answer to all the *Matt 25:31–46* awakenings by which God had prepared his people for it. He came into the world to reveal God's love to us. God so loved the world:

John 3:16; Matt 5:17; Rom 8:3–4

240. See footnote 246n235 on Jonah 4:6.

241. Hamann assumes the following translation of 2:12: "But the Lord will cut off anyone who does this from the tents of Jacob, both he who awakens and he who answers, and he who presents an offering to the Lord of hosts."

he came into the world to fulfill the law, to atone for the desecration of his holy name and the spots by which our sins obscured his qualities, to suffer the punishment for them on our behalf, to vindicate[242] the God of righteousness and his forbearance, to send us his Spirit who would lead us into all truth and convict the world of sin, righteousness, and judgment, and let his whole life be a lesson and example of humility and a penance for our pride.

1 Pet 2:24

John 16:7–13

The last verse of the revelation of the Old Testament corresponds with the end of the revelation of the New Testament.[243] John supplements and responds to God's threat in Malachi: lest I come and strike the earth with a curse. How does this uncertainty about God's coming awaken repentance? How threatening is it? How comforting John is: "He who testifies to these things says, 'I am coming, certainly and soon.' Amen. Yes come, Lord Jesus."

Mal 4:6

Rev 22:20

Could the Jews pray with such confidence for God's coming and long for it as we Christians and the church of Christ here do through the mouth of his elder and beloved disciple?

2 John 1; John 13:23

MATTHEW 1:1

Here we see the mystery of the Holy Trinity figuratively: Jesus Christ, David, and Abraham. Also Saul, David, Solomon; Abraham, Isaac, Jacob.

MATTHEW 1:2, 3, 5, 6

We see how the Holy Spirit points back to the prophecies in the stories of the Old Testament. He mentions Judah's connection with his brothers, Tamar, Ruth, and Uriah.

242. In his claim that Jesus "rescues" God's righteousness by showing that God was righteous in his previous forbearance and in justifying sinners, Hamann echoes Paul's words in Rom 3:25–26.

243. The uncertainty is whether God will come in judgment or salvation, and to whom.

MATTHEW 1:17

We see how exactly God arranges the periods of time in symmetry and correlation. We see how he makes significant knots in the course of the ages that human reason cannot foresee. The era of Abraham ends with David, who ushers in a new age that ends with the apparent disappearance of the Jewish people in the Babylonian captivity, both of which were unforeseen in Abraham's days. This can be regarded as the *flood for the sins of the Jewish people*. Enoch and Elijah were forerunners for them, and the call of Abraham and
Gen 12:1–3; Matt 2:15 the call of our Savior from Egypt followed the flood. The time from the flood to the call of Abraham corresponds quite closely with the time from the Babylonian captivity to the birth of Christ. The end
Gen 11:1–9 of the construction of the tower of Babel and the destruction of Babylon also occur in the interim between both ages.

MATTHEW 1:19

Solomon was born from an adulteress and the mother of our Savior
2 Sam 12:24 was regarded as one by her bridegroom. How often we humans err! How often we slander God in our neighbor, when we think that we act justly, yes, more generously than other people! How we all, in our natural blindness, banish God's blessing for our home and our souls, God's Spirit and his work, the Son of God and the Savior of his people from their sins, out of shame, out of shrewdness like Joseph, yes, out of compassion. Nothing but an angel of the Lord is able to instruct us and throw light for us on the true matters that we should be ashamed of when we apply and use our natural virtues. For even what is good in our nature is against us; it contributes to what is bad for us. God's instruction in sleep and a dream makes us wiser and more successful than the wakefulness of reason and our natural abilities and good intentions.

MATTHEW 2:4

Herod's true purpose was to exterminate *Christ*. He was not ignorant of him, even less the Jews who recognized Herod as the Messiah and put their hopes and expectations on him as such.

MATTHEW 2:16, 17, 18

The murder of the children in Bethlehem was one of the signs that were linked with the birth of Christ. These innocent martyrs were the prophets and fulfillers of the prophecy that had come to pass. Here I recall the story in 1 Kings 13 and think that I have come across an explanation of the relationship between them both. A prophet comes to Bethel and announces the birth of a child who would be a king and a type of Christ (Zech 12:11).[244] Idolatrous *1 Kgs 13:2* Jereboam stretches out his hand against him who would immediately after speak the good message to him that he would be healed. *1 Kgs 13:5–6* He asked the prophet to join him just as Herod asked the wise men to return to him. Both had the command to return home by another way. *1 Kgs 13:7–10*

A prophet receives the report of the prediction that had been made to King Jereboam, just as the scribes and priests are here summoned together by Herod. His character presents their mentality very well among the Jews. This lying prophet receives God's word just as they told Herod the prophecy of Bethlehem. The donkey that would be spared was saddled by the prophet himself, and the corpse of the killed man together with the donkey was not touched by the lion. *1 Kgs 13:23–24*

The old prophet regards this murder as God's confirmation that the prophecy would certainly be fulfilled. Even so, these children, by their death, confirm the certainty of the report that the wise men had brought about the birth of the child. Just as Rachel is presented lamenting, so we hear the prophet who was responsible for the death of that prophet, lamenting: "Oh, my brother! My brother!" *1 Kgs 13:30* Just as David's lament over his son expresses God's sorrow, so I *2 Sam 19:1* believe that I hear the voice of the Redeemer in the cradle for his brother of the same age. In the old prophet we likewise see Herod, who pretended that he wanted to pay homage to the child when he sought to murder him; and this old man likewise reported a lie

244. This seems to be a mistaken citation for either Zech 12:10 or 9:9–11.

as a vision and then spoke what God would do, just as Herod did what God had promised through his prophets.

MATTHEW 3:4

Locusts appear so often as an image of divine punishment and represent the armies of the Almighty that John's nourishment by them and wild honey was a prophecy that foretold the nourishment of *2 Kgs 1:8* Christians, just as his clothing pointed back to Elijah, and the place where he stayed was like the wilderness that had to be crossed *before the promised land* represented the law, and the promised land the gospel, and repentance, the way of the kingdom of heaven.

MATTHEW 3:14

And do you come to me? Indeed, God and his Son are still so gracious today. He comes to us when we need him as if he needed us.

MATTHEW 3:16–17

These two verses tell the greatest event that has ever happened on our earth and in nature. They include more in them than when *Gen 1:1* Moses says: "In the beginning God created heaven and earth." *God* himself *man*; in the form of a poor man, in his own land, with his own people, he who had to flee as a child so as not to be killed, steps into the Jordan, like the leper Naaman, like one member of the brood of serpents and vipers that tries to escape God's wrath by *Matt 3:7; 12:34; 23:33* the fulfillment of all righteousness, allows himself to be immersed for forgiveness by the hand of a sinner. Behold! Heaven was opened above him, the Spirit of God appeared like a dove and settled on him, and, behold, a voice from heaven that says: "This is my beloved Son, with whom I am well-pleased." My soul, do not forget what the Lord your God has done.

MATTHEW 4:2

Gen 7:4; Exod 24:18; 34:28 These forty days are like the rain of the flood, the stay of Moses on Mount Sinai, the journey in the story of Elijah. We can therefore see *1 Kgs 19:8* how important the story of Jesus in these days, how much depends on them, from the fact that God's Spirit pointed to them so often in the Old Testament and kept them, as it were, always in mind.

MATTHEW 4:3, 6

This was the hard touchstone with which Satan began, and which, in the last moments of his life and on the cross, Satan used so vehemently against him (Matt 27:40, 42).[245]

MATTHEW 4:11

Heaven and earth are astonished at our indifference, at our hard heart of stone and bestial lack of reason with which we examine, despise, yes, reject a work that was done for our very best. It is such an amazing, awesome, great, and wonderful mystery with its whole blessing just for us. What a monstrosity is a human being, and what *1 Tim 3:16*
an inhuman monstrosity is a dead Christian!

MATTHEW 4:13, 18

Jesus our Savior chose a town by the lake as his place of residence. Here we find four fishermen whom he makes his apostles, and he calls the preaching of his teaching parabolically fishing for people. This belongs together with the remarks that I have made about the sea in a number of passages in the Old Testament and its use as an image of Satan's realm.

Here our Savior gives a sign of the power that he has over the souls of people that God does not use, at least rarely so, with as much control as the seducer presumes to exercise over our spiritual powers. The reasons for this are doubtless mysteries of God's wisdom and love for us. The impact of the divine call is so much more wonderful because it does not just come to workmen who love their livelihood very much and do not give up their source of food to satisfy a mere suggestion, but also because the management of fishermen and lake-fishermen seems to be, above all else, unsuited

245. A touchstone tests and so proves the purity of gold or silver. The touchstone for Jesus was the temptation to put his own salvation before the salvation of the world and use some other way to save it than by his death on the cross.

for such a calling. These people have an inherited love for water as their element and, like huntsmen, a special liking for its challenges.

Here our Savior calls brothers—brothers—the first two throw out their nets. They hear God's voice: "Follow me." They leave the nets that they have *cast out* and follow him.

The last two who are with their father *mend nets*; from that we should conclude that they previously had a large catch. Jesus calls them; *immediately* they leave their ship, their house and homestead, and father and follow him.

The first apostles and the teachers in the early church seem to be represented by those who cast out the net of the gospel, while their successors only needed to repair it.

MATTHEW 4:24

The Redeemer presents himself to the world as a charitable physician, and the sicknesses of the body belong to the ultimate purpose of his redemption because they are parables for the operation of the ailing soul. Among the many troubles by which the dominion of Satan was evident in our Savior's times, three especially are noted here: *demon-possessed* people, whose soul was perhaps less fettered and whose body Satan therefore regarded as his own, so that it was nothing better than a stage for the slavery of souls; *lunatics,*[246] people whose conceptions and acts did not depend on the will of their souls but on external impressions, people who were therefore not in a self-conscious state, acting in deep sleep as though they were completely awake, and, despite their deep sleep, are as active as if they were awake; cripples with a *paralysis of our limbs* that makes us unable to use them. Taken together, all three show the corruption, the misery, that our sin has inflicted on us. Once Satan has disabled us so that we cannot use our own limbs, it is easy for him to govern them instead of us. Then the moon takes the place of our souls. Finally, Satan himself replaces the soul of the sinner.

246. Literally, "the moonstruck." This term, which comes from the ancient notion that certain kinds of insanity were caused by the phases of the moon, is here taken to refer to somnambulism. It was also used in Matt 17:15 for epilepsy.

These are the unhappy people who seem to possess a demon rather than a human soul.

MATTHEW 5:16; 6:1

Our Savior always says, "your Father in heaven," when he wants to distinguish him from another father whose power we should avoid. *John 8:38, 41*

MATTHEW 9:34–35

How excellently the second verse refutes the slander of the first verse. The Pharisees seem to be so convinced of the explanation of the miracles of Jesus that they repeat them often, while the evangelists repeat them to show how this shameless theft claims God's honor and grace for itself in a most abominable way, in order to frighten people from doing the same.

MATTHEW 10:6

Which land can take pride in such a patriot, such a lover of the fatherland, such a human friend, as the land of Israel? How is it possible to regard the Jews without pity? The cruel treatment of this people seems to belong to the sins that the heathen committed against them. Have we not also been the murderers of this friend of humanity? Do we not, we Christians who call ourselves by his name, perhaps surpass their stubbornness, ingratitude, and hardheartedness?

MATTHEW 11:19

Wisdom discloses herself to no others than her children. She has not written, taught, bled, or triumphed for any others than them. Whoever would be her child will find all her treasures no richer and more wonderful than the power of imagination is able to reach. Who but a true Christian understands the prayer of Jesus at the end of the chapter and hears the echo of its sense in his heart?

MATTHEW 14

In this account of John's death, our Savior's death is prefigured. Fear of the people delayed his murderers for a while until the birthday of *Exod 4:22–23; 13:11–15; Matt 26:17–19* the firstborn was celebrated, the Passover. Then Jesus was offered up to please them and because of Jewish custom. The daughter brings John's head to her mother who had previously instructed *Mark 6:17–18* her. Herod's incest and his adultery with his brother's wife are only a new similarity.

MATTHEW 14:13

Our Savior took many voyages on ships, and his teaching was also widely spread by shipping. He wanted to sanctify all that was needed for human travel, especially those that poor people had to use.

MATTHEW 14:19

We saw the head of John on a platter given to the daughter, who brought it to her mother. Here we see our Savior giving the loaves to the disciples, who gave them to the people.

MATTHEW 6:26

Sowing, reaping, gathering into barns, like the fool in Luke 12:18.

MATTHEW 6:28

Worry about clothes is a female characteristic. So, since spinning is a female activity, our Savior associates it with lilies.

MATTHEW 7:7

Matt 7:11 The difference in the reception of good gifts and in prayer for them lies in these three expressions. Some matters must only be brought to God and sought for from him. Others must be brought with fervor, with the diligence that is due to something precious that has been lost. Still others with vehemence, like Jacob: "I will not let you *Gen 32:26* go, my God, until you bless me."

MATTHEW 1:18–25

We are God's fiancées. The adultery of sin, our intercourse with the spirits of darkness, separates us from God, just as Joseph here intended to separate himself from Mary. God does not once again recognize our soul as his lawful wife until the Firstborn is formed in us, until Jesus is brought forth in us and we have been born again by the Holy Spirit.

Hos 2:21–22; Gal 4:19; Col 1:15, 18

John 3:5–8

MATTHEW 3:11

Whose shoes I am not worthy to carry (Eph 6:15). The preaching of repentance, which John the forerunner has been sent to do and which he alludes to here, is the preparation for the gospel of peace. Just as John acknowledged that he was unworthy to baptize our Savior, so here he also acknowledges that he is just as unworthy of the high calling that God had chosen him for, to complete the stewardship of the law and be the forerunner, the messenger of the new covenant.

Mal 3:1

MATTHEW 9:21

My most loving Savior! I do not just take hold of your cloak but of your body and blood that I have received as a pledge of your wonder-working grace.

MATTHEW 2

How remarkably God lets an opportunity arise at the birth of his Son to call the attention of the Jews and their teachers to the time, place, and circumstances of Christ's promised birth. The murder of the children was not enough to make them think. Even though we see much that was extraordinary which could have, at that time, given the Jews' reason for reflection, it was all lost. Yet, in contrast, the sight of the child and his mother, whom the wise men had made inquiries about and whom they now found unrecognized and in conditions that could be regarded as contrary to their expectation and reason, was not able to mislead them or make them coldhearted (2:10).

MATTHEW 4:1–11

The temptation of our Savior must be taken together with the story of Adam's fall. Our forefather was in the garden that God had planted, with an abundance of the loveliest fruits. We see our Redeemer in the wilderness. In preparation for it, He, apparently, had chosen forty days of fasting in the wilderness to observe it so much more stringently. We should not envisage the fasting of our Savior according to the empty misconceptions of our monks nor compare his solitude with theirs, with the result that his life in the wilderness would be as empty as the ground on which he stood.

Here all the advantages that Satan has over us in our isolation, with his arrows that no mortal would be able to ward off, particularly when we are depressed, were given to the seducer to have over our Savior.

We have been so little born for loneliness that the mere footsteps of a person serve to encourage us; the mere traces left by our kind affect how we think and feel. Here our Savior is located in a place of social and natural solitude. We see nothing but stones all around him. We feel all the demands of our human nature more acutely when we are left to our own resources (4:2)[247] and the less we are able to satisfy them. Here we should contrast the hunger of our Savior with the arrogance that drove Adam to eat from the
Gen 3:6 forbidden tree. It was not hunger or lack of food but contempt for God's command, contempt for God's word and faith in the serpent's deductions, in his promises that it would be well worth trying to become equal with God.

In all these attempts that seem to be so beyond human nature, what would have been more natural than to make it easier through a miracle of divine omnipotence? What would have been more human than to use the opportunity that Satan gave to bolster human powers, in order to convince him that the Redeemer was God's Son? No! Here was the moment in which a man had to empty himself
Phil 2:6–7 of the divinity that he had not stolen for himself, to atone for the

247. Hamann mistakenly cites 4:21.

transgression of Adam who, in compliance with the serpent, had desired to be equal with God. No! God, who performs so many miracles to please any poor person, does not think it worth letting the prince of hell see his almighty power, which Satan would only feel from him as a Judge and a Conqueror. *Gen 3:5, 22*

Jesus uses no other weapon than God's word. Its power is in the use that he made of it in this extraordinary situation for all those who would be sanctified and blessed by using it for themselves in the same circumstances. It was Satan, it seems, who was keen to know nothing else except whether Jesus was God's Son. He employed a dangerous situation for that; he attacked him in the weakness of hunger to solicit a miracle from him so that he would no longer be uncertain about who Jesus was.

He suggests the opportunity for a second miracle from him by trying to clear the way for it with a prophecy. This prophecy had to do with the Messiah. Here the devil wanted to disguise himself as an angel of light. When this test failed for him, he seemed almost to have a suspicion about his divinity. He boldly takes off his mask out of desperation to gain certainty or out of contempt for a person whom he began to regard as a mere man. We should note the suitability of the place, the holy city, the pinnacle of the temple; all these were things that were supposed to hide him from our Savior as the seducer of men. As soon as he shows himself as such to our Savior, Jesus opposes him with his human nature that had been given for the exercise of our powers over all the beasts of the field and the most cunning of them. He says, "Away with you!" He accompanies his departure with another arrow from the quiver from which he had hit the tempter. The victory of a human being over the devil is easiest when he most clearly reveals and shows himself for what he is. The Ten Commandments, which we speak against him, which are written in our hearts, are able to drive him away.[248] Here the highest mountain is not as dangerous for us as when he tempts us by the needs of our nature, so that through the *1 Cor 11:14*

248. This refers to the paraphrase of the first commandment that was used by Jesus in Matt 4:10.

neglect of our duties we seem to have no other purpose than to make bread from stones, and when he tempts us by confidence in our powers, especially by vain confidence in our spiritual powers, he sets our feet, as it were, on the pinnacle of the temple and makes it our calling to throw ourselves down from it.

MATTHEW 5

The blessing of the new covenant is quite unlike the signs of blessing that God gave to the patriarchs.

MATTHEW 5:5

Here the meek can particularly be contrasted with the spirit of those times when the name of the Romans had associated the government of the earth in a common misconception with the specter of conquest.

MATTHEW 5:12

In your sorrow rejoice in my poverty with the meekness of the Spirit which knows no right for recompense, which does not even consider it worth resisting evil and injustice (5:38, 42). Do not just rejoice in your hunger and thirst, in your mercifulness, purity of heart, peacefulness, yes, in the persecutions of the world, but be extraordinarily joyful. Let your joy abound! The land of Canaan has not been promised to you, not the place through which our fathers were led to follow God, suffer for him, trust in him. The time of shadows has ended; the rosy dawn is here and it announces the radiance of the sun. Can't you fools and heavy-hearted people believe that my Father is pleased to let you see a few short, changing days here on earth? The reward that your fathers could know only in their temporal happiness would not be worth his effort. I am no longer showing you the sky, so that like Abraham you may count its stars; your sight will reach further! Beyond the foothills of the visible creation lies your fatherland, whose King you see before you. There is your reward. Great as heaven, great as its Lord!

MATTHEW 5:13–14

You are the salt of the earth. Is it not Wisdom herself who speaks to her children as children? What picture could be so easy, so common as this? This extraordinary, fruitful, and sublime concept here shows the office of the apostles, their dignity, the status that they would have in the world and the benefit that the world would have from them, their duties, their importance, and the greatest responsibility that they would assume for themselves even when they would like to keep their duties out of sight.

You are the light of the world. How precisely our Savior here explains the inherent impossibility that they would remain hidden from the eyes of the world. In addition to this reason, which he borrows from the nature of things and explains further with such a beautiful picture from nature, he also mentions the wisdom of God, who could not let it remain hidden but instead wanted it to shine on the lampstand for the benefit of the world. Jesus therefore impresses on them their commitment to good works, to a pure way of life, for the glory that God would finally have in their life as his ultimate purpose. As Lord of the world, God had tried to glorify himself in the old covenant through the miracles for the human race. Now his glory on earth depends on your good works. Your miracles will themselves be nothing but good works, works of love, alms for those who are lame, blind, sick, yes, even dead (Acts 3:6). Through your good works, God will no longer be known as the Lord of nature but as the Father of mankind; and his name will be revealed to the world just as he glorified it formerly on the field of battle with Joshua[249] through the staff of Moses.

1 Cor 2:7; Col 2:3; Prov 4:18; 6:23

Exod 17:8–16; compare 14:4, 17–18

After this, our Savior explains the purpose of his incarnation to his disciples, to fulfill the law. He unlocks its mystery for them in its unchangeable nature. He compares it with the law of nature and shows its superiority over the will of God that had produced nature and through which it was preserved. It is in God's power to abolish the laws that establish heaven and earth; but no single

249. Hamann calls him Joash.

letter, yes, no single stroke of a pen in the laws that are based on his holiness, can be deleted. The preservation of the laws of nature depends on their fulfillment. How could God, who had revealed his wisdom and almighty power, disown his love and benevolence and holiness? An unholy God! What blasphemy, what a contradiction! How could a God who had done so much to provide people with every possible proof for some of his attributes keep the greatest of them hidden, disowned, yes, unable to be used by mankind, yes, deadly and hostile to them? No, great God, you desire that your will should be done on earth as in heaven. The law must be fulfilled completely. you forgive us humans when we call your power into question, when we misunderstand your omniscience, like Sarah, your omnipresence, like Jacob, when we doubt your providence and love for human beings. You forgive us when we only acknowledge you as a glorious God and try to please you like our forefathers, because we consider you a good God and avoid what is evil, like Joseph, because it offends your holiness.

God has expressed this Spirit of holiness in his law, and our Savior discloses it here to us in a number of cases which we cannot read without trembling. Thus, the law itself is only a shadow of the
Heb 10:1; compare Col 2:16–17 perfection that we have obtained. The purity of the law and its holy meaning could only be revealed by him who came into the world to fulfill it through his life and suffering. Just as God's wisdom is
Rom 11:33 unsearchable, so he hides himself from human beings, so that they remain unknown to themselves. The more the knowledge of God increases and the brighter it becomes, we see our misery with so much more despair. The greatest light from God and the greatest sense of our unworthiness were not revealed to any of us before the fulfillment of our redemption. Here we have the solution for what Moses told us about God's command in Exodus 19:20, 24: God wants to reveal his law; he fences in the mountain; he commands the Jews to separate themselves from it. He seems to be afraid that they will come any closer. The ignorance of Moses about God's thoughts keeps him calm. God knew his holiness. He takes pains

to fence it in, so that it does not break out. Go back; tell them, so that I do not break out.

Holy! Holy! Holy is God the Lord of Sabaoth! All lands are full of his glory! *Isa 6:3*

In the contemplation of this, all human reason is lost. How right is the ecstasy of the English poet: the whole creation disappears; everything is nothing but God and me:

Thou, thou art all; nor find I in the whole
Creation aught, but God and my own Soul.[250]

Let us silently revere the arrangement of God's mercy that acts with such mysterious righteousness and fairness towards sinners and the devout. A sinner does not know God; he does not know his own misery, his own corruption, the horror of his own sins; he does not know the punishment, the eternal unhappiness that cannot but follow them. The sinner does not know his Redeemer; he does not know his salvation, which he spurns. Here we see a chain of errors in which there is a kind of relief for him.

The devout person, the believer, knows God; he knows his misery and corruption, but also the value and fruits of the great redemption, which makes the knowledge of God even more valuable for him and transforms his misery into perfection. He knows his Redeemer and the salvation that he has gained and prepared for him. What a house of truth and peace is the soul of the Christian! What a foundation! How one plank is held by another! What a rock that defies the gates of hell and seems to be made for the eternity that God has promised! *Matt 16:18*

MATTHEW 5:23

With great power our Savior here tries to moderate the holiness of the law for human beings and make its rays less harmful for the eyes of his weak hearers through the clouds that he gives for them by showing them the application by which they in their human weakness could come as close as possible to the holiness of the fifth

250. Edward Young (1681–1765), "The Consolation: Night 9," *Night Thoughts*, lines 1586–91.

commandment.[251] It would be his calling to fulfill the whole law. As
for them, God, however, would be satisfied with the kind of fulfillment that he gives as an example. It is not possible for us humans
to keep such close scrutiny of all our thoughts, the emotions of the
heart, that a countless number of them would not be manslaughter
in God's eyes. So God instituted sacrifices in which he required the
blood of animals instead of their blood. If you, therefore, go to present such a sacrifice (the reference to this event is unique because
he also reminds his hearers of the satisfaction and fulfillment of the
law which was prefigured by the sacrifices), if you then are engaged
in this kind of enactment, our Savior moderates it still more: If you
remember any sin (God will also overlook the sins that you have
forgotten), then leave your gift before the altar. God will gladly see
you delay the service that you intended for him, in order to do what
is righteous to your neighbor. You cannot love him as long as you do
not love your neighbor, and this love for your neighbor requires a
sign of your love for him from you. Let God wait; first hurry to make
a friend of your brother; then he as a reconciled brother will also
show himself as God reconciled to you. Go quickly, while you are
Matt 5:24 still going on your way with your brother, while you are still living
on earth and are able to do so. When both of you appear before
the Judge, then it will be too late to think of a favorable settlement;
then you must depend on his judgment. Every new picture that
our Savior uses gives a new reason. In matters that have to do with
your souls, you must use the same shrewdness as in your worldly
Luke 16:1–9 dealings—have the same fear of God that you have of your temporal
judge, fear the enemy of your souls, the ferocious lion, more than
1 Pet 5:8 you fear a ferocious brother, fear the punishment that awaits you
in God's judgment more than what an earthly judge can inflict on
you. If you waste the time, there will be no escape for you until you
Matt 5:26 have paid the last penny. Because you are unable to do that, I have
Matt 20:28 come into the world. If you want to discard my ransom payment,

251. This is commonly regarded as the sixth commandment, "Thou shalt not kill," in the Reformed tradition.

then everlasting, eternal damnation is as certain for your souls as an obliteration of heaven and earth.

MATTHEW 5:29–30

Nothing is more natural for a man than the love of his own body and its members. Nothing is more painful and uncomfortable than to lose one of them or to experience the mutilation of one of them. Our Savior employs these reasons with such severity in order to dramatize the baseness of sin and the rigor by which the law commands it to be uprooted, along with the greatness of the punishments that are inflicted on its transgressors. The law condemns everyone who looks at a woman with a lustful eye just as rigorously as an actual adulterer. Zaleucus punished adulterers with the loss of both their eyes.[252] The law of my heavenly Father cannot punish it in any other way than with the wages of all sin, hell. Should you not do the same *Rom 6:23* thing to preserve your body that this blind heathen did with the eye of his son? Would you not, like him, gladly tear out your eye, your best eye that misled you into sin, your eye that begot sinful lust in your soul, and throw it away from you, rather than see your whole body tormented for eternity in hell? You poor person, your hand would have performed this necessary cruelty in vain on your sinful eye! This hand would deserve a similar punishment. If you too should ruin your eye with this hand to save your body and its other limbs, would you not just as willingly chop off your own hand and throw it away from you, and consider it better to be mutilated with your eyes and hands than to see your body, all your limbs, tormented in hell? Would not all the limbs be missing if you did this? Would you not, with the loss, with the painful, unnatural loss of them all, likewise have to suffer the loss of what you believed you would gain by their loss? If your body therefore is unable to redeem itself, even if you should treat it ever so cruelly, what can

252. Zaleucus, a legendary Greek lawmaker who lived in Locri in southern Italy during the seventh century BC, compiled the first written code of law in Europe. When his own son was found guilty of adultery, Zaleucus is said to have insisted on the removal of one of his own eyes so that his son could keep one of his.

you do for your soul? With what foolhardy means do you then believe that you will find the redemption of an immortal spirit?

Yet, even if somebody would be able to atone for his own sins by his self-annihilation, which is itself also a sin and humanly impossible, do you think that the law would be fulfilled? How would you atone for the sins of others that you are accountable for under the law? I tell you that if a husband whom God in his law permits to divorce his wife abuses his freedom, he will, in God's judgment, be held guilty for all those sins that his divorce has caused. He will be punished as an adulterer for the sexual immorality of his wife, and he will be to blame that the man who marries his divorced wife is also an adulterer in God's eyes.

MATTHEW 5:33

Truth is only sacred for you when you bind it with an oath. I tell you, all your speech in which yes is not yes, no is not no, and all your dealings which need more conditions, evasions, and assurances than these expressions that state the approval of your judgment and the thoughts of your hearts, are sins in God's eyes. They presuppose that you diverge from the love for truth and righteousness
Eph 4:20–25 with which God has created you.

Do not think that you can use heaven or the earth or Jerusalem or your life and head to confirm your lies and cloak your deception and unrighteousness! It is truth and holiness that make heaven God's throne and the earth God's footstool, Jerusalem the city of the great King and your life and head! Am I not in the form of a man on your account? How little you acknowledge your own worth in God's eyes! My suffering will disclose all this to you! Let me ask you, you who use your head as a pledge for your deception and injustice or for your frivolity: How far does your control extend over it? Are you able to produce a white or black hair, a tiny change of color in this product of its impurity?

MATTHEW 5:38, 42

You regard the law of retaliation as a sacred law of nature. How little you know it! What if this right of retaliation were enacted with your debts, your sins; what if God would avenge your sins, just as you avenge the failures of your neighbor! Let his patience with you be an example for your patience with your brother. Is it a miracle that you can live together honestly and peacefully with your offenses against God every moment in your thoughts, words, and deeds, especially in those that you consider lawful or innocent, as I have shown you? Is it a miracle that you want to resist the evil person that God tolerates? Is it a miracle that even the observance *Matt 5:39*
of some commandments, the imperfect observance of them, should give you such pride that you demand the greatest justice from your neighbor? To be sure, your neighbor may strike you even though you are innocent. He may corrupt the laws by bribery, or pervert them in order to harm you with your possessions. He may use compulsory measures to acquire what you are not obliged to give. He may wish to grab from you what he should ask for, or try to beg you for your money under the pretense of borrowing it, or, even more, seek your company out of self-interest. Even so, think how much better it is to be abused than to abuse. Give such a person something more in addition so that he receives the payment for his offense, and regard this as a thank offering that God pays him because he has removed the opportunity and desire[253] for you to do additional harm, for it is not the result of your will but of circumstances that you are not the abuser instead of him, but a fortunately abused person. You don't know the danger that is associated with always opposing an evil person. Every so often we ourselves become unjust in wanting to prevent others from being unjust. We ourselves become sick when we want to be physicians for others. Do not resist an evil person. The hand of God can turn the poison that your neighbor tries to administer to you into a means for your health. He can turn his curse into a blessing for you. He intends to

253. Literally, "the heart."

Gen 50:20 do evil for you and God intends something good for you. At the very least, your patience will be rewarded by God and contribute to the shame and dishonor of your neighbor. In the last two cases our Savior provides special disclosures of the human heart. We have an unfortunate sharp-sightedness in cleverly assessing the intentions of our neighbor and the nature and manner of his engagement with us. The mere appearance of insincerity is enough for us to turn far away from our duties to him. My brother demands something that I am not obliged to give, or he makes empty promises about it to me. This makes us turn against him and our own duties to him. So we think that we have the right to do the opposite of what he demands, or to refuse to give him what he has asked for. Our brother pursues us. He knows that we have the means, and we know what he needs. So we avoid him as much as possible and don't let him get too close to us.

MARK 4:20

To *receive* and *understand* the word.[254] What belongs to taking in and understanding the word? A prepared field; repentance, a contrite heart, a broken spirit. This is the plough and harrow of the Holy Spirit (8:17). *Ps 51:17; Isa 57:15*

MARK 4:24, 25

Hearing and *having*. Only the soil that receives the seed after appropriate preparation becomes fruitful and gains full ears instead of a single grain. Where that is missing, the grain and its fruit are lost.

MARK 4:34

This is what the Holy Spirit still does, and this is the leisure, the rest, of a Christian. *John 16:12–15; Heb 4:1–13*

254. The reference to understanding comes from Matt 13:23.

MARK 5:15

It is extraordinary to see what a conflict of emotions arose in people's minds at the miracles of our Savior. At the end of the previous chapter, we see people frightened, yes, more frightened at the calm from the wind than they were afraid of the storm. Here we see the inhabitants of a town shocked at the restoration of an unfortunate man. The natural person has so little comprehension, so little proper feeling for God's works. Should not a storm be more fearful than calm from the wind, a raving madman than a reasonable creature? The reason for this is just as great a miracle as the cause of these emotions or the Savior's miracle itself. Should we not assume that Satan made use of this fear, this astonishment, to numb sound reason and reflection in people and the souls of sinners? He employs the affective mechanism by which exaggerated emotions end in the apathy and exhaustion of souls. This is like the joy with which we see the seed of the divine word sprout as quickly as it withers in stony souls.

Mark 4:41

1 Pet 1:23; Mark 4:5–6, 16–17

MARK 5:30

Even though our divine Savior as a man could feel and be aware of the hand of faith that tried to touch just his clothing, he was not satisfied until he discovered her. How much more cause do we now have to trust in him to accept those who reflect on their misery and seek to approach him as their physician, their only physician?

MARK 6:16

Here Herod, who announces the resurrection of Jesus, seems, like Saul, to be among the prophets.

1 Sam 10:11

MARK 8:1–8

The miracle of the twelve baskets that were left over precedes the seven baskets. Both are prophecies of how we see the seven elders of the church after the twelve apostles. By themselves both these numbers seem to have a certain solemnity in common life: the

Mark 6:41–44

Acts 6:5

number of months that make up a year and the number of days that make up a week. Both are divine institutions.

MARK 8:18

Our eyes, ears, memory have been given in vain to us as long as our hard heart, the unprepared heart, is in us by which we cannot receive or understand the divine seed.

Mark 4:14; Luke 8:11

MARK 9:37

To welcome a child in the name of Jesus, as a creature for whom Jesus died and suffered, a creature that is his redeemed property, that therefore belongs to him; this is why I love that child and show him the way to the good shepherd. I have patience with his weakness and tolerate it, just as my Savior tolerated the blindness, the hardness of his disciples, yes, just as he must tolerate my own blindness. All this because the child belongs to Jesus and I am his disciple (9:41), a helper of the good shepherd by bringing his lambs to him and gathering the lost sheep into his fold.

John 10:12

John 10:16; Matt 10:6; 15:24; 18:12–14

MARK 9:49, 50

We are all sacrificial victims of sin and so of death. As such, the fire of hell is our end and recompense. Our gracious Redeemer was the sacrificial victim for us. Just as the Levitical sacrifices prefigured him and were taken in his place by God, so his offering in our place was regarded by God. But we owe ourselves as offerings to our Savior and God the Father, not like the offering that he was but like those that prefigured him. We get away with salt rather than fire, with the awareness of our misery and of what Christ suffered for it, with faith and the acceptance of his gain for us, which could not happen without pain and vulnerability; but in this is our preservation and the aroma that makes us acceptable as an offering to the Most High God as images of his Son. Thus no offering is acceptable that does not have the right salt for it, a sense of our sin and faith in the One who puts out the fire of sin. This salt is the only antidote to pride, envy, and all sins. His disciples were to seek to keep it in themselves

Exod 29:18, 25, 41; Rom 12:1; Eph 5:2

and have peace with each other. His disciples were to be even more intent on keeping this salt in their souls because God had chosen them personally as the salt of the earth through which he make his sacrificial death best available to the world. They were to take up his cross on themselves before all other people and display his life before all the other people of the world by copying his conduct, because they were to be an instrument of redemption, just as salt belonged to the offerings that prefigured it.

Matt 5:13

Matt 16:24

Lev 2:13; Ezek 43:24

MARK 10:18

Nothing, no good, except One, a single Being, God! If only we could believe this truth about ourselves, with what eyes would we see ourselves and all of nature? Actually, the existence of every finite being is already evil (Isa 45:7).

LUKE 2:46[255]

The loss of our blessed Savior for three days prefigures his death and resurrection.

LUKE 2:52

This is the order that the teaching and life of Jesus wanted to reintroduce into human nature. As Christians, our growth in wisdom and years were meant to go equally hand in hand with each other, in favor with God and man. Lord! If your will would be done on earth as in heaven, what a heaven this earth would already be!

LUKE 5:19

How badly the Jews misused the roofs of their houses for the idolatry of the stars.

Jer 19:13; 32:29; compare 7:18; 44:15–25

255. Rather than 2:4, 6 as in the text.

LUKE 5:36, 39

Nothing elevates the divine character of our Savior's teaching more than that he always appeals to observations of the natural world, common events, judgments of taste, the management of domestic affairs and domestic prudence to demonstrate and explain it.

LUKE 8:19

From him will be taken away what he thinks that he has.

LUKE 10:25–27

THOUGHTS ON THE SENSE OF THIS PARABLE[256]

The purpose of this parable is to show the nature of faith. It comes to the help of all self-righteousness and is grounded only on the love of a Redeemer. Faith in this Redeemer is and can make us fruitful in all good works. It can give us power to fulfill the law and love our neighbor.

That this parable has to do with the salvation of the human race may be deduced from the question which includes the application that our Savior makes: Who, O man, O sinner, O Christian, is your neighbor? Who is it that had mercy on you when you lay
Ezek 16:4–6 in your blood, when the elders of creation, like Cain, let the earth drink it up? Is it not your God who is your husband (Isa 54:5)? Is this not the primary relationship that a person has with himself and his Creator? Is it not the closest relationship? Did God not leave
Gen 2:24 heaven and everything to cleave to his wife? Did he not share your fate, your poverty, your sin and shame?

John 8:48 Was not Jesus reproached as a Samaritan on your behalf? And
Gen 4:12–14; Luke 9:58 one of us? Did he not become a vagrant traveler on your behalf? and with what discomfort? Did he not come where you were, see you like Adam among the trees, like Nathaniel under the fig tree,
Gen 3:8; John 1:48 take pity on you? Did he not only come where you were but also

256. The freestanding text of this reflection on the parable of the Good Samaritan is found on four separate pages that differ in form and style from the rest of this work. It was subsequently included here when this work was published.

he himself came to you, to you—bound your wounds? "I the Lord am your healer" (Exod 15:26). Did not the foremost signs in his life have to do with fulfilling this word? Did any sickness at all, yes, even a legion of demons, ever make it powerless? He poured oil and wine—both of them daughters of his own press, fruits of his righteousness which alone can ease your pain and cleanse your wounds. Did you have power to come to him by yourself and enter the city of refuge, the inn, that he has sought out and prepared for you? No! He lends you his strength, not the strength of an earthly king. The God of Israel has no delight in horses and strong legs. He lends you the animal by which he himself made his entrance as a humble and gentle-hearted King. His payment, his undertaking, the care for you in his absence, the promise of his return, and the cancellation of all your debts.

Luke 8:30

Num 35:6–34; Deut 19:1–13

Ps 147:10

Zech 9:9; Matt 21:5

Neither priest nor Levite, neither Moses nor Samuel, neither the law nor the prophets, neither the zeal of the Jews nor the wisdom of the Greeks—nothing could, nothing would help you. The priest seems to avoid the sight of you out of sympathy and sensitivity. The Levite examines you more closely—his curiosity does not help you at all (cf. Job 5:7).

So we have died to the law that was given by angels and administered by Levites. We are betrothed to him who was made sin for us, who became a Samaritan for us, who was raised from the dead so that we might bear fruit for God (Rom 7:4),[257] the fruit of the love by which he loved us, the fruit of the mercy that he has shown us. He brought us to the faith that confesses him as our Neighbor, as our Physician, with the mouth and the heart. Faith is the going and doing likewise, by which alone we inherit eternal life. This concluding statement is the right answer for the ignorant, proud unbelief of the scribes. Our Savior is the Samaritan. In every sinner he suffers what he has done for us and expects from us (Matt 25:35, 40). See too Hervey's "First Conversation."[258]

Rom 7:4; Gal 3:19; Hos 2:21–22; 2 Cor 5:21

John 8:48

Rom 10:8–10

257. The German text has Sam 7:4.

258. James Hervey, *Meditations and Contemplations (London, 1752)*, 1–2.

Faith is the hand that receives everything from Jesus and gives everything to him. I am the half-dead man who owes his life to none other than the merciful Sin-Bearer. Neither the priest, nor the Levite, nor the Samaritan in my breast, but he himself, formed in *Gal 4:19* my soul through the Holy Spirit, must pour his oil and wine in the wounds, and I must care for him in the humble state where I shall find him in the soul of my neighbor. Just as everything in heaven and earth was created through him and for him, so everything in us also comes from him and flows back to him.

Our Savior therefore is our true Neighbor that faith alone can teach us to love. He has ascended, yet nevertheless he remains *Matt 28:20* with us all our days until the end of the world. We do not have *John 12:8* him with us by himself, but we always have the poor with us in whom he waits for the same mercy from us that he has shown us. *Rom 8:39* He is so near to us that nothing can separate us from him. Bone of *Gen 2:23* our bone, flesh of our flesh. Our gratitude for what our Savior has done for us, our awareness of our corruption, the enjoyment of his grace cancels enmity with God. Because everybody bears his image, there should be no hatred of anybody, no murder of a brother. The mercy that has been shown to us through Jesus, while we were still *Rom 5:10* enemies, shows us our neighbor as our own likeness, a creature in whom our Savior, who has redeemed us, has the same interest as in us—whatever you do to the least—(a cup of cold water in my name) *Matt 25:40; 10:42* you have done to me. Christ is therefore our Neighbor—he who has had mercy on us. We must love him as we love ourselves because *Gal 2:20; Rom 6:4* he died in our place. He lives in us, and we have been buried and raised with him.

To obtain eternal life we must do what he has done—practice mercy. He lives in every person, in the least of them. (He is the *1 Cor 15:45* second Adam.) He lives as a stranger, a sick person, as an infant *Matt 2:16–18* that was persecuted by Herod, and so on.

Every sinner bears the image of the crucified Savior. "See the *John 19:5* man," says Pilate. See how God says, "See, Adam has become like *Gen 3:22* one of us." We do not just bear the image of God but also the image of the Sin-Canceller on us. Every folly, imperfection, weakness, sin

against our neighbor is a nail in the cross, a drop of blood from the face of Jesus for a Christian, that squeezes out the prayer for him:
"Father, forgive him; they do not know what they are doing!" Judge *Luke 23:34*
the murderer who has so mauled your image, your Son. Forgive *John 8:44*
the priest, forgive the Levite, and let me pour out your own oil and wine that have enriched me on your wounds, rather than mock your nakedness, and let me quench your lament about your abandoned state with vinegar and gall on the field of battle for my human
neighbor. *Matt 27:46, 48*

LUKE 13:1–9

How beautifully the following parable illustrates this admonition to repentance! Your righteousness does not preserve you, but the intercession of the faithful Gardener and the experiment of his forbearance and mercy with which he decides to conclude after so much futile effort.

LUKE 13:12

Our merciful Savior called this woman because she apparently could not see him on account of her sickness. Here in London and not more than once in my life I have seen an example of this kind of sickness. A person with a rather brisk gait who walked so bent over with his body and head that he could almost have used his hands rather than the stick that he had.

LUKE 14:1

Our merciful Savior always used the Sabbath to do good, while on every occasion his enemies made its holiness a pretext to lie in wait for him and distort his love for humanity into an offense.

LUKE 14:28, 31

The religion of our Savior does not balk at the arithmetic of either architects or diplomats, because the Creator of heaven and earth and the Lord and wise Regent is author of them both (Prov 11:24; 13:7; 14:15). It is the product of the greatest Merchant and the masterpiece of wisdom and intelligence. The foundation of the Christian church is therefore prefigured in the conquest of Canaan (Deut 20:5).

LUKE 16:18

Should adultery here be taken in the same figurative sense as in the prophets? The Pharisees committed a double sin against God: They had forsaken the law of Moses; instead of it, they turned their
Matt 15:1–9; Mark 7:1–16 statutes into God's commandment. They also now constantly tried to assert the law of Moses against the teaching of Jesus. They had divorced themselves from the law of Moses, and now, when our
Matt 5:17 Savior had come into the world to fulfill it on behalf of mankind, they wished once again to take it as their lawful wife.

LUKE 17:25

God! Your mysteries are great! Who is able to perceive them? Who is able to fathom them? Not just the suffering of our Savior but also the rejection by the generation in which he lived were conditions for redemption and his glorious revelation.

LUKE 22:4

Going his way.[259] This is one of the usual expressions in Scripture that have a special sense. The enemy sows seeds, and went his way (so also Matt 13:25)—to his own place. In the Old Testament this expression occurs more frequently and with just the same sense.

LUKE 17:5, 10

How can our faith be strengthened? Through the contemplation of our imperfection. If we were able to fulfill all laws ever so exactly, we would, of course, thereby earn nothing from God. Since the opposite of this occurs, we realize the need for an alien, higher, divine merit that makes us worthy in God's eyes. The righteousness of our works makes us feel discouraged, yes even if it were perfect,

259. Translation in the KJV.

without trust in God. So sin makes faith worthy for us, and the anxiety of repentance strengthens the hand of faith to reach out to Jesus to gain rescue and help for ourselves, as it were, by his merit.

LUKE 20:1–8

Just as faith is based on the resurrection of Jesus together with the testimony of the Spirit who inspired Moses and the prophets and makes it credible in our souls, so the baptism of John and the gospel of our gracious Savior were similar divine revelations, a helpful resource for mankind. If a person suppresses this Spirit, no miracles are strong enough to convince him, but he, like Pharaoh, becomes more obstinate. Here the Pharisees use their reason, they draw sly conclusions, they deny their own thoughts, they make a pretense of ignorance that they do not have, an ignorance that is the result of the greatest reassurance of our blind reason. They themselves answered their own question. They were able to resolve it if they had only wanted to do so. The closer they are to the truth, the more adamantly they deny it as the only pretext to escape it. For us, this incident portrays the miracles that Satan is capable of producing when we make room for them.

LUKE 14:12–14

(1) The Pharisees had a general expectation of a temporal redeemer and hope for a kingdom of this world. (2) They therefore imagined his court with sheer luxury, an array of pleasure, a series of feasts and banquets, and, in addition to that, the stupidities of life in an earthly court. (3) Because of God's patience and the miracles of his guidance of them, the Jews had strange ideas about him and themselves. They conceived of him as a temporal monarch who chose his favorites capriciously and excluded others from his consideration. God's management and revelation of himself in the Old Testament in sensory and visible pictures was grossly misunderstood and so widely misused that poor people and cripples were regarded as specifically designated outcasts from God's provision. They therefore would have little to hope for in the kingdom of the Messiah.

(4) Yes, resident gentiles had the right to be guests in their feasts, *Exod 12:48; Num 9:14* which was not just based on kindness but also on religion. Because these were associated with his kingdom, we can well imagine that they constantly kept the royal table of their Messiah in mind in their feasts (14:15; cf. Gen 43:25).

Two Dissertations on certain passages of Holy Scripture. Viz the first on Luke XIV.12.13.14—and the Second on Rom. XIII.1.2.3.4. wherein the Cavils and objections of the late Mr. Chubb in the first vol. of his posthumous works, viz Remarks on the Scriptures *are particularly considered and refuted by Josiah Tucker. A. M. Vicar of All Saints in Bristol. London 8°. 1749.*[260]

The author notes how all these prejudices that had given occasion to this instruction by Jesus had ceased, because we have no festive meals of a devotional nature except the Holy Supper, to which sinners are invited by God himself and all appear as believing sinners. I would like to add a few extra thoughts.

It was the Sabbath day (Luke 14:1). The dispute about rank must not just have been a matter of earthly folly, because our Savior castigated it, but it seems as if they considered a higher place as a superstitious sign of the future honor that they would enjoy in the *Luke 14:7–11* kingdom of heaven. The dispute about rank was therefore simi- *Luke 18:9–14* lar to the prayer of the Pharisees. That dispute was a part of the superstition that was based on an earthly conception of the kingdom of heaven, just as all their pride was based on the perfection of their works and the merit from them. The teaching of our Savior *Luke 14:7–11* about it was not a prescription for prosperity but an article of faith. *Luke 14:16–24* So the following prescription for their meals with guests is hardly restricted to those who attended that meal but is as much a parable as the following parable of the banquet. God wanted to teach them *Luke 14:12–14* how their meals should be arranged if they were to symbolize the devotion of their faith in the kingdom of heaven. They had to be like the kingdom of heaven. And in what did that consist? Precisely

260. Hamann is quoting the English title of this book.

in the guests that our Savior tells the Pharisees to choose, because they were to be guests of God in heaven.

JOHN 1:48, 50

Nathaniel may have observed the fig tree that was about to bud as he sat under it and may have wanted to make the comparison that our Savior seems to use with so much delight because all three evangelists have included it. God! You have given us a sign of summer in the budding of the fig tree. When will we see the signs of this approaching kingdom where the hope for such sweet fruit will be prepared for us? Or Nathaniel may have had a vision under the fig tree of the appearance of the Savior and his divine calling, because Jesus says: "You shall see greater things than these."

Matt 24:32; Mark 13:28; Luke 21:29–30

JOHN 9

How splendidly the miracle of this man born blind corresponds with the blindness of the Jews in the previous chapter and their judgments of him with those that they make of Jesus. Some said: "It is he"; others said, "He is like him." The one who knew best said, "I am the man." In Mark 6:15 people say: "He is a prophet or someone like a prophet." The disagreement in 9:16–17 drove them to ask the blind man himself of his own judgment. After that, they declined to pass their own judgment because it suited them best to deny that he had been blind. So they go to the parents of the man born blind. What curt conclusions fear inspires in them in order to dismiss them. He is our son, he was born blind—these were the two reasons why they appealed to his parents. How they embellish the stubbornness of the unbelief and prejudice with hypocrisy and the mask of religion: "We know that this man is a sinner. Give the glory to God!" The truth knows how to distinguish and separate all the tricks and traps of malice and wickedness, all the sophistries of the scribes and hypocrites, so simply. Doubt is cast on him as a person; then, when this got nowhere, due to his blindness and the truth of his testimony, and when nothing could also be made of it,

John 9:9

the final resort was to the nature of the miracle. The free thinkers of our times are such fools. How will they accomplish anything if these hairsplitting enemies used all their wits in vain? The answer of the man born blind in 9:30–33 explains what Jesus said to his disciples in 9:3: "That the works God might be revealed in him."

JOHN 10:10

Not just life, but also more, abundant life. From his fullness we have
John 1:16 all received, grace upon grace.

JOHN 10:17

God loves his Son for our sake, on account of the love that he had for us, on account of the death that he died in our place and for our
1 John 4:8, 16 good. God is love.

JOHN 11:4

This sickness is our original sin, and death is its penalty and consequence.

JOHN 11:5, 6

This love detained Jesus for two days in the place where he was. These two days were the time that had to be fulfilled before Jesus came into the world.

JOHN 12:29

We see how the most trivial details in sacred Scripture are prophetic. Two aberrations of human reason that continue to our times are alluded to here: explaining the voice of God by natural actions or by a lesser miracle. Instead of seeing and believing, the people imagine the sound of thunder or the voice of an angel. This is also the effect that God's revelation has on sinners and devout people. The unbeliever hears a thunderstorm, a thunderclap, while a believer and Christian hears the voices of an angel speaking to him.

JOHN 15:15

The communication of God's thoughts was the daily business that our gracious Savior shared with his disciples on earth. He revealed himself to Abraham like this when he wanted to let Sodom and Gomorrah be destroyed and he rescued Lot. This therefore is most *Gen 19:1–29* likely the day that Abraham saw, the day that brought him joy. *John 8:56*

JOHN 19:12

The emperor's friend. This is the same emperor about whom Jesus said, "Give to the emperor what belongs to the emperor and to God what belongs to God." The prince of this world; the children *Matt 22:21* of mankind to whom the earth has been given. *John 12:31; 14:30; 16:11*

JOHN 19:26, 27

Our Savior bequeathed his beloved disciple to his mother.

JOHN 21:13

After Jesus had been the master of the banquet, he here becomes the waiter. After the flood, all animals were blessed for human *John 2:8–10* use. Our Savior has especially decided to sanctify the food from *Gen 9:3* the rivers and the sea.

JOHN 4:15, 16

There seems to be no connection between the answer of our Savior and the request of the Samaritan woman. We see how God takes us on detours to bring us so much more quickly to the goal of our wishes and his holy will. What was the water that quenches the thirst of our souls? Faith in Jesus. The sham righteousness and the superstition of human darkness is the opposite of this. This is what we must renounce if our eyes would be opened to know our Savior more intimately: first as a prophet, and gradually as the true and only God who humbles himself to death on the cross to be the Mediator of the sinful world and the highest righteousness. That's how faith was engendered in this Samaritan woman; that's how her longing to drink was fulfilled in deed and in truth, a longing that at first was only a misunderstanding in her which our Savior clarified through her apparent misunderstanding. The spring of living water is explained through what Jesus says about his food in 4:34.

JOHN 4:52, 53

John recounts this as the second miracle in Galilee. In the first it is said: "My hour has not yet come." Here we discover what our Savior said would happen in the hour that he had spoken of.

JOHN 5:1ff[261]

The circumstances of this account make it noteworthy. Here there is a contrast between a mediated and an unmediated miracle. It was mediated because an angel and pool were God's instruments for healing all kinds of sicknesses. But it was connected with a certain time in the year and certain conditions. In this the power of the angel over natural forces is like the prophets. Both are limited and dependent on means and conditions. The Creator alone is Lord and the Master of nature; his will and word is sufficient for it. "Let there
Gen 1:3 be light and there was light" = "Stand up, and he stood up." Thus the language of Moses agrees with the language of the evangelists. The faith of the apostles could perform exactly the same miracle
Acts 2:43; 3:6; 5:15 in the name of Jesus. Yet this distinguishes it from the miracles of the Old Testament: human lovelessness for a time frustrated God's mediated miracles. How often this poor paralyzed man had seen the pool in motion and its effect on his infirm colleagues; in vain he may have asked for their help. When God himself offers us his help, we look around for people, friends, and more distant aids
John 5:7 (5:38). For years the effect of sin had pursued this poor man, and the transgression of natural and divine laws had stunk for him. Nothing except an unmediated miracle can free us from the yoke that we have submitted to so frivolously and willingly. "Do you want
John 5:6 to be made whole?" Your almighty power, O God, seems to wait for nothing except our will in order to reveal its greatness. "Sin no

261. This unit as well as the following five units are found only in some manuscripts.

more from now on." Was this reminder necessary for a man who had for so long suffered punishment for it, who could live for his God as a recreated person? Was not the reminder itself based on the omniscience of the almighty Physician? *John 5:14*

JOHN 5:16, 18

The good that our Savior had done seemed to deserve death. Now the witness to the truth that Jesus gave earned his punishment in the eyes of the Pharisees.

JOHN 6:21

Jesus is a fellow traveler with his disciples. The force of the storm was transformed into a calm sea. As soon as he got into the ship, they reached the shore where they wanted to disembark. So great is our safety in the midst of danger; with such great speed we reach our harbor in his company!

JOHN 9

The story of the man born blind describes the miserable subterfuges of unbelief for us in most vivid color—the unhappy effort that it makes to restore the witness of the senses, healthy reason, and the conscience; as well as the play of passions, the sophistry of willful blindness and obstinacy.

ACTS 1:18

Just as Judas portrays Satan for us, so we also see Satan's punishment foreshadowed in him. What the enemy did through his agents is here attributed to Judas—his sin was that he wanted to buy and take ownership of the earth through the sin and death of human beings. His judgment will be a fall, a terrible fall. He will burst open and his bowels would gush out—the secret wickedness of his bowels will be revealed; its prey will escape from it and reach a terrible end, and all his children would fall as his bowels and be punished like him.

ACTS 2

The confusion of speech was an act of God to scatter mankind; the gift of speech was an act of the Holy Spirit to unite mankind. We do not just hear our own tongues, but we hear the mighty works of God speaking in them (2:11).

ACTS 2[262]

The confusion of languages is a story, a phenomenon, a continuing miracle, and a parable through which God continues to speak with
Gen 11:1–9 us. The very reason that people with the same language often do not understand each other correctly and relate two completely different ideas with the same external written sign and spoken sound, means that we can express the same mental picture with completely different signs. Here we discover a feature of both the divine image and the fall. The first belongs to the freedom of Adam in naming
Gen 2:19–20 the animals as he wished. Through the second, the abuse of this freedom has grown, together with all the inconveniences that have arisen from it. With the outpouring of the Holy Spirit, we thus see that all the hearers among the apostles saw the same ideas in their minds. This may be deduced from the external effects that the Holy Spirit reports through the mouth of Luke. Each person believed that he heard his own native tongue. The same ideas and perceptions occurred to each of them that usually happened through the impact of known words.

We see our habit of explaining God's deeds by natural causes in the example of ascribing the finger of the Holy Spirit to the effects
Luke 11:20; Acts 2:13 of sweet wine.

The usual offense for unbelief is the lowliness of the means that God uses for his purposes. Here it was that they were Galileans.

The curiosity to know how something is unleashes its subsequent doubt, with its eventual question of why, and for what.

The dogmatists are the greatest mockers of God's wonderful works. All events are fulfillments of God's word and his secret will

262. This was written on two sides of a separate page.

(2:16). There is no sign that occurred on earth without a miracle in heaven.

ACTS 2:19

Blood—the death of the Savior. Fire—the outpouring of the Holy Spirit. Smoke and columns as is written in the prophet,[263] partly the apostles who like the clouds were pillars of the early church, *Exod 13:21; Gal 2:9* partly the judgments that would be executed on Jerusalem and the prince of the world. *John 12:31; 14:30; 16:11*

ACTS 2:20

By the sun and the moon, we can properly understand the two natures in Christ. The first was obscured in the human nature that bled to death.

ACTS 2:24

The story of the raising of Lazarus explains this passage. Lazarus was alive but came from the grave bound in cloth. We therefore see *John 11:44* the cloths and especially the head cloth wrapped up together in the empty tomb of our Savior. *John 20:6–7*

ACTS 2:36

This Jesus whom you crucified, God has made Lord and Christ. How terrible is the first fact for his enemies; how comforting is the second fact for his friends and the disciples of Jesus.

He is the Lord of heaven and earth, who, however, has been anointed as a man for this lordship, for this kingdom, and he sends us the same Holy Spirit that anointed him, with the same oil by which God anointed him, to make us the kind of people that he *Acts 10:38* is—God! Who is not shocked by this extravagant grace? He anoints and consecrates us, like Jesus, as kings in heaven and priests of God. *1 Pet 2:9; Rev 1:6; 5:10*

263. Here Hamann recalls the Hebrew text of Joel 2:30: "I will give signs in heaven and earth, blood and fire and columns of smoke," and identifies the columns with the apostles as the pillars of the church.

ACTS 9:18

Everyone carries these scales that were evident in Saul, and every devout Christian feels them fall off by repentance for sin and faith in Jesus. These were therefore required by God for fish that were clean[264] because our Savior would receive the blind, the sick and sinners, rather than those who could see, the healthy who were without scales, without sin. *Matt 9:12*

ACTS 9:31

The fear of God and the comfort of the Holy Spirit, these are the senses and feet of the inner person for the spiritual life and for devout conduct. *Eph 3:16*

ACTS 10:6

We see how the Holy Spirit mentions the lodging place of his apostle, its business, and even its location! Yet there are still Christians who are able to deny his providence and government.

ACTS 12:3

Here we also see traces of how piously eager Satan is to make people observe the celebrations and authorized festivals of the Lord.[265]

ACTS 15:23–29

This church order is a model of simplicity, clarity, moderation, and Christian intelligence. How natural is its effect on the minds of its readers (15:31)!

ACTS 15:37ff

The failures of the leading apostles are disclosed very accurately and truthfully without judgment. No decision is made here about which of the two was right or wrong. We discover some clues in

264. For Hamann the mention of scales recalls the definition of clean, edible fish in Leviticus 11:9–12 and Deuteronomy 14:9–10 as those that had scales.

265. This cryptic remark compares Herod's use of the Passover to kill James and arrest Peter to Satan's promotion of religious observance to accomplish his purposes.

incidental details. Barnabas took Mark, Paul chose Silas. We also see that he reveals the reason for his unwillingness with Mark. Paul's departure was accompanied with the special commendations of the brothers.

ACTS 18:14–17

Gallio is an example of those people who know their duties and appeal to their knowledge of them, but also know how to use their duties as a cloak for their negligence and injustice, who trivialize a matter without listening and examining it so that they can shrug it off, people who want to have the opportunity to be of use in matters that concern them and are shown to be just as careless and unjust in these matters. In this man who judged them, the Jews could see a similarity to their own wisdom and fairness in opposing the apostles and their teaching.

ACTS 17:21–22

Curiosity is a kind of superstition and idolatry. Socrates,[266] on whom the fashionable philosophers[267] agreed to confer the title of a wise man, confessed that he knew nothing. Solomon, to whom the Spirit of God awarded this title with greater justification, has left us a testimony in Ecclesiastes that is even sadder. Nothing new—and labor, sorrow, pain to be wise. The father of the new philosophy was *Eccl 1:9–18* forced to forget, renounce, and reject all that he knew and regarded this as the only means to discover the truth.[268] Yet this truth is also nothing but an edifice of re-polished and reclaimed errors. If curiosity is a mother or wet-nurse of knowledge, we can easily draw a conclusion about its fruit from its root and sap.

---

266. See page 244n237 for Mic 7:1.

267. Hamann mentions *die Weltweisen*, the sarcastic designation that Luther coined in his translation of 1 Cor 1:20.

268. This refers to the French philosopher and mathematician Rene Descartes (AD 1596–1650) and his *Meditations on the Foundations of Philosophy*. In this famous thought experiment, he attempted to forget all that he knew and so abstracted his mind from his body and its senses in a quest for intellectual certainty. He concluded that he could be certain about nothing except himself as a thinker.

All natural knowledge is revealed. The nature of objects supplies the *matter*, and the laws by which our minds[269] perceive, think, infer, judge, and compare supply the *form*. All natural knowledge is therefore as old as nature itself, and since nature cannot be changed, no innovation can, in a strict sense, occur in our perception of it. The part of the earth that we call the new world is a sensory example of the misunderstanding that the use of speech causes in our ideas, or, even more, of how the weakness and vagueness of our thoughts debase our words and how through the same deception we accept counterfeit coins as genuine and valuable. Thus we do not encounter anything new in the course of nature, or within the horizons of our reason and every reasonable creature. That must happen outside this domain. If we are to discover and know something new, or something more than what is old, God has to alter the course of nature, or set us in another visual field, or extend it for us. What is itself new cannot appear in the dress of what is old, just as what is old can hoodwink us by the appearance of something new, for we see nothing except the surface, and we see this surface itself often only in darkness and through a mist. It is God alone who can produce something new that reveals something new to us, who can teach us to distinguish and discern it.

Isa 42:9; 43:19; 48:6; 65:17; 66:22 God explicitly attributes all this to himself, and Ecclesiastes seems mainly to have been written by Solomon, so that he, the wisest of all seekers of wisdom, would point to the revelation of God in the flesh and the proclamation of his kingdom as the only
1 Tim 3:16 innovation that would be significantly, generally, and really new for the earth and its inhabitants, yes something that would never cease to be new. Thus God let a rumor of this new thing spread over the earth so far in advance: the angels were the messengers from heaven that had to announce it as a great joy which was of vital importance
Luke 2:10 to all people. The proclamation of the gospel was therefore called *the*
Acts 9:15 *joyful news of God's kingdom* (Luke 8:1). God's prepared instrument,

269. German, souls.

the student of Gamaliel, *Paul*, who was considered worthy of rap- *Acts 22:3*
ture into the third heaven, knew nothing except Christ crucified. *2 Cor 12:2; 1 Cor 2:2*

This therefore is the only reason why God has planted the instinct for curiosity in us. This is the only thing that can satisfy it and transform our *curiosity* into *wisdom*. This is the thirst that we feel, despite our original sin, a thirst that is increased by every earthly fountain, a thirst that magnifies our ardor without quashing it in order to quench it. This is an itch that becomes more dangerous, ablaze, and widespread with all external gratifications and
earthly drugs, an itch that cries out for the balm of Gilead and does *Jer 46:11*
not produce relief and healing in us, but a craving and refreshment of a completely opposite kind. This is the thirst of a sick person, that is heightened by a drink. This is the thirst of a tired person, a parched person who has a pure spring, with cooling and reviving nectar, for his refreshment. For the more he drinks, the more it flows, and it is impossible to drink too much from the spring that preserves our thirst for sweetness and richness and energy.

ACTS 17:23

This is one of the countless contradictions that we discover in our nature and are unable to resolve. Reason is inclined to serve an unknown God, but to *know* him as infinitely remote. It does not want to know him, and what is even more astonishing, when it does
know him, it ceases to serve him. This is why God reveals himself *Rom 1:21–25*
late in time and so slowly, for he knows that the knowledge of him
is an offense, a stumbling block for mankind. He knows that he is *1 Cor 1:23*
foolishness and a thorn in the eye for people as he reveals himself and makes himself known to them. When Jesus said that he was
God's Son and disclosed the most comforting, most important, and *Matt 26:63–64*
newest truth, the Jews picked up stones—they therefore tore their *John 8:59; 10:31*
clothes and damned him as an evildoer. The devout Athenians were *Matt 26:65*
ready to fall down before an unknown God, but as soon as this unknown God was disclosed to them, they wanted to have nothing to do with him. They made fun of him and believed that they

were hearing insignificant things rather than something new, things that were not worth studying and knowing in their coherence—it did not matter whether and when they gained any further insights about them.

ACTS 27, 28

These two stories about Paul's journey by ship and his arrival in an unknown island are prophecies of the spread of the Christian religion by ship and its fate in America. The murderous plan of the Roman soldiers to execute all prisoners prefigures the cruelties
Acts 27:42 that were partly carried out on the inhabitants of the new world. The fourteenth night when they believed that they had come closer
Acts 27:27 to land corresponds with the time of the discovery of new lands. The action of Paul in gathering wood for a fire is noteworthy. The
Acts 28:3–6 viper that latches onto his hand from the heat of the fire; the judgment of the islanders on him; the length of time and the curiosity with which they waited for his death—and the sudden reversal of their judgment—all prefigure the gospel and the story of its spread and propagation. Everywhere in the story of the Jewish church we discover that it prefigures the Christian church. Its split with the Samaritans has also occurred in Christianity. The Protestant and Roman churches agree in many chief articles. What Moses was in the one, Peter is in the other.[270] The division [between the Jews and the Samaritans][271] was over the canon of the divine word.[272] The reliance [of the Roman church][273] on human ordinances and their pride in the saints is similar to the reliance of the Jews on Abraham and their forefathers. There have been some scholars that have uncovered the similarity of the papal church with heathen religion. I am surprised that they have not discovered the main features of Judaism in the Roman superstition since we cannot read the gospel

270. Hamann aligns Moses with the Jewish church and Peter with the Christian church.

271. Hamann says "their division."

272. Only the Pentateuch was accepted by the Samaritans as God's word.

273. Hamann implies this without holding that Protestants were at all similar to the Samaritans.

writers without employing the zeal that our Savior shows against the Pharisees and the scribes over the errors that we see with our own eyes. *Matt 23:1–32*

Just as God permitted the superstition of the papacy to reach their highest degree in order to cause a new division of the church through it, so some scholars think that the increasing superstition will produce the same effect.[274] The Christian religion has been spread in the same way by its adherents as the Jewish faith through the captivity of its people and its consequences. Their sins and inclinations are similar means in the hands of God's providence. Through their punishment, other people are taught, warned, and blessed. What mysteries eternity will reveal to us of God's management of his household!

ACTS 3:6

Faith is active in love, love that chooses all the means that God entrusts to times and circumstances. In the very beginning, the church needed miracles; these therefore were the "alms" of the apostles.[275] In God's wisdom they ceased; he has placed in our hands and entrusted to us so many more temporal and external means by which we can show our faith just as powerfully and glorify his name just as perfectly. Let us perform miracles with the unrighteous Mammon that has, in our times, made so many lame, blind, possessed, and crippled people. Let us perform miracles with it, use it in the name of Jesus and to glorify him, distribute some of our goods as God's faithful stewards, and let the world see our good works, so that the world may praise the Father and Redeemer that we believe in and whom we honor by confessing him with our mouths. Because divine Providence has inaugurated a different order in external matters and the course of the world, we must turn the word of Peter around: "I cannot perform any miracle, but what I can and what I

Gal 5:6

Luke 16:9–11

1 Pet 4:10

Matt 5:16; 1 Pet 2:12; Rom 10:9–10

274. Here Hamann seems to refer to the increase of superstition in Europe with its nominal adherence to a liberal form of Christianity.

275. The alms of the apostles were the miraculous deeds of mercy that they performed and gave as gifts of mercy to people in need.

have I will contribute willingly with joy and faith in the Redeemer of my soul and of my fellow creatures, and let everyone enjoy it who can lay a claim to it."

ROMANS 1:16[–2:29]

The gospel of Christ is the might and power of God for the salvation of all those who believe; and in this gospel the justification of God is revealed from faith to faith. Through justification by God, all the attributes of his great will are understood—his truth, his holiness, his righteousness, his mercy. Yet through justification by God our human state is also understood as the only order and condition in which God wills to accept us as justified, in which God wills to forgive and can forgive our weak and sinful nature. In this we have the power of God for salvation, and without this authority no one can obtain salvation. In the gospel of Christ, we find the strongest and most sensory and most extravagant revelation of the nature of God's will and all its moral attributes, and the purpose of this shocking revelation is comforting for us, because it happened for our sake. We have been changed, as it were, into mere spectators of what we as his creatures owed to God and what we had earned by our disobedience. God came as a man into the world to show us the first in his life, the second in his suffering. Neither sin nor death, neither the law nor its curse, is there for those who believe that God so loved
John 3:16 the world that he gave his only-begotten Son; those who believe that he had been sent by God to convince us of this love with which he loved us; those who believe that the Father himself wanted to love him more for our sake if we would receive him as the Son of the Most High, as the King of heaven and the Savior of the world. Without this faith we are condemned, fallen, lost creatures; through this faith everything is forgiven for us, all perfection is reckoned to us, there
Rom 8:1 is nothing to be condemned in us, but God's good pleasure in his
Matt 3:17; Luke 2:14 Son rests on us. You would think that reason would be inclined to recognize and accept a teaching before all others that seems to have been made for the imperfection of our nature and to have raised it, in such an easy, and, let me say, probable and only possible way,

to the dignity that our fancies dare to wish for. Despite all that, nothing is harder and more impossible for the natural person than this faith. How much time God took to prepare his people and the whole human race for it!

Adam did not *believe* that he would die. The first world did not have any more than a single man who *believed* that it would be drowned in water. The story of the people of Israel—yes, even the disciples of our Savior—is nothing but the saddest story of unbelief. By contrast, sacred Scripture shows us how God led people from *faith* to *faith*, step by step, until the revelation of the One through whom we alone could gain righteousness and salvation. After the fall into sin and the flood, his highest purpose seems to have been no other than this, to regain his credit and the faith of his own people who had mistrusted him as a liar and had therefore been disobedient to him. You will bring forth children in pain—thistles and thorns and the sweat of the face; they all were prophecies of saving faith in its spiritual sense. But the letter of these prophecies served to prepare them for it. Their experience soon showed Adam and Eve how truthfully God had spoken. The flood was meant to confirm Noah's faith, while their unbelief drowned his contemporaries. God created the alternation of days and nights, the seasons, and the rainbow as signs of his faithfulness and marks of the faith that gained God's promises. What did Abraham's faith consist of? He believed God concerning his son and his land. All revelations of the future, all temptations, all miracles, all blessings, all punishments were aids to prepare people for saving faith in the merit of our gracious Redeemer through their trust and faith in God's promises and threats in temporal things and worldly events.

Gen 2:17

Heb 11:7

Gen 3:16, 18

Gen 12:7; 13:14–16; 15:5–6, 18

Adam did not believe God—about what? That he would really die. This is the second point of unbelief and the second reason for saving faith. Why the eviction from Paradise? Why the flood, the persecutions, the trouble, the sad end of this life, the captivity, the desert, the wars, the alternating and unequal happiness in them? Why the law, the curses and the blessings? *From faith to faith.* See these stages in the chapter 11 of the Letter to the Hebrews. We have the sounds of thunder in Moses and the milder drops of divine comfort and his promises in the prophets. All this is given in order to reveal sin to us and show how impossible it is to please God in it, or else to escape divine punishment and its curse and show it visibly to the world in temporal events and actions.

Faith in Jesus Christ is therefore based on the truth of human misery, the curse, the condemnation which is our natural state in the sight of God, who is just, holy, and implacable with sin. The antidote for this terrible truth lies in the joyful news and proclamation of Christ, the proclamation that he has taken on himself the curse for us and has compensated for our inability to please God with our mutilated and corrupted nature by the perfection that properly belongs to the supreme Being, the proclamation that all this did not just occur in human nature but also in its name.[276] Human righteousness and salvation is thus to be sought in no other name than in the name of this great and gracious will.

The first of these basic truths of faith—namely, the irreconcilability of God with sin, the estrangement of human nature from its author, and its abominable deviation from the fairness that every natural person can sense is necessary—is revealed to the heathen by the application of their reason, by their consideration of nature and the visible world and their reflection on it. For the Most High intended to impress traces of his attributes on its creation, marks of invisible things and spiritual creatures, rules for his government, laws for his wisdom and ways. We discover that all the virtues of individuals and entire societies are expressed in the animals, and all their vices, such as laziness, impurity, and falsehood; so too the riches and waste of divine generosity, together with thrifty frugality and special attention to the smallest worm and the tiniest conditions of its existence. The whole physical nature of a person from his conception to his decay is a typological account of it, and the only key to the knowledge of it and of redemption. All our limbs are keys for the soul that exist in an amazing correlation with notes

276. That is, in the human name of Jesus.

that can only be heard. Neither the wood nor the strings nor the fingers are its harmony; unnoticed, their combination produces the harmony.

The gentiles recognized God and had insights that we Christians read about with amazement; yet, despite that, they fell into the most vulgar idolatry, into the most abominable abuses and vices of the flesh. Why did God allow this? As Moses says, to know what was in the human heart, to make the horror of the heart visible and evident to men, to reveal the shamefulness and harmfulness of their sin. *Deut 8:2*

Just as the gentiles were encouraged by God to consider nature and sharpen their reason, so he gave the Jews the law. For what purpose? To show them the same thing that the gentiles had gained by their reason. In addition to their obstinacy, they themselves became greater sinners in God's eyes by breaking his law, misusing it for their pride, and observing the outward sign of God's covenant[277] instead of keeping his commandments. *Rom 2:17–29*

Paul therefore makes an earnest appeal to the Jews and the gentiles not to pass judgment on each other. Your reason and your conscience condemn you, you gentiles; still much more the law condemns you, you Jews. The first of these is the law of the gentiles, which is just as holy for God as the revealed law of the Jews. What does the gentile do who passes judgment on a Jew and thinks that we would have kept the law better if God had given it to us? How could he have had so much patience with this stiff-necked people and so little for us poor gentiles in revealing himself to us so late in time? Consider, you gentile, that you despise God's riches in generosity, patience, and forbearance. Consider that you have abused it for your own self-preservation through the transgression of the natural law in your heart: yes, consider that God wants to use and has used his patience with the Jews even more to bring you to repentance. *Rom 2:1* *Rom 2:14–16* *Rom 2:4*

I have tried to unpack the arrangement of the first two chapters here only for myself. In the Bible we find just the same regular disorder that we discover in nature. All methods of interpretation should

277. This refers to circumcision (Gen 17:11; Rom 2:25–29; 4:10–12).

be regarded as the handcarts of reason[278] and its crutches. The imagination of a poet has a thread that is invisible to the common eye and appears to be a masterpiece to experts.[279] All hidden artifice is governed by the nature of the imagination. In this respect sacred Scripture is the best example and finest touchstone for all human criticism.

ROMANS 2:20

The whole law of Moses is only a form of the knowledge and truth that would be revealed through Christ; the letter of the law is a mere offprint of it. The circumcision of the foreskin was a mere symbol that distinguished the Jews from other nations and yet, by itself, did
Rom 2:25–29 not make them any more worthy in God's eyes.

ROMANS 3

"'What advantage then does our law give us,' say the Jews, 'and
Rom 3:1 how has our circumcision helped us?'" See for yourselves the many
good things that God has done for you: the miracles, the name that
he made for you and the gentiles, the honor to be his people, the
outstanding revelation that he has granted to you, his choice of you
Deut 7:6 before all other nations for him to spread the knowledge of himself
through you and to allow the blessed offspring of the woman to be
Luke 1:42 born from your race. See the advantage that you have because your
Messiah, whom you crucified, also begins to usher in the kingdom of
Acts 2:32 heaven with you; because in his life he sought for nothing as much
Matt 15:24 as to gather the lost sheep of Israel and gave his first commandment
Luke 24:47 to his messengers to begin their proclamation in Jerusalem.

Since his people did not want to believe, should God therefore give up the whole world and not attempt to proclaim his Son to the

278. This refers to the small four-wheeled carts that were used as playthings by children who pulled each other around in them.

279. This seems to be an allusion to the ball of thread that Ariadne, the daughter of Minos, King of Crete, gave to Theseus to find his way out of the labyrinth of the Minotaur after he had killed him. The thread of Ariadne is a common term for the application of logic to solve a complex puzzle, such as the way out of a maze. Here, however, Hamann uses it for the application of the imagination rather than reason in the interpretation of literature.

other nations that had not yet known him, nations that had been reserved by him for the revelation of himself to them now at the end of days? (3:3)

But perhaps the unbelief of the Jews was a means of God to reveal his providence, justification, and love for humanity even more. Can God then at all punish this unbelief by which he is glorified? Could Satan then credit God with all his wickedness? Could God then be no Judge? (3:5)

So, what advantages did the Jews have that they could appeal to against other nations? None! The law was only given to them in order to justify God's wisdom in the government of the world and show how incapable anybody was of living for himself and even more incapable of keeping the easiest laws of a God that were all based on his temporal blessings, the greatest differences from the nations, the greatest hopes and threats and everything. The whole world must therefore admit that it is sinful and guilty; the majority that had submitted to the direction of reason and natural revelations and the minority that enjoyed direct dependence and fellowship with the supreme Being. It was all in vain. Israel had nothing except sin; God had nothing but punishment, miracles, and patience. Apart from the law, Israel was as idolatrous and corrupt as the gentile world; yes, more corrupt and much more culpable. For the more a sinner receives blessings, so much greater is the guilt. The more acquainted and obligated and closer a sinner is to God, so much greater is the judgment on him. We Christians have good reason to tremble when we compare ourselves with the blindness of the Jews. How happy are the Jews that are blameless and the blind nations that are still heathen in comparison with a Christian who confesses his Savior with his mouth but defames him in his heart and life!

ROMANS 3:31

There is no greater proof of the holiness and eternity of the law
than the necessity of our gracious Savior to fulfill it and atone for *Matt 5:17*
our transgression and inability to keep it. Thus faith in this Fulfiller
of our righteousness confirms the law that serves us only as our *Matt 3:15*

Gal 3:24 guardian, just as Pharaoh made the[280] daily quota of work and the
Exod 5:4–18 punishment for failing to meet it so much harder in order to make
the promise of Moses and redemption by him, which were both
fulfilled in Christ, so much more agreeable.

ROMANS 5:1–2

Under the law we were nothing but transgressors; faith in Jesus
Heb 9:11–12 Christ, the sacrifice of our high priest before God, has made him our
Friend. He no longer regards himself as our Judge but us as those
Isa 62:12 redeemed by his Son. Our fear of God and his righteousness that
weighed down on us as fallen and lost creatures has ended. Instead
Heb 4:16 of this fear, faith gives us access to God's grace and joy in hope.

ROMANS 5:3

Under the law, all adversities, all public plagues in the land, and all domestic chastisements were promised as its penalties and realizations of its curse. How disheartened this must make the believing Jew, how fearful, how servile! The cross of faith is the pride of a Christian, his school, a pledge of the future glory that will be
2 Cor 1:22; Eph 1:14 revealed in us.

ROMANS 5:5

Just as the apostle Paul previously commented on the difference of the adversities that occur for Christians and Jews, so he explains the excellence of the hope of a Christian until verse 11. Hope is still too little; the cross of Christians produces joy for them. How could the Jews rejoice in God when they were experiencing the adversities that he has to consider as his punishments for them? What a Christian suffers is not a punishment of the law. How could God punish the sins that were all atoned for in his Son and all forgiven in him?

280. The text has "our."

ROMANS 5:15

However varied, however severe the consequences of sin may be, they do not match the blessing of redemption, the free gift of the forgiveness of sins and justification before God. God has permitted all people to become wretched through the sin of one man, so that he might show his grace and the free gift by his grace through one Man so much more gloriously and extravagantly. What is a sinner compared to him? What are the offenses of a sinner compared with his expiation for them? What is the injustice that we have done to God compared to what has been done for us by God in this innocent Guarantor? How must this offense against the God-man be *Heb 7:22*
avenged and compensated on our behalf, not only by the payment of our guilt but also by the premium of the incomparably greater treasures that belong to our Savior as God and man?

The first gain from God's atonement for sin is that the wages of sin was death. Atonement has not just given us life but also an *Rom 6:23*
even higher treasure in addition to a new life, a state that we could never have gained from what was appointed to us in creation (5:15).

ROMANS 5:16[281]

One sin condemns us all; this gift of justification makes us righteous, even if our sins are like the sand of the sea.

ROMANS 5:20[282]

Sin turns us all into the slaves of death and Satan; if sin has such great power, our gracious God will be so much more powerful. Instead of slaves we ourselves will be kings, abundantly rich in grace. We will, in God's eyes, possess such great merit that he can never properly repay and reward it. His Son and with him everything! This we are; this we own!

281. Hamann mistakenly cites this as 5:21.

282. Hamann mistakenly cites this as 5:31.

ROMANS 6:4[283]

The judgment and imperfection of sin cannot be lost as much as rescued through redemption.

Thus we see how fortunate the consequences of sin, its punishments, are for us. What seemed to be strict righteousness, yes cruelty, that was inflicted on us poor, blind, seduced sinners, has been transformed into grace and blessing. Yes, God's wisdom made the curse of sin so terrible by giving the law to spread it so much more, so that the blessing of the Sin-Blotter would turn out so much greater, so much more general, so much more amazing for the good of mankind.

How satisfied a poor subject would be to let himself be flogged by his master if he knew that each blow would soon be paid and credited with a large sum of money! God allowed the human race to fall into a pit for a short time. He purchased them and gave them a short time to recover, in order to bring them back into another prison[284] and finally to produce such a great transformation from it as in the life of Joseph.

Gen 37:12–28; 39:1–41:45

ROMANS 6:14

As long as the law had been given as a prescription for mankind, the author of sin always used our flesh and blood for disobedience and our disobedience as the reason for our condemnation. His power over us Christians has ended; he can now no longer accuse us before God as breakers of the law. Thus faith in our Savior by which his neck is broken now stands in his way, and his one concern now is to obscure it, to drive it from the center of the Christian religion and from the hearts of God's children, in order to foil what Jesus has gained, through unbelief in human souls.

283. Hamann cites this as 4 instead of 6:4.

284. The other prison seems to be physical death and burial.

ROMANS 7:8

In this passage we see explicitly how Satan uses the law to raise up the desires against it and to multiply the transgression of the law. Without the law, we would not know about another will that contradicts God's will.

ROMANS 7:11

Satan even uses his craftiness to lead us into the transgression of the law and its punishment in order to kill us. The law of God was given so that by it the works of the devil would be revealed in human souls, so that people would know their thoughts and their heart, or, rather, recognize the one who dwells in the heart and turns us into rebels by the law of our will for the best that is at work in our members. Thus it is also said, a sword will pierce through your own soul, so that the thoughts of many may be revealed. Our Savior himself was destined to be the downfall of sin, an offense, the testing of the spirit world and its human offspring. The fool, as Scripture calls him despite his cleverness, digs his own pit and falls into the traps that he has set for others.

Rom 7:21–23
Luke 2:35
Ps 14:1
Ps 7:16; cf. 57:6

ROMANS 7:24

Wretched man that I am! Who will deliver me from this body of death? Apart from the body, nothing belongs to death and nothing falls prey to the enemy of mankind in keeping with God's promise that gave him the dust as his food. *So it seems that the power of Satan extends only as far over the souls of Christians as the soul depends on the body, on its sinful instruments, on the workshop of the brain and the bodily images of the imagination, on the terrors and needs of our nature.* Thus, it is said, they have eyes and do not see; ears and do not hear. That is why the power of Satan is called *flesh*, indwelling sin that opposes God's Spirit that dwells in the souls of believers (8:9). It is called *a law in the members*, *sin* in general, *death*. Just as in the beginning Satan was described as mere, cunning animal by Moses, so God's Spirit did not think it worth naming him, to humble his

Gen 3:14
Matt 13:13–16

soul; instead, he named and regarded him as something secondary to human nature, like the apostle here in 7:20, something decrepit,
Eccl 1:14; 2:11, 17, 26 something futile, just as Solomon did.

This is the reason for laziness, indolence, cold jabs at goodness, temptations, foolish thoughts, silly whims in prayer, distractions, temptations of sleep and hunger, spiritual hypochondria, inordinate desires and slavish cravings in fashions, comforts, pastimes, habits:
Rom 7:24 this body of death has as many members of death as the natural body.

Rom 8:11 When God's Spirit dwells in our souls, the furthest borders of our domain enjoy the spiritual, divine, supernatural peace that is higher than all reason, peace that guards our hearts and senses,
Phil 4:7 our emotions[285] and thoughts, the senses of the mind and the soul. The enemy finds the coasts of the soul laid waste for him, nothing that gives any livelihood for him, everything dead and arid for him.

ROMANS 13

Here we see what the Christian religion provides for the subjects of a kingdom. We see how irresponsibly the authorities and princes act that do not respect them publicly and do not try to gain their affection by their good example.

1 CORINTHIANS 1:17

Not eloquent wisdom[286]—The cross of Christ would be disempowered by it. God! What depths of your wisdom! The preaching of the cross, the power of God, Christ himself the might and wisdom of God; on the other hand, his teaching for those who would be lost is folly, mockery—a stumbling block, an offense. In God's children this teaching would be more powerful than any miracle. Its weakness would be strength and God's folly would be a wisdom that would shame the wit of all people, all intellectuals.[287] What an irresistible spirit is Paul's testimony in 1:27–28!

---

285. Or "affects."

286. Literally, "wisdom of speech."

287. The German "Geister," spirits, echoes the use of "esprit" in French for people with lively minds.

1 CORINTHIANS 1:21

The wisdom of this world would not reach far enough for it to know God. God acted to make this so in his wise counsel, with unfathomable forethought—then it pleased God to save those who believed through the folly and simplicity of preaching.

1 CORINTHIANS 6:12

This is an important, basic rule that governs the use of Christian freedom and limits our assessment of customs and temporary fashions. The first test is the *benefit* that I gain by doing this or that. In countless cases we will find that many polite deeds and morally indifferent things damage our health, our attentiveness and concentration, our precious time, and so on. The second test is the reign of prejudice, of agreeableness with the wish to be like the world, and of slavery to custom, so that indifferent things become indispensable for us, the necessities of life become the conditions for our contentment.

2 CORINTHIANS 1:9

The law lets us hear and feel the answer of death and the curse in ourselves, so that we would not build on and trust in our own powers, our works, our own righteousness, but in God and his Son whom he offered up for us and in whom we have risen to new life.

2 CORINTHIANS 1:21–22

God is pleased with the truth that so many, countless promises have gained their fulfillment through Jesus. He *confirms* every believer in Jesus, he *anoints* him, he *seals* him, he gives him the *guarantee of the Spirit* in his heart.

2 CORINTHIANS 2:2

If a mere person, a mere apostle, can be so kindly minded to his flock, how must God himself then be? If his image and his inscription has so much radiance in earth and clay, how must he himself be when he impresses himself on us and shares himself with us? If *2 Cor 3:2–4:15*

we are grieved through penitence, who could make us glad except
2 Cor 7:10 the One who has produced this divine grief in us for our salvation?

2 CORINTHIANS 2:11

This is an important part of the knowledge of a Christian[288] that teachers should excel in more than others. God has not only revealed the mysteries of heaven, the depths of our hearts, but also the secret ways of hell.

2 CORINTHIANS 8:14

In this way God knows how to produce equality though opposite means in the management of his household. He wants to share his rule with us. He wants us to make up for him when he seems to have been too frugal or too wasteful.

2 CORINTHIANS 8:24

We see how excellently faith and the teaching of Jesus know how to make use of human passions, just as they also transform our weaknesses into praise and use them to do good.

2 CORINTHIANS 11:26

The apostle Paul lists his dangers from his *countrymen*—and from false *brothers* or friends. A traveler learns to recognize the first and to be even more on guard against them than strangers.

GALATIANS 3:19[289]

The law was added because of transgression. Our Savior himself says that he has come into the world to remove all excuses for sin (3:22).

GALATIANS 4[:3, 9]

The elements are the basic principles of the world. They are called elements because they are weak and beggarly, nothing but the mere letter of the alphabet—mendicant and derived from the images of

288. Paul refers to the need for forgiveness to foil the devil.

289. Not 3:9 as is cited by Hamman.

the senses, from their promises and threats—they are called *worldly*, because the prince of this world would be deceived by them, and because they, like Goliath's sword, were his own product that would serve as an antidote for mankind and as death for him.

John 12:31; 14:30; 16:11

1 Sam 17:51

EPHESIANS 1

What riches are in this chapter!

EPHESIANS 3:8

The example of his own humility that the apostle here shows is an excellent hint by which the gentiles would recognize God's grace; not Israel's obstinacy, nor the worth of the gentiles, their great dignity, but God's wise counsel and the treasures of his grace.

EPHESIANS 3:10

Through the church God's manifold wisdom would be revealed to the spirits of heaven, the angels, a revelation that would glorify God's righteousness to good people and evil people.

EPHESIANS 6:12

It is more than flesh and blood, says the apostle, that wars against God, his Holy Spirit, and the inner person.

EPHESIANS 4:16

Christ is the head; the church is like the members of his body. Here Paul describes this body: the whole body is joined and knit together—fitly, skillfully, as is appropriate—it has been put together firmly, and the tie, the glue for this firmness, is what every member supplies through its effective operation as each part is able. This is the origin and purpose of the growth of the whole body—to be built up in love (4:29). Just as everyone nourishes and cares for his own flesh, and its members do the same for each other, so too the Lord of the *church*. Thus the arrangement and physical[290] management

Eph 5:29

290. The German text uses the adjective "animal" to refer to the body of the person as an animate creature.

of our body is also a prophecy; everything was created by him who
John 1:3 has redeemed us. If he had not decided to redeem us, nothing would exist. This life that was in him and in his love is the light for man-
John 1:4 kind. The light is everything that makes this manifest and present for human sight, everything that discloses hidden things.

EPHESIANS 5:6

On account of empty words God's wrath comes on the children of disobedience. That is why Solomon calls the seducer and his off-
Gen 3:15; Rev 12:17; Prov 18:6, 7 spring a fool with his lips. Thus in 2:2 he is called the prince of the power of the air who does not deceive and cannot deceive by anything except castles in the air, by wind and emptiness.

PHILIPPIANS 2:20[291]

Here the apostle gives excellent testimony to Timothy: he will be *naturally*[292] concerned for your condition. He does not know anything better than this; he cannot be otherwise; he lives for this; it is his instinct. "All seek their own interests," Paul had to lament on
Phil 2:21 that occasion, "not those of Jesus Christ." This friend of the apostle regarded nothing as his own; nothing belonged to him except the Good Shepherd's flock and care of it and the spread of his teaching through preaching and living. These are his father, his mother, his bread, his sheep—so it was natural that he loved this flock as much as other people loved those things that they could not at all do without. This means he was naturally wise—without coercion, without vanity, untiringly, without selfishness in claiming this as his own.

PHILIPPIANS 2:27–28

We see how faith gives thanks to God for his grace and benefits to others, how it feels relief from its own pains in the joy of others. The natural person grumbles and is annoyed at the good luck of others.

291. The reference to Philippians is missing. The following reflections on Philippians were written on a single sheet and misplaced by the original editors from their proper context because they mistook 2:20 as a reference to 2 Timothy. Paul's friend Timothy is mentioned in Philippians 2:19.

292. Hamann follows the translation of this adverb in the KJV.

He considers that he is exempted from God's providence and that his preservation is a reward for his own virtue. He is flattered by the cross that is suffered by others and regards the good that his neighbor enjoys as something stolen from him.

PHILIPPIANS 3:8

I consider everything as manure in order to gain Christ. This does not just show the worthlessness of temporal things but also the use that God makes of them by granting them and withdrawing them from us. Both serve only as manure for our hearts to soften them and make them attentive to the love of God in Christ Jesus. All temporal changes, all fluctuations in scarcity and plenty, are like the manure that a gardener uses to prepare the soil and nourish and sustain the seed. They are trials by which our patience and faith and *Luke 13:8* hope are strengthened and increased (4:8). David says, "I have seen the end of all perfection; your law is exceedingly broad." *Here we see* *Ps 119:96* *how kindly our religion and our ethics are in their extent and breadth. We as Christians can make use of everything and sanctify everything in such agreeable, easy freedom.* Whatever is true in all knowledge that is understood and in all acts that are willed, whatever is worthy of honor, whatever is fair and right, whatever is pure, whatever is pleasing and lovely, whatever belongs to a good name and wellbeing, whatever contributes to the perfection of public and domestic life, whatever is able give you a public reputation that is appropriate to you as Christians—make all that the object of your reflection, assessment, comparison, imitation and behavior. *Phil 4:8*

PHILIPPIANS 3:10, 17

Does all the freedom of prosperity, all the flatteries from the most refined wit and ethical taste, come close to the grandeur and simplicity to which the love of Christ, the love of our neighbor and love for humanity, raises us and directs us?

COLOSSIANS 3:3–4

We are *dead* here on earth and our life is hidden with Christ in God. When Christ our life appears, we too will appear with him in glory.

This is the redemption that we long for while we still feel the Rom 7:24 misery that this body of death produces in us. See Rom 8:19, etc. The Holy Spirit of promise who has sealed our faith for salvation is the guarantee of our inheritance until the actual *delivery* and *acquisition* of the possession that has been purchased for us—to the praise of God's glory (Eph 1:14).

1 THESSALONIANS 2:15

They displease God and are hostile to all people. Thus the fear of the Lord is not just the beginning of wisdom but also the beginning Ps 111:10; Prov 1:7 of all love. It is light for our understanding, warmth for our heart. What a friend of mankind our Savior was! How his apostle shines!

1 THESSALONIANS 2:16

Our sins against our neighbors fill up the cup of wrath in God's hand until it overflows on us. The true nature of Satan lives on in his children; he lives without hope, and he, too, does not grant it to people. The Jews themselves did not want to be saved, but it irked them that the gentiles would be saved. If Paul's teaching was wrong, did it deserve to be rejected? Where did the compassion for the gentiles, their greatest enemies, come from, that they would not let them have this error, this madness, this offense? *Whatever horrifies us and whatever we regard as harmful, we prefer to see in the hands of our enemies.* Because a person acts so unreasonably, because he contradicts himself so blindly and punishes his own lies, there is so little that is coherent and conclusive in blind reason and the passions of the heart. Satan hinders us—2:18.

2 THESSALONIANS 2:3

The fall into sin, every divine miracle, the giving of the law, and the incarnation and suffering of our divine Redeemer all have the same ultimate purpose and the same effect. Heaven was put to the test and purged in the church on earth. The whole of creation existed in preparation for the work of its new days, and this in separation. The man of sin,[293] the son of perdition, Judas is the new prototype, and the whole story of our Savior's life and the Jewish people until the destruction of Jerusalem is a prophecy that must be compared with the Revelation of John and the prophets of the old covenant. As in nature, God repeats himself in Scripture, in the government of the world, in building up his church, in the alternating course of time—it at least seems so to us, and it is necessary for us to see repetition. It is not the same fruit that every spring produces, yet it is still the same fruit; it is not the same body that we deliver from its mother's body and sow in the womb of the earth, yet it is the same body; it is not the same river that seems to swallow up itself, yet it is the same. Whoever is able to explain a ray of the sun has the answer to the riddle of all nature. Yes, the Spirit that searches the depths of the Godhead puts a mysterious word in Samson's mouth, a mysterious word that is explained by a rather insignificant event, a word whose meaning was revealed through the same mystery that Paul was an apostle of and that he calls his gospel (Rom 16:25–26).[294] How Satan wants to gnash his teeth at the pride of this mortal who had been his faithful subject! It is no wonder that he takes vengeance on Paul through his angels for regarding this gospel as his own, the gospel that grinds him to dust and shames his arrogance.

Gen 1:3–19

1 Cor 15:35–44

1 Cor 2:10

Judg 14:5–18

2 Cor 12:7

1 TIMOTHY 2:15

Since the woman brought the curse of death on the human race, so, on that account, she has been appointed to restore it again. Yes, she had to give birth to the Savior himself; and the raising of children is a blessed task that suits her better than her husband. The first impressions of God and of the fear of him, the first fervent

293. Here Hamann prefers the variant text instead of "the man of lawlessness."

294. Samson's slaughter of the lion with his bare hands and his provision of honey from its carcass as food for his parents mysteriously foreshadows Christ's defeat of the devil and his delivery of salvation in all its sweetness through the proclamation of the gospel.

prayers, are now a blessing for her. It is obvious that Paul does not
here speak about eternal salvation, but about temporal happiness,
advantages, and benefits. "Godliness also holds promise for this
life," says the apostle in 4:8, and in the same way he says in 4:16,
"Pay attention to yourself and your teaching. Persist in this, for
by so doing you will save both yourself and those who hear you."
Neither our own salvation nor the salvation of others rests on what
we do and on attentiveness to what we do, but *this attention to ourselves and the teaching of the gospel is a splendid thing and the only
means to keep ourselves in saving faith and encourage others to receive
it.* Thus, in this mention of salvation Paul thinks only about the
advantages of a good conscience, the advantages from the exercise
of his office and its effect on the souls of his hearers. A certainty
that we ourselves are a sweet aroma of Christ to the Most High
2 Cor 2:15 God among those who are being lost—a greater ease and joy in
the exercise of our vocation, a greater blessing from it—are these
not blessed things? Yes, has not a greater reward been promised
for them in heaven? A woman can also take special comfort in
the fact that her comfort and her joy will be very great if she may
be able to say at their appearance with her Savior: "Here Lord,
Heb 2:13 are those that you have given me. I am happier than you, because
John 17:12 none is lost, not a single one." These are the works that will praise
a devout woman in the gates of heaven in keeping with the words
of King Lemuel in Proverbs 31:31.

TITUS 1:12

We see how for a Christian all means are sanctified for their use in
the spread of the gospel. A knowledge of the moral character and
a taste for the manners of people are especially necessary for this.
The poets who elucidate and depict the mentality and tendencies
of people and a nation most faithfully and vividly are helpful in
this and the best proof of it. The testimony of the human arts, sciences, and history all serve as a seal, the human seal of revelation.
As Christians, we have as little reason to neglect and abandon them
2 Tim 4:13 as Paul his overcoat in Troas. Paul honors a poet by calling him a

prophet of his people. True poetry is a natural kind of prophecy. Its basis belongs, or should belong to the province of reason, and its content is a task of the imagination. Experts say mythology is the soul and inspiration of a poet.

PHILEMON

We see how the pastoral office in the church does not give us the least privilege in worldly disputes.[295] We see how careful Paul is in making the least forceful use of the gospel for himself. Good works should not be rejected by us. The office of preaching should be regarded as too holy for it to be used to settle worldly disputes. Religion has nothing to offer and prescribe concerning the legal right of a master over his servant, the legal right of a believer over his debtor. Obey the government, obey unusual rulers, it says, be subject to all worldly order. This letter of Paul is a splendid example of the modesty, the fear that we need in keeping the limits of our office before our eyes, so that we do not misuse it for our own purposes, wishes, and self-interest, even when we have the apparent right to do so. While love is pleasing to God, untimely zeal is always more dangerous and sinful. The mentality that we find in Paul is not inherent in the natural person. The more wit, the more understanding we have, the more shameless are the turns that we take to make ourselves agreeable to our neighbor. Our neighbor does not owe us anything; does God, despite his greatness, his righteousness and his grace, compel people? Our neighbor does not owe us anything unless he wishes to. How modest this mentality makes us when we resort to the other important principle that we, we ourselves as Christians, owe everything to our neighbor. Even

Rom 13:1–7; Titus 3:1; 1 Pet 2:13

295. In this letter Paul addresses Philemon as a pastor and regards his runaway slave as a fellow Christian, a brother in Christ. Paul therefore appeals to Philemon to exercise his pastoral office appropriately and modestly, without misusing his pastoral authority to insist on his legal rights as a master and owner to punish Onesimus. As a Christian Philemon was bound by the law of love to his neighbor, and his debt of love to his brother in Christ (Rom 13:8), to forego his rights and grant what is best and most useful for Onesimus by emancipating him and receiving him as a physical and spiritual brother. Thus here Paul neither sanctions nor denounces slavery; he, in fact, circumvents it by offering to compensate Philemon for his losses and pay for the emancipation of Onesimus.

though our brother can demand everything from us, we do not have the least right to take anything from him. Even though all of heaven is ours, we may not even take the dust of our feet with us
Matt 10:14 from the house that refuses to hear God's word from our mouths.

We see what weapons a Christian has against his neighbor: the example of humility, renunciation, selflessness, magnanimity that is expressed so kindly, so powerfully in Paul, humility that is greater than all laws of human fairness, all notions of wittiness and flattery, all cunning tricks of the smart world.

1 PETER 1:25

1 Tim 3:16 God's revelation in the flesh is the center of everything. This is the content of God's whole word. Yes, it is the reason why it was given to us.

1 PETER 2:17

Value all people greatly and highly. Vain reason teaches us to hate and despise people under the appearance of virtue. It makes fun of the defenselessness of those who are simple and evil. It is proud of the difference that it discovers between itself and its neighbor and
Matt 7:3 is blind to the plank in its own eye. Nothing but Christ's Spirit and the gospel can make us true philanthropists, good citizens, good neighbors, good companions, and people who are fit and well-qualified for all the ties of the natural world and human order.

1 PETER 3:4

We see how the courage of wild horses, the fierce fire and the continual blaze in our thoughts and deeds that we regard as noble and great and as the impulse of a heroic soul, is the opposite of the gentle-minded, quiet, peaceful, patient, tolerant, untiring spirit of faith that is precious in God's eyes. How ridiculous, how tasteless it seems to the world, its conquerors, its great minds,[296] when the King of heaven makes his royal entry on the foal of a burden-bearing

296. Literally, "great spirits," a term that was used for the leading thinkers of the Enlightenment in France and Germany, the fashionable intellectuals.

donkey! How ashamed Satan should be when he hears his own children mocking and laughing at God's deeds that he himself cannot think of without shuddering!

1 PETER 3:6

The last words of this verse seem to refer to the agitated emotions of Eve as she heard the serpent speaking, when fear and amazement, horror and astonishment had overcome her capacity for reflection.

1 PETER 4:11

Holy Scripture should be our dictionary, our linguistics, on which all the ideas and language of Christians should be based and from which they should be derived and composed.

2 PETER 1:20

The prophecy of Holy Scripture does not come from any *individual person* or from human *interpretation*. The deeds of Abraham and the miracles of Moses and the history of Israel are not its content. It does not deal with particular people or particular nations or even the earth by itself, but it foresees higher, more general, heavenly things. If Moses would have decided to write at his own impulse, like Caesar[297] or Homer,[298] we would probably have expected nothing but a collection of original documents and reports from him. It is not Moses and Isaiah who have left behind their thoughts and the events of their time as earthly authors and writers for future generations or their people. It is the Holy Spirit who has revealed
himself through the mouth and pen of these holy men. The Spirit *2 Pet 1:21*
who hovered over the waters of the young, unformed earth, who *Gen 1:2*
overshadowed Mary and acted so that a Holy One would be born, *Luke 1:35*
the Spirit who alone is able to search out and discover the depths

297. The reference is to Julius Caesar and his famous book *The Gallic Wars*. In it he recounts his role in the Roman conquest of the Gallic tribes in present day France and Belgium.

298. Homer is the reputed author of the classical Greek epic poems, the *Iliad* and the *Odyssey*.

1 Cor 2:10 of the Godhead. This should move us to read the divine word with very great reverence and enjoy it too.

1 JOHN 1:1

The testimony of ears, eyes, and touch is the foundation of the gospel. How could any revelation be more certain than this!

1 JOHN 1:4

That your joy may be full. What can be more gracious than this final purpose of God? And what should move us more to receive the preaching of faith than its purpose to pour out the fullness of truth, grace, and joy into our souls.

1 JOHN 1:8, 10

We do not owe our happiness to our works or our perfection but to our awareness and confession of sin. This is a riches that is based on our needs, a righteousness and holiness that has its source in our sins, a salvation that flows from our condemnation! How comforting, how acceptable, how serious this should be for us!

1 JOHN 2:11

What would flood us with more confidence, more affection and enthusiasm for any religion than the One that requires no other service except love for our neighbor as the touchstone for perfection? What a God, who commands nothing more for us than to love ourselves and our neighbor as a mark of the love that we have
Matt 22:37–40 for him, bringing it into the light of day in this way and testing our own condition with it.

1 JOHN 2:12–14

I write, says John, to young and old, to fathers, young people, and children. All these differences have ended through our loving Redeemer. There are no longer any children in knowledge. We are all children in heart, in simplicity, in innocence, in unity. We old

people, we fathers, are children of the heavenly Father. We are all
children of one household, sheep of one shepherd, one fold, one
pasture. You infants, you know your Redeemer; in your hearts as in *John 10*
ours, the Spirit cries, "*Abba*! Father!" We old people do not know *Rom 8:15; Gal 4:6;*
more than you know: "God so loved the world." We know noth- *John 3:16*
ing, we all know nothing except Jesus and him crucified. So rejoice; *1 Cor 2:2*
again I say it, rejoice. I have nothing more to write to you than what *Phil 4:4*
I have written to you, and I will never grow tired of writing this to
you; I write it to you anew, so that your joy may be full. Your sins *1 John 1:4*
are forgiven for his name's sake. We know Jesus for whose sake they
have been forgiven for us; however, it is he who created heaven and
earth for us; he who came on earth; he whom we have heard, seen, *1 John 1:3*
and on whose bosom we have reclined; he who taught us to know *John 13:23*
the Father in himself; he who has made us conquerors of the evil
one; he who makes us strong so that we may still conquer him and
daily participate in his victory over him; he (gives) his word to us, *1 Cor 15:57*
the almighty word that speaks and makes everything happen, and *Ps 33:9*
the Spirit of the word, through whom he called the heavens into
existence and through whom he rose from the dead and is exalted
to sit at the right hand of his Father and our Father. *Ps 33:6; Rom 8:11; Eph 1:16–23; 1 Tim 3:18; 1 Pet 3:18; John 20:17*

1 JOHN 2:17

You all know your Father. You will be immortal, perfect, holy, as *1 John 1:13*
he is and you are. For how can you die, how can you be unclean, *Matt 5:48; 1 Pet 1:16*
how can you be weak when God's word is in you? So do not love
the world. It is passing away together with its desires, and you will *1 John 2:15*
lose your immortality, your innocence, your Father, your Advocate,
his word, and his Spirit, if you try to stand on common ground
with it and degrade, pardon, and poison yourselves through it.

1 JOHN 2:20

By faith we participate so fully in the divine nature that we already *2 Pet 1:4*
here on earth enjoy its omniscience and the anointing of the heavenly kingdom.

1 JOHN 2:25

Gen 12:7; Exod 3:8 What is his promise? Canaan, a land flowing with milk and honey.
The food and clothing that was given to Jacob and a fellow traveler.
Gen 28:20 Dear God! A person knows so little about the purpose of his call; he
knows so little about what God is and what it means to have God
as his Friend and his Father.

1 JOHN 3:1

The world does not know God; it crucified his only begotten Son
Matt 3:17 with whom he was well-pleased—how would it know his children?

2 JOHN [1–2]

John calls the *truth* what other apostles call the gospel, the preaching
of Jesus, faith in him, and so on. From this we see that the truth of
doctrine does not rest on words and formulae but on its spirit, its
sense and concepts. If these agree with God's word, then we can allow
everyone to have his own expressions. Love itself often includes the
Gal 5:6 concept of faith and is nothing else than faith that is active; it is the
Col 3:14 breath, or life and the clothing of faith.

2 JOHN 11

Just as John is a great preacher and such a splendid example of love, so we also see that this love must be governed by love for the truth and that it must agree with faith and the love of God. This love must not extend to the enemies of God outside the church and his secret enemies in the church that the following letter gives us an example of. We love our neighbor because of God, and brotherly love is the fruit of God's love in us.

3 JOHN 9–10

Here we see from John's example that love for our neighbor, as the Holy Spirit intends it, is not weakness, childish fear, or impotence. We see that when it excuses faults, it knows how to distinguish faults from evil. We see that it tolerates faults patiently and leniently, but opposes wickedness emphatically and ardently.

HEBREWS 7:19[299]

The purpose of the law was to usher in a better hope and share it with mankind; a hope that brings us near to God and lets the Jews, as those who came first, share in its fulfillment (10:1).

HEBREWS 9:23

Everything was a shadow, sketches, earthly engravings of heavenly, spiritual things. In 9:10 they were called carnal practices; they are the same things that the apostle calls the *first principles of the world, earthly elements.*

HEBREWS 9:26

There is no longer any sin, any death, any curse for those who believe in Jesus Christ.

HEBREWS 10

How great is the grace by which God's Spirit permits the apostle to speak to the world on behalf of the divine Reconciler—this man, this human being—how greatly this must humiliate God's enemies who have always regarded us as grasshoppers. *Num 13:33*

HEBREWS 11:3

Without faith we cannot even understand creation and nature, hence the efforts to remove God's word and will, to explain what exists by hypotheses and probabilities, and the many doubts that have been raised about the story of Moses.

HEBREWS 11:35

The apostle crowds his witnesses so closely together that the Christian reader can scarcely catch his breath for them. Faith, says the apostle, raised dead people—yet the same faith that made mothers and children grateful for a new life was strong enough to despise this life when a tyrant and the prince of this world offered

299. Hamann is following the order of Luther's translation, which gives Hebrews, James, Jude, and Revelation as the last four books of the Bible.

John 12:31; 14:30; 16:11 it to believers as a reward for their apostasy. For them, death was then faith in a better life, and this faith helped them to experience death and torture without weakness. Contrast gives a special force to the thoughts and expressions of the apostle in the reversal and reflection that it causes.

JAMES 2:6

What good does a rich person do for you? What do you find worthy of honor about him that you treat him with respect and deference? What harm does a poor person do to you that you despise, yes, hate and insult him, because you can do it with impunity? He goes out of the way for you and blesses you. When the rich person shows off with the insults that he inflicts on you, he is your oppressor rather than your benefactor.

JAMES 2:14

Here faith is taken in the same sense as it often appears in Paul's letters, *2 Tim 2:13* the pattern of healthy teaching, the questions and answers that we can follow about the content of the gospel.[300] Without faith that *Matt 7:21; Luke 6:46* comes from the heart and the Holy Spirit, this teaching is no better than to say "Lord! Lord!" An active faith shows its life through *Gal 5:6* love. The illustration in the following verses explains the apostle's meaning even more clearly. Not the love of the lips, not the faith of the lips, but the work of faith and the labor of love (1 Thess 1:3).

JAMES 4:11

Whoever speaks evil against his brother and passes judgment on his brother speaks evil against the law and judges the law. The law is the will of the Lawgiver. Whoever blames his will by saying that God has authorized him to uphold the transgressor and judge the evil done by his neighbor injures God and the wisdom of his will.

---

300. Here Hamann alludes to the use of asking questions and providing answers in traditional catechesis and in Luther's Small Catechism.

JAMES 5

In this chapter I discover the Spirit of the prophets in the old covenant who always targets the author of sin and always sees further than temporal enemies and the temporal redemption of Israel.

In the whole of this letter there are traces of this: the tongue as a special member that is used by the seducer as its master; the faith of the devil who trembles in the midst of faith, Wisdom that acknowledges no other Author than God, the widows and orphans who everywhere represent the human race; the reward of him who pulls a sinner from the jaws of Satan.

Jas 2:19; Jas 1:5; 3:15–17

Jas 1:27

JUDE 4

We see how the heresies that Satan invented as hindrances to the Christian faith have been taken up into the plan of God's wisdom to purge and preserve and spread it.

REVELATION 1:1

This prophetic book differs from the books of the old covenant. It is a revelation that our Redeemer has disclosed to us as he has received it from the Father (John 16:13; also 15:15).

REVELATION 1:3

Blessed are those who read with faith, who hear with faith, who understand and accept—those who hold the word in themselves with an honest and good heart, so that it bears fruit with patience (Luke 8:15).

The time is at hand and near—soon—Scripture teaches us Christians how to tell time, its whole duration, by God's reckoning. As his children, we should also try to learn his way of reckoning in it. Our life is like the duration of the whole world, nothing more than a *Today* before God. What is our death? We must see it, at least, as near as any future moment. Is it we who die? No, it is the world that dies for us, passes away for us, the dust on which we rest our heads. Thus the death of every man is the time when this revelation is partly fulfilled in every human soul. In this sense

it is literally true that the time of fulfillment is near, and it should
make us attentive for the end of the world that ceases to be for us
1 John 2:17 at death, that passes away and is no more, and makes us ready to
travel on.

REVELATION 1:4

How imperfect and insufficient human ideas are to imagine heavenly and spiritual things! God's eternity cannot be grasped except through parts of time, through the combination of three moments that we, in our imperfection, must distinguish from each other and compare with each other. God's unchangeable nature, in which, as James says in 1:17, there is no shadow from turning or reversing, cannot be made clear to us apart from the transience of earthly things. In our conceptions, the past precedes the present; with God the present is foundation for the past and the future. What is able to give us a more wonderful and more mysterious idea of God's unchanging nature and his extravagant greatness and his unsearchable height than this annihilation of all human ideas, and this transcendence of them? In this name of God, we do not just discover
a picture of the Holy Trinity but also of our divine Redeemer in
Matt 28:20 particular. *He is*—I am with you for all days to the end of the world.
He was—the word became flesh and dwelt among us full of grace
John 1:14 and truth. *He will be*— Behold I am coming; it is written about me
Ps 40:8; Rev 22:20 in the book. Yes, come, Lord Jesus! Amen!

How little we still know about God and the mysteries of his Being and his Kingdom, and how hard it is for us to fathom the little that has been revealed to us. Here we find seven spirits that are before God's throne. The seven spirits are called seven eyes on a stone that God himself has engraved, the eyes of the Lord that range to and fro
through the whole earth (Zech 3:9; 4:10). Thus God has decided
Gen 1:1–2:3 to sanctify this number by the creation of the world, by signs in the
See Exod 20:8–11; 34:18; Lev 8:33–35; 23:23–43 service that was instituted by Moses, and by the number of churches

in Asia Minor. It has also been observed in the genealogies and the number of generations that preceded the fullness of time.[301] *Gal 4:4*

REVELATION 1:5

Jesus Christ, the Faithful Witness, who sealed his testimony with his death, who came into the world to reveal the Father and glorify him, and who frees us from sin and death through faith in him and his testimony—the firstborn from the dead, *Col 1:18* who died in order to satisfy God's righteousness as an offering for sin and was raised because everything had been completed for us to rise to a new life through him—the ruler of kings on earth, who has been anointed by God and appointed by God as the Judge of the world and the angels. *John 19:30; Heb 10:14; Rom 6:4; Acts 10:42; 17:31*

REVELATION 1:7

He is coming with clouds; they are the dust of his feet, says the prophet. *Dan 7:13; Nah 1:3* The pictures in the Bible surpass the loveliest flowers in beauty. But their sense is obscured by the eating of the fruit. *Gen 3:6–7* Anyone who sees the approach of an army sees so much less of it the larger it is and the quicker it marches. Yet without seeing it we are certain of its arrival. How? By the dust, the clouds that make it impossible for us to see it, the clouds that make what is invisible to our eyes so much more visible and nearer for the expectation and conjecture of faith. All the great judgments, the miracles that precede the Last Judgment are nothing but clouds, the dust of his feet that permits us to expect and see his appearance, even though we do not yet see him.

REVELATION 2:2, 6

The heretics of the early church are to be regarded in the same way as the Canaanites and pagan people that remained in the promised land. Both were instruments of Satan by which God chose to test, refine, and glorify his people.

---

301. This refers to the genealogy of Jesus in Matthew 1:2–17, which follows the genealogy of David in 1 Chronicles 1–2. It mentions fourteen (7x2) names from Abraham to David, from David to the exile, and from the exile to Christ.

3

THOUGHTS ON THE COURSE OF MY LIFE

In the multitude of my thoughts within me (and about me myself) thy comfort[s] delight my soul.[1]
— *Psalm 94:19*

Like the Confessions of Augustine, this best-known work of Hamann relates the circumstances of his so-called conversion, his spiritual awakening. He pictures his life as a journey and his awakening as a discovery of the significance of his life. This account of his life is a personal confession, a conversation with God and himself that begins and ends with prayer to God the Father. In it he engages in three kinds of confession: a confession of his sins, a confession of thanksgiving for God's saving word, and his confession of faith in the Triune God. That is, Hamann confesses his faith in God the Father for the revelation of himself to humanity; faith in Jesus for his incarnation and work as a needy man for needy people, whom he has redeemed by his blood; and faith in the Holy Spirit for providing an offensive book for us proud people as his word in which seemingly trivial, contemptible events tell us the story of heaven and earth. Hamann completes his confessional biographical

1. Here Hamann translates the KJV into German with his own addition to the text.

sketch by claiming that the course of his life shows how useful the practice of godly piety was for his delivery from silly, little bad habits and the transformation of his petty weaknesses into something beneficial and beautiful for him.

Yet despite its personal, autobiographical character, the most significant and often overlooked feature of this confession is its concentration on God's word and its impact on him rather than the spiritual awakening and transformation that he experienced so momentously. Unlike similar confessions that were prized by his Pietist contemporaries, he does not present his experience as an example of a true conversion for the self-appraisal of others to be emulated by others but as evidence of the gospel's transformative power.

LONDON, 21 APRIL, 1758

1 Sam 7:12 *Hitherto hath the Lord helped me.*[2]

I was born on 27 August 1730 in Königsberg in Prussia.[3] The following day, as far as I know, I was brought to the washing of
Titus 3:5 Holy Baptism by my devout, upright parents[4] who showed their Christian care for me in this way. God allowed me to enjoy the honor and privileges of a firstborn son. Like Jabez, I have been
1 Chr 4:9 a son of grief and pain for my mother. She also provided another son for my father, my younger brother. We, whom God has graciously preserved since he had given us life, were the whole wealth of our parents.

My richly loving Father in heaven! How should I begin to thank you for the abundant blessings with which you have adorned me as

2. Hamann once again translates the English text of the KJV into German and personalizes it by changing "us" into "me."

3. Königsberg was the capital of East Prussia from the Late Middle Ages until its annexation by the Soviet Union in 1945, the expulsion of its German population, and its renaming as Kaliningrad. As a Lutheran university city it was a prominent intellectual and cultural center in Eastern Europe. With its port on the southeastern corner of the Baltic Sea it was also a center for trade and commerce.

4. Neither of his parents were born in Königsberg. His father, Johann Christoph Hamann (1697–1766), came from Lausitz, and his mother, Maria Magdelena née Nuppenau (1699–1756), came from Lübeck. His brother was Johann Christoph.

with a wreath already in the circumstances of my birth? A healthy body, which you formed in secret—a soul to which you freely gave a heavenly place of honor and the pledge of salvation, by washing away my inherited sin[5] and receiving me into the covenant of your Son and the lap of the church, already before I was aware of its existence, just as you already prepared the milk in my mother's breasts, before I recognized the thirst and need and taste for it; parents whom I remember most fondly and cannot pass over without a tender sense of love and gratitude; parents through whom you first decided to reveal yourself to me, who, as they were able, undertook to bring me to you; my parents, blessed by you in temporal matters, who always pointed to their own life as a proof of your wise, generous rule and commended it to us. You have privileged me to witness the departure of my mother who has now entered your rest—her good works will have followed her. The merit of your Son makes up for what is imperfect in us and what we lack in goodness; thus the salvation that he has gained is the reward that compensates abundantly for the world's ingratitude. If my father is still alive, then let his old age be blessed. Comfort him in the distress that without doubt has pressed down on him on my account. Comfort him with the same Spirit that has raised me up, the Spirit whose oil alone can make our faces radiant and gladden and refresh our hearts more than new wine and fine wheat. Let the misery of his present troubles become light under your wings.[6] If this prayer, my God, is wrong, then make his joy full through the conversion of a penitent sinner,[7] whom he had believed he would lose on earth, in order to find him once again in the home of your children! Hear me, my God, for the sake of your dear Son. Amen!

Jer 3:4, 19; Ps 139:15

Eph 2:6; 2 Cor 1:22; Eph 1:14

Rev 14:13

Ps 104:15

Ps 91:4

I was sent to school early by my parents. They both were enemies of sloth and friends of divine and human order. They were not satisfied with the apparent fulfillment of our duties to them and

5. This recalls Eph 5:26 and Titus 3:5 and alludes to baptism as God's covenant with the baptized person.

6. Here Hamann alludes to the occupation of Königsberg by Russian forces early in 1758.

7. Here Hamann is speaking about his own conversion.

the mere formality of education which so many parents let their children enjoy for the sake of appearances. They wanted what was best for us, and they themselves did as much as their circumstances and insights permitted them to do. Our teachers had to give them an account of our diligence and performance; at home we were schooled under the oversight, the strict oversight and example, of our parents. Telling lies, being evasive, and stealing sweets were the three main things that were not excused, things that we were never allowed to disregard. We could boast about doing too much in our education rather than doing too little. The greatest art of education is the proper arrangement of a household and its management, just as the lavish praise of parents and the severe blame of children by parents produce the basic defect in it. Our home was always was a place of refuge for young people who studied at the university and traded on their poverty. They were always welcome and were at times deliberately recompensed for instructing us; by giving us extra tutorials with revision and preparation for school, they were also our companions who helped us pass the time and supervised us; as we grew older, they became confidants and good friends. We enjoyed these advantages as long as we remained at home, and whenever I returned home again; they included the study of languages—Greek, French, and Italian—as well as music, dancing, and drawing. Even though we were strictly and rightly curtailed in our dress and in other foolish things, we were allowed and encouraged to indulge in these activities.

The good intentions of my dear parents would have been better accomplished and their generous inclination would have been better applied if they would have had good advice in choosing how to do this, and if we would have had more accountability to guide us in what we did. Yet experience has taught me how superior their insights and principles and heartfelt impulses were to their children, compared to countless other parents, as I have frequently thought back over it and engaged in self-examination.

My schooling occurred in three stages. The first was in a gathering of children of both sexes and all ages under the direction of a defrocked priest named Hoffmann. He laid the foundation of my education, and I was a student of this man for seven years. After that he believed that he had brought me as far as was necessary for a child to become a young man all at once; or, perhaps, this was nothing but an admission that he was unable to take me any further. Even though the memory of his instruction is dim, I know that he, extraordinarily, tried to teach me Latin without learning any grammar.

From here I came into the hands of a teacher who held a public office; as a sideline he ran a little school that consisted of two round tables. His name was Röhl. He was the head teacher of the school in Kneiphoff;[8] his stepson was his assistant. This man was most successful and experienced. Yet both of them relied on mere pedantry and humdrum pedagogics. When he accused me of knowing nothing, because I did not understand his method of instruction, I was suddenly displaced from the little hill where his predecessor had set me. With this man I began to use Donat as a textbook[9] and whipped through a number of the most prominent and difficult Latin and Greek authors several times with a boldness that he himself admired. (He taught me their literal sense and a way of determining it which is not to be despised and which I myself have copied). He flattered me and himself for producing a great Latin and Greek scholar; I could translate a Latin author into German without understanding his language and what it meant. So my Latin and Greek compositions were bookish exercises, juggling tricks, through which memory gorges on itself and the other powers of the soul disappear, because it fails to find any wholesome, proper sap to nourish it. His son advanced me very far in arithmetic. Yet all this is lost if children do not learn to exercise their own judgment as they do it without attention and understanding. It is like learning music; the ears and the sense of hearing need to be taught,

8. Kneiphoff was the island on the Pregel River where both the cathedral and university of Königsberg were located.

9. This ancient Latin grammar which had been written in the fourth century by Aelius Donatus, the teacher of St. Jerome, became the standard in the Middle Ages.

instructed, and practiced, rather than just the fingers. Anyone who has learned to play a piece of music, or a hundred pieces of music, no matter how quickly and correctly, without a feeling for its harmony, plays it like a dancing bear rather than like the most unhappy violinist who knows how to express his own misery.

Let me add a few remarks here. The first is that I believe I have weakened my memory and my head badly by heaps of unnecessary school work and that my natural vitality and ability have suffered somewhat from it. An even greater evil is that these methods have obscured all sense of order in me, I should rather say, all comprehension of it and its threads and all pleasure in it. I discovered that I was overwhelmed with a mass of words and things without realizing what they meant, why they were, how they fitted together, and how they were to be used. I always tried to heap up more and more things on each other without selection, examination, and reflection. This plague spread out over everything that I did until at last I saw that I was in a labyrinth[10] where I could not discover any way out or any way in, nor any footprints to follow. Meanwhile, even though I found that I was actually more advanced in some subjects than I needed to be, I was thereby completely left behind in much more useful and necessary subjects, such as history and geography, without the slightest notion of prose composition and the art of poetry. I have never been able to make up properly for my lack of history and geography, and have acquired a taste for prose and poetry far too late. I find it very hard to arrange my thoughts in an ordered way in speaking and in writing and to express them easily.

A competent teacher must go to school with God and himself if he wishes to exercise his office with wisdom. He must imitate him as he reveals himself in nature and in sacred Scripture, and be able to teach both equally in our souls. Almighty God, for whom it costs
1 Cor 6:20 nothing, for whom nothing is too expensive for human beings, is the thriftiest, slowest God. His rule for agriculture, and the time that he

10. Here Hamann alludes to the story in Greek mythology of the maze that housed the Minotaur built in Crete by Daedalus. The Athenian hero Theseus and his companions escaped with the help of a ball of silken thread provided by Ariadne, the Cretan princess.

waits patiently for its fruits, should be our guide. It is not a matter of what fruit, or how much fruit, but it is all about how it is produced. Both children and we too know that! He tells his disciples that, in that hour when you need to speak, it will be given to you first and foremost *how* to speak and then *what* to say.[11] This order seems to be back to front for us human beings; yet it is to some extent proper to God and sanctified through his own ways. *Luke 8:15*

To the pure all things are pure. Our natural sense of taste can distinguish between the goodness of different foods; natural judgment can determine their relationship. But thanksgiving and God's will, by which and with which we enjoy these foods, is the work of faith alone and the condition for divine blessing. We do not sow the full plant and all its fruits, but nothing more than the smallest part of it, the seed; and this itself is so superfluous that its body must decay before it can sprout. Yet even this does not sprout, unless the soil has been prepared and it is planted in the right season. Thus the growth of the seed depends more necessarily on these conditions than on its own nature. *Titus 1:15*

The methods that we use to teach children cannot be too simple; yet even if they are simple, there is still always much that is superfluous, lost, and ephemeral in them. But they must be rich in what they produce, diverse and fruitful in their application and practice. As soon as children have been taught to read, examples should be chosen for them—not just the best books first, or for learning how to read—to receive light in their understanding and virtue in their hearts. Yet, even if learning to read itself is the main purpose, it must be regarded as a secondary purpose that prepares for the exercise of attentiveness with the senses, the opening and enlightenment of concepts, the awakening of feelings, and the portrayal of good inclinations. So the study of foreign languages should be used as an aid to understand the mother tongue better, to become fruitful in thinking with it, to analyze it, to compare its expressions with other expressions and to note their difference. In short, what looks

11. Matt 10:19: "Do not be anxious about how you are to speak or what you are to say, for what you are to say will be given to you in that hour."

only like memory work should be used as a preparation and exercise for all the powers of the soul and for higher, more important, more profound, yes more spiritual things. The lack of this in teaching makes the learning of languages so hard, so dry, so irksome, so seemingly futile and useless.

What connection and affinity do children who will become householders, shepherds, artisans, and so on, have with the deeds of Greek and Roman heroes, foreign people, their customs, and so on? This practice is even less excusable because there are good examples of discourse in the world on moral rules, stories and the like that promote purity, diversity, and elegance through their content and usefulness. A landowner should make use of the writers about agriculture as textbooks for Latin rather than the life story of Alexander[12] and the letters of Pliny.[13] I have always wished for a selection from Latin books on economics as as models for the use of language in poetry and prose, like the excellent collection by a French writer which I have put to good use. In this way Latin would be easier to learn, more interesting and useful, not only for a young nobleman, but also for many children of citizens, and insights into economics that are so relevant to the general public and individual citizens would hereby be spread.

I myself have used this observation partly in teaching writing, for the same examples set for children to copy in writing should also be used as exercises to teach them to read. Yes, in writing the eye must be kept steady in order to gain visual judgment and attentiveness. Perhaps the consideration of my own education distracts me with extensive side-tracks. Yet this is such an important task; I
John 21:15 still always find in me a gentle call to feed God's lambs that I cannot resist the temptation to follow the inclination of my heart which gives me so much to write on this topic.

12. Hamann refers to Alexander the Great, who lived from 356–323 BC and established a Greek empire that stretched from Greece to India.

13. Pliny the Younger, who lived from AD 61 to about 113, was a Roman official whose collection of essays were used to teach Latin prose composition.

I believe that the practice of writing comes at the cost of much time, much effort, and boredom. Yes, for some it is even much more detrimental, the earlier they are introduced to it. It damages good health, because this task requires sitting still for a long time, a requirement to do nothing or at least to be idle in thinking, while the hand must be kept annoyingly busy. What pleasure does a child have in being able to form an "a" or a "b"? Are years required to become skilfull in copying twenty-four letters? Could we not instead let children begin with painting and drawing, with the hieroglyphic art of writing? Since we all born to imitate, it would be easier to do this by imitating the natural world: the sense and discernment of the eye, the sense and taste for proportion and visible beauty, the comparison of similarities and dissimilarities which provide such a great benefit in the ability to think. A sharp and critical eye for natural and artistic products would be *more useful* in assisting all tradesmen in the perfection of their trade; it would be an immense advantage for travelers; a general pastime for women and young people; it would influence and prepare us to write neatly and quickly. Yes, this part of the art of writing would be learned easier and more quickly. The history of the arts and human nature in them seems to confirm this even more. Were not painters the first writers and poets, and orators the first authors? The perfection of the world seems to entail alienation from nature. How unnatural have fads and fashions made us, and how hard it is for us in our times to return to the simplicity and innocence of the old customs.

My dear, respectable father partly recognized what was missing in the schooling that I had received. He engaged a most distinguished teacher to make up for that by asking the private tutor for a pastor's widow to let me have special instruction together with the sons of this generous woman. Instead of satisfying myself with the pure milk of the gospel, I fell away into another byway with my *1 Pet 2:2*
curiosity and precocious interest in all heresies and errors. In this way the enemy of our souls and everything good tried to choke the divine wheat with his weeds. I filled my head with the names and *Matt 13:25*
absurd controversies of all the fools who became heretics or made

others heretics in order to distinguish themselves. What an effort is needed for God and his Spirit just to clear away the rubbish under which Satan buries our souls, when we think that we are building on them together with him!

In this household I with my brother had the misfortune of being infected by a child who had been born with an infectious rash that could not be healed but led to his early death. The hats that we wore unwittingly helped the child to cover up himself and it. We both suffered from it for a long time with trouble and distress for our deceased mother. It resisted the strongest means of treatment even for the removal of venereal disease. We were often kept from school for weeks. Mercifully, God cured both of us from it. I thank him once again that he always wants to be my physician for as long as I travel as a pilgrim on this infectious earth, with the poison of sin in my blood and heart and in the uncouth generation of sinners. I bear the mark of my recovery from this infection on my bald head from which the hair that was enclosed by the brim of my hat has fully fallen out. We scrubbed ourselves, and the follicles of hair were full of pus; the stink was unbearable; my now deceased mother was not put off by it but endured it often on our behalf, with tears at our pain and disfigurement. Thank God, my hair that dropped out is the only thing that I have, until now, lost from my body. This is the only sickness that is worth noting for its duration and severity in my life to now. During it I often suffered from sharp attacks of dizziness and faintness from which I have, thank God, experienced almost nothing more when I was away from home.

Before this affliction by God, my father employed a lout as an apprentice who taught me to become just like him physically. Thereafter he visited our house and pretended to have resided in Sweden. God forgive him and me! The example of this sad experience has been good because it has made me as strict and careful as possible at the association of children with employees and domestic servants. I have attempted to keep my eye on this in both households where I was a private tutor. I now realize that Satan's moral teaching and casuistry makes some sins trivial for us in comparison with others. My reason regarded prostitution as an all too human and pardonable transgression. I had read the story of Joseph without profiting from it. Yes, I held that prostitution was a means *Gen 39:2–20* for virtue to escape the misfortune of an unhappy marriage, or the perjury of adultery. So little does a person discern what is of God's *1 Cor 5:11* Spirit. I came close to committing adultery in Riga. I have been tempted by flesh and blood as well as by witty banter and what I felt,[14] and up to now God has graciously protected me from the snares of prostitutes, I might add, miraculously so. Let him give me grace to protect myself from every defilement of body and spirit, and make this earthly vessel, that he wishes to make holy by his *2 Cor 7:1; 4:7* dwelling in it, a member of Christ's body and preserve it free from *1 Cor 6:19* all impurity and without any blemish. *1 Thess 5:23*

Before I come to the last stage of my education, I will add a consideration about the small groups and extracurricular tutorial classes with which many are so infatuated that they openly prefer them. That is not what I think is best. I believe that teaching a middling number of children requires much more effort and diligence than a larger one, and that a smaller number is dangerous for the moral development of the children, because they more easily become familiar with each other, and this familiarity therefore increases the opportunity for its abuse as well as also for envy and hatred, which is not so damaging to larger groups of students, serving more for competition and encouragement.

My father, my respectable father, removed me rather painfully from this kind of education which had made him so hopeful and perhaps too hopeful for my progress in learning. He finally decided to enroll me in a public school, making a lucky choice with the

14. In German the untranslatable rhyme "Witz und Herz" means "wit and heart."

school in Kneiphoff.[15] I saw that the students who were below me received freedom in their study and now I had to be satisfied with taking my place in the second grade rather than the sixth grade, where I had Latin authors that were so easy for me to explain that I did not need to prepare them in order to outdo the others. I came to school there just before the public examinations. This was why the principal rather cleverly put me in that class well below what I claimed to have learned. Here I too had the chance to make a beginning with history and geography as well as essay writing. Dr. Salthenius, the principal of this school, was a worthy, well-educated, devout man with rare and unusual gifts, who possessed faithfulness and wisdom and honesty alike in his office.[16] Apart from him, I owe very much to two capable teachers, Buchholtz[17] and Herold,[18] both now pastors, the one in the old city and the other in the country. They were likeable and devout twins, good examples in what they were like, both together and taken separately.

In my first promotion after the school examination in which I came first, I entered the first class, a distinction that my fellow students did not begrudge me. Before my experience of this little joy, I had to stay away from school for quite some time on account of my infection. Here I received the foundational concepts of philosophy and mathematics, theology and Hebrew. Here a new field for distraction lay open for me, and my brain became a stall in an annual market with quite new wares. I brought this whirlwind with

15. Together with Altstadt and Löbenicht, Kneiphoff was originally one of three towns that came together in 1724 create the new city of Königsberg. It was located on an island in the Pregel River where both the cathedral and university of Königsberg were located. Significantly for his later development, Hamann's father did not enroll him in the Pietist school that Kant attended but in this old orthodox cathedral school where Hamann received a sound grounding in the Bible and Lutheran doctrine.

16. Salthenius was the son of a pastor in Sweden who rather foolishly made a pact with the devil in his youth (which he later renounced). He was a teacher of logic, metaphysics, and theology.

17. Buchholz (1719–73) was a teacher in the cathedral school from 1743 to 1748 and then became the pastor of the church in the suburb of Altstadt.

18. Herold (1716–79) taught in the school from 1743 to 1751 before he became a pastor elsewhere in East Prussia.

me into university where it actually belonged. There I was enrolled as a student on March 30, 1746.[19]

I became a student of Knutzen,[20] famous in all branches of philosophy, in mathematics, and in tutorials on algebra. As well as that, I became a member of a society for physics and theology which was set up under him but was never actually constituted. All these opportunities to learn and become useful were offered to me with all too little faithfulness, order, and benefit. I realized all too little that I was wasting the bitter sweat of my father and the sweet hope that he would see the fruits from what he had expended with so much pleasure and self-denial of necessities. Hear, God, and forgive! Restore to him what his own child has destroyed—do not hold it to my account, nor let the punishment that I deserve be too heavy for me. Grant me remorse and sorrow, so that I acknowledge it, and do not let it be acknowledged too late.

The memory of a less famous teacher is much more pleasant for me. God made him live in oppressive, miserable, dark circumstances; he deserved a better fate; he possessed qualities that the world does not value and so does not reward. His end was like his life, unnoticed, yet I do not doubt that it was blessed. His name was Rappolt,[21] a man who possessed a clear-sighted ability to assess natural phenomena reverently and simply, the modesty of a Christian philosopher, and an unusual ability to imitate the spirit and language of Latin authors. May you, O God, let your blessing and the blessing of their father rest on his sons![22]

---

19. Hamann studied at Albertina, the University of Königsberg, which was founded by Duke Albert of Prussia in 1544 and named after its founder. It is the world's second Lutheran University. According to the records of the university, he was accepted as a student of theology on April 25, 1746.

20. Martin Knutzen (1713–55), a Pietist rationalist and the teacher of Kant, was the well-known professor of logic and metaphysics with a special interest in mathematics and astronomy and the relation of the body to the soul.

21. Karl Heinrich Rappolt (1702–53) was a professor of physics at the University of Königsberg. An enthusiast for the poetry of Alexander Pope, he also taught English and gave lectures on English literature.

22. Some of what follows from here on has been partially influenced by the translation of selections from this work by Roland Gregor Smith in *J. G. Hamann 1730–1788: A Study in Christian Existence with Selection's from His Writings* (London: Collins, 1960), 140–57.

Meanwhile, as I drifted around in the forecourts of academic disciplines, I lost the call that I thought I had to the study of theology. I found an obstacle in my speech, my poor memory, and many other sham obstacles in my way of thinking, such as in the corrupt morals of pastors and my high regard for what their duties were. Of course I thought that I was right in my thinking because I regarded myself as the giver and author of what belonged to the pastoral office. I forgot the source of every good thing from whom
Jas 1:17 I could expect and claim all that I lacked, so that with his help I could have overcome every obstacle that lay in my way.

As a student I enjoyed the outstanding love of my godfather and confessor[23] in whose house I dined weekly with his sons, most of all the theologian Dr. Lilienthal, who like his father became famous for his writings.[24] Thus I also had two free meals with an opportunity to learn and to wean myself from the shyness that I retained for a long time and still sticks with me. Without any doubt I could have used these comforts better than I did, and I have incurred the appearance of ingratitude for myself for some of them.

My previously mentioned godfather gave me various important books as gifts. He also gave me introductory instruction in Christianity and confirmed me with a large number of others on the Sunday after Easter in 1743 or 1744, if I am not mistaken. I remember that I came to the altar during the seventh verse of the hymn, "*O Lord How Great Is Your Wrath*":

You feed each little sheep so well
And hold it close to you;
Your arms are filled with many lambs,
You care for all the weak.
No one can snatch one from your hand

23. Hamann's godfather was Michael Lilienthal (1686–1750), a prominent theologian with an interest in philosophy, languages, and history, who was the dean of the local cathedral.

24. Theodore Christopher Lilienthal (1717–1781) was a prominent professor of theology and pastor in Königsberg who wrote a well-known apologetic handbook of the Bible in sixteen volumes.

That you have marked with your own blood
And paid your life for ours.
Since you have claimed us for yourself
And made our cross so light for us,
We give our all to you.[25]

I now return to the sequence of my life. What took away my taste for theology and all serious subjects was a new inclination that awoke in me for antiquities, for critical analysis; for the fine, decorative arts as well; for poetry, novels, philology; for French authors and their talent for writing, painting, portraying, pleasing the imagination, and so on. May God forgive me for the abuse of my natural powers, which would perhaps have been improved and been made beneficial for the world and myself by their proper application in a first-rate manner, yes powers which I had dedicated to the service of his house and his work on earth, powers which I have mangled and spoilt so completely. The waste of time, the expense for my father, his hope that he would have a staff for his old age with his children. My gracious God! Hear and forgive me. Amend what I have spoilt, if it is not too late, and make the next year, which you grant me, so much more blessed. Let all my errors produce what is best for me; let them all now at last serve to make me wise, and to warn others, with so much greater force and zeal, against the reefs on which I myself was wrecked. *Rom 8:28; Ps 90*

So for the sake of appearance, I enrolled in the study of law. In my foolishness I indulged my sense of grandeur and superiority by studying, as I was inclined, as a pastime for the love of the arts and sciences themselves, rather than in order to make a living. I imagined that it would be better to be a martyr than a day-labourer and hireling of the muses.[26] What nonsense is expressed in well-rounded

25. This little-known penitential hymn, which was composed by Bernhard Derschow (1591–1639), a pastor and professor of theology in Königsberg, has not been translated into English.

26. In Greek mythology the muses were the daughters of Zeus who taught people the arts of civilization by inspiring artists to compose music, poetry, and literature. A hireling of the muses is an uninspired hack writer who composes poetry and literature for pay.

and resounding words! So I attended lectures on *the Institutions and Pandects*[27] without preparing for them and summarizing their content, without any serious intention and commitment to become a lawyer, just as I had none and showed none to be a theologian.

Meanwhile I had always considered taking up a position as tutor in a household in order to find whether it was suitable for me and try out my freedom in the world. In my mind my dependence on my dear parents restricted me financially, and I wanted to manage my own money. For my own good I had been kept a little too short of it, and I learned to be careful with it a little too late, when I had my own. Maybe there was also no divine blessing on my income, which makes what is little into more than enough. Disorder, the gen-
Mark 6:35–44 eral flaw of my mentality, a false sense of generosity, love that was too blind, pleasure in the opinions of others, and carelessness that sprang in part from inexperience and ignorance were all to blame.

Unwittingly, chance came to help me in my plans. A pastor who belonged to a group of household tutors and had taught us to play the piano came from Latvia to visit his parents in a small town and his friends in Prussia.[28] He came to our house. I sensed that there was an extraordinary change in his attitude and conduct with me because I held a very favorable preconception of Latvia and the Latvian way of life on account of some friends that came from there. He was looking to fill several vacancies in Latvia. With some others one was on the estate where he himself was the pastor. Even though the conditions of employment were not entirely favorable, an only son, a very wealthy house, his proximity, and some other additional things moved me to accept this position. Despite the misgivings of my parents and the predictions of trouble from the woman that I would have to serve, I decided to work there.

When I left my parents' home in November 1752, my now deceased mother broke down with grief, my father himself accompanied me to the gate of the city, and an elderly, honest, intelligent

27. This was a legal textbook that consisted of selections of cases from collections of Roman law.

28. This pastor was Johann Gottlieb Blank (1723–1764).

Swabian called Wagner, our neighbour and the owner of a book-shop, traveled with me for a mile and returned to the city by foot the next day. I had the good fortune to have a good friend Gericke[29] as my travelling companion, whose half-brother offered me many friendly services in Courland, just as I enjoyed remarkable generosity and love in the house of both his parents in Riga.[30]

Despite the late time of the year, the weather and the journey were exceptionally good. Our crossing of the lagoon was very successful,[31] and the company of a salesman who got married during my time in Riga and began his own business was very stimulating and pleasant.[32] We also had an Armenian merchant who traveled through all countries without understanding any of their languages. He took great pleasure in chatting, cheering us up with his signs and gestures and our misunderstanding of them. He pursued astonishing moderation in his lifestyle and thereby possessed an ever so wonderful cheerfulness and freshness of body and spirit, even though he did not seem to be young any more.

In Riga I stayed with a compatriot of my father who had for a very long time come and gone as a trusted guest in our house.[33] Thereupon I took my journey to the estate where Baron Budberg lived in Kegeln, twelve miles from Riga.[34] On a Saturday I reached the pastorate of the estate in Papendorf, and on the following Sunday saw the family to whose house I would belong: a child aged nine who looked rather shy, awkward, and delicate;[35] his young

---

29. Johann Christoph Gericke (1696–1759) was the son of a pastor from Pernigel in Latvia who eventually became a pastor in Riga.

30. Riga, the present capital city of Latvia, was the main port on the eastern side of the Baltic Sea and the center of trade between Russia and Germany. It was at that time part of the Russian Empire.

31. This refers to the Kurskiy Zaliv, the enclosed Kurisch Bay on the Baltic Sea north of Königsberg.

32. The salesman was a man called Eckart.

33. The host was the crown lawyer Philipp Belger.

34. Kegeln, now Kiegeli, is located near Papendorf, now Rubene, northeast of Riga.

35. This son was called Waldemar Dietrich. He later became a student of Lindner in Riga and a friend of Herder.

sister; and an orphaned girl who was being brought up by the baroness. My beginning in this my new calling was rather difficult. I had to educate myself, my underage pupil, and an uncouth, coarse, ignorant mother. Like a spirited horse with a plough, I went at it with much enthusiasm, good intentions, little discretion, with too much confidence in my own self and little regard for human folly on account of the good that I did, or wanted to do. By nature we are inclined to overestimate our efforts, to expect results from them as an inevitable consequence, to weigh and evaluate other duties according to our own prejudices and inclinations.

A farmer cannot expect a yield of a hundred percent just from
Luke 8:8 careful husbandry; the soil, the weather, the quality of the seed, pests, things that escape our attention, play their part, and over all there is the blessing of divine providence and government. I felt that my actions should have been recognized and, at times, admired by others; yes, they should have put them to shame. All these are sordid motives that disorder and disgrace our powers. God showed me much unending grace. He gave me more patience than I was ready to receive, more wisdom, more success, all of which I may have credited to my own account, but which may have been the result of the prayers of my devout parents and the forbearance of his divine patience and grace. My unsociable, odd way of living, which was partly a pose, partly false cleverness, partly a result of the inner unrest that plagued me for a very long time in my life, my dissatisfaction and inability to put up with myself, my conceitedness in regarding my own self as an enigma—all these did much damage and made me obnoxious. I wrote two letters to the baroness about the education of her child which were meant to arouse her conscience. Misunderstood, they poured oil on fire when she received them. So I was unexpectedly sacked, even though I had not been in the house for half a year. I received some compensation for the humiliation of my pride through the affection of the child and the flattering notion that I either suffered innocently or was repaid with evil for good. I wrapped myself as far as I could in the cloak of religion and virtue, so as to cover up my nakedness with it, but I fumed

with rage to avenge and justify myself. This was an act of folly that in time I myself recognized and so dispersed like a cloud of smoke.

Then I spent a few months in Riga, used up the little money that I had received, and also put myself in debt to my landlord who was the same compatriot of my father with whom I had stayed on my arrival. This time was divided between desolate, misanthropic diligence and excessive indulgence in pleasure and sloth. My money melted away up to the last ducats which I foolishly spent on some useless books. On the one hand I lived carelessly. On the other hand I made futile attempts to get a new position. God had mercy on me, and made use of the brother-in-law[36] of the baroness herself to open up the door of a very favorable opportunity for me in Courland when I was on the brink of poverty and had already spent many sleepless nights on that account. I felt my embarrassment so much more strongly because I had no friend to open up to and the house where I was staying was quite sick of me. By this ingratitude to them I committed a grave offense against my good-hearted parents. It is true that these people were very self-serving and boastful about their good works. This, however, should not belittle the good for us that we enjoy from the hand of a neighbor. Our vanity makes us quibble far too much about motives and the way that people put us under obligation with the result that we have less reason to be grateful. I repaid them in like kind, and admit this with shame and regret, even though I did not realize that I had deliberately acted in this way, yet partly out of ignorance and partly out of necessity.[37]

Thus in 1753 I arrived in Courland in the most beautiful time of the year at the home of General Witten and his wife, who was born the Countess von Lacy.[38] They had two sons. I followed two

---

36. Hamann inserts "N.B." above "brother-in-law" to emphasize the importance of this man as his confidant.

37. For some reason Hamann adds: "NB. Privy Councillor von Campenhausen." He was the father-in-law of Hamann's former student, Waldemar von Budberg.

38. The duchy of Courland was the fertile area south of the River Düna which since 1561 had been a Lutheran principality under Polish control. It is now the southern part of present day Latvia. Christoph Wilhelm von Witten (1703–61) was the owner of a feudal estate near Mittau with its residence in Grünhoff.

tutors who had worked here at the same time, one a coarse windbag and the other a man with a shallow brain. Here I found two children quite different in temperament from the baron; they required more discipline, attention, and rigor, and showed more promise, because the older child possessed great ability. Yet I could never be as satisfied with his inclinations as I had been with my first pupil. God also showed me immensely much grace in this house with the children and parents as well as the members of the household. I also overrated my services to them and made too many demands in return for them. Because I felt dissatisfied, impatient, overstretched, I found it hard to last for a year, until with much grief, discontent, resentment, and, in part, outrage, I returned to Riga once again.

Apart from the extraordinary kindness that I enjoyed in this house from the parents and children, except for my departure, I became good friends with Major von Oven, a very worthy man from Westphalia who combined unusual emotional intelligence with genius,[39] whose kind, profitable, cordial company I was often very lucky to enjoy. May the dear God reward and govern him, and make him fully happy and at peace. We were both similar with our good intentions and distractions, in our wishes and our failure to fulfill them.

Apart from him, Bassa, a man born in Turkey, was a brotherly minded friend to whom I, unfortunately, have been rather ungrateful. May God give me grace to be on good terms with him and reward him all the good that he has done for me in every possible way with a very sincere, loyal, and tender heart!

I spent just as many sweet hours in my association with Mr. Parius, a regimental surgeon in the Russian army, and with the well-educated, kind Master Haase[40] who, with his much greater accomplishments, much lesser advantages, and much higher and more general talents, taught me, sadly in vain, by his example to live more contentedly and humbly.

---

39. This term refers to the exceptional supernatural creative gifts given to a person at birth.

40. Haase, a pastor, is called Master because he held earned the degree of Master of Arts.

With sadness I here especially recall the friendliness of Dr. Lindner[41] in Mitau,[42] whose steady, intimate acquaintance I am flattered to claim and so all the more regret his condition because I am now only too like him.[43] May the Highest bless his cross, just as he has blessed mine in order to bring me to the recognition of the one needful thing and my own self. May he comfort him with the *Luke 10:41* same comfort with which I have been comforted and grant him the *2 Cor 1:3–5* same earnest desire for self-amendment with which I call on God's Spirit and his guidance as the only way to avoid sin and deliver him from the wrong ways into which it eventually brings us. Hear, hear me, God, for the sake of your Son and your holy name. Amen!

So well into summer in 1755 I returned once more to Riga, filled with contemplation and reflection about my own confusion, yet also filled with hope and contentment that the presence of my two friends promised me. The first of them was my friend Berens, whom God used as a special instrument.[44] I cannot yet discern the purpose and goal of this, even though I live with full trust and confidence that his wise providence, which uses people to tie the knots in our life, knows how to undo them for his glory and what is best for us. This extraordinary friend had been my favorite in Königsberg; from there he had gone on journeys from which he had returned again

41. From 1753, Ehregott Friedrich Lindner, the younger brother of his close friend Johann Gotthelf Lindner, worked as a doctor in Mitau. He accompanied Hamann at the end of his life on his trip to Westphalia in 1789.

42. Mitau, which lay on the River Drixe, about fifty miles south west of Riga, was the capital of Courland.

43. Hamann implies that the younger Lindner has had a financial or spiritual crisis that is similar to his own experience.

44. Johann Christoph Berens (1729–1792), the fourth of fifteen children, came from a prominent merchant family in Riga. He studied law in the University of Königsberg from 1748 to 1751 where he became a close friend of Hamann. Together with him and Lindner, he established a weekly magazine called Daphne which promoted the cause of the Enlightenment. After his return to Riga he established a circle of like-minded, enlightened intellectuals and joined in the operation of the family firm with the rest of his family. He arranged for Hamann to be employed in it in 1756 and sent him on his mission to London in 1757. After Hamann's return to Riga from London, Berens fell out with him over what he considered his newfound irrational religious fanaticism, called off Hamann's engagement with his sister Katharina (1727–1805), and prevailed on Kant to straighten out their friend's misguided views. That resulted in Hamann's composition of his first published work called the *Socratic Memorabilia* in 1759.

with much profit and evident benefit.[45] God knows why he was so taken in by me; he who searches and tests hearts and knows how to use them has had his wise purposes for us by bringing us both into temptation through the other. I believe in God's providence in this drama as a Christian for whom his providence has promised to account for each of the hairs on his head. This friend had not in the least forgotten me, and his friendship towards me had changed so little that he hurried to meet me as soon as he could. On that account, in an express coach that had been dispatched, which set the whole house in Grünhof in turmoil, he unexpectedly came to Mitau in the same night. I jumped from bed in order to get dressed, hurried to meet him, and found him fast asleep. His welcome was so exceptionally affectionate and friendly that I was too embarrassed to respond to him immediately or to engage with him. He dazzled me with his views, his proposals, his ideas about the world, new disciplines, the prevailing taste of the present century, and so on, and a hundred witty asides that a sociable heart and a fruitful imagination is able to produce.

Ps 7:9; Rom 8:27

Matt 10:30; Luke 12:7

The second friend whom I had chosen as my host was the older Lindner, a good friend with whom I had lived in fraternal intimacy from my first year at university.[46] He had now become the principal of a school in Riga. I was the Lepidus in this triumvirate.[47] Yet our friendship bubbled equally strong in the three of us. We were on fire to see and enjoy each other.

How much dross there is in our best natural and artistic impulses! How spoiled must the soil be that turns and changes the

45. This refers to his journey as a student to the University of Göttingen and elsewhere in Germany.

46. Johann Gotthelf Lindner (1729–1776) was the son of a Lutheran pastor in Pomerania. Even though he was a year younger than Hamann, he was the leading light in his circle of friends at the University of Königsberg. After graduation he took up a position as a teacher in the cathedral school in Riga in 1753 and became its rector in 1755. He became a full professor of poetry in 1765 and the director of the German Society in 1766. After gaining a doctorate in theology with a dissertation on poetry in the Bible in 1773, he became the pastor and school inspector of the Löbenicht parish in Königsberg.

47. Lepidus was the weaker party with Anthony and Octavian at the temporary division of the Roman Empire into three parts in 43 BC.

best seeds of wheat into weeds! How easy it is to corrupt nature itself!

I arrived at a time when the people in Riga enjoyed country life on their estates, and I was lucky to make use of the spa of the spring at Pyrmont together with the Berens family. My health had suffered so badly, partly by my work at school, partly by my obsession with trivial matters, and partly by the tumult of emotions which constantly tossed my mind to and fro like a little boat on a stormy sea, that this *Eph 4:14*
was a very welcome occasion for me. Even though I had every reason to be contented, I could not yield to enjoyment in the company of the most high-minded, liveliest, best-hearted people of both sexes. My brain saw a fog of ideas around it that it could not separate; my heart felt emotions that it did not know how to explain; it felt nothing but mistrust of myself or others, nothing but anguish at how I should approach them or disclose myself to them. I remained in this state for most of my time in the household where I was the greatest admirer, hero-worshipper, and friend of all who belonged to it.

How is it possible that I could be taken to be a clever, let alone a useful person, when it was never possible for me to show what I am and what I can be? This is a mystery that I have never been able to understand nor explain. That is why I regard all these things partly as intimations, partly as the work of God's hand that lay heavy upon me, so that I could not discover my own self in the midst of all the *Ps 32:4*
good that I experienced from other people. I regard all the unrest in which I lived as the result of all that, and I take comfort that God will now put aside the rod under which I groaned without recognizing it and will reveal his gracious will to me to which I now surrender myself completely. I have been a premature fruit in all my deeds *Luke 8:14*
and actions, in all my undertakings and projects, because they were all attempted and begun without God; they have fallen into a hole instead of reaching completion. In the end, wounded and bleeding, I kicked against the goad which I did not want to recognize; and I *Acts 26:14*
pray for nothing more than that the gracious God, who pardons the penitent, believing sinner and forgets what has happened, would *Luke 15:7; Jer 31:34; Heb 10:17; Rom 6:4*
let my future life be new and holy.

So I lived in Riga and enjoyed many happy hours and many pleasant interactions in the house of my friend where I was regarded as a brother, yes almost as an older brother.[48] Since school dust had become odious to me, I thought that I should fit in with the taste of the time by working usefully in trade and in economic and political matters. The knowledge of these disciplines pleased me because they were new and influential for human life. I could have chosen these secondary matters more aptly than metaphysical and fanciful systems. But it was ill-advised to begin a new building and to relocate myself all at once from a cell into business affairs that required more facility and practice and leadership, or, even more, *hands-on management*.

During this time I was happy to see my first student, the young Baron Budberg, in my friend's house. I was tracked down through my successor. I welcomed him wholeheartedly and would gladly have assisted him in his instruction. But it seemed that this had formerly been the reason for a coolness in our friendship and had produced a rather bad impression as an attack in the mind of the young man. My friend seemed to regard my attentiveness to the young baron as interference and criticism, and the baron repaid me with hatred and contempt. We were perhaps all caught in a misunderstanding that became harmful to all three of us and caused the greatest offense to the one that we tried hard to help and please.

As time went on, I became more depressed, because I saw no way for me to make an honest living and be used as I wished and preferred. Once again God took up my cause in an extraordinary and surprising way. I was called back most urgently, with an offer that met all my demands, to that same house in Courland that I had left with some rash and hurtful words. My need for employment, my self-complacency, and, in some measure, reason and prudence counselled me to accept the summons. So towards the end of the same year I returned and was welcomed back to Courland and Grünhoff.[49]

48. His friend was either Johann Christoph Berens or Johann Gotthelf Lindner.

49. This was the name of the family estate in Courland.

At the beginning of the year in 1756 I received the sad news from my dear father about the ill health of my mother, and not much later the tactful directive to come home if I still wanted to see her and fulfill her wishes in that regard. This made for new anxiety at the prospect of losing my dear mother and some reflection on my own condition and the little comfort that she would have in it if she saw me once again. I procured a sum of about 150 Albertsthaler[50] for myself but no overcoat for the trip, putting myself in such a large debt for a silly, painful trip to Riga in order to see my friend whom I found unwell; I was more in the way and trouble than a relief for him. My honest Bassa lent me this money with whom I subsequently fell into deeper debt, even though I was not able to pay him for my previous trip and have still not done enough for him (which I cannot think about without pain and sorrow).

My heart and my sense of duty, however, called me back home. I reported this to my friends in Riga who gained a clear understanding of my situation and took me up into their employment, business, and family. I had much resistance in entering this. Yet it was a comfort, because I believed that I would discover God's providence, and I thought that I would ingratiate myself to myself and my parents. So I hoped to reach them on the Nativity of John the Baptist,[51] and, with a heavy, doubtful heart, entered into the terms of a contract with the Berens family. I would take the trip at their expense to be cheered up and return to their family business with more ability to command respect and with increased competence.[52]

By God's extraordinary blessing I was released from the house in Courland for false reasons and without sincerity in my promises that I would return, which was a blatant lie and contrary to what I envisaged and intended. Early on Sunday, the fourth day of the journey, I was lucky to reach Trutenau where I was picked up in a

---

50. This was a large silver coin that had been issued in Holland by Albrecht VIII in 1616. From there it spread to Denmark and Prussia.

51. That is, on June 24.

52. The trip at the beginning of his employment by the Berens family was a business journey that brought him to England.

carriage by my cousin Zoepfel and my brother, who fainted when he saw me once again. For twenty weeks God, my dear God, permitted my now deceased mother to wait for me, before he took her to himself. Weeping, my aged father, who had been watching for me at the window, gave me a sad welcome. I saw my mother, my now deceased mother, whom God had repeatedly and miraculously raised from chronic ill health and her death bed, even though her children, or at least I, did not ask or thank him for that. She received me less enthusiastically than I thought she would, because the day before she had suffered a sudden turn and God had redoubled the pace of her steps to the grave. She admitted that there was nothing more in the world for her to enjoy. In our first moments together she reprimanded me for the tone of my voice, which appeared to her to have changed and not become more manly. She was all skin and bones, and her features had become so completely distorted by her painful, protracted time in bed that I could not look at her without natural sympathy for her. I am loathe to admit that my heart was much less tender than it should have been, and that, despite the near prospect of losing her from the world, I was about to abandon myself to other distractions. Meanwhile I was lucky that she was pleased with my physical care, and preferred to ask me to lift her up and put her right in her bed. Our gracious God summoned her after a few days, during which, for hardly a week, I had been a witness who shared in her cross and in the burden of my old, respectable father. When I saw her die—with much emotion and many reflections on death—I saw the death of a Christian. In the pangs of her death the Highest granted her a *calm appearance,* her heart was *softly and gently* broken, and she passed away like a light, without *residual pain* on account of *the innocent blood that you shed*
Matt 26:28 *for her.*[53] I attended her funeral with unspeakable sorrow and sadness which seemed to melt my heart; but, regrettably, soon I once again found comfort in the world and the whims of my good luck.

53. The phrases in italics come from Bartholomew Ringwaldt's funeral hymn "Herr Jesu Christ, ich weiss gar wohl, dass ich einmal muss sterben," which, though included in 14 German hymnals, has no known English translations.

After this I freed myself entirely from my ties in Courland. I received the money and authorization for my journey, which I undertook after a long delay, half with sadness and half with the contentment from a false hope, which our flesh and blood and Satan never fail to provide so that he can leave us so much more naked and then mock us for our gullibility. I mounted the mail-coach to Danzig early in the morning on October 1, 1756, after taking leave from my father in his bed. I can only pray to God for him and can now only commend him to our heavenly Father.

I remained in Danzig for a mail-day and went from there to Berlin. On the way I passed through a terrible storm which did great damage; then, praise God, I reached Körlin unharmed and with much good fortune, and stopped there for few days.[54] My travelling companion from Danzig to Berlin was a Jew, a pleasant, sociable young man, who lived in Halberstadt; he was a good fellow traveler for me, because like me he had gone to university and had gone into trade. In Körlin I went to church and heard an edifying sermon from the pastor. This little town was rather run down, and the inn was wretched; we were the first people to stay so long in it. The innkeeper was a barber, and his wife was most kind-hearted to me, because she believed that I was much like her pastor who had edified me without knowing at all about this.

Then I reached Berlin on October 14 where, on account of my old father, I found an unusually warm reception from Privy Counsellor Ursinus as well as from Count von Fink. Besides that, at the recommendation of my friend in Riga many favors were shown to me by the houses of Merk and Guzkowsky.[55] I enjoyed this place very much because it was the first large city that I had seen, and I found some good old friends in it: Rutzen, Pastor Reinbeck,[56] and

54. Körlin was a small town close to Kolberg in the Baltic Sea in Pomerania.

55. These were two merchant houses in Berlin that had trading links with the Berens family. Later in this account Hamann notes that Mr. Merk commissioned him to deliver a sum of money for him to someone in Hamburg.

56. Reinbeck (1727–1805) was the archdeacon of St. Peter's Church and member of the church consistory in Berlin.

Reusch,[57] who were all pleased to see me; I got to know my friend Sahme[58] and the Jew Moses[59] among the scholars together with another man of his faith who emulated his ability, Professor Sulzer, who introduced me to the Academy;[60] Ramler, a young French academic who was a Swiss citizen; and Merian, who introduced me to Premontval. Nevertheless I could not enjoy any of this; I was utterly inhibited and anxious about myself, pensive without thinking, restless and dissatisfied like a refugee from a bad conscience (Gen 4:12).

On November 23 I left Berlin where I stayed far too long for my project and much too idly for a long time, and went to Hamburg where Mr. Merk wanted me to deposit a sum of gold coins, which caused me much distress because on the first night the lock of my trunk came off; however, I managed to deliver it safely to Hamburg. From there I hurried to Lübeck where I arrived on Sunday morning the 28th and dismounted at the home of my generous maternal uncle.

I wished to spend the winter there as a guest of my blood relatives; my unexpected visit produced as much amazement as joy. Praise God, they were all pleased to see me, and I have good reason to be proud of the affection and friendship with which I was received into my uncle's house and by most of my other relatives; the memory of my parents was altogether blessed and fortunate for me. I was treated well in the household of Roed and better than I deserved by Karstens, a proven friend. Often my old aunt reminded me quite often of my deceased mother; they were much alike and had always loved each other as sisters.

---

57. Reusch was the son of the deacon in Königsberg.

58. Sahme was the son of the arch-deacon in Löbenicht, a parish in Königsberg.

59. Moses Mendelsohn (1729–1786) was a prominent Jewish philosopher and ardent advocate of the Enlightenment in Berlin. Hamann later crossed swords with him in his famous tract *Golgotha and Scheblimini*.

60. Sulzer, a professor of mathematics in the Joachimsthal Gymnasium, was a member of the Academy for the Sciences in Berlin together with the poet Ramler, the Swiss philosopher Merian, and the mathematician Prémontval.

The gentle delights of blood ties were, to some extent, new feelings for me, because my parents had met and discovered each other as strangers in Königsberg. I found myself in the company of good, contented people and gave in too much to sloth and its pleasures. I strained as hard as I could to be satisfied and followed every possible distraction—all for nothing! "The worm does not die" (Mark 9:48)—how could any sinner take fright at the worm of a bad conscience without thinking of the fire that cannot be quenched. The first threat of an undying worm alone is punishment and agony enough without the fire of damnation!

I left Lübeck on January 24 with tears and a thousand heartfelt well-wishes, accompanied by my cousin and friend from a club for half the way to Hamburg where we stayed with the old, honourable Commander Brandenberger, a distant cousin, who had distinguished himself in the competitions for the poets of Lower Saxony with some successful poems. Then on the 27th I reached Jenner and set out for Bremen in good winter weather. Then a strong thaw occurred. However I found a young traveling companion from Hamburg called Reich who kept me company, since he too wished to go to Amsterdam. We took a special mail coach in order to go the quickest and safest way. The first days we traveled in unusual danger because everything was inundated and no road was to be seen. After our departure on the 9th we passed through Delmenhorst, Wishausen, Kloppenburg, Löningen, Vosselohe, Lingen, Neuhus, Hartenberg, and Zwolle to Amsterdam, where we arrived on the 17th.

In the inn where we stayed I met a rogue, a fellow citizen who knew our house well and had been our customer. His name was Klein. He was a thorough-going, slippery scoundrel who enticed his fellow citizens so as to mislead and deceive them. He brought us to a disreputable inn where we could easily have gotten into financial trouble because he was in league with the proprietor. He put everything on credit, even though he did not have a coin on him to pay. I paid for him, and after a few days he left with the money, having meanwhile put himself abjectly in debt everywhere.

My time in Amsterdam was just as wasted. I was confused and did not know whether to investigate business opportunities or matters of scholarship. I had lost all my previous, much-vaunted knack of finding acquaintances and friends of my own standing and mentality. I believed that everybody shunned me, and I myself shunned everyone. I cannot give any reason for it, except that God's hand was heavy on me (Ps 32:4), because I had banished him from my eyes and forsaken him. I had confessed and invoked *Rom 10:10; Rev 3:16; Mark 7:6* him with a lukewarm heart and with only my mouth. My ways did not please him. Despite his reminders and promptings, I did *Ps 32:5* not acknowledge my guilt. I also sought more and more distraction, but this too in vain. I would at last almost have disowned my sense of taste just to escape from myself. For most of my life I have found this as the basic reason why I had misused, belittled, and scorned all the good that God had conferred on me. So I set out to try my luck. Wherever I went, I always took with me my self-accusation that whatever change I had now made I had not done the right thing. So I had to use each change only as an aid to seize a better chance to make a fortune for myself, and I would have done this if I had found an opportunity for me to satisfy my friends. All for nothing; no one was able recognize me; no one wanted to recognize me. I had to run to the end of my course and see the outcome of my rash wishes, my foolish preferences, my extravagant fancies.

At last I got my wish to go to England with the most liberal set of requirements. The final destination that had been set for me inspired my one and only hope, a hope that was propped up by my ridiculous preference for that country which I had always regarded as my homeland, the right place and base for my adventurous way of thinking and living.[61]

---

61. The exact purpose of Hamann's visit to London is a matter of some conjecture. The Berens family seems to have commissioned him to engage in secret political and trade negotiations with some British officials for direct trade between Russia and London through the Russian-controlled city of Riga, apart from Prussian interference and control. That secret project was undermined by the Seven Years' War from 1756–1763, the alliance of Great Britain with Prussia against France, and the Russian occupation of East Prussia in 1758.

I left Amsterdam by a barge on Maundy Thursday or Good Friday,[62] which I thought was not necessary for me to observe as a holy day, because it is not regarded as a festival in England and Holland, and I celebrated the first days of Easter in the greatest disorder and mental oppression. Then I headed for Rotterdam, where I stayed in the best inn, called Swienshoeft, the Pig's Head. There I came upon a young Englishman looking for company and traveled with him from Amsterdam to Leiden. This suited me very well as I already had indulged in flattering delusions of my acquaintance with him, an acquaintance that ended badly. We chartered a yacht for Helvoetsluys where on the same day, April 16th, a Saturday, the packet-boat left, and, accompanied by a rather large crowd that included a young man from Bremen who was going to England to learn English where he thought of studying at a university, we arrived by a fair wind at Harwich on Sunday evening, without me feeling an attack of seasickness apart from dizziness and some nausea. On the morning of the following Monday, we hired a coach, I and my English companion whose surname was Shepherd, a university student who had also gone on a visit to Holland and benefited from it as little as I had, because he did not understand any language except English. He was, if I am not mistaken, a Roman Catholic. In the morning I discovered him praying on his knees; I was partly surprised and partly edified by his devotion. He offered to bring me to London for two guineas as the payment of all tolls and other expenses. I gave them to him. But half the way there he gave me back about half a guinea in deep distress and said that I should pay the rest myself. I had so much sympathy for his anxiety and so much scorn for his behaviour that I did not press him for further compensation. He perhaps had done it out of necessity, because at my arrival in London I had to advance him a shilling, which I would not see again any more than him.

Late in the evening of April 18th, 1757, we reached London, where I spent a very restless night at the inn with my companion

62. That is, April 7th or 8th.

from Bremen, because in our eyes it appeared to be a den of murderers and seemed to be full of riffraff. Our room was so insecure that anyone who did not want to wake us up through the door could climb in through the window. In London all windows can be pushed open.

I had a breathing space for a few days before I attended to my business. I found a good inn together with my companion from Bremen who was accompanied by a guide and friend, a young merchant engaged to his sister. After hiring a footman, the first foolish thing that I did was to visit a quack, who, I heard, could heal every speech impediment.[63] He lives in Islington. I made inquiries about him at the German inn where he was quite well known, and people told me he had performed some cures that had made him famous. But they could not see why I needed him. I went and found an old man who examined me and could see nothing wrong with my vocal organs. As condition for my cure he required me to stay in his house and pay a large sum of money. For a fixed period I would not be allowed to speak at all until I learned to spell out each syllable. I was not able to find out anything else about his method. So I had to begin my business with my old tongue and my old heart.

When I disclosed the nature of my business to the people I was directed to meet, they were astonished at the seriousness of my proposals, even more at how they were pursued, and perhaps, most of all, at the choice of the person who had been entrusted with them. After they had recovered from their surprise, they began to smile—blatantly showing what they were thinking—at those who had sent me, and why I had come, and why they felt sorry for me. All this unsettled me and also enraged me. Finally I worked at a petition to the Russian ambassador—that was all I could do![64] He deprived me of any hope that something could be done and gave me every additional assurance of his eagerness to help me, so that his eagerness might be credited to him if something should eventuate.

63. Hamann suffered from a stutter that prevented him entering public life as a pastor or a lawyer.

64. The Russian ambassador was Alexander Gallitzin.

There are certain situations and certain affairs that can be managed best and most honourably if we do nothing or as little as we can. If we took everything as seriously as possible, then we would first have to give up our contentment and tranquillity, and then expose ourselves to great danger and likely liability for making enemies and becoming victims of our good will and powerlessness. That is the situation of a minister of state who regards the gross betrayal of his duties and the honor of the one that he represents, and so on, as shrewdness and foresight, the minister who puts his own security before the interests of others, the minister who regards each difficulty as an impossibility. So I believed that I had to manage my business just by these rules, doing as little as I could so as not to heap up my expenses and expose and disgrace myself by taking rash steps. I had to regard this little thing as the only thing that was suitable and practical for me. So I went about depressed, reeling to and fro, with nobody to confide in, nobody who could advise or help me.

I was close to despair, and I tried to ward it off and suppress it with mere distractions. Blindness, frenzy, even sacrilege seemed to be the only remedy for me. Let the world go as it goes—slandering confidence in providence that helps in a wonderful way, take with you everything you chance upon, in order to forget yourself—this was a system by which I wanted to organize my conduct. Even though it fell down with every unsuccessful attempt, I built it up again for the same purpose. My purpose was nothing but taking an opportunity—each good opportunity, each good opportunity. God knows what I would not have considered in order to pay off my debts and be free once again to embark in a new folly.

So I gave up everything. My futile attempts at keeping watch with letters and assurances of friendship and gratitude were a mere show, rotten wood, will-o'-the-wisps with the swamp as their mother. My good humor and heroic courage were nothing but the fancy of a knight errant and the bells on my fool's cap.

In Berlin I foolishly took up lessons for a week from Baron, a teacher of the lute. My respectable father reminded me that I should think of my vocation and my eyesight and punished me because of that. This had been in vain. Satan tempted me once again with the lute, which had made trouble for me in Berlin, because I had unwittingly ruined an instrument borrowed from a poor student named Viermetz who nourished himself with its music. I had not compensated him for it, but had, instead, felt hurt in my heart by his diffident and touching sensitivity. Thus I began once again to make inquiries about a lute, as if my happiness depended entirely on this instrument for which I have so little musical aptitude. It was not possible to find one. People told me that there was only one player of the lute in London, who could have made lots of money with it but now lived as a lord. I was on fire to get to know this son of the white hen,[65] and I got what I wished. How much I was punished through this man! He became my confidant. I went about daily with him and moved to live close to him. He had his own house and kept a prostitute; he offered me everything. No matter how much my first assessment of him had kept me away from him and despite the many reservations I had about his character, he smoothed it all out. I believed I had now found what I wanted—he can make you famous! You now have at least one friend to go around with! You have a house where you can amuse yourself! You can practice the lute and do what he does! You can become as happy as he is! I thank my dear God that he loved me even more, and he freed me from a man to whom I had chained myself, like a mill-slave, in order to walk with him the same way of sin and depravity.

In my association with him, my blind heart got me to focus on my intention to instill good taste and right principles in an uneducated, unprincipled man. Blind as I was, I wanted be a guide to
Matt 15:14 another person, or perhaps instruct him on how to sin stylishly and divert reason to what was evil; I ate for nothing, I drank for nothing, I curried favor for nothing, I raced around for nothing. For nothing I alternated between gluttony and reflection, between reading and revelry, between industry and complete sloth. I strayed in both for

65. This is a proverbial description of a lucky child, born, as it were, with a silver spoon in its mouth.

nothing in both. For three quarters of a year I changed my place of residence almost every month. I found rest nowhere; deceitful, mean, selfish people were everywhere.

Finally I received the last stroke that led to the exposure of my friend, who had already given me much evidence for suspicion, which I had suppressed. I discovered that he was kept in a disgraceful way by a rich Englishman. He called himself Senel and pretended to be a German Baron von Pournoaille. He had a sister in London who called herself Lady von Perl. She, presumably, was kept in a similar way by the Russian ambassador and had a son under that name. I was horrified at this rumor and wanted to be sure about it. Long before this, he had entrusted a pack of letters to me. Despite their alleged importance, he had forgotten to ask for their return. I too do not know from what intimation I had not returned them to him, even though it never occurred to me to abuse his trust. Since the letters were rather loosely sealed, I could not now resist the temptation to gain certainty from them. So I broke their seals, making the excuse that if I would not find anything in them with regard to his supposed offense, I would return them to him with a frank confession of what I had done in my curiosity and swear total secrecy to him about the rest; but I would also renounce my friendship with him if I discovered other secrets which went against my principles. Sadly, I found too much that convinced me of his disgraceful behavior. They were disgusting, ridiculous love letters written in what I knew was the hand of his supposed good friend.

I was rather uneasy about the steps that I had to take but shrewdly believed that I was forced to keep back some of the letters that contained the greatest proofs of his offense and to leave the use of them for the right time and the right circumstances. He had stayed for some time in the country with his companion and paymaster in evildoing. When he came back, he asked rather discreetly for the return of his letters, which I handed back to him with some unease and he received with just as much unease and even more. I wanted to open up to him and form my own opinion about it. So I was happy to be once again on the same footing as before, even though my heart was not in it any more. It seemed that he had only wanted to spare me, in order to discover whether I knew anything about the secret of his wickedness. Since I appeared to have been set at ease about it, he believed that he could gradually withdraw himself adroitly from me. I prevented him by making another decision to write to the Englishman, whom I knew, to set before him the disgraceful nature and danger of his association with his fellow villain. I did this as emphatically as I could, but failed to achieve my goal. I did not separate them; they joined together to silence me.

Meanwhile, because I had no one to keep me company, I shifted to a coffee-house in order to gain some encouragement to engage in public life and perhaps thereby become known and build a bridge to success. This was always the main purpose of all that I did. It was too expensive and seductive for me to stay there any longer. Reduced, like evaporating water, to a few guineas, I had to make another change. Fearful and anxious, I left to find a new room. God was so gracious that he let me find one in Marlborough Street with Mr. and Mrs. Collins, very honest, good people, where I have been since 8 February this year, 1758. Both of them are young people who make it a point of honor to tell everybody that they had been in service and had started a little business which God had visibly blessed; they acknowledged this with gratitude, persistent industry, and humility. It was a special favor of God in his providence that he let me find this house in which I live most inexpensively and contentedly, because I do not need to be afraid of being overcharged by a single cent, and enjoy the best service free of charge. I wondered why God did not let me find this house earlier, which could have rescued me sooner. He alone knows the time, the best time to show us the beginning of his help; we who deserve nothing but wrath and the misfortune that we strive for grumble with God about why he will not help us earlier, we who
Exod 16:7–8 do not want to be helped.

In the coffee-house where I had previously stayed, I was constipated for up to eight days at a time and had an amazing hunger that could not be satisfied. I guzzled down the local strong beer into me like water. Thus my good health during all the disorder in my way of living and my state of mind was, without any doubt, a miracle from God, like my life and its preservation. Even though I have been in this house for nearly three months, I have had, at the most, four full meals. My only nourishment is porridge and coffee once a day. God has made this diet unusually successful, and I intend with his help to maintain it as long as possible. Necessity has been the strongest incentive for this diet, which, however, has been perhaps the only way to restore my body from the results of its gluttony.

Here I have gone through 150 pounds sterling, and I *can* and *will* not go further into debt. In all, my debts in Latvia and Courland amount to more than 300 pounds. I don't have any more money and have given my watch to my landlord. The company of the previously mentioned rogue has cost me much useless expenditure. My moving about frequently from place to place has cost me just as much. I have also purchased two suits, one with a rather richly embroidered vest, and a heap of books.

In this house I wanted to cut myself off from all company and to seek comfort from nothing apart from all my books, quite a few of which I had not yet read, or at least read uselessly, without much reflection and proper application. At the same time, God inspired me to purchase a Bible, looking around for it with much ardor until I found one that suited me.[66] I had until now been a rather indifferent owner of it. My isolation, the prospect of abject poverty and beggary, in despair I, at times, fought hard for this, because I regarded it as a way of encouragement to make a lucky strike. Yes,

66. On pages 44–47 of their introduction to the *London Writings*, Bayer and Weissenborn consider which version of Bible this was. Hamann seems to have bought the KJV as published in the Oxford Bible of 1755. It is listed in the Biga catalogue of books for auction from his library. From his comments in his "Biblical Meditations" it is evident that he also consulted the Hebrew and Greek text as he read. As he explained in his comment on 2 Kings 25:15, he attempted to "remain as close as possible" to the robust language of the original text in translating what it said (p. 160). Hamann also draws on Luther's German translation, with its distinct ordering of the New Testament books.

I wanted poverty for myself with a wicked intention to put the gracious God of my previous life, who had at all times stood by me in my need, to the test in a new way, deliberately, with sinful audacity, in short, the barrenness of my circumstances and the magnitude of my worries took away any taste for my books. They were poor
Job 16:2 comforters, these friends that I thought I could not do without and whose company had so charmed me that I looked at them as the only support and ornament of human destiny.

In the tumult of all my passions, which so overwhelmed me that often I could hardly breathe, I kept on praying to God for a friend, a wise, sincere friend, such as I could no longer envisage. Instead of that, I had tasted, tasted enough, the bitterness of false friend-
Ps 69:21 ship and the unlikelihood of a better friendship. A friend who could give me a key to my heart, the thread that would lead me out of my labyrinth was a wish that I often had, without understanding and discerning its content rightly.

Praise God! I found this friend in my heart, who crept in just
Gen 1:2 when I most felt its emptiness, darkness, and desolation. By this time, if I am not mistaken, I had read through the whole of the Old Testament once and the New Testament twice. So as I wanted to make a new beginning, it seemed as if I became aware of a veil over
1 Cor 2:13–16 my reason and my heart, which had at first closed this book for me. I therefore set out to read it with more attention, in a more orderly way, and with more hunger; and to write down my thoughts that occurred to me as I read it.

This beginning, when I still brought rather imperfect and unclear ideas about God's word to my reading of it, was nevertheless made by me on March 13 with more sincerity than before. The further I went, the newer it became for me, the more divine was my experience of its content and effect. I forgot all my books about it; I was even ashamed that I had ever compared them to the book of *God*, had ever set them side by side, and had ever preferred any other book to it. I found the unity of the divine will in the redemption of Jesus Christ, so that all history, all miracles, all the commandments and works of God converge at this central point, in order to lead the human soul out of the slavery, bondage, blindness, folly, and death of sin to the greatest happiness, the highest blessedness, and a reception of such good gifts that their greatness, when they are revealed to us, must shock us more than our own unworthiness or the possibility of making ourselves worthy of them.

I recognized my own offenses in the history of the Jewish people. I read the story of my own life and thanked God for his forbearance with this his people, because nothing but such an example could justify a similar hope for me. Above all else, I made an extraordinary discovery in the books of Moses that in some cases the Israelites, however uncouth a people they may appear to us, sought from God nothing but what God wanted to do for them. They acknowledged their disobedience just as vividly as any penitent sinner and also forgot their penitence just as quickly. Yet in the anguish at their sin they called for nothing but a Redeemer, an Advocate, a Mediator, without whom they could not rightly fear him, nor rightly love him.

In the midst of these reflections, which seemed rather mysterious to me, I read the fifth chapter of the Fifth Book of Moses[67] on the evening of March 31 and fell into deep meditation. I thought about Abel and God's word about him: "the earth had *opened its mouth* to receive your *brother's blood*." I felt my heart thump, I *Gen 4:11* heard a voice groaning and wailing in its depths like the voice of blood, like the voice of a murdered brother, who wanted to avenge his blood, even though I, at times, did not hear it and continued to shut my ears to it. It said that this was what made Cain restless and unable to escape.[68] At once I felt my heart flowing, it poured itself out in tears, and I could no longer, I could no longer hide from God that I was the killer of my brother, the murderer of his only begotten Son. Despite my great weakness, despite the long *John 1:14* resistance which I had, until now, put up against his witness and

67. That is, Deuteronomy. The fifth chapter of Deuteronomy repeats the Ten Commandments.

68. Gen 4:12. Here Hamann diverges from Luther's translation and the KJV by replacing *flüchtig*, "fleeing, being a fugitive," with *unflüchtig*, "unable to flee, unable to escape."

his tender touch, the Spirit of God kept on revealing to me, still
more and more, the mystery of divine love and the benefit of faith
Rom 8:16–17, 26–30 in our gracious, only Savior.

With sighs that were brought before God by an Interpreter,
Rom 8:26 who is dear and precious to him, I went on reading the divine
2 Tim 3:16 word, enjoying the same assistance as that by which it was written
as the only way to receive the understanding of it. With God's help
I brought my work to completion on April 21, with unusually rich
comfort and uninterrupted refreshment.

Praise God, my heart felt more at rest than ever before in my
life. In the moments when depression wanted to arise, I was overwhelmed with a sense of comfort, the origin of which I cannot
credit to myself, and which no one is able to pour into his neigh-
2 Cor 1:2–5 bor so abundantly. I was shocked by its overflow. It swallowed up
all fear, all sadness, all mistrust, so that I could not find any trace
of them in my soul any longer. I pray that God will bless the work
Phil 1:6 that he has begun in me, bless my weak faith through his word and
gracious Spirit—the abundant Spirit of God, the Spirit of peace
Phil 4:7; John 14:27 that passes all understanding and is not the kind of peace that the
world gives, the Spirit of love without whom we are nothing but
2 Tim 1:7 God's enemies—how can anyone who hates this Benefactor love in
Rom 5:5 the temporal world? The Spirit of hope that does not disappoint us
like the shadow-play of fleshly fancies.

Matt 13:45–46 Since I have received that great kindness, the priceless pearl, the
prize for which God gave me birth, how should I now doubt his
government of my whole life? I have reached its goal. I surrender
myself to his will which alone is good. I now recognize, all too well,
Mark 8:34 the blindness and corruption of my own will, not to deny it. My sins
are debts of infinitely greater significance and consequence than
my temporal debts. The gain of the whole world would not pay for
the first of them. If, on account of four hundred shekels, Abraham
had to hear these words from Ephron, a Canaanite, "What is that
between me and you?" should God not allow a Christian to think
more magnanimously than a heathen, since the Christian has been
put right with him in the main issue? What would it cost God to

throw in something little for her or him? The three hundred pounds are his debt.[69] He will deal with me like Paul with Philemon's slave and know how to settle it in keeping with his wisdom. *Phlm 10–21*

I have set down these thoughts about the course of my life for myself and my dear father and brother and would therefore like them to be read by them and my closest friends.[70] In them I have spoken with God and with me myself. I have justified God and accused myself with self-denunciation and self-disclosure, all to the praise of the only good God, who has forgiven me by the blood of his only begotten Son and the witness that the Spirit of God confirms in his word and in my heart. God has poured me out from one container into another, so that I should not accumulate too many dregs and become irredeemably bitter and rancid. All must work for what is best for us. Since the death of sin brings us life, so all its sicknesses must promote our experience of God, serve as an illustration of it, and be for the glory of God. Anyone who compares the map of Israel's travels with the course of my life will find how exactly they correspond. I believe that by the grace of God the end of my pilgrimage will usher me into the promised land even if I would not have had the time and chance to make up for the disordered things and damages that I have done to others. My friends would be more grief-stricken if I died in the poison of sorrow and despair. My good health and my life, I repeat, are also a wonder and a sign that God did not despair of my recovery, or of my future usefulness in his service. "My son! Give me your heart!" Here it is, my God! You demanded it, as blind, hard, rocky, perverse, and stubborn as it was. Purify it, create it anew, and let it become the workshop of your good Spirit. When it was in my own hands, it deceived me so often that I no longer wish to acknowledge it as my own. It is a leviathan that you alone can tame by your indwelling let it enjoy peace, comfort, and salvation.

1 John 1:7
Rom 8:16
Rom 8:28
Prov 23:26
Ps 51:7, 10–11
Compare Job 3:8; 7:12; 41:1–34; Isa 27:1

69. This refers to the unpaid debt that he had acquired in Latvia and Courland.

70. He refers to his two best friends, J. C. Berens and J. G. Lindner.

I conclude, from the evidence of my own experience, with heartfelt and sincere thanksgiving for his saving word which I have tested and found to be the only light by which we not only come to God, but also get to know ourselves. It is the most precious gift of God's grace that surpasses the whole natural world and all its treasures as much as our immortal spirit surpasses the clay of our flesh and blood. His word is the most amazing and venerable revelation of the most profound, most sublime, most wonderful mysteries of the Godhead, whether it be in heaven, on earth, or in hell, the mysteries of God's nature, attributes, and his great, bountiful will chiefly toward us poor people, full of the most significant disclosures throughout the course of all the ages until eternity. His word is the only bread and manna for our souls, which a Christian can no more do without than the earthly man can do without his daily necessities and sustenance. Yes, I confess that this word of God accomplishes just as great miracles in the soul of a devout Christian, whether he be simple or learned, as those described in it. I confess that the understanding of this book and faith in its contents can therefore be gained by no other means than through
1 Pet 1:21 the same Spirit who inspired its authors, and that his unutterable sighs which he creates in our hearts are of the same nature as the inexpressible images that are scattered throughout Holy Scripture with a greater richness than all the seeds of the natural world and
Rom 8:26 its realms.

Secondly, I confess with my heart and my best understanding that without faith in Jesus Christ it is impossible to know God and what a loving, unutterably good and generous being he is, he whose wisdom, omnipotence, and other attributes seem to be only, as it were, instruments of his love for humanity. I confess that this preference for people, the insects of creation, belongs to greatest depths of divine revelation. I confess that Jesus Christ was not only
Phil 2:7–8 pleased to become a man, but also a poor and most wretched man. I confess that for us the Holy Spirit has published a book for his word, in which, like a fool or a madman, yes like an unholy and unclean spirit, he turned proud reason's children's stories, trivial,

contemptible events, into the history of heaven and God (1 Cor 1:25). I confess that this faith shows us that all our own deeds and the noblest fruits of human virtue are nothing but the sketches from the finest pen under a magnifying glass or the most sensitive skin as seen under it. I confess that it is therefore impossible for us to love ourselves and our neighbor without faith in God which *Matt 22:37–40* his Spirit produces and without the merit of the only Mediator. In *1 Tim 2:5* short, a person must be a true Christian to be a proper father, a proper child, a good citizen, a proper patriot, a good subject, yes a good employer and a good employee. I confess that every good deed, in the strictest sense of the word, is impossible without God, and that he indeed is its only author. *Jas 1:17*

So I hand over to him all the consequences of my sins, since he has taken on himself their burden. May God comfort my father and, as I have asked him to pardon me for his grief at my thoughtlessness and forgetfulness of his love, so may God also share with him the fruits of this pardon. I can't reach out to do that, and he may be in a state in which the most obedient son can be no joy and help for us ... Thus may God be his Father, whether he lives as an old man in the fury of war, or as a rejuvenated angel in the land of peace.

May God alone guide and rule my dear brother, protect him from my follies, excesses, and offenses, and make him a useful instrument in the household of his Son, Jesus Christ.

May he let my friends think of me without worrying about me or cursing me.[71] May their good plans for me be rewarded openly by our good God, so that they do not shut their hearts against others through my abuse of their love. May he let them feel the same riches of the Spirit and grace that the loss of their kind pro- *Eph 1:7; 2:7* vision has gained for me.

Loving God, the Father of those whom you have created and redeemed! All my desires are known to you; my help comes from you alone. You have for so long seen and heard and forgiven my *Ps 121:2*

71. His two closest friends were Johann Gotthelf Lindner and Johann Christoph Berens. Here he likely refers most directly to the members of the Berens family who had financed his trip to England.

See 1 Kgs 8:29–30 sins. See and hear me now as well and forgive them: yet not my will but yours be done. Amen.[72]

Luke 22:42

Give me understanding from on high,
That I do not rest and rely
Upon my own will.
May you be my friend and faithful adviser
Of what is right for me to do.

Give to me the noble light
That reaches from your face
Into pious souls
And there awakens the power of true wisdom
Through your own power.

Test all things well, and inspire in me
What is good for me. Keep far from me
What flesh and blood would choose.
May the highest goal, the noble part,
Be your glory and love.

So now be yourself, my soul,
And trust in him alone
Who has created and redeemed[73] *you.*
Let happen what will happen,
Your Father from on high
Knows what to do in all matters.

Ended April 24, 1758

72. The first three stanzas that follow are taken from Paul Gerhardt's hymn, "Ich weiss, mein Gott, dass all mein Tun," 8, 7, 9. None of its fourteen stanzas seem to have been translated into English but all of them are included as number 1300 in the Breslau hymnal of 1903. The fourth stanza comes from Paul Fleming's travelling hymn, "In allen meinen Thaten," 15. The whole hymn is also included as number 190 in the Breslau hymnal of 1903.

73. Hamann adds "and redeemed" to the text of the hymn.

APRIL 25[74]

Godliness is useful for all things. The course of my life provides me with two special applications for the significance of this truth. First, it reaches into our smallest deeds and searches out the old disorders up to the most imperceptible failure and makes it better in an equally imperceptible manner. Satan and our flesh make us depend on them through countless trifles and follies which are rather indifferent and insignificant in themselves but are only wrong in our desire for them. Without knowing how, I have for a short time escaped from bad habits: snuffing tobacco and getting up late after staying up late, which has been so harmful for my eyes. Snuff may be as indifferent as can be, but one must also consider how incomprehensible it is that we are silly enough to become so accustomed to this powder that the lack of it makes us dissatisfied, clumsy in thinking, and in greater need for it than the basic necessities for life, yes as severe as hunger and thirst. How often similar desires for such things hamper us in prayer itself and in the divine service. *1 Tim 4:8*

The second application is the comfort that faith alone can give us concerning the smallest accidents in our life—yes, even more about its twists and the breaks in it. Thus I hope that my disorder and the spread of my lustful plans can, by God's will, become profitable and useful for him ... or, at least, that the rubbish dump can soon be cleared away by him. Even if I, like Nehemiah (2:1–2), regard it with dread and sorrow, it would cost God little to put up a new, better building for him to show his glory in the place of the decrepit, ruined building.

You alone, Lord,
Clear away from us all blocks and stones.[75]

Yes, the whole Bible seems to have been written for just this purpose, to teach us the kingdom of God by way of trivial details. He is a God who hears the thoughts and words of a midwife when

74. This was added the day after the completion of main text.

75. This is a quotation from an unidentified source.

we enter the world and writes them down (Gen 38:27–30), and the rather insignificant exchange of words between Leah and Rachel about the mandrakes that Reuben had found (Gen 30:14–15). Our religion is arranged so completely to meet our needs, weaknesses, and deficiencies that these are all transformed into blessings and things of beauty—all against our will as unconverted people—they are all transformed, even what was and is against our will, with
Rom 8:31 us as believing children of God. Everything that was unlikely and ridiculous to our earthly reason is indispensable and irrefutably certain and comforting for a Christian. Whatever reason suppresses, whatever it makes doubtful and discouraged, lifts us up and makes us strong in God.

Today I visited the preacher at the Savoy Church, Mr. Pitius,[76] a devout, righteous pastor whose words I heard, understood, and received with much emotion. He took away from me all hope of finding employment here, without making me feel downcast by this, because I believe that I cannot be helped by people but by God. If our soul first finds its center in him, then it no longer abandons him in its motion. It remains true to him, like the earth with the sun, and all other inclinations are governed, like the moon, by the original, proper influence of this orbit and its course.

In a sleepless night in London, I, with painful reproaches for my ingratitude, remembered how I had forgotten my deceased aunt who had loved her nephews with such motherly affection.[77] May God reward her in eternity for all her love, just as he has graciously forgiven her for the frailties of her love and me for profaning her remembrance by my disloyalty and thoughtlessness.

---

76. Johann Reichard Pitius was the pastor of St. Mary's German Evangelical Lutheran Church in Savoy from 1742—1768.

77. Here Hamann seems to refer to his mother's sister, whom he visited in Lübeck on his way to London.

4

THOUGHTS ON CHURCH HYMNS

Here Hamann meditates devotionally on six hymns that all reflect on the hidden glory of Christians who have been made in God's image for participation in the communion of the Son with the Father by the Holy Spirit. The centerpiece of these meditations is a sermonic reflection on Christ's exaltation on Ascension Day, 1758, with 1 Corinthians 4:6 as the text. In it Hamann notes that "God became a son of man and an heir of his curse and death and fate, so that the man would become a son of God, an only heir of heaven, as closely united with God as the fullness of divinity dwelt bodily in Christ." By Christ's kenosis, his self-emptying, we have theosis, our participation in his divine life, since we, by faith, share in his divine nature (2 Pet 1:4). By our sacramental union with him, he and all that belongs to him are ours, just as we and all that belongs to us is his. Hamann therefore exclaims in amazement at this great exchange:

> *How human, how weak and lowly God makes himself on our account! How small he makes himself, and how proud he makes a human being! He himself became a man to make us gods; he gives us all that he has. What could be dearer than his Son and his Holy Spirit? All that God has is mine—and what was the purpose of that? He says, "My son, give me your heart."*

He concludes with this description of what the Lutheran scholastic theologians termed "mystical union":

This true union with God is a foretaste of heaven. It is heaven itself. It is the last rung on the ladder which unites earth as a footstool with God's throne. This participation in the divine nature is the final goal of God's incarnation. They are both equally great mysteries, which are nevertheless prefigured by human nature and its parts.

THOUGHTS ON THE HYMN: "I AM GOD'S IMAGE AND GLORY"[1]

APRIL 29, 1758

Gen 1:27 *I am God's image.* He created me in his image. This would endure.
By the great work of redemption, he renewed it. He also extinguished sin. The Spirit of God has restored it again through faith in my Savior and Creator. Now God sees himself in my soul, as it were, with the Trinitarian radiance of his being. My former existence that I received from him was a shameful blot on his holiness and wisdom, a reproach of his divine attributes rather than the glorification and revelation of them as in the rest of creation. The high
1 Cor 6:20; 7:23 price that he paid to purchase me contributed to a new death for
me, because I denied the divinity and glory of the second Creator, just as I had blasphemed the first Creator.[2]

In vain God's Spirit hovered to and fro without descending any-
Gen 1:2 where in my heart. It waited in vain, like Noah's dove—this noble
Gen 8:8–9 guest—to be admitted out of pity. This blessed One of the Lord[3]
stood outside with the camels and waited, as it were, for permission to come under a roof that would be blessed by his message and
Gen 24:31 dealings. Let me, my God, never forget this proclamation of your
name in my soul. You have favored me with the same manifestation

1. The author of this 1652 hymn, "Ich bin Gottes Bild und Ehr," is unknown. It is number 784 in the Breslau hymn book of 1903 for Silesia. See also the entry for this hymn at hymnary.org, which gives the German text and notes its inclusion in the *Kirchenbuch der Ev.- Luth.-Christus Gemeinde*, published in New York in 1864.

2. The second creator is the Holy Spirit.

3. This is an allusion to Ps 118:26 and the use of that verse in the liturgy for Holy Communion.

that Moses saw (Exod 34:6). Without this forbearance, without this attentive, long-suffering God, no one would be saved (2 Pet 3:15). Without it, the Triune God would not have disclosed any of his attributes[4] so eagerly in my own[5] life and carefully for my own good only, since there would have been no revelation that showed me his likeness, and this would have been too incomplete for me to be fit to be the book of his name and his works. Let my heart be the workshop of your Holy Spirit, who has stamped everything that my heart feels, imagines, and desires with your image and inscription *Mark 12:16*
for the remembrance of all your benefits and promises.

1. *I am God's image and glory* (John 17:22).[6]

Just as the image refers mainly to our creation, the glory, the honor that we offer to God, is the result of our salvation. The merit of Jesus does not just cover our nakedness but also infinitely surpasses its shame by the full value of his suffering and life that faith owns for itself completely.

I am his child. What more could I desire?

The Spirit of adoption cries out "Abba! Dear Father!" (Gal 4:6) *Rom 8:15*
This is the chief benefit from the indwelling of the Holy Spirit. If we were able to assess this threefold string of pearls that consists of our creation, redemption, and regeneration, how shocked we would be at our riches! How shocked we would be that a Christian could lack any blessing and that he could wish for anything else than what he already possesses.

Christ is my kinsman;
My status is glorious.[7]

4. The German text has "your attributes."

5. Or "special."

6. We are setting off the texts that Hamann quotes with italics. His underscores within quotes are rendered as bolds.

7. Alternate reading "supremely precious."

If a person could choose his lot at birth, he would no doubt select great parents and as an important family as he could find. Yet no one can make this choice except the only one with whom God is well-pleased (Matt 3:17), the one that Solomon discovered by faith (Eccl 7:28).[8] He chose very poor blood-kinship for himself. Just as our Savior disowned his mother, sisters, and brothers and only regarded those as his closest friends who heard his word and
Matt 12:47–50; Luke 8:19–21 did his will, so let us accept this forefather of our family and our happiness as our mother, sister, and brother in the place of all other ties of blood. How great an honor it is to have the greatest Monarch of heaven and earth and the Lord of all heavenly and earthly possessions as such a Blood-friend!

Christ is my adornment and dress
Here on earth and there in eternity;
I rejoice greatly in him.

If we would prefer to have famous parents and blood relatives out of ambition, we would do so even more out of vanity. What distinguishes children of high rank from children of low rank? Not nature, which favors the low-born;[9] it gives them the healthiest bodies, the best nourishment from the true milk of their mother, the best nurture from their own parents rather than hired foster care. What then is the difference? The cradles of the high-born are
Luke 2:7 not mangers; their swaddling cloths are not silk. People rock them, sing for them, play with them to keep them in a good mood; everybody laughs with them and bounces them; nothing is too expensive for their needs, their amusement. The extravagances of childhood therefore often prefigure a short life or miserable old age. In Christ the adornment—the clothing, the joy, the provision for the needs and wellbeing of our souls—is much more glorious. He lavishes much more on us with the robes of his salvation and the joy of
Isa 61:10 his righteousness. From his fullness, which is inexhaustible, which

8 This puzzling remark refers to Jesus as the only man that Solomon found in all his search for wisdom who himself was the answer to his quest for understanding.

9. Or "the last-born."

becomes ever richer for us the more diligently we use it, from this fullness we receive grace upon grace, light and life. *John 1:16*

> 2. *God has made me righteous;*
> *Christ has brought me salvation.*

How many unhappy people look in vain for help from their relatives in a royal court, or else from investments and prestige. We see so many unhappy people with gold and silk clothing—and in places for worldly enjoyment, who have lost the taste for it. Where does this come from? All temporal misfortune comes from sin and its consequences, such as a bad conscience, sickness, the lack of love and rage against our fellow-creatures, the discomforts of old age, extravagant desires, and so on. How blessed and exceptional it would be to know nothing of this curse. What you wish for, you human being, is the happiness of a Christian. He no longer has any sin, he no longer has any Judge, he has a Savior who is his God, became a sinner, and is the Judge and the Savior of sinners. *2 Cor 5:21; 1 Tim 1:15*

> *God is no longer angry with me;*
> *I am blessed for ever and ever.*

It is such a blessing to have God no longer as our enemy. That gives us certainty and contentment, despite the rage of all creatures, no matter how great and frightful they may be. God's wrath turns the whole of nature into a corpse; yet at his smile it wakes up, like the flowers of spring from the mud of ebbing winter. It is *no longer possible* for God to be angry with me.

> *God holds me in his lap;*
> *I am God's houseguest;*
> *my place of residence is in heaven's palace.* (Eph 2:19)

God has been my midwife; he has nourished me with the pure milk of his gospel. He has given me many different proofs of his grace, providence, and my election as pledge and down payment of his divine calling of me. I am his houseguest. I live on the food from his table and drink from his cellar; his Spirit is my waiter and butler. *1 Pet 2:2* *Eph 1:4; 2 Cor 1:22; 5:5; Heb 3:1*

He saw me standing in the marketplace of this vain world; he set me
Matt 20:3–4 to work in his vineyard. Like Adam, my present vocation is now in
Gen 2:15 Paradise. I walk about in his word as I seek to plant a little slip from
it here and there in my soul and prune off as many wild shoots as I
Eph 2:6, 19–20 can. My place of residence is in heaven's palace. The earth is a wil-
Exod 16:12–31; John 6:29–35 derness; without manna I would go hungry; my need for food has
performed the same miracle on my heart of stone that the staff of
Ezek 36:26; Exod 17:5–6; Rom 5:20 Moses did on the rock. Where sin abounded, there grace abounded
even more. My treasure, my fatherland, is in heaven; that is where
Matt 19:21; Heb 11:16; Col 3:1–2 my heart and mind are fixed. In my Father's house there are many
rooms; every resident has a place, a throne,[10] that waits for him
John 14:1–3; 17:24 and is prepared for him.

> 3. *God never forsakes me;*
> *He gives me what I long for;*
> *All that God has is mine.*

God cannot be unconcerned with his creatures. Is there not patience and mercy and leniency in his wrath? Is not the goal of it and end of it *blessedness and immortality*? How comforting it should be for us to have a God who is so great, so awesome, so generous, a God who *leaves behind* a trace of his close presence and special attention that follows us in our steps just like our own shadow?[11] And why is that? So that his help would not seem to be far from us, on account of our weak sight, which would reckon that he had vanished if he were too remote from us. So he acts as if his arm could not reach any further than ours, as if he needed to be just as near to us as we needed to be to him. How human, how weak and lowly
Phil 2:7–8 God makes himself on our account! How small he makes himself,
and how proud he makes a human being! He himself became a man
Ps 82:6; John 10:34 to make us gods;[12] he gives us all that he has. What could be dearer

10. Literally "a chair, a seat."

11. See the meditations on Gen 33:2, 14 and Gen 33:14 in "Biblical Meditations of a Christian."

12. This is also an allusion to the famous assertion of Athanasius: "He was made man so that he might make us gods" (*De incarnatione* 54,3).

than his Son and his Holy Spirit? *All that God has is mine*—and what was the purpose of that? He says, "My son, give me your heart." *Prov 23:26*

> *Christ's baptism washes me clean;*
> *I am God's holy shrine.*[13]
> *Christ adorns me with honor,*
> *He gives himself to me as my possession.*

How it must have gladdened God, who had grieved that he had made mankind, to recognize himself in them, to see his image new, *Gen 6:6* clean, and with fresh radiance, and all this for mankind to be dedicated and consecrated to him (John 10:35–36)! How agreeable to God were all the little things that people dedicated to him! Just as his Son noticed the two tiny coins of the widow, so he was eager *1 Cor 4:7* to receive everything that was dedicated to him. If, by faith in the divine Propitiator, a handful of flour and a portion of sacrificial meat served to offer a restful aroma again and again for his never-ending enjoyment of its fragrance and to show his favor to a person with food for refreshment and invigoration, how must the person be in *Lev 3:1–17; 7:11–18* his sight who gives back to God all that he is and all that he has received from him, the person who consecrates himself to him after being washed and made clean in Christ's baptism? Yes, he must be adorned—adorned with the *glory* of his dear Son. God no longer has *John 17:22; 2 Thess 2:14; 2 Pet 1:3* any Son; his Son has sold himself for us. He left heaven on account of the earth and his Father in heaven on our account and has given himself to us as our possession. How good it must be for God the Father to find his Son, whom he had given up as lost, in our heart, in the temple and sanctuary of our heart. The Savior employed so many arts of love to make us so much more acceptable to his Father, to make us appear before God the Father by faith in him with so much more joy, with so much more adornment and glory. The one that he had afflicted so severely and had chosen to be such a terrible Judge now seems to see himself shamed by us, because he has transformed us so unexpectedly into a new creature and meets us in such a close friendship with his Jonathon. *2 Cor 5:17; 1 Sam 18:1–4*

13. Or "sanctuary."

Luke 23:39–43; Eph 1:3; 1 Pet 1:20–21

Does this blessing belong to me only yesterday and the day before that? Is it my repentance that gains it for me? Does this blessing and blessedness depend on the age of my weak faith? The thief on the cross believed for a few minutes; the most perfect Christian for a few more; yet both did so equally powerfully and strongly enough to gain eternity for themselves. God rewards our faith with eternity because he credited it to us from eternity. Our whole life may be regarded as a transgression of our baptismal covenant; if we lay hold of it in faith, the credit of our divine Redeemer replaces our whole life, and we receive the purity that baptism is meant to produce and preserve in us. Not our baptism but Christ's baptism is the time of our rebirth.

Luke 3:21–22; John 8:56; Eph 1:3–6; 1 Cor 6:11; John 1:16; Matt 28:10; John 20:17; 1 Cor 6:15; 12:12; John 15:5

This is a wonderful mystery that God deigns to reveal so solemnly on earth that we cannot envisage this event without spiritual trembling and rapture and read the account of it without adoration, the same adoration with which Jesus rejoiced in the Spirit and thanked God the Father, the Lord of heaven and earth (Luke 10:23). Here all those who listen to his Son and are washed in his baptism are acknowledged as God's sons by the Father himself, those with whom he is well-pleased and on whom his Spirit descends. If Abraham saw the day of Jesus, then God himself certainly saw his day and all the sons of this day from eternity, *washed clean* from eternity in the baptism of Christ—from eternity as holy shrines of God, adorned with the honor of his only-begotten Son, full of grace and truth, as his brothers, his limbs and branches.

4. God's love dwells in me;
His grace is my banner.[14]

Acts 17:28; Luke 2:12; 2 Kgs 4:10

Paul says, "We live and move and have our being in God." The God who is everywhere does not apparently want to be at home anywhere except with us. Thus he who created the whole world chose a manger. This very Lord wants to be our guest; like Elijah, he puts up with a tiny room. Why was that? To reveal his love to

14. Or "standard."

us and bless all that belongs to us, to help us to bear every cross as long as we dwell in this tent, to transform its pain into joy by a wonderful dispensation, like that which Elijah's hostess experienced with the bestowal of a son and his awakening by her Lodger. That is how blessed and delighted we should be by God's love, how great and strong by God's grace. Here on earth we still fight the Lord's battles for the conquest of Canaan. Our victory is quite certain with our Conqueror, who has trampled all our enemies under his feet and has done everything to grant us the honor of a triumph, like Joab with David.

Matt 16:24
2 Cor 5:4
Num 21:14; 1 Sam 18:17; 1 Cor 15:57
Ps 110:1; Eph 1:22; 2 Sam 12:26–31

Christ has chosen me;
He has betrothed himself to me,
He has pledged himself to me;
I am his treasure and bride;
His eye gazes on me.

The book of Esther, the book of Ruth, and the Song of Solomon give an exposition of these blessings (Eph 5:32). We always have the love of a bride for her Savior, and the charms, youth, and purity of a bride in the sight of the Bridegroom of our souls. His eye can never see enough of us; we never get sick and tired of following him with our love and delighting in his enjoyment of us. This marriage of the human race, or, much more, the church of God and Jesus with her Savior, is, without doubt, much more than a mere figurative representation of divine love and tenderness; it is a picture of a *greater mystery*, like the birth of our loving Savior. He did not want to appear on earth like any other human being; he chose a virgin mother and her offspring, so that he would be portrayed as a natural man by the supernatural, secret overshadowing of the Holy Spirit, and be born in a natural way. Thus, just as Mary became a mother and yet remained a virgin because she did not know any man, so we must envisage the spiritual marriage of the church with her bridegroom Jesus. The fact that we are already able to feel the raptures of heavenly love for our Savior here on earth is, by faith, a foretaste of our future blessedness.

Eph 5:32; 1 Tim 3:16
Luke 1:35
Luke 1:27

5. My rest remains undisturbed.

This rest is the philosophers' stone.[15] Teachers of ethics look for it and promise to discover it, just as the opposite of rest is a problem that mathematicians struggle to solve. Just as a body does not seem to lose its gravity in its center of gravity, so the soul enjoys its lightness by itself, or else gathers its gravity at the single center of all its powers; where they have flowed out from, there they try to reunite. This rest is the first stage[16] of happiness; it is nothing except
Gal 5:22 the peace of the Spirit in God and with God.

My pleasure lasts forever,
My delight does not pass away.

The transience of things that give us pleasure and the instability of our taste for them deceive us continually. We are deprived of them—or else we have enough of them. The object of pleasure is like a flower with its transience; we either exhaust it or else discover the deficiencies and imperfections that spoil our enjoyment of it. The application of these observations flows for itself from the object and nature of faith.

I do not ever come into judgment
Christ himself is the Man
Who has done enough for me.
No trouble[17] touches me.

Even though rest may occur with sin, every desire would end with its object and something new would replace it. We see how all the short happiness of earthly living becomes bitter at its end and the anticipation of a reckoning for it. Both the divinity and humanity of our blessed Savior are equally comforting. The latter is more visible for us in our senses and suitable to our nature for so much greater glory over our spiritual enemies and so much

15. See page 14n35 in "Biblical Meditations."

16. Or "degree."

17. Literally, "plague."

greater glorification of God who has decided to create our poor human form as the instrument for such astounding signs and wonders and works. Thus our divine Redeemer so self-evidently calls himself the Son of Man and the apostle Paul often calls him the *Man* with the pride and audacity of faith, the *Man* who has trodden the winepress for us all, who, like David, is worth ten thousand men. Did he not carry all our trouble? Has he not taken enough on himself? Did he not heal them all? Were any of them too heavy for him? What will this Man not do for his brothers, since he now sits at the right hand of his Majesty, the right hand of his Father?

Rom 5:15; 1 Cor 15:21, 45, 47; 1 Tim 2:5; Isa 63:3

2 Sam 18:3; Isa 53:4, 11, 12; Matt 8:17

Heb 1:3; 8:1

6. So I am always cheerful,
Because Christ cares for me,
And his heart loves me forever;
Yes, because he gives himself to me completely.
Awake, my spirit; do not put off
Loving God, your good portion,
Always for your salvation.

THOUGHTS ON THE HYMN: "O LOVE, YOU HAVE MADE ME TO WEAR"[18]

APRIL 30

Yesterday I wrote down some meditations on the hymn: "I am God's image and glory." The author of it and this hymn are not known to me. I only wish to begin with the observation that he has woven his song, like the robe of Jesus, our Savior, in one piece from top to bottom with the name of Christ and what he accomplished. This mighty, comforting, only-saving, wonder-working name is the true

John 19:23

18. An English translation of six verses from this hymn, "Liebe die du mich zum Bilde," by Johann Scheffler (1653–1737) is given in *The Lutheran Hymnal*, number 397. See the entry for "O Love, who formedst me to wear" at hymnary.org., which gives the tune, cites Catherine Winkworth's translation along with alternative versions, and links to forty-three English hymnals that contain the song.

shibboleth of faith.[19] The so-called natural Christian cannot pronounce it. He regards its repetition by an enlightened, anointed Christian as an abuse, an offense, an act of desecration.

Rom 8:15 Repentance alone teaches us to stammer this "Abba." The faith that moves mountains, that storms heaven, that treads the earth and its prince under its feet, that possesses the key to God's heart and all his treasures and riches is nothing but the use of the name *Matt 17:20; 21:21; Ps 44:5; 91:13; Luke 10:19; Rom 16:20; John 14:13–14; 16:23–24; 1 Cor 1:22–2:4* of Jesus. This is the wisdom and almighty power of God; without it he himself is unable to save us. The first comfort, the Alpha and inexpressible glory and blessedness that no human ear has heard and no human eye has seen and no human sense and heart can conceive, the highest enjoyment and the Omega of our delight and joy, *Heb 13:8* is the name of Jesus Christ, yesterday and today and for all eternity.

The eagle has been used as a symbol for John, the evangelist and prophet. His letters, the letters of this elder of the church of Jesus may be compared with the wings of a dove covered with silver, with feathers of yellow and gold (Ps 68:13). Just as John the Baptist is called the voice of the preacher in the wilderness: "Repent and *Matt 3:2–3* prepare the way of the Lord," so, in contrast with the Baptist, this devout man is truly the voice of an intimate disciple in new Zion: "Beloved, let us love one another, for love is of God; God is love, and whoever abides in love abides in God. We love him, because *1 John 4:7, 16, 19* he has first loved us." These are the yellow-gold feathers from the wings of a dove, covered with silver, which the spiritual author enjoys holding in the light so as to show the variety and beauty of its radiance at the change of light and take delight in it from a number of excellent points of view.

> 1. *O Love, you have made me to wear*
> *The image of your Godhead here.*

The love of God is the foundation for creation. In particular God chose the human family, the youngest and smallest part of it, *Deut 7:6–7* to reveal his love for it and his great, glorious name to all the other

---

19. This was the test word that Jephthah used in Judg 12:4–6 to distinguish the fleeing Ephraimites (who could not pronounce the *sh*) from his own men.

families of creatures, to greater worlds, yes even to the inhabitants and princes of heaven. This love moved him to impress his image on us in creation. God has exactly the same love for every individual person that he had for the whole human family. This image of the Godhead, O Love, is only revealed by faith that combines the grace of God the Father, the love of the Son, and the fellowship, the intimacy of the Holy Spirit in our souls.

Exod 20:2; 34:5–7

Eph 3:10–11; Phil 2:10

1 Cor 13:13

> *O Love, you took such gentle care*
> *After the fall for my salvation.*

In Adam we were created; in Adam we fell. In the fullness of time, we were born and brought all his sin, his impurity, and curse with us into the world as a sign that we were his children. Yes, our whole life was a continuation and confirmation of his fall. Since we did not thank God for his image, each of us set up the image of the enemy with our own hands in Adam[20] and for the duration of his life. Yet God's love for Adam and me never ended; he let us both live. Was this not love? Yes, he purposely permitted us, like ignorant children, to spoil a masterpiece of his hand because he had intended a better gift for us in its place. How ancient my duties to God are! Now the miracles of my body and the way that it has been built appear to be quite natural to me since I contemplate it as a bit of dust from the same clay that God formed to be the human family tree.

Gal 4:4

Rom 1:21–23

Gen 2:7

> 2. *O Love, you have chosen me,*
> *Even before I had been created.*
> *O Love, you were born as man*
> *And made like us in every way.*

In love God gave us our existence and bound it up with a special sign of his exceptional love. When we were hardly aware of our existence, we abused it in defiance of its Author and our own selves, because God had especially intended to distinguish our nature by

20. Here Adam is the name for all humanity.

its careful connection with his own infinite being. God did not just love us so much that he was willing to forgive our terrible affront to him; our freedom to do so was a mystery of even greater love.

As wonderful as God's love seems to be in this contrast, another contrast follows here in the new creation. God did not just love us in
John 3:16 time when he gave his only-begotten Son, so that, like us, he would be sin on our behalf and the offering for it; he loved us from eternity
2 Cor 5:21; Eph 1:4 in his Son and chose us in him. Nothing but love in creation, in the fall, in the incarnation, yes until the bosom of eternity. It is here that my years began in God and in the love of his Son; his election of me in Jesus is my true birthday and the first moment of my existence. This election in Jesus moved God to create me in Adam, to make his only-begotten Son like me, and produce the salvation that he had also intended for me in the fall of my physical forefather, in the sinful generation of my birth, and in the course of the unbelieving, disobedient, and ungrateful life that I had led for so long, he had waited patiently for my return and had run, with inexpressible love, to meet me on my way home as his lost son.

Luke 15:11–32

O Love, I give myself to you
To remain yours eternally.[21]

3. *O Love, in time you suffered*
And died on my behalf.
O Love, you have fought for me
To gain eternal delight and blessedness for me.

We human beings can get as little an idea of sin's abomination as of death from it. No one except a true Christian can imagine a shadow of sin in the suffering of our great Savior and the treasures that follow from it. In particular there are three treasures. First, all punishment has been completed and endured in our place. Great as this may be, there would be little help for us in this. We have enemies that have always persecuted us; God's vengeance could not have defended us from them. We are now safe from our enemies;

21. This is the refrain that comes at the end of each verse.

they have been conquered—yes even more than that, these mighty foes have been laid low in our name, and their homes, their thrones, and all their property will belong to us. This is the eternal delight and blessedness that our Savior has fought to win for us. Third, through this glorious victory he has obtained the Father's kingdom *1 Cor 15:57* and the reign over everything in heaven and earth that we will also share with him. Yes, he has become our Brother and has humbled himself as far as the death on the cross to make us co-heirs with him. *Matt 28:18; 2 Tim 2:12; Heb 2:17; Phil 2:8; Rom 8:17*

> 4. *O Love, you are Strength and Life,*
> *Light and Truth, Spirit and Word.*

Through the revelation of our Savior in the flesh and the proclamation of his love, the life in God, the truth, and the word together with its Spirit have been given and distributed for empowerment and clear enlightenment. Arise from the dead and Christ will shine on you. In him is life, and the life is the light of mankind; he is the *Eph 5:14* light that enlightens everyone that comes into the world; he is the *John 1:4, 9* way and the truth and the light. He is the truth that alone can set us free; into it no one can guide us except the Spirit of truth, free- *John 14:6; 8:32* dom, and adoption. *John 16:21; Rom 8:15–16, 21*

> *O Love, you have given yourself completely*
> *To me to be my salvation and soul-stronghold.*

The love of Jesus for us human beings moved God to create us, because the magnitude and benevolence of his Being could not be expressed and glorified only through creation. Yes, he created us because his love was, to some extent, obscured by the limitations of finite things. It was presented and appeared in an inaccurate light. Every finite being is imperfect; like its very existence, the happiness of its existence depends on no other being than its Creator. Any finite creature that would like to be much closer than us to God in the ladder of being would be just as unhappy if it wanted to regard itself separated from its Creator and Lord and independent, like a branch cut off from its vine stock. Thus, through its mysterious closer relationship with the Highest Being, the smallest, most finite and weakest creature is able to become happier than a cherub or seraph that makes itself a god. The heavens will see this mystery in mankind.

The compassion of God's Son for our misery under the curse of
Heb 4:15 divine righteousness and the tyranny of proud, unrighteous spirits moved our Savior to hand himself over to the wrath of the Father and the wickedness of his creatures for my salvation, so that the Father would be reconciled and their wickedness would be punished and avenged, and that these enemies would see us in the wounds of Jesus and be afraid of us as if we were in too high a place, an insurmountable rock for them. This refuge of our souls is faith in
Deut 34:1–4 him; it is the mountain where we can enjoy the prospect of heaven. It is a stronghold against our enemies and a feast for our eyes rather than the barren wasteland where we had to travel here for a while.

> 5. *O Love, you have bound me*
> *Body and soul under your yoke;*
> *O Love, you have conquered me,*
> *Enrapturing my heart.*

How gracious God is in sending the cross to his own people! This is the only school that can lead us to God and to hold fast on God. Our flesh and blood are too unruly to govern themselves. So what is called a yoke, a burden, by God himself is the only, easiest
Matt 11:29–30 means for the salvation of our souls. It is the best and most convenient way, the straight pathway to heaven, which would become much more difficult and uncertain for us in good times on earth and in the intoxication and gluttony of good luck. We should be suspicious of all earthly possessions because they are handed on by the greatest sorcerer and poisoner ... Jesus says, "I am gentle and humble in heart." A little donkey is splendid and gallant enough
Matt 21:1–5; Num 22:27 for his royal entrance. Even though it was a foal, he did not use Balaam's stick. Like Jacob he follows in the footsteps of his flock and
Gen 33:14 his children and lets Esau trot ahead with his crowd of horsemen.

O Love, you have conquered me! Our Savior is like the poor widow who complained for a long time in the ears of the unjust judge until

he heard her. He does not grow tired of looking for every lost sheep Luke 18:1–5
and every lost coin for a long time until he finds it, until the person Luke 15:1–10
cannot hide himself any longer, until he cannot keep running away
any longer, until, like Saul, he is touched by David's friendliness, 1 Sam 24:8–22
until that person promises to turn back to him and decides to follow
him, chooses him as his guide and companion, and entrusts himself
entirely to him. Like Boaz, he does not take any rest until he has
done his work with us and until he possesses the heart of the sinner, Ruth 3:18
in order to make his happiness so much greater and more certain.

> 6. *O Love, you love me eternally,*
> *You intercede for my soul.*

The Gardener says, "Father, let it be for this year also. I take responsibility for it. It does not have enough manure. It does not have enough attention. Give it another year." Every moment that God gives to the sinner, every new day of reprieve, is a loving offer and query of God whether he will be determined to love what he has saved, and whether he wants to regard eternal blessedness important enough and prevent eternal damnation. The fact that you are not now cut down is the result of the intercession of your faithful Savior who has sought to save you eternally and is intent on planting you, if possible, in his paradise. *Luke 13:8* *Rom 8:34; Heb 7:25*

> *O Love, you have paid the ransom*
> *And plead powerfully for me.*

It is with some awe that we hear Abraham bargaining with the Hittites for a plot of land in Genesis 23. How precious must our ransom be for the Father, the Father who took such great interest in the blood of Abel? How will his own heart not defend a sinner for whom his Son speaks? Surely our enemies must have received it with great embarrassment and silent confusion, just as the Pharisees saw the payment for their murder of Jesus thrown down before them by the man who was the instrument for it. *Matt 20:28; 1 Pet 1:18–19* *Gen 4:10; Heb 11:4; 12:24* *Matt 27:3–5*

7. O Love, you wake me up
From the grave of mortality.

1 Cor 15:21–22 Just as we were created in Adam, so we will also rise with him.
The sign and seal of this resurrection is the risen Savior, who has
not disowned his love for his disciples in his exalted state but has
doubled its tenderness. He withdrew from the whole earth just to
enjoy them alone and is still with them to the end of the world. He
accompanies us on our journeys, like the disciples on the road to
Luke 24:15–16 Emmaus. Even though our eyes are closed, he appears to us in our
John 21:4–13 vocation, like his disciples with their catch of fish. He asks to be
John 21:9 our guest. He serves a meal for us. He produces coals and bread; he
appears to us in our sinful ways and removes the scales of our blind-
Acts 9:3–9; 17:19 ness from our eyes by the grace of his divine work and Holy Spirit.

O Love, you will surround me
Lev 23:39–43 *With the leafy bower of glory.*

Here the same thing happens for the devout Christian as for Peter
on the Mount of Transfiguration: "Lord, it is good to be here. Let us
make huts, one for you and one for me. Provide us with branches
Matt 17:4 so that we may dwell here." He did not know what he was saying.
The hymn writer seems to have copied the confusion of Peter rather
aptly. He follows divine love up to its throne. He envisages that he has
been awakened from the long sleep of death and is surrounded, all at
1 Cor 2:9 once, by a radiance that his eyes have never perceived. He imagines
that he dreams of Tabor and thinks of heaven. He wants to have the
Ps 92:12; Ezek 31:8–9 same glorious foliage that the cedars have around God's throne, in
order to build a booth for himself. He does not recognize, after his
own transformation, his own eminence and grandeur in bearing the
crown and the scepter.

O Love, I give myself to you
To be yours eternally. Amen. (Song of Songs 4:16)

THOUGHTS ON THE HYMN: "MY SPIRIT AND MIND REJOICE GREATLY"[22]

MAY 1

1. *My spirit and mind rejoice greatly*
In God who has blessed me
In Christ his Son, Luke 1:46; Eph 1:3
Whom he has sent
From his throne
As my best portion and salvation.

The exalted joy of a Christian that fills his whole soul, every spiritual and bodily blessing, all salvation, the best portion of heaven, the fat of the kidneys and the diaphragm that contains the heart and the entrails of divine mercy,[23] the ornament of his throne, and the scepter of divine rule over the whole world are included in the sending of his only-begotten Son and in its purpose and effects on our souls.

2. *He has chosen me before the world began* Eph 1:4
And numbered me with his children;
He will never leave me.
The fullness of his grace
Gives what I desire.
His love is without measure.

His love began before I existed. Yes, he preferred my nature, no matter how wretched and corrupt it was, to all other natures.

22. This hymn, "Mein Geist und Sinn ist hoch erfreut," is ascribed to the Pietist pastor Johann Friedrich Stark (1680–1756). The hymn appears in numerous eighteenth and nineteenth century German hymnbooks. Hymnary.org gives no English translations, but cites its appearance in a Mennonite hymnal published in the United States: *Gesangbuch in welchem ein Sammlung geistreicher Lieder befindlich* (Elkhart, Indiana: 1880 and 1918).

23. The kidneys of an animal and the fat that covered them were regarded as its essence, its most sensitive and vital part. They were reserved for God from a peace offering and presented to him as a well-pleasing offering on the altar (Lev 3:3–5, 9–11, 14–16). The diaphragm of a mammal separates the heart, the seat of thought and feeling, from the entrails, the seat of love, affection, and compassion.

He counts the stars and the sand by the seashore, the sparrow
Ps 147:4; Isa 40:26; Gen 22:17; Matt 10:29–30 and the hairs of my head—everything can be counted except the good things that his children will enjoy and the length of years that they will live. What I wish for cannot be as insatiable as his love is immeasurable. For my sake he became a Creator; for my sake the Creator became a creature. That is, God's omnipotence worked to become rich. Like a father for his children, a father who scrimps and saves during his life so that he can give them so much more for their enjoyment after his death, he, seemingly, eked out a poor living for a while, out of love for us, to unlock it all unexpectedly, all suddenly. Our share that we received at birth seemed to be too small for him. He therefore did not rest until he found a way of adopting his most distant, remote, and impoverished friends and appointing them as his heirs.

3. Though I am an unworthy sinner,
His love remains intact.
It lifts, it carries, it endures.
So I am not struck
By his wrathful judgment
That I should have deserved.

Our unworthiness, yes, an even greater impediment than this for us, the curse upon us that did not just exclude us from God's good gifts but had also, even more, subjected us to the wrath, the eternal wrath, seemed to be the greatest impossibility that lay, like fetters and chains, on God's will, no matter how good he wanted to be with us. Just this constitutes the mystery of God's wisdom in uniting things that seem to exclude each other, contradict each other, nullify each other—this is nothing else than creating *out of nothing*. No one except God can do this, creating what is *evil* and making it an enemy, creating darkness and forming the light (Isa 45:7). This is a love that had nothing to bear, nothing to lift, noth-
1 Cor 13:7 ing to endure with us, yet, even so, it had, through such a love, to make us worthy of a love with which he loves his own great, infinite
Gen 2:7 self—not to create an angel but to steal a clod from the earth that

had become a firebrand of hell and transform it into a cedar of heaven, into more than an angel—that means to create something infinitely more than an angel. *Ezek 17:22–24*

4. In Christ he does not regard
The wrong that I have done
When my faith takes hold of him,
And I hate all the sin
That is still found in me
With earnestness and disgust.

Without doubt there were many great, mighty spirits in heaven and on our earth that, like Sarah, laughed at this divine will, because what God intended to do seemed to be incomprehensible, unlikely, yes, foolish to them. No, reason, which must here give way, cannot comprehend this miracle. The faith of a simplest Christian surpasses the shrewdness of the most cunning beasts of the field. Yes, God has so graciously put the miraculous staff of his wisdom and power, of this abundant blessedness, into the hand of every person to bring about God's will for him. We need even less exertion than Moses to be a god to Pharaoh and Aaron. Repent and believe that your Savior and your God and your Father is love—truth—and life. So you have become a child of God from a slave of sin and an heir of blessedness from an earthworm and a prey of hell. *Gen 18:12* *Gen 3:1* *Exod 4:17* *Exod 4:16; Matt 3:2*

5. He gives me his Spirit,
Who shows me the way to life
And pours his love into my heart;
He reduces
And sweetens
My pain and my sorrow.

God is incomparably more benevolent in grace than in nature. He has made us lords of the blessed soil of the earth and gives us seed with its produce, but at the same time he also makes his sun shine on them and gives the early and later rain in its season. Thus his blessing comes from above and below to be united for *Deut 11:14*

our blessing and our joy. The way to heaven would still be too hard for us, but he gives—he gives—his Spirit as a true companion, guide, and fellow traveler through the desert of this life, the Spirit who feeds us, gives us water to drink, strengthens our feet, so that
Deut 8:3–4; Rom 5:5 they do not swell, and does not let our clothes grow old. The Spirit pours the love of God into our hearts by his communion, his conversation, his disclosures and revelations of God and his land; he
Num 13:23–27; Gal 5:22 gives us his fruit as a scout who is more loyal to his companions than to his master; like Rahab he provides help from all danger by
Josh 2:1–7 his good counsel and instruction. The bad weather that breaks on us is transformed into sunshine by his companionship; the sorrow that is poured out over our frame is burnt into dust and ashes by his comfort in our hearts, and in his chalice even the sadness of our sins becomes a drink that heals and refreshes us. My pain and sorrow are not just reduced but also sweetened.

6. He is my very best Friend,
Who is always true and kind to me;
No one else is like him.
Will he ever leave
The one who knows
And owns him as his Father?

We see how true is what the poet says in one of his *Night Thoughts.*

The ***smoothest*** *course of Nature has its Pains*
And ***truest*** *Friends, thro' error, wound our Rest.*
Without Misfortune, what Calamities?
And what ***Hostilities****, without* ***a Foe****?*[24]

I have tasted the honey and the thorn of earthly friendship; and my friends are now feeling nothing but the latter from me at present. The wounds that I have inflicted on their tranquility, their

24. Edward Young (1681–1765), *Night Thoughts*, "The Complaint," Night One, lines 277–80. Hamann quotes these lines in English. Hamann emphasizes four words in this verse by writing them in bold print.

possessions, and perhaps even their reputation have hurt them and will hurt them for a long time. Even though I have not ceased to be their friend, they have received all kinds of hostilities from me. This is no surprise when I compare my life with my very best Friend, my debts and my misuse of his generosity and patience with his good deeds. How true it is that we find no one else like him. What bliss it is to know him, to call him Father, in Spirit and in truth. *John 4:23* The confidence of a Christian that he is not forgotten, not forsaken by God, rests only on knowing this God, knowing him in his Son Jesus and on naming God by calling him Abba with the Spirit from his mouth in Jesus. *Rom 8:15*

7. I have and I hold him,
I give myself completely to him
Apart from him I want to know nothing
Since I have him
As my grave,
I can easily do without everything.

The previous verse shows us the reason for our confidence, the rock on which a Christian builds his comfort and hope; apart from it everything is sand and all people are miserable comforters. Faith turns death in the pot into a tasty meal and a salty, bitter *Job 16:2; 2 Kgs 4:40–41* spring into healthy, refreshing water. Thus we do not find any true contentment, satisfaction, satiation, plenty, and fullness apart from *Exod 15:23–25* God and his Son. The thirst for knowledge is, without doubt, one of the strongest, most dreadful and most voracious impulses in a person who swallows up rivers, like Behemoth, and never grows tired of swallowing them (Job 40:23). When this thirst is quenched through Christ the crucified, when we are satisfied to know only him and nothing but him, how unimportant, how easy it must be *1 Cor 2:2* to do without everything else?

8. Since he is my life, comfort and light,
My rock, my salvation, I do not prize
Heaven itself and the earth

If this were a matter of singular significance in the eyes of Christians, God would not let them perish. Is not everything that God does and has chosen to do also the wish of a Christian? Is it not evident that God thinks, lives, and acts in him, and he in God? Everything that is not appropriate for us is transient; it is nothing, too, in God's eyes. But everything that has to do with us is a concern of the special providence and reign of God. Not just confidence in God—a Christian does not even need this, because he is unpretentious, content, and satisfied, because he has the best portion that
Luke 10:42 he prefers before everything else. He cannot just be satisfied but also unconcerned about himself. Since he can do without heaven
Ps 73:25 and earth, how much more can he do without a handful of gold,
2 Cor 5:1–4 the thirst for honor, the earthly tent of his body?

Because I sense
That without him
Ps 73:25–26 *Nothing good can be my portion.*

It is not ignorance, not the lack of senses or judgment, that inspires this exalted mentality in a Christian. It is the taste of the master at the wedding in Cana; he alone samples the wine and declares that it is *good wine* that our Savior has made, and he dis-
John 2:1–10 owns the goodness and spirit of the first wine.

9. He is my greatest good;
My heart rests in his heart;
I sleep in perfect peace.

What is the origin of unevenness in human tendencies and their changes, the complaints about the capriciousness of fate, the disturbances, the suspicions and hatred of rivals, and the envy of competitors? The highest good is the only thing that can obscure all others, that can share itself with everyone and is as inclined to share itself as it is able, that cannot be paid for but only given as a gift. Whoever possesses this highest good has done what he needs to do. He has reached the ultimate goal of his life and has completed his earthly day's work. He has peace and rest. He has his treasure and his heart in a place where it is not exposed to any danger. For him life on earth is a dream, and he sleeps through the storms that terrify others. His harbor is everywhere, because every departure from the world is nothing but waking up to a better life, the last sleep of temporal existence.

Matt 6:19–20

Matk 4:35–41

We always remain,
Both here and there,
United and unseparated.

This true union with God is a foretaste of heaven. It is heaven itself. It is the last rung on the ladder which unites earth as a footstool with God's throne. This participation in the divine nature is the final goal of God's incarnation. They are both equally great mysteries, which are nevertheless prefigured by human nature and its parts. It is a much more perfect union than the union of the soul with the body. Since the soul is nothing but a breath of God in comparison with God, we shall become so very great through him, so very blessed in him. As the body stands in contrast with the soul, as a clod of clay stands in contrast with the breath of God, so human nature, with all the unified, purified, transfigured powers of humanity, stands in contrast with the Godhead. If the limits of our members and our physical senses with their perceptions impede the buoyancy that our souls here already have, how can we surpass that and gain any notion of a being that will be one in God, just as the Father is in the Son and the Son is in the Father (John 17:21)?

Isa 66:1

2 Pet 1:4

Gen 2:7

10. He blesses me when I am cursed,
And when the enemy seeks to harm me,
He will never succeed.
He sets me free
And stays with me
So that I can sing joyfully.

If the curse of our temporal enemies tears down our tents, the blessing of our Father builds castles and principalities for us in heaven. Every tear will not just be wiped away here on earth with

Isa 25:8; Rev 7:17; 21:4; Isa 66:13 the tender hand of a mother; it is transformed into jewels in the place where it is shed and gathered to make our transfiguration so much more joyful, radiant, and transcendent. Yes, these enemies of the human race are our benefactors; they unite us ever more closely with God. He loves us so much more, the more we are
Matt 5:10–11 hated and persecuted on his account. Despite their superiority that makes them lords and masters and despots of our fate, we, instead of being their slaves, become their conquerors and victors. Already here we can sing greater and more momentous songs of triumph
Exod 15:1–18; Judg 5 than Moses and Deborah. With much jubilation we will carry our palm branches in eternity and play laurel-covered harps as psalm-
Rev 7:9; 5:9; 15:2–3 ists who have been crowned.[25]

> 11. *It will be well with me eternally;*
> *With my eyes I will see him,*
> *The source of all joy.*
> *Yes, I believe*
> *My heart will feast*
> *On him without end.*

Every Christian is his own prophet. How should the lord and partaker of eternity, the son, the friend, the heir of the great Monarch be a stranger to heavenly mysteries and future blessedness? The eternal wellbeing that he predicts for himself consists of nothing else than seeing the source of joy for himself with his own eyes. As modest as this wish of a Christian, this faith of a Christian, appears, so unfathomable and unattainable is its occurrence. My heart will, I believe, feast on him eternally. How poor the bills of exchange[26] for spiritual riches appear! How inexpressible are the amounts that will be cashed through them!

---

25. In ancient Greece musicians who won a musical competition were crowned with laurel wreaths as a mark of divine honor. Their harps and lyres were decorated with pictures of laurel leaves that were sacred to Apollo, the god of music. The picture here is that Christians are honored because they play God's harps that commemorate his victory (Rev 15:2).

26. Bills of exchange were early letters of credit that functioned like a bank check.

12. No human ear has ever heard
What has been kept for me by God; 1 Cor 2:9
I see it already now by faith (1 Sam 9:23–24)
And I rejoice greatly
That no enemy
Can ever take that away from me.

Scripture and the apostle who spoke from his own experience tell us that our language and its concepts and signs are not just unable to receive and reflect any impressions of this blessedness, but, even more, if they could do so, our ear and its hearing are too weak to understand it and they would be deafened and destroyed by it. Faith alone receives its radiance without it becoming detrimental to us and without us becoming truly aware of it, like the face of Moses that the children of Israel ran from, even though he himself was unaware of why. *Isa 64:3–4; 2 Cor 12:1–4* *Exod 34:29–30*

"You, you O God, you yourself prepare a table before *me* in the presence of my enemies." So sings David in the delightful psalm: "The Lord is my Shepherd." This presence of my enemies is the spice of the table that God himself prepares; their sight is the salt that makes every morsel tastier for a Christian. But this presence of our enemies is also an instruction for our conduct, a warning for us to be vigilant, an encouragement to glorify God in us in defiance of our enemies. Thus here on earth a Christian always needs the presence of his spiritual enemies, so that he does not become complacent and does not forget himself, so that he is as untiring in looking to God as they are in looking out for the tiniest acts of carelessness, inattention, and recklessness to gain an advantage over him. Thus, as long as we live here on earth, our enemies are necessary and useful to exercise and sharpen the vision of our faith, to heighten our joy at their futile attempts to harm us, the joy of our battle against them. *Ps 23:1, 5*

ON ASCENSION DAY[27]
MAY 4, 1758, LONDON

A STAGE

We have become a spectacle to the world,
to angels and to people. (1 *Corinthians* 4:9)

If they had known the Lord of glory, the rulers of this world would not have crucified him. If they had discerned the wisdom of God in the mystery, the hidden plan that God had decreed before the creation of the world for the glorification of believers, they would not have crucified the Lord of glory, nor would they have persecuted his servants and stewards with equally blind rage (1 Cor 2:7–8). We Christians see that the crucified Jesus is the Lord of glory from the event and sign of his glorious ascension into heaven that the church commemorates today. What a spectacle for the world, the angels, and people was the cross! The King of a nation that God had now
Deut 7:6 chosen as his own from all families on earth. We read that he was
John 19:19–20 their King in three languages. This King hangs as a criminal, mocked by his people, forsaken by God and exposed to all his enemies as the object of their malice. All this crowd that surrounds him and the number of arrows that were shot at him prove the greatness, importance, and the eminence of him as a person (2 Chr 18:29–31).

He who thirsted and was denied something to drink, yes—what was even crueler, he who was offered gall instead of wine has places of honor to confer in paradise and in God's kingdom. What a double drama on majesty and humiliation, of divinity and the lowest degree of human misery! What a drama for the Creator and all the dominions of creation! The world, the angels, and people have a part to play in this mystery as spectators, actors, scriptwriters. It

27. Just as Hamann had earlier interrupted his reflections on the Pentateuch after Genesis and before Leviticus in his "Biblical Meditations" with an excursus on the Sermon on the Mount on Maundy Thursday, he here interrupts his reflections on hymns on Ascension Day with an excursus on the participation of all Christians in the exaltation of Jesus. He may do so because all the hymns that he ponders have to do with the heavenly blessings that he has received from his exalted Lord for his life on earth.

is accomplished—this word of dénouement[28] that the Man of God cried out on Golgotha stunned all of nature, created a new heaven and a new earth, glorified God, glorified mankind. It revealed to the world, angels, and mankind that *God is righteous* and that all those who believe in him will *be righteous* (Rom 3:26). God's throne is based on this judgment and its revelation. The scepter of heaven and earth depends on the perfection of these divine attributes.[29] The reign and kingdom of God was conditional on his power to uphold it and on the glory by which it was upheld, confirmed, and revealed. God has carried out all this in the form, the nature, and the name of human beings. The results of this gracious choice by God in assuming our humanity are shown in the resurrection, which confirms our redemption and liberation, and is revealed even more richly in the ascension of our Savior, which convinces us of the glory to which we will rise and by which we will be glorified.

Ps 97:2

Here our nature becomes a new stage for the world, the angels, and people. It is not heaven that descends to the earth to see God bleeding, it is not hell that stands united around the tree of the curse, to crucify the Lord of glory, but the Mediator of our race, the firstborn of mankind. He makes his entrance into heaven as a Conqueror, a Victor, an Overcomer of God's enemies. He appears before God's throne, accompanied by captivity that he leads captive and by those who have been redeemed by God that he himself has set free. He bases his intercession on the marks of his wounds, the blood that flowed from them, his love for us as our Brother, as our Bridegroom, as our Benefactor, our innocence, our suffering, the merits that the faith which he gives us wraps us up in, the righteousness, the truth, the love of God. In the Spirit David saw the King of Glory, God, making his entrance as a Man with great uproar and tumult. "Who is the King of Glory? The Lord strong and mighty, the lord mighty in battle. Lift up your heads, O you gates, up, up, you eternal doors, that the King of Glory may come

Deut 21:23; Gal 3:13.; 1 Cor 2:8

Col 1:15

Isa 62:12

28. The German *Losungswort* is the technical term for the statement in a play that disentangles and explains all the intricacies of its plot.

29. This refers to God's justice and righteousness.

in. Who is the King of Glory? The Lord of hosts! He, he is the King
of Glory. Selah" (Ps 24).

Heb 1:3 God has set him at the right hand of his majesty. the angels see
our Redeemer as a man with the portrayal of his love for us on his
1 Tim 3:16 glorified body. God has given him a name that is above every name,
so that every knee in heaven and earth will bow at the name of Jesus
as his subjects, to show the homage and subordination that they
Phil 2:9–10 owe to him. Is not this the name by which we pray to God and are
John 14:13 heard by him, no matter what we pray for? Our faith in him and
Gen 1:28; Ps 8; Eph 2:6–10 his name makes us almighty; it makes us creators, the lords of creation. Yet, what is this compared to the fullness of grace that was
Rom 5:17 unlocked for us through him, so that we receive grace upon grace
John 1:16; Matt 1:23 from it. Our Immanuel, our Brother and Friend, reigns in heaven;
human nature is crowned in him, adored in him, revered in him.
Matt 28:18 In this Plenipotentiary, in this Firstling,[30] God welcomes our entire
race as well as the recovery of his righteousness and the revelation
of his love in our race. He has glorified himself in us; in the story of
our fall and our redemption he has publicized the supreme majesty
1 Tim 3:16 of his being and his will to the world, to angels, and to people. The
greatest sinner who repents and believes in him gives God greater
Luke 15:7 glory than the sky with its stars is able to declare his fame.

Heb 2:17 As the God who condescended to be like us in every way had
no place where he could lay his head, and did not enjoy the com-
Luke 9:58 forts that the animals looked for in their nests and holes, so the Man
had to be raised above all finite creatures, exalted and glorified in
God himself. God became a son of man and an heir of his curse
and death and fate, so that the man would become a son of God,
an only heir of heaven, as closely united with God as the fullness
of divinity dwelt bodily in Christ.

Who can think of his blessedness without trembling and shaking with fear at the calling of a Christian? How incomprehensible

30. The term for the firstborn male animals, Israelites, and the first fruits of the harvest that belonged to God (Exod 13:2; 23:19). Since they were holy to God, they had to be presented as offerings to him. In 1 Cor 15:20 and 24, the risen Lord Jesus is regarded as the first human offering to God that sanctifies all his disciples.

is the prize that is kept in store for us? How the eyes of the world, of angels, and people are fixed on the hope and promise of faith? The envy of infinitely greater rivals surrounds us for two reasons, the love of God for us and our unworthiness of it. Yes, they are not rivals—they are afraid of us as their future judges. *Matt 19:28; 1 Cor 6:2*

Sinner, think of the mockery that your subordinates inflict on you, you who have been called by God to be a king, His anointed one, in order to judge and condemn the devil. Tremble when you fall into his clutches; think of your Redeemer whose suffering foreshows your agony. "Behold the man." See yourself in this moving portrait *John 19:5* of scorn and cruelty. The spirits of darkness will never distort the fact that you are their king. So take fright at the greatness and dignity of your calling and the peril that is attached to its rejection.

On the other hand, we can look at God, his heaven, and its hosts with great delight. Our Savior continually reminds God of the human race and urges him to remember it. We have been engraved *Isa 49:16; Hag 2:23* on his hands, a jewel on the ring of his finger. In our name he carries the rule of the world on his shoulders. God sees us portrayed *Isa 9:5* on the breastpiece of our High Priest. Our Savior and Redeemer *Exod 28:15–29* cannot make any movement without us and the hearing of our needs by him and his Father, like the bells of Aaron. The Father cannot embrace his only-begotten Son, like Isaac with Jacob, without smelling *Exod 28:33–35; Luke 15:20* the smell of his clothes and being reminded of the venison that he loved to eat, and blessing him and us in him (Gen 27:27). He says, "See, the smell of my Son is as the smell of the field that the Lord has blessed" (Gen 27:27).

Thus, just as he sits on the throne of heaven as a man, so he is with each and every one of his believers everywhere and at all times with his divine presence. He is visible in heaven but invisible *Matt 28:20* here on earth, so that our heart, like his, would be there where our treasure is, our body on earth but our citizenship in heaven. Yes, *Phil 3:21* so that we will enjoy him visibly with a glorified body and be certain of our own body, he feeds us with his own body and blood as a pledge of the meal that we shall have at our disposal at the heavenly table and on our wedding-day. *1 Cor 11:23–26; John 6:54–58; Rev 19:7–9*

We see grave ministers, generals who have become stiff and grey, adopt the tricks of nurses and babysitters, flattering trifles, to please the crown prince of their monarch. In what more lovely light can we consider the angels as our guards and attendants, as spirits who happily put up with the weakness of our childhood by moving in with us as friends, darlings, and favorites of our blessed Redeemer and Creator? How significant for them are all services that they are able to perform for us? We can see how crowded the
Isa 66:1 highways are, the royal roads from the throne to the footstool, from his palace to his sheep fold (Lev 26:22).[31] Every stone that is the main pillow for a Christian is the kind of ladder that Jacob saw in
Gen 28:10–22 his dream. The angels are pleased with the appearance of our body, because he deigned to carry this heavenly glorified frock-coat from the earth as his festive robe that the wide expanse of heaven carpets with radiant blue and the sun has given its coat of gold:

> *This Heav'n-assum'd*[32] *majestic robe of earth*
> *HE deign'd to wear, who hung the vast Expanse*
> *With Azure bright, and cloth'd the Sun in Gold.*[33]

While the disciples gazed on high with firmly fixed, unaccustomed eyes towards heaven, their company increased with two men in white robes who stood by them (Acts 1:10).[34]

Jesus was taken up into heaven, to return again as the same loving Jesus. The Mount of Olives was as far from heavenly Jerusalem as
Heb 12:22 from earthly Jerusalem. The way to both is nothing but a Sabbath day's journey (Acts 1:12).

The conquering and triumphant church is only a story higher than the militant church on earth (Acts 1:13). The unity of love, the

31. This allusion to John 1:51 envisages Jesus as the way by which the angels descend to attend to us and ascend to usher us into the Father's presence.

32. Hamann has "affuen'd," a misconstrual of the eighteenth century English printing convention of rendering *s* with type that looks like *f*.

33. Edward Young, *Night Thoughts*, "Narcissa," Night Three, lines 193–95.

34. These two men were angels.

zeal for prayer, and the presence of God is a threefold blessing that is common to both (Acts 1:14).

He has only been withdrawn from our sight. There is nothing but a cloud, the dust of his feet, that makes him invisible.[35] He is in us, closer than if we saw him outside of us with our eyes. He is our heart, whose movement is our life, whose pulse we feel. He is our eye, the light of our whole being that reveals everything to us without revealing himself. He is the soul of faith in whom we live and move and have our being. Can we be satisfied seeing his picture? The word of God and the testimony of the Holy Spirit reflect it back to us and let us see its reflection as in a clear mirror.

Acts 1:9; Nah 1:3

Acts 17:28

My Savior, do not let my vain reason that at your ascension still lets itself be duped by temporal happiness, like one of the people from Galilee that were flattered by earthly hopes, gape at the clouds on high. Strengthen my faith in the salvation of my soul that was purchased by your suffering. Let me rise from the grave of sin and wait with joy and comfort for your coming in death. Let me eagerly pray for your Spirit and your grace in my room, together with your apostles in union with you. My soul has been a stage for a show to the world, the angels, and people. The world has seen its comedies and tragedies conjured up on it like a puppet play. Satan can take pride in it as a battlefield where many a good thought and resolution, many a warning and inspiration have remained. Good and bad people can likewise take pride in triumphing over my duties, my calling, and my conscience. The drama of my sin and the bitter, heavy suffering to atone for it, and the wickedness of the Place of the Skull,[36] have been staged long enough on it. In vain my heart has been dedicated as your temple and house of prayer through baptism and so many repeated vows. Let this den of robbers and table of exchange for delusion be uprooted and overturned and destroyed.

Acts 1:10–11

Matt 6:6; Acts 1:14

Matt 21:12–13; John 2:13–21

35. See Hamann's comments on Rev 1:7 in the "Biblical Meditations of a Christian."

36. This is the literal sense of the word Golgotha (Matt 27:33; Mark 15:22; John 19:17), the hill where Jesus was crucified, the place that Luke calls the Skull (23:33). By his use of the term Hamann may allude to the human brain and its abuse of reason to justify sin and reject the lordship of Jesus.

Transform it into a new stage on which the world sees itself and me
Gal 6:14 crucified, on which your good angels long to look with pleasure at
the mysteries of your gospel by the Holy Spirit (1 Pet 1:12).

Let the name of my heavenly Father be praised and known and
hallowed by a new life and genuine human love.[37] Your kingdom
1 Cor 2:4 come, in power and the Spirit rather than in show and words. Let
1 Thess 2:12 me be a citizen of the future kingdom to which we have been called
and let me be anointed for that by faith in your saving Son though
God's Spirit. Your will be done, on earth as in heaven—my whole
life depends on your gracious will; your holy, good will is its happiness.[38] Let this fountain of my life and the outflow from it also be
the guideline and river bed for it to run in, without deviating to the
Prov 4:20–27 right or the left. Give us today our daily bread—and give us power
through your word and your Holy Spirit to live in keeping with your
holy name, your kingdom, and your glory. Your bread is the staff of
our life and our powers. Both accomplish nothing unless you give
us the nourishment for them. And forgive us our debts as we forgive
our debtors—God's compassion for poor debtors is already evident
in the laws of Moses. May God let all my spiritual and material debts
be wiped out! Together with the joy of your forgiveness, let me also
enjoy the satisfaction of repaying my human creditors! Let these
petitions be as powerful and heard by you as the petition for daily
bread is in your eyes that comes urgently to you from the mouth of
Ps 147:9 a young raven! Let the word of your Savior which promises us all
Matt 6:33 temporal things as a simple addition to God's kingdom and the word
of your apostle Paul that encourages us to hope for the fruit of piety
1 Tim 4:8 for our temporal life as well, *once again—once again*—be fulfilled and
praised by me! Lead us not into temptation, but deliver us from all
evil. Our whole life is an ongoing enactment of redemption and is
in need of an eternal Redeemer. Let all temptations be overcome
for us by faith and all evil blossom for good by your government.
When we too are at enmity with ourselves, grant us peace in ourselves with peace in you. For the kingdom, and the power, and the

37. In this paragraph, Hamann is praying the Lord's Prayer (Matt 6:9–13), interpolating his own petitions.

38. Or "success."

glory are yours, forever. Amen. Let us in faith call you the Lord of this kingdom; through faith let us obtain power in it and the hope of being an heir of glory. Amen! *Rom 8:17*

FRIDAY MORNING
MAY 5, 1758

Yesterday God let me celebrate Ascension Day with much grace. Because I devoted the day to resting, I excused myself to him for taking my temporal rest earlier than usual. Without light I went to bed. My heart kept conversing with the angels that surround us human beings. In the darkness the fiery arrows of the evil one seem to be greater in number and brighter for us. They are difficult for us, even though they are not any more dangerous for us than in the night of bondage to sin. We endure them like the belching of an upset stomach that shows us the ferment in it, but also, at the same time, relieves us of it. This effect shows the positive determination and power that it uses to relieve itself of its infection. Our gracious God overlooks this weakness in us, just as we make allowance for the weakness of a close friend without any apology from him and letting our visits be spoiled by it. Thus, I rose above the prose of (angel) fear (as the poet calls it)[39] and addressed my invisible company with bold confidence in their fellowship as they whispered to me some of their thoughts, their perceptions, some tuneful sounds of their glowing devotion. Then this passage that I had read a previous evening in Young's *Night Thoughts* occurred to me:

> *O Thou bleeding Love!*
> *Thou **Maker** of **new** morals to Mankind!*
> *The **grand Morality** is Love of Thee.*[40]

---

39. Probably a reference to a line from Edward Young: "That prose of piety, a lukewarm praise," from *Night Thoughts*, "The Christian Triumph," Night Four, line 645. Young is contrasting the prosaic religion of "cold-hearted, frozen, formalists" to the poetic religion of heart-felt, passionate faith.

40. Edward Young, *Night Thoughts*, "The Christian Triumph," Night Four, lines 781–83. Hamann adds this paraphrase of the previous English lines in German:

> *O bleeding Love!*
> *You Creator of a new ethics for mankind!*
> *The foundation and peak of the most exalted*
> *morality is to love **you**; is **your love**.*

My imagination helped me see this picture of bleeding love more vividly than ever before. It was portrayed before my eyes in soft outline and color. I saw it dripping with all sensitivity, sympathy, and comfort from faith, with thirst and thanksgiving. I thanked him for the drops of blood that I believed I was seeing. I thanked him, now *for the first time*, for eyes that could see his running tears. I asked that this picture of his bleeding love would appear at my death to comfort me. Thus I fell asleep and enjoyed the peace and balm of death in its shadow. I awoke and celebrated its blessing with the wish and the hope for the resurrection.

> 9. *O Jesus, let me in the Spirit*
> *Rise and live with you,*
> *Until you finally exalt me*
> *And give me the crown*
> *That you have prepared for me*
> *Hereafter in the kingdom of glory.*
> *Lord, hear! and let my pleading*
> *Be heeded!*[41]

The characteristics of a clean animal represent the nature of a
Deut 14:6–8 Christian for us. It chews its cud; its hoofs are cleft. A Christian wants to enjoy the taste of the food properly that nourishes his soul; he therefore does not grow tired of ruminating on it. By chewing, the food is not just prepared for nourishment, but the means to assimilate it itself provides nourishment and enjoyment.[42] Every word of God is a seed that produces fruit for him; for him, therefore, meditation does not have to do with the seed only, but, especially, with the fruit and the powers that lie in it. These powers are released by rumination; they are let loose by thinking this way and that. This rumination is the preparation of the field, the nurture of

---

41. Here Hamann quotes the ninth verse of the hymn "Ach Gott, mich drückt ein schwerer Stein," by Lorenz Lorenzen, a music director and cantor in Bremen, 1660–1722.

42. Here Hamann recalls the traditional Christian comparison of meditation on God's word with rumination of a cow on its cud.

what has been sown, by which every mustard seed becomes a tree in our souls.

The cloven hoof expresses the nature of faith in just as sensory terms. The different ways that we move and the dexterity and firmness of our grip and hold on something are the results and advantages of these cloven hoofs. These are the fingers, the sinews of faith, the tendrils by which a grape vine twists and winds around what is able to hold it up, the senses by which our soul receives the impressions of the physical world through which nature affects the spirit and the spirit affects nature and joins them both together.

THOUGHTS ON THE HYMN: "I THANK YOU, DEAR LORD"[43]

The offering that I brought to God this morning also served as my breakfast. As priests we live from the fruits of the altar on which we serve God. I have been edified in a special way by the hymn: *1 Cor 9:13* "I Thank You, Dear Lord." To some extent our Savior approves of the world's taste for old wine (Luke 5:39). In this psalm we find the strength and purity of the Spirit in an old, smoked wine skin of our mother tongue, which makes its content so much more worthy of honor and more powerful. *Mark 2:22*

1. *I thank you, dear Lord,*
That you have guarded me
And led me during this night.[44]

The Christian appears here like a grey Eliezer,[45] an old, trustworthy servant and steward for the Ancient of Days, who bows *Dan 7:9, 13, 22*

43. This morning hymn was written by Johann Kolross, a teacher in Basel (1487–1558). It was inspired by Luther's morning prayer in his *Small Catechism*. Hymnary.org gives the original text and cites its appearance in sixteen German hymnbooks, but records no English translations. The reflections that follow were most likely written on Friday, May 5.

44. Hamann misquotes this line of the hymn, which reads "in the danger of this night."

45. Eliezer was Abraham's "steward" (Gen 15:2), "the chief servant of his household" who was "in charge of all that he had," whom Abraham commissioned to find a wife for Isaac (Gen 24:2–4).

before the father of his family and the master of his house with *Gen 15:2; 24:2–9, 34–41* reverence and intimacy, simplicity and sincerity.

On his harp the spiritually gifted Paul Gerhardt speaks to the *Job 7:20* faithful Watcher of mankind about the danger of every night.[46] Today when the dark shadows surrounded me completely, Satan wanted to have me; but God prevented it. Yes, Father! When the cursed one wanted to devour me, I was on your lap—your wings enclosed me. You said, "My child, just lie down! Scorn him who would deceive you. Sleep well! Don't be alarmed! You will see the sun." Your word has come true, I can still see the light—I have been freed from trouble; your protection has made me new.

I lay so hard this night,
Surrounded by darkness.
Yet you, Lord my God,
Have helped me to escape
From great danger.

A hard bed—Genesis 28:11. In prison, in the chains of darkness, in great danger, from enemies that crawl to devour the dust of the earth where the head of the poor rests (Amos 2:7).[47]

Every night is also like the night spent by Peter in prison; every *Acts 12:6–8* awakening is a redemption like his. A light that shines for us (Acts *Mark 8:22–25* 12:7). A touch from God that opens our eyes. The chains of sleep that fall down from all our limbs. A command to get dressed, put on shoes, wrap our clothes around us, follow his angel: God performs all these miracles of the night and of his loving provision for us, even though we are unaware of it. Every night is Abraham's *Gen 15:12–16* vision of Egypt and slavery and darkness in both (Acts 12:9). These are the times of deep sleep that sinners who are in deep sleep, like

46. Here Hamann quotes verses 2–5 of Gerhardt's morning song: "Wach auf, mein Herz, und singe." See hymnary.org/text/awake_my_heart_be_singing for an English translation of the hymn by J. Kelly (1867).

47. Here Hamann alludes to God's judgment on the serpent in Gen 3:14. See his comments on Amos 2:1 in "Biblical Meditations of a Christian" where he remarks that Satan devours people by reducing them to dust once again.

Nebuchadnezzar, cannot remember, that no one but God is not only able to relate, but also interpret (Gen 15:12; Dan 2).

> 2. *With thanksgiving I will praise you,*
> *My God and Lord,*
> *There high above in heaven.*

Praising God with thanksgiving; God himself is greatly praised in judgments and punishments, in the suffering of the godly and the torment of the godless. The weeping and gnashing of hell are nothing but praise, the terrible praise of divine righteousness and holiness. From this preserve us, dear Lord God. The thirst of the *Matt 8:12; 13:42* rich man is a praise of the good things that he enjoyed in his life and a praise of the sores and death of poor, miserable Lazarus who was comforted in Abraham's lap. All praise on earth is nothing but a *Luke 16:20–22* key-note that we sound by which we anticipate singing and making music to God in that life. All praise is nothing but a vow to God to praise him finally there in heaven. *Ps 30:12; 52:9*

> *Grant me the day as well.*
> *I do not wish to ask you for anything*
> *But that your will be done.*
> *Lead me in your morality*
> *And break my will.*

Grant me *the day* where I shall praise you forever, the light where I shall enjoy you forever without sunset or clouds; and let every day *Isa 60:19–20; Zech 14:8* that you give me on earth be a pledge, a down payment, a morning of the longer day of eternity—let my whole life be nothing but the morn- *2 Cor 1:22; 5:5* ing business for this great, glorious day of praise and happiness by getting up from the sleep of sin, washing myself in the blood of your Son, putting on the clothes of righteousness and holiness around me, *Eph 4:24; Col 3:12–14* strapping on the sword of your Spirit, spreading some grains of incense in your praise, and slaughtering some offerings here on *Eph 6:17* earth as tokens of my future service,[48] and thereby let me keep

48. This refers to the burning of incense and presentation of a lamb in the divine service by the high priest each morning and evening (Exod 30:7–9, 34–37; 29:38–46).

Exod 12:11 myself ready to travel and set out on the Sabbath's day journey to *Acts 1:12; Heb 4:9–16; 12:22* heavenly Jerusalem together with your Holy Spirit. Give me too *the day* on which I now live in its morning and I now have at hand.

3. So that I do not turn away
From your right path, O Lord,
May the enemy not fool me,
So that I do not go astray.

The right path where God leads us with his moral instruction is the royal highway (Num 20:17; 21:22). We read how the enemy seeks to fool us by a remarkable example from this same book in Numbers 14:39–45 where he used the appearance of faithfulness, obedience, and trust to make the Israelites new transgressors and greater rebels than by their previous mistrust in him.

Preserve me with your goodness,
I ask you diligently,
From the devil's craft and rage
By which he attacks me.

We could not ask God for our creation; we do not know the misery of our sin to call on him for our redemption. We therefore *Eph 2:8–10* were created by grace and redeemed by grace. Through faith we know that we were nothing, yes, we had stumbled into the greatest void of blessing, goodness, and happiness. Yes, all the curse, death, and misery that was possible for us in our existence lay on us. But *John 1:16–17* we also know that through faith, such fullness of grace and truth, such rich, such abundantly rich life, imperishable and eternal life, *John 10:10* has been won for us. The preservation of this twofold life in God, this twofold treasure, must be the *diligent prayer* of a Christian.

4. Grant me the faith
In your Son Jesus Christ.
Forgive me my sin too
Always here at this time of life.
You will not refuse to give

What you have promised.
Since he has borne my sin,
Free me from its burden.

5. *Give me the hope as well*
That does not disappoint; (Rom 5:5)[49]
With it a Christian love
For those who hurt me;
So that I may display it only,
Do not let me seek my own good in it, (1 Cor 10:24)
But love each person as myself
In keeping with ***all*** *your will.*

6. *Let me confess your word*
Before this evil world (Rom 10:9–10)
And call myself your servant;
You do not want me to fear power or money,
Which would soon lead me away
From your clear truth,
And separate me
From the Christian congregation.

What a kernel of knowledge lies in these broken shells! How these words strain, wearily and beyond their power, to pull its load and its riches! What a full, shaken, and overflowing measure is presented by every line! How fruitful the Spirit of the divine word makes us in sublime, surpassing, lively thoughts and sentiments! Power and money are the main-springs and the mark of fashion and prestige for all people; honor, eminence, and the security of power: riches, treasure, and everything that money can buy, the selfishness of greed as well as the vanity and lust that cost people so dearly, for which all people strive and on which the envy, the diligence, the thoughts and desires of the human heart are set. The weak Christian fears all this. A greater degree of faith is required to be able to scorn them fearlessly and use them fearlessly. He enjoys

49. Unlike the biblical references in the notes, this and the following references were inserted as part of the text by Hamann himself.

his faith and lives in it with a clarity that cannot be muddied by *Rev 22:1* anything. He is like the sea of glass in the revelation of John, with *Gen 1:2* no darkness on the face of the deep. The sun shines through it completely; it never loses its reflection in it.

Just as love for the neighbor seems to decrease more and more in the world, so we now see little brotherly love. The church is represented to us in vain as a body and our union like the ligaments of *Rev 21:2, 9; 22:17; Rom 12:4–5; 1 Cor 12:12–13* its limbs. It is called the bride of the Savior in vain. What's more, the union of his love that is extended to all its members should draw us closer to each other. For God's sake we should all love each other as sons of one Father, servants of one Master, clients *Eph 4:4–6* of one Benefactor, since this love should be the measure of those who belong to him and a benefit to us. The love with which God blesses us will be measured by how much we seek to bless each other. How much more should we love ourselves for Christ's sake, who, by the example of his eagerness to serve, has shown us the *Jas 2:8* royal commandment in a light that should make us alarmed at ourselves! How pleasing it must therefore be for God and Jesus when we, by our obedience, our good will, make this rare attempt to be an eager, persistent beginner as a member of his body, a friend and attendant of his betrothed bride, a persistent, faithful companion in the Christian congregation!

7. Let me complete the day
In the praise of your name.

Our whole life is a story of divine mercy and love. We complete our daily work; we bless and extol it when we receive that love and appropriate it for ourselves, the love that moved him to be our Creator and Redeemer. Only this love can make us a creature that *Gen 1:31* he regards with pleasure and seals with the word: "It is very good" *John 19:30* and the word of the second creation: "It is completed." By the completion of every day and every hour that is lived in God and Jesus, his name is hallowed, praised, and glorified. Our whole life is the fulfillment of this praise and of God's name in us.[50]

Let me never turn from you,
But be faithful to the end.
Protect my body and life
And the fruit of the land;
All that you have given me
Remains in your hand.

My body and my life and my fellow creatures depend on these. The common storehouse must have priority over our own pantry and kitchen.[51]

8. *I give you praise, Lord Jesus,*
For all ***the good deeds***
That you have done ***everywhere***
for ***me all my days.***
I want to praise your name,
Since you alone are good;
Feed me with your body,
Give me your blood to drink.

9. *The glory is yours only!*
The honor is yours only!
No one restrains your vengeance!
Let your blessing come to us!
So that we may sleep in peace,
With grace—to us—come quickly!
Give us the weapons of faith
Against the devil's crafty arrow. Amen.

50. The meditation in this section hinges on the meaning of *Vollendung* and its verb in Greek as both completion and fulfillment.

51. Because Hamann places this remark alongside this verse and verses 8 and 9 alongside each other, this remark could refer either to verse 7 or verse 8.

MAY 6, 1758

The following hymn[52] is a setting of a jewel from the dowry that is sung about in the wedding song of Solomon 2:16: "My Lover is mine and I am his."

> 1. *You, the sages of this age, always restrict*
> *Your friendship to those that are like you*
> *And deny that God associates*
> *With those who cannot match him.*
> *God is everything, and I am nothing;*
> *I a shadow—He the source of light,*
> *He still so strong, I so feeble-minded,*
> *He still so pure, I so vile,* (1 Cor 12:22–27)
> *He still so great, I so small:*
> *"My Friend is mine, and I am his."*

Friendship has been compared with love that occurs among equals or makes people equal. It has been deduced that it is rare, because it is a kind of knowledge; because it is a flower of virtue that teaches us to deny our innate selfishness and pride. If an enlightened understanding—a pure heart—belongs to our perceptions, then it lies beyond the domain of our natural powers. Only the knowledge of God and Jesus can disclose to us the unique object of our affection, the thing that is uniquely worthy of love. Thus Paul says: "Whoever has no love for the Lord Jesus is *anathema, maran-atha*: Let him be cursed. Our Lord, come!" (1 Cor 16:22). He is blind, he does not know God, he has no conception of what is good, he has no feeling as a creature, let alone a human being. He is a curse for those who know him and associate with him. He is like a serpent in their bosom, an adder that blocks their ears against the voice of the greatest charmer; how poisonous, how deadly must such a person be for all those who trust him? (Ps 56:4–5). He is like a viper by

52. The hymn is "Beschränkt, ihr Weisen diese Welt" by Christoph Wegleiter (1659–1706). Hymnary.org gives the German text and cites its appearance in thirteen German-language hymn books published in the US but records no English translations.

the path that bites the horse's heels with its poison, so that the rider falls backward (Gen 49:17).

Secondly, what has greater power to exploit our selfishness and overcome our pride than the greatness and love of the Highest Being that tries to trap us in our own snares? What greater goal can human pride discover than the one that transfers him from the dust that he is ashamed to lie in, to the pinnacle of all grandeur and glory? *Matt 4:5–10* What greater prospect of riches and treasure is it possible to survey than on God's mountain where faith exalts us, which is promised to all those who adore God in Spirit and truth and serve him with all their heart in his Son with all powers of sanctification? *John 4:23–24*

> 2. *My Joel,*[53] *my Immanuel,*[54]
> *My Mediator was able to find the means*
> *To unite himself with my hard-pressed soul*
> *That had turned away from him.* (Song 1:5–6)
> *My Solomon,*[55] *my Jonathon,*[56]
> *My bridegroom* (Isa 54:5)*—my God and Man*
> *Came from heaven to earth*
> *To become my Bosom—and Blood*[57]*—Friend,*
> *One body and one spirit—one flesh and one bone:*[58]
> *"My Friend is mine, and I am his."*

---

53. Jesus is called the poet's "Joel," a Hebrew name that means "the Lord is God."

54. Jesus is called the poet's "Immanuel," a name which means "God with us" (Isa 7:14; Matt 1:23).

55. The poet call Jesus his "Solomon," his man of peace (1 Chr 22:9), because he does not just, like Solomon, teach divine wisdom but is also greater than Solomon because he embodies it (Matt 12:42; 1 Cor 1:30; Col 2:3).

56. The poet calls Jesus his "Jonathon," David's intimate friend, because of the great love that Jesus has for him (1 Sam 18:1; 20:16; 2 Sam 1:26).

57. The two rhyming German pair of words, *Muthsfreund* and *Blutesfreund*, which usually describe the friendship of kindred spirits and that of close relatives, here describe the intimate spiritual friendship of the Christian with Jesus through their redemption by his blood and inner transformation by his Spirit.

58. Hamann writes these references: "(Gen 2:23; Judg 9:2; 2 Sam 5:1; 19:12; 1 Cor 12:27; Rom 12:5; Eph 4:16; Eph 5:29-31; 1 Cor 6:17; Phil 2:5)."

My God and Man! This contrast is just as moving as that of the English poet:

My sacrifice! My God! What things are these![59]
My sacrifice! My God! What awesome mysteries.
My God! And Man! What a depth of the divine love for humankind![60]

We are not just blood-friends but also bosom-friends of Christ. The apostle Paul says this in 1 Corinthians 2:16: "We have the sense of Christ."[61] Jonathon foreshows this double friendship splendidly. The Holy Spirit gives testimony to this (1 Sam 18:1). The soul of Jonathon was knit to the soul of David, and Jonathon loved him as
1 Sam 18:1 his own soul, as his own blood, as his own life. Their story is the story of friendship itself. The third and final testimony is David's anguished cry in his ode of lament in 2 Samuel 1:26: "I am distressed; I have been made unhappy by your death, my brother Jonathon. (He has borne our sicknesses and carried our sorrows;
Isa 53:4; Matt 8:17 he had to suffer and die for us.) You have been very pleasant and lovely to me; your love for me was wonderful—much, much more wonderful than all sexual love, than all the love of women."

3. *The God who gave me his Son*
Grants everything to me with his Son (Rom 8:32),
Not just his cross—not just his grave (2 Kgs 23:17–18),
Also his throne and his crown (Song 3:2).
Yes, what he says—has—and does[62]
His word—and Spirit—His flesh and blood;
What he has gained and won in battle (Josh 11:23);
What he has accomplished and suffered,
He bestows it all on me:
"My Friend is mine, and I am his!"

59. Edward Young, *Night Thoughts*, "The Christian Triumph," Night Four, line 596. Hamann quotes this line in English. He gives the reference "*Night* 4. pag.89."

60. These two lines are a paraphrase in German of the English text.

61. The usual English translation is "the mind of Christ." Hamann follows Luther and the Vulgate with this translation that puts the emphasis on perception rather than cognition.

62. Hamann writes these references: "(John 15:15–16; 16:13, 15; 1 Cor 3:21–23)."

What blessings, what worlds, what eternal blessings of salvation and happiness depend on the cross, on the dry wood that the Prince of Life was nailed on. This stake has become the doorpost of *Acts 3:15* heaven; it is the post of the narrow gate that leads to life; on it the *Matt 7:14* Spirit lets his ear be pierced as a sign of the bodily service that he owes to his Lord and Redeemer. On his grave, see 1 Kings 13:31 and *Exod 21:6* 2 Kings 13:20–21. The Mary who anointed Jesus teaches us how precious this grave and linen cloths of the risen Savior are. She broke *John 20:6–7* her crystal flask so as not to withhold a single drop of her expensive perfume; and, even much more than that, by his extraordinary approval our Savior agrees with her prophetic act and instructs his disciples about his burial and the splendid, lovely fruit of his grave with the aroma and the costliness of the nard perfume. If the cloths *Mark 14:3–9; John 12:1–8* of the apostle performed such miracles (Acts 19:12), how powerful must the cloth be that wrapped the body of him whose name, by itself, was effective to such a vast and remote extent? *Acts 3:6, 16; 4:12*

> 4. *I find profit, delight, and honor*
> *To the highest degree in our covenant;*
> *He requires nothing more from me*
> *Than faith, and I nothing else than grace.*
> *O what a good choice that is provided for us!* (Song 5:9; etc)
> *Away with regret and bargaining! I take delight*
> *In him—and he is satisfied with me.*
> *In both of us there thus remains, united,*
> *One heart and mouth—one Yes and No!* (2 Cor 1:18–22)*:*
> *"My Friend is mine, and I am his"!*

The suitability of our religion for all our inclinations, impulses, and natural needs, this exact correlation of its truths and disclosures with our greatest defects and tiniest imperfections, as well with our highest and most extravagant wishes, is the source of uncommonly fruitful and delightful meditations—and besides that, it is convincing proof that our religion has the same Author as the natural world. Just as the whole design of nature is based on the external bodily needs and comforts of human beings, so the whole design of grace is based on the nature, the defects, and the secret demands of our souls and our immortal spirit. In short, all the benefits that I enjoy through creation for my temporal life are nothing but silhouettes of incomparably higher benefits that my soul recognizes, receives, and enjoys in redemption for my spiritual life. So the soul can live as little without faith as the body without the products of nature.

If this is the true light, the only light, by which we must regard religion, then we would soon be convinced of its divinity, necessity, and sociability. The perfection of our existence depends on the knowledge of God in Christ Jesus. How should its happiness not be bound up with the perfection of our existence? My gracious God, give me faith and increase my faith in you and in Jesus Christ, the One whom you have sent. Without you, I am nothing; you are my whole self. Without you, it is impossible to know you and come to you. In your Son and the proclamation of his gospel, you have
Luke 12:52; Matt 16:19 granted us the key of all knowledge and with it the key of heaven. Let this be our wisdom and power and glory.

5. *He can truly satisfy* **the spirit of all Christians**
By feeding them with his love.
We dare not be jealous or envious
Of the highest good with each other. (2 Cor 9:8, 10, 11, 12)
Its abundance is not at all exhausted
By our uttermost enjoyment. (2 Kgs 4:6; Luke 4:25–27)
So I will not begrudge it at all to anyone, (Luke 4:25–27)
But I will make it my own for everyone.
Bicker, you world, over mine and yours. (John 18:36)
"My Friend is mine, and I am his."

6. *My Friend is the spirit of my soul;*
My friend is the life of my life.

**The double Son, the made and the re-made! And
Shall heaven's double property be lost?**[63]

For him who calls me his,
And no one else, I strive;
To him I devote myself, as he to me, (Song 8:6)
Him whom I love, as he loves me, (Gal 2:20)
From whom I can desire nothing more (Song 7:10)
He who can grant me nothing better.
This light extinguishes all make-believe:
"My Friend is mine, and I am his."

Without God, our soul is nothing but a dead wick; he is the One who must light our lamp. The Lord my God will lighten my darkness (Ps 18:28). He is the flame as well as the oil and the Spirit that awakens and nourishes this flame. He is the breath of our life and its kidney fat.[64] Everything is his, from the hair on our head to the heels with which we trample down the serpent and the head of its offspring. Since the body is his temple, we can say, as rightly as David in Psalm 29:9, that every bit of dust, every little speck, *every whit*[65] of it, declares his glory; it is a syllable, an iota of his glorious name.[66] He alone is love, expert in love and worthy of love. He has withheld nothing from me; all that is his is mine. And I cannot think of anything greater and better than what he has purchased for me and offers to me. By this sun of blessing and grace and truth every other light is extinguished and darkened; yes, every good thing borrows its light from him, like the light of the moon.

Gen 3:15; Rom 16:20

1 John 4:8, 16

John 16:14–15; John 8:12

Jas 1:17; Rev 21:23

63. Hamann injects and underscores these lines in English from Edward Young, *Night Thoughts*, "The Christian Triumph," Night 4, lines 471–72. He added the reference "Young. pag. 85. Tom.3."

64. See note 60.

65. Rather strangely Hamann writes "every whit" in English even though it is not the translation that is given in the KJV. The Hebrew word that he translates means "all of it," which he understands as "every bit" or "every jot."

66. Or "jot." Like iota, the smallest letter in the Greek alphabet, *jod* is the smallest letter in the Hebrew alphabet. It is the first letter of the holy name YHWH, which is invoked fifteen times in Psalm 29.

7. For me heaven is dreary without him,
And earth the open jaws of hell;
But his love can transform
The wilderness into Eden. (Deut 2:7; Ezek 36:35)
For me, without him, despite its extent,[67]
Time is too long, the world too narrow.
If enemies and friends flee,
If angels turn away from me,
I am truly isolated
But not alone: (John 16:32)
"My Friend is mine, and I am his."

8. *Take all that I have,*
Give me nothing that I ask for,
Exclude me, strip me, (Num 20:26, 28)
Take the clothes from me and the skin from my flesh,
(Job 1:21; Luke 10:30)
Yes, take food and drink and what you will,
(Deut 12:15, 22; cf. Song 2:9)
My Friend remains my be-all and end-all.[68] (Ps 4:7; 16:5–6)
Should the world steal everything from us,
Should it leave me nothing but my faith,
Then nothing remains, except my One and All:
"My Friend is mine, and I am his."

9. *His is my body and my soul*
That he created and redeemed.
Here he nourishes and anoints them with his oil,
Until he comforts both there eternally.
His is my mind, his are my senses,

67. Hamann includes the following explanation of what is meant by *extent*: "Here extent is understood as greatness, the greatness of a group and a place, or the size of both. See Deut 2:14." Hamann seems to presuppose the following translation of Deut 2:14: "The time in which we came from Kadesh-barnea until we crossed the brook of Zered was thirty-eight years, the extent of the whole generation of the fighting men in the army."

68. The literal sense of the rhyming German phrase "Hüll und Füll" is "outer covering and full content."

His is all that I am.
Yes, all that I have around me and in me
Is a gift of his grace.
It also frees me from ingratitude:
"My Friend is mine, and I am his."

The payment for our possessions that we have received on credit becomes so much more frightening the greater it is; like the bill of debt in the hands of a creditor, it discourages us so much more. Nothing but Christ's credit can give us poor people relief from it. If we belong to him, everything is paid for, everything belongs to us, we have the title for his property, the possession and use of all his goods. Everything that we thank God for in Christ's name is as good as purchased by us. Everything that we ask him for is as good as given and Amen.

10. *My work is his, my fame is his.* (Eph 2:10; Rom 9:23)
He looked for me before I found him. (John 15:16; 1 John 4:10, 19)
I have him as my possession,
And sadly nothing else than sin and shame.
Yet my Friend has also taken up this burden
On himself together with the cross,
And, to abolish my hostility, (Eph 2:14–16)
He interred my much-repented guilt
And punishment in the shrine of his grave.
"My Friend is mine, and I am his."

We know the tender attentiveness of divine friendship; with much flattery we recognize and respect it in the great people on earth. He pursues us, he goes before us, he runs towards us, he interprets our contempt for him as stupidity. The word *shrine* has lost its true meaning almost completely in German; the English language, which has retained it, can give us its sense. *Shrine* describes everything that contains a consecrated and holy thing. Thus it is a common figure of speech for an altar, a temple, a sacristy, the outward service, and so on. The grave of our Savior resembled the altar of burnt offering for the divine service of the Levitical priests, which was hollow, so that the ashes could fall down into it. Thus the ashes of our natural unworthiness lie interred in the altar of his grave, in its sanctuary, just as our bodies rest and rot away in churches.[69] Sin and punishment, its cause and its effect are interred.

> 11. *His is my good fortune and my time;*
> *His is my dying and my living.*
> *It is dedicated to his service and glory,*
> *Determined by him and devoted to him.* (Phil 2:13)
> *What I do and leave undone*
> *Comes from him, and returns to him.*
> *His too are all my sorrows* (Isa 53:4; Exod 3:7)
> *That he gently takes to heart;*
> (John 11:36; Luke 19:41, 42; Phil 2:27–28)
> *He feels and senses my pain.* (Deut 30:1–10; Josh 7:25)
> *"My Friend is mine, and I am his."*
> (Isa 63:9; 2 Thess 1:6; Judg 10:16)

His soul was squeezed by the misery of Israel, like a crying, sobbing person who cannot draw breath. The need to groan in distress is shown sensibly and graphically by the curtailment, the contraction of the soul, of life, of breath.[70]

> 12. *Let every enemy rage and storm!*
> *He does not surprise me much at all.*
> (Ps 56:11; 112:7; 118:6; 2 Sam 16:5 etc.)
> *Since the Judge is my best Friend,*
> *The world's trumpet does not frighten me.*
> *Should earth and heaven break and roar,*
> *Should my body and soul faint and fail,*
> *If my bones too would decay,*

---

69. This refers to the ancient custom of burial in a vault under a church.

70. This insertion explores the literal and metaphorical sense of the startling application to God of the Hebrew verb for *constriction* in Judges 10:16.

My motto still remains and can be read,
Set as a seal on my tombstone:
"My Friend is mine, and I am his."

5

DEUTERONOMY 30:11–14 TOGETHER WITH ROMANS 10:4–10

It is uncertain whether this is meant to be a new document or the conclusion for Hamann's "Thoughts on Church Hymns," since it comes after the meditation on Saturday May 6 and concludes with a verse from a well-known Lutheran hymn on the incarnation. In its form, this is a scripted sermon on these two texts. Here Hamann explores the correlation between God's creative word and receptive faith in both the order of creation and the order of redemption. He explores what could be called the theological anthropic principle. Just as the whole universe is fine-tuned in all its parts to support human life on planet earth, so God has created the human soul in Christ's image for life by faith in him here on earth. We therefore have a fine match, a wonderful correspondence, an inseparable, asymmetrical correlation between God's incarnate Son and each embodied human soul, between Jesus, the creative, life-giving, enlightening word of God and the faith that is created by God's word to receive life and light from him. God's cosmic will and purpose are focused on his Son, the word incarnate, and on the human reception of light and life through faith in his word. God's perspective coincides with our human perspective in the creative, redemptive word and in the faith that is created and maintained by the word in the human heart for a receptive life with God.

MAY 7, 1758

Christ is the end of the law for righteousness to everyone who believes. For Moses writes about the righteousness that comes by faith, that the person who does these things shall live by them. But as for the righteousness that comes through faith he says this, "Do not say in your heart, 'Who will ascend into heaven' (that is, to bring Christ down), or 'who will descend into the abyss' (that is, to bring Christ up from the dead)?" But what does he say? "The word is near you in your mouth and in your heart" (that is, the word of faith that we preach). Because if you confess the Lord Jesus with your mouth and believe in your heart that God raised him from the dead, you will be saved. For with the heart a person believes for justification and with the mouth confession occurs for salvation. [Romans 10:4–10][1]

The word of omnipotence and love has created the world, and
through it everything was created. In him was life, and the life was
John 1:3–4 the light of mankind. This is the true light that gives light to every-
John 1:9 one who comes into the world. Yet the word of omnipotence and
love is the faith by which light and life are also able to arise in our souls rather than only outside of us. Thus faith preserves us; everything for which he made us is preserved for us, in the strictest sense, through it. We have the same right to it as if we ourselves were the creator of everything.

If we take the torch of the divine word and faith into nature in order to recognize and adore its Creator, will we not discover that his love for us has constructed the entire project, as a whole and in every detail, so that all the wheels of natural phenomena have been assembled just as we would have wished them to be designed if he had entrusted us with their arrangement? The deeper our times penetrate into the mysteries of natural science, the clearer and more unanimous is its testimony of nature. Is not its body more perfect than a different and better construction for it which the most famous dissectors of nature are able to imagine? Is not the movement of

1. The quotations in the Romans passage are taken from Deuteronomy 30:11–14.

the earth, the sun, the moon, and the stars arranged for the greatest benefit, use, and comfort of people?

No one except a Christian grasps the reason for this and understands the mystery of creation through faith in the God-Man (Heb 11:3). The God-Man, the word revealed in flesh, God's Son, who, from eternity, had chosen the mystery of his incarnation and redemp- *1 Tim 3:16; John 1:3*
tion in human form, is the Creator. Even though he was only born in the fullness of time, he regarded himself as our Brother with our *Gal 4:4*
flesh and blood and created in our name, fashioning the whole of nature in the shape[2] and after the likeness and image of the human nature that he would assume out of the love with which he cre- *Phil 2:7*
ated Adam in the image of God. We wanted to exist—we received *Gen 1:27*
our existence. We wanted the happiest existence for ourselves—we would not have attained this if we were the first-born of creation; *Col 1:15*
this rank would have made us the unhappiest creatures. We did not possess this wisdom, but our Father, the Creator, knew this in his Son, and our Brother, the Son, knew this in his Father and our Father. They knew that in the sequence of divine miracles the youngest, the last in creation, would be the first. This is the secret *Matt 19:30*
and hidden wisdom that no one but God's Spirit could devise in the depths of the godhead (1 Cor 2:10), the wisdom which God had foreordained for our glory (2:7) and about which the mind of Christ alone can instruct us (2:16).

The omnipotence and love in creation spoke through our mouth and from our heart.[3] Everything happened as we would have wished it to be, as we could have spoken it. What happier invention than to replenish our powers by way of sleep? The first tired person would have wished for such a way to satisfy the needs of his nature. He would not have wished for it in vain, but we received it in the most perfect way that was at all possible to devise. That first person would have wished to have a kind of alternation in time in which he

---

2. Or "figure."

3. In his reference here and throughout to "mouth" and "heart"—that is, language and faith—Hamann is alluding to Deuteronomy 30:14, as also quoted in Romans 10:8: "But the word is very near you. It is in your mouth and in your heart, so that you can do it."

could be without the sun for some hours and enjoy a softer light, stillness, and so on—he would not have wished in vain; he received such an alternation by the motion of the sun and the earth. In short: all the delights, comforts, and benefits that we enjoy as the lords
Gen 1:28; Ps 8:3–8 of the earth and which all our subjects share in keeping with their position and diversity seem to flow from a human perspective and, if I may speak humanly and foolishly like this, from a human heart, or else to express it better, that God the Creator of all things wanted to become, and has become, the most loving Son of Man who, like all children, shared our flesh and blood (Heb 2:14).

The power and the wisdom that created the world is so close to us that it is in our mouth and heart. The power and wisdom for our salvation is even so much closer in the human mouth and heart. If creation is a human work, what would redemption not be that concerns us so much more closely?

We poor people could, too, as little create the natural world[4] for ourselves as we could redeem ourselves and our creatures. The God-Man shows that he is able to do both in miracles and mysteries, and both are granted to us by faith in Jesus Christ. Both nature in its creation and grace presuppose God's incarnation. Through faith in Jesus Christ everything is available that we would be able
Eph 3:20 to ask or desire from God for our existence and its happiness. We could not pray to God to give us a body and all the conditions for its preservation. We could even less pray to God to give us a soul with his image, and to restore it with so much glory, if we would be too weak to preserve it from the envy of the enemy. At that time, we knew about nothing that would allow us to fall in order to soar up to a higher level, nothing that would shorten our earthly life, which sin would make such a frightful burden. But God could have activated everything in our mouth and heart if one of our race could have been preserved who would later share its curse. Yes, with the recognition of our sin, we, like the Israelites in Deuteronomy 5:25–29 and 18:15–19, feel the need for a mediator. The law is a guardian to

4. Literally, nature.

bring us to Christ; repentance discloses the treasures of comfort, the indispensable need for a high priest like our gracious Savior. Faith convinces us that nothing but a God who is love can calm us, can make us righteous and accept us. *Gal 3:24*

Thus, like nature, grace is a creation, a fulfillment of our own thoughts and wishes. Grace presents all of it to our soul as something complete and present, so that without it our soul would not be able to enjoy its existence, its life, and its salvation. Just as nature has in advance prepared and anticipated all that the voice of our bodily needs would require from the Creator, so grace has slaughtered a victim and set the table for us. We need to do nothing but follow her[5] invitation to participate in the supper, which she got up early to prepare, earlier than we were aware of our existence and our future hunger and her prevenient love. Yes, we were awakened from the womb of the night for life in order to participate in this banquet. *Prov 9:1–6*

Nothing can so clearly present the meditation of a Christian on his graciously restored nature as the story of Adam. He falls into a deep sleep. God uses the time of this deep sleep when Adam is unaware of himself in order to introduce a helper to him, a playmate, in whom he would see himself depicted in softer, lovelier, and livelier light. Adam cries out: "This is flesh of my flesh, bone of my bone." *Gen 2:18–23*

God used the deep sleep of sin to prepare and introduce a radiant image of a restored person in his Son Jesus Christ. He is flesh of our flesh and bone of our bone. He is the right that we have to it, the right by which faith, seemingly, steals him from the hands of our dear God, in order to embrace him and appropriate him for itself only, thereby apparently denying God possession of him, because he had misappropriated a rib from our body that belongs to us and that we therefore regain and reclaim for ourselves as our rediscovered possession. As suddenly as Adam's admission gushed from his heart and issued from his mouth, so close has the word of faith in our divine Redeemer been set for us. Adam seemed to see *Eph 5:27*

5. The feminine forms in this sentence refer to wisdom personified as a noble woman, the patron of a young student.

that a dream picture or presentiment was fulfilled in Eve, as if she was what was still missing for his happiness, as if God had promised her to him or owed her to him.

The nature of faith is therefore expressed as vividly and sensibly as possible in this confession and appropriation by Adam. We would like to go even further. How did Adam recognize his flesh and bones? Ask Thomas what moved him to cry out: "My Lord and
John 20:28 my God!" Ask Mary Magdalene, who refers even more to Adam's story! As soon as she hears her name spoken by the gardener, she cries out with the same joy as Adam: "Rabboni!" (John 20:16). Ask your own heart how it recognizes the voice of the blood that speaks
Heb 12:24 more powerfully than the blood of Abel.

Faith matches God's thoughts. How does faith match God's thoughts? How did God match Adam's thoughts? Adam's thoughts were God's and God's thoughts were his. What moved the gracious God to form Eve? Because the wish to have such a creature as this helper lay in the mouth and heart of Adam. We are naturally inclined to wish for and ask for everything that seems good to us from him who is able to grant it to us. It is remarkable that God utters the word in Adam's mouth and heart as a wish to be freed and removed from something dangerous and bad.[6] It therefore was the speech about an imperfection that would be removed through Eve, like something bad that would be taken away and rectified by her. Adam therefore found the word in his heart and mind by which he claimed Eve for himself. He saw nothing else than that the need of his nature had been satisfied by God's love and provision: God had anticipated his wishes; he had surpassed them.

Faith discovers this is so in even greater measure in Jesus Christ. Everything that we lack, yes more than we can ask and hope and
Eph 3:20 wish, is offered to us in him. All impurity is washed away in him; all guilt is paid for in him; the mouth of all enemies is shut up and everything that we lack is supplied through him. Our dominion is not just restored in him, but its limits, certainty, and standing are

6. Here Hamann refers to Adam's exclamation in Gen 2:23 that corresponds with God's remark in 2:18 that it was not good that man should be alone.

heightened. All darkness in our understanding of God, his works and his ways, and of ourselves and the contradictions in our nature vanish. We break through the limits of the knowledge of our senses with which the greatest philosophers in the world shackle themselves so as not to go astray. Faith knows no other limits except spiritual, heavenly, eternal things, sees the decrees of God's love in the heart[7] of his only-begotten Son, enjoys him with its mouth, and feels the presence of the Most High God and his Spirit in its heart.

The word that is so near to us is not just faith in Jesus Christ but Christ himself, the word that came down from heaven and brought us truth and life, the power to hear and act. Christ, who came into the world to destroy the works of Satan and entered into his land of death and hell for us and returned from it in this journey with the message of his triumphant victory over our enemies and the fruits of his resurrection, with the spoils from our enemies and his judgment on them. When we confess this self-subsistent word with our mouth and accept him in our heart, when we believe in the preaching of the gospel, when we recognize the purpose of our redemption in his incarnation and its completion in his resurrection, it is as if we had climbed up into heaven to plead for God's Son to come down and had explored the depths of hell, like Jonah, to bring him back again. The former is nothing but an intention for the latter actions, an intention that God accepts as its enactment. Was it possible that Simeon could die before he came to see the Savior as a child? Was it not Simeon's faith that, to speak in human terms, bound our Savior to his word? Does not every Christian believe what Simeon believes? Was it possible for Zechariah to speak before the prophecy of the angel was fulfilled by the birth of a son? John's birth had to follow to remove the punishment of his father's unbelief and confirm it as a sign of faith.

Deut 30:14; John 1:1–18
1 John 3:8
1 Cor 15:55–57
Rom 10:10
Jonah 2:3; Rom 10:6–8
Luke 2:25–35
Luke 1:57–80

The word, God's Son, the object of our faith is near—in the mouth—we cannot pray except in his name and in the Spirit of his mouth. Yes, this same Spirit that teaches us to pray gives us the food

John 14:13; 15:16; Rom 8:26–27; Jude 20

7. Literally, "bosom" or "lap."

for our souls and the hunger for him in the divine word. The Spirit
Gal 4:19 forms him in *our heart,* acts so that Jesus may gain shape there, pre-
pares the heart and voices the sighs that we do not utter and we are
Rom 8:26 unable to utter. So that One is in our mouth and heart in whom we
Acts 17:28 live and move and have our being, and only his Spirit can make the
testimony of his love for humankind and our salvation in him so
understandable and pleasing to us that we hear it in faith and live
Rom 8:16 by faith according to it.

The word comes from heaven—from the good land beyond the
Jordan, the lovely hill country and Lebanon that Moses so earnestly
asked God to see without being heard (Deut 3:24–25). So it comes
from a very remote, better land that is our fatherland, God's kingdom! Like cold water for a thirsty soul, so is good news from a far
country (Prov 25:25). The preaching of Jesus consisted of nothing
except the most joyful news of the kingdom of heaven (Luke 8:1)
Luke 2:10–11 that the angels were glad to deliver as its lovely messengers.

The word comes from beyond the sea—like richly laden merchant ships that convey wares and goods from afar (Prov 31:14). The
draught of fish from a ship has been recorded in his story among
John 21:1–14 his most outstanding miracles. He knew the inhabitants of the sea
and had them so completely under his control that at his command
they hung themselves on the hook of his disciple in order to pay the
Matt 17:24–27 money of the tax for himself and his disciples. He spoke to turn the
Matt 8:23–27; Job 41:34 greatest storm into calm from the wind and sent Leviathan, the king
over all the sons of pride, at his command as an insect, a buzzing
Isa 7:18 fly (Ps 104:25–26).

Faith therefore represents everything. Even though faith seems
to be the littlest thing, God has made it the condition for our salva-
1 Cor 12:3; Gal 3:2 tion. Only God's Spirit can produce faith in us. This fruitful Spirit
makes a mustard seed of faith so powerful that it can move moun-
Matt 17:20 tains and transform the tiniest little seed into the largest plant and
Matt 13:31–32 a tree in God's garden.

I am convinced that every soul is a stage for the great wonders
that are contained in the history of creation and the entire Holy
1 Cor 4:9 Scripture. The course of the life of every Christian is included in the

daily work of God, in his covenants with people, in transgressions, warnings, revelations, miraculous preservations, and so on. For a Christian, who has passed from the death of sin into a new life, can *John 5:24* the preservation of Jonah, the raising of Lazarus, the healing of the cripple, and so on be conceived as greater miracles? Does not the *Jonah 2:1–11; John 11:17–44; Matt 9:1–8* Savior himself say: "Which is easier, to forgive sins or to say: take up your bed and walk?" May you, my Savior be praised for all the signs and miracles of your love!

Let us increase in your love
And in knowledge of you,
In order to remain in faith
And so serve you in the Spirit
That we may here taste
Your sweetness in our hearts
And always thirst for you.[8] Amen.

8. This is verse 3 of the hymn "Herr Christ, der einig Gottes Sohn" by Elizabeth Kreutziger (1505–1536). It was translated into English by Arthur T. Russell in the nineteenth century as "The Only Son from Heaven" (*The Lutheran Service Book* #402).

6

FRAGMENTS

Gather up the fragments that remain, that nothing be lost.
—John 6:12

MAY 16, 1758
LONDON

In these ten fragments, Hamann reflects briefly on a number of questions that are both philosophical and theological. The introduction explores our human dependence on the five senses, which are compared to the five loaves that Jesus transformed into twelve baskets full of leftover scraps after the feeding of the five thousand in John 6. Apart from the senses and their illumination by the Holy Spirit, reason is blind and faith—which comes from hearing—could not exist. Our knowledge is therefore limited and partial. So, for example, we cannot even know ourselves apart from God and our neighbor; only through Jesus—who has become our neighbor—do we truly get to know ourselves and God. But that only partially as we are known fully only by God. Hamann concludes: "Here we live on scraps. Our thoughts are nothing but fragments. Yes, our knowledge is patchwork." After that introduction, we have some reflections on the connection between self-love and freedom, the human desire for what is best, God's natural revelation in human history, the origin of evil, the link between laws and human freedom, the role of fear in salvation, the physical conscience of the body, the prophetic vocation of humankind, the body as clothing for the soul, and the dependence of the state on the industry of its subjects.

EXPLANATION OF THE TITLE

A crowd of people was fed abundantly by five barley loaves; this small measure is so bountiful for the multitude in the desert that more baskets remained full of left-overs than the loaves that they received. We see just the same miracle of divine blessing in the many sciences and arts. What a storehouse the history of learning provides! And on what are they all based? On five barley loaves, *the five senses which* we have in common with the irrational animals. Not only the warehouse of reason but also the treasury of faith rests on this floor.

John 6:1–13

Our reason resembles Tiresias, that blind soothsayer from Thebes, to whom his daughter Manto described the flight of birds; he prophesied from what she reported.[1] *"Faith," says the apostle, "comes by hearing," by the hearing of God's word (Rom 10:17). Jesus says, "Go, and tell John what you* ***hear*** *and* ***see****" (Matt 11:4).*[2]

Human beings enjoy infinitely more than what they need, and waste infinitely more than what they enjoy. How spendthrift nature must be for the sake of her children! How great is the condescension by which she disregards the scale in the relationship between our number and our needs and adjusts herself in her expenditure according to our hunger and the arrogance of our desires! Must she not be the daughter of a richly loving Father and of a Friend of humanity?

How much more do human beings sin in their complaints about the prison of the body, the limitations placed on them by their

1. Tiresias, a figure from Greek mythology, was, as a child, changed from a male to a female and then back again. He therefore was called to settle a dispute between Zeus and his wife Hera about the intensity of male and female sexual pleasure. When he declared that a woman's orgasm was nine times as strong as that of a man, Hera punished him by making him blind and Zeus rewarded him with a long life and the gift of prophecy. When Tiresias was a woman, he became the mother of Manto, who also was a prophet and who assisted her blind parent in the practice of augury based on the observation of birds.

2. Hamann emphasizes the paragraph by putting lines in the column on both sides. His additional underscores are represented here by bold type.

senses, the imperfection of the light, when at the same time they damn their senses by the insatiable lusts of their flesh, their preference *1 John 2:16* for sensual predilections, and their pride in the very light that they belittle. Even though the *visible* world may be a desert in the eyes of a spirit created for heaven, the loaves that God here serves up for us may seem to be unimpressive and meagre, and the fish may be ever so tiny, yet *they are blessed,* and we with them, by an *Gen 1:22; John 6:11* almighty, wonderworking, mysterious God, whom we Christians name as our God, because he has revealed himself as such in the greatest humility and love.

Is it not our spirit itself that divulges this proof of its high origin in the depths of its misery and that raises itself up as a creator above the impressions of the senses by making them fruitful and building them up as a scaffold to climb up into heaven? Or when it makes idols for itself *Gen 11:3–4* *for which it burns bricks and gathers stubble? Is it not a miracle of our* *Exod 5:5–19* *spirit itself that it transforms the poverty of the senses into such wealth that must astonish us by its wide distribution?*[3]

But our soul becomes just as guilty of dissipation in the nurture of its powers as through the body. Besides the moderation that our neediness should prescribe for us, we should not censure thrifty attention to gathering the fragments that fall down in the heat of our appetite which we do not think it worth the trouble to notice because our appetite sees more before it. *Here we live on fragments. Our thoughts are nothing but fragments.* Yes, our knowledge is patchwork. With God's help, I intend to weave a basket in which I will *1 Cor 13:9* gather up the fruits of my reading and reflection as loose and mixed thoughts. In order to gather together those with the same content at one time, I shall number them.

§ 1

Is not self-love quite evident in our idea of freedom? This self-love is the heart of our will, from which all inclinations and desires arise and converge like our arteries and veins. We can no more *think*

3. Hamann emphasizes this paragraph by putting a line on both sides of this paragraph.

without being conscious of ourselves than we can *will* without being conscious of ourselves.

A Japanese person sees his idol as closely connected with his ideas and inclinations as a Russian sees his beard and an Englishman his Magna Carta.[4] A superstitious person, a slave, and a republican therefore fight with similar fury and profit for the object of their self-love, on the same basis of freedom and the same zeal for it.

Why does trade increase the love of freedom? Because it increases the assets of a nation as well as of every citizen. We love what we own. Here freedom is thus nothing but self-interest and a branch of self-love for our own goods.

Hence there is such a close resemblance between the effect of self-love and freedom. Yes, the former governs the latter, as Young says:

> Man, love thyself;
> In this alone, free agents are not free.[5]

Just as all our cognitive powers have self-knowledge as their object, so our inclinations and desires have self-love as their object. Self-knowledge is our wisdom, self-love our virtue. As long as a person cannot know himself, there remains no possibility for him
John 8:32 to love himself. So the truth alone can make us free; this is the teaching of heavenly wisdom that came into the world to teach us
See Jas 3:17 to know ourselves and love ourselves.

Why can a person not know his own self? The reason for this must lie only in the state of our souls. *Nature, which instructs us about what is invisible in reliable riddles and parables,* shows us from the relations on which our body depends how we can understand the relation of our spirits to other spirits. Just as the body is subject to the laws of external things—air, earth, and the effect of other bodies—so we must conceive our soul similarly. It is exposed to the continual influence of higher spirits and connected with them.

4. The Magna Carta of 1215 is the foundational English legal code which establishes the rights of citizens for freedom, property, and their place in feudal society.

5. This is an English quotation from "Night VII. Infidel Reclaimed," from *The Complaint: or Night-Thoughts on Life, Death and Immortality* by Edward Young (London 1742–45).

Without any doubt, this, therefore, is what makes our own self so uncertain that we cannot recognize, distinguish, or even define it.

The impossibility of knowing ourselves can result from our fundamental nature as well as in its particular arrangement and condition. Thus the movement of a clock presupposes its proper construction and the condition that it must be wound up. *If* our nature depends, in an especially exact way, on the will of a higher Being, then it inevitably *follows* that we must use an understanding of it in order to explain our nature; *the more light* we receive as we consider this Being, *the more* our own nature must understand itself.

Our life is the first of all goods and the source of happiness. When we take our life into consideration, then its constitution shows us what makes for our happiness. It is so contingent that countless accidents may rob us of it, and we have as much power over it as every external thing may boast of. The whole host of hostile causes which can suspend and break the tie of the soul with the body nevertheless remains under the government of him to whom we owe our life. All intermediate instruments remain in his hands. The same condition applies to happiness. From this we may see how our self is so necessarily grounded in its Creator that we do not have the knowledge of our self at our disposal, *and that, in order to measure its circumference, we must penetrate to the bosom of the Godhead* *John 1:18*
that alone can ascertain and solve the whole mystery of our being.

The first cause of all things on which we depend so immediately must therefore unavoidably come to our help if we wish to understand our own self, our nature, destiny, and limitation. Next to this first cause belongs the knowledge of all intermediate beings which stand in connection with us; they, by their effect on us, help to produce our knowledge or are able to change it. We may call all these observations, taken together, *the condition of human nature in the world*. For me to fathom my own self it is not enough just to know what a person is, but also to know his state. Are you free, or a slave? Are you underage, an orphan, or a widow? How are you regarded by the higher beings that claim to have authority over you, oppress you, cheat you, and seek to gain from your ignorance, weakness, and folly?

From this we may see how many factors determine our self-knowledge, and that our self-knowledge is impossible, or most inadequate and deceptive, as long as they are not disclosed and revealed to us. We may see *that reason can grasp nothing except an analogy,* in order to receive a rather indistinct light, and that we, by observing the plan of divine creation and its government, can be brought only to conjectures, which may be used to make a particular sketch of his secret will for us.

Our life consists of a union of a visible part with a higher Being that we can infer only from its effects. This union is, to some extent, handed over to our own will, and subject to countless many other contingencies, both remain, *in an incomprehensible and hidden way,* under the government and providence of the One who gives us life and preserves it according to his will. These and other similar concepts are pointers that we must pay attention to, in order to reach conclusions about our own self.

In order to make the knowledge of ourselves easier, my own self is visible in every neighbor as in a mirror. As the image of my face
Prov 27:19 is reflected in water, my *I* is projected back in every fellow person. In order to make this *I* as dear to me as my own self, providence has sought to combine so many advantages and comforts in the human society.

Thus God and my neighbor are part of my self-knowledge, my self-love. What a law, what a delightful Law-giver, who commands
Matt 22:37–39 us to love him with all our heart, and our neighbor as our self! This is the only true human self-love, the highest wisdom of a Christian's self-knowledge, who not only loves God as the highest, most gener-
Mark 10:18 ous, the one and only good and perfect Being, but also knows that this God has, in the strictest sense, himself become his neighbor, and the neighbor of his fellow man, so that we might have every possible reason to love God and our neighbor.

Thus we see that only in our faith do heavenly knowledge, true happiness, and the highest freedom of human nature combine.

Reason, spirits, ethics are three daughters of a true doctrine of nature, which has no better source than revelation.

§ 2

How frightened we should be by the greatness of our nature when we consider that the choice not only of what is good, but also of what is best is the law of our will? The construction of every creature is related to its destiny. Is not this calling a prophecy of the highest happiness?[6]

§ 3

According to Roman law, soldiers were not allowed to buy land as a hereditary estate in the country where they were waging war.[7] We see here a Roman law that condemns the Christian, called to be a warrior here on this earth, who wants to be a settler on it. In the histories, laws, and customs of all nations, we find what we may call the common sense of religion. Everything is alive and full of hints about our calling and the God of grace. Our consideration is very biased if we limit God's working and influence exclusively to the Jewish people. By their example, he has merely wished to explain to our senses the hiddenness, the method, and laws of his wisdom and love, and has left us to apply this to our own life and to other matters, nations, and events. The Apostle says explicitly to the citizens of Lystra that God has given the heathen just as good a testimony and a witness to himself. Well, what did that consist of? *Acts 14:15–17*
He did good to them—*he made himself known to them as love and the God of love.* He gave them rain from heaven and fruitful seasons *1 John 4:8, 16*
and filled their hearts with food and gladness (Acts 14:17). Here it is evident that this rain and these fruitful seasons do not just have to do with the weather, they also show the working of the Spirit who communicates good thoughts, emotions, and impulses to us, the Spirit who was conferred in such a distinct way to the Jews that

6. Hamann emphasizes this whole paragraph by putting a line in the column on both sides.

7. Hamann gives an unidentified Latin reference to Roman military law: "L. 9. II. <qui testamenta facere [?]> de re militari et L. 13. II eodem."

it is even said that the women needed the help of the Spirit to spin *See Exod 31:1–3; 35:25, 30–35* wool for the tabernacle.

If the smallest bit of grass is a proof of God, how should the *Matt 6:30; 1 Pet 1:24–25* smallest actions of people be less important? Did Scripture not select the most despised nation, one of the smallest nations, and its worst, yes its most sinful actions, in order to clothe God's providence and wisdom in them and to reveal him in such humiliating images? Thus nature and history are the two great commentaries on God's word; and, on the other hand, this word is the only key to unlock both of them for us. *What does the difference between natural and revealed religion wish to tell us?*[8] If I understand it correctly, the difference between them is no more than the difference between the eye of a person who sees a picture without understanding the least about painting and drawing or about the story that is presented, and the eye of a painter, the difference between natural hearing and a musical ear.

Could we not say the same thing of Socrates,[9] when he referred to his guardian spirit, that was said of Peter: "he did not know what *Mark 9:6* he said," or of Caiaphas, who prophesied and proclaimed divine truths, even though neither he nor his hearers perceived the least *John 11:49–52* of what God was saying through them? The remarkable stories *Acts 7:54–8:3; 9:1–19; Num 22–24* of Saul and Balaam show that the revelation of God lies before our eyes even in the midst of idols, yes even in the instruments of hell, and that he even uses them to be his servants and slaves, like *2 Chr 36:11* Nebuchadnezzer.

An English clergyman first tried to introduce the anointing of grace into natural philosophy.[10] We still lack a Derham to

8. Hamann emphasizes this sentence by putting lines in the columns on both sides.

9. Socrates, who lived from 470–399 BC, was championed by Hamann's intellectual contemporaries for his rational pursuit of truth. But he himself spoke about his inspiration by his genius, his tutelary spirit. In his *Socratic Memorabilia* of 1759, one year after the *London Writings*, Hamann would turn the tables on the Enlightenment rationalists by using Socrates as a figure to critique their certainties through the philosopher's conviction of his own ignorance.

10. William Derham (1657–1735) was an Anglican priest, prominent scientist, and well-known natural philosopher. Here Haman refers to his book *Physico-Theology or Demonstration of the Being and Attributes of God from His Works of Creation*, which was published in London in 1713 and in a German translation in Hamburg in 1764.

uncover[11] *the God of Holy Scripture to us rather than, so to say, the God of naked reason for us in the realm of nature, someone who shows us that all the treasures of nature are nothing but an allegory, a mythological picture of heavenly systems, just as all events in world history are silhouettes of more mysterious actions and revealed miracles (Jer 32:20).*

§ 4

What question has given the philosophers of this world[12] more to do than the origin of evil or the toleration of it? God himself says: "I create what is evil." *If we had the right conception of these matters* Isa 45:7
or tried to acquire it for ourselves, we would not let ourselves be confused or offended by how this is expressed. Good and evil are actually only general terms which indicate nothing more than a relationship of our self to other objects and their reflexive relationship, so to say, to us. Thus, we therefore stand connected with other things; not only our true being and actual nature, but also all its possible variations and nuances rest on this nexus.

Our life needs to be maintained and repaired by nourishment. This depends on the fruits of the earth, and they, to some extent, depend on our industry and the course of nature. So laziness is a moral evil and overpricing is a physical evil. Yet we call them both evil, because through them the connection is broken that we, in part, depend on for our existence and its preservation.

Our health is a good which consists in the harmony of our bodily frame and its union with the soul.

So everything that is able to destroy or change our health is called an evil; on the other hand, whatever maintains or restores it is a good. Our health and life can therefore cease to be a good as soon as both infringe on a higher order which stands in a closer relation with our spiritual nature.

---

11. Hamann emphasizes the rest of this sentence by putting a line on both sides of this paragraph.

12. Here Hamann borrows the term *Weltweisen* from Luther's translation of 1 Cor 1:20 which the NIV translates as "the philosopher of this age."

In the chain of created things, a person is a very remote link from the great original Being by whom all things exist and through whose word they all came to be. He may be ever so weak compared to the whole nexus; yet even so, everything depends on God. He who holds the whole chain in his hand holds him in his immediate care, according to the laws by which all intermediate beings have their origin and goal in him.

Nothing throws such an extraordinary light on the whole nature of
Mark 10:18 *things as the great truth of our Savior: "No one is good but God alone."*[13] So instead of asking, "Where does evil come from?" we should turn the question around and be astonished that finite creatures are able to be good and happy. In this we have the true mystery of divine wisdom, love, and omnipotence. This philosophical curiosity which is puzzled and unsettled so much by the origin of evil should almost be *regarded as a dim awareness of the divine image in our reason*, a conclusion about what was earlier from what came later,[14] whose true sense is understood when it is reversed, but in whose transposition there is also a cabbala,[15] a hidden sense.

There is nothing more than a single connection that God has made as a law for our nature and our happiness. Whatever a person does against this correlation dissolves the common bond, the harmony, *the peace by which all external things are too weak to act on him,*[16] *and he is strong enough to resist the violence of all things that attack him in order to crush him. Yes, he is not just strong enough to resist them, but also to overrule their combined power.*

Imagine a mighty monarch who has sacrificed a favorite to the fury of his courtiers, in order to avenge himself on them through that man's son. The father is banished and suddenly removed from the vengeance and power of his enemies. His immature son remains

13. Hamann emphasizes this sentence by putting a single line in the column on both sides.

14. Here Hamann quotes the Greek axiom υστερον προτερον, "later-earlier," which Aristotle rules logically out of order.

15. This is the Hebrew term for the Jewish mystical tradition that teaches a system of esoteric theosophy based on a mystical interpretation of the Old Testament.

16. Hamann emphasizes the rest of this paragraph by putting a single line in the column on the left side.

in the kingdom, and all of the courtiers vent their fury at this child in order to torture the father doubly in him and avenge themselves even more cruelly on his heir. To that child the monarch discloses the fate of his father, the wickedness, the power, and craftiness of his enemies, and also a part of the secret why he cannot speak up publicly for his father and him too, why he had to forbid the son to remain in the court. Yet he also gives him an assurance that he can go everywhere unafraid, because has appointed an unknown friend to be with him wherever he goes and to watch the steps of his enemies. The monarch gives the child an assurance that he will put a mark on him which everyone must honor and which no one can erase or steal from him except the child himself, with his own hand or his own will or his own disobedience and contempt for the warnings and aids which he had entrusted to him to use.[17] The monarch gives the child an assurance that his father's absence will only last for a short while, and that he intends to lead the son incognito to his father's place of residence. Then, after the completion of some urgent matters, he wants to recall them both publicly to his kingdom and publicly declare them his friends and successors or co-rulers, and at the same time carry out the punishment of their enemies.

Let us follow this child as his enemies lie in wait for him, doing everything to win him over with blandishments and threats. Now they ridicule the sign on his forehead, now they urge him to wipe it off as a stain, now they promise to give him savories and mountains of gold so as to get him to do this by himself. Suppose that the enemies succeeded so far as to make the mark unrecognizable or temporarily invisible. After that, they merely wait to carry out their desire for revenge. Then, when the child discovers their cruelty and the danger for him, the unknown friend comes to save him from their clutches. Even though the way is short, it appears to be threatened by inner anxiety, fear, and the incessant attacks of his enemies in which his previously unknown friend always appears

17. This is an allusion to the sign of the cross that was placed on the forehead in the rite of baptism as a mark of ownership by Christ.

at the right time to prevent him from dying. With his presence, all nightmares and bogymen vanish.

Taking this fictitious analogy even further, let us suppose that the child carries this mark on his forehead without knowing it, and that no other hand except his own could extinguish it. Suppose that it was his duty not to touch his forehead with his hand or be persuaded by any argument to do so, even though he did not know the reasons or the existence of the mark and the respect that his enemies had to have for it. He only knew that the consequences of his disobedience would thereby be disclosed.

So this immature son is now travelling—he has the monarch's commands and promises. There is the place of residence where he will find his father, and the protection of the unknown friend that he actually had to rely on in every besetting danger: hope, childlike love, and trust are his pride, joy, and strength.

Imagine that the human race and every person is in a similar situation! Imagine that their life, security, and eternal happiness depend on their victory over all difficulties! Imagine that they would not only forfeit their happiness by their transgression of this stipulation, but would also fall into the worst misery. Imagine that they must be kept in constant fear, anxiety, and danger, and need deliverance in each moment, so that they are not lost eternally! Then the question about the origin of evil will be seen from a quite unfamiliar point of view.

§ 5

The more I reflect on the concept of freedom, the more it seems to me to agree with all observations about it. Let me give just two of them. It is agreed that there can be no freedom without laws, and we declare those countries to be free states in which both the people and their prince are subject to laws.

Laws only have all their power from the *basic instinct of self-love, which makes rewards and punishments work as motivations.* A law is never as unsettling and hurtful as the sentence of a judge that is based on what is fair. On the one hand, the law does not touch my self-love at all and deals only with my action; it therefore treats me the same as everyone else in the same situation. On the other hand, we always regard an arbitrary, illegal sentence as slavery, because it is resisted by self-love which reacts negatively to it. Through the law, I am informed about the consequences of my actions. So my imagination cannot deceive me with flattery and suspicious thoughts about the fairness of our prince or our judge.

Yes, in a free republic the judge, by his example, shows me that the law commands him to pronounce this sentence on me just as it commands me to endure it. In this we have the advantages of political freedom. Everyone knows the consequences of their actions, and no one can transgress them without punishment, because nothing but the will of the law can restrict me, and this will is as *well-known* as it is *unalterable*. In all instances, the will of the law is before me as a support for my self-preservation and self-love. That is why we appeal to laws and why we fear them.

We may add that the laws that we ourselves make, out of our self-love, never seem onerous for us, and that the greatest prerogative of a free state is that it is its own lawmaker. Thus, laws do not *restrict freedom*, but they provide me with those cases and actions that have advantageous or disadvantageous consequences for my self-love. This insight therefore determines our inclinations.

The Stoic principle that a virtuous person alone is free and that every evildoer is a slave is also understood in the light of this explanation. Lusts and vices hamper our knowledge; *their false judgments therefore confuse our self-love*. We believe that we act for what is best for us, for our pleasure and our honor, and choose means that contradict these ends. Is this self-love? ***Where there is no self-love there can also be no freedom.***[18]

§ 6

When we consider how much strength, spiritedness, and speed, which we otherwise do not have, the fear of extraordinary danger gives us, we understand why a Christian is so very superior to a

18. This sentence has a double underlining.

natural, secure person, because he seeks his salvation with fear
Phil 2:12 and trembling.

§ 7

My stomach complains at intemperance; every member has its feeling which warns it against what is harmful: this is its physical conscience.

§ 8

What is the origin of the high regard for the arts of divination and of the great number of them, which are based on nothing but the misunderstanding of our instinct or our natural reason? We are all able to be prophets. ***All natural phenomena are dreams, visions, riddles, which have their meaning, their secret sense. The book of nature and the book of history are nothing but ciphers, hidden signs, which require the same key that interprets Holy Scripture and is the purpose of its inspiration.***[19]

§ 9

The body is the clothing of the soul. It covers its nakedness and shame. Lustful and ambitious people ascribe their vicious inclinations to their blood and nerves. The body also serves to preserve the soul, just as clothing protects our bodies from external attacks by the air or other natural forces. This necessity of our nature has preserved us, whereas higher, lighter spirits fell without any redemption. *The hindrance of our clothes, which makes us a little heavier* and restricts us a little in the use of our limbs, does not extend as much to what is good for the soul as what is bad for it. How disgusting a person would be, if, by chance, his body did not keep him within limits!

§ 10

The common good of a state is sustained by the alms of its subjects. Every shard of industry is blessed by God for its general wealth and nourishment.

---

19. Hamann emphasizes this paragraph by putting single lines in the columns on both sides of it and adding another line in the left column for the last two sentences.

7

MEDITATIONS ON NEWTON'S ESSAY ON PROPHECIES

In these meditations Hamann interacts with Thomas Newton (1702–1882), the Anglican bishop of Bristol. In response to Lord Bolingbroke's critical mockery of Biblical prophecy in "Letters on the Study and Use of History" (London, 1735), Newton published an apologetic work in three volumes called "Dissertations on the Prophecies, which have remarkably been fulfilled, and at this time are fulfilling in the world" (London, 1754–1758). Hamann notes that the Old Testament does not just record some Messianic prophecies, but that it is entirely prophetic. He shows how the Holy Spirit revealed himself in his word in the form of a servant and became embodied in the Old Testament in anticipation of God's incarnation in Jesus, just as our spirits are enfleshed in our bodies.

Every Biblical story is a prophecy that would be fulfilled through all centuries and in every human soul. We only need to open the Bible to believe and feel[1] the omnipresence and omniscience of God's Spirit. Every story not only bears a human image, a body that is dust and ashes and nothing, the letters of the senses, but also a soul that is the breath of God and an exhalation from his mouth, the light and the life that shines in the darkness and cannot be comprehended by the darkness. God's Spirit, revealed in his word as

Gen 1:27; 3:19 *Gen 2:7* *John 1:5*

1. Or "experience."

Phil 2:7 self-subsisting[2] in the form of a servant, is flesh and dwells among
John 1:14 us full of grace and truth.

I. ABOUT THE STORY OF NOAH[3]

As people of the natural world, our life, work, yes, even our mere
Acts 17:28 existence, occur by God's will and omnipotence. As God's influence is so great and his union is so true in faithful people, in every
2 Pet 2:5 preacher of righteousness who like Noah has been preserved in the
Gen 6:8; Heb 11:7 floods of wrath and rescued from them through faith, so the event
of the great flood is nothing but a symbol, a parable, a shadow by
which God chose to reveal himself to the human race. The mysteries
Matt 13:31–32 of the kingdom of heaven lie hidden like a grain of seed in this story
of Noah, the mysteries of the two branches of the human family
tree, the branch from the woman or the branch from the offspring
Gen 3:15 of the serpent, and, at last, the mysteries of every human soul and,
particularly, the miracle of its redemption.

Gen 9:21, 24 The patriarch who rests, is drunk, and wakes up from his sleep,
is a symbol of God and his voice in the wilderness—a preacher of
Isa 40:3; Matt 3:3; 2 Pet 2:5 righteousness is his sleep, his drunkenness, his judgment and sentence on his children (John 15:1; Ps 78:65).

Gen 9:25 Why is Canaan cursed instead of his father? The Son of Man
2 Cor 5:21; Gal 3:13 was made sin for us, the curse and sacrifice for sin. But through his
sacrifice the curse and penalty for sin fell back on its author and his
offspring. The blood of God's Son proves to be life for the faithful
and eternal damnation for impenitent sinners.

Gen 9:26 Blessed be the Lord, the God of Shem! Not for Shem's righteousness but for God's mercy. The mystery of the incarnation and
the mystery of faith by which we can alone be saved is contained
Eph 1:22; 4:15; Col 1:18; compare Luke 3:36–37 in these two words. Shem is the body with Christ as its head, and
its union is expressed in several ways, the unity of the believer in
Christ and through the unity of his Spirit in God (John 17:21). So
too the words of Shem's God express the union of the two natures
in Christ and in us as long as we live in our lowly state.

---

2. Or "someone separate."

3. The numbering of this and the following sections refer to sections in Newton's study.

The indwelling of the Holy Spirit as well as the spread of the church among the nations is contained in the blessing of Japheth. Both Japheth and God dwell in the tents of Shem.[4] Both are true; the words of the Holy Spirit are like the wheels in Ezekiel's vision that run in all directions without needing to turn around. *Ezek 1:15–21*

The curse of Canaan may be compared to the story of the raven that Noah released and Proverbs 30:17.[5] *Gen 9:25; 8:12*

The ark is a symbol of our Savior. Both Ham and Japheth came out from it (Gen 9:18). Behemoth is also a creature of the word by which all things were made (Job 40:19). Compare this with 1 John 2:19. *1 Pet 3:20–22* *John 1:3*

The tongue is a fire that sets the wheel of nature on fire and rests on the fire of hell (James 3:6). The serpent speaks, Cain speaks, Ham *told* his brothers outside. All our thoughts are tongues of lies and the spirit of murder (Ps 73:9). *Gen 3:1; 4:8; 9:22*

God's nakedness, the shame of creation,[6] is the human race,[7] the fall into sin.

Drunken Noah is also a symbol of the human race. Its natural corruption is expressed through intoxication and its correlated insensitivity to its own shame. Do we not, with Ham, mock our own nature and the nakedness of our Father among the uncivilized barbarians? What did Shem and Japheth, the Jews and wise gentiles, achieve? Did the law and the philosophy of both reach far enough to compensate for the fall of Adam? They both went backwards (Isa 44:25). They both did not know the corruption of their nature—they did nothing except spread a cover, a cloak over it. That's how much their shoulders were able to carry. Their righteousness, their strength, their wisdom went no further than that! *Gen 9:21* *Gen 9:23*

4. This is a deduction from the fact that the pronoun "he" in Genesis 9:27 could refer grammatically either to God or to Japheth.

5. The point of the comparison is that, like the dove that did not return to the ark, Canaan left the people of God.

6. Or "the pudendum."

7. Or "human sexuality." The German word *Geschlecht* is also the term for sex.

When our conscience wakes up in us from the slumber and deep sleep of sin, it does not curse the Man, like Noah, but blesses the
Gen 9:24–26 God of Shem and the victory of our Lord Jesus Christ.

Gen 9:24 Noah woke up, and knew what his youngest son had done. The
Gen 1:23–28 beasts of the field were made before people, yet as their subjects. Noah knew—he did not experience it.[8]

The word of Hannibal: "I perceive the fate of Carthage,"[9] which
Eph 2:2; Num 22:28 Livy reports in book 27, was the voice of the spirit that rules in the air. Like Balaam, it speaks the words that God puts in its mouth.
1 Sam 10:12 Like Saul, Satan too belongs among the prophets. In the children of
2 Pet 2:5 unbelief, he himself is a preacher of righteousness and announces the fire for his sins on himself like Judah. He will be judged from his own mouth, ruined by his own lies, trapped in his own snare, and become his own murderer.

The nakedness of his father, which Ham mocks and ascribes
Gen 9:22 to wine, is a mystery of God, like all sins, because God used them to reveal his wisdom, power, and righteousness. The spirit of Ham resorted to the same mockery when it heard the disciples speak-
Acts 2:13 ing in tongues.

II. ABOUT THE PROPHECY OF ISHMAEL (PAGES 46, 47)

It is as little a wonder that the spirit of the serpent, the tempter, continues his role in the human race and will never cease to speak and
John 8:44 work in us and through us as a liar and murderer, as that Ishmael's spirit and reign should still exist in his children and descendants. The whole of creation is the trunk of a tree that is spread out with countless branches. Taken together, the whole of the human race must appear depicted to us in the same way, and every single nation in it, yes, every person, as a seed of grain which contains the entire design of all creation.

8. In other words, Noah knew it by revelation rather than sensory experience.

9. In Latin he says, "agnosco fortunam Carthaginis."

Ishmael was given to Abraham by God. He was called into existence as wild ass. God will humble him before his brother.[10] Ishmael is nothing but a name, a shadow, a type, a sign given by God. *Gen 16:12*

Sarai is dissatisfied with God, whom she blames for her infertility. She wants to be built up[11] through her maid like Adam, and Abram listens to his wife. Superior through the generosity of her mistress whom she despises, through the indulgence of her master and new husband. Hagar runs away and is angry at the harshness that she deserved to experience. This harshness of Sarah occurred with Abram's agreement and permission. *Gen 16:2* *Gen 3:6* *Gen 16:5–6*

Ishmael the archer was the head[12] of those who wounded Joseph (Gen 21:20; 49:23; compare Isa 21:17).

We discover Hagar and Ishmael as far from each other as our Savior was from his disciples in the Garden of Gethsemane (Luke 22:41).

The author quite often repeats the observation that individuals represent whole peoples and nations. Nevertheless, he always remains with the outer shell of the story. Legions of spirits and their story, the name of God and his will and reign through Leviathan and his conqueror, lie sketched in the darkness with the story of every person. The Spirit is the historian of the Bible unless we see him hovering on the water, we discover nothing but waste, emptiness, and darkness over the depths. *Job 40:23–24*

IV. JACOB'S PROPHECY[13]

A dying person is like Noah waking up from intoxication. What belongs to our senses, the produce of our vineyard, makes our head swim so much that we are not conscious of ourselves. Happy is the person who, when he wakes up, finds a cover over him that *Gen 9:24*

---

10. The Hebrew verb that is usually translated by "dwell" can also mean "to lay low," as in Ps 68:18.

11. Hamann alludes to the pun in the Hebrew verb which can mean to be built up as well as to have a child.

12. Or "leader."

13. In this section Newton examines Jacob's prophecies concerning his sons in Genesis 49:1–27. Here Hamann refers to the prophecy in 49:7 that, like Levi, Simeon would be scattered among Israel.

removes eternal shame and disgrace from him and recognizes how *Gen 9:23* much he needed it.

The author quotes the Targum that very many members from the tribe of Simeon were distributed as scholars and teachers.[14] Did we not see how the Greeks, who had given their name to an empire, experienced the same fate as learned slaves in Rome and everywhere? Do not the Jews, according to the testimony of Basnage, book 7, chapter 33, section 15,[15] still take pride in being witnesses to the unity of God throughout the whole world? See the author, page 53.

VIII. PROPHECY ABOUT THE JEWS

The Jews still always remain a mirror in which we see God's mysteries in the redemption of the human race as a riddle. In 1 Kings 8:50–51, Solomon still continues to pray for them. David still always lives, who at that time prayed for God's tolerance when they should become old and their strength would fail them (Ps 71:9; 59:11). For our sake they were struck, so that we would marvel at the wealth of his patience and the riches of divine forbearance in their pres- *Rom 9:22* ervation and would thereby be led to repentance.

Is it not the same unbelief that reigns in us, and should we not learn from its penalties for this nation to fear for ourselves? Have we not crucified God's Son as they have? Do we not build the tombs *Matt 23:29* of the prophets that they have put to death?

Obad 10, 15 Can we Christians read Obadiah without dismay? Are not the gentiles threatened with just the same end, we gentiles who have been in the same olive tree whose branches were discarded and *Rom 11:24* chopped off by God through our hands? This was what he threatened to do to the Edomites and what he did to the Romans.

14. He refers to the Jerusalem Targum, the Aramaic paraphrase of the Hebrew Bible that was used liturgically for synagogue services in Palestine.

15. Jacques Basnage, a French Reformed theologian, 1653–1725, wrote a comprehensive historical supplement to Josephus in seven volumes. An English translation of it appeared in London in 1708, called *The History and Religion of the Jews from the Time of Jesus Christ to the Present*.

Has Jesus ceased to be a king of the Jews? Has the inscription on his cross been changed? Do we not therefore persecute him in his people? Is not our faith just as much a table as their law, which has become a snare?[16] If Abraham's children were so punished, who did not do as he did, what kind of judgments await us who name God our Father and his only begotten Son and slander his teaching and his works through our unbelief and obstinacy?

John 19:19

Ps 69:22; Rom 11:9

Matt 3:9–10; John 8:39–41

16. By this image from Psalm 69 David, the Messianic king, compares false teachings to a poisoned meal that ensnares those who offer it to ensnare others.

8

FURTHER THOUGHTS ON THE COURSE OF MY LIFE

These entries revolve around Hamann's decision to ask for the hand of Katharina Berens in marriage and the refusal of permission to marry her. This untitled section consists of three units: a report from May 29 on his decision to leave London for Riga; entries after his return to Riga from June 25 to the last day of 1758; and a prayer for New Year's Day 1759.

MAY 29[1]

I began this week with a visit to Pastor Pitius.[2] God graciously granted me to gain his help officially once again, for I had been much awakened by hearing this devout man preach on the gospel reading for yesterday about the rich man and happy Lazarus. *Luke 16:19–31*
Because he announced that there would be Communion for his congregation next Sunday, I, as I had so often already previously done, asked God to invite me to his table.

I was in deep trouble because I had no more than a half a crown in my purse and my watch worth four pence was already with my landlord. All too disconsolate physically, I therefore visited this man and opened my heart and disclosed my condition to him. He urged me to leave England. God gave him much grace so that he spoke to my heart and also helped me to hear him and answer him. I stayed with him for a long time and was not aware of it until I noticed his

1. This section has this date as its heading. The day was the Monday after the Feast of the Holy Trinity, 1758. The title was added later to indicate that it is a continuation of the earlier autobiographical narrative.

2. Johann Reichard Pitius was the pastor of St. Mary's German Evangelical Lutheran Church in Savoy from 1742 to 1768.

great embarrassment, which drove me away from him. I left him in good spirits, which seemed to make him somewhat dismayed at me.

My God, your ways of mercy and truth are so full of love! You have had to do so many wonderful things so that I would learn to believe what I already knew as a child, what every child knows and no one truly believes unless God produces and grants this faith to him. I mean the simple truth: "Apart from me you can do nothing." I mean the only comfort: "I will never leave you nor forsake you."

John 15:5; Josh 1:5; Heb 13:5

It was not in vain that I was banished by the embarrassed demeanor of this guileless Israelite. Hardly had I left with a few steps from where he lived in Savoy when I heard a man call my name. Unexpectedly, he addressed me in a friendly, pleasant way. Since I had always supposed that he disliked me, I had avoided him as much as possible. It was the secretary of the Russian ambassador, Mr. Luders, who addressed me. He had received letters from my friend in St. Petersburg and heartened me quite anew with his observations and news. He was pleased with the happy accident of finding me by chance because he had been anxious about me and wished to find me.

John 1:47

I wanted to run back to the city with him when another just as noteworthy happening called me back again, which I will remember as long as I live. Because the pavement was very narrow, I stepped aside so that I could speak with my companion so much more comfortably. All at once, without realizing it, I lay on the ground near a post on which I could have smashed my head or put my arm out of joint so suddenly that it was a wonder how I did not lose my hat and wig and, at least, make myself look ridiculous to the onlookers, even though I got away without any damage. Because I had become dirty, I therefore had to turn back again, with much heartfelt emotion that this fall seemed to preach to me, and with much joy and comfort from such extraordinary protection and such a happy resurrection. All this so that I would return home, where I again returned clean because I resolved, as I went, to put myself in order.

I went out again immediately after my midday meal, unaware of what made me do it, to look up the father of a young English man that I had got to know in Riga, where I could hear something new from home or with whom I could perhaps find an acquaintance and friend who would provide me with a place to stay, if it came to the worst, or, at least, support me with good advice. After much asking around, I eventually found Mr. Vernizobre. As soon as I mentioned my name, he received me joyfully and congratulated himself that he would be able to delight my father with the news that he finally found me.

I read an English letter from my brother with a note from my old, honorable father. But I could not understand it. My heart was so overwhelmed with emotion that I did not know what I was reading and thus had to postpone this task. God gives me hope that I may be allowed to see my father once again, just as he showed me grace by letting me embrace my mother before she died. God has laid a cross on him with the loss of his memory. My father, do I not deserve the punishment that you bear! I have commended him to God and trust that he will do all things well and carry it out wonderfully. The testimony of the Holy Spirit does not depend on our *Ps 37:5*
memory, and when we forget everything Jesus the crucified makes *Rom 8:16*
up for all wisdom and all power, all reason and all senses. It is more *1 Cor 2:2*
possible to live without a head or a heart than without him. He is the head of our nature and all our powers, the source of all motion that can as little stand still in a Christian as the pulse in a living person. A Christian is the only living person, an eternal, undying, living person, because he lives and moves and has his being in God
and with God, yes, for God. *Acts 17:28*

By his extraordinary grace, God permitted me to attend the Holy Supper on June 4. I was much restored by it and strengthened for spiritual life with God. May the Spirit of God who truly brings Jesus to our remembrance not only preserve the memory of his death but also give me power to show and proclaim the death of the Lord in
my life and conduct until he comes. Amen. *John 14:26; 1 Cor 11:23–26*

My decision to return to Riga has become ever more fixed. I have written to all my friends and already taken leave of them. What encourages me even more in this right way that I have again found are the hindrances and stumbling blocks that Satan tries to throw in the way for me. Help me, my loving God, to clear them away and overcome myself and the world. All good success and all comfort in failure depend only on you!

THE TWENTY FIFTH OF JUNE: ON THE FIFTH SUNDAY AFTER TRINITY LUKE 5:1

This is most likely the last Sunday that I will commemorate in England. God too shared his blessing with me in the sermon for today through the mouth of his devout servant, whom I was able to hear with much personal relevance, comfort, and joy. The gospel is so much more relevant for my departure because I will be trav-
Luke 5:1–11 elling by ship.[3] His introduction came from Ecclesiastes 9:7: "The Lord approves what you are doing."[4]

He presented five rules for home and life from the story of the gospel by which our vocation would be blessed and all our works would be made pleasing to the Lord:

1. Meditation on God's Word. This is no hindrance for us in our vocation but increases God's blessing on it and clears away the obstacles of laziness, disorder, excess, and so on.

2. Faithfulness and diligence in our undertakings. The fishermen whom Jesus had chosen to be his disciples were engaged in their vocation.

3. Courage in their temptations.

   (a) A whole night's lost labor.

   (b) The improbability of God's ways and the fear of venturing out on the high sea.

---

3. This was the Gospel reading for that Sunday.

4. The Old Testament reading that was assigned for this Sunday was Eccl 9:7–10.

(c) The tearing net.

(d) The sinking ship. All these were temptations that the disciples could have allowed to overwhelm them, but they overcame them with a simple faith.

4. The humility with which we must receive and recognize all God's benefits. "Depart from me, for I am a sinful man," says Peter. It was not their obedience but their perseverance that gained this reward.

5. The denial of all temporal advantages and the renunciation of them for the salvation of our souls and out of obedience and gratitude for God's love, just as the disciples here forsook everything.

The service in the afternoon ended with the hymn that I ruminated on for eight days: "I cry to you, Lord Jesus Christ."[5] The last two verses describe the sinews and muscles of faith as they are in life. May God graciously hear my prayer and grant me wisdom and faith to cling to his grace with his good Spirit and not let him go until he has heard and blessed me. Amen! In the name of Jesus. Amen! *Gen 32:26*

I had to leave London unexpectedly on June 27, because I was shocked by the news that my shipping agent had left. I reached Gravesend that night where I was threatened by a sailor who, I can only deduce, intended to take what belonged to me. Just then, an Englishman came from an inn nearby and took care of me by showing where to go. We had to sail on a warship and wait for a rendezvous with the other ships so that we only took to sea on July 8. On Sunday July 16, I was much unsettled by a rather strong opposing wind and storm and the peril of the Kattegat[6] but was comforted and encouraged by the reading of Psalm 42.

---

5. Catharine Winkworth's English translation of this hymn written by Johann Agricola (1494–1566) is provided in the *Evangelical Lutheran Hymnary*, number 255, under the title "Lord, Hear the Voice of My Complaint." See hymnary.org for the German texts and English translations.

6. The Kattegat is the stretch of sea on the west between Denmark and Sweden.

By the grace of God, I arrived in Riga on July 16 after leaving London on June 27 and disembarked to meet with Mr. Karl Berens, who welcomed me most amicably and affectionately.[7] Despite *Phil 2:13* my distraction, God granted me to will and to act, so that I then attended the Holy Supper on the following Sunday after July 19 when I was surprised and moved, because God received me with the same gospel of Peter's large catch of fish that I heard when I took leave from England on the fifth Sunday after Trinity.

On the day of my arrival, I immediately hurried to visit my old friend Lindner, who shocked and delighted me with the news that my brother had been called as a long-awaited coworker with him at the local cathedral school. He had first arrived safely after travelling from October 16–27.

God be thanked and praised for all the mercy that he has shown so richly to us both. For the sake of his dear Son Jesus Christ, may he also hear my daily prayer for my only brother that he has put in my mouth! May he grant him the strength needed for his calling and the will and zeal to use it faithfully! May he give him grace to *Mark 9:36–37* receive the children in the name of Jesus and feed them. May God prepare and equip him to be a faithful shepherd of the sheep and *John 10:12; 21:15–17* lambs that he has entrusted to him. May he give him the blessing of the fourth commandment on all his undertakings and let it *Exod 20:12; Eph 6:1–2* accompany him in all his ways—and allow us to both enjoy it for the sake of the perfect obedience of his dear Son Jesus Christ! May our hearts also be united in true brotherly love through him, so that we do not become stumbling stones to each other on our journey but mutually encourage each other to follow the true voice of the *John 10:27* Good Shepherd, our Savior, always deny ourselves more and more, take up his cross, and walk in his footsteps that he has marked with *Matt 16:24; 1 Pet 1:17–19; 2:21* his precious blood. Amen!

On my arrival, my brother pleased me with a present from our father, which he had been instructed for us to share with each other. The charitable gift of this honorable old man moved me so much

7. Karl was the second oldest son of Arend Berens, the head of the merchant family that had sent Hamann on his mission to London.

more because with it I was able to discharge my debt to my dear friend Bassa. May God reward my dear father and unassuming believer—and let me be increasingly delivered from my habitual disorder by my experience of it and gradually instructed and trained in the wise stewardship of temporal blessing!

My dealings in the house of my benefactor had until now been negotiated only by letter with his brother at the instruction of the oldest daughter of the head of the family and some help from his younger brother, George, who was in charge of the finances of the firm.[8] God had until now visibly blessed these efforts. May he be thanked and praised for that from my heart in the name of his dear Son Jesus Christ! Furthermore, may he let me draw grace upon grace from his fullness and grant me the assistance of his good Holy Spirit in all my works. May he let everything prosper for his glory and the salvation of my soul and other souls, make me a good steward of the talent that he has lent me, and let my faith be increasingly active and fruitful in unfeigned love for my neighbor with the good works that he has prepared for me and are pleasing to him in the Son, whom he loves, my High Priest and Advocate!

John 1:16

Luke 19:11–27

Gal 5:6; Eph 2:10

Col 1:10; Heb 4:14; 1 John 2:1

God used the exchange of letters with my friend in a special way to preserve me watchfully from the leaven of unbelief and hypocrisy. May he reward this so very wholesome scrutiny of me with all spiritual blessing for his own soul!

Luke 12:1

On December 6, the second Sunday in Advent, God gave me grace to attend the Holy Supper, since the day before I had been deeply moved when I went to confession with Pastor Essen, who took the place of my sick father confessor, Pastor Gericke. I repeated my filial thanksgiving to God for his mercy by which he had awakened me for this holy deed and allowed me to complete it and enjoy its peace and fruit.

8. The benefactor is Arend Berens Jr. (1723–69) who managed the family merchant firm after the death of his father. His brother is either the second son Karl (1725–89) or, more likely, Hamann's close friend Johann Christoph (1729–83). The oldest daughter Katharina (1727–1805) was the woman Hamann hoped to marry. His mission to London seems to have been negotiated by her with the help of Johann Christoph and the younger brother George (1739–1813).

December 11 was a day of repentance. I spent the evening writ-
Ps 51:3; Luke 18:13 ing a letter with contents that shall always be very momentous. May God be merciful to me a sinner and not let me myself be cast away
1 Cor 9:27 when I preach to others!

On December 13, the third Sunday in Advent, I experienced some dark misgivings at dinner caused by the condition of my friend—I seemed to sense something similar with his sister without being able to say why it was so. I asked their permission to write as gently as possible to their brother and offered to be helpful to them in doing this.[9] And they seemed quite inclined to accept this offer.

In December 14, I ate by myself upstairs and worked on the promised letter, which seemed to turn completely wrong, because it struck me that my hand always wrote different words and thoughts than what my head thought. I sent down what I had written and was uneasy about the reception of my impressions. So when I went out, I spoke to them, partly so that I could apologize and partly so that I could explain it somewhat further. Their reception struck me as distressed. That evening I came home to eat and was driven to my room earlier than usual by extremely dark misgivings, where I went to bed at rest and was comforted after the reading of some chapters from Job and some Psalms (12–20 if I am not mistaken). On climbing in, I was conscious of that and wished that I could fall asleep in tranquility.

I am not able to put into words exactly what I experienced shortly after that. With God's help, I will do it in order to preserve my memory of it as much and as truthfully as I can, because this event became the basis for part of the decision that I did not think I was able to make. I thought about the fate of my friend and thanked God for having spared me similar temptations of the flesh and asked him to do so in the future. As far as I know, I had not fallen asleep. I do not know anything at all about whether I was properly awake, or how. I heard a voice in me that asked me about my decision to take a wife—and out of obedience to him, I did not speak a word;

9. The letter was to his friend Johann Christoph, who disapproved of Hamann's relationship with Katharina.

but it struck me as if I sprang up with a shout and cried out: "If I must, give me no one else than the sister of my friend."[10] It seemed to me as though I heard the joyful assurance with a solemn voice that it was she who was meant for me, kept so long and wonderfully—I had initially renounced marriage for rational, foolish reasons.[11] I had gladly wished to adopt celibacy as chastisement for the sins of my youth and asked God to make my body a sacrifice that would be living, holy, and well-pleasing to him. Yes, that was so because *Rom 12:1*
God had watched over me with special care through his angel so *Ps 91:11*
that I could not sin by any sexual intermixture.[12] Abraham believed without wavering. Even if my body should have died, does God not *Rom 4:19–21*
give, and can he not give, children to the solitary person from stones that he can awaken? Search me, O God, and know my heart! Try *Heb 11:12; Matt 3:9*
me and know how I think! And see if there be any evil way in me, and lead me on the eternal way (Ps 139:23, 24)!

The Lord redeems the soul of his servants, and all who trust in him will have no guilt (Ps 34:22). On St. John's Day, December 15, after I had commended myself and my girlfriend to the mercy of God, who lets all human work perish and does not want to let those who wait on him and trust in his goodness be put to shame, *Ps 25:3*
I got up with the thought that I would marry. This was on my mind when she received my first morning greeting since she had perhaps just been busy writing a letter to her brother. On December 16th, I wrote a letter to my father that reached him on the 22nd, and on the 27th I received his response in which he pointed me to God. On the 28th, I announced my decision in a letter to my friend. God gave his grace to my letter. The next morning, I sent it down to his sister. In the afternoon, I received a letter that was addressed to her that arrived with my name on it. When I handed it over to her, she told me that she was hopeful.

10. Hamann here refers to Katharina Berens, the older sister of his friend Johann Christoph.

11. Literally "out of reasonable follies."

12. This term seems to refer to homosexual intercourse.

The last day of 1758 was full of extraordinary scenes between
Mr. Arend Berens and me.[13] I listened to him speaking to me like
1 Sam 10:12 Saul among the prophets. Hezekiah said of a day: "This is a day of
trouble and abuse and disgrace; children have come to the point of birth, and there is no strength left to deliver them" (2 Kgs 19:3). I was unusually moved by the change of mind and the favorable impressions that I seemed to notice in him. I had no peace downstairs where I had eaten my supper, and on the last evening of this year I went cheerfully to die in bed that night if God would be so gracious as to rescue the soul of this brother.[14]

1759[15]

Father, since you are reconciled through the blood of your dear
Rom 5:9–11 Son, let this year be blessed for all our souls. In it give our hearts
Ezek 11:19 of flesh a new mind and a new, sure spirit. Cast us not away from
Ps 51:12–13 your presence and do not take your Spirit away from us. Let your
finger write the whole of Psalm 51 in my heart and have mercy on me. you will punish our sins with a rod and our iniquity with stripes, but you will not remove your grace from us and let your truth fail us. You will not profane your covenant and alter what has gone from your mouth. Once for all, you swore by your holiness: "I will not lie to David. His offspring shall endure forever and his throne before me like the sun. Like the moon it shall endure forever and be as sure as the witness in the clouds. Sela" (Ps 89:32–37). Turn to me and be gracious to me. Strengthen your servant with your power and give help to the son of your maid. Show me a sign that it will turn out well for me that those who hate me may see it and be put to shame, because you, Lord, stand up for me and comfort me (Ps 86:16–17).

---

13. This was Arend Berens Jr., the oldest son in the family and the head of the family firm after the death of his father.

14. At this point Hamann was still hopeful that he would be able to marry Katharina Berens. But that did not happen because this "brother," the third son, his friend Johann Christoph Berens, refused to give his approval.

15. This prayer was composed on New Year's Day.

Let my father, brother, benefactors, and friends, and especially those with whom I live, rejoice in your love and rich blessing. Preserve them in your good favor. Give them your peace, life, and kindness. May the good work that you have begun in some of their souls be brought to completion by your Spirit and strengthen what *Phil 1:6* has become weak in me and others. Let us not abandon our first love. Give us ears to hear; help us to fight and conquer; give us the *Rev 2:4* hidden manna to eat; let us receive a good testimony; and let a new name be written with the testimony that no knows except the one *Rev 2:17* who receives it.

O God of love, watch over my heart and the heart of my sister. Sanctify and purify our hearts of all fleshly thinking by your Holy Spirit. If it is your gracious will, let the promise of Psalm 128 be fulfilled in us. Let all who pass by call out to us: "The blessing of the Lord be upon you; we bless you in the name of the Lord!" Those *Ps 129:8* who wish to vindicate me must rejoice and be glad and always say: "May the Lord be highly praised, who delights in the welfare of his servant!" Let us soon hear this congratulation from the mouth *Ps 35:27* of our absent brother and let him feel its truth and power in his heart! Amen!

9

PRAYER

No date is given for this comprehensive series of eight prayers in which Hamann prays for himself and his needs, his father, his brother, his former fiancée Katharina Berens, his friends and relatives, his country and household, all households and their members, and for his own empowerment by the Holy Spirit in prayer, baptismal piety, and faithful participation in the sacrament of Christ's body and blood. These prayers culminate in the Lord's Prayer, the Aaronic Benediction, the benediction for peace from Philippians 4:7, the Trinitarian benediction from 2 Corinthians 13:14, a prayer for Christ's help from Psalm 118:25–26, the prayer for Christ's return from Revelation 22:20, and the sinner's prayer from Luke 18:13. While they seem to originate from his time in London, Hamann subsequently reworked them and used them in his morning and evening devotions. This is a fitting conclusion to his London Writings, which come from the time when he himself learned to pray in a new way to God the Father through his Son by the inspiration of the Holy Spirit.

Lord, hear my word, consider my speaking, listen to my cry, my King and my God, for to you I will pray. *Ps 5:1–2*

Let the speaking of my mouth and the conversation of my heart before you be well-pleasing to you, my refuge and redeemer. *Ps 19:14*

I praise and glorify you, dear heavenly Father, for all your mercy and faithfulness with which you have guarded and protected me

this day.[1] Accept my thank offering from the hands of my high priest
Heb 4:14–15; 1 John 2:1 and advocate, Jesus Christ, and for his sake also forgive me all my
sins. Let my conscience be washed clean from all the dead works of
Heb 9:14; Rom 13:12; Eph 5:11 darkness. Into your hands I commend my spirit. You have redeemed
me, O Lord, you faithful God.

Ps 31:5 For the sake of your name, complete the good work that you
have begun in my soul. Give me your Holy Spirit to rule and guide
Phil 1:6; Ps 23:3 me on the level path that leads me into all truth, the Spirit that
John 16:13; John 14:26; John 17:17; 1 Thess 5:23 reminds me of it. Sanctify and cleanse me through it. Make me free
and fruitful in all good works that are well-pleasing to you in your
dear Son, Jesus Christ. Guard me, so that I do not grieve and anger
your Spirit, and, instead, make me attentive and obedient to his
John 8:32; Col 1:10; Eph 4:30 gracious influence and his winsome voice. Give your angels charge
over me, to guard me in all my ways and carry me on their hands,
so that I do not dash my foot on any stone [and to guard all those
Ps 91:11–12 who are mine, so that they may preserve me from sin and shame,
from harm and danger. Let your angels this night also be a wall of
2 Kgs 6:15–17 fire and a barricade of chariots around us and our belongings.][2]

If it is your will, wake me up tomorrow morning at the right
time for your praise and service. Prepare and equip me for what
Ps 37:5; Mark 7:37 you have called me to do [and may everything be committed to
you. You will do all things well. You will never leave us or forsake
Josh 1:5; Heb 13:5 us.] May the Lord our God befriend us and establish the work of
our hands; yes, you want to establish the work of our hands to
Ps 90:17 your glory and the salvation of our souls. I also commit to you
Ps 37:5; 55:22; 1 Pet 5:7 all my cares and concerns and cast them in your lap. You will do
what is good and will never leave nor forsake us. Amen.

Have mercy on my father. Be gracious to him. Forgive us all our
Matt 6:12 sins. Bless and strengthen him in soul and body, and, as long as
it is your gracious will, let him live to your glory and the blessing
of his family. Complete the good work that you have begun in his

---

1. In the line above "this day" Hamann adds "this night and reviving me again healthy and joyful this morning" to show that he used this prayer in the morning as well as in the evening.

2. This sentence and the other sentences in brackets, as well as some words and phrases, were added in subsequent copies of the prayer.

soul and let your dear Son Jesus Christ be revealed and glorified in
him. Draw him to yourself with the cords of your love and give him *Phil 1:6*
patience to overcome the sufferings of this present time. Through *Hos 11:4;*
the trials that you will still inflict on him, let him be prepared for *Rom 8:18*
your appearance. Draw him away from all earthly things and let
his treasure and his heart be with you in heaven. Let him see and *Matt 10:21;*
taste how friendly the Lord is and thereby cleanse and purge his *Col 3:2*
heart from all anger, hatred, and the root of bitterness. *Ps 34:9; 1 Pet*

Rule the hearts of all the people that deal with him and espe- *2:3; Eph 4:31; Heb 12:15*
cially those who depend on him, and let my heart be filled with
love, respect, and obedience to him. Give me grace to follow the
example of the subordination of my Savior and also let my treatment of him be in keeping with your holy word and will. Let his *Luke 2:51*
rod and staff comfort him through the dark valley, lead and guide *Ps 23:4*
him with your wise counsel, and finally receive him into glory, and *Ps 73:24*
also let those whom you have given to him soon be united around
your throne, so that they can praise you in eternity for the riches
of your patience, forbearance, and mercy by which you have preserved us here and brought us to yourself. Amen. *Rom 2:4*

Have mercy, too, on my brother. Be gracious to him and forgive us
all our sins, and do not let the guilt, shame, and punishment of them *Matt 6:12*
come on us. Let us grow and increase in your fear and knowledge, *1 Tim 2:5*
and let your love and the love of our Savior, Mediator, and Advocate *Col 1:11*
be poured out richly in our hearts through your good Spirit. Let *Rom 5:5*
us remember Jesus Christ, who was crucified and is risen, and his
intercession at the right hand of the majesty on high to comfort and *2 Tim 2:8; Heb*
gladden us. Let him be revealed and glorified in our souls as our *1:3; Rom 8:34*
wisdom, righteousness, holiness, and redemption. Make us ves- *1 Cor 1:30*
sels of glory and mercy rather than vessels of wrath and dishonor. *Rom 9:22–23*
[Prepare us for yourself as the people you want us to be.] Unite our
hearts so that we may not be like a stumbling stone to each other,
but may rather encourage each other to follow the voice of Savior,
the Good Shepherd, always deny ourselves more and more, take *John 10:16*
up his cross on us, and tread in the footsteps that he has marked *Matt 16:24*
with his precious blood. Amen. *1 Pet 2:21; 1 Pet 1:19*

Matt 6:13 Have mercy on her as well.[3] Protect us from the evil one, and
2 Pet 3:14 give us grace to keep ourselves unspotted by the world. Keep our
spirit, together with our soul and body, guiltless until the day of
1 Cor 1:8; 1 Thess 5:23 your coming. Prepare our body as an offering that is living, holy,
Rom 12:1 and well-pleasing to you. Unite us in your love and let everything
Rom 8:28 serve what is best for us. Amen.

Have mercy on my kin friends and soul friends, my acquain-
2 Pet 3:9 tances and relatives. Let none of them be lost. Bring us all to a
knowledge of our corruption and open our eyes so that we may see
Ps 119:18 the wonders in your law and the source of our salvation which you
have prepared for us in Jesus Christ. Let us all obtain grace upon
John 1:16 grace from his fullness. Repay them richly for their magnanimity
to us, and let our faith also prove to be living and active to them in
Gal 5:6 hearty, brotherly love. Let all the needs of their souls and bodies
be under your care. Reveal yourself to them as a reconciled God
and gracious Father in Christ Jesus, and make us all members of his
Rom 12:4; 1 Cor 12:12; Ps 100:3; John 15:5 body, sheep of his pasture, and branches of your vine.

Be merciful to our enemies. Forgive them and let our hearts be
reconciled to them in the love with which you loved us while we
Rom 5:10 were still your enemies and you did not stop having mercy on us
and receiving us in grace.

I commit to you all the misery and corruption in the world. More and more destroy the reign of Satan in us and through us, and let your kingdom and the kingdom of your dear Son grow and increase in our hearts. Take care of the public needs that weigh on many countries. [Give us arable land and] protect the land that is under cultivation among us. Bless and protect our country, our city, and our house.

Matt 21:13 Make our hearts a place of prayer for yourself. Remove all the
Eph 6:11 weapons of Satan and undo all his cunning schemes to turn it into
a robbers' den.

Give our fathers and protectors wisdom, patience, and love to manage their house and rule in a godly way. Grant us all an

3. This seems to refer to Hamann's would-be fiancée, Katharina Berens.

obedient heart, and let the love of our Savior be poured richly *1 Kgs 3:9*
into our hearts. Let your name be poured out among us like per- *Rom 5:5*
fumed ointment, and let the glorious light of the gospel always arise *Song 1:3*
among us more and more, and give us grace to produce its fruit with *2 Cor 4:4*
patience. Preserve, increase, and protect your little band among us, *Luke 12:32*
and may there soon be one flock and one shepherd. By genuine *John 10:16*
repentance and an unfeigned, true faith in Jesus Christ, your dear
Son, our Lord, prepare us too for the judgments that our sins have
deserved. [Do not punish us in your anger and discipline us in your
wrath, and let our present circumstances and troubles serve to glo- *Acts 26:20; Ps 6:1*
rify your name and to the salvation of our souls.]

Give us grace that we may lead a quiet and peaceful life in all
godliness and honor under the authority of those whom you have
set over us. Bestow on them a wise heart to govern and guard your *1 Tim 2:2*
people. *1 Kgs 3:9–12*

Have mercy on our king. Let all his policies flourish to your glory and the common good. May your dear Son, Jesus Christ, be glorified in him, his own soul be drawn to you through the signs and wonders of your love, and many be awakened and attracted to righteousness and the confession of your name and the teaching of Jesus Christ by his example. Amen.

Be merciful to all fathers and mothers, all teachers and students, all widows and orphans, all those who are sick and dying, pregnant women and infants, travelers by land or by sea, those who are tempted, forsaken, imprisoned, impoverished, needy, and distressed. Have mercy on them. Let your gracious, holy will be known and praised by all and revealed and glorified through all people. Amen.

My Savior, intercede for me before your heavenly Father. Give
me the Spirit of sonship and prayer who may call out in my heart, *Rom 8:34; 8:15*
"Abba, dear Father!" May he come to help me in my inability and
unworthiness with his inarticulate sighs. Let me detest and throw *Rom 8:26*
off the filthy rags of my own righteousness. Clothe me with the *Isa 64:6; Col 3:8*
white silk of a righteousness and holiness that was gained for me
at such great cost. Let me enter into your strength and power, walk *Eph 4:24*

Gen 17:1 uprightly before you, and be devout. Give me the shield of faith to
Eph 6:16 quench all the fiery arrows of the wicked one. May you yourself be
Gen 15:1 my shield and my very great reward. Stay with us when the evening
comes, and help us bravely here contend, through life and death
to you ascend.[4]

[Through your good Spirit] renew my baptismal covenant and
give me grace and power to live more worthily and properly in it.
Help me to resist and renounce the devil and all his works and ways,
to put off the old self with all its desires, and, instead, put on the new
Eph 4:22–24 self, created after God's likeness in true righteousness and holiness.

May I, since I am redeemed by the Lord, live for him and
Isa 35:10; 62:12; Rom 14:8 die for him, and while I still live may I live only by faith in my
Gal 2:20 Redeemer. May I look to Jesus, the founder and perfecter of my
faith, who, since he truly wished to have joy, endured the cross
and despised the shame. Help me to put off all the clinging sin
that holds me back and makes me weary in the race [battle] that
Heb 12:1–3 has been set before me. May you yourself sprinkle my conscience
Heb 10:22 with your precious blood and—[5]

Give me your body to eat and your blood to drink for the for-
1 Cor 11:23–25 giveness of my sins, for the strengthening of my faith and my spiritual life, for the remembrance of your love and the kindling of a
true, heartfelt, ardent love in response to it. Let me also here already
Heb 6:5 now taste the powers of the coming world, and let my way of life
Phil 3:20 be with you in heaven. Usher me soon into your glorious kingdom
which you have prepared for us from eternity to eternity. Amen.

Father of us all, you who are in heaven,
hallowed be your name,
your kingdom come,
your will be done on earth as in heaven.
Give us this day our daily bread,
and forgive us our debts as we forgive our debtors.

4. This is a paraphrase of last two lines of Luther's Pentecost hymn "Komm, Heliger Geist." See *Lutheran Service Book*, page 497, verse 3, lines 7–8.

5. The em dash indicates that these two paragraphs belong together.

Lead us not into temptation,
but deliver us from the evil one.
for yours is the kingdom and the power and the glory,
from eternity to eternity. Amen. *Matt 6:9–13*

The Lord bless me and keep me;
the Lord make his face shine on me and be gracious
to me;
the Lord lift up his face on me, and give me his peace. *Num 6:24–26*
Amen.

The peace of God which surpasses all reason, guard our hearts and senses in Jesus. Amen. *Phil 4:7*

The grace of our Lord Jesus Christ, the love of God the Father, and the fellowship of the Holy Spirit be with us all. Amen. *2 Cor 13:14*

Lord Jesus, help! O Lord let everything turn out well.

Blessed is he who comes here in the name of the Lord. Amen. *Ps 118:26*

Yes, come, Lord Jesus! Amen. *Rev 22:20*

God, be merciful to me, a sinner. Amen. *Luke 18:13*

SELECT BIBLIOGRAPHY

Alexander, W. M. "Johann Georg Hamann. Metacritic of Kant." *Journal of the History of Ideas* 27, no. 1 (1966): 137–44.

———. 1966. *Johann Georg Hamann: Philosophy and Faith*. Martinus Nijhoff: The Hague, 1966.

———. "Sex in the Philosophy of Hamann." *Journal of the American Academy of Religion* 3 no. 4 (1969): 331–40.

Alfsvåg, Knut. "Christology and Critique in the Thought of Johann Georg Hamann." In *Christology as Critique: On the Relation between Christ, Creation, and Epistemology*. Eugene, Oregon: Pickwick Publications, 2018.

———. "Imagination and Critique in the Work of Johann Georg Hamann." *Mishkan* 80 (2019): 68–80.

Anderson, Lisa Marie, ed. *Hamann and Tradition*. Topics in Historical Philosophy. Evanston.: Northwestern University Press, 2012.

Bayer, Oswald. *A Contemporary in Dissent: Johann Georg Hamann as a Radical Enlightener*. Translated by Roy A. Harrisville, and Mark C. Mattes. Grand Rapids, Mich.: Eerdmans, 2012.

———. "God as the Author of My Life-History." *Lutheran Quarterly* 15 (2001): 45–58.

Beech, Timothy. *Hamann's Prophetic Mission. A Generic Study of Three Late Works against the Enlightenment*. Manley: London, 2010.

Berlin, Isaiah. *The Magus of the North: J. G. Hamann and the Origins of Modern Irrationalism*. New York: Farrar, Strauss, and Giroux, 1993.

Betz, John R. *After Enlightenment: The Post-Secular Vision of J. G. Hamann*. Oxford: Wiley-Blackwell, 2012.

———. "Enlightenment Revisited: Hamann as the First and Best Critic of Kant's Philosophy." *Modern Theology* 20 no. 2 (2004): 291–301.

———. "Glory(ing) in the Humility of the Word: The Kenotic form of Revelation in J. G. Hamann." *Letter & Spirit*, 6 (2011): 141–79.

———. "Hamann before Kierkegaard: A Systematic Theological Oversight." *Pro Ecclesia* 16 no. 3 (2007): 299–333.

———. "Hamann's London Writings. The Hermeneutics of Trinitarian Condescension." *Pro Ecclesia* 14 no. 2 (2005): 191–234.

———. "A Radically Orthodox Reformer: J. G. Hamann as a Metacritic of Enlightenment and Secularization." *Modern Theology*, 33 no. 4 (2017): 64–77.

———. "Reading 'Sibylline Leaves': J. G. Hamann in the History of Ideas." *Journal of the History of Ideas* 70 no. 1 (2009): 93–118. Reprinted in a slightly different form in L. M. Anderson (ed.), *Hamann and Tradition*, Evanston: Northwestern University Press, 5–32.

German, Terence. *Hamann on Language and Religion*. Oxford: Oxford University Press, 1981.

Goesser Assaiante, Julia. *Body Language: Corporeality, Subjectivity, and Language in Johann Georg Hamann*. Studies on Themes and Motifs in Literature, vol. 111. New York: Peter Lang, 2011.

Green, Garrett. 2000. "Against Purism: Hamann's Metacritique of Kant." In *Theology, Hermeneutics, and Imagination: The Crisis of Interpretation at the End of Modernity*. Cambridge, UK; New York: Cambridge University Press, 2000.

Griffith-Dickson, Gwen. "God, I and Thou: Hamann and the Personalist Tradition," in L. M. Anderson (ed.), *Hamann and Tradition*. Evanston: Northwestern University Press, 2012.

———. "Johann Georg Hamann." *Stanford Encyclopedia of Philosophy*. Edited by Edward N. Zalta, 2017. https://plato.stanford.edu/archives/fall2017/entries/hamann/.

———. *Johann Georg Hamann's Relational Metacriticism*. Berlin/New York: de Gruyter, 1995.

Hamann, Johann Georg. *Writings on Philosophy and Language*. Edited and translated by Kenneth Haynes. Cambridge Texts in the History of Philosophy. Cambridge, UK; New York: Cambridge University Press, 2007.

Harrisville, Roy A. "Johann Georg Hamann, Biblische Betrachtungen." In *Promising Faith for a Ruptured World. An English-Speaking Appreciation of Oswald Bayer*. Eugene, OR: Wipf and Stock, 2019.

Leibrecht, Walter. *God and Man in the Thought of Hamann*. Translated by J. H. Stam and M. H. Bertram. Philadelphia: Fortress, 1966.

Lowrie, Walter. *Johann Georg Hamann: An Existentialist*. Princeton: Princeton Theological Seminary, 1950.

Milbank, John. "Knowledge: The Theological Critique of Philosophy in Hamann and Jacobi." In *Radical Orthodoxy: A New Theology*. Edited by John Milbank, Catherine Pickstock, and Graham Ward. London: Routledge, 1999.

O'Flaherty, James C. "Hamann's Concept of the Whole Man." *German Quarterly* 45 no. 2 (1972): 253–69.

———. *Johann Georg Hamann*. Boston: Twayne, 1979.

———. "Language and Reason in the Thought of Johann Georg Hamann." *Lutheran Quarterly* 2 no. 4 (1988): 457–75.

———. *Socratic Memorabilia: A Translation and a Commentary*. Baltimore: Johns Hopkins University Press, 1967.

———. "Some Major Emphases of Hamann's Theology." *Harvard Theological Review* 51 no. 1 (1958): 39–50.

———. *Unity and Language: A Study in the Philosophy of Johann Georg Hamann*. Chapel Hill: University of North Carolina Press, 1952

Pan, David. "Language and Metaphysics in Johann Georg Hamann's *Aesthetica in Nuce* and *Philologische Einfälle und Zweifel*," Monatshefte 106 no. 3 (2014): 351–75.

Smith, Ronald Gregor. "The Hamann Renaissance," *Christian Century* 77 no. 26 (1960): 768–69.

———. *J. G. Hamann: A Study in Christian Existence with Selections from His Writings*. Collins: London, 1960.

Sparling, Robert Alan. *Johann Georg Hamann and the Enlightenment Project*. Toronto: University of Toronto Press, 2011.

Swain, Charles William. "Hamann and the Philosophy of David Hume." *Journal of the History of Philosophy* 4 (1967): 343–51.

Terezakis, Katie. "Language and Immanence in Hamann," *Graduate Faculty Philosophy Journal*, 27 no. 2 (2006): 25–50.

———. "Words and the Word: J. G. Hamann, Trojan Horse at the Gates of the Enlightenment." In *Edinburgh Critical History of Christian Theology.* Edited by Daniel Whistler. Edinburgh: Edinburgh University Press, 2017.

Vaughan, Larry. *Johann Georg Hamann: Metaphysics of Language and Vision of History.* Frankfurt: Lang, 1989.

Von Balthasar, Hans Urs. *The Glory of the Lord: A Theological Aesthetics* Vol. 3. Translated by Andrew Lowth. Edinburgh: T&T Clark, 1986.

Von Lüpke, Johannes. "Metaphysics and Metacritique: Hamann's Understanding of the Word of God in the Tradition of Lutheran Theology." In *Hamann and the Tradition.* Edited by L. M. Anderson. Evanston: Northwestern University Press, 2012.

Yamato, Lori. 2012. "Rhapsodic Dismemberment: Hamann and the Fable." In *Hamann and the Tradition.* Edited by L. M. Anderson. Evanston, IL: Northwestern University Press, 2012.

SUBJECT AND AUTHOR INDEX

Aaron, 64, 154, 391, 401, 469

Abel, 25–26, 29, 99, 212

Abraham (Abram), 19, 38–45, 48, 53–54, 58–60, 81, 86, 91–92, 97, 129, 147, 209, 227, 231, 251, 262, 283, 292, 314, 323, 364, 378, 387, 407, 453, 465

Academy for the Sciences (Berlin), 352

Adam, xx, 15, 17–23, 26–27, 43, 71, 86–87, 122, 146, 149, 173, 233, 260–61, 274, 276, 286, 295, 376, 384, 388, 426, 429–30, 453

Aesop, 2, 226

Africa, 34–35

Alexander, W. M., xxx

Angels, xvi, xix, xxi, 30, 43, 66–67, 69, 82, 91, 77–78, 80–81, 83, 90–91, 95–96, 101, 115, 125, 145, 164, 166, 179, 182, 220, 231, 247, 252, 261, 275, 282, 284, 290, 323, 366, 390–91, 398–401, 403, 408, 420, 432, 465, 470

Animals, 2, 21, 25, 28, 33, 61, 68–69, 73, 77, 92, 95, 101–2, 115–16, 152, 157–58, 162, 175–76, 181–82, 184–85, 192, 198, 205, 211–12, 219, 226, 233, 244, 266, 275, 284, 288, 296, 304–5, 406, 436

Archimedes, 33

Aristotle, 14, 247, 444

Art, 152, 328, 332, 339, 347, 442. *See also* Music.

Atonement, xxi, xxvi–xxvii, 62–66, 126–27, 132, 301. *See also* Redemption; Sacrifice, of Christ.

Augustine, St., vi, 325

Babel, xix, 36–37, 100, 152, 252

Baptism, xxii, 178, 247–48, 259, 326–27, 377–78, 403, 445, 469, 474

Baron (lute teacher), 357–58

Barth, Karl, v

Basnage, Jacques (theologian), 454

Bassa (friend), 344, 349

Bayer, Oswald, vii, xxix–xxx, 287

Beauty, 20, 78–79, 98, 114, 134, 201, 219–20, 323, 332, 370, 382, 388

Belger, Philipp (family friend), 341

Berens, Arend (friend's father), 463

Berens, Arend, Jr. (friend's brother), 464, 466

Berens, Johann Christoph (friend), vii, ix–x, xii, xxviii, xxxi, 345, 365, 366, 463–64, 466
Berens, Karl (friend's brother), 462–63
Berens, Katharina (would-be fiancée), x, xxxii, 345, 464–66, 469, 472
Betz, John, iv, v, vi, x, xxx
Bible, xii, xiii–xiv, xix, 1–2, 6–15, 18, 68–69, 75–76, 88, 98–99, 100–101, 110–12, 115, 118–19, 136, 141, 158, 160, 169, 175, 191, 198–99, 209, 224, 228, 231, 235, 237, 238, 256, 344, 357, 361; condescension of the Holy Spirit, xx–xxiii, 1–2, 12, 15, 118, 128–29; Hamann's reading of, viii–ix, xiv–xv, 6–8, 361–66; Hamann's versions of, viii, 104, 361; imagery of, xiv, 13–14, 74–75, 115–16, 255–57, 322–23, 366, 369–70; Inspiration of, vi, xviii–xxiii, 1–3, 8, 314, 446; interpretation of, xvi, 1–3, 14, 48, 67, 297–98, 314, 446; language of, xix, xxi, 14–15, 161, 194, 204–5, 227, 314, 397; and nature, xvi–xviii, 1, 8–9, 12–15, 32–33, 118–19, 137, 311, 248, 263; reading of, viii, 1, 5, 81, 87–88, 92–94, 106, 163, 279, 312, 331; reading with imagination, xiv–xv, 5, 8, 14, 297–98; 442; typology in, xiv, 5, 78, 155, 204–5, 423, 453. *See also* Word of God.
Blackmore, Richard, 35
Blank, Johann Gottlieb (pastor), 340
Body, vi, xv, 6, 17, 23, 27, 29, 48–49, 44–45, 76, 86, 92, 136, 137, 145, 156, 166, 176, 209, 237, 267, 207, 267–268, 303, 307–308, 310, 311, 327, 361, 380, 382, 383, 395, 400, 402, 412, 417–23, 425–26, 435–38, 448, 449–50, 465, 472, 474
Bolingbroke, Henry St. John, Viscount, 11, 13, 449
Brandenberger, Commnander (relative), 353
Bucholz (teacher), 336
Budberg, Baron (employer), 341
Budberg, Waldemar Dietrich von (pupil), xxxi, 341–42, 344, 348

Caesar, Augustus, 60
Caesar, Julius, 60, 315
Cain, viii, xxiii, 22, 25–29, 89, 78, 100, 148, 212, 236, 274, 363, 451
Campenhausen, von, Privy Counsellor (pupil's relative), 343
Catechism, Luther's Small, xii, 206, 320, 407
Catholicism, 26, 37, 83, 210, 292, 355
Christianity, 61, 223, 257, 292, 302, 304, 321, 338
Church, xii, 48, 64, 82, 106, 141, 155, 162, 165, 171, 176, 177, 194, 225, 244, 251, 256, 278, 287, 292, 307, 310–311, 318, 322–23, 327, 351, 382, 402–3, 412; Catholic, 37, 292, 281–82; Lutheran, 37, 370, 362; Protestant, 292
Collins, Mr. and Mrs., vii, xxxii, 360

Communion, Sacrament of Holy, xii, 34, 59, 124, 135, 142, 211, 290, 373, 401, 457, 459, 462, 469, 474

Condescension of God, vi, xv, xxi, xviii, xix–xxiii, 2, 8, 11–12, 15, 17, 22, 37–38, 42, 45–46, 68, 77, 110, 129, 152, 154; of the Father, xx, xxi, 34, 118; of HolynSpirit, xx, xxi–xxii, 1–2 11–12, 118; of the Son, xx–xxi, 118, 283–84, 319, 400

Confession: of faith, 113, 241–43, 366, 411–12, 429,; rite of, xii, 338, 457–58, 463; of sin, 49, 112, 136–37, 149, 322, 314, 325

Creation, xvii–xviii, xxi–xxii, 1, 14–20, 31, 33, 67–68, 80, 86–87, 91, 97, 98–100, 119, 122, 131–33, 151–53, 218–19, 220, 224, 226, 231, 238, 265, 274, 295, 297, 311, 319, 322, 372, 382–383, 398–99, 410, 412, 417, 425–30, 432, 439–40, 451. Nature.

Cross, xx, 51, 63, 194, 203, 225, 254, 283, 300, 304, 309, 339, 345, 350, 378, 379, 385, 386, 398, 417, 421, 445, 457, 462, 472, 474

David, xxii, 1–2, 23–24, 43, 53, 126–44, 163–64, 188, 224, 323, 379, 415, 416, 454; as Psalmist, 17, 21–22, 39, 72, 114, 139, 165, 195–96, 309, 316, 399, 419, 466; as type of Christ, 126–27, 139, 144, 253, 381, 387, 416

Death, 9, 18, 21, 26, 42, 45, 49, 53–55, 61, 85, 93–94, 116, 122, 126, 128, 136–140, 141, 145, 149, 173, 175, 194, 203, 205, 219, 222, 225, 232–34, 249, 253, 259, 282–85, 291, 301, 307, 311, 319–20, 321–23, 334, 350, 362–63, 365, 385, 390, 400, 403, 406, 409–10, 416, 431, 433, 439, 474

Derham, William (scientist), 443

Derschow, Bernhard (hymnwriter), 339

Descartes, René, 14, 37, 290

Devil (Satan), xx, xxiii–xxv, 8, 27, 32, 57, 67–71, 73–74, 76, 78–81, 87–90, 91, 95–98, 101–10, 114–18, 125, 128–31, 133, 166–68, 177, 180, 183–88, 195, 204–5, 209–10, 224, 228, 230–31, 233, 235–37, 239–40, 244–45, 254–57, 259–62, 285, 288, 299, 301–4, 310–11, 314, 321, 336, 351, 358, 369, 401, 403, 408, 410, 413, 431, 452, 459, 472, 474. *See also* Serpent.

Disease: *See* Sickness.

Disrobing and Transfiguration (1786), xvi

Divine Service (Lutheran liturgy), xii, 40, 166, 421; attendance at, 351, 457, 460, 463

Donatus, Aelius, 329

Eckart (travel companion), 347

Enlightenment, vi–vii, 6, 9–10, 12, 234. Rationalists; Reason.

Enoch, 30, 161, 252

Esau, 45, 54, 80, 153, 175, 241, 386

Essen, Pastor, xii, 463
Eve, 22–24, 295, 314, 429–30
Evil, 7, 21, 25, 27, 45, 34, 63, 95, 125, 131, 164–65, 180–81, 188, 198–99, 208, 240, 241, 245, 247, 248, 264, 269, 273, 291, 307, 314, 307, 318, 342, 358, 390, 404, 405, 435, 443–44, 446, 465, 475; incoherence of, 70; origin of, 443–46
Ezra, 8, 171–72, 177, 178

Faith, vi, ix–x, xiv–xv, xxi–xxii, xxiv, xxvi–xxvii, 8, 11, 16, 30, 54, 57–58, 61, 69, 71, 76, 80–81, 85, 91, 101, 103, 104, 108, 122, 124, 133, 135–38, 143, 150, 154, 165–66, 170, 176, 179, 181, 186, 191–92, 200, 207, 227, 231, 244, 247, 260, 272, 274, 276, 279–80, 284, 288, 292–96, 306, 310, 312, 314 317–23, 325, 364, 366, 374, 378, 379–84, 391, 396–97, 400, 403–5, 410–14, 417, 429, 425–33, 436, 440, 457, 461–63, 474. *See also* Justification.
Fall, xxiv, 15, 19–24, 35, 63, 69, 71, 145, 183, 214, 216, 260, 286, 294–95, 451
Fink, von, Count (family friend), 351
Fontaine, Jean de la, 2
Freedom, 29, 33, 68, 68, 104, 124, 155, 173–74, 223, 220, 268, 284, 286, 305, 309, 399, 411, 437–40, 446–47, 470
Gallitzin, Alexander (Russian diplomat), 356
Gallitzin, Princess, xxxiii
Gerhardt, Paul (hymnwriter), 43, 292, 325
Gericke, Johann Christoph (pastor), 341, 463
Gideon, 61, 107–8
Gildemeister, Karl Hermann, xxix
God: attributes of, 12, 22, 41, 69, 75, 145, 166, 181, 186, 191, 245, 264, 294, 296, 366, 372, 399; as author, xviii, 1,8; hiddenness of, 22–23, 126, 142, 204, 263–64, 398, 426, 440–41, 444, 448, 450, 467; judgment of, 20, 23, 42–43, 67–69, 74–75, 84, 87, 94, 96, 104, 109–10, 116, 99–100, 105, 110–13, 116–17, 124–25, 129, 173–74, 183, 194, 176–79, 182, 184–85, 190–91, 193, 196, 200, 221–22, 285, 287, 299, 302, 323, 455, 473; providence of, x, 7, 162, 186, 196, 218, 230, 264, 293, 309, 345, 346, 349, 360, 394, 442; Trinity, xviii, xx, xix, xxii, 37, 55, 122–23, 136, 174, 252, 322, 372. *See also* Condescension of God; God the Father; Grace; Holy Spirit; Love; Revelation; Son of God
God the Father, vi, xiii, xviii, xx–xxi, xxvii, 2, 8, 19, 54, 61, 76, 77, 97, 118, 120, 122, 126, 131, 134, 136, 138, 176, 227, 246, 257, 272, 277, 294, 366, 373, 377, 381, 383,

385–87, 391, 395, 401, 424, 408, 412, 426, 455, 470, 472, 474
Goethe, Johann Wolfgang von, v
Golgotha and Scheblimini, 352
Gospel, 38, 46, 79, 130, 140, 155, 157, 178, 253, 256, 259, 279, 291, 292, 311, 318, 320, 325, 333, 404, 418, 431, 457, 460, 462. *See also* Law, and Gospel
Grace, ix, xv, xxi, xxiv, xxvi–xxvii, 53, 72, 74, 94, 102, 104, 111, 124, 127, 138, 140, 143, 144, 146, 155, 158, 165, 170, 172–73, 177–80, 190, 198, 200, 204, 211, 232, 257, 259, 282, 287, 301, 307, 308, 315, 319, 355, 344–45, 365, 376, 383, 391, 400, 405, 410, 419–21, 457, 459, 462, 463, 465.
Greeks, 60, 108, 275, 329, 332, 454; language of, 60, 328

Haase, Master (friend), 345
Hamann, Elizabeth Regina (daughter), xxxii
Hamann, Johann Christoph (brother), ix, xxviii, 327, 350, 365, 366, 459, 462, 467, 472
Hamann, Johann Christoph (father), vii, ix, x, xxviii, xxxi–xxxii, 327, 333–37, 339–41, 348–50, 365, 366, 292, 363, 366, 471–72
Hamann, Johann Georg: childhood of, vii, xxxii, 327–38; chronology of life, xxxi–xxxiii; as civil servant, v, x, xxxii–xxxiii; conversion of, vii–ix, xi–xiv, xxvii, 361–66; education of, vii, xxxi, 329–40; and Katharina Berens, x, xxxii, 457, 464–66, 472; literary career, v, x, xxxii; in London, vii, ix, xii, xxvii,xxxi–xxxii, 355–70, 457–61; reputation, v–vii. See titles of individual works.
Hamann, Johann Michael (son), xxviii, xxxii
Hamann, Magdalena Katharina (daughter), xxxii
Hamann, Maria Magdalena (mother), vii, xxxi, 326, 334, 349–50, 352, 459
Hamann, Marianne Sophie (daughter), xxxviii
Heaven, x, xvii, xx–xxi, xxiv, 3, 14, 31, 37, 46, 54, 59, 61, 76, 81–82, 87, 89, 91, 97, 99–100, 106, 116–17, 121, 124, 125, 129, 134, 152, 154, 161, 171, 174, 183, 194, 197, 220–21, 224, 229–32, 239, 288, 253–54, 262, 263, 269, 276, 286–87, 306, 307, 311–12, 314, 366, 371, 376, 378, 388, 391, 395, 409, 415, 418, 420, 431, 437, 450, 471, 474
Hegel, Georg Wilhelm Friedrich, v
Hell, x, xxiv, 27, 31, 79, 81, 87, 102, 105, 112, 171, 173, 176, 150, 203, 206, 208, 221, 239, 245, 249, 261, 267, 306, 366, 390, 399, 409, 431, 442. *See also* God, judgment of.
Heraclitus, 16
Herder, Johann Gottfried, v, xxix, 341
Herod, 12, 130, 142, 178, 220, 252, 258, 271, 278

Herodatus, 12
Herold (teacher), 336
Herostratus, 9
Hervey, James (author), viii, 7, 275
Heumann, Christoph August (theologian), 59
History, viii, xvi–xix, xxi, xxiii, 9, 40–41, 46, 53, 60, 68–70, 84, 118, 137, 169, 178, 181, 229, 231, 312, 314, 330, 333, 336, 362, 432, 442, 448
Holy Spirit, vi, xiii, xv, xx, 2, 3, 75–76, 81, 82, 94, 103, 109, 113, 118, 120–21, 123, 132, 140–41, 152, 159, 171, 173–74, 176, 178, 199–200, 207, 251, 270, 286–88, 307, 338, 372–73, 377, 379, 380, 383, 403, 409, 416–17, 331–32, 451, 470, 472, 473–74, 475; and Scripture, xiv, xv, xviii–xxvii, 1–3, 8, 12, 75, 81, 102, 118, 118–19, 131–32, 134, 139–41, 200, 228, 231, 251, 270, 314, 319, 366, 403, 449
Homosexuality, vii, 66, 358–59, 465
Hume, David, vi
Hymns, xii, xvi, xxix, 56, 58, 338–39, 351, 368, 371–423, 433, 462, 473

Idolatry, 17, 26, 39, 40, 71, 80, 83, 122, 153, 179, 233, 236–37, 253, 273, 289, 297, 299, 442
Image: of God, xix, 15, 18, 22, 30, 64, 74, 87, 142, 246, 276–77, 305, 372–73, 377, 382–83, 425; imagery in Scripture, xiv–xvii, xxv, 58, 70, 155, 244, 254, 366, 442
Imagination, vi–vii, xiv–xvii, 8, 14, 17, 19, 56, 114, 205, 209–10, 282, 297–98, 313, 322, 339, 373, 388, 406, 425, 446–47. *See also* Image, imagery in Scripture.
Isaac, 54, 152, 203, 230, 251, 401, 407

Jacob, xx, 36, 45–49, 54–56, 177, 250, 251, 258, 264, 318, 386, 401, 453
Jacobi, Friedrich Heinrich, v, xi, xxviii–xxix
Jesus Christ, iv, viii–x, xii–xiii, xvi, xviii–xix, xxi–xxvii, 2, 5, 48, 51, 52–61, 71, 76, 80, 100, 105, 107 121–23, 127–28, 136, 136–41, 143–44, 161, 167, 189, 144, 159–60, 207, 221, 225, 230, 240, 243, 246, 251–53, 256, 259–60, 263, 274–77, 280, 287–88, 293–94, 297, 300, 302, 305–10, 318–19, 322–23, 335, 373–403, 407, 410, 412–17, 425–33, 436, 445, 450–52, 459, 461–63, 466, 470–72, 475; atonement of, 63, 65, 126, 132; divinity of, 126, 134, 175, 209; 400; as Redeemer, viii, xxiv, xxvi, 2, 34, 42, 48, 51–52, 71, 75, 92, 102, 121, 126, 128, 131, 140, 141, 172, 174, 194, 200, 209, 253, 256, 260, 265, 272, 274, 293, 310, 306, 321, 322, 363, 378, 381, 400–401, 404, 412, 417, 371; resurrection of, 54, 122, 126,

134, 194, 224, 184, 271, 273, 431, 472; as Savior, ix, xix, xxvii, 18, 23, 41, 51, 52, 53, 55, 58, 61, 75, 78, 79–81, 92, 95, 100, 103, 107, 111–26, 129–34, 136–38, 175–80, 183, 250, 260, 280, 241, 250, 256–57, 260, 271–73, 277, 278, 280, 294, 295, 294, 299, 301–3, 306, 311, 364, 372, 374, 375, 377, 379, 384–88, 401, 403, 407, 412, 417, 421, 429, 433, 444, 451, 453, 462, 471–73. *See also* Son of God

Jews, 9, 12, 17, 36, 40, 44, 46–49, 51, 60–61, 65–67, 69, 75, 84, 102, 108, 110, 117, 128, 130, 138, 140–42, 154, 175, 176, 178, 225, 231, 252, 259, 264, 273, 279, 281, 291–92, 298–300, 319, 441, 451,454; unjust mistreatment, 158, 257, 297, 458

Joseph (Mary's husband) 259

Joseph (son of Jacob), 48–52, 57–58, 104, 121, 161, 252, 264, 303, 335, 453

Judah: son of Jacob, 49–53, 100, 161, 252; kingdom of, 115, 131, 178; tribe of, 100, 103, 168

Justification: by faith, 294, 299–301, 425; of God's ways, 109, 191. *See also* Faith, justification by

Kant, Immanuel, v, vi, x, xxxii, 336, 337, 345

Karstens (relative), 352

Kierkegaard, Søren, v, 80

Kleuker, Friedrich, xxviii–xxix

Knutzen, Martin (professor), 337

Königsberg, Prussia, vi, x, xxxi–xxxii, 327, 329, 336, 341, 345, 351, 353; University,of (Albertina), xxix, xxxi, 337–40, 346, 346

Kreutziger, Elizabeth (hymnwriter), 433, 472

Lacy, von, Countess (employer), 343

Language, vi, xix, xxi, 14, 36–38, 108, 160, 194, 204–5, 224, 227, 234, 247, 284, 286, 314, 319, 332, 341, 355, 397, 421

Latin, 2, 160, 329, 332, 336, 441, 452

Law, 47, 138, 160, 181, 380, 435, 440, 441, 446–47, 451; of God, 24, 29, 36, 53, 59, 65–66, 89, 103, 108, 115, 150, 166, 170, 178, 184, 208, 231, 264, 266–67, 299–300, 303, 309, 320, 440, 472; and Gospel, 60, 65, 77, 157, 254, 207, 218, 222, 234–35, 239, 241, 243–44, 319, 425, 428–29; natural, 29, 77, 125, 137–38, 159, 263, 269, 284, 290, 296–97, 311, 314, 441, 444, 446–47

Leah, 370

Leibnitz, Gottfried Wilhelm, 37

Lilienthal, Michael (godfather), 338

Lilienthal, Theodore Christopher (theologian), 338

Lindner, Ehregott Friedrich (friend's brother), 345

Lindner, Johann Gotthelf (friend), vii, ix, xii, xvi–xvii, xxviii, xxxi–xxxii, 341, 345, 345–48, 365, 366, 462

Loehe, Wilhelm, v

London Writings: chronology of, xi–xii, xxxii; and Haman's thought, iv–vii, xv–xvi, xxviii–xxx; key metaphors and themes of, xvi–xxvii; manuscripts of, xxviii–xxix; nature of, xi–xvi; origin and purpose of, vii–x; publication of, xxviii–xxx; style of, xiii–xiv, xvi–xvii

Longinus, Dionysius, 18, 24, 79

Love, 179, 184, 169, 212, 309, 253; for God, 38, 68, 76, 85, 92, 116, 172, 197, 276, 363, 380, 382, 414, 415, 440; of God, ix, xxii, xxvi–xxvii, 11, 41, 47, 56, 90, 94, 109, 194, 206, 212, 235, 250, 255, 264, 277, 283, 234, 238, 275, 307, 358, 364, 366, 368, 379, 381–91, 396, 399–401, 405–6, 412, 334–35, 338–39, 341, 343–44, 346, 352, 458, 461, 467, 472, 473; human, x, 35, 61, 68, 101, 120, 255, 263, 268, 309, 313, 317, 318, 340, 359, 370, 375, 402, 330, 414; between men and women, xxxii, 67, 127, 416, 429; of neighbor, 116, 191, 238, 266, 274–76, 292, 309, 306, 320, 367, 382, 412, 440, 463; between parents and children, 25, 43, 45, 52, 73, 149, 171, 272, 338, 352, 366; of self, 17, 91, 193, 209, 367, 412, 437–38, 440, 446–47

Lowrie, Walter, v, xxx

Luders, Mr. (secretary to Russian ambassador), 458

Luther, Martin, xii, 26, 206, 407, 474; his translation of Bible, viii, 7, 83, 143,180, 289, 319, 361, 363, 416, 443

Lutheranism, v, vi–vii, xii, xix, xxi, xxxi, 37, 83, 160, 210, 326, 336, 337, 343, 346, 370, 381, 425, 433, 457, 461, 474

Marriage, ix–x, xxxii, 20, 49, 95, 97, 121, 178, 378, 400, 414, 457, 465

Mary (mother of Jesus), 26, 130, 174, 259, 387

Melchizedek, 39–42, 162

Mendelsohn, Moses (philosopher), 352

Merian, Johann Bernhard (philosopher), 352

Metzke, Erwin, xxix

Moser, Carl von, iv

Moses: as lawgiver, viii, 8, 12–18, 21, 26–28, 32, 37–45, 48–49, 66, 68, 79–80, 84, 97, 148, 153, 176, 194, 206, 226, 236, 254, 278, 284, 296, 298, 303, 314, 363, 395, 425; as prophet, 9, 20, 23, 44, 73, 75, 81, 85, 86, 100, 101, 103, 106, 111, 124, 153, 154, 156, 174, 177, 180, 216, 224, 264, 265, 275, 279, 291, 296, 300, 314, 319, 322, 372–73, 391, 397, 432. *See also* Law, of Moses

Music, 28, 165–66, 319, 340, 358, 396, 407, 409, 442. *See also* Hymns.
Mystery: 2, 14, 16, 18, 35, 59, 84, 88, 98, 104, 112, 114, 118, 119, 122, 132, 191, 204, 247, 255, 278, 292, 306, 311, 322, 378, 379, 386, 395, 399, 416, 426, 439, 443, 444, 454

Nadler, Josef, v, xxix
Nature, 8–9, 14–15, 27, 29–30, 63, 67, 77, 81, 88, 191–93, 147, 152, 167, 184, 191–92, 202, 214–15, 218, 226, 245, 247, 249, 255, 263, 269, 273, 284, 231, 290, 291, 311, 319, 331, 333, 276, 297–98, 311–12, 317,324, 333, 407, 425–28, 438, 442–43, 451; book of, xvi–xviii, 137, 153, 191, 448; human, vi, xxv–xxvi, 10, 12, 18, 34–35, 36, 48, 63, 68, 83, 93–94, 97–98, 101–2, 109, 110, 119, 122, 127, 145, 157, 164, 175, 187, 205, 210, 213, 229, 252, 261–62, 273, 287, 291, 294–96, 304, 383, 389, 395, 400, 427, 431, 439–40, 443, 452, 459
Newton, Isaac (scientist), 9, 14, 37
Newton, Thomas (theologian), ix, 5, 449–55

O'Flaherty, James, xvii, xxx
Oven, von, Major (friend), 344

Parius (friend), 344
Paul , St. (the Apostle), iv, 3, 14, 24, 25, 40, 71, 78, 289, 300, 306, 308, 312, 313, 314, 320, 365, 381, 404, 414,
Paul, Jean, v
Perl, von, Lady (Senel's sister), 359
Peter, St. (the Apostle), 19, 85, 93, 242, 408, 442, 462
Phaedrus, 2
Pilate, 12, 142, 276; wife of, 51
Pitius, Johann Reichard (Pastor), xii, 370, 457
Pliny, 332
Pope, Alexander, 337
Postmodernism, v–vi
Prayer, ix, xi–xiii, xv, xxv–xxvii, 41, 81, 100, 106, 150, 171–72, 177, 196, 199, 212, 221, 236, 243, 258, 277, 304, 311–12, 325, 327, 342, 369, 410, 431–32, 454, 462, 469–75
Prémontval, Pierre le Guay (mathematician), 352
Prophecy, xxiii, 3, 9, 48, 57, 71, 75, 171, 177, 194, 199, 221, 223, 230, 241, 253, 261, 311, 313, 431, 449, 359–61
Protestantism, 291
Ptolemaic model, 10, 137
Rachel, 55, 124, 253, 370
Ramler, Karl Wilhelm (poet), 352
Rappolt, Karl Heinrich (professor), 338
Reason, vi, x, xiii, xv–xvi, xix, xxi–xxii, 9, 16, 26, 30, 32, 37, 39, 46–47, 68, 85, 88, 91, 96, 101, 118, 122, 127, 133, 137, 154, 156, 167, 186, 189–90, 197, 204, 213, 216, 218, 224, 237, 248, 252, 255, 259, 265,

271, 279, 285, 290, 294–99, 310, 313, 358, 362, 391, 436, 440, 443, 444, 59, 475
Rebekah, 46, 55
Redemption. *See* Jesus Christ, as Redeemer
Reinbeck, Pastor (friend), 351
Reusch (friend), 351
Revelation (of God), vi, xix, xxiv, 2, 8–14, 17, 21, 23, 66, 75, 83—84, 86, 143, 174, 177, 179–80, 188, 191, 205, 218, 224, 230, 232, 237, 248, 264, 282, 290, 297–99, 308, 314, 331, 366, 372, 392, 399, 400, 452; in Bible, xiv, 2, 8–15, 87, 179, 251, 279, 366; in Christ, 47, 66, 157, 195, 278, 294–95, 385; in nature, 8, 14, 36, 108, 205, 290, 331, 426, 441
Riga, Latvia, vii, ix–x, xxxi–xxxii, 335, 341, 343, 345–49, 354, 457 459
Roed (relative), 352
Romans, 2, 34, 130, 138, 169, 262, 292, 332, 340, 346, 441, 454
Romanticism, v
Roth, Friedrich, xxix
Rutzen (friend), 351

Sacraments: *See* Baptism, Holy Communion.
Sacrifice, 148, 158, 180, 205, 266, 444; of Christ, 92, 123–25, 134, 273, 450; in Old Testament, 115, 127, 165, 168, 266, 272
Sahme (friend), 352
Salthenius, Dr. (teacher), 336
Sarah, 31, 36, 45, 106, 112, 211, 311, 360
Satan: *See* Devil (Satan).
Schlegel, Friedrich, xxix
Schumacher, Anna Regina (common law wife), x, xxxii
Science, 6, 32–33, 148, 339, 426, 436, 442–43. *See also* Enlightenment, Nature, Rationalists, Reason
Scripture: *See* Bible.
Senel, Baron von Pournoaille (friend), 359
Senses, vi, xiv–xv, xxv, 12, 18, 20, 37, 46, 58, 74, 84, 89, 96, 101, 111, 113, 118, 123, 127, 143, 152, 156, 157, 201, 204–5, 214, 216, 238–39, 247, 279, 285, 304, 307–8, 315, 330, 355, 380, 382, 395, 407, 420, 431, 435–36, 441, 449, 453, 459, 475
Serpent, xxiii–xxiv, 80, 88–89, 96, 100, 104, 108, 114–15, 119, 124, 129, 145–47, 150, 152, 163, 168, 199, 201–2, 214, 223, 226, 314, 419, 450–51. *See also* Devil (Satan).
Shaftesbury, Anthony Ashley Cooper, Earl of, 11 Sickness, 7, 65–66, 107, 129, 136–37, 142, 145, 156, 159, 195, 202, 227, 256, 263, 269, 275, 277, 282, 284–85, 288, 291, 334–35, 335, 265, 375, 417, 463, 473
Sin, ix, xix, xxiv, 21–25, 32, 42, 49, 51, 55, 57, 63–64, 67–68, 71–72, 78, 94, 96, 105, 107, 118, 121, 136, 138,

141, 144, 153, 156, 157, 159, 162, 173, 187, 188, 197, 199, 202, 204, 206, 213, 214, 219, 224, 229, 231, 232, 245, 252, 255, 256, 265, 267, 269, 272, 278, 289, 282, 284–85, 288, 294–97, 311, 307, 323, 428, 433, 436, 442, 451–52, 365, 461, 464, 466, 470, 472, 473

Smith, Ronald Gregor, xxx, 337

Society, 19–21, 172, 349

Socrates, iv, 16, 247, 289, 442

Socratic Memorabilia (1759), x, xvi–xvii, xxxii, 247, 345, 447

Solomon, xxv, xxvii, 42, 48, 82, 145, 149–55, 179, 201, 205, 216, 218, 222, 229, 241, 251, 289, 290, 304, 308, 374, 379, 414, 454

Son of God, vi, ix, xvi, xviii, xx–xxi, xxvi, 2, 47, 52, 56, 59, 63, 75, 77, 82, 85, 86, 94, 110, 113, 122–26, 136, 153, 207, 252, 254, 259, 272, 277, 282, 291, 294, 298, 300, 305, 318, 327, 345, 364, 365, 366, 371, 377, 378, 383, 384, 386, 389, 389, 393, 395, 401, 405, 407, 410, 415, 416, 419, 427, 429, 431, 450, 454, 462, 466, 469–73. *See also* Jesus Christ.

Soul, viii, xi, xiv–xvi, xviii–xix, xxi, xxiii, xxv–xxvi, 18, 22–23, 44, 47, 55, 57, 62, 65, 75, 82, 92, 94, 97, 102, 107, 124, 127, 132, 135, 145, 156, 163, 165, 176, 180, 199–202, 206, 211, 212, 224, 240, 247, 252, 257, 259, 265, 266, 267, 271, 276, 279, 284, 293, 296, 302–4, 313, 314, 322, 364, 373, 376, 379, 370, 383, 386, 387, 389, 395, 403, 407, 415–16, 418–20, 422, 426–29, 432, 438, 443, 448, 449, 461, 463, 467

Sulzer, Johann Georg (mathematician), 352

Temple, 243, 422; body as, 419; heart as, 154, 175, 228, 377, 403; pagan, 26; of Solomon, xxvii, 48, 82, 115, 152, 154–55, 165–66, 179, 233, 249, 261

Truth, 35, 38, 41, 61–62, 67, 75, 78, 82, 84, 88, 89, 102, 129, 138, 165, 216, 186, 201, 211, 232, 243, 247, 251, 265, 268, 273, 279, 283, 289, 296, 298, 305, 315, 318, 322, 369, 379, 385, 391, 399, 411, 415, 417, 419, 431, 438, 442, 449, 458, 466

Ursinus, Privy Counsellor (family friend), 351

Vernizobre, Mr. (father of friend), 459.

Vilmar, August, v

Voltaire, 9, 11, 13

Wagner (neighbor), 341

Wegleiter, Christoph (hymnwriter), 414

Weissenborn, Bernd, vii, xxix–xxx, 287

Wisdom of Solomon (Apocrypha), xxv, 42, 205

Wisdom, iv, xxii, xxiv–xxv, xxx, 10, 11, 6–8, 17, 20, 52, 59, 66, 69, 82, 94, 104, 109, 131, 133, 190, 191, 186, 191, 192, 195, 197, 200, 201, 209, 212, 214, 216, 217, 219, 221, 234–35, 246, 255, 263, 264, 274, 275, 277–78, 289, 291, 302, 304–5, 307, 410, 320–21, 322, 336, 342,364, 366, 367, 372, 382, 390, 398, 418, 427, 428, 452, 459, 461, 373–74

Witten, Christoph Wilhelm von (employer), xxxi, 343

Word of God, viii, x–xiv, xvi–xviii, xxi–xxii, xxv–xxvi, 2, 8–15, 13–14, 18, 47, 52, 45, 63, 67–68, 75–76, 79, 82–83, 89–92, 96, 98, 99, 102, 107, 111, 114, 118, 129, 133, 134, 150, 156, 171, 178, 190, 193, 200, 214, 219, 248, 253, 260, 270–71, 284, 286, 291, 314, 317, 376, 385, 403, 406, 411, 460. *See also* Bible; Son of God.

Worship: *See* Divine Service.

Young, Edward (poet), viii, 8, 265, 392, 402, 405, 416, 419, 438

SCRIPTURE INDEX

This index includes the Biblical allusions identified in the text with margin notes and footnotes.

OLD TESTAMENT

Genesis

1:1 .... 89, 99, 254
1:1–2:3 322
1:1–2:4 14
1:2 .... 15, 93, 98, 102, 111, 173, 315, 362, 372, 412
1:3 284
1:3–5, 6–8, 9–10 87
1:3–19 311
1:4 .... 16, 53, 133
1:4, 10, 12, 18, 21, 25 16
1:4, 6, 7, 14, 18 53
1:4–10 151
1:5, 8, 10 15
1:5 21
1:6–10 89
1:7 111
1:14–19 87
1:16 17
1:20 15
1:20–31 87
1:22 .... 15, 437
1:23–28 452
1:26 15
1:27 .... 15, 372,427, 449
1:28 ...... 16, 33, 87, 145, 400, 428
1:31 .... 16, 53, 412
2:1–3 87
2:3 17
2:7 .... 2, 17, 23, 31, 86, 118, 199, 383, 390, 395, 449
2:8, 9, 15 19
2:9 .... 19, 75, 119
2:15 .... 19, 376
2:16–17 58
2:17 .... 93, 103, 146, 193, 295
2:18 .... 20, 27, 86
2:18–23 429
2:19–20 .... 21, 286
2:21–23 .... 21, 23
2:23 .... 23, 276, 415, 430
2:24 274
3:1 .... 68, 73, 97, 112, 191, 212, 391, 451
3:1–2 97
3:1–7 .... 119, 191
3:3 21
3:5 22
3:5, 22 261
3:5–6 96
3:6 .... 20, 260, 453
3:6–7 323
3:7–8 .... 21, 27
3:8 274
3:9 26
3:9, 13 22
3:10 27
3:10–12 26
3:12 .... 58, 186
3:14 .... 241, 303, 408
3:14–15 100
3:14–19 96

3:15......48, 52, 69, 73, 76, 88, 89, 90, 104, 107, 114, 115, 117, 119, 124, 129, 147, 168, 199, 214, 222, 226, 308, 419, 450
3:16....... xxxiv, 23, 78, 175
3:16, 18........................219
3:17–19.............20, 26, 71
3:18, 23
3:19............................. 241
3:21............................... 23
3:22 276
3:23 23
3:24..................24, 47, 75
4:1 24
4:2............................... 25
4:4 25
4:8...................... 100, 451
4:8–10...........................92
4:8–9 212
4:9.........................26, 116
4:10 387
4:10–11.........................99
4:10–14.........................26
4:11........................xv, 363
4:12 ....xv, 352, 363
4:12–14 274
4:12–17 116
4:13 186
4:13–14 22
4:15 27
4:17 28
4:17–22 236
4:20............................. 28
4:22............................. 28
4:23............................. 29
4:24 29
5:1.................................15
5:1–6:3 29
5:21–24 30
5:24....................... 31, 161
5:28–29.........................60
5:32.............................. 32
6:1–4 30
6:1–13...........................89
6:2 117
6:4............................... 29
6:5–7 19
6:6 377
6:8 450
6:11–12 31
6:14–22.........................76
6:17 32
6:18 32
7:4..............................254
7:11 200
8:7–11.......................... 33
8:8–9 372
8:9...............................175
8:12............................ 451
9:1–16......................... 33
9:2 33
9:3 .... 33, 283
9:4..............................200
9:4–6 34
9:6................................15
9:8–16.........................200
9:9–17 209
9:18 451
9:21............................ 451
9:21, 24 450
9:22 .... 33, 451, 452
9:23 ....451, 454
9:24....................452, 453
9:24–26 452
9:25 ....450, 451
9:26............................450
9:26–27 34
9:27 ....33, 451
10:9 .... 90, 116
11:1–9 ....36, 252, 286
11:3–4 437
12:1–3 ....19, 40, 90, 252
12:1–4.......................... 53
12:3.............................. 33
12:7 ....53, 295, 318
12:7, 8........................... 53
12:10–20 38
12:13 48
13:4, 18......................... 53
13:5–12 230
13:8..............................38
13:9......................... 38, 53
13:10, 14 53
13:13 39
13:14–16.....................295
13:17 38
14..................................39
14:8–17, 21–24 42
15 41
15:1 474
15:2.............. 81, 407, 408
15:5........................ 19, 133
15:5–6, 18...................295
15:12 .... 41, 409
15:12–14 227
15:12–16 408
16:2 453
16:5–6 453
16:12.......................... 453
17:1 ....225, 474
17:11 297
18........................ xxx, 42
18:1 58
18:6–8..........................58
18:12...........................391
18:16–21...................... 41
18:18.......................33, 90
18:22–32 41
18:32.......................... 239
19 42
19:1–29....................... 283
19:26 ....42, 87
19:30–38 43
19:33–36..................... 129
20:1–18.......................148
20:3 129
20:6............................. 53
20:16 .... 134, 142

21:1–20 152
21:20 453
21:22–26 97
21:25–31 203
21:25–34 203
22 43
22:9–10 46
22:13 54
22:17 19, 133, 209, 390
22:18 33, 90
23 43, 54
23:8 201
24 44
24:2–9, 34–41 408
24:31 372
24:62–67 46
25 44
25:27, 29–33 60, 133
25:29–34 45
25:30 54
26:4 33
26:17–22 203, 230
27 45
27:27 401
27:34–40 152
27:43 54
28:6–9 45
28:10–17 177
28:10–22 402
28:11 47, 408
28:12 73
28:14 33
28:17 46
28:20 318
28:20–22 46
29 46
29:31 46
30:14–15 370
31:14–16 55
31:20 55
31:32 55
31:35 55
31:39, 40 55
32:10 52
32:12 209
32:22–31 109
32:25–26 232
32:26 258, 461
33:2, 14 47, 376
33:14 56, 376, 386
33:19 47
34 48
37:12–28 302
37:33 48
37:35 49
38 52
38:5 56
38:9 49, 57
38:24 50
38:26 131
38:27–30 370
38:28–30 50
39:1–41:45 302
39:2–20 335
39:5 50
39:12 51
39:22–41:57 221
40 51
40:8 57
40:20 194
41:9 52, 57
41:32 57
41:54–57 52
43:8 57
43:25 280
45:1 57
45:12 58
45:24 58
48:8–20 161
49:9 161, 162
49:1–27 453
49:17 415
49:23 453
50:20 270

Exodus

1:6 104
1:15–22 67
2:11–15 38
3:2–3 84
3:7 422
3:8 59, 318
4:1–5, 17, 20 166
4:16 391
4:17 391
4:22–23 232, 258
5:2 10
5:4–18 300
5:5–19 437
7–11 227
7:5–12, 15–20 166
7:8–12 10
7:8–8:19 156
8:5–6, 16–17 166
8:15 118
8:16–19 10, 125, 226
8:18–19 84
9:22–23 166
10:9, 24–26 116
10:12–15, 21–23 166
10:21–23 202
11:5 125
12:1–18, 27 38
12:11 176, 410
12:31–32 116
12:48 280
13:1–2, 11–17 29
13:2 400
13:11–15 258
13:21 170, 287
13:21–22 7
14:4, 17–18 263
14:15–29 125
14:27–28 120
15:1–18 396
15:11 153
15:23–25 393
15:26 275
16 100

16:3 210
16:7–8 360
16:12–31 376
16:33–34 154
17:1–7 100
17:5–6 376
17:8–16 263
18:4 81
19:16–18 59
19:20, 24 264
20:2 383
20:5–6 206
20:8–11 322
20:12 462
20:15 210
20:21 154
21:6 417
22:26–27 112
23:15 64
23:19 .... 29, 400
23:29–30 103
24:15–18 188
24:18 254
28:6–14 135
28:15–29 401
28:33–35 401
29:18, 25, 41 272
29:38–46 409
30:7–9, 34–37 409
31:1–3 442
32:1–6 108
32:30–34 99
33:16 153
34:5–7 383
34:6 .... 246, 373
34:11–16 177
34:18 322
34:28 254
34:29–30 397
34:33–35 134
35:25, 30–35 442

Leviticus

2:13 273
3:1–17 377
3:3–5, 9–11, 14–16 389
3:5, 16 63
3:11 63
3:16 63
4:1–5:13 63
5:14–6:7 63
6 64
7:11–18 377
7:20–21 64
8:33–35 322
10:9–10 64
12 64
13:12–13 64
13:18–44 65
13:45 212
16:9–10 65
16:31 65
16:33 65
17:11 .... 34, 92, 200
18:1–5 65
18:22, 23 66
18:24–25 67
19:5 68
19:19 68
19:29 69
19:33 69
23:7 71
23:11 71
23:23–43 322
26:13 71
26:15 71
26:16 72
26:17 72
26:18 72
26:19 72
26:22 .... 73, 402
26:25 74
26:29 74
26:30 233
26:31–33 75
26:32 75
26:33 75
26:34–35 75
27:10 77
27:24 77

Numbers

6:24–26 475
9:14 280
11:1 157
11:4–6, 31–34 210
13:23–27 392
13:30 78
13:33 .... 81, 319
14:3 171
14:24 78
14:39–45 410
17:10 154
20:18, 20 78
20:17 .... 79, 150, 410
20:21 54
20:26, 28 420
21:8 86
21:14 379
21:22 .... 79, 150, 410
22–24 .... 180, 442
22:4 81
22:21–34 226
22:27 386
22:28 452
23:11 202
31:28–30 116
35:6–34 275

Deuteronomy

1:33 77
1:36–38 78
2:4 78
2:6, 28 79
2:7 420
2:10–12, 20–23 78
2:14 420

2:24–25 78
2:26 79
2:27 79
2:31 80
3:21 80
3:23–25 81
3:24 81
3:24–25 432
3:25 81
4 82
4:2 21
4:6 82
4:7 11, 82, 215
4:7–8, 33–35 153
4:11 59
4:12 83
4:13 83
4:32 84
4:33 84
4:34 85
4:37 90
4:39 91
4:40 91
5:5 92
5:6–21 26
5:14 226
5:25–29 428
6:16 85
7:3–4 177
7:6 298, 398
7:6–7 382
7:7 12
7:22 92, 103
8:1 93
8:2 93, 110, 297
8:2, 16 85
8:3 94
8:3–4 394
8:4 205
9:4–6 12
10:14 88
10:18 94
11:14 94, 391
12:6 116
12:15, 22 420
13:13 151
14:6–8 406
14:7–8 100
16:3 94
18:15–19 428
19:1–13 275
19:15–21 95
20:1–4 95
20:5 278
20:5–9 95
21:23 399
23:15–16 95
24:5 95
24:6 96, 101
24:7 96
24:12–13, 17 112
25:3 96, 184
25:4 226
25:5–10 49
25:13, 14 96
26:2, 10 246
27:17 96
27:24 97
27:25 97
28:13 97
28:26–51 97
28:68 101
29:11 101
30:1–10 422
30:11 98, 102
30:11–14 xvi, xxix, xliv, 98, 425–33
31:30 99
32:1–3 111
32:2 164
32:5 99
32:6 99
32:13 102
32:35 215
33:6 100
33:7 100
33:8 100
33:9 100
33:16 84
34:1–4 386

Joshua

1:5 458, 470
1:18 101
2 104
2:1–7 392
5:9 102
5:12 102
6:25 104
7:25 422
8:1–29 102
10:13 139
11 102
11:15 102
11:23 416
13:8–19:51 103
15:16–19 103
17:12–13 103
24:2–4 40

Judges

1:7 103
1:12 103
1:21 103
1:24, 25 104
2:10 104
2:14 104
3:15 104
3:19–23 104
3:31 104, 105
4:4–24 105
4:15 109
4:17–22 105
5 396
6:39–40 62
6:6 106
6:11 106
6:37, 39 107
7:5 107

7:16 107
7:17 107
7:19 107
7:20 107
8:4–7, 13–16 107
8:18 107
8:20 108
8:21 108
8:24–27 108
8:27 108
9 116
9:2 415
9:9, 11, 13 119
10:15 108
10:16 .... 108, 422
12:4–6 382
14:5–18 311
14:8 219
14:18 112
16:4–22 112
19:22 109
20:47 110
21:6 109

Ruth

1:1 110
1:20–21 112
2:1–9 112
2:2–3 111
2:5, 6, 9, 15, 21 115
2:8–8 112
2:14 112
2:17 111
2:18 112
3:3 112
3:15 113
3:18 .... 113, 387
4:11–12 113
4:13 111
4:14–16 113

1 Samuel

2:8 .... 125, 132, 182, 209
2:12–17 114
2:13 115
2:31–33 115
3:2, 3 115
3:11–14 115
4:13 117
4:18 117
4:20 117
5:4–5 142
7:12 325
7:15 117
8 117
8:11–18 118
9 118
9:2 119
9:23–24 .... 209, 397
10 118
10:1 123
10:2 124
10:3–4 124
10:6–7 124
10:11 .... 202, 271
10:11, 12 125
10:12 .... 452, 466
10:22 126
10:25–27 126
13:14 129
15:23 162
17:40, 49 133
17:51 .... 129, 133, 307
17:54 135
18:1 .... 415, 416
18:1–4 377
18:4 126
18:17 379
19:7–10 127
19:12 127
19:13 127
20:1–17 127
20:12–17 127
20:16 415
20:18 127
20:26 127
20:35–36 128
20:37–39 128
21:9 128
21:10–15 215
21:13–15 .... xxxii, 2
22:2 129
22:5 130
22:22 130
23 130
23:6, 9 135
23:7 130
23:15–18 130
24:2 130
24:8–22 387
24:11 130
24:12 131
24:17 131
25:22 132
25:27 133
25:29 133
25:37 135
26:3,4 133
27:12 133
28 134
28:15–19 134
28:20 134
29 134
29:5 134
30:2 135
30:7–8 135
30:11 135
30:12 136
30:13 136
31 136
31:4–5 211
31:9–10 138

2 Samuel

1 137
1:14 138
1:18 .... 139, 155
1:21 141
1:26 .... 415, 416
2:19–28 139
2:23 140
2:26–28 139

3:6–19 140
3:6–21 140
3:8–11 140
3:17–30 141
3:22–27 140
3:27–29, 38–39 140
3:29 141
3:29, 36–37 141
3:31–34 141
3:33–34 141
4:5–12 ....141, 142
5:1 415
5:6 142
5:8 142
5:23 144
6:1–4 144
6:6–10 144
6:11–12 144
6:20 144
7:5–16 174
9:6 144
9:8 144
9:10 145
12:5 127
12:5–7 50
12:24 252
12:26–31 379
16:5 422
16:21 146
17:23 187
18:3 381
18:18 176
19:1 253
19:12 415
23:6 151
24:17 226

1 Kings

3:9 473
3:9–12 473
3:16–27 148
3:27 149
5:5 150
5:6 150
5:7 151
5:18 151
6:7 151
6:9–16 82
7 152
7:1–7 155
7:14 ....152, 153
7:29 152
7:36 152
7:40 153
7:46 153
8:1 154
8:9 154
8:10–11 154
8:12 154
8:22 154
8:23–53 154
8:29–30 368
8:50–51 454
9:12–14 151
10 155
10:14–11:18 155
10:15 155
10:21 60
10:26–29 155
11 155
11:1–8 155
11:41 155
13:2 253
13:5–6 253
13:7–10 253
13:23–24 253
13:30 253
13:31 417
14:10 158
15:23 156
17 156
17:1 141
17:4–7 161
19 157
19:8 154
19:11 185
21:21 158
22:21–23 84

2 Kings

1:8 254
2:1–11 31
2:8, 13–14 166
2:11 161
4:6 418
4:10 378
4:40–41 391
6:15–17 470
9:8 158
10:32 157
12:3 157
13:20–21 417
17:9 157
17:35 158
19:3 ....158, 466
20:2 159
22:7 158
22:14 159
23:17–18 416
23:34 159
24:4 159
24:14 159
24:17 159
25:1–21 115
25:4–5 160
25:15 160
25:27–30 ....161, 194

1 Chronicles

4:9–10 161
5:1–2 161
10:13 162
11:6 143
12 165
12:18 162
12:32 162
19:5 162
21:1–2 162
21:4 163
21:11 162
21:12 163
21:15 164
21:17 164

21:23 164
22:9 415
23:5 164
23:11 165
26:1 165

2 Chronicles

16:2–3 156
16:9 31
16:12 156
18 166
18:18–22 180
18:20–21 166
18:23 166
18:26 166
18:29–31 398
18:33 167
21:9–10 167
26:10 167
28:20 167
28:22 167
30:6–10 168
32:8 168
32:21 168

Ezra

4:1 168
4:4 168
4:6–16 169
4:11 169
4:14 170
4:22 169
7:6 170
7:9 170
7:23 170
8:24–30 170
8:29 171
9 171
9:1–2 177
9:5–15 171
10:1–17 177
10:44 171

Nehemiah

1:3 171
1:4 172
1:5 172
1:6 172
1:8–9 172
1:10 172
2:1 173
2:1–2 369
2:2 173
2:3 173
2:4 173
2:7 169, 174
2:8 174
2:10 175
2:13 175, 176
2:14 175
2:15 176
2:19 176
2:20 176
4:17 176
4:18 177
4:21 177
5 177
5:15 177
5:19 177
6 177
6:1 177
6:7 178
6:8–9 178
7:3 178
8 8
8:1, 3 178
8:5 178
8:10 178
9 179
9:20 171
9:21 179
9:29 179
9:30 179
9:32 180
13:2 180
13:8 180
13:26 180

Esther

1:15 180
2:7–10 180
2:22 181
5:1–7:10 222
5:9–13 182
6:1–4 182
7:8 206

Job

1:7 203
1:9–19 241
1:10 182
1:13 184
1:15, 17 184
1:16, 19 184
1:20 185
1:21 185, 420
1:22 186
2 186
2:2 203
2:3 187
2:7 188
2:8 187
2:9 187
2:9–10 186
2:11–13 186
2:13 188
3 188
3:3 189
3:8 198, 365
3:14–19 189
3:25 199
4 190
4:7 190
4:17–18 190
4:19–21 190
5:7 275
7:12 365
7:20 408
9:6 209
9:13 225
15:2 213
16:2 362, 393

16:20 6
26:11 209
26:12 225
33:15 234
33:23–28 .... xxxvi, xxxviii, 99
38:1 188
38:4–38 205
38:8–11 244
38:11 208
38:39–39:30 205
38:41 106
39:14–17 22
39:18 192
39:19 192
39:19–25 192
39:30 192
40:15–41:34 205
40:19 ... 192, 202, 358, 451
40:19–24 244
40:23 393
41:1 198
41:1–34 .... 205, 365,
41:22 204
41:31 209
41:34 432
42:3 187
42:10, 12 188

Psalms

1:1 193
1:4 250
2:3 193
2:7–8 193
3:3 194
3:5 194
4:1 194
4:4 195
4:8 194
5:1–2 469
5:3 195
5:6 195
5:10 195
6:1 473
7:9 346
7:16 303
8 .... 87, 145, 400
8:3–8 428
8:5 93
8:6 44
11:2 128
12–20 464
14:1 303
18:28 419
18:42 143
19 216
19:6 138
19:14 469
22:13 73
23:1, 5 397
23:3 470
23:4 471
23:5 .... 72, 80
24 400
29:9 419
30:12 409
31:5 470
31:16 235
32:4 .... 72, 347, 354
32:5 354
33:6 317
33:9 .... 81, 317
34:9 .... 249, 471
34:22 465
35:27 467
37:5 .... 459, 470
40:8 322
42 461
42:1 111
44:5 382
45:1 114
45:8 59
48:2 59
50:21 22
51 466
51:3 464
51:7, 10–11 365
51:12 .... 125, 135
51:12–13 466
51:17 270
52:9 409
55:22 470
56:4–5 414
56:11 422
57:6 303
59:11 454
60 39
63:1 111
64:3 128
66:9 199
68:13 382
68:18 453
69 455
69:1–2 81
6:21 362
69:22 455
70:13 472
71:9 454
73:9 451
73:22 22
73:24 471
73:25 394
73:25–26 394
74:14 198
75:3 209
78:65 450
78:72 20
82:1–6 231
82:6 .... 16, 375
86:16–17 466
87:3 59
87:4 225
88:10 21
89:10 225
89:27 232
89:32–37 466
90:4, 12 91
90:12–15 117
90:17 470
91:4 327
91:11 465
91:11–12 470

91:13 382
92:12 388
94:10 21
94:19 325
95:7 139
97:2 399
100:3 472
102:6–7 6
103:14 17
103:20–21 88
104:6–9 244
104:15 327
104:25–26 432
104:29–30 19
105:18 201
108 39
110:1 .... 59, 379
110:4 40
111:10 310
112:7 422
115:16 16
118:6 422
118:25–26 469
118:26 .... 372, 475
119:18 472
119:96 309
119:105 .... 69, 189
121:1 86
121:1, 2 59
121:2 367
125:2 59
126:5 79
127:2 21
128 467
129:8 467
139:7–12 75
139:15 327
139:23, 24 465
140:3 148
141:5 195
142:4 196
143:10 171
144:8, 11 196
145:18 .... 11, 215
146:4 196
146:9 226
147:4 390
147:9 .... 106, 404
147:10 275
148:14 11

Proverbs

1:7 197
1:8 197
1:9 198
1:10 198
1:15–19 198
1:20–22 199
1:33 199
2:2–5 199
2:6 199
2:14 204
2:16–19 198
2:17 199
3:2 200
3:16 200
3:20 200
3:22 200
3:27 201
4:12 201
4:18 263
4:18, 19 201
4:20–27 404
4:22 202
5:1–6 202
5:1–14 198
5:6 202
5:9 202
5:15–18 203
5:22, 23 203
6:1 203
6:6–8 205
6:6–11 203
6:12, 13 203
6:16–19 204
6:21 204
6:22 205
6:23 263
6:23–36 198
6:27, 28 205
6:29, 30 206
6:34 206
7 206
7:4 206
7:4–27 198
7:6–23 207
7:22–23 208
8:9 222
8:13 208
8:20, 21 208
8:29 208
9:1 209
9:1–6 429
9:2 209
9:13–19 198
9:17 209
10:6 211
10:8 211
10:9 211
10:11 211
10:12 212
10:18 212
10:19 212
10:26 214
10:29 214
11:8 214
11:11 215
11:24 277
12:10 226
13:7 277
14:15 277
16:1 242
16:6 215
16:33 218
23:26 365
24:17–18 229
25:2 219
25:17 215
25:25 .... 215, 432

29:13 241
30:8–9 218
30:17 451
31:14 432
31:31 312

Ecclesiastes
1:4 216
1:5 215
1:9–18 289
1:13 216
1:14 304
1:15 216
1:17–18 217
2:2 217
2:10 217
2:11, 17, 26 304
2:12 217
2:18 218
2:24 218
2:25 218
2:26 219
3:1 219
3:11 219
3:14–15 220
3:15 235
3:19 220
4:8 220
4:13 220
5:1–6 221
6:2 221
6:8 221
7:16 221
7:20–22 222
7:28 374
8 222
8:15 222
9:4–6 222
9:7–10 460
9:11 223
9:12 223
9:14–15 223
10:19 223
12 223

Song of Solomon
1–8 224, 379
1:3 473
1:5–6 415
1:7 201
2:9 420
2:14 110
2:16 414
3:2 416
4:11 59
4:16 388
5:9 417
7:10 419
8:6 419

Isaiah
1:2 99
1:3 126
1:31 224
2:4 224
3:12 224
4:1 224
4:2 59
5:2 63
5:14 201
5:26 225
6:2–3 86
6:3 87, 134, 265
6:13 216
7:4 225
7:6 225
7:14 415
7:18 432
8:14 103
9:5 401
9:6 33
10:33–34 216
11:1 216
11:2 62
11:5 81
14:12–14 87
14:12–20 145, 146, 161
14:13–14 224
21:16 225
21:17 453
25:7 153
25:8 396
25:11 225
27:1 198, 230, 365
28:19 7
29:13 221
30:7 225
30:23–24 226
35:10 474
40:3 450
40:3–5 155
40:4 59
40:5 48
40:26 390
41 39
41:2 225
42:3 187
42:6 36
42:9 290
43:19 290
44:25 35, 451
45:7 273, 390, 443
48:6 290
48:19 209
49:6 36
49:16 401
50:7 62
51:9 225
52:7 215
53:4 127, 416, 422
53:4, 11, 12 381
53:7 143
54:5 274, 415
57:15 154, 270
57:20 230
59:1 7
60:1 48
60:19–20 409
61:10 112, 374
62:10–12 155
62:12 300, 399, 474
63:3 381

63:9 422
64:3–4 397
64:6 473
65:2 235
65:12 110
65:17 .... 31, 290
65:20 71
66:1 .... 395, 402
66:2 231
66:13 396
66:22 290
66:25 81

Jeremiah

1:18–19 227
2:11 227
2:12 227
2:13 210
2:31 227
3:4, 19 .... 7, 94, 327
5:22 .... 209, 244
6:19 32
7:18 273
7:28 227
7:30 228
17:13 175
19:13 273
23:12 228
28:10–14 193
31:34 347
32 228
32:20 443
32:29 273
38:11 228
38:11–13 .... xxxii, 2
44:15–25 273
46:11 291

Ezekiel

1:5–10 237
1:15–21 451
11:5 228
11:19 466
12:22 228
16 36
16:4–6 274
16:44 228
17:22–24 .... 216, 391
18:2, 25 228
18:14 228
18:23, 32 42
20:6 53
24:27 229
25:3 229
26:2 229
26:10 229
27 229
27:28 230
28 230
28:2, 6, 9 231
29:3, 9 230
29:14, 15 230
31:8–9 .... 231, 388
33 231
33:11 42
33:32 231
34:4 231
36:26 376
36:35 420
37:6 232
43:19 232
43:24 273
44:9–16 232
44:18 232
44:31 233

Daniel

1:2 233
1:4 233
1:8 233
1:8–16 241
1:15 234
1:17, 20 234
1:19 234
2 409
2:1 234
2:4 234
2:5 235
2:11 235
2:14 235
2:15 235
2:23 236
2:24 236
2:25 236
2:27 236
2:28 236
2:31 236
3:5, 7, 10 236
3:15 237
4 237
4:7–8 250
4:17 237
4:19–27 237
4:33 237
4:33–37 237
7:9, 13, 22 407
7:13 323
7:15 237
9:24 95
9:27 228
11:31 228
12:11 228

Hosea

1:10 209
2:21–22 .... 86, 259, 275
4:1 238
4:13 238
11:4 .... 238, 471

Joel

1:2–7 225
1:4 238
1:10 238
1:12 238
2:1–11 225
2:23 239
2:30 287
3:13 239
3:15 239

Amos
1:1 ... 239
2:1 ... 240
2:1 ... 408
2:6 ... 240
2:7 ... 240, 241, 408
2:8 ... 241
4:2 ... 241
4:6 ... 241
4:7 ... 242
7:7–8 ... 158
8:8 ... 230
8:11 ... 141

Obadiah
1 ... 242
1–21 ... 242, 454
3–16 ... 242
10, 15 ... 454
21 ... 242

Jonah
1:3, 5 ... 242
1:6 ... 242
1:9 ... 243
1:12 ... 243
1:13 ... 243
1:17 ... 243
2:1–11 ... 433
2:3 ... 431
2:6 ... 243
2:9 ... 244
2:10 ... 244
3:1–2 ... 245
4:1, 2 ... 245
4:5 ... 245
4:6 ... 246, 250
4:7–8 ... 246

Micah
7:1 ... 246, 289
7:2 ... 247
7:3 ... 247

Nahum
1–3 ... 247
1:3 ... 323, 403
2:1 ... 215

Habakkuk
2:3 ... 248

Zephaniah
1:3 ... 248
1:6 ... 248
1:9 ... 248
2:3 ... 248
3:7 ... 249
3:9 ... 249

Haggai
1:5, 6, 9 ... 249
2:23 ... 401

Zechariah
3:9 ... 322
4:10 ... 322
9:9 ... 275
9:9–11 ... 253
11 ... 71
12:10 ... 154, 171, 253
12:11 ... 253
14:8 ... 409

Malachi
1–4 ... 250
3:1 ... 259
4:2 ... 87
4:6 ... 251

NEW TESTAMENT

Matthew
1:1 ... 251
1:2, 3, 5, 6 ... 251
1:5–6 ... 113
1:17 ... 252
1:18–25 ... 259
1:19 ... 252
1:23 ... 400, 415
2 ... 259
2:1–2 ... 175
2:1–12 ... ix
2:2 ... 170
2:4 ... 252
2:13–15 ... 130
2:15 ... 252
2:16–18 ... 130, 253, 276
3:2 ... 391
3:2–3 ... 382
3:3 ... 450
3:4 ... 254
3:7 ... 79, 254
3:9 ... 465
3:9–10 ... 455
3:10 ... 31
3:11 ... 259
3:14 ... 254
3:15 ... 299
3:16–17 ... 254
3:17 ... 294, 318, 374
4:1 ... 130
4:1–11 ... 180, 255
4:2 ... 254
4:3 ... 109
4:3, 6 ... 255
4:4 ... 94
4:5–10 ... 415
4:10 ... 261
4:11 ... 255
4:13, 18 ... 255
4:17 ... 62
4:24 ... 195, 256

5 262
5–7 59
5:1 59
5:2–3 59
5:5 262
5:10–11 396
5:12 262
5:13 273
5:13–14 263
5:16 .... 257, 293
5:17 .... 36, 251, 278, 299
5:23 265
5:24 266
5:26 266
5:29–30 267
5:33 268
5:38, 42 269
5:39 269
5:48 317
6:1 257
6:6 403
6:9–13 .... 81, 404, 475
6:10 87
6:11 241
6:13 .... 77, 242, 472
6:19–20 395
6:26 258
6:28 258
6:28, 31, 32 24
6:30 442
6:33 404
7:3 .... 96, 314
7:7 258
7:11 258
7:12 212
7:13–14 160
7:14 .... 31, 417
7:15 198
7:21 320
8:12 .... 62, 409
8:17 .... 142, 175, 381, 416
8:23–27 .... 115, 432
8:27 209
9:2 195
9:6 195
9:12 .... 65, 143, 288
9:15 95
9:21 259
9:32 195
9:34–35 257
10:6 .... 257, 272
10:14 314
10:19 331
10:21 471
10:29–30 390
10:30 346
10:42 276
11:4 436
11:19 257
11:23 52
11:25 119
11:29–30 .... 227, 386
12:6 152
12:20 187
12:22 195
12:25 37
12:29 203
12:31–32 141
12:34 254
12:36 213
12:38–41 245
12:39–40 246
12:42 .... 153, 155, 415
12:47–50 374
13:1–9 .... 98, 115
13:13–16 303
13:23 270
13:24–30 64
13:25 .... 278, 374
13:27–28 88
13:31–32 .... 22, 432, 450
13:37–41 29
13:38 62
13:42 409
13:45–46 364
14 258
14:13 258
14:19 258
15:1–9 278
15:8 221
15:14 358
15:24 .... 272, 398
15:32–39 52
16:4 .... 245, 246
16:16 243
16:18 265
16:19 .... 106, 418
16:24 .... 273, 379, 462, 471
17:1–9 124
17:4 388
17:15 256
17:20 .... 382, 432
17:24–27 432
18:12–14 272
19:17 42
19:21 376
19:28 401
19:29 93
19:30 427
20:3–4 376
20:28 .... 16, 266, 387
21:1–5 386
21:5 275
21:10 178
21:12–13 403
21:13 472
21:21 382
22:4 209
22:21 283
22:29 142
22:36–40 116
22:37–39 .... 193, 440
22:37–40 .... 316, 367
23:1–32 293
23:27 101
23:29 454
23:33 254

24:15 228
24:17–18 158
24:32 281
24:38 29
25:31–46 250
25:33 139
25:34 61
25:35, 40 275
25:40 276
26:17–19 258
26:26 .... 80, 135
26:28 .... 82, 350
26:63 109
26:63–64 291
26:65 291
27:2–10 54
27:3–5 387
27:14 142
27:19 51
27:24–25 159
27:25 128
27:33 403
27:34 .... 63, 173
27:40 131
27:40, 42 255
27:45 139
27:46, 48 277
27:48 63
27:59–60 54
28:8–17 57
28:10 378
28:18 .... 121, 385, 400
28:18–20 79
28:20 .... 51, 75, 81, 276, 322, 401

Mark

1:32 195
2:3–4 195
2:9 195
2:22 407
3:21–22 129
3:27 203
4:1–2 101
4:5–6, 16–17 271
4:14 272
4:20 270
4:24, 25 270
4:34 270
4:35–41 395
4:41 271
5:11–13 230
5:15 271
5:30 271
6:15 281
6:16 271
6:17–18 258
6:35–44 340
6:41–44 271
7:1–13 130
7:1–16 278
7:6 354
7:37 470
8:1–8 271
8:14–21 61
8:18 272
8:22 195
8:22–25 408
8:34 364
9:5, 6 .... 36, 242
9:6 442
9:17–20 195
9:36–37 462
9:37 272
9:48 .... 75, 353
9:49, 50 272
10:18 .... 273, 440, 444
11:15 180
12:16 373
13:28 281
14:3–9 417
14:29 100
14:52 51
14:55–59 84
15:22 403
16:15 79
16:17–18 125
16:18 152

Luke

1:27 379
1:35 .... 174, 315, 379
1:42 .... 201, 298
1:46 389
1:57–80 431
1:78 .... 195, 202
2:7 226
2:8–14 175
2:10 290
2:10–11 432
2:12 378
2:14 294
2:22–23 175
2:25–35 431
2:32 36
2:35 .... 62, 303
2:46 273
2:51 471
2:52 273
3:3–6 157
3:21–22 378
3:36–37 450
4:25–27 418
5:1 460
5:1–11 460
5:19 273
5:31 11
5:36, 39 274
5:39 407
6:31 212
6:46 320
8:1 .... 290, 432
8:8 342
8:11 .... 52, 133, 272
8:14 347
8:15 .... 321, 331
8:19 274
8:19–21 374
8:30 275

9:58 274, 400
10:17 16
10:19 79, 193, 382
10:20 193
10:23 378
10:25–27 274
10:30 420
10:41 345
10:42 394
11:13 8
11:20 286
11:47–51 159
12:1 463
12:6, 24 226
12:7 346
12:32 473
12:52 418
13:1–9 277
13:8 309, 387
13:12 277
14:1 277, 280
14:7–11 280
14:12–14 279, 280
14:16–24 95, 280
14:17 209
14:26 100
14:28, 31 277
15:1–2 129
15:1–10 387
15:7 53, 347, 400
15:7, 10 121
15:11–32 7, 134, 384
15:16 102
15:20 401
16:1–9 266
16:8 145
16:9–11 293
16:18 278
16:19–31 457
16:20–22 409
16:22–31 188
17:5, 10 278
17:10 7
17:25 278
17:27 29
17:37 192
18:1–5 387
18:9–14 280
18:13 464, 469, 475
19:4 144
19:11–27 463
19:11–48 144
19:41, 42 422
19:41–44 140
20:1–8 279
21:29–30 281
22:4 278
22:20 209
22:31 86, 141, 241
22:41 253
22:42 368
22:43 51
22:44 71, 100, 232
23:7–11 12
23:9 142
23:23, 39–43 51
23:31 240
23:34 277
24:15–16 388
24:15–27 121
24:25 59, 214
24:32 23
24:33 214
24:39 76
24:45 214
24:45–49 178
24:47 298
24:50 100

John

1:1 83
1:1–18 431
1:3 155, 308, 427, 451
1:3–4 426
1:4 308
1:4, 9 385
1:5 83, 449
1:9 426
1:14 xv, 152, 231, 235, 322, 363, 450
1:16 282, 375, 378, 400, 463, 472
1:16–17 410
1:17 232
1:18 439
1:29 49
1:32–33 62
1:47 458
1:48 274
1:48, 50 281
2:1–10 394
2:8–10 283
2:13–21 403
3:5–8 259
3:14–15 86
3:16 94, 124, 212, 251, 294, 317, 384
3:35 176
4:15, 16 283
4:16 100
4:23 393
4:23–24 415
4:24 165
4:52, 53 284
5:1 284
5:6 284
5:7 284
5:8 195
5:14 285
5:16, 18 285
5:24 433
6:1–13 436
6:11 437
6:12 435
6:21 285
6:29–35 376
6:32–51 100
6:54–58 401
7:37–38 100

8:9, 59 ... 61
8:12 ... 419
8:32 ... 385, 438, 470
8:34 ... 68
8:38, 41 ... 257
8:39–41 ... 455
8:44 ... 67, 76, 88, 195, 212, 229, 277, 452
8:48 ... 274
8:56 ... 42, 283, 378
8:59 ... 291
9 ... 281, 285
9:6 ... xxxii, 2
9:9 ... 281
9:39–41 ... 143
10 ... 317
10:1–21 ... 226
10:10 ... 282, 410
10:12 ... 272, 462
10:16 ... 272, 471, 473
10:17 ... 282
10:18 ... 137
10:27 ... 462
10:31 ... 291
10:34 ... 376
10:35–36 ... 377
11:4 ... 282
11:5, 6 ... 282
11:36 ... 422
11:44 ... 287
11:49–51 ... 229
11:49–52 ... 442
12:1–8 ... 417
12:8 ... 276
12:29 ... 282
12:31 ... 73, 88, 94, 107, 115, 116, 141, 147, 167, 183, 195, 242, 283, 287, 307, 320
13:21–30 ... 116
13:23 ... 251, 317
13:34–35 ... 58
14:1–3 ... 376
14:6 ... 120, 385
14:13 ... 400, 431
14:13–14 ... 224, 382
14:16–17, 26 ... 153
14:17 ... 75, 102
14:23 ... 82
14:26 ... 459, 470
14:27 ... 364
14:30 ... 73, 88, 94, 107, 115, 116, 141, 147, 167, 195, 242, 283, 287, 307, 320
15:1 ... 450
15:5 ... 378, 458, 472
15:15 ... 283, 321
15:15–16 ... 416
15:16 ... 421, 431
15:26 ... 88, 102, 153, 174, 207
16:7–13 ... 251
16:11 ... 73, 88, 94, 107, 115, 116, 141, 147, 167, 195, 242, 283, 287, 307, 320
16:12–15 ... 270
16:13 ... 71, 76, 88, 176, 321, 470
16:13, 15 ... 416
16:14–15 ... 419
16:21 ... 385
16:32 ... 420
17 ... 212
17:12 ... 86, 312
17:17 ... 470
17:21 ... 76, 395, 450
17:22 ... 373, 377
17:24 ... 376
18:1 ... 79, 176
18:9 ... 86
18:36 ... 79, 418
19:5 ... 276, 401
19:12 ... 283
19:17 ... 403
19:19 ... 455
19:19–20 ... 398
19:23 ... 138, 381
19:26, 27 ... 283
19:30 ... 412
19:34 ... 245
19:34–37 ... 138
20:6–7 ... 287, 417
20:15–16 ... 144
20:16 ... 430
20:17 ... 317, 378
20:20, 24–27 ... 176
20:20, 25 ... 58
20:22 ... 18, 86
20:27 ... 76
20:28 ... 207, 266, 430
21:1–14 ... 432
21:4–13 ... 388
21:9 ... 388
21:13 ... 283
21:15 ... 333
21:15–17 ... 462
21:25 ... 83

Acts

1:9 ... 403
1:10 ... 402
1:10–11 ... 403
1:12 ... 410
1:13 ... 402
1:14 ... 403
1:18 ... 285
1:18–19 ... 54
2 ... 286
2:1–4 ... 171, 178
2:13 ... 286, 452
2:19 ... 287
2:20 ... 287
2:24 ... 287
2:32 ... 298
2:33, 47 ... 176
2:36 ... 287
2:40 ... 99
2:43 ... 125, 284
3:6 ... 263, 293, 417
3:6, 16 ... 417

3:15 .... 110, 417
4:4 176
4:12 417
4:30 125
5:12 125
5:14 176
5:15 284
6:5 271
6:7 176
7:25, 26 38
7:54–8:3 442
8:18 471
8:18–24 49
9:1–19 442
9:3–9 388
9:15 290
9:17 171
9:18 288
9:31 .... 176, 288
10:6 288
10:38 287
10:42 323
12:3 288
12:6–8 408
14:17 441
15:23–29 288
15:37ff 288
17:19 388
17:19–21 12
17:21–22 289
17:23 291
17:28 .... 378, 403, 432, 450, 459
17:30 148
17:31 323
18:14–17 289
19:6 171
19:12 417
20:28 95
22:3 291
26:14 347
26:20 473
26:24–25 129
27 292
27:42 292
27:27 292
28 292
28:3–6 292

Romans

1:16–2:29 294
1:21–23 383
1:21–25 291
1:22 140
2:1 297
2:4 .... 297, 471
2:5 214
2:14–16 297
2:17–29 297
2:20 298
2:25–29 .... 297, 298
3 298
3:1 298
3:3 299
3:5 299
3:23 202
3:25–26 251
3:26 399
3:31 299
4:10–12 297
5:1–2 300
5:1–11 189
5:3 300
5:5 .... 300, 364, 392, 411, 471, 473
5:9 91
5:9–11 466
5:10 .... 276, 472
5:15 .... 301, 381
5:16 301
5:17 400
5:20 .... 301, 376
6:4 .... 276, 302, 323, 347
6:5 82
6:14 302
6:23 .... 267, 301
7:4 275
7:8 303
7:11 303
7:21–23 303
7:24 .... 303, 304, 310
8:1 .... 55, 294
8:3–4 251
8:5 31
8:6 88
8:9 96
8:11 .... 304, 317
8:14–17 76
8:15 .... 171, 317, 373, 382, 385, 393
8:15–16, 21 385
8:16 .... 365, 432, 459
8:16–17, 26–30 364
8:17 .... 120, 121, 385, 405
8:18 471
8:19 310
8:22 226
8:26 .... 364, 366, 473
8:26–27 .... xxxvi, 155, 174, 431
8:27 346
8:28 .... 235, 365, 372, 339
8:31 370
8:32 416
8:34 .... 99, 387, 471, 473
8:39 276
9:22 454
9:22–23 471
9:23 421
9:24 155
9:32–33 103
10:4–10 .... xvi, xxix, xliv, 98, 425–33
10:5 66
10:6–8 431
10:8 .... 11, 427
10:8–10 275
10:9–10 .... 293, 411

10:10 .... 354, 431
10:17 436
11:1 216
11:9 455
11:11–12, 25–32 110
11:17–24 216
11:24 454
11:28 140
11:33 .... 83, 264
12:1 .... 272, 465, 472
12:1–2 75
12:4 472
12:4–5 412
12:5 415
12:19 215
13 304
13:1–7 313
13:12 470
14:8 474
16:20 .... 382, 419
16:25–26 311

1 Corinthians

1:8 472
1:17 304
1:18–25 9
1:20 .... 289, 443
1:21 305
1:22–2:4 382
1:23 291
1:25 .... xxxi, 3, 367
1:27–28 .... 78, 219, 223, 304
1:27–30 204
1:28 3
1:30 .... 415, 471
2:2 .... 291, 317, 393, 459
2:4 404
2:7 263
2:7–8 398
2:8 399
2:9 .... 90, 388, 397
2:9–10 75
2:10 .... 311, 316, 427
2:14 204
2:16 416
3:16 .... 96, 174
3:21–23 416
4:7 377
4:9 .... xxv, 398, 432
5:7 34
5:11 335
6:2 .... 35, 401
6:3 .... 125, 142
6:11 .... 75, 378
6:12 305
6:15 378
6:17 415
6:19 .... 75, 228, 335
6:20 .... 15, 331, 372
7:23 372
9:13 407
9:27 464
10:4 100
10:24 411
11:14 261
11:23–25 474
11:23–26 .... 401, 459
12:3 432
12:12 .... 378, 472
12:12–13 412
12:22–27 414
13:7 390
13:9 437
13:12 83
15:20, 24 400
15:21–22 388
15:21, 45, 47 381
15:35–44 311
15:45 276
15:55, 57 137
15:55–57 431
15:57 .... 68, 71, 79, 83, 89, 93, 105, 317, 379, 385
16:22 414

2 Corinthians

1:2–5 364
1:3–5 345
1:9 305
1:18–22 417
1:21–22 305
1:22 .... 176, 248, 300, 327, 375, 409
2:2 305
2:11 305
2:15 312
2:16 .... 62, 141
3:2–4:15 305
3:12–18 153
4:3–4 134
4:4 .... 84, 87, 473
4:7 .... 154, 335
5:1–4 394
5:4 379
5:5 .... 375, 409
5:13 134
5:17 377
5:21 .... 53, 108, 118, 275, 375, 384, 450
6:7 89
6:15 .... 37, 110, 125, 126, 140, 151
6:16 174
7:10 .... 61, 65, 124, 306
8:14 306
8:24 306
9:8, 10, 11, 12 418
10:4–6 .... 133, 157
10:5 154
11:14 .... 67, 231
11:26 306
12:1–4 397
12:2 291
12:2–4 14
12:7 311

Galatians

2:9 287

2:20............276, 419, 474
3:2............432
3:12............66
3:13............399, 450
3:16............245
3:16, 29............214
3:19............59, 275, 306
3:24............129, 300, 429
4:1–3............116
4:3, 9............306
4:4............152, 162, 178, 323, 383, 427
4:5–7............76
4:6............317, 373
4:19............259, 276, 432
5:6............293, 318, 320, 463, 472
5:22............380, 392
6:14............404

Ephesians

1............307
1:3............378, 389
1:3–6............378
1:4............375, 384, 389
1:7............367
1:13............248
1:14............300, 310, 327
1:16–23............317
1:22............162, 379, 450
2:2............88, 107, 110, 116, 151, 308, 452
2:3............124
2:6............121, 125, 162, 367,
2:6–10............400
2:6, 19–20............376
2:7............367
2:8–10............410
2:9............56
2:10............421, 463
2:14–16............421
3:8............307
3:10............59, 307
3:10–11............383
3:12............56
3:16............288
3:17............154
3:20............428, 430
4:4–6............412
4:11–16............22
4:14............347
4:15............71, 450
4:16............307, 415
4:20–25............268
4:22–24............474
4:24............112, 409, 473
4:30............173, 248
4:31............471
5:2............272
5:6............308
5:11............470
5:14............385
5:26............178, 327
5:27............429
5:29............307
5:29–31............415
5:30............470
5:32............379
6:1–2............462
6:11............473
6:12............307
6:14, 17............126
6:15............259
6:16............90, 128, 474
6:17............76, 80, 128, 409

Philippians

1:6............113, 364, 467, 470, 471
2:5............415
2:6–7............260
2:7............16, 427, 450
2:7–8............56, 118, 175, 366, 376
2:8............110, 203, 385
2:9–10............400
2:10............383
2:12............448
2:13............422, 462
2:15............99
2:20............308
2:21............308
2:27–28............308, 422
3:8............309
3:10, 17............309
3:20............474
3:21............16, 176, 401
4:4............317
4:7............304, 364, 469, 475
4:8............309

Colossians

1:10............463, 470
1:11............471
1:15............53, 87, 90, 119, 232, 399, 427
1:15, 18............259
1:16............155
1:18............162, 323, 450
2:3............154, 263, 415
2:16–17............264
2:17............151
3:1–2............376
3:2............471
3:3–4............310
3:8............473
3:10............142
3:14............318

1 Thessalonians

1:3............320
2:3–10............228
2:12............404
2:15............310
2:15–16............140
2:16............310
5:23............335, 470, 472

2 Thessalonians
1:6 422
2:3 310
2:14 377

1 Timothy
1:15 375
2:2 473
2:5 .... 367, 381, 471
2:15 311
3:9 16
3:16 .... 66, 157, 195, 235, 255, 290, 314, 379, 400, 427
3:18 317
4:8 .... xvli, 249, 369, 404

2 Timothy
1:6 171
1:7 364
2:12 .... 125, 385
2:13 320
3:15 8
3:15, 16 8
3:16 364
4:13 312

Titus
1:12 312
1:15 331
3:1 313
3:4 245
3:4–7 178
3:5 326

Philemon
1–25 313
10–21 365

Hebrews
1:1–2 59
1:3 .... 87, 381, 400, 471
1:3–4 59
1:14 .... 73, 82, 121
2:2 59
2:4 .... 125, 171
2:13 312
2:14 428
2:14–15 68
2:17 .... 385, 400
3:1 375
4:1–11 75
4:1–13 270
4:9–16 410
4:12 .... 47, 84, 111
4:13 111
4:14 .... 54, 463
4:14–15 470
4:15 .... 175, 386
4:16 300
6:4–5 94
6:5 .... 81, 474
7:1–10 40
7:3 161
7:19 319
7:22 301
7:25 .... xxxvi, 99, 155, 387
7:26 62
7:26–27 54
8:1 381
9:11–12 300
9:14 470
9:15 209
9:23 319
9:26 319
10 319
10:1 .... 44, 59, 151, 264, 319
10:10 154
10:14 323
10:15–18 132
10:17 347
10:22 .... 178, 474
11:3 .... 319, 427
11:4 .... 25, 387
11:5, 13–16 30
11:7 .... 295, 450
11:12 465
11:13 30
11:16 376
11:35 319
12:1 213
12:1–3 474
12:9 120
12:15 471
12:18–21 59
12:22 .... 195, 402
12:22–24 82
12:24 .... 99, 209, 387, 430
13:5 .... 458, 470
13:8 382

James
1:5 321
1:17 .... 338, 367, 419
1:27 321
2:6 320
2:8 .... 212, 412
2:14 320
2:19 .... 75, 79, 321
3:1–12 213
3:6 451
3:15–17 321
3:17 438
4:11 320
5 321
5:20 212

1 Peter
1 69
1:12 .... 40, 85, 86, 404
1:16 317
1:17–19 462
1:18 66
1:18–19 .... 34, 92, 387
1:19 .... 200, 471
1:20–21 378

1:21 ... 366
1:23 ... 133, 193, 271
1:24–25 ... 442
1:25 ... 314
2:2 ... 118, 333, 375
2:3 ... 471
2:9 ... 121, 198, 287
2:12 ... 293
2:13 ... 313
2:17 ... 314
2:21 ... 462, 471
2:24 ... 251
3:4 ... 314
3:6 ... 315
3:18 ... 317
3:18–22 ... 76
3:20–22 ... 451
3:22 ... 16
4:8 ... 212
4:10 ... 293
4:11 ... 315
4:13 ... 93
4:19 ... 19
5:7 ... 470
5:8 ... 73, 81, 183, 266
5:9 ... 93

2 Peter

1:3 ... 377
1:4 ... 142, 317, 371, 395
1:19 ... 177, 195
1:20 ... 315
1:21 ... 8, 315
2:5 ... 450
3:7, 9 ... 219
3:9 ... 472
3:14 ... 472
3:15 ... 373

1 John

1:1 ... 76, 316
1:3 ... 317
1:4 ... 316, 317
1:7 ... 365
1:8, 10 ... 316
1:9–2:2 ... xxxvi
2:1 ... 463, 470
2:9 ... 83
2:11 ... 316
2:12–14 ... 316
2:14 ... 89
2:15 ... 317
2:16 ... 114, 437
2:17 ... 317, 322
2:19 ... 451
2:20 ... 317
2:25 ... 318
3:1 ... 318
3:8 ... 431
4:7, 16, 19 ... 382
4:8, 16 ... 212, 282, 419, 441
4:10, 19 ... 421
5:6 ... 245
5:7–8 ... 76

2 John

1 ... 251
1–2 ... 318
11 ... 318

3 John

9–10 ... 318

Jude

4 ... 321
6 ... 231
20 ... 431

Revelation

1:1 ... 321
1:3 ... 321
1:4 ... 322
1:5 ... 34, 75, 162, 323
1:6 ... 125, 287
1:7 ... 323, 403
1:8 ... 53, 163
1:16 ... 47, 139
2:1 ... 139
2:2, 6 ... 323
2:4 ... 467
2:7 ... 75
2:14 ... 20–22
2:16 ... 47
2:17 ... 467
3:12 ... 209
3:16 ... 354
5:6, 9, 12 ... 139
5:9 ... 34, 396
5:10 ... 125, 287
7:9 ... 396
7:9–12 ... 166
7:15 ... 82
7:17 ... 396
9:1–2 ... 87, 146
9:3 ... 225
12:7–9 ... 183
12:7–17 ... 245
12:9 ... 163
12:10 ... 95, 109, 215, 241
12:11 ... 80
12:17 ... 67, 73, 76, 90, 104, 107, 117, 124, 129, 168, 214, 224, 308
14:4 ... 177
14:13 ... 327
15:2–3 ... 396
15:8 ... 154
17–18 ... 237
19:1–8 ... 99
19:7–9 ... 401
19:9 ... 121
19:10 ... 48
20:1–15 ... 142
20:2–3, 10 ... 245
20:6 ... 125
20:7–10 ... 142
20:10 ... 81, 136
20:10, 14, 15 ... 93, 126

21:1 .... 31, 245
21:2, 9.......................... 412
21:3..........................82, 152
21:4 396
21:23.......................... 419
22:1.......................... 412
22:2 119
22:2, 14, 19 75
22:13.......................... 53
22:16 177
22:17.......................... 412
22:18 21
22:20..................251, 322, 469, 475

GOD'S WORD
A Guide to Holy Scripture
CHRISTIAN ESSENTIALS
JOHN W. KLEINIG